RULES OF PROCEDURE AT THE UN AND AT INTER-GOVERNMENTAL CONFERENCES

This new third edition is a comprehensive manual of the rules of procedure and conduct of business at the UN General Assembly, at international conferences and at assemblies of inter-governmental organisations such as the World Health Organization. It examines the legal basis of these rules, the history of their development and the attempts at their codification. At the heart of the book is an examination of the practical applications of rules of procedure. Procedural rulings, updated to October 2016, are quoted from the records of UN General Assembly meetings, from assemblies of international organisations and from treaty-making conferences. This book is of interest to those involved in international law, international relations and international organisations. It also serves as an indispensable practical guide for delegates to the UN General Assembly and to international inter-governmental conferences. The first edition of this book was awarded the American Society of International Law Special Award.

ROBBIE SABEL is Professor of International Law at the Faculty of Law, Hebrew University of Jerusalem, and a member of the Permanent Court of Arbitration, The Hague. He is a former counselor for Political Affairs at the Israel Embassy, Washington, DC, and later served as the legal adviser to the Israel Ministry of Foreign Affairs and Deputy Director General for Arms Control and Disarmament of the Ministry.

RULES OF PROCEDURE AT THE UN AND AT INTER-GOVERNMENTAL CONFERENCES

ROBBIE SABEL
Hebrew University of Jerusalem

CAMBRIDGE
UNIVERSITY PRESS

CAMBRIDGE
UNIVERSITY PRESS

University Printing House, Cambridge CB2 8BS, United Kingdom

One Liberty Plaza, 20th Floor, New York, NY 10006, USA

477 Williamstown Road, Port Melbourne, VIC 3207, Australia

314–321, 3rd Floor, Plot 3, Splendor Forum, Jasola District Centre, New Delhi 110025, India

79 Anson Road, #06-04/06, Singapore 079906

Cambridge University Press is part of the University of Cambridge.

It furthers the University's mission by disseminating knowledge in the pursuit of education, learning, and research at the highest international levels of excellence.

www.cambridge.org
Information on this title: www.cambridge.org/9781107172722
DOI: 10.1017/9781316779323

First published 1997
Second edition 2006
Third edition 2018

Printed in the United Kingdom by Clays, St Ives plc

A catalogue record for this publication is available from the British Library.

Library of Congress Cataloging-in-Publication data
Names: Sabel, Robbie, author.
Title: Rules of procedure at the UN and at inter-governmental conferences / Robbie Sabel.
Other titles: Procedure at international conferences
Description: Third edition. | Cambridge, United Kingdom ; New York, NY : Cambridge University Press, 2018. | Revised edition of: Procedure at international conferences. 2nd edition. 2006. | Includes bibliographical references and index.
Identifiers: LCCN 2017026230 | ISBN 9781107172722 (hardback)
Subjects: LCSH: Conference proceedings. | Congresses and conventions. | International agencies – Rules and practice.
Classification: LCC JZ4850.S23 2018 | DDC 060.4/2 – dc23
LC record available at https://lccn.loc.gov/2017026230

ISBN 978-1-107-17272-2 Hardback

CONTENTS

PREFACE TO THE THIRD EDITION

Although the book examines the theory, history and development of procedure at conferences, the emphasis of this third edition is more on the book serving as a practical manual for those attending the UN General Assembly or international conferences.

In recent years there have been far fewer international law-making conferences than in the past, so that most of the recent precedents quoted are from debates at the UN General Assembly or from annual conferences of UN specialised agencies. This third edition contains some 250 new rulings and opinions on procedural issues, updated to October 2016. They are nearly all available online so that readers who wish to can easily access the full record of any procedural ruling.

Several international law luminaries and friends who helped and encouraged me in earlier editions have since unhappily passed away; I treasure the memory of Sir Eli Lauterpacht, Meir Rosenne, Shabtai Rosenne and Louis Sohn.

I also want to thank some of those who helped with the present edition: Eli Alook of the Israel Civil Aviation Authority; Dorota Lost-Sieminska of the International Maritime Organization; Markus Pallek and Stadler Trengove of the UN Office of Legal Affairs; Doron Peer, my law assistant at the Hebrew University; Mathieu Vaugeois of the International Civil Aviation Organization; and Nili Zentler of the Israel National Library.

As in past editions, special thanks to that wonderful personality at Cambridge University Press, Finola O'Sullivan, who, together with Abdus Salam Mazumder, Rebecca J. Roberts and Sarah Starkey, have enabled this project to come to fruition.

Finally, thanks again to my wife Ruthie for her understanding and forbearance.

ABBREVIATIONS

AJIL	*American Journal of International Law*
BYIL	*British Year Book of International Law*
CTBT	Comprehensive Test Ban Treaty
EC	European Commission
EU	European Union
ECOSC	United Nations Economic and Social Council
FAO	Food and Agriculture Organization
GAOR	General Assembly Official Records
IAEA	International Atomic Energy Agency
ICAO	International Civil Aviation Organization
ICC	International Criminal Court
ICJ	International Court of Justice
ICLQ	International and Comparative Law Quarterly
ICRC	International Committee of the Red Cross
ILC	International Law Commission
ILO	International Labour Organization
IMF	International Monetary Fund
IMO (IMCO)	Inter-Governmental Maritime (Consultative) Organization
INMARSAT	International Maritime Satellite Organization
ITU	International Telecommunication Union
NGO	nongovernmental organisation
NPT	Nuclear Non-Proliferation Treaty
PCIJ	Permanent Court of International Justice
PLO	Palestine Liberation Organization
RCADI	*Recueil des Cours (Collected Courses), Academic de Droit International*
UN	United Nations
UNCIO	1945 United Nations Conference on International Organization
UNCITRAL	United Nations Commission on International Trade Law

UNEP	United Nations Environment Programme
UNESCO	United Nations Educational, Scientific and Cultural Organization
UNGA	United Nations General Assembly
UNIDO	United Nations Industrial Development Organization
UN Jur. Y.B.	*United Nations Juridical Yearbook*
UNTS	*United Nations Treaty Series*
WHO	World Health Organization
YBILC	*Yearbook of the International Law Commission*

Unless stated otherwise, reference to the United Nations rules of procedure of the General Assembly is to the rules in the General Assembly and not to the equivalent rules in committees.

Unless using a direct quotation, reference to the number of a specific rule of procedure is always to the rule of procedure as it appears in the 2016 version, UN Doc. A/520/Rev.18 (2016), and not to the numbering of the rule as it was when the statement referred to was made.

INTRODUCTION

A 1953 study defines the rules of procedure of a conference as 'all the rules and practices which determine the status of each of the participants in an international conference and the conduct of the discussions until the conference adopts its final decision'.[1] The temporary nature of conference procedural roles was emphasised by Tammes in a lecture at The Hague Academy in 1958: 'The conference is a preparatory phase in a law making process; a passing event doomed to be buried in archives together with all its rules and its organisational structure and leaving behind nothing except the living results.'[2]

An examination of state practice at international conferences[3] reveals, however, that the rules of procedure and their interpretation follow remarkably consistent patterns. Conferences and assemblies of different organisations tend to reach similar conclusions on procedural issues. Oppenheim's *Treatise* states that 'the degree to which they [conferences] follow a similar pattern and the frequency with which they are held is such that they may be regarded in some sense as one of the regular institutions of the international community'.[4] Conferences do not in fact draft rules of procedure *de novo* without reference to previous practice. The fate of

[1] C. Chaumont, 'The Evolutionary Aspect of International Organisations and International Cooperation', 5 *UNESCO International Social Science Bulletin* 258 (1953 No. 2).

[2] A. J. P. Tammes, 'Decisions of International Organs as a Source of International Law', 94 RCADI 306 (1958 II).

[3] Reference is made throughout this book to 'conferences' and not 'congresses'. Pastuhov, writing in 1945, could even then state that 'the word "congress" as the designation of an assembly of plenipotentiaries has today become more or less obsolete'. Vladimir D. Pastuhov, *A Guide to the Practice of International Conferences* (1945), p. 9. See also Shabtai Rosenne, 'Conferences and Congresses, International', in *Encyclopedia of Public International Law*, ed. R. Bernhardt, vol. I (1992), p. 739 at p. 740.

The term 'international conference', as used in this study, refers to inter-governmental conferences, that is, conferences of representatives of States. As to whether the term can also be applied to non-governmental conferences, see Yuen-li Liang, 'Notes on Legal Questions Concerning the United Nations, What Is an International Conference?' 44 AJIL 333 (1950).

[4] *Oppenheim's International Law*, eds. R. Jennings and A. Watts, 9th edn, vol. I (1992), p. 1184.

rules of procedure of past conferences is not quite as morbid as Professor Tammes feared.

Parliamentary procedure is a vital element of all democratic institutions. During a UN Security Council debate, US Representative Senator Moynihan described due procedure as 'not an aspect of governance, it is the essence of government'.[5] In national parliaments experienced legislators excel in using procedural techniques against their political rivals. In the realm of the study of international law, procedure at international conferences – except for questions of voting[6] – tends, however, to be a neglected topic. Even regarding international organisations, where there is a relatively rich literature, Jenks could write in 1958 that the 'parliamentary law of international organisations has attracted very little attention'[7], and Detter writes that the 'Rules of Procedure of international organisations have not attracted the interest of international lawyers'.[8] Notwithstanding the lack of academic interest, it has been pointed out, I believe validly, that 'the development of procedure and the development of [international] collaboration are interdependent'.[9] No international organisation or international conference can carry out its function without clearly defined rules of procedure. Procedural debates have been termed 'time-consuming', 'rather uninteresting and profitless';[10]

5 Official Records UN Security Council, 1870th Meeting, para. 94, UN Doc. S/PV.1870 (1976).

6 See, for example, the seminal study, Louis B. Sohn, 'Voting Procedures in United Nations Conferences for the Codification of International Law', 69 AJIL 310 (1975).

7 C. Wilfred Jenks, *The Common Law of Mankind* (1958), p. 24.

8 Ingrid Detter, *Law Making by International Organisations* (1965), p. 52.

9 Chaumont, 'The Evolutionary Aspect', at 265.

10 The quotation is taken from the following comment by Hambro:

> The rules of procedure play an important part in the day-to-day work of the organs of the United Nations. They are necessary for the orderly conduct of business and to ensure fair play in the Organisation. But on the whole they do not play a preponderant part. There are certain delegates who love the sport of raising technical points of order. And a nervous chairman or president trembles when a number of delegates simultaneously stand up in different corners of the room and shout 'point of order!' One sees happy smiles on the faces of some of the adepts at this sport once the going is good, particularly in the legal committee, where it has been developed into a fine art. But the wise chairman tries to avoid this sport which is time consuming and, on the whole, rather uninteresting and profitless. A presiding officer who knows his rules and applies them impartially is generally spared

Edvard Hambro, 'Some Notes on Parliamentary Diplomacy', in *Transnational Law in a Changing Society, Essays in Honour of Philip C. Jessup*, eds. Wolfgang Friedmann, Louis Henkin and Oliver Lissitzyn (1972), p. 281.

nevertheless procedure, in any organisation, is integrally linked to due process and Jenks's statement on this issue is worth quoting at length:

> [D]ue process requires regularity of procedure. A proper forum, freedom of speech and a fair hearing are important elements in, but they do not exhaust the requirements of, regularity of procedure. The inclusion in the agenda in accordance with recognised rules of questions which it is desired to raise, respect for time limits designed to secure due notice of such questions, the despatch of business in an orderly manner, and respect by international bodies for their own terms of reference and the limits of their constitutional power are not tedious technicalities which it is legitimate to sweep aside in the name of a higher morality. They are essential ingredients of substantial justice on which all members, whether directly involved in the matter or not, are entitled to rely as guarantees that, before being called upon to participate in a decision which may have far-reaching implications, they will be able to ascertain and give responsible expression to the considered views of their government or other constituents.[11]

In ascertaining the functions of rules of procedure, the definition proposed by the Secretary-General of the UN in 1953 seems particularly apt: 'The rules of procedure are intended to protect the rights of individual Members. They are equally intended to permit an orderly conduct of business.'[12] In attempting to apply this maxim to international conferences one author comments:

> The drawing up of suitable rules of procedure, combining as far as possible the conflicting national practices and affording an adequate guarantee of fair play to all concerned and of orderly proceedings, is also one of the manifold problems which from the very outset confront those who are responsible for the organisation of international conferences.[13]

A detailed knowledge of procedure can be a keen tool for a delegate attending a conference. Righter, in a 1995 book, quotes an anonymous Swiss diplomat as telling her, 'Western defeats on procedural motions

[11] Jenks, *Law in the World Community* (1967), p. 114.

[12] Measures to Limit the Duration of Regular Sessions of the General Assembly: Memorandum by the Secretary-General of the United Nations, Annex VII, Agenda Item 50, 1952–1953, para. 27, UN Doc. A/2206 (1952). See also Louis B. Sohn, 'Editorial Comment, Due Process in the United Nations', 69 AJIL 620 (1975) at 621; Henry G. Schermers and Niels M. Blokker, *International Institutional Law: Unity within Diversity*, 5th rev. edn, para. 1205 (2011).

[13] William O'Davoren, *Post-War Reconstruction Conferences: The Technical Organisation of International Conferences* (1943), p. 4.

are . . . the result of carelessness', adding that 'experts on locust control are rarely masters of parliamentary tricks'.[14] On the early years of the UN, Peterson writes, 'The most effective delegates were those who could steer deliberations through procedural motions, submission of amendments or alternate draft resolutions, or attempts to transform others' drafts through motions to delete particular pieces of a draft.'[15] Fitschen writes of the UN General Assembly (UNGA) rules of procedure that '[d]elegations can utilise them as a political instrument to determine the direction or speed of GA organs on important substantive issues or even to prevent debate or action concerning a matter altogether'.[16]

States frequently choose to contest an issue through the use of procedural motions, rather than contesting the substance of the issue. Such a choice may be made when a State estimates that it is easier to garner support for its position on an ostensibly neutral procedural issue rather than on the substance. The word 'ostensibly' is used since States involved are cognisant of the substantive issue behind the procedural debate, but nevertheless prefer to leave the substance in the background. Delegations may also have flexibility on procedural motions that they do not have on the substance. Rosenne, referring to an Israeli effort to gain support in advance for a procedural motion at the 1958 Law of the Sea Conference, writes, 'Questions of procedure, and especially hypothetical ones, are usually left to the delegations on the spot, and it is unusual for instructions to be sent from a capital about a hypothetical procedural vote in a remote conference.'[17] Procedural decisions are taken by a simple majority, while in treaty-making conferences issues of substance are usually decided by a two-thirds majority. Thus, for this reason as well, States may at times choose to contest an issue on procedural grounds, rather than as a substantive issue.[18]

This study commences with a historical review of the development of rules of procedure and the attempts to draft model codes. Chapter 2 deals with the adoption by conferences of their rules of procedure. Chapter 3 examines why States attending a conference are obliged to comply with the

[14] Rosemary Righter, *Utopia Lost: The United Nations and World Order* (1995), p. 135.

[15] M. J. Peterson, 'General Assembly', in *The Oxford Handbook on the United Nations*, eds. Thomas G. Weiss and Sam Daws (2007), p. 101.

[16] Thomas Fitschen, 'Article 21', in *The Charter of the United Nations, A Commentary*, eds. Bruno Simma et al, 3rd edn (2012), p. 690.

[17] Shabtai Rosenne, 'Israel and the First United Nations Conference on the Law of the Sea: The Straits of Tiran', in *An International Law Miscellany* (1993), p. 723 at p. 757.

[18] See Shabtai Rosenne, *Developments in the Law of Treaties 1945–1986* (1989), p. 244.

rules of procedure and whether certain rules of procedure have become international law. This is followed by the main body of the study, which consists of an examination of the procedural practice of States at international conferences since the end of the Second World War.

It must be stated at the outset that procedural decisions are usually a reflection of the political reality at an assembly or conference. States nevertheless tend to follow precedents in procedural matters: such precedents carry particular weight if they are accompanied by a reasoned decision of an experienced presiding officer, are an opinion of a legal adviser or form part of a consistent pattern of procedural behaviour.

This study gives examples of procedural issues from the UNGA, whose rules of procedure have been described as 'the fullest and the best developed system of procedural norms of international organisations'.[19] Emphasis is placed on those issues that are relevant to all international conferences and assemblies; hence subjects such as the distribution of agenda items to specific committees are not dealt with in this study. Procedural rulings and practices are also brought from the practice of assemblies of international organisations, in particular the assemblies of IAEA, ICAO, ILO, IMO and WHO. Here again examples are only brought of procedural issues that are germane to other assemblies and to international conferences and not those issues particular only to a specific organisation. As treaty-making conferences publish full records of their deliberations, most of the examples of conference practice are taken from the records of such conferences.[20,21]

[19] Jan Kolasa, *Rules of Procedure of the United Nations General Assembly: A Legal Analysis* (1967), p. 111.

[20] Law-making conferences tend to be more respectful of procedural standards than other conferences. It is interesting to note in this context the conclusion of the Institut de Droit International in its resolution on 'The Elaboration of General Multilateral Conventions and of Non-Contractual Instruments Having a Normative Function or Objective', 62 *Yearbook of the Institute of International Law* 274 (1987 II) at 278 (Cairo Session):

> The elements which help to identify a resolution as [having a normative function] include, *inter alia*: . . . (b) respect for procedural standards and requirements.

Judge H. Mosler, replying to a questionnaire on a draft to the above resolution, pointed out that 'the procedural conditions of resolutions are less strict than those for the elaboration of multilateral conventions'. 61 *Yearbook of the Institute of International Law* (1985 II) at 268. See also Rosenne: 'I believe that treaty-drafting is a much more careful operation than resolution drafting.' *Developments in the Law of Treaties*, p. 275.

[21] Many records of conferences state curtly that a 'procedural debate occurred', without giving even a summary report. One author writing a handbook on conferences advises, 'Debates on questions of procedure which do not affect the substance of the issues under consideration, should especially be summarised in a succinct manner.' O'Davoren, *Post-War*

Each headlined paragraph in the study usually deals with a specific issue of procedure. Paragraphs commence by giving first the text of the rule of procedure in the UNGA and then the relevant proposal of the UN Model Conference Rules.[22] The UN Model Rules themselves are a useful source of practice since the drafters attempted to incorporate conference practice into the rules they drafted. After the text of the rule, examples are quoted of procedural decisions and statements on the issue taken from the records of UNGA practice and then from conferences, followed by examples from the practice of international organisations. Where relevant, the author's comment is added as to the predominant international practice.

This book is intended both as a study of the issue and as a practical manual for the use of delegates to the UN, as well as diplomats, lawyers and other participants at international conferences and assemblies. It demonstrates that, as regards procedure at conferences, universal State practice appears to be developing. As far back as 1926, a member of a committee of the League of Nations studying the possibility of codifying rules of procedure commented, 'Whatever the subject before the conference, there were certain principles [of procedure] which were invariably identical.'[23] That committee itself reached the conclusion, as regards rules of procedure, that 'a certain number of practices have grown up and these reappear at each conference and are handed on from one to the other'.[24] Some ninety years after the League of Nations report, certain rules of procedure have achieved near-universal application and may well by now have the status of customary international law.

Reconstruction Conferences, p. 105. Modern UN conferences, unless they are treaty-making conferences, do not normally publish records of the debates, but only of resolutions and recommendations that were adopted.

22 Draft Standard Rules of Procedure for United Nations Conferences, Report of the Secretary-General, UN Doc. A/40/611 of 11 September 1985 (hereinafter referred to as 'the UN Model Rules').

23 M. Fromageot, member of the Committee of Experts for the Progressive Codification of International Law, Report to the Council of the League of Nations on the Questions Which Appear Ripe for International Regulation, Questionnaire No. 5, Procedure of International Conferences and Procedure for the Conclusion and Drafting of Treaties, quoted from Shabtai Rosenne, ed., *League of Nations Committee of Experts for the Progressive Codification of International Law (1925–1928)*, vol. I (1972), p. 236.

24 Committee of Experts for the Progressive Codification of International Law, Report to the Council of the League of Nations on the Questions Which Appear Ripe for International Regulation, Questionnaire No. 5, Procedure of International Conferences and Procedure for the Conclusion and Drafting of Treaties, Annex to Questionnaire No. 5, Report of the Sub-Committee, p. 107, League of Nations Doc. C.196.M.70.1927.V [CPD 95(2)] of 20 April 1927.

1

Historical Development of Rules of Procedure of Conferences and Attempts to Establish Model Rules

1.1 Development of Conference Rules of Procedure

Sohn points out that at the 1868 Geneva Conference 'a distinction seems to have been made for the first time between matters of substance and questions of procedure'.[1] The Congress of Berlin of 1878, however, is usually regarded as the first conference where a clear distinction was made between decisions on substance and those on procedure. It was there that Bismarck declared, 'In the interest of accomplishment, resolutions concerning procedure not touching questions of substance should be held to be decisions of the Congress when approved by a majority vote, unless the minority should register formal protest.'[2]

Despite these two examples and additional cases of adoption of ad hoc procedural decisions, Pastuhov writes that it 'was not the practice of diplomatic conferences held prior to the twentieth century to adopt formal rules of procedure for conducting their business'.[3] Although the First Hague Conference of 1899 voted on procedural issues, it did not have a formal set of rules of procedure; the first conference with a formal set of rules of procedure appears to have been the Second Hague Conference of 1907. The rules of the Second Hague Conference consisted of twelve short articles dealing with its structure and organisation. Only two dealt with the process of conduct of business and voting.[4]

[1] Louis B. Sohn, 'Voting Procedure in International Conferences for the Codification of International Law, 1864–1930', in *Jus et Societas: Essays in Tribute to Wolfgang Friedmann*, ed. Gabriel M. Wilner (1979), p. 278 at p. 279.

[2] British and Foreign State Papers, LXIX 892 (translated from the French original).

[3] Vladimir D. Pastuhov, *A Guide to the Practice of International Conferences* (1945), p. 122 n. 1.

[4]

Article 8

Each delegation has a right to only one vote. The vote is taken by roll call according to the alphabetical order of the Powers represented.

The draft rules of procedure of the International Naval Conference held in London in 1908 and 1909, proposed by the United Kingdom as the convening State, had four articles,[5] and the final rules of procedure consisted of nine articles, of which only one (article 5) could be considered as dealing with the actual conduct of business.[6]

The rules of procedure of the 1919 Paris Peace Conference consisted of fifteen articles, of which perhaps three could be considered as dealing with the conduct of business.[7]

Article 9

Every proposition of a resolution or vœu to be discussed by the Conference must, as a general rule, be delivered in writing to the president in order to be printed and distributed before being brought to discussion.

The Proceedings of the Peace Conference, Translation of the Official Texts, prepared in the Division of International Law of the Carnegie Endowment for International Peace, *The Conference of 1907*, vol. I, Plenary Meetings of the Conference (1920), p. 53.

[5] 1. Plenipotentiary and non-plenipotentiary delegates have equally the right of speaking in the discussions of the Conference.
2. Secretaries of the delegations may accompany the members of their delegations at all the sessions of the Conference.
3. The sessions of the Conference are not public. Its deliberations remain strictly confidential.
4. The French language is recognised as the official language for the deliberations and acts of the Conference. Speeches delivered in another language are given orally in outline in French.

The Declaration of London February 26, 1909, A Collection of Official Papers and Documents Relating to the International Naval Conference held in London December, 1908–February, 1909, ed. James Brown Scott (1919), Annex B, p. 13.

[6] 5. Tout nouvelle proposition et tout amendement à discuter par la Conférence doivent, en règle générale, être remise par écrit au Président. Si la proposition ou l'amendement n'a pu être distribué avant la séance, la Conférence ne peut s'opposer à une demande d'ajournement à une séance ultérieure.' Quoted from n. Hill, *The Public International Conference* (1929), Appendix F 243.

[7] Rules of procedure of the Paris Peace Conference of 1919.

X

With a view to facilitate discussion any Plenipotentiary wishing to propose a resolution must give the President twenty-four hours' notice thereof, except in the case of proposals connected with the order of the day and arising from the actual discussion.

Exceptions may, however, be made to this rule in the case of amendments or secondary questions which do not constitute actual proposals.

XI

All petitions, memoranda, observations and documents addressed to the Conference by any persons other than the Plenipotentiaries must be received and classified by the Secretariat.

Such of these communications as are of political interest will be briefly summarised in a list circulated to all the Plenipotentiaries. Supplementary editions of

With the exception of the rules of the General Conference of the ILO,[8] the rules of procedure of the Assembly of the League of Nations apparently are the first occurrence of detailed instructions and rules as to the conduct of business. They consisted of twenty-eight articles subdivided into sub-articles. These rules are the direct predecessors of the rules of procedure of the UNGA. The rules of the UNGA, in turn, have served as the model for all subsequent international conferences and for the UN Model Rules.

The contrast between the detailed rules of the Assembly of the League of Nations and the scant rules of the preceding congresses and conferences is so great that it raises doubt as to whether the League rules were derived from the rules of previous conferences. It has been suggested that their primary source was parliamentary procedure, a source that was familiar to the draftsmen of the Covenant and of the rules of procedure of the League. Prélot, in his lecture at the Hague Academy, states that the rules were adopted practically *en bloc* from various parliamentary procedures.[9]

The rules of procedure of the Assembly of the League of Nations contain such terms as 'calling a speaker to order', 'rising to a point of order' and 'moving the previous question'. The appearance of such terms for the first time in the rules of procedure of an international conference points clearly to their parliamentary ancestry. The rules appear to have been influenced primarily by British parliamentary procedure, but certainly not exclusively so.[10]

> this list shall be issued as such communications are received. All these documents shall be deposited in the archives.
>
> XII
>
> All questions to be decided shall be discussed at a first and second reading; the former shall afford occasion for a general discussion for the purpose of arriving at an agreement on points of principle; the second reading shall provide an opportunity of discussing details.

English version quoted from 13 AJIL Official Documents 109 (1919) at 111.

Marston writes that the basis of these rules was a semi-official document 'Sur le Congrès de la Paix' prepared by French diplomats. F. S. Marston, *The Peace Conference of 1919, Organisation and Procedure* (1944), p. 35.

8 Butler points out that the ILO rules of procedure were in fact 'the first set of international standing orders ever framed'. Harold B. Butler, 'The Washington Conference', in *The Origins of the International Labor Organisation*, ed. James T. Shotwell, vol. I (1934), p. 305 at p. 315. However, because of the unique structure of the ILO, the rules of procedure are themselves of a very particular nature.

9 Marcel Prélot, 'Le droit des assemblées internationales', 104 RCADI 476 (1961 III) at 477.

10 Many external features of similarity might suggest that procedure in the various democratic assemblies is practically uniform. To a considerable extent this similarity is imposed by the nature of the task at hand. To some degree, however, it is traceable to the fact that

Kolasa, in his book on the rules of procedure of the UNGA, argues, however, that although there was borrowing from parliamentary procedure, the rules of procedure of the League were in fact a continuation of previous international practice. Kolasa cites the unanimity rule of the League as support for his view that this was international practice and not parliamentary procedure.[11] Although Kolasa is undeniably correct as regards the genealogy of the unanimity rule, an examination of the procedural rules of the League Assembly would appear to support the statement by Noel-Baker that the composition and work of the League 'bear hardly a trace of the old diplomatic conferences of the past'.[12]

At the 1945 United Nations Conference on International Organization at San Francisco, the Secretariat introduced its proposal on the procedure of that conference by stating, 'The following rules of procedure relating to discussion, to motions and to the appointment of subcommittees have been widely applied in connection with international conferences in the past.'[13] An examination of the provisional rules of procedure of the UNGA, as prepared by the Preparatory Commission,[14] however, shows them to be nearly identical to the rules of the League of Nations, and there appears to have been little input from the procedure of other international conferences. Oscar Schachter, the executive secretary of the first conference convened by the UNGA, explained to the conference that the provisional rules of procedure were based on the rules of procedure of conferences called by the UN Economic and Social Council (ECOSOC).[15]

procedure in a great many parliaments developed out of that in the British Parliament. Joseph J. Senturia, 'Parliamentary Procedure', in *Encyclopaedia of Social Sciences*, vol. XII (1933), p. 455.

[11] 'This [the adoption of rules of procedure of the League of Nations] not only followed the earlier international practice, but that only the experience of previous international gatherings and the actual existing patterns and precedents established at earlier international debates made it possible to find an easy and fairly straightforward solution to the procedural problems of the League of Nations.' Jan Kolasa, *Rules of Procedure of the United Nations General Assembly, A Legal Analysis* (1967), p. 42.

'Therefore it must be stated and stressed that irrespective of the indisputable direct borrowings from the procedural practice of national parliaments, the rules of procedure of the League Assembly are, as in principle they should be, a natural link in the chain of development which began in the 19th century with international conferences and the first international organisations.' *Ibid.* at p. 46.

[12] Philip Noel-Baker, 'League of Nations', in *Encyclopaedia of the Social Sciences*, vol. IX (1933), p. 289.

[13] UNCIO, Doc. 332 EX-SEC/8, 13 May 1945.

[14] Report of the Preparatory Commission of the United Nations, PC/20/C.I, sec. 3 (1945).

[15] 1950 Conference on Missing Persons, UN Doc. A/CONF.1/SR.1, para. 23. The UNGA, in its Resolution 366 (IV) of 3 December 1947, instructed ECOSOC to 'prepare, or request the Secretary-General to prepare, provisional rules of procedure for the conferences'.

In the drafting of the UNGA rules of procedure, there does not appear to have been any direct borrowing from parliamentary procedures.[16] However, when, in 1954, the Sixth Committee of the UNGA was debating the issue of correction of votes, delegates freely turned to parliamentary procedures for guidance. The UK delegate suggested applying a system adopted in the French National Assembly,[17] and the delegate of Peru referred generally to parliamentary procedure.[18] The UNGA requested the secretary-general to 'obtain information concerning the existing rules and generally accepted practices of other intergovernmental organisations *and of national legislative assemblies*' [emphasis added).[19] The representative of Belgium at the Sixth Committee, however, sounded a caveat:

> The United Nations was not a parliament, and the rules applicable to a legislative assembly might be quite out of place in the world body. A member of parliament was responsible only to himself, while the vote of a representative in the General Assembly was binding on his government.[20]

Hovey, writing in 1951 about the UNGA, commented that the spirit of accommodation in parliamentary rules of procedure was lacking in the UN and that,'[i]n a body whose Members are sovereign states dedicated to mutually uncongenial ideologies, it would be optimistic to presuppose "the courtesy of generous minds"'.[21] Chaumont, in an analysis written in 1953, compares the rules of procedure of the US Senate, which preserve the individual freedom of action of Senators, with the more restrictive rules of the US House of Representatives and the British House of Commons, whose rules limit individual rights in favour of efficiency and the rights of the majority. He then states,

> When parliamentary practice was transferred to international organisations, with the preparation of their rules of procedure, a particular stage in parliamentary development was taken as the model. It is understandable that this stage was marked by a certain liberalism, half way between the extreme freedom of the American Senate and the strict organisation of the British House of Commons.[22]

16 Although there was indirect borrowing via the rules of procedure of the League of Nations.
17 UN GAOR, 6th Committee, 9th Session, 438th Meeting, para. 32, UN Doc. A/C.6/9/SR.438 (1954).
18 *Ibid.* at para. 26.
19 UNGA Resolution 901 (IX) of 14 December 1954.
20 Mr De La Vallée Poussin, UN GAOR, 6th Committee, 9th Session, 438th Meeting, para. 25, UN Doc. A/C.6/9/SR.438 (1954). The debate was on the issue of the correction of votes.
21 Allan Hovey Jr, 'Obstructionism and the Rules of the General Assembly', 5 *UNESCO International Organization* 515 (1951 No. 3) at 529.
22 C. Chaumont, 'The Evolutionary Aspect of International Organizations and International Co-operation', 5 *UNESCO International Social Science Bulletin* 258 (1953 No. 2) at 271.

Chaumont adds that the result of the changes made to the original draft rules of the UNGA procedure was 'to strengthen the power of the majority to the detriment of individual members'.[23]

1.2 Proposals for Drafting Model Codes of Conference Rules of Procedure

1.2.1 League of Nations Codification

In 1925 the Committee of Experts for the Progressive Codification of International Law[24] decided to include in its list of issues of international law that might be ready for codification this question: 'Whether it is possible to formulate rules to be recommended for the procedure of international conferences and the conclusion and drafting of treaties, and what such rules should be'.[25] The committee stated from the outset that there was 'no question of attempting to reach by way of international agreement a body of rules which would be binding obligatorily upon the various States'. The object of the study was 'to put at the disposal of the States concerned rules which could be modified as they chose in each concrete case but whose existence might save them much discussion, doubt and delay'.[26]

To that end, a subcommittee was formed that submitted a report stating inter alia that a 'certain number of practices have grown up and these reappear at each conference and are handed on from one to the other'.[27] The report continues, 'The process of evolution has not yet ceased, however. To realise this, it is sufficient to study the history of recent conferences and to observe that the procedure, while in general following established precedent, has been modified in detail by the application of special provisions *in concreto*.' Nevertheless the report reached the conclusion that certain categories of rules of procedure were 'the application of certain fundamental

[23] *Ibid.* at 262.

[24] Described by Rosenne as 'that early predecessor of the International Law Commission'. Shabtai Rosenne, ed., *League of Nations Committee of Experts for the Progressive Codification of International Law (1925–1928)*, vol. I (1972), p. v.

[25] Committee of Experts for the Progressive Codification of International Law, Meeting of 8 April 1925. Report to the Council of the League of Nations on the Questions Which Appear Ripe for International Regulation, Questionnaire No. 5, Procedure of International Conferences and Procedure for the Conclusion and Drafting of Treaties, p. 105, League of Nations Doc. C.196.M.70.1927.V [CPD 95(2)] of 20 April 1927.

[26] *Ibid.*

[27] *Ibid.* Annex to Questionnaire No. 5, Report of the Sub-Committee, pp. 106, 107.

principles generally recognised as forming part of existing international law (customary law, "*opinio necessitatis*")'.[28] The report enumerated a list of procedural issues that the subcommittee considered could be codified, and States were asked to comment on the list.

Among the States submitting comments was Germany, which commented, 'Conditions differ so greatly that it would appear to be desirable to retain some measure of freedom in organising international conferences.'[29] The Austrian comment was that 'the questions of international law set out in the questionnaire may be settled by international agreement, provided the future rules are conceived as a *jus dispositivum* which would not limit the independence of States'.[30] The British comment was that it did not 'consider the procedure of international conferences . . . to be a subject of international law whose regulation by international agreement is desirable and realisable'.[31] Denmark replied that it was not 'entirely convinced that present-day necessities warrant an endeavour to codify these points in an international convention'.[32] The French Government was of this opinion: '[I]t appears desirable and practicable to draw up for the use of international conferences and Foreign Offices a body of rules which would serve as a guide except as otherwise agreed in some particular case.'[33] The Italian Government stated that it saw 'no objection, in principle, but does not consider the matter to be of any urgency'.[34] Norway was in favour provided that 'the rules to be established should not in any way limit the freedom of Governments'. The Norwegian Government added that even nonbinding rules would 'tend to develop a correct and uniform practice'.[35] The Netherlands was of the opinion that, leaving aside all questions of urgency, 'it should be possible to reach an agreement on the main points'.[36] The Swedish and US Governments were doubtful whether such codification was desirable.[37] The analysis of these comments, submitted by a member of the subcommittee, reaffirmed that the objective of the committee had been 'to put at the disposal of States rules in the form of *jus dispositivum*, which they could apply or modify as they chose in each concrete case'.[38] The report reached the conclusion that the issue was 'sufficiently ripe' for an international agreement,[39] and the Assembly of the League decided to authorise the

[28] *Ibid.* [29] *Ibid.* at p. 130. [30] *Ibid.* at p. 138. [31] *Ibid.* at p. 145.
[32] *Ibid.* at p. 151. [33] *Ibid.* at p. 165. [34] *Ibid.* at p. 171. [35] *Ibid.* at p. 178.
[36] *Ibid.* at p. 181. [37] *Ibid.* at pp. 238, 237. [38] *Ibid.* at p. 271.
[39] *Ibid.* at p. 7, Report to the Council of the League of Nations, signed by H. L. Hammarskjöld, Chairman of the Committee of Experts, 2 April 1927.

Secretariat to prepare a study of the issue. Nevertheless, no further study was undertaken, and the issue was in effect deferred *sine die*.[40]

Manley Hudson commented negatively on the work of the Committee of Experts, as regards procedure. He stated,

> A collection of these *règlements* might serve as a source of suggestion and guidance to future conferences. But it seems to be very debatable whether it is possible to go further than to place before the bureau of a conference more than such a collection, whether indeed the subject is one which lends itself to any conventional regulation, facultative or otherwise. Most conferences will prefer to shape their organisation and procedure to meet conditions which cannot be foreseen.[41]

Writing in 1946, Kunz commented on the report of the Committee of Experts that it had 'led to no results but the progress made in this matter since the Paris Peace Conference renders the question again timely'.[42]

The Committee of Experts also dealt with issues relating to the conclusion of treaties, and these issues were included in the 1969 Vienna Convention on the Law of Treaties.[43]

Hill, writing in 1929, commented that 'the rules of an international conference are complex neither in form nor in substance . . . they are ordinarily comprehended within ten or twelve concise articles'.[44] Assuming that Hill's comment reflected the accepted view at the time, the issue was clearly not ripe for model rules to be prepared.

Doubt continues to be expressed as to whether the field of rules of procedure in international forums is in fact ripe for any form of rigid drafting or codification.

1.2.2 UN Codification

In 1952, the Report of the Secretary-General, in examining the proposal to produce a *répertoire* of procedure of the Security Council, commented,

> The view has repeatedly been expressed in the Security Council that the Council is, and should remain, the master of its own procedure. It has been indicated that the Council should not commit itself to procedures which

40 9 *League of Nations Official Journal* 123 (1928). Rosenne, *Committee of Experts*, p. 219.

41 Manley O. Hudson, 'Editorial Comment, Procedure of International Conferences and Procedure for the Conclusion and Drafting of Treaties', 20 AJIL 747 (1926) at 748.

42 Josef L. Kunz, 'Book Review, "A Guide to the Practice of International Conferences", by Vladimir D. Pastuhov', 40 AJIL 230 (1946).

43 8 ILM 679 (1969).

44 Hill, *Public International Conference*, p. 63.

> in practice might prove to be excessively rigid, since each dispute with which the Council has to deal has unique characteristics. Attention has been drawn to the danger that any premature formalisation of the procedures of the Council might impede the latter in the discharge of its responsibilities under the Charter. Such an attitude, it has been contended, corresponds to the very nature of the work of the Security Council.[45]

The report continues:

> [T]he *répertoire* should avoid taking any position, even in the manner of classifying and presenting the material, on the question whether the practices of the Council constitute precedents which have any binding character for the future.
>
> [T]he *répertoire* should present, in readily accessible form, all the relevant data regarding the practice and procedure of the Council, but should not itself constitute a work of codification or interpretation. It should be left entirely to the reader to draw conclusions as to the interpretation of the Charter and the provisional rules of procedure.[46]

In 1953, W. R. Sharp of Yale, on behalf of UNESCO, prepared a 'check list' for possible 'case studies of the conditions under which contentious rules of procedure are applied, and of the resultant impact on decision making'.[47] There does not appear, however, to have been any follow-up to this research.

The 1971 UN Committee on the Procedure and Organisation of the General Assembly discussed the possibility of producing a manual on procedure. It was argued in favour of such a manual that it would be of assistance to chairmen, but it was argued in opposition that it 'would be an interpretation of the rules of procedure that would limit a Chairman's freedom of action'.[48] The Committee made no recommendation. It also discussed the possibility of preparing a repertory of practice of the rules of procedure. The representative of the secretary-general pointed out that 'it would not be appropriate to ask the Secretariat to make a selection from

[45] Ways and Means for Making the Evidence of Customary International Law More Readily Available: Report of the Secretary-General, UN GAOR, 7th Session, Annexes, para. 102, UN Doc. A/2170.

[46] *Ibid.* at paras. 103, 106.

[47] W. R. Sharp, 'A Check List of Subjects for Systematic Study of International Conferences', 5 *UNESCO International Social Science Bulletin* 322 (1953 No. 2).

[48] Para. 338 of the Report of the Special Committee on the Rationalisation of the Procedures and Organisation of the General Assembly, UN GAOR, 26th Session, Supp. No. 26, UN Doc. A/8426 (1971).

among the various precedents'.[49] The committee decided that, in view of the lengthy nature and financial implications of the proposed repertory, it would not recommend such a project.[50]

In 1977, the UNGA began a review of the multilateral treaty-making process.[51] In 1980, the secretary-general produced a report on the subject that referred to the possibility of convening treaty-making conferences within the framework of the General Assembly.[52] A working group was formed[53] that proposed formulating model rules of procedure for treaty making within the framework of the UNGA. It also proposed that the model rules of procedure be practically identical with the rules of procedure of the General Assembly.[54] However, the proposal was not included in the final report of the Working Group issued in 1984[55], and there was no General Assembly endorsement of the proposal, nor does there appear to have been any follow-up to the proposal.[56] However, the 1994 UNGA instructed the Sixth Committee, when drafting a treaty,[57] to do so in accordance with rules of procedure of the UNGA subject to a few changes.[58] The resolution thereby clearly reflected the recommendations of the 1984 Working Group.

In 1980, the UNGA requested that the UN secretary-general propose draft standard rules of procedure for special conferences of the UN.[59] The Secretariat presented its report to the 1981 UNGA.[60] Although the draft

49 *Ibid.* at para. 343. 50 *Ibid.* at para. 344.

51 UN GAOR, 32nd Session, Agenda Item No. 124, UN Doc. A/32/143 (1977). The proposal was the initiative of Eli Lauterpacht, at the time the Australian representative to the Sixth Committee. UN GAOR, 6th Committee, 30th Session, 1541st Meeting, para. 16, UN Doc. A/C.6/30/SR.1541 (1975). The initiative was adopted by the UNGA in Resolution 34/402 of 21 September 1979.

52 UN Doc. A/35/312 and Add.1 and 2 and Add.2/Corr.1 (1980). The substance of the report was prepared by Paul Szasz.

53 Pursuant to UNGA Resolutions 36/112 of 10 December 1981 and 37/110 of 16 December 1982.

54 UN Doc. WG Working Paper No. 7/1983, reproduced in WG Report II, Annex, part B.

55 UN Doc. A/C.6/39/L.12 (1984).

56 The issue is analysed in Paul C. Szasz, 'Reforming the Multilateral Treaty-Making Process: An Opportunity Missed?' in *International Law at a Time of Perplexity, Essays in Honour of Shabtai Rosenne*, eds. Yoram Dinstein and Mala Tabory (1989), p. 932. The references to UN Working Papers are taken from the article.

57 Resolution calling for a study of the non-navigational uses of international watercourses, on the basis of the ILC draft. Annex to UNGA Resolution 49/52 of 9 December 1994.

58 The changes refer to the basic proposal, order of discussion, drafting committee and the need to attempt to reach consensus.

59 UNGA Resolution 35/10C of 3 November 1980.

60 Draft standard rules of procedure for United Nations Conferences, Report of the Secretary-General, UN Doc. A/36/199 and Corr. 1 (1981).

text prepared by the Secretariat does not state explicitly that it is a codification of practice, it does state that 'it has been found advisable to include certain additional details based on the actual practice of United Nations conferences and organs'.[61] The draft text was not limited to 'special' conferences, but was proposed to apply to all UN-convened conferences.[62] It is referred to hereinafter as the 'UN Model Rules'. The UNGA decided, a number of times, to defer consideration of the report.[63] Comments were received from a number of States and a revised draft was presented in 1982,[64] but again consideration of the report was deferred.[65] No action appears to have been taken on the subject by the General Assembly since 1985.

States have clearly shown a lack of enthusiasm about adopting the UN Model Rules. A study of the comments received shows that nearly all of the comments by States refer to the convening of conferences or to issues of participation. There is remarkably scant commentary on the provisions dealing with the conduct of business. It may be that no conclusion can be drawn from the silence of those States that refrained from making any comments. However, the fact that those States and organisations that did comment refrained, in near totality, from commenting on the provisions concerning the conduct of business may perhaps lead to the conclusion that those provisions are not controversial.

Other attempts at standardisation of rules of procedure include the ICAO 1967 model text of rules of procedure for 'Meetings in the Air Transport Field'[66] and the UN standard 'Rules of Procedure for United

[61] *Ibid.* at para. 2.

[62] Paul Szasz informed me that the UN Secretariat made the deliberate decision to ignore the wording of the UNGA Resolution, which referred only to 'special' conferences.

[63] UNGA Resolution 36/427 of 10 December 1981.

[64] Draft standard rules of procedure for United Nations conferences, Report of the Secretary-General, UN Doc. A/37/163 (1982); Draft standard rules of procedure for United Nations conferences, Report of the Secretary-General, Revisions to the draft proposal, UN Doc. A/C.6/37/5 (1982).

[65] UNGA Resolution 37/428 of 16 December 1982. The comments appear in Draft standard rules of procedure for United Nations conferences, Report of the Secretary-General, Addendum, UN Doc. A/38/298/Add. 1 and 2 (1983). UNGA Resolution 38/427 of 19 December 1983. Draft standard rules of procedure for United Nations conferences, Report of the Secretary-General, UN Doc. A/C.6/39/6 (1984), reported that no comments had been received. UNGA Resolution 34/419 of 13 December 1984. The comments are reported in Draft standard rules of procedure for United Nations conferences, Report of the Secretary-General, UN Doc. A/40/611 (1985); Addendum, UN Doc. A/40/611/Add.1 (1985).

[66] ICAO Doc. 8683 (1967), reprinted September 1985.

Nations Pledging Conferences'. As regards the latter, the use of standard rules has led to a considerable saving of time and effort, obviating the need for preparation and approval of rules of procedure each time anew.[67]

Although the UN Model Rules have not enjoyed explicit State support, their provisions, at least those regarding the rules of conducting business, broadly reflect State practice and have served as the basis for the rules of procedure for most diplomatic conferences convened since then.

[67] UN Doc. A/33/580 (1979), UN Sales No. E.79.I.17. Rule 1 states: 'These rules of procedure shall be applicable to all pledging conferences convened by the United Nations, except as otherwise decided by the organ under whose authority the Conference is convened.' They were in fact adopted by a 1995 non-pledging conference (International Meeting on Mine Clearance, Geneva, 5–7 July 1995, UN Doc. SG/CONF.7/4, para. 14 [1995]).

2

Adoption of Rules of Procedure

2.1 The Adoption of Conference Rules of Procedure

The principles behind the adoption, by conferences, of their rules of procedure have generated very little debate at conferences, nor have they generated much academic discussion. For example, Schermers simply states. 'The power to make its own rules of procedure is inherent in every organization',[1] though later in his study of the subject, he adds that rules of procedure 'must be followed as long as they have not expressly been amended. This requirement lends rules of procedure a special status.'[2] This absence of debate is remarkable as the issues involved touch on some fundamental principles of international law, including the process of formation of custom, treaty-making procedure and the role of tacit consent.

2.2 Independence of an International Conference

An international conference of plenipotentiaries, unless it is a subsidiary organ of an international organisation, is an independent body. 'No existing agency has the power to lay down rules of procedure or determine the competence and organisation of conferences in general.'[3] The Secretary-General of a conference convened by the League of Nations informed a delegation that '[a]ccording to the procedure followed at all conferences held under the auspices of the League of Nations, the Conference alone has sovereign powers; it may take whatever decisions it thinks fit'.[4] Rosenne

[1] Henry G. Schermers and Niels M. Blokker, *International Institutional Law, Unity within Diversity*, 5th rev. edn, p. 756 (2011).

[2] *Ibid.*, p. 760.

[3] F. S. Dunn, *The Practice and Procedure of International Conferences* (1929), p. 17. The book was written in 1929; thus the context is conferences convened by the League of Nations.

[4] The representative of the United States to the Conference for the Suppression of the Illicit Traffic in Dangerous Drugs, quoting the Secretary-General of the Conference, Records of the Conference for the Suppression of the Illicit Traffic in Dangerous Drugs (Geneva, 8–26 June 1936), Text of the Debates, LN Doc. C.341.M.216.1936.XI, p. 23.

writes, 'The experience of the Convention on the Status of Refugees suggests that a Resolution of the General Assembly, whatever its persuasive value, cannot bind an ad hoc diplomatic conference, which has an autonomous existence of its own and is, in the words of a representative of the Secretary-General, a 'sovereign body.'[5] A recent comment on this issue is that 'the relationship with the international organization does not prevent such conferences of disposing freely, and in an autonomous and final way, of the task entrusted to them'.[6]

This independence has not always been regarded as self-evident. In 1947, the UNGA requested the Secretary-General to prepare, in consultation with ECOSOC, draft rules for the convening of conferences.[7] The Secretary-General gave his opinion: 'Where a decision of the Council [ECOSOC] on a particular question can be regarded as a condition precedent to the decision to call the conference, such a decision, it seems, should bind the conference.'[8] The draft was prepared by the Secretary-General, approved by ECOSOC[9] and included a clause (Rule 11) that provided that decisions of the Council (ECOSOC) would be binding on all States and organisations attending the conference.[10] The Sixth Committee of the UNGA discussed the ECOSOC draft. The representatives of the United States and the United Kingdom, inter alia, supported the clause as to the binding nature on a conference of ECOSOC decisions. The US representative argued, 'If draft rule 11 were deleted, that would be tantamount to saying in the Charter and other documents that certain rules were to be laid down but that international conferences, for instance, could proceed to disregard them and do as they please.'[11] The representative continued, stating, 'There was nothing harmful in adopting draft rules of the type under discussion, which would be binding upon a State and consequently would limit its sovereignty.'[12]

France, which was among the States opposing the clause, commented that 'it would give the Council, a body of only eighteen out of the fifty-nine

[5] Shabtai Rosenne, 'United Nations Treaty Practice', 86 RCADI 281 (1954 II) at 320.

[6] Santiago Torres Bernárdez, 'The Organs of International Organizations', in *A Handbook of International Organizations*, ed. René-Jean Dupuy, 2nd edn (1998), p. 134.

[7] UNGA Resolution 173 (II) of 17 November 1947.

[8] ECOSOC, Seventh Session, Draft Rules for the Calling of International Conferences, Rule 'O', Comments, UN Doc. E/836 (1948).

[9] UN Doc. A/943 (1949), approved by ECOSOC Resolution 220 (VIII) of 2 March 1949.

[10] *Ibid.*, Rule 11.

[11] UN GAOR, 6th Committee, 4th Session, 194th Meeting, p. 350, para. 49, UN Doc. A/C.6/4/SR.194 (1949).

[12] *Ibid.* at para. 55.

Member States of the United Nations, absolute powers in all matters affecting conferences'.[13] The Argentine representative argued that 'sovereign States could not be bound by decisions of the Council'.[14] The representative of the USSR proposed deleting the clause,[15] arguing that 'it was contrary to all precedent to apply stringent restrictions to an international conference'.[16] The Soviet proposal was adopted, and the clause was omitted from the final text.[17]

At a very early UN-convened conference, the 1950 Conference on Missing Persons, a representative, speaking on a point of order, asked 'whether the Conference was entitled to depart from the terms of reference set forth in General Assembly Resolution 369 (IV)' (the resolution that had referred the draft convention to the UN members). The president ruled that 'the Conference could, if it wished, extend the application of the convention, but that it was not bound to do so by the provisions of Resolution 369 (IV)'.[18]

During the ILC discussions on the law of treaties, some jurists seemed to contend that, in theory, the UN could set preconditions for conferences it convened. Bartoš stated, 'It was a practice recognized in international law that the negotiators attending a conference had the right to propose or to accept in advance the conditions under which the conference would work: such rules were tacitly accepted by the participants.'[19] Sir Gerald Fitzmaurice, speaking as Special Rapporteur at the ILC discussion on the law of treaties, stated, 'On the other hand it could perhaps be held with equal force that the United Nations was not bound to convene any conference and that, if it did so, it could lay down certain conditions for the conduct of the proceedings.'[20]

Even though the overwhelming majority of conferences are now convened by the UN, there does not appear to have been a recent attempt to deny the independent nature of an international conference. However, the Secretary-General of the UN has defined the task of the UN Office of Legal Affairs as including 'preparing draft rules of procedure

[13] *Ibid.* at p. 349, para. 34. [14] *Ibid.* at para. 38. [15] UN Doc. A/C.6/L.72 (1949).

[16] UN GAOR, 6th Committee, 4th Session, 194th Meeting, p. 349, para. 46, UN Doc. A/C.6/4/SR.194 (1949).

[17] *Ibid.* at p. 352, para. 96.

[18] Summary Records of the 4th Meeting of the 1950 Conference on Declaration of Death of Missing Persons, para. 5, UN Doc. A/CONF.1/SR.4 (1950).

[19] *Ibid.*

[20] 488th Meeting, [1959] 1 YBILC 41, para. 55. See also Rosenne, 'United Nations Treaty Practice', at 320.

and advising United Nations organs and conferences on the conduct of business'.[21] Szasz points out that in UN-convened conferences the Secretariat and usually the premises are under the authority of the UN, and hence, in his opinion, the conference cannot in fact act in violation of a UNGA resolution or contradict instructions of the UN Secretary-General.[22]

2.3 Independent Right of Conferences to Adopt their Own Rules of Procedure

The UN Model Rules propose:

> *Rule 1*
>
> *Applicability of these rules*
>
> These rules of procedure shall be applicable to all conferences convened by the United Nations pursuant to a decision taken after 31 December –, unless the convening organ authorizes a conference to adopt its own rules of procedure or to the extent it otherwise prescribes.

In his commentary on the UN Model Rules, the Secretary-General states,

> The draft rules annexed hereto are so formulated that, if approved by the General Assembly, they will automatically govern all conferences hereafter convened by any organ of the United Nations, except to the extent otherwise specified by the convening organ.[23]

The Secretary-General provides no authority for this radical proposal except to state that the approach is similar 'to the approach taken in respect of United Nations pledging conferences'.[24]

The Ukrainian Soviet Socialist Republic commented on this draft article that

> the standard rules may serve simply as recommendations. It would be advisable to clarify in the draft rules the division of powers between the 'convening organ' and the 'United Nations Conference' and to establish the criteria and the extent to which the convening organ may predetermine the choice of rules of procedure of the conference. It would hardly be

[21] Secretary-General's Bulletin, Organization of the Office of Legal Affairs, UN Doc. ST/SGB/1997/8, 15 September 1997.
[22] The late Professor Paul Szasz in conversation with the author, 26 April 1996.
[23] Draft Standard Rules of Procedure for United Nations Conferences, Report of the Secretary-General, UN Doc. A/40/611, para. 9 (1985).
[24] *Ibid.* at note 7 to para. 9.

> appropriate to establish . . . that the standard rules take precedence over the rules of procedure adopted by each individual conference.[25]

The proposal of the UN Model Rules does not reflect existing practice. The practice is that, where a conference of plenipotentiaries is convened by the UN (or in the past by the League of Nations), the convening body prepares provisional rules of procedure.[26] The conference, although usually adopting the provisional rules as its own provisional rules, does this as an independent act of the conference and not by virtue of it being convened by the UN.[27] Dunn states that this was the rule for League of Nations conferences.[28]

[25] Draft Standard Rules of Procedure for United Nations Conferences, Report of the Secretary-General, Addendum, UN Doc. A/38/298/Add.1 (1983).

[26] At the 1950 Conference on Missing Persons, the Legal Adviser to the UN informed the Conference that 'the Secretariat had thought it advisable to prepare provisional rules of procedure'. UN Doc. A/CONF.1/SR.1, para. 18 (1950).

A UNGA Resolution approved draft rules for the calling of international conferences by ECOSOC (UNGA Resolution 366 (IV) of 3 December 1949). Rule 7 of the rules states:

> The Council:
> (a) Shall prepare, or request the Secretary-General to prepare, provisional rules of procedure for the conference.

[27] At the 1950 Conference on Missing Persons, the representative of Greece argued that as the Conference had been called by the UNGA, '[l]egally, therefore, it should observe the rules of procedure of the General Assembly' (UN Doc. A/CONF.1/SR/.1, para. 22 (1950)). There was no recorded support for this view. Sir Gerald Fitzmaurice, speaking as Special Rapporteur at the ILC discussion on the law of treaties, explained, 'For example, conferences convened by the United Nations did not automatically follow the rules of procedure of the General Assembly. The 1958 United Nations Conference on the Law of the Sea had adopted its own rules and, although they were similar to the voting procedure of the General Assembly, they might in theory have been different' (484th Meeting, [1959] 1 YBILC 25, paras. 37, 38). Fitzmaurice goes on to state that 'there was no provision in the Charter which laid down a voting rule for conferences held under the auspices of the United Nations' (488th Meeting, [1959] 1 YBILC 41, para. 49). He comments later that 'it was doubtful whether, for example, the United Nations, in the absence of any express provision in the Charter, was competent to lay down in advance obligatory voting rules for a conference which it convened' (*ibid.* at para. 55). He again states that 'everyone had agreed that the international conferences . . . would always have the right to adopt whatever voting rule they preferred' (*ibid.*, 490th Meeting, p. 47, para. 8).

Bartoš states, 'If an international organization convened a conference, the participating States were free to accept or not to accept the rules proposed by that organization' (*ibid.* at p. 44, para. 25).

Khoman was of the opinion that 'the question of the rules of procedure could be set aside and left to the decision of each international conference, on the principle that every independent organ was master of its own procedure. That was implicit in the Special Rapporteur's redraft for sub-paragraph (ii) that stated that 'unless the conference . . . decides to adopt another voting rule" (*ibid.* at p. 46, para. 52).

[28] Dunn, *The Practice*, p. 32.

The 1949 draft ECOSOC rules for convening international conferences referred to earlier contained a clause (Rule 6) stating that the ECOSOC Council could 'prescribe rules of procedure' for a conference.[29] This text was amended in the Sixth Committee of the UNGA[30] to read:

> *Rule 7*
>
> The Council:
>
> (a) Shall prepare, or request the Secretary-General to prepare, *provisional* rules of procedure for the conference.[31] [Emphasis added]

Sohn comments that the changes in Rule 6 and the deletion of Rule 11 from the ECOSOC rules for convening conferences 'confirm the autonomy of international conferences in deciding on their rules of procedure, and provide no guidelines as to the voting rules to be followed'.[32]

During the debate in the ILC on the law of treaties, Fitzmaurice commented that

> so far as the United Nations was concerned, whether or not it had the power to lay down an a priori rule for conferences convened by it, it had deliberately chosen, so to speak, not to exercise that power . . . the invariable practice had been to leave the matter to the decision of the Conference itself.[33]

Ago was of the opinion that 'a technical international organization such as the International Telecommunication Union might call an international conference on the basis of a pre-established voting rule, although the constitution of the organization was silent on the matter'.[34] Waldock pointed

29 UN Doc. A/943 (1949), approved by ECOSOC Resolution 220 (VIII) of 2 March 1949.

30 UN GAOR, 6th Committee, 4th Session, 197th Meeting, p. 369, para. 52, UN Doc. A/C.6/SR.197 (1949).

31 Report of the 6th Committee to the 4th Session of the UNGA, p. 204, Annex, Agenda Item 52, para. 23, UN Doc. A/1165. Approved by UNGA Resolution 366 (IV) of 3 December 1949.

32 Louis B. Sohn, 'Voting Procedures in United Nations Conferences for the Codification of International Law', 69 AJIL 310 (1975) at 317.

33 490th Meeting, [1959] 1 YBILC 48, para. 14.

34 *Ibid.* at p. 49, para. 20. Morgenstern writes that

> the Standing Orders of the World Employment Conference held in June 1975 were established by the Governing Body of the International Labour Office. The view was strongly expressed by some that the accredited representatives of member States meeting in a conference had an inherent power to determine and alter rules of procedure. In practice, however, one particular contentious point was reviewed by the Governing Body itself.

Felice Morgenstern, 'Legality in International Organizations', 48 BYIL 241 (1976–7) at 252.

out that the UN Secretary-General prepares draft provisional rules of procedure for conferences, but 'it is left to the conference to decide whether to adopt the suggested rule or replace it by another'.[35]

During the Third Law of the Sea Conference, the President of the Conference proposed that the Conference apply the UNGA rules of procedure prior to the adoption of its own rules of procedure. The representative of Japan pointed out that 'the rules of procedure of the General Assembly should be applicable within the Conference only to the extent that, and in cases where, the Conference agreed to that procedure on a case by case basis'.[36] The delegate of France stated, in a similar vein, that 'the Assembly rules were being applied by consensus, and if there was any objection to the application of any rule, it would not be applied'.[37] The Special Representative of the Secretary-General to the Third Law of the Sea Conference (the then-Legal Counsel of the UN, Mr Stavropoulos), when commenting on this question, did not attempt to claim that there was any obligation to apply the UN's rules of procedure to the Conference. Mr Stavropoulos said that all past international conferences had applied the rules of procedure of the General Assembly pending the adoption of their own rules, usually as the fourth item of their agenda. A number of the Assembly rules were obviously not applicable to the Conference, and the President had made it clear that the Conference would be governed only by the applicable rules.[38]

In 1980, the ILC submitted to the UN Secretary-General comments on the review of the multilateral treaty-making process. In these comments the ILC remarked, 'Each United Nations codification conference ... approves its own rules of procedure.'[39] In the 1988 UN Convention against Illicit Traffic in Narcotic Drugs and Psychotropic Substances, the President of the Conference commented that 'the Conference, according to international law and State practice, enjoyed a collective form of sovereignty, whereby it was free to decide its own procedure'.[40]

Szasz is of the opinion that the UN has the authority to establish rules of procedure for conferences that it convenes, although in practice the UN

[35] First report on the law of treaties, by Sir Humphrey Waldock, Special Rapporteur, [1962] 2 YBILC 41, UN Doc. A/CN.4/144 (1962).

[36] Official Records of the Third Law of the Sea Conference, vol. I, p. 13, Summary Records of the 5th Plenary Meeting, para. 18, UN Doc. A/CONF.62 (1973).

[37] *Ibid.* at p. 15, para. 41. [38] *Ibid.* at p. 13, para. 54.

[39] Review of the Multilateral Treaty-Making Process, Report of the Secretary-General, Addendum 1, Observations of the International Law Commission, para. 95, UN Doc. A/35/312/Add.2 (1980).

[40] UN Doc. E/CONF.82/SR/6, p. 5, para. 32.

delegates most of its authority in this respect to the conference.[41] Szasz further points out that where the UN has failed to establish rules for the three major issues of composition, decision making and terms of reference, this has led to paralysis and delay.[42] It appears to this author, however, that this cannot be a general rule for it is not applicable in the, admittedly few, cases where conferences are convened by a State and not by the UN. It would appear therefore that a conference of plenipotentiaries may override any preset conditions regarding rules of procedure.

Within the UN Organisation it is the Office of Legal Affairs that has the task of preparing draft rules of procedure and advising United Nations organs and conferences on the conduct of business.

2.4 Majority Required to Approve Rules of Procedure

Conferences usually adopt their rules of procedure by acclamation, with votes normally being conducted only on proposals to amend specific rules. The question of what majority is required to adopt rules of procedure thus rarely arises. Since the invariable rule in conferences is that procedural issues are decided by a simple majority,[43] it could thus be argued that the majority required for adoption of rules of procedure, as in other procedural issues, should be a simple majority. Since rules of procedure usually include rules stipulating that a two-thirds majority is required for certain decisions,[44] the result is that a simple majority of States attending a conference enacts rules stipulating the need for a two-thirds majority on certain issues. This becomes an anomaly where the rules of procedure, adopted by a simple majority, stipulate that they can only be amended by a two-thirds majority.[45]

The issue of the majority required for approval of rules of procedure came up for discussion at the ILC, in the context of the discussions on the codification of the law of treaties. The Special Rapporteur, Sir Gerald Fitzmaurice, pointed out, regarding States voting against the rules of procedure, that 'those who had voted against them would, by continuing to participate in the conference, have tacitly consented to the procedure that had prevailed, and that acquiescence could be considered as "common consent"'.[46]

[41] In a conversation with the author, 22 April 1996. [42] *Ibid.*
[43] With the exception of motions for reconsideration.
[44] For example, reconsideration of a decision. [45] See Chapter 21.
[46] [1959] 1 YBILC 21, para. 58.

Verdross stated, 'Any international conference which was not governed by the constitution of an international organization could be convened only by agreement among *all* the participating States. Logically, therefore, the rules of procedure of such a conference would also require the agreement of *all* the participating States.'[47] Verdross, however, acknowledged the practice that 'the rules of procedure were adopted by a majority vote . . . any participating State was free not to accept them and to withdraw from the conference before the actual proceedings began'.[48]

The discussions in this respect in the ILC centred not so much on the adoption of rules of procedure in general but on the question of what majority was required to decide the voting rule for adoption of a text. The 1959 session of the ILC proposed the following article:

> *Article 6(4)*
>
> The adoption of the text takes place as follows:
>
> (c) In the case of multilateral treaties negotiated at an international conference . . . by such voting rule as the Conference may, by a simple majority, decide to adopt.[49]

The ILC commentary stated that there 'was general agreement that the rule of the simple majority as the basis of the adoption by the conference of its rules of procedure, including its *substantive* voting rule, was the only practicable one'.[50]

Waldock, in his first report, maintained the Commission's 1959 draft text with minor drafting changes.[51] During its 1962 session the ILC however changed this text to read:

> *Article 5*
>
> (a) In the case of a treaty drawn up at an international conference convened by the states concerned . . . by the vote of *two-thirds of the states participating in the conference* unless by the same majority they shall decide to adopt another voting rule.[52] [Emphasis added]

[47] Verdross, 'ILC Discussion on the Law of Treaties', [1959] 1 YBILC 45, para. 32.

[48] *Ibid.* at p. 25, para. 31.

[49] Report of the ILC to the UNGA covering the work of its Eleventh Session, [1959] 2 YBILC 100, UN Doc. A/4169 (1959).

[50] *Ibid.* at p. 100. [emphasis in original]

[51] First report on the law of treaties, by Sir Humphrey Waldock, Special Rapporteur, [1962] 2 YBILC 39, UN Doc. A/CN.4/144 (1962).

[52] Report of the ILC to the UNGA covering the work of its Fourteenth Session, [1962] 2 YBILC 166, UN Doc. A/CN.4/144 (1962).

The ILC commentary explains, 'The rule in sub-paragraph (a) takes account of the interest of minorities to the extent of requiring at least two-thirds of the States to be in favour of proceeding by simple majorities before recourse can be had to simple majority votes for adopting the text of a treaty.'[53]

The Secretary-General commented on Article 8(2) of a later draft, substantially identical to Article 5(a) presented earlier,[54] that 'para. 2 of Article 8 is not in accordance with the practice of United Nations conferences, under which the adoption and amendment of the rules of procedure, including the rules relating to voting, normally take place by a simple majority of representatives present and voting'.[55] At the 1969 Vienna Conference on the Law of Treaties, the representative of the Secretary-General – the Legal Adviser, Mr Stavropoulos – commented that 'the rules of procedure of conferences were adopted by a simple majority because, under the United Nations Charter, decisions on procedural matters were normally adopted by a simple majority, and that rule had been automatically extended to United Nations conferences'.[56] Notwithstanding the comments by the Secretary-General of the UN and his representative, the final text of the Vienna Convention on the Law of Treaties reads:

Article 9

1. The adoption of the text of a treaty takes place by the consent of all the States participating in its drawing up except as provided in paragraph 2.
2. The adoption of the text of a treaty of an international conference takes place *by the vote of two-thirds of the States present and voting, unless by the same majority they shall decide to apply a different rule*. [Emphasis added]

Sohn comments on this clause that its adoption was due to the need to safeguard the sovereignty of States against imposition of a voting rule that a large number of them might dislike; the general feeling that the voting rule is more substantive than procedural; and the desire for an 'elegant'

[53] *Ibid.* at p. 167, para. 5.

[54] Report of the ILC to the UNGA on the work of the second part of its Seventeenth Session, [1966] 2 YBILC 194, UN Doc. A/6309/Rev.1 (1966).

[55] Comments on the final draft articles on the law of treaties, prepared by the ILC at its Eighteenth Session, Report of the Secretary-General, UN GAOR, 22nd Session, Annexes, Agenda Item 86 at p. 14, UN Doc. A/6827 (1967).

[56] Official Records of the 1969 Vienna Conference on the Law of Treaties – 2nd Session, Committee of the Whole, 84th Meeting, p. 217, para. 43 (1970).

solution, providing parallel rules for both voting questions that might be faced by a conference.[57]

The issue of the majority required for adopting rules of procedure arose at the Third Law of the Sea Conference. The representative of Venezuela remarked that 'an effort should be made to reach a consensus on the draft rules of procedure. However, if it proved impossible to reach a consensus, a vote would have to be taken by a simple majority.'[58] The President, basing himself on UNGA procedure, confirmed that matters of procedure are decided by a simple majority.[59] The representative of Australia submitted that 'the adoption of the rules of procedure was a very important matter requiring, under Rule 85 of the Rules of Procedure of the [UN] General Assembly, a two-thirds majority'.[60] The US representative argued, 'It would be a very unfortunate beginning for the Conference if rules of procedure concerning such fundamentally important questions as that of the decision-making process were adopted by a simple majority.'[61] After further discussion, the Conference adopted an Argentinian proposal, amended by Kenya, by which

> the rules of procedure of the [UN] General Assembly should be applied to the adoption of the rules of procedure of the Conference, it being understood that their adoption would be by a decision taken by a simple majority, unless the Conference decided that it constituted an important question requiring a decision by a two-thirds majority.[62]

In the event, the Third Law of the Sea Conference adopted its rules of procedure by consensus.[63]

COMMENT

As stated earlier, Article 9(2) of the 1969 Vienna Convention on the Law of Treaties stipulates:

> The adoption of the text of a treaty of an international conference takes place by the vote of two-thirds of the States present and voting, unless by the same majority they shall decide to apply a different rule.

[57] Sohn, 'Voting Procedures in UN Conferences', at 332.

[58] Official Records of the Third UN Conference on the Law of the Sea, vol. I, p. 27, Summary Records of the 9th Plenary Meeting, para. 56, UN Doc. A/CONF.62 (1973).

[59] *Ibid.*, vol. I, p. 31, Summary Records of the 13th Plenary Meeting, para. 11.

[60] *Ibid.*, vol. I, p. 31, Summary Records of the 13th Plenary Meeting, para. 16.

[61] *Ibid.*, vol. I, p. 26, Summary Records of the 9th Plenary Meeting, para. 43.

[62] *Ibid.*, vol. I, p. 32, Summary Records of the 13th Plenary Meeting, para. 30.

[63] *Ibid.*, vol. I, p. 58, Summary Records of the 20th Plenary Meeting, para. 85.

Ostensibly this rule does not apply to the adoption or changing of other stipulations of the rules of procedure nor to rules of procedure of non-treaty-making conferences. Nevertheless, since nearly all rules of procedure contain stipulations as to a two-thirds majority for certain decisions (for example, reconsideration), it is submitted that it would be logical to require that all rules of procedure, if not adopted by acclamation, need a two-thirds majority for their adoption.

3

Rules of Procedure and International Law

3.1 The Obligation of States Attending a Conference to Comply with the Rules of Procedure of that Conference

States attending international conferences apparently accept as axiomatic the requirement to comply with the conference rules of procedure. A State not wishing to abide by the rules of procedure has the option of not attending the conference. As a practical matter, a State would be in an intolerable situation if it chose to attend a conference, but flouted its rules of procedure.

There is a question, however, of whether such compliance, apart from being necessary on a practical level, is also obligatory under international law. For example, would it be a violation of international law if, after the conclusion of a conference, a State flagrantly decided to publish the records of a closed session or of a vote in a secret ballot?

In regard to the obligatory nature of rules of procedure, there is a distinct difference between the assemblies of international organisations and independent international conferences.

3.1.1 Obligation of States to Comply with the Rules of Procedure of an Assembly of an International Organisation

In an assembly that is a subsidiary body of an international organisation,[1] the source of a State's obligation to abide by rules of procedure is the law

[1] For definition and evolution of the phrase 'international organisation', see Abdullah El-Erian, 'First Report by Special Rapporteur to the International Law Commission on "Relations between States and Inter-Governmental Organizations"', [1963 II] 2 YBILC 159 at 162 (UN Doc. A/CN.4/161 and Add.1); Ingrid Detter, *Law Making by International Organizations* (1965), p. 19.

of treaties.[2] The statute, constitution or charter of an organisation is a treaty, although a treaty of a special type,[3] and States members of such an organisation are bound, under international treaty law, to comply with the provisions of such statute, constitution or charter. Furthermore, international organisations are independent entities possessing the implicit authority to draw up their rules of procedure[4] and some writers see the enactment of such rules of procedure as international legislation.[5] Skubiszewski refers to rules of procedure as 'the oldest law originating in international organization'.[6] Schaefer writes, 'The frequent disputes among member States [of the UN] about the interpretation of certain rules, in particular in the political organs of the GA, indicate the opinion of member states that the Rules of Procedure contain legal norms which have to be respected.'[7] And in a later edition of the same book, Fitschen writes that the rules of procedure 'have legal character inasmuch as they bind the members participating in the proceedings of the GA'[8]

2 See Gerald Fitzmaurice, 'Report to the International Law Commission on the "Law of Treaties"', G. G. Fitzmaurice, Special Rapporteur, 'Draft Text of Articles of Code' [1956 II] 2 YBILC 108 (A/CN.4/101) Article 3; Philippe Cahier, 'L'ordre juridique interne des organisations internationales', in *A Handbook on International Organizations*, ed. René-Jean Dupuy (1988) p. 244; Joël Rideau, *Juridictions internationales et contrôle du respect des traités constitutifs des organisations internationales* (1969) pp. 33–4; Rudolph Bernhardt, 'International Organizations. Internal Law and Rules', in *Encyclopedia of Public International Law*, ed. Rudolph Bernhardt, vol. V (1983), p. 142.

3 Rosenne points out the differences between regular multilateral treaties and the constituent instruments of international organisations: see Shabtai Rosenne, *Developments in the Law of Treaties 1945–1986* (1989) p. 181; see also Detter, *Law Making*, p. 54.

4 See *Reparation for Injuries Suffered in the Service of the United Nations*, Advisory Opinion of 11 April 1949, 1949 ICJ Reports, p. 174; *Certain Expenses of the United Nations (Article 17, paragraph 2 of the Charter)*, Advisory Opinion of 20 July 1962, 1962 ICJ Reports, p. 151.

5 Philip C. Jessup, 'Parliamentary Diplomacy, An Examination of the Legal Quality of the Rules of Procedure of Organs of the United Nations', 89 *RCADI* 181 (1956 I) at 204; Hans Kelsen, *The Law of the United Nations, A Critical Analysis of Its Fundamental Problems* (1951, 6th printing 1966) p. 194; H. Waldock, 'General Course in Public International Law', 106 RCADI 100 (1962 II); Rosalyn Higgins, *The Development of International Law through the Political Organs of the United Nations* (1963) p. 4; Henry G. Schermers and Niels M. Blokker, *International Institutional Law, Unity within Diversity*, 5th rev. edn, (2011).

6 Krzysztof Skubiszewski, 'Enactment of Law by International Organizations', 41 BYIL 198 (1965–66) at 226.

7 Michael Schaefer, 'Article 21', in *The Charter of the United Nations, A Commentary*, ed. Bruno Simma (1994), p. 361 at p. 362.

8 Thomas Fitschen, 'Article 21', in *The Charter of the United Nations, A Commentary*, ed. Bruno Simma *et al*, 3rd edn (2012), p. 690.

Other writers see the obligation to comply with rules of procedure of organisations as deriving from customary law.[9]

3.1.2 *Obligation of States at an International Conference to Comply with the Rules of Procedure Adopted at that Conference*

States attending an international conference are bound by the rules of procedure of the conference. Morgenstern writes, 'Rules of Procedure are the "rules of the game". It is normal, in games, for these rules not to be changed in the middle of a match.'[10] A State that is dissatisfied with a rule of procedure may propose to the conference that it change the rules. A State may decide to leave the conference in protest at the adoption of certain rules of procedure or their application.[11] However, for as long as a State participates in the conference, it is bound by the rules of procedure, although it may have voted against adopting some or all of the rules. Scelle wrote in 1953 that the rules of procedure of an international conference 'may be regarded as the first expression of an international legislative power, since they are imposed on the minority'.[12] One recent writer, however, is of the opinion that rules of procedure are 'social (professional) norms' or 'instrumental rules' which may not be 'a legal obligation' and that terms used in rules of procedure 'derive their full meaning from the context in which they are used and from practices concerning them'; the issue thus is 'less a question of *obligation* than of *meaning and implication*'.[13] The present author, however, is of the opinion that there is a legal obligation to comply with rules of procedure of conferences and that there appear to be five possible sources for such obligation. The possible sources examined

[9] Cahier writes that 'il est possible aujourd'hui d'affirmer qu'il existe en droit international une règle coutumière qui accorde aux organisations internationales un pouvoir général d'établir des règles nécessaires à leur fonctionnement interne', and furthermore 'la *coutume* peut être une source de l'ordre juridique interne des organisations internationales'. Cahier, 'L'ordre juridique', p. 249.

[10] Felice Morgenstern, 'Legality in International Organizations', 48 BYIL 241 (1976–77) at 251.

[11] During the ILC discussion on the law of treaties, at its 489th Meeting, Bartoš stated that 'in any case it was open to the dissenting minority to withdraw from a conference which had approved rules [of procedure] by a majority decision'. [1959] 1 YBILC 44, para. 25.

[12] Georges Scelle, 'The Evolution of International Conferences', 5 *UNESCO International Social Science Bulletin* 241 (1953 No. 2) at 247.

[13] Maurice Mendelson, 'Book Review, "Robbie Sabel, Procedure at International Conferences"', 10 *European Journal of International Law* 478 (1999). [emphasis in original]

are treaty, voting, tacit consent, general principles of law and customary international law.

3.1.2.1 Do Rules of Procedure at a Conference Constitute a Multilateral Treaty?

Where the conference is not a subsidiary body of an international organisation no umbrella treaty exists as a source of authority for rules of procedure.[14]

One possible source of authority could be that the rules of procedure of each conference constitute in themselves a multilateral treaty valid for the duration of the conference. Rules of procedure do not come within the usual format of an international agreement, but this does not necessarily imply that they cannot constitute a binding agreement.[15] The hypothesis that rules of procedure are multilateral treaties encounters, however, several difficulties, in that rules of procedure of a conference:

Do not state that they are an agreement or a treaty;
Do not have the form or structure of a treaty;
Come into effect by voting and not by signature or ratification;
Can be amended by a vote;
Are not given to reservations, although no mention of this issue is to be found in them;
Bind all States attending a conference, including States that were not present when the rules were adopted, and furthermore bind a State that may have voted against their adoption;[16]
Are not regarded by States as treaties in that they are not registered with the UN under Article 102 of the UN Charter, nor do they appear in national registers of treaties in force;

[14] See William L. Tung, *International Organization under the United Nations System* (1969) p. 98.

[15] The Vienna Convention on the Law of Treaties:

> *Article 2 (1)(a)*
>
> 'treaty' means an international agreement . . . whatever its particular designation.
>
> *Article 3*
>
> The fact that the present Convention does not apply . . . to international agreements not in written form, shall not affect:
>
> (a) the legal force of such agreements.

[16] Jessup comments, 'No Member of the United Nations has ever maintained that it was not bound by a rule of procedure because it had voted against its adoption.' Jessup, 'Parliamentary Diplomacy', p. 203.

In addition, States that have constitutional requirements for entering into international obligations do not apply these requirements to rules of procedure of conferences.

No State acts as depository.

It thus seems difficult to treat rules of procedure of a conference as constituting an international agreement.

3.1.2.2 Can Voting for a Resolution Be Considered as a Legal Commitment to Comply with the Resolution?

Some authorities view approval of certain resolutions as akin to adopting an agreement.[17] Lachs wrote that although UN Resolutions

> with some exceptions . . . cannot be viewed as creative of legal rights or obligations[18] [however] almost all Members of the United Nations attached to it [the UN Declaration on the Law of Outer Space[19]] an importance similar to that resulting from a legally binding instrument, assimilating it, as it were, to the latter. Thus, by expressing their will to be bound by the provisions of the document in question, they consented so to be bound, and there is no reason why they should not be held to it, for their intention seems to be clear, the question of form ceases to be of essence.[20]

Castañeda writes, 'There is no legal reason why a vote in an international organ cannot be, *in principle*, an equally licit and effective way of expressing consent to an agreement, when the circumstances in which it is cast prove that the vote is a clear manifestation of the wish to be bound.'[21] Castañeda, however, adds that the 'multilateral executive agreement does not yet constitute a legal category or phenomenon generally accepted in the theory and practice of an international organization'.[22]

There does not appear to be State practice supporting such a theory of 'multilateral executive agreements'. An executive agreement comes within the definition of a treaty in the 1969 Vienna Convention on the Law of Treaties. Many States have simplified legislative requirements for approval of executive agreements, but nevertheless require

17 This issue differs from the theory that some UNGA resolutions may be of binding character.

18 Manfred Lachs, 'The International Law of Outer Space', 113 RCADI 1 (1961 III) at 96.

19 '1963 United Nations General Assembly Declaration of Legal Principles Governing the Activities of States in the Exploration and Use of Outer Space' (Resolution 1962 (XVIII) of 13 December 1963).

20 Lachs, 'The International Law', p. 98.

21 Jorge Castañeda, *Legal Effects of United Nations Resolutions* (1969), p. 153.

22 *Ibid.* at p. 160.

formal approval procedures that go beyond voting at an international conference.[23] Furthermore, the assumption is that States are bound to comply with the rules of procedure even if they voted against them, abstained, were absent during the vote, or joined a conference after the rules of procedure had already been approved.

3.1.2.3 Does Tacit Consent Constitute the Basis of the Obligation to Comply with Rules of Procedure?

A State attending a conference undeniably consents tacitly to abide by the rules of procedure of the conference. The State always has the option of leaving a conference, and by continuing to participate, the State implies that it accepts the 'rules of the game'. Regarding States voting against the rules of procedure, Fitzmaurice points out that 'those who had voted against them would, by continuing to participate in the conference, have tacitly consented to the procedure that had prevailed, and that acquiescence could be considered as "common consent"'.[24] Detter quotes Bartoš as authority for stating, 'States who agree to remain at the international conference obviously [give] a sort of implied consent to the adoption of the Rules in question. In this way, the rule of unanimity would always prevail, although in a disguised manner.'[25] In a footnote, Detter adds, 'With the theory of tacit consent it would be possible to find common consent in all cases: if States stay on in a conference after a majority decision they thereby give their implied consent.'[26] Tunkin refers to 'acquiescence' by States in regard to acceptance of rules of procedure.[27] Common sense seems to support the thesis that there is such acquiescence or tacit consent to be bound by the rules of procedure. Furthermore, tacit consent or acquiescence may be relevant in determining the existence of custom or may serve as a procedural 'estoppel'. Nevertheless, international law does not, it is submitted, recognise mere tacit consent or acquiescence by a State as a source of obligation in international law. Although international lawyers of the *positivist* school regard consent as basic to all international obligations, Brierly is, it is submitted, correct when he states that 'consent cannot of itself create an obligation; it can do so only within a system of law which declares that consent duly given, as in a treaty or a contract, will be binding on

[23] See generally Thomas Buergenthal, 'Self-Executing and Non-Self-Executing Treaties in National and International Law', 235 RCADI 303 (1992 IV).

[24] 483rd Meeting of the ILC, [1959] 1 YBILC 21, para. 58.

[25] Detter, *Law Making*, p. 53. [26] *Ibid.*

[27] ILC discussion on the law of treaties, [1959] 1 YBILC 25, para. 35.

the party consenting.'[28] The conservative international lawyer, in seeking to determine a source of obligation, must conduct his[29] search in accordance with the list of sources enumerated in Article 38(1) of the Statute of the International Court of Justice.[30] Tacit consent does not appear in that list.

3.1.2.4 Are General Principles of Law the Source of Authority for the Obligation of States to Comply with Rules of Procedure?

Certain procedural rights of delegations may well be so basic and fundamental that they should be considered as general principles of law. There does not, however, appear to be clear authority for such a statement.

Morgenstern comments, 'It has been suggested in recent years that international organizations have an obligation to comply with certain basic, generally accepted principles of law.' She concludes, however, by stating that '[p]erhaps the most that can be said at this stage is that various organizations have indeed adopted texts which raise the issue of due process.'[31]

Jessup writes, 'When one turns to the ordinary rules guiding proceedings in debate, one finds in all parliamentary bodies sufficient similarities to induce the adoption of such expressions as "the general principles of parliamentary law."'[32] Referring to the discussion in the UN on the report on correction of votes, Jessup comments. 'This report and the discussions

[28] Andrew Clapham, ed, *Brierly's Law of Nations*, 7th edn (2012), p. 51.

[29] Whenever 'he' is used, the intention of course is to refer either to 'he' or 'she'.

[30] Article 38(1) of the Statute of the International Court of Justice:

1. The Court, whose function is to decide in accordance with international law such disputes as are submitted to it, shall apply:
   a. international conventions, whether general or particular, establishing rules expressly recognized by the contesting states.
   b. international custom, as evidence of a general practice accepted as law.
   c. the general principles of law recognized by civilized nations.

The categorisation into the three sources referred to in Article 38(1) of the Statute of the ICJ follows conservative legal thinking.

McWhinney criticises such conservatism and writes, 'When ordinary common sense and the will of the parties coincide, why should the court stand in the way of recognition and acceptance of that fact in legal terms by doctrinaire judicial insistence on continued deference to abstract legal formalism and the positivists' closed categories of formal sources of principles and rules of international law?' Edward McWhinney, *United Nations Law Making* (1984), p. 44.

[31] Morgenstern, 'Legality', p. 253.

[32] Jessup, 'Parliamentary Diplomacy', p. 220.

lend some support to the idea that there are "general principles of parliamentary law."'[33]

Regarding specific rules of procedure, it may be that a rule could be considered a general principle of law where it is common to most parliamentary-type organisations throughout the world[34] or of a nature essential to allow States to express their opinions and participate in deliberations at international conferences.

It is submitted that 'rules of procedure which suppress or seriously restrict the right of an individual State to express its opinion and present its proposals'[35] would be a violation of the general principles of law. It is further believed that the principles of those rules of procedure that set out the rights of delegations to make statements, present amendments and move motions may well be considered as general principles of law. Schermers writes that the rules on the order of voting are 'so widely used that they may be seen as general principles of international institutional law, which means that they must be applied even in meetings which have no rules of procedure'.[36]

3.1.2.5 Customary International Law as the Source of Authority for the Obligation of States to Comply with Rules of Procedure

A possible source of authority for an obligation of States to comply with rules of procedure is customary international law. It would be logical to assume that there is a customary rule to the effect that States attending conferences are bound by the rules of procedure for so long as they attend a conference, even if they were not party to the adoption of the rules. There is, however, a dearth of scholastic or judicial authority for such an assumption.

[33] *Ibid.* at p. 225.

[34] Jessup writes, 'Because the discussions are carried on under the fixed rules of procedure which in many respects are analogous to the rules of parliamentary law which govern the debates of most national legislative or parliamentary bodies, the adjective "parliamentary" is descriptive and appropriate.' *Ibid.* at p. 186.

[35] The wording is taken from Conforti's statement that 'we must consider as conflicting with the Charter, first of all, those violations of the rules of procedure which suppress or seriously restrict the right of the individual state to express its opinion and present its proposals'. Benedetto Conforti, 'The Legal Effect of Non-Compliance with Rules of Procedure in the UN General Assembly and Security Council', 63 AJIL 479 (1969) at 485.

[36] Henry G. Schermers, 'The Chairman of an International Organ', 34 *German Year Book of International Law* 296 (1991).

Customary international law[37] has generated a great deal of academic scholarship[38] and jurists find in it many uncertainties.[39] It is, however, clearly part of modern international law[40] and Article 38(1)(b) of the Statute of the International Court of Justice enjoins the Court to apply 'international custom, as evidence of a general practice accepted as law'.[41] Custom[42] is generally accepted as comprising State practice[43] and *opinio juris*. Legal authorities tend to commence any examination of the element of 'State practice' by distinguishing it from usage. State practice that clearly

[37] Kunz defines custom as 'a procedure for the creation of norms of general international law'. Josef L. Kunz, *The Changing Law of Nations* (1968) p. 338. Wolfke distinguishes between 'customary rule' or 'international custom', which he defines as the 'ought' aspect and 'custom', which he considers the 'is' or 'practice' element. Karol Wolfke, *Custom in Present International Law*, 2nd edn (1993) p. xx. O'Connell, however, reaches a different conclusion. He writes, 'The word "custom" stands for the proposition that the practice is actually productive of law' and 'Perhaps it may be said that "practice" is evidence of the act of creation, "custom" is the result.' D. P. O'Connell, *International Law*, 2nd edn, vol. I (1970) p. 9.

In the present study, to prevent ambiguity, as far as possible I refrain from using the word 'custom' and use either customary international law or customary rule as denoting both elements, namely the 'ought' and the 'is'.

[38] Of recent scholarship see in particular three books: G. M. Danilenko, *Law Making in the International Community* (1993); Mark E. Villiger, *Customary International Law and Treaties* (1985); Wolfke, *Custom*.

[39] Kelsen refers to the fact that 'the customary process in international law is one characterized by many uncertainties'. Hans Kelsen, *Principles of International Law*, 2nd rev. edn, ed. Robert W. Tucker (1966), p. 448. Other writers comment in a similar vein. See, e.g., Sir Hersch Lauterpacht, *The Development of International Law by the International Court*, rev. edn (1958) p. 390; Anthony A. D'Amato, *The Concept of Custom in International Law* (1971), p. 5; Wolfke, *Custom*, p. xiv.

[40] 'It [the ICJ] relies on customary international law constantly and as a matter of course – a fact which explains the inconspicuous character of the process.' Lauterpacht, *The Development*, p. 392.

[41] This definition has been subject to much criticism on the ground that one would expect a practice to be evidence of a custom and not vice versa. It has been argued that since customary international law is binding international law, it makes little sense and is tautologous to state that it is evidence of a practice accepted as law. See: Danilenko, *Law Making*, p. 76; Georg M. Schwarzenberger, *International Law*, 3rd edn, vol. I (1957), p. 39; Michel Virally, 'The Sources of International Law', in *Manual of Public International Law*, ed. Max Sørensen (1968), p. 130; Wolfke, *Custom*, p. 8; *Oppenheim's International Law*, eds. R. Jennings and A. Watts, 9th edn, vol. I (1992) p. 26; H. W. A. Thirlway, *International Customary Law and Codification* (1972), p. 47.

[42] There is a great deal of discussion among jurists as to the place of custom as a 'source' of international law, but I believe a discussion of the issue of sources of international law would be beyond the scope of this study. Kelsen's comment on this issue is that it is 'a figurative and highly ambiguous expression'. Kelsen, *Principles*, p. 437.

[43] '[T]he practice of states; that is to say, we must look at what states do in their relations with one another.' Clapham, *Brierly's Law of Nations*, p. 59.

has no legal significance is described as 'mere habit or usage'.[44] In international conferences the issue is described by one expert:

> Thus if over a long period of time, international conferences were consistently opened by three taps with a gavel, no one would be able to seek legal redress if a particular conference were opened by the ringing of a bell. For it is not apparent that anyone would be inconvenienced or damaged by this change. On the other hand if we suppose that over the same period of time the practice were universally followed of transacting business in plenary sessions only when a quorum were present, there might be room to claim custom.[45]

State practice must be accompanied by *opinio juris*,[46] namely, State practice should have occurred in a way that shows a general recognition that a rule of law or legal obligation is involved. The ICJ definition in the *North Sea Continental Shelf Cases* of *opinio juris* as 'a general recognition that a rule of law or legal obligation is involved'[47] reflects a broad consensus among authorities and writers.[48]

The present author shares Prosper Weil's apprehension that 'the degree of generality required of a practice, to enable it to serve as the basis of a customary rule, has been steadily diminished . . . The result is a danger of imposing more and more customary rules on more and more States, even against their clearly expressed will.'[49] Notwithstanding this caveat, it is relevant to point out that States have been consistently complying with rules of procedure of international conferences for nearly a hundred years. The question then arises as to whether there is *opinio juris* accompanying

44 *Ibid.*

45 F. S. Dunn, *The Practice and Procedure of International Conferences* (1929), p. 20.

46 Or, in full, *opinio juris sive necessitatis*, translated in James Fox, *Dictionary of International and Comparative Law* (1992), as 'opinion that an act is necessary by rule of law'.

47 *North Sea Continental Shelf Cases (Federal Republic of Germany/Denmark; Federal Republic of Germany/Netherlands)*, 1969 ICJ Reports, p. 43.

48 *The Lotus Case*, PCIJ (1927) Series A, No. 10, pp. 18, 28; *Asylum Case (Colombia/Peru)*, 1950 ICJ Reports, p. 276: quoted with approval in the *Morocco Case*, 1952 ICJ Reports, p. 200; *North Sea Continental Shelf Cases*, 1969 ICJ Reports, p. 44; *Case Concerning Military and Paramilitary Activities in and Against Nicaragua (Nicaragua v. USA)* (Merits), 1986 ICJ Reports, pp. 97–98.

See also Bin Cheng, 'Epilogue on the Nature and Sources of International Law', in *International Law: Treaty and Practice*, ed. Bin Cheng (1982), p. 223; O'Connell, *International Law*, p. 6; 'The Restatement (Third) of the Foreign Relations Law of the United States', Art. 102(2).

49 Prosper Weil, 'Towards Relative Normativity in International Law', 77 AJIL 413 (1983) at 435.

such State practice. The innumerable occasions when delegates at conferences call upon other delegations to abide by the rules of procedure would appear to be ample manifestations of the acceptance of *opinio juris* in this regard. It is submitted that the State practice of complying with rules of procedure at international conferences fulfils the criteria for *opinio juris*. There is the element of 'obligation' referred to by the ICJ and most authorities. It has the 'oughtness' referred to by O'Connell.[50] There is the 'expectation of pattern and uniformity' referred to by McDougal.[51] There is the 'implied consent' or 'acquiescence' referred to by other authorities. At the very minimum there is the presumption that 'constant', 'uniform' State practice is accompanied by *opinio juris*.

The fact that a certain State practice takes place at an international conference neither negates nor necessitates it being transformed into custom. Where the application of a rule occurs in the assembly or conference hall, then the declarations of States and their votes at the assembly or conference as regards such a rule could legitimately be regarded as actual State practice. States regularly make statements and declarations, submit diplomatic notes, and so on, and such verbal acts can also constitute practice.[52] According to Wolfke, such verbal acts have the limited effect of giving rise 'only to customs of making such declarations, etc., and not to customs of the conduct described in the content of the verbal acts'.[53]

[50] O'Connell, *International Law*, p. 6.

[51] Myres S. McDougal, 'The Hydrogen Bomb Tests and International Law of the Sea', 49 AJIL 356 (1967) at 358 n. 7.

[52] Akehurst writes that 'it is artificial to try to distinguish between what a State does and what it says', and 'all that is needed is that the claim or assertion must be phrased as an assertion of *lex lata* and must be acquiesced in by the other States concerned'. Michael Akehurst, 'Custom as a Source of International law', 47 BYIL 1 (1974–75) at 3, 5. In Akehurst's book, edited by Malanczuk twenty-five years later, the statement appears as: 'The better view therefore appears to be that State practice consists not only of what States do, but also of what they say.' *Akehurst's Modern Introduction to International Law*, 7th rev. edn (1997), p. 43. Villiger, *Customary International Law*, p. 7, supports this view, as does Rudolf Bernhardt, 'Customary International Law', in *Encyclopedia of Public International Law*, ed. R. Bernhardt, vol. I (1992), p. 900, and Rudolf Bernhardt, 'Custom and Treaty in the Law of the Sea', 205 RCADI 247 (1987 V) at 267.

Sinclair's opinion is that '[t]he better view would appear to be that State practice covers *any act or statement* made by or on behalf of a State from which its view can be inferred about the existence or content of a rule of international law.' Sir Ian Sinclair, *The Vienna Convention on the Law of Treaties*, 2nd edn (1984), p. 254. [emphasis added]

Onuf writes, 'State agents know that "verbal acts" constitute the bulk of what they do in the name of the state.' Nicholas G. Onuf, 'Book Reviews and Notes', 88 AJIL 556 (1994) (reviewing Wolfke, *Custom*).

[53] Wolfke, *Custom*, p. 42.

If States consistently, over a period of time, adopt certain procedures at conferences, it could well be argued that in such cases it is the behaviour of the States at the conference by their statements and by their voting that constitutes State practice. Such State practice would still require the element of *opinio juris* to transform it into customary international law.

The ICJ has held that the behaviour of States in relation to UN resolutions can, at times, be considered as expressing a legal opinion, an *opinio juris* as regards a legal norm encompassed in such resolutions.[54] A State making a declaration as to *opinio juris*, or voting in favour of such a resolution, may or may not be making it *bona fide*, but the fact that the declaration is made at an international assembly or conference does not, *per se*, void any legal significance of such a declaration or vote.[55]

3.2 Are Procedural Precedents Binding?

Erskine May, writing about the English Parliament, notes, 'The House of Commons has its own body of case-law. This consists principally of rulings given by the Speaker in answer to questions raising points of order on current business.'[56] Is such a statement, however, relevant to international law where precedents, as such, are not a formal source of law[57] and

[54] *Military and Paramilitary Activities in and against Nicaragua (Nicaragua v. United States of America)* (Merits), 1986 ICJ Reports, pp. 99, 100, 102. Although see D'Amato's cogent criticism of this decision in Anthony A. D'Amato, 'Trashing Customary International Law', 81 AJIL 101 (1987).

Akehurst states, 'A State voting in favour of such a resolution (declaratory of customary law) must be regarded as accepting that the resolution is declaratory of customary law, in the absence of a statement to the contrary.' Akehurst, 'Custom', pp. 1, 7. See also Samuel A. Bleicher, 'The Legal Significance of Re-Citation of General Assembly Resolution', 63 AJIL 444 (1969) at 447.

[55] Thirlway writes, 'There would appear to be no objection of theory to the assertion that a General Assembly resolution may be evidence of the *opinio juris* with regard to *a practice of which there is, apart from the resolution itself, adequate evidence of usage*' (emphasis added). Thirlway, *International Customary Law*, p. 66. See also Krzysztof Skubiszewski, 'The Elaboration of General Multilateral Conventions and of Non-Contractual Instruments Having a Normative Function or Objective, Resolutions of the General Assembly of the United Nations, Definitive Report and Draft Resolution', 61 *Yearbook of the Institute of International Law* 325 (1984 I) at 327.

[56] *Erskine May's Treatise on the Law, Privileges, Proceedings and Usage of Parliament*, eds. Sir Donald Limon and W. R. McKay, 22nd edn (1997), p. 7.

[57] Judge Azevedo of the ICJ states, 'Precedents, whether isolated or repeated, prior or subsequent to the Request for Opinion, cannot prevent an organ, even the one which created them, from determining the extent to which they can be legally relied upon ... It is always possible to retrace one's steps.' Competence of the General Assembly for the Admission of

not every consistent recurring pattern of State behaviour attains the status of customary international law? 'International law knows no rule of *stare decisis*',[58] and although the ICJ and international arbitrators base their decisions on precedents, this is not done on any stated assumption that precedents as such are binding on them.[59] The fact that States, or rather individuals acting on behalf of States, tend to be conservative in their behaviour and to follow precedents[60] and previous patterns of behaviour does not, in itself, have legal significance in international law.

a State to the United Nations, 1950 ICJ Reports, p. 4 at p. 24, Dissenting Opinion of Judge Azevedo.

Rosenne writes that 'the inherent fluidity of international relations and the variable circumstances in which the interpretation [of the UN Charter] is required leave little room for consistency'. Shabtai Rosenne, *The International Court of Justice, An Essay in Political and Legal Theory* (1961), p. 215.

Castañeda points out that '[n]aturally, precedents are frequently invoked in the United Nations because the logical, juridical, or factual premises on which resolutions are based usually have an objective value transcending the concretely determined case. But United Nations practice does not reveal that the organs respect these precedents as a matter of legal obligation.' Castañeda, *Legal Effects*, p. 131.

58 Lord Denning in *Trendtex Trading Corporation v. Central Bank of Nigeria*, [1977] QB at 554.

59 The ICJ tends to follow its previous decisions, but it is not formally bound to do so. Article 59 of the Statute of the ICJ states, 'The decision of the Court has no binding force except between the parties and in respect of that particular case.' Article 38 (l)(d) of the Statute calls upon the Court to apply, 'subject to the provisions of Article 59, judicial decisions . . . as subsidiary means for the determination of rules of law'.

Clearly, according to the Statute, the common law rule of *stare decisis* does not apply. See definition of *stare decisis* in *Black's Law Dictionary*, 8th edn (2004). Nevertheless, the ICJ tends to cite its previous decisions in support of its rulings or to distinguish previous decisions where it deviates from them. Such distinguishing was done, for example, in the *Barcelona Traction, Light and Power Company Limited* (Preliminary Objections), Judgment (1964 ICJ Reports, p. 29) where the Court distinguished the circumstances from those in the case of the *Aerial Incident of 27 July 1955 (Israel v. Bulgaria)* (1959 ICJ Reports, p. 127).

Apparently, there is no instance where the Court has invoked Article 59 in order to ignore a previous decision. See also Shabtai Rosenne, 'Article 59 of the Statute of the International Court of Justice Revisited', in *International Law in an Evolving World, Liber Amicorum in Tribute to Professor Eduardo Jiménez de Aréchaga* (1994); Shabtai Rosenne, *The Law and Practice of the International Court of Justice*, 2nd rev. edn (1985), p. 611; N. Singh, *The Role and Record of the International Court of Justice* (1989), p. 185; D'Amato, *Concept of Custom*, p. 248; Wolfke, *Custom*, p. 139; Richard D. Kearney, 'Sources of Law and the International Court of Justice', in *The Future of the International Court of Justice*, ed. L. Gross (1976), p. 698; D. Pratap, *The Advisory Jurisdiction of the International Court* (1972), p. 257; Michla Pomerance, *The Advisory Function of the International Court in the League and UN Eras* (1973), pp. 361–364.

60 Wolfke uses the word 'precedent' in the sense of 'every act, single manner of acting of any organ (or even private person) which can have any significance for the creation or application of international law in the future'. Wolfke, *Custom*, p. xix.

Nevertheless, delegations at international meetings assume they are bound to follow practice. At a 1998 meeting of a UNGA committee, a delegation explained, in regard to a procedural issue, that 'traditional, customary practice acquires a kind of valid legal force'.[61] Regarding the UNGA rules of procedure, Fitschen writes that 'the repeated application of new procedural methods created precedents which later became generally accepted practice without any formal decision by the GA'.[62]

In matters of procedure, as in other matters of international relations, diplomats are usually comfortable when they are following precedents. At a 1980 meeting of the UNGA, during a very lengthy procedural debate, the representative of Spain quoted 'precedents' from other UN committees.[63] The representative of India retorted:

> I am sure that the representative of Spain, with his vast experience in the United Nations, would recognize the differing interpretations and the differing situations which have arisen in various committees in the many years of the existence of the United Nations, and I am sure he would not like me to quote precedents from other committees which may have pointed in a different direction.[64]

The representative of Singapore appealed to the representative of India to reconsider his position on the procedural point in issue and pointed out that

> [e]very deliberative body has its ground rules, and it is important that those ground rules be defended. If we don't defend them when they happen to be inconvenient to our particular point of view on one occasion, there is no gainsaying that the precedent created or the exception made will later be invoked to haunt us on another occasion. Therefore, both on the grounds of justice and of convenience, I think that the best course for all of us to pursue is to try and comply with the ground rules of our own deliberative body.[65]

At a 2008 session of the Third Committee of the UNGA, a debate took place on the procedure of holding separate votes. All speakers referred to previous practice of the Committee, and one delegate 'asked for

[61] The delegate of Chile, UN GAOR, 1st Committee, 53rd Session, 23rd Meeting, p. 6, UN Doc. A/C.1/53/PV/23 (1998).

[62] Fitschen, 'Article 21', p. 692.

[63] UN GAOR, 1st Committee, 35th Session, 48th Meeting, p. 11, UN Doc. A/C.1/35/SR.48 (1980).

[64] *Ibid.* [65] *Ibid.* at p. 22.

clarification regarding the Committee's practice, since on previous occasions a different interpretation had prevailed'. The Secretary of the Committee referred to 'well-established practice of all the Main Committees of the General Assembly and of the Assembly itself at its plenary meetings.' One delegate commented that 'although it might have been past practice', 'the practice had rightly been considered regrettable and had therefore been abandoned'.[66]

Hovey, writing in 1950 on the work of the UNGA, stated, 'As the Assembly has gained in experience, it has tended increasingly to resolve old problems by precedent. Over the period of four regular and two special sessions, there has been a distinct reduction in the time lost in procedural discussion.'[67]

Werners, writing in 1967, commented that 'delegates are sometimes very careful in introducing innovations on procedure, because these innovations can constitute a precedent, to which the presiding officer can refer in the future'.[68] Bailey, writing in 1964, pointed out that

> the United Nations began with only a few exact precedents. With the steady accumulation of a body of precedents, presiding officers have increasingly been called upon to interpret the Rules and the customary practices rather than to establish new precedents.[69]

In a 1994 commentary, Schaefer writes, in relation to the UNGA, that 'the repeated application of new procedural methods created precedents which later became generally accepted rules without a formal amendment of the Rules of Procedure'.[70] In a 2012 commentary, Fitschen writes, 'A great number of procedural methods that are being followed today have developed over the years in the practical work of organs of the GA according to their day-to-day requirements.'[71] At the Preparatory Conference for the 1979 Weapons Conference, the representative of Yugoslavia argued that, in relation to decision-making procedures, 'A precedent should therefore

[66] UN GAOR, 3rd Committee, 63rd Session, 45th Meeting, UN Doc. A/C.3/63/SR.45, paras. 74–82. For the substance of the dispute see *infra* Chapter 17.1.6.

[67] Allan Hovey Jr, 'Voting Procedure in the General Assembly', 4 *UNESCO International Organization* 412 (1950 No. 1) at 427.

[68] S. E. Werners, *The Presiding Officers in the United Nations* (1967), p. 190.

[69] Sydney D. Bailey, *The General Assembly of the United Nations, A Study of Procedure and Practice*, rev. edn (1964) p. 112. In the earlier, 1960, version of the book, Bailey included the phrase 'though there are certain generally accepted practices relating to the organization and procedure of intergovernmental conferences'. *Ibid.* at p. 122 (1960). This phrase is omitted from the revised 1964 edition.

[70] Schaefer, 'Article 21', p. 361.

[71] Fitschen, 'Article 21', p. 691.

be sought in similar United Nations Conferences', and 'to abandon the traditional two-thirds majority formula would be to create a precedent that could have far-reaching consequences for other United Nations bodies and conferences'.[72] Nevertheless, a committee reported to the IMO Council meeting in 2000 that it did not recommend adopting an ITU procedural practice as a precedent as 'it was the prerogative of each agency to decide its own rules of procedure, ITU was entitled to restrict the right to submit conference proposals to Member States, although that was not IMO practice'.[73]

At a 1975 ICAO Conference, the President was asked a question on application of rules of procedure and responded that, to find the answer, '[t]he Director of the Legal Bureau and he had checked the minutes of some previous air law conferences.'[74] The relevance of precedent was emphasised at a 2003 session of the UNGA involving an irregularity involving the elections to the International Criminal Tribunal for Rwanda. The President stated, 'We do not have a precedent that could help us to move on. Let me stress that we are now establishing the precedent for any future elections.'[75]

Szasz, when he was at the Office of the Legal Counsel of the UN, was asked to give an opinion on a particular procedural practice of the UNGA. He commented,

> [I]t could either be said that it is an accepted practice of the Assembly in interpreting rule 74 or that, as the President has just pointed out, the Assembly is master of its own procedure *and there is no rule that is specifically contravened by this interpretation*.[76] [emphasis added]

International organisations, like States, are not bound by precedents; yet, here as well, precedents carry weight. Szasz writes,

> [O]nce a senior IGO [intergovernmental organisation] has taken a certain decision, often after much travail, it will later repeat or apply that decision by analogy, and so will other organs of the same IGO and even of other organizations. This is so because at such junctures the individual representatives who are called upon to approve the later decision are generally

72 UN Doc. A/CONF.95/PREP.CONF./1/SR.10 (1978).
73 IMO Council, C85/SR.1 (2000) p. 8.
74 Third Meeting of the Commission of the Whole, ICAO Doc.9154-LC/174, p. 29 (1975).
75 UN GAOR, Plenary, 57th Session, p. 8, UN Doc. A/57/PV.80 (2003).
76 UN GAOR, Plenary, 37th Session, 111th Meeting, paras. 82, 83, UN Doc. A/37/PV.111 (1982).

comforted by the fact that their government had approved the earlier one, and thus it seemed politically safe to do so again.[77]

During procedural debates at conferences, it is frequently argued by delegations that 'the rules of procedure should be regarded as the creature of the conference and not as its master'.[78] Yet rules of procedure require normative power if they are to fulfil the dual functions of protecting 'the rights of individual Members' and allowing 'an orderly conduct of business'.[79] The two postulations, it is believed, are compatible.

Studying records of conferences reveals that, except on the rarest of occasions, conferences respect the basic rights of individual delegations. The rights respected include the right to submit proposals and amendments; the right to move procedural motions; and the right of delegations to state their position, explain their vote and exercise the right of reply.

Regarding the element of the 'orderly conduct of business', here again conferences, although independent entities, do not operate in a legal vacuum. It has been claimed that before the adoption of its rules of procedure, a conference has no such rules.[80] This claim, it is submitted, is without substance. If it were true, early sessions of international conferences would be disorderly and chaotic; in practice, they are usually orderly and businesslike. The Preparatory Conference for the 1979 Weapons Conference was, at its early meetings, unable to adopt rules of procedure.[81] The delegate of Spain cautioned that 'it would be inadvisable to hold a general debate until the Preparatory Conference had adopted its rules of procedure, since problems might arise in the course of the debate which could be solved only by reference to the rules of procedure'.[82] In fact, the Conference conducted itself without procedural difficulties. Delegations in such circumstances nearly always respect the authority of the president, are orderly in requesting the floor, raising points of order and following

[77] Paul Szasz, 'General Law Making Process', in *United Nations Legal Order*, eds. Oscar Schachter and Christopher C. Joyner, vol. I (1995), p. 35 at p. 65.

[78] The representative of the Philippines, Official Records of the 1958 Law of the Sea Conference, Committee I, vol. III, p. 114, para. 5, UN Doc. A/CONF.13/39 (1958).

[79] Measures to Limit the Duration of Regular Sessions of the General Assembly: Memorandum by the Secretary-General of the United Nations, Annex VII, Agenda Item 50, 1952–1953, para. 27, UN Doc. A/2206 (1952). Quoted in the introduction to this study.

[80] The delegate of France, Official Records of the Third Law of the Sea Conference, vol. I, p. 11, Summary Records of the 4th Plenary Meeting, para. 28, UN Doc. A/CONF.62 (1973).

[81] At a later stage it adopted rules of procedure other than those referring to the decision-taking process.

[82] UN Doc. A/CONF.95/PREP.CONF./I/SR.2, para. 28 (1978).

other accepted norms of behaviour that allow an international conference to proceed in an organised fashion.

An analogy may perhaps be drawn from the procedure of international tribunals. Sandifer, writing on the laws of evidence of tribunals, concludes,

> A further by-product of this pattern of agreement on the basic character and purpose of international proceedings pertaining to evidence has been the development of what is tantamount to a customary law of evidence. While most of the tribunals involved are *ad hoc*, dependent only on the agreement creating them and bound by no rules of precedent from other tribunals and cases, they inevitably borrow from each other and from the principles of municipal law. The basic rules and principles thus applied have become, in effect, rules of the international forum, optional, it is true, but persuasive and weighty, pressing in the direction of uniformity of practice.[83]

Sandifer's comment is also valid, it is believed, for practice regarding rules of procedure at international conferences.

In 1980, the Canadian Government, in comments to the UN Secretary-General, posed the following questions:

> Are there uniform rules of procedure developing in certain areas? Is there some scope for codifying some non-contentious rules for all multilateral treaty-making conferences convened by the United Nations? What contentious areas could be resolved in a forum outside the conference? What matters have to be left for each conference to resolve on its own?[84]

It is submitted that there exists sufficient State practice and *opinio juris* to answer the Canadian query by stating that certain rules of procedure are by now customary international law.

For at least the last eighty years, States have consistently applied certain rules of conference procedure under the conviction that they were obliged to do so. A recent writer states, 'Sous certaines resérves aisément compréhensibles (vote, par exemple), la procedure paraît très souvent substantiellement identique.'[85] There are, it is submitted, rules

[83] Durward V. Sandifer, *Evidence before International Tribunals*, rev. edn (1975), p. 457.

[84] UNGA, 35th Session, Agenda Item 105, Review of the Multilateral Treaty-Making Process, Report of the Secretary-General, Addendum, Comments of the Canadian Government, para. 16, UN Doc. A/35/312/Add.1 (1980).

[85] Joe Verhoeven, 'The Normative and Quasi-Normative Activities', in *A Handbook of International Organizations*, ed. René-Jean Dupuy, 2nd edn (1998), p. 432.

of procedure that are applicable in situations where a conference has not yet adopted its rules of procedure or has adopted only partial rules. This consistent practice, under a sense of obligation, raises the possibility that certain rules of procedure are by now customary international law and binding even if not adopted by a conference. The nature of such rules, if they exist, is clearly that of *jus dispositivum*, and a conference can decide to change or waive them.[86]

3.3 Disclaimers as to Setting a Precedent

Because of the tendency to follow precedent, representatives of States affirm explicitly at times that an action on a specific issue is not intended to serve as a precedent. Szasz refers to the fact that representatives of international organisations 'often self-consciously and meaninglessly assert that they are not establishing a precedent'.[87] Such statements are not infrequently made regarding procedural behaviour at conferences.[88]

At an early session of the UNGA, the President made a ruling that a resolution after being adopted by a committee no longer had specific sponsors. The President introduced his ruling by stating explicitly that he wished 'to make a statement for the record and, if the Assembly agrees, to set a precedent'.[89] A delegation did object, and the President consequently stated that he did 'not want to set a precedent. We have more important work to do than to set legal precedents.'[90] The President was, of course, incorrect at the outset in stating that he was creating a precedent for only subsequent behaviour could determine if his ruling was to be used as a precedent.

At the Preparatory Conference for the 1979 Weapons Conference, the Secretary-General presented a set of draft rules of procedure, but added

[86] See discussion of the issue in Chapter 21.

[87] Paul C. Szasz, 'Centralized and Decentralized Law Enforcement: The Security Council and the General Assembly Acting under Chapters VI and VII', in *Allocation of Law Enforcement Authority, Proceedings of an International Symposium of the Kiel Institute of International Law, March 23 to 25, 1994*, ed. Jost Delbrück (1995), p. 17.

[88] See, for example, statements of the representatives of the United Kingdom, Belgium and the United States at the 1973 Geneva IMCO Conference, where they declared that their agreement to certain arrangements 'did not constitute a precedent for other UN bodies whether permanent or ad hoc'. Summary Records of the 2nd Plenary Meeting of the UN/IMCO Conference on International Container Traffic, p. 12, UN Doc. E/CONF.59/PV.2 (1973).

[89] UN GAOR, Plenary, 5th Session, 304th Meeting, paras. 92, 93, UN Doc. A/PV.304 (1950).

[90] *Ibid.* at para. 101.

'these rules would not necessarily constitute precedents for those that this Conference is to propose'.[91]

The drafters of the rules of procedure of the 1995 NPT Review Conference were apparently very much aware that in practice States follow precedents, for they added two disclaimers regarding the setting of precedents. In a footnote to the article on the financial arrangements for the Conference, the rules state, 'It is understood that the financial arrangements provided by rule 22 do not constitute a precedent.'[92] A further disclaimer appears in a footnote to the rules on voting, stating, 'This rule is without prejudice to rules which may be adopted for future conferences.'[93] It is far from apparent, however, that such disclaimers can prevent States from attempting to make future use of such precedents.

The Third Law of the Sea Conference took the unusual step of voting that its President, Mr Amerasinghe, continue as President although he had ceased to represent his country, Sri Lanka. The question of this vote serving as a possible precedent was raised, and the Special Representative of the Secretary-General replied that 'as far as the legal implications of the appointment of the President and the possibility of setting a precedent were concerned, it was not for the Secretariat to predict how the Conference's decision might be interpreted in the future by other United Nations bodies'.[94]

Regarding the use of consensus at the 1986 Conference on Treaties between States and International Organisations, the Mexican delegate stated that his delegation's agreement to adopting the rules of procedure 'did not, however, mean that the agreement reflected in . . . constitutes a binding precedent for the adoption of resolutions and decisions of the United Nations and its organs, commissions and committees'.[95] The Egyptian delegate to the same conference stated that 'while his delegation was able to accept the rules of procedure, including . . . , for the special purposes of the Conference, it considered that they should not be deemed to constitute a precedent for all international meetings'.[96] The UNGA,

[91] Provisional rules of procedure, Note by the Secretary-General, Article 1, UN Doc. A/CONF.95/PREP.CONF./2 (1978).

[92] Footnote to Rule 12 of the rules of procedure of the 1995 NPT Review Conference, Doc. NPT/CONF.1995/28 (1995).

[93] *Ibid.*, footnote to Rule 28(3)(h).

[94] Official Records of the Third Law of the Sea Conference, 90th Plenary Meeting, vol. IX, p. 17, para. 143, UN Doc. A/CONF.62 (1978).

[95] Official Records, 1986 Conference on Treaties between States and International Organisations, 1st Plenary Meeting, UN Doc. A/CONF.129/16, para. 30.

[96] *Ibid.* at para. 33.

in a resolution dealing with invitations to NGOs to attend a special session on Environment and Sustainable Development, declared that its decision 'will in no way create a precedent for other special sessions of the Assembly'.[97] In fact, it did serve as a precedent for subsequent special sessions. In a 2016 session of the Third Committee of the UN General Assembly on the issue of holding two simultaneous debates on the same subject, a delegate commented that 'exceptional cases were understandable but no precedent should be set'.[98]

COMMENT

It is the conclusion of this author that there is a rule of customary law obliging States to comply with rules of procedure of a conference for so long as they attend it. There does not, however, appear to be explicit authority for expounding such a rule. The absence of supportive authority may well be because of the axiomatic nature of the proposed rule and the lack of interest that international lawyers have shown in the rules of procedure of international conferences.

It is believed that State practice at conferences, coupled with *opinio juris*, can and has attained for certain specific rules of procedure the status of customary law. The acid test would be prior to a conference adopting its rules of procedure or where there is a lacuna. If, in such circumstances, States comply with certain rules of procedure under the assumption that they are so obliged, then we have a rule of customary international law.

The bulk of this study examines specific rules of procedure, attempting to verify if different bodies apply similar rules and follow similar interpretations. In some of the rules examined there does not emerge any clear sense of consistent behaviour and interpretation. However, as regards many rules, clear consistent patterns of behaviour and interpretation emerge. Such rules have, it is submitted, become customary law. Customary rules are needless to say *jusdispositivum* and therefore can, 'by agreement, be derogated from in particular cases, or as between particular parties'.[99] However, where conferences make such changes, it is done as a deliberate act by a conference deciding to diverge from a customary rule.

97 Draft decision submitted by the President of the Assembly, UN Docs. A/51/L.70 (1997), A/51/467 (1997).

98 The Delegate of Algeria, UN Doc. A/C.3/71/SR.45, p. 11, para. 65.

99 *North Sea Continental Shelf Cases (Federal Republic of Germany/Denmark; Federal Republic of Germany/Netherlands)*, 1969 ICJ Reports, p. 42.

4

Invitations, Participation and Credentials

4.1 Invitation and Participation

4.1.1 Who Issues the Invitations?

In his classic book on the Congress of Vienna, Harold Nicolson writes, 'The first two problems which face any international Conference are "Who is to issue the invitations?" and "Who is to be invited?"'[1]

Where an individual State convenes a conference, that State issues the invitations.[2] Nowadays, however, most conferences are convened by the UN or by other international organisations, and it is these organisations that issue the invitations. The European Community has also convened UN conferences.[3]

4.1.2 Participation of States

Law-making conferences are open to participation by all States. The only recent exception was the 1997 Oslo Mine Ban Conference where participation was limited to those States that had agreed in advance to the principles of the antipersonnel mine ban, set out in the 'Brussels Declaration'.[4]

An early application of the principle of universality concerned the invitations issued to the 1899 Hague Peace Conference, which were addressed to the representatives of all the Powers of Europe, America and Asia represented at St Petersburg.[5] Issuing such invitations was intended

1 Harold Nicolson, *The Congress of Vienna: A Study in Allied Unity: 1812–1822* (1946), p. 134.

2 For example, Switzerland in the case of the 1974–1977 Humanitarian Law Conference. Rule 1(3) of the rules of procedure of the 1997 Mine Ban Treaty Conference referred explicitly to 'an invitation from the Norwegian Government' (APL/CRP.2). Rule 1(4) of the rules of procedure of the First Meeting of States Parties to the Mine Ban Treaty referred to invitations to attend to be issued by 'the Host Government'.

3 Third UN Conference on the Least Developed Countries, A/CONF.191 (2000).

4 UN Disarmament Yearbook, vol. 22:1997, UN Publication Sales No. E.98.IX.1 (1998), p. 107.

5 F. De Martens, *La Conférence de la Paix à la Haye, étude d'histoire contemporaine*, ed. Arthur Rousseau (1900), p. 8.

to allow what was regarded at the time as universal participation. During the early years of the UN, the criterion for invitation to conferences was the so-called '1949 Vienna' formula, namely inviting States that were members of the UN, or of a UN specialised agency, or parties to the Statute of the International Court of Justice.[6] This formula permitted the participation of the Federal Republic of Germany, South Korea and South Vietnam and prevented the participation of the German Democratic Republic, North Korea and North Vietnam. The issue, however, is now not relevant, and the principle of universal participation in law-making conferences is generally applied.

The UN Model Rules propose:

Rule 16
Invitations

1. Except as otherwise prescribed by the convening organ, the following shall be invited to participate fully in the Conference:
   (a) All States;
   (b) ...
2. Except as otherwise decided by the convening organ, the following entities shall also be invited to participate, without the right to vote, in the Conference:[7]

   ...
3. Except as otherwise specified by the convening organ or by these rules, neither the preparatory organ nor the Conference shall have authority to make decisions concerning participation in the Conference.[8]

In international organisations, non-member States are often invited to participate as observers.[9] At an IMO Council meeting, the question arose as to whether observer States, invited to attend 'on a matter of concern to them' should also attend a closed meeting dealing with the appointment of

[6] From a conversation of the author with the late Paul Szasz, 22 April 1996. Szasz adds that the same formula was used for guiding the UN when acting as depositary. When universal participation was thought to be vital, the UN was not appointed as sole depositary, thus allowing departure from the Vienna formula.

[7] The proposed provisions as to invitations not involving full participation reflect recent UN practice. The provisions have been omitted here as they will necessarily depend on the nature and subject of individual conferences.

[8] This proposed article is a clear infringement of the independence of an international conference and does not reflect State practice.

[9] On observers see Rüdiger Wolfrum and Christiane Philipp, eds., *United Nations: Law, Policies and Practice*, new rev. English edn (1995), pp. 936–945 and bibliography listed there.

the Secretary-General of the organisation. The Council decided that they could attend.[10]

4.1.3 *Multiple Accreditation of States*

A 1967 opinion of the UN Office of Legal Affairs states, 'In no event may one individual be permitted to represent two States members of a UN organ, as multiple voting is contrary to the concepts underlying UN proceedings.'[11] However it is quite common for a delegate to speak on behalf of more than one State or organisation.

4.1.4 *Participation of Non-State Entities*

Provisional conference rules of procedure often list inter-governmental organisations invited to attend the conference, and approval of the rules of procedure by the conference entails approval of such invitations. Where no such list is included, the decision as to issuing such invitations is made by the conference itself.[12]

In recent years there has been increased participation by NGOs in international conferences and in UNGA special sessions. Non-State entities invited to conferences organised by the UN are invited 'as observers without the right to vote'.[13] This formula is applied by UN-sponsored conferences to 'Entities',[14] 'Intergovernmental organizations and other entities that have received a standing invitation to participate in the capacity of observers', 'Associate members of regional commissions', 'Representatives of specialized agencies', 'Representatives of other intergovernmental organizations' and 'Representatives of interested UN organs'.[15] Such

[10] IMO C 89/SR.8, p. 4 (2002).

[11] Memorandum to the Secretary General, UN Conference on Trade and Development, "Question of Dual or Multiple representation in UN Organs", 16 May 1967, http://legal.un.org/ola/media/GA_RoP/GA_RoP_EN.pdf

[12] See, for example, Rule 44(3) of the Draft Rules of Procedure, 2005 Review Conference of the Parties to the Treaty on the Non-Proliferation of Nuclear Weapons, NPT/CONF.2005/1 (2004).

[13] For a recent example, see Provisional Rules of Procedure of World Conference on Disaster Reduction, UN Doc. A/CONF.206/PC(II)/2/Corr.1, 30 August 2004.

[14] The former Trust Territory of South West Africa (Namibia) was treated by the UNGA as a particular case: see UNGA Resolution 844 (IX) (1954).

[15] See, for example, Rules 60–64 of the Provisional Rules of Procedure of the International Meeting to Review the Implementation of the Programme of Action for the Sustainable

participation usually includes the right to attend open meetings, to make statements and to submit documents.[16] Observers do not have a right of 'introduction of substantive proposals or procedural motions, the raising of points of order, the circulation of communications as official documents of that organ and the exercise of the right of reply'.[17] The rules of procedure of the 1986 Conference on Treaties between States and International Organisations included a detailed list of rights granted to observers.[18] The 1997 Ottawa Mine Ban Treaty Conference formulated the 'general rights of observers' as follows: they 'May not participate in decision-making', 'May not make any procedural motion or request, raise points of order or appeal against a ruling of the Chairman' and 'May not introduce proposals or amendments to any proposal'.[19] The rules of procedure of the 2004

Development of Small Island Developing States, UN Doc. A/CONF.207/2, 2 November 2004.

16 See, for example, Rule 44(1) of the Draft Rules of Procedure, 2005 Review Conference of the Parties to the Treaty on the Non-Proliferation of Nuclear Weapons, NPT/CONF.2005/1 (2004).

17 UN Office of Legal Affairs, 'Letter to the Director, Office of International Standards and Legal Affairs, UN ECOSOC,' 29 September 1995, 1995 UN Jur. Y.B. 438, ST/LEG/SER.C/33.

18 1. . . .
   (a) To participate in public and private meetings of the Conference, the Committee of the Whole, sub-committees and working groups, as well as the process leading to general agreement;
   (b) To submit documents for circulation;
   (c) To intervene in the debates;
      – To exercise the right of reply in accordance with rule 22;
      – To explain their positions on any matter on which a decision has been or is to be taken;
   (d) To submit substantive proposals, which as such may only be put to the vote subject to rule 63 if a formal request is made by a State to that effect. If the proposal has been circulated in writing, the formal request shall be circulated in the same manner;
   (e) To submit procedural motions, including those referred to in rules 23, 24 and 25, which may not be put to the vote unless supported by a State.

2. Representatives of the organizations participating in the Conference in accordance with paragraph 1 of this rule may not:
   (a) Object to any procedural motion put forward by a representative of a participating State;
   (b) Prevent on their own the achievement of general agreement or participate in any vote.

19 Rule 47, Rules of Procedure, Diplomatic Conference on a Convention on the Prohibition of the Use, Stockpiling, Production and Transfer of Anti-Personnel Mines and on their Destruction, APL/CRP.2 (1997).

Mine Ban Treaty Review Conference omitted the rule that observers may not 'introduce proposals or amendments to any proposal'.[20] The provenance and intention of this omission are not apparent.

4.1.4.1 Participation of 'Palestine'

The UNGA has granted the PLO,[21] subsequently titled 'Palestine',[22] observer status that was then upgraded with 'additional rights'.[23] The additional rights include 'the right to co-sponsor draft resolutions and decisions on Palestinian and Middle East issues', qualified by the phrase, 'such draft resolutions shall be put to the vote only upon request from a Member State'. 'Palestine' also has a 'right of reply' and 'the right to raise points of order related to the proceedings on Palestine and Middle East issues', qualified by the phrase, 'provided that the right to raise such a point of order shall not include the right to challenge the decision of the presiding officer'. The UNGA resolution upgrading the status adds that the rights do not include 'the right to vote or to put forward candidates'.[24] By inference the rights do not include the right to submit procedural motions.

In 2012 the UN General Assembly granted 'Palestine' "non-member observer State status"[25]. This resolution has had political repercussions, but has not changed the status of Palestine as regards conduct of business at the General Assembly.[26] Until recently conferences had not generally followed the UNGA precedent in granting this upgrading, but had invited 'Palestine' under the general rubric of 'entities, intergovernmental organizations and other entities that have received a standing invitation from the General Assembly to participate in the capacity of observers in the session and work of all international conferences convened under its auspices'.[27]

[20] Rule 24, Rules of Procedure, First Review Conference of the States Parties to the Convention on the Prohibition of the Use, Stockpiling, Production and Transfer of Anti-Personnel Mines and on their Destruction, APLC/CONF/2004/PM.2/L.3, 15 June 2004.

[21] UNGA Resolution 3237 (XXIX) of 22 November 1974.

[22] UNGA Resolution 43/177 of 15 December 1988.

[23] UNGA Resolution 52/250 of 7 July 1998.

[24] *Ibid.*, Annex, Article 8.

[25] UN Doc. A/RES/67/19.

[26] 'The rights and privileges of Palestine in the work of the United Nations remained the same as they were enhanced by resolution 52/250, which gave Palestine maximum rights without becoming a Member of the United Nations.' http://palestineun.org/status-of-palestine-at-the-united-nations.

[27] See, for example, Rule 60 of the draft provisional rules of procedure of the International Meeting to Review the Implementation of the Programme of Action for the Sustainable Development of Small Island Developing States, UN Doc. A/CONF.207/2, 2 November 2004.

In view of the 2013 Report of the UN Secretary-General, Palestine is now invited to UN conferences with the status of a State.[28]

4.1.4.2 Participation of the European Union

Since 2010 the European Union (EU) has been granted special rights of participation in the UNGA. The EU is

1. (a) Allowed to be inscribed on the list of speakers among representatives of major groups, in order to make interventions;
   (b) Invited to participate in the general debate of the General Assembly, in accordance with the order of precedence as established in the practice for participating observers and the level of participation;
   (c) Permitted to have its communications relating to the sessions and work of the General Assembly and to the sessions and work of all international meetings and conferences convened under the auspices of the Assembly and of United Nations conferences, circulated directly, and without intermediary, as documents of the Assembly, meeting or conference;
   (d) Also permitted to present proposals and amendments orally as agreed by the States members of the European Union; such proposals and amendments shall be put to a vote only at the request of a Member State;
   (e) Allowed to exercise the right of reply regarding positions of the European Union as decided by the presiding officer; such right of reply shall be restricted to one intervention per item.
2. The representatives of the European Union shall be ensured seating among the observers.[29]

[28] Status of Palestine in the United Nations Report of the Secretary-General, 8 March 2013,

> 7. With respect to conferences convened under the auspices of the General Assembly and other United Nations conferences, as a non-member observer State of the United Nations and a member of UNESCO, the State of Palestine may participate fully and on an equal basis with other States in conferences that are open to members of specialized agencies or that are open to all States. Arrangements are being made to ensure the full participation of the State of Palestine in conferences convened on that basis. UN Doc. A/67/738 (2013).

[29] UN Doc. A/RES/ 65/276.'Participation of the European Union in the work of the United Nations', Annex A.

The representatives of the EU, however, do not have the right to vote, to co-sponsor draft resolutions or decisions, or to put forward candidates.[30]

The rights granted to the EU have caused some resentment among other regional groups. For example, the representative of the Caribbean Community (CARICOM) speaking at a 2011 session of the UNGA Third Committee remarked that that the EU 'could not take priority over other major groups'.[31] The delegate from Singapore at a UNGA 2014 made a similar comment. stating 'ASEAN would request that an ASEAN State member, when speaking on behalf of the group, speak before the European Union if the latter is represented by the EU observer delegation'.[32] The President of the meeting responded that the 'General Assembly takes note of the statement'.[33]

The EU is granted the right to 'full participation' in a number of UN conferences.[34] Furthermore, the EU is a member of FAO and is a party to a number of international treaties,[35] and hence it could be logically argued that in conferences drafting multilateral treaties, the EU should enjoy a status equal to that of States. However, the UN Office of Legal Affairs gave its opinion, in 1993, that there was no basis for going beyond the previous practice of full participation whereby the 'EEC was explicitly excluded from holding office, from being counted for quorum purposes and from making such procedural motions as moving for adjournment of debate, closure of debate or suspension or adjournment of the meeting'. The Office recommended that the European Community 'shall not have the right to vote but may submit proposals which may be put to the vote on request of any member' and it 'should not in our view be placed on the same level as members with regard to such procedural matters as the right to put proposals to a vote'.[36] Notwithstanding this opinion, at many conferences the EU has been granted the right of 'full participation', rather than the more limited observer status enjoyed by other international organisations. The right of 'full participation' has included the right to make statements in

[30] *Ibid.*

[31] UN Doc. A/C.3/66/SR.2 para. 14. The representative of Mexico made a similar point at a 2008 meeting of the UNGA First Committee, UN Doc.A/C.1/63/ PV.1p. 5.

[32] UN Doc. A/69/PV.70 p. 20. [33] *Ibid.*

[34] See 'Letter from UN Office of Legal Affairs to the Director of International Standards and Legal Affairs, UNESCO', 29 September 1995, Comments on some procedural questions, www.un.org/en/ga/about/ropga.

[35] See comments on this issue in United Nations Treaty Collection, 'Summary of Practice of the Secretary General as Depositary of Multilateral Treaties' Prepared by the Treaty Section of the Office of Legal Affairs, ST/LEG/7/Rev.1, para. 98 (1999).

[36] See Office of Legal Affairs comments of 26 January 1993 on Draft Report on the Rules of Procedure of the Commission on Sustainable Development, 1993 UN Jur. Y.B. 415.

right of reply, whereas in the case of international organisations the right is at the discretion of the President.[37] The EU has been granted a right to raise points of order, but that does not include challenging a decision of the Chairman.[38] The right of full participation does not normally include the right to submit proposals to the vote nor to participate in voting. However, a right to vote has been granted in certain WHO and FAO conferences.

This formula that has been used concerning such voting rights: a regional economic integration organization, on matters within its competence, shall exercise its right to vote with a number of votes equal to the number of its Member States that are Parties to this Convention. Such an organization shall not exercise its right to vote if any of its Member States exercise its right, and vice versa.[39] In the WHO the practice is that the representative of the State holding the Presidency of the Council of the EU provides information 'for which items competency was shared and to explain which items were specific to either the EU or the European Community'.[40]

The EU has also counted for a quorum according to this formulation:

> For the purposes of determining a quorum for a decision to be taken on a matter within the competence of a regional economic integration organization, that organization shall be counted to the extent of the number of votes it is entitled to cast in accordance with [the relevant article of the Convention concerned].[41]

According to internal EU regulations, 'The Commission is responsible for negotiating international agreements.'[42] Where a delegation from the EU participates in a conference, it submits credentials signed by the President

[37] See, for example, Rule 24 of the draft provisional rules of procedure of the International Meeting to Review the Implementation of the Programme of Action for the Sustainable Development of Small Island Developing States, UN Doc. A/58/567, 11 November 2003.

[38] ECOSOC Decision 1995/201 of 8 February 1995.

[39] Article 23, 2001 UNEP Stockholm Convention on Persistent Organic Pollutants (2001); WHO, Draft Rules of Procedure for the Conference of the Parties, WHO Framework Convention on Tobacco Control, WHO Doc. A/FCTC/IGWG/1/4 (2004). A similar formula was used in the FAO 2002 World Food Summit, WFS, Five Years Later, 2002/2, Rule 30 (2002).

[40] WHA 59/2006/REC/3 (2006), p. 14.

[41] WHO, Draft Rules of Procedure for the Conference of the Parties, WHO Framework Convention on Tobacco Control, WHO Doc. A/FCTC/IGWG/1/4 (2004).

[42] *The European Convention*, The Secretariat, CONV 161/02, 3 July 2002, para. 14. Under the Treaty establishing a Constitution for Europe, the responsibility might be transferred to representatives of the Union as part of a proposed 'Union External Action Service', European Parliament, Committee on Constitutional Affairs, Provisional Draft Report 2004/2207(INI), 22 February 2005.

of the Commission.[43] This is usually stated explicitly in the rules of procedure, but an FAO conference adopted a more general formulation whereby credentials of a 'Regional Economic Integration Organization' should be signed by 'the head of the executive body of the Member Organization concerned'.[44]

4.1.4.3 Participation by NGOs

Recent years have seen a marked increase in the involvement of non-governmental organisations (NGOs) in international conferences. UN practice has been to invite to conferences those relevant NGOs that have consultative status with ECOSOC; other NGOs are invited on a 'no-objection' procedure by the bureau of the conference.[45] However, the 2001 UNGA, convened in a special session, decided to reinstate a representative of an NGO who had been removed from the list of observers on the basis of the 'no-objection' rule.[46] The 2001 World Conference Against Racism was markedly liberal in its policy as to inviting participation of national institutions and NGOs involved in human rights issues.[47] At IMO conferences the issuing of such invitations is at the discretion of the President or Chairman.[48] NGOs that are invited to attend conferences enjoy access to

[43] See, for example, Rule 3 of the draft provisional rules of procedure of the International Meeting to Review the Implementation of the Programme of Action for the Sustainable Development of Small Island Developing States, UN Doc. A/58/567, 11 November 2003.

[44] Rules of Procedure of the World Food Summit, WFS, Five Years Later, 2002/2, Rule 2 (2002).

[45] See Report of the Bureau of the Preparatory Committee for the high level international inter-governmental event on financing for development on modalities of the participation of all relevant stakeholders in the substantive preparatory process and the high-level inter-governmental event on financing for development, UN Doc. A/AC.257/6 (2000); UNGA Resolution 54/279 of 30 June 2000, UNGA Resolution 55/245B of 7 August 2001; debate on the issue in the UNGA, UN Doc. A/58/PV.44, 27 October 2003. Invitations to the Ottawa Mine Treaty Review Conference were issued by the coordinating committee of the conference, 'subject to approval of the Review Conference', Rule 1(4) First Review Conference of the States Parties to the Convention on the Prohibition of the Use, Stockpiling, Production and Transfer of Anti-Personnel Mines and on their Destruction, APLC/CONF/2004/PM.2/L.3, 15 June 2004.

[46] UN GAOR, 26th Special Session, 1st Meeting, UN Doc. A/S-26/PV.1 (2001). The session dealt with HIV/AIDS, and the NGO concerned was the International Gay and Lesbian Human Rights Commission.

[47] Rules 63–66, Rules of Procedure, 2001 World Conference against Racism, Racial Discrimination, Xenophobia and Related Intolerance, UN Doc. A/CONF.189/2 (2001).

[48] For example, Rule 58, Rules of Procedure, IMO International Conference on the Establishment of a Supplementary Fund for Compensation for Oil Pollution Damage, LEG/CONF.14/2 (2002).

open meetings and distribution of documents, but can only address the conference with the explicit permission of the conference.

4.2 Credentials

Delegations attending a conference are obliged to be equipped with documentation from their State authorising them to represent that State. If they are to sign a treaty, they need full powers to that effect.[49]

The Legal Counsel to the UN defined credentials for the UNGA as

> a document issued by the Head of State or Government or by the Minister for Foreign Affairs of a State Member of the United Nations submitted to the Secretary-General designating the person entitled to represent that Member at a given session of the General Assembly. Unlike the acceptance of credentials in bilateral relations, the question of recognition of a Government of a Member State is not involved, and substantive issues concerning the status of governments do not arise.[50]

Where the European Union is invited, the credentials are signed by the President of the Commission.[51]

4.2.1 Submission of Credentials

The UNGA rules of procedure state,

> *Submission of Credentials*
> *Rule 27*
> The credentials of representatives and the names of members of a delegation shall be submitted to the Secretary-General if possible not less than one week before the opening of the session. The credentials shall be issued either by the Head of the State or Government or by the Minister for Foreign Affairs.

[49] Rosenne writes, 'The credentials of a delegation to the Conference are therefore adequate for signature of the Final Act, but for signature of the treaty itself formal powers are needed (they may be incorporated in the credentials of the delegation).' Shabtai Rosenne, *Practice and Methods of International Law* (1984), p. 39.

[50] Statement by the Legal Counsel (of the UN) submitted to the President of the General Assembly, 11 November 1970, 1970 UN Jur. Y.B. 169, 170.

[51] See Rule 3 of the draft provisional rules of procedure of the International Meeting to Review the Implementation of the Programme of Action for the Sustainable Development of Small Island Developing States, UN Doc. A/58/567, 11 November 2003.

The UN Model Rules propose,

Rule 18
Notification of Delegations

1. The names and titles of the members of the delegation of each participant and observer shall be submitted to the Executive Secretary, if possible not less than one week before the date on which the Conference is scheduled to be convened.
2. In respect of a treaty-making conference, the convening organ may specify that the representatives of States shall submit credentials issued by the Head of the State or Government or by the Minister for Foreign Affairs;[52,53] except if such credentials specify otherwise, they shall remain valid for all sessions of the Conference, unless they are withdrawn or replaced by new credentials. Credentials shall be submitted to the Executive Secretary, who shall report thereon to the Conference if it so requests.

The introduction to the UN Model Rules states, regarding the draft article on credentials,

> The proposed rules are expected to lead to considerable administrative savings, both for States and for the Organization, through three related but independent proposals for the modification relating to the present routine requirement for the submission and examination of credentials. These proposals would:
>
> (a) Require the presentation of credentials only for certain treaty-making conferences, while eliminating this requirement for other types of conferences; the practice of requiring credentials, which originated at a time when long-range communications were such that it was not

[52] The UN Model Rules in a footnote comment that '[s]uch a requirement would make the Conference one of plenipotentiaries. Whether or not credentials are required for a treaty-making conference, representatives desiring to sign any treaty instrument promulgated by the Conference will have to submit full powers acceptable to the depositary.'

[53] The 1969 Vienna Convention on the Law of Treaties states,

Article 7
Full powers

2. In virtue of their functions and without having to produce full powers, the following are considered as representing their State:

...

(a) representatives accredited by States to an international conference or to an international organization or one of its organs, for the purpose of adopting the text of a treaty in that conference, organization or organ.

always possible to check whether a person appearing at an intergovernmental conference actually represented the authority that allegedly dispatched him, no longer has much relevance in an era of instant world-wide communications;

(b) Eliminate the need to establish a Credentials Committee, by transferring the most critical function of such a body – the examination of challenged credentials – to the General Committee while abolishing the function of routinely examining unchallenged credentials;

(c) Abolish the requirement for the automatic examination of all credentials which frequently introduces an unnecessarily contentious element into a non-political conference, while still retaining the possibility of challenging the participation of any delegation.

4.2.2 *Invalid Credentials*

4.2.2.1 Credentials Not Signed by the Correct Person

Credentials may be invalid as a result of being signed by a person other than the Head of State or Government or Minister of Foreign Affairs.[54] Credentials have been held to be invalid where signed by ambassadors, officials of the Ministry of Foreign Affairs or ministers other than the Minister of Foreign Affairs.[55] The General Assembly of the International Seabed Authority allows credentials to be signed by a person authorized by the Minister of Foreign Affairs;[56] however, the UN Office of Legal Affairs comments that it should not be cited as a precedent 'in favour of UN bodies taking similar decisions'.[57]

[54] Or in the case of a regional integration organisation, by the competent authority of that organisation. UN Office of Legal Affairs, 'Memorandum to the Coordinator, Ozone Secretariat UN Environment Programme', 28 September 1993, 1993 UN Jur. Y.B., ST/LEG/SER.C/31.

[55] UN Office of Legal Affairs, Memorandum to the Assistant Director in charge of the International Trade Relations Branch, Department of Economic and Social Affairs, Question of Issuance of Credentials by Permanent Representatives to the UN, Rule 27 of the Rules of Procedure of the General Assembly, 25 February 1964, http://legal.un.org/ola/media/GA_RoP/GA_RoP_EN.pdf.

[56] RULES OF PROCEDURE OF THE ASSEMBLY OF THE INTERNATIONAL SEABED AUTHORITY, Rule 23, 'The credentials shall be issued either by the Head of the State or Government, by the Minister for Foreign Affairs or person authorized by him or, in the case entities referred to in article 305, paragraph 1 (f) of the United Nations Convention on the Law of the Sea, by another competent authority', www.isa.org.jm/files/documents/EN/Regs/ROP_Assembly.pdf.

[57] UN Office of Legal Affairs, Letter to the Senior Legal Officer, UNCTAD, Geneva, 'Rule 13 of the Rules of Procedure of UNCTAD Authorities Issuing Credentials', 2 May 1966, http://legal.un.org/ola/media/GA_RoP/GA_RoP_EN.pdf.

The unique tripartite composition of the ILO International Labour Conference causes special problems relating to the approval of credentials. The claim has frequently been raised that certain worker or employer delegations are not representative. At the 2004 session, the International Labour Conference broadened the mandate of the credentials committee, on an interim basis, with a view to ensuring that delegations were independent and representative.[58]

Although it is usual to send telegraphic or faxed copies of credentials prior to the opening of a conference, they must be followed by submission of the actual signed text and are invalid if this is not done. In practice the Secretariat of a conference immediately advises delegations of any fault in their credentials so as to allow rectification prior to submission of the report.

4.2.2.2 Credentials Not Signed in the Capital

At an IAEA Conference, a number of Arab States queried the credentials of the Israel delegation on the grounds that they had been signed in Jerusalem, which was not recognised as Israel's capital. The Legal Adviser of IAEA gave his opinion that the rule of procedure dealing with credentials

> does not require that credentials must be issued in the capital of the issuing State. In fact it makes no reference to the place where such credentials are to be signed at all. Nor does international law impose any requirements regarding the place of signature of credentials. Therefore the place of signature is irrelevant to the validity of the credentials, such validity depending solely upon whether they have been signed by the proper authority. Likewise, the acceptance of credentials does not mean that the accepting authority takes in any way a position with respect to the status of the place of signature either under international or national law.[59]

4.2.2.3 Competing Credentials

Where there are rival authorities submitting competing credentials, it would be logical to apply a criterion of effective control to determine which credentials are to be accepted.[60] In reality the decision is regarded

[58] International Labour Conference, Provisional Record of the 92nd Session, 16th sitting, 15 June 2004, Provisional Record 23/22.

[59] IAEA General Conference, 43rd Regular Session, Examination of Delegates' Credentials, Report of the General Committee, para. 6, GC(43)/33, 30 September 1999.

[60] See Felice Morgenstern, *Legal Problems of International Organizations* (1986), p. 57.

as a political issue. The issue has arisen at the UNGA as regards representatives of Congo (where a decision was taken by the General Assembly),[61] Kampuchea[62] and Afghanistan[63] (where decisions were taken by the Credentials Committee). The question of the representation of China arose in the Credentials Committee at the Fifth Session of the UNGA, but subsequently was generally dealt with directly as a political issue of the Assembly and not as an issue of the report of the Credentials Committee.

4.2.2.4 Invalidating Credentials on Political Grounds

In a 1986 report of the UNGA Credentials Committee, the US representative pointed out, 'If members of the Committee failed to recognize the technical nature of the credentials exercise and rejected the credentials of a country's representative merely because they did not like its Government's policies, it would lead to chaos in international relations.'[64] The Netherlands representative at the same committee added that it was not the task of the committee 'to make political judgements regarding the Governments that issued the credentials'.[65] Blum writes that where there is 'only *one* Government claiming to represent a Member State, the credentials issued for its UN delegation cannot be challenged on grounds of legitimacy',[66] and Fitschen emphasises that the credentials committee 'has no authority to cast a political judgment on any government issuing a letter of credentials'.[67] The opinion of the UN Office of Legal Affairs is that 'the United Nations itself is not in a position to consider the constitutionality of a regime in deciding whether or not to accept persons accredited to it'.[68] A contrary view appears to be supported by Jhabvala, who writes that 'effective control' is a condition precedent, but beyond that there is a

[61] UNGA Resolution 1498 (XV) of 22 November 1960.

[62] Report of the Credentials Committee to the 34th Session of the UNGA, UN Doc. A/34/500 (1979).

[63] There was a challenge by a rival government, but no alternative credentials were submitted. UNGA Resolution 51/9B of 17 December 1996.

[64] Report of the Credentials Committee to the 41st Session of the UNGA, UN Doc. A/41/727, para. 13 (1986).

[65] *Ibid.*, para. 19.

[66] Yehuda Z. Blum, *Eroding the United Nations Charter* (1993) p. 38. See also Malvina Halberstam, 'Excluding Israel from the General Assembly by a Rejection of Its Credentials', 78 AJIL 170 (1984).

[67] Thomas Fitschen, 'Article 21', in *The Charter of the United Nations, A Commentary*, ed. Bruno Simma *et al*, 3rd edn (2012) p. 700.

[68] 'Practice of the United Nations in cases of challenged representation of a member state – General Assembly Resolution 396 (V) of 14 December 1950, Office of Legal Affairs Memorandum to the Under-Secretary-General for Political Affairs', 1997 UN Jur. Y.B. 468.

'legal gap' that grants States 'wide political discretion' to refuse to recognise credentials.[69]

States wishing to reject credentials on political grounds have usually limited themselves to having their reservations to the credentials of a particular State reflected in the records of the credentials committee. There have, however, been cases of the General Assembly being asked to reject credentials. Such proposals have been submitted *inter alia* regarding Hungary,[70] Portugal,[71] South Africa,[72] Israel[73] and Cambodia.[74] Certain Arab and Muslim States utilise an explanation of their vote on the report

[69] Farrokh Jhabvala, 'The Credentials Approach to Representation Questions in the United Nations General Assembly', 7 *California Western International Law Journal* 615 (1977) at 637.

[70] From the 11th to the 17th Sessions, the UNGA decided to take no action on the credentials submitted on behalf of Hungary.

[71] The credentials were approved 'on the clear understanding that they represent Portugal as it exists within its frontiers in Europe and that they do not represent the Portuguese dominated Territories of Angola and Mozambique nor could they represent Guinea-Bissau, which is an independent State'. UNGA Resolution 3181 (XXVIII) of 17 December 1973.

[72] No action was taken on the South African credentials from the 20th to the 25th Sessions of the UNGA. Commencing at the 25th Session in 1970, the credentials were rejected, but the ruling was that 'rights and privileges of membership' were not affected, UN Doc. A/PV.1901 (1970). At the 29th Session of the UNGA, when the Credentials Committee disapproved the South African credentials, the President of the Assembly ruled that 'the General Assembly refuses to allow the delegation of South Africa to participate in its work', UN GAOR, Plenary, 29th Session, 2281st Meeting, para. 159, UN Doc. A/PV.2281 and Corr.1 (1974). The UN Office of Legal Affairs submitted its opinion, regarding the South African issue, that 'a subsequent session [of the UNGA] is not bound by any decisions of a previous session regarding credentials'. Memorandum (by the Office of Legal Affairs) to the Under-Secretary-General for Political and General Assembly Affairs, 27 August 1975, 1975 UN Jur. Y.B. 168.

[73] Proposals were submitted to amend the report of the Credentials Committee by rejecting the credentials of Israel. However, on each occasion a procedural motion was passed under Rule 74 to take no action (adjourn the debate) on such proposals. This was done at the 37th Session of the General Assembly by a motion submitted by Denmark, Finland, Iceland, Norway and Sweden, UN Doc. A/37/L.11 (1982). At the 38th Session of the UNGA it was done by raising a point of order, UN GAOR, Plenary, 38th Session, 34th Meeting, para. 43, UN Doc. A/38/PV.34 (1983). This procedure was followed at subsequent sessions, where such an amendment was proposed. From the 45th Session the practice has been for the Plenary to postpone *sine die* consideration of the report of the Credentials Committee. See, for example, UN Doc. A/45/PV.36, p. 41 (Provisional) (1990).

[74] As regards the 'Cambodian' issue (Democratic Kampuchea), amendments were introduced to the Plenary of the UNGA, proposing the rejection of the credentials of the representative of Democratic Kampuchea; the amendments, however, were defeated. UN Doc. A/35/L.5 and Add.1 (1980); UN Doc. A/36/L.2 and Add.1 (1981); UN Doc. A/37/L.8 and Add.1 (1982).

of the credentials committee to make a reservation that the adoption of the report should not be 'construed as recognition of Israel'.[75]

The use, for political ends, of the procedure for the approval of credentials has occurred occasionally at assemblies of international organisations,[76] but rarely so at international conferences. O'Davoren wrote in 1943, 'It very seldom occurs in ordinary international conferences that the credentials of delegates are questioned, and the adoption of the report of the credentials committee is as a rule a pure matter of form.'[77] This statement continues, usually, to be valid.

4.2.3 Credentials Committee

The UNGA rules of procedure state,

> *Credentials Committee*
>
> *Rule 28*
>
> A Credentials Committee shall be appointed at the beginning of each session. It shall consist of nine members, who shall be appointed by the General Assembly on the proposal of the President. The Committee shall elect its own officers. It shall examine the credentials of representatives and report without delay.

[75] See, for example, statement by the Islamic Republic of Iran at the 73rd Session of the UNGA, UN Doc. A/57/PV.75 (2002), and at the 43rd General Conference of the IAEA, GC(43)/OR.10, p. 21, para. 111 (1999).

[76] See, for example, IAEA Resolution GC(XXVI)/RES/404 of 24 September 1983, which accepted the report of the Credentials Committee 'with the exception of the credentials of the delegation from Israel'. This Resolution was adopted on the last day of the 26th General Conference. Consequently, at the 27th General Conference, the representative of Iran commented that 'Israel had participated in all the conferences' meetings and votes.' 'In order to prevent similar cases in the future', the Iranian delegation proposed that Rule 28 of the rules of procedure be amended to read: 'The credentials of delegations must be approved not later than the end of the second day of the regular session' (GC(XXVII)/OR.253, para. 63 (1984)). The representative of Norway on a point of order 'moved that no action be taken on the proposal by the delegate of the Islamic Republic of Iran to the effect that the credentials of the delegate of Israel be rejected' (GC(XXVII)/OR.256, para. 6 (1984)). The Norwegian motion was approved.

At the IAEA 29th General Conference, the US threatened to suspend its participation in the agency if the Israel credentials were rejected (GC(XXIX)/GEN/R.47, para. 7 (1985)). The Credentials Committee limited itself to recording the reservations and Israel's credentials were approved.

[77] William O'Davoren, *Post-War Reconstruction Conferences, The Technical Organisation of International Conferences* (1943), p. 80.

The general rule is that a delegate cannot represent more than one State, but an exception has been made allowing a delegate of Andorra to vote on behalf of Israel in a vote that took place on the Jewish Sabbath.[78]

The UN Model Rules propose eliminating the need for a credentials committee.

The practice of conferences is that the presiding officer proposes to the conference the composition of the credentials committee, and this is normally approved without a vote. The composition of the credentials committee usually reflects the political status quo at the most recent UNGA.

The Credentials Committee of the UNGA at its 1981 session refused to allow a representative of South Africa to present his delegation's position on its credentials. The Chairman stated that it was not the policy of the Committee to allow nonmembers to participate in the work of the Committee.[79]

4.2.3.1 Physical Examination of Credentials by Credentials Committee

A 1985 legal opinion of the UN Office of Legal Affairs states, 'The Credentials Committee does not normally itself physically examine credentials submitted by States. It only does so exceptionally in individual cases if the need arises. All credentials received are however available for examination by any member of the Committee who may wish to do so.'[80]

4.2.3.2 Report of Credentials Committee

The rules of procedure of the UNGA and of UN-convened conferences call upon the credentials committee to report 'without delay'. Nevertheless, the practice has developed that credentials committee reports are often submitted towards the end of proceedings. This practice has been used to ensure that controversial credentials issues are deferred to the end of the session or conference at which time approval of credentials loses its relevance.

78 See Section 14.2.12, 'Voting on Behalf of More than One State'.

79 Third Report of the Credentials Committee to the 35th Session of the UNGA, UN GAOR, Agenda Item 3, Annexes, para. 4, UN Doc. A/35/484/Add.2 (1981), approved by the UNGA, Resolution 35/4C of 2 March 1981.

80 Replies (by the UN Office of Legal Affairs) to a questionnaire concerning the practice of the General Assembly with regard to the examination of credentials, 12 February 1985, 1985 UN Jur. Y.B. 128, 129.

4.2.4 *Which Body Should Decide Disputes as to Credentials?*

A 1950 UNGA Resolution resolved that 'when any such question [more than one authority claiming to be the government] arises, it should be considered by the General Assembly'.[81] The Legal Adviser to the UN comments, 'It is clear from this Resolution that the General Assembly considers itself the organ best suited to clear the controversy where more than one authority claims to be the Government entitled to represent a Member State of the United Nations.'[82]

When the issue of two conflicting credentials for the delegate of Panama arose in the UN Security Council, the Secretary-General reported to the Council that 'credentials have to be reported upon by the Secretary General but that the determination as to their approval has to be made by the Council itself'.[83]

The UN Model Rules propose,

Rule 19
Objection to a Delegation

1. If an objection is raised against the participation of a delegation, such objection shall be considered by the General Committee, whose report thereon shall be submitted to the Conference.

4.2.5 *Provisional Admission*

The UNGA rules of procedure state,

Rule 29
Provisional Admission to a Session

Any representative to whose admission a Member has made objection shall be seated provisionally with the same rights as other representatives until the Credentials Committee has reported and the General Assembly has given its decision.

The UN Model Rules propose,

Rule 19

2. Pending a decision of the Conference regarding an objection against the participation of a delegation, the latter shall be entitled to participate

[81] UNGA Resolution 396 (V) of 14 December 1950.
[82] 1979 UN Jur. Y.B. 167. [83] UN Doc. S/21047 (1989).

> provisionally in the Conference with the same rights as other delegations within the same category.

In a 1993 opinion, the UN Office of Legal Affairs advised that 'the practice of the Credentials Committee is to accept provisional credentials, i.e. those not signed by the Head of State or Government or by the Minister for Foreign Affairs, "on the understanding that formal credentials for representatives . . . would be communicated . . . as soon as possible"'.[84] The IAEA has an identical provision, *mutatis mutandis*, in its rules of procedure.[85] At a 1993 committee meeting of the General Conference of the IAEA, the question arose as to whether the rule on provisional admission applied to delegations whose members had not submitted proper credentials, yet to whose credentials no objection had been made. The Legal Adviser stated that the rule as to provisional seating applied to such delegations.[86]

4.2.6 *Credentials of Observer Organisations*

In a 1975 note, the Office of Legal Affairs of the UN stated, 'The letter from an observer organization or movement designating a representative or representatives does not constitute "credentials" within the meaning of the relevant rules of procedure and is not examined by the Credentials Committee established at the session or conference.'[87]

[84] UN Office of Legal Affairs in a Memorandum to the Coordinator, Ozone Secretariat, UNEP, 28 September 1993, 1993 UN Jur. Y.B. 427.

[85] Rule 29 of the rules of procedure of the General Conference of the IAEA, IAEA Doc. GC(XXXI)/INF/245/Rev.1 (1992).

[86] IAEA Doc. GC(XXXII)/GEN/OR.66, paras. 13, 16 (1993).

[87] UN Office of Legal Affairs note for the use of the UN Secretariat, 1975 UN Jur. Y.B. 166. This may no longer be valid for credentials of the European Union.

5

Presiding Officer and Other Officers of the Conference

5.1 Presiding Officer

Bailey writes that 'an incompetent presiding officer can, single-handedly, create procedural chaos if he does not understand the Rules, or does not enforce them, or acts in a dictatorial or partisan manner'.[1] Delegations to conferences are apparently aware of the dangers pointed out by Bailey since, although the appointment of presiding officers is dictated by political considerations, the tacit understanding among delegations is to appoint competent individuals. The records of conferences show that it is very rare that this tacit understanding is violated.

5.1.1 Appointment of Presiding Officer

One of the earliest discernible practices of international conferences was the practice of appointing a senior representative of the host country as the presiding officer, or at least as the presiding officer of the opening session. President Wilson, in his speech nominating Clemenceau as President of the Paris Peace Conference, referred to the election of a representative of France as being 'in conformity with usage'.[2] Clemenceau, in his opening speech at the Conference, referred to his being chosen President as a 'lofty international tradition and time honoured courtesy shown towards the country which has the honour to welcome the Peace Conference in its capital'.[3] Kolasa, referring to the development of conferences in the second half of the nineteenth century, writes that 'the President of each conference

[1] Sydney D. Bailey, *The General Assembly of the United Nations, A Study of Procedure and Practice*, rev. edn (1964), p. 111. On the importance of an effective presiding officer, see also André Lewin, 'Le Président', in *La Charte des Nations Unies, commentaire article par article*, ed. Jean Pierre Cot and Allain Pellet (1985), p. 419.

[2] 'The Paris Peace Conference', 139 *International Conciliation* 27 (June 1919) at 28 (p. 813 of the volume).

[3] *Ibid.* at 30 (p. 816 of the volume).

was invariably the representative of the country where the conference was held'.[4]

O'Davoren wrote, in 1943, that '[w]hen a conference is held in a certain country on the invitation of its Government, it is customary to elect as president a representative from that country.'[5] Pastuhov wrote in 1945, 'In the case of conferences convened by a particular state or by a group of states, the prevalent practice is that the country serving as host to the conference supplies the president of the conference.'[6] Pastuhov quotes the following reference from the first volume of the journal of the UN Conference on Food and Agriculture: 'In accordance with established practice, the President of the United States of America, as Chief of State of the Country serving as host to the Conference, has designated . . . as temporary President of the Conference.'[7] Wood and Serres, writing in 1970, could still state that the 'opening session of the conference . . . is presided over by the representative of the country in which the meeting is being held, which is referred to as the host country'.[8]

The opening session of the 1945 San Francisco Conference was presided over by the US Secretary of State, while the working sessions, at the insistence of the Soviet Union, were presided over by representatives of the four Powers (China, UK, USA, and USSR).

The rules of procedure of the 1946 Paris Peace Conference stipulated,

> *Rule II*
>
> The Chairmanship of the Conference will be held in the first place by the representatives of the host Government and thereafter in turn by each of the Members of the Council of Foreign Ministers in the French alphabetical order.[9]

The Brazilian delegation proposed that the representative of the host government be the sole chairman, justifying its proposal by stating that it would be in harmony with diplomatic usage. It was also perfectly natural that the representative of the State on whose territory the conference

[4] Jan Kolasa, *Rules of Procedure of the United Nations General Assembly, A Legal Analysis* (1967), p. 31.

[5] William O'Davoren, *Post-War Reconstruction Conferences, The Technical Organisation of International Conferences* (1943), p. 70.

[6] Vladimir D. Pastuhov, *A Guide to the Practice of International Conferences* (1945), p. 89.

[7] *Ibid.* at p. 86. A US representative also presided over the 1944 Bretton Woods (IMF) and Chicago (ICAO) Conferences.

[8] John R. Wood and Jean Serres, *Diplomatic Ceremonial and Protocol, Principles, Procedure and Practices* (1970), p. 176.

[9] Collection of Documents of the Paris Conference, C.P.(C.R.) 2 A.(d), at p. 151.

was being held should act as President. This was not only a natural mark of courtesy towards the inviting government, but the practical advantages of the system would also be taken into account, and these included primarily the fact that unity of policy in directing the work of the conference would thus be assured.[10] The Brazilian proposal was not adopted.

Practice, although not consistent, appears to show that it is the convening State, and not necessarily the State of the venue, that is being honoured. The Peace Conferences of 1899 and 1907 were held in The Hague. The presidency, however, was granted to Russia, presumably in view of the Tsar's initiative in convening the conferences, although a representative of the Netherlands was elected honorary president. The 1957 Brussels Conference on Maritime Law was presided over by a representative of Belgium,[11] and the 1954 Hague Conference was presided over by a representative of the Netherlands. The 1949 Geneva Conference and the subsequent 1974–1977 Geneva Humanitarian Law Conferences, which were convened by the Swiss Government at the initiative of the ICRC, were presided over by representatives of Switzerland.

Scelle, writing in 1953, states,

> The appointment of the president and the selection of the site of the conference were once the prerogative of the convening government. Nowadays these are merely matters of diplomatic courtesy. The host government presides over the inaugural meeting, at which the guests are welcomed; but the conference subsequently continues its work under a president of its own choice.[12]

At the First Session of the Assembly of the League of Nations, a representative of Switzerland was appointed honorary president. However, this practice was not continued. Conferences convened by the UN are opened by the Secretary-General of the UN or his representative as acting or temporary president, and the permanent president is then nominated and elected. The United States and Switzerland have neither claimed, nor been granted, the presidency of UN or League of Nations conferences convened in New York and Geneva, respectively. Two of the earlier conferences held by the UN in Vienna, the 1961 Vienna Conference on Diplomatic

[10] *Ibid.* at p. 96

[11] Conférence Diplomatique de Droit Maritime, Dixième Session, Bruxelles 1957, Doc. No. 10. Royaume de Belgique, Ministère des Affaires Etrangers et du Commerce Exterieur (1958), p. 25.

[12] Georges Scelle, 'The Evolution of International Conferences', 5 *UNESCO International Social Science Bulletin* 241 (1953 No. 2) at 247.

Relations and the 1963 Vienna Conference on Consular Relations, after being opened by representatives of the Secretary-General, were presided over by a representative of Austria. In the speeches nominating the President, reference was made to Austria as host State. The Vienna Conference on the Law of Treaties was convened, however, on the understanding that 'no claim would be laid for the election of an Austrian national as president'.[13] Most of the later UN conferences held at Vienna did not elect an Austrian president. The 1968 Teheran Conference on Human Rights,[14] after being opened by a representative of the Secretary-General, elected a representative of Iran as the President, but in the nominating speech no reference was made to Iran as the host country. The various sessions of the Third Law of the Sea Conference did not elect representatives of the host States as presidents.

The Assembly of the League of Nations elected presidents who were not members of a delegation.[15] The practice in conferences and in the UNGA is, however, that presiding officers are elected from among members of State delegations. A notable exception was when the President of the Third Law of the Sea Conference, Amersinghe of Sri Lanka, continued to serve as president, even though he was removed from his country's delegation to the Conference.[16]

SUMMARY AS TO PRACTICE

Where a conference is convened by the UN, there is no convening State, and such conferences are opened by the Secretary-General of the UN or his representative. Where a UN conference is convened at a UN office (New York, Geneva or Vienna), there is no practice of granting the host State any preferential standing in election of the president. When the UN convened a conference outside New York, Geneva or Vienna, there was in the past a practice of electing a representative of the host State as president, but this practice appears to have lapsed. Regarding the (few) non-UN conferences,[17] the practice continues of electing a representative of the host or convening State as president.[18] A recent

13 Shabtai Rosenne, *The Law of Treaties: A Guide to the Legislative History of the Vienna Convention* (1970), p. 58.

14 UN Doc. A/CONF.32.

15 Conversation with Shabtai Rosenne, 3 July 1995.

16 The Third Law of the Sea Conference, in a closed session, requested Amerasinghe to remain as President.

17 Principally, as regards the laws of war, at The Hague and, as regards humanitarian law, in Switzerland.

18 The 1997 Oslo Mine Ban Treaty, however, was chaired by the South African ambassador to the UN.

innovation is replacing the term "Chairman" with the gender-neuter term "Chairperson".[19]

5.1.2 *Obligation of Impartiality of the Presiding Officer*

The question of the impartiality of a presiding officer is rarely raised at international meetings.

The propriety of a presiding officer officiating on an issue involving himself arose at the Third Law of the Sea Conference. The issue of the continued presidency of the Conference was discussed,[20] and the President informed the Conference that 'he had felt it would be improper for him to remain in the Chair while that question was discussed'. '[H]e had designated the Vice-President to act as President during the consideration of that question.'[21]

At a 1981 meeting of the UNGA, the representative of Israel questioned the propriety of the representative of Iraq presiding at a debate on the issue of the Israel attack against the Iraqi nuclear reactor. The Iraqi President ruled that there was no inappropriateness involved. His ruling was not challenged.[22] At another meeting of the same session, the representative of Israel again questioned the propriety of the representative of Iraq presiding at a debate on the Palestine question. The Iraqi President once more ruled that there was no inappropriateness involved.[23] His ruling was not challenged. At a 2008 meeting of the UNGA the representative of Morocco strongly criticized the President (from Nicaragua) for using 'flagrantly partisan terms' as regards Western Sahara, but no action was requested.[24]

The issue of presidential impartiality has arisen at several ILO Conferences. At a meeting of the 1951 session of the ILO Conference, the representative of Bulgaria questioned the impartiality of the President.[25] The President replied, 'I am entirely at the disposal of the meeting. I shall leave the presidential chair if the Conference so wishes.'[26] At a meeting

19 See for example the World Conference on Disaster Reduction (2004) UN Doc. A/CONF.206/PC (1) 2*.

20 When the President, Mr Amersinghe, ceased to represent his country, Sri Lanka.

21 Third Law of the Sea Conference, Plenary, 7th Session, 88th Meeting, Official Records, vol. IX, p. 3, UN Doc. A/CONF.62/SR.88, para. 1 (1978).

22 UN GAOR, Plenary, 36th Session, 52nd Meeting, para. 6, UN Doc. A/36/PV.52 (1981).

23 UN GAOR, Plenary, 36th Session, 80th Meeting, para. 11, UN Doc. A/36/PV.80 (1981).

24 UN GAOR Plenary, 63rd Session, 41st Meeting, p. 8. UN Doc.A/63/PV.41 (2008).

25 ILO Conference, 34th Session, Geneva 1951, Record of Proceedings, 14th sitting, p. 228.

26 *Ibid.* at p. 229.

of the 1963 ILO Conference, the President, explaining why he was asking to be excused from presiding over the debate on South Africa, stated,

> As you will remember, two years ago I piloted through this Conference the resolution calling for the expulsion of South Africa for its apartheid policy. Last year in my speech I made it plain that my Government was bent on seeing that the Conference carried out that obligation. Through the good will of all members I have been elected President of this august assembly for this year. You will agree with me that it would not be right that the principles that must guide one in the job of President should be allowed to take second place to other considerations. Because of this I am asking leave to be excused from presiding over this Conference when a matter over which I feel very strongly indeed is going to be debated. In a word, I refuse to be an accuser and a judge in my own case. I think I have your permission, and accordingly, I am asking one of my Vice-Presidents to take the Chair.[27]

At the 1989 World Health Assembly, during the debate on the proposal to admit Palestine as a member, a delegation pointed out that the President, who was from China, should 'personally appreciate its importance, because for years the People's Republic of China was prevented from joining the WHO'.[28] The Director-General of WHO retorted that 'we have no nationality – neither the President nor myself has a nationality. As long as we sit on this rostrum, he has no nationality.'[29]

As a largely symbolic gesture of impartiality, the rule of procedure in the UNGA and in conferences, except those convened by the ICAO, is that the presiding officer, although he is usually head of his State's delegation, does not himself vote, but a member of his delegation votes in his stead.[30]

5.1.3 *Functions of the Presiding Officer*

The UNGA rule states,

> *General Powers of the President*
> *Rule 35*
>
> In addition to exercising the powers conferred upon him elsewhere by these rules, the President shall declare the opening and closing of each plenary meeting of the session, direct the discussions in plenary meeting, ensure observance of these rules, accord the right to speak, put questions

[27] ILO Conference, 47th Session, Geneva 1963, Record of Proceedings, 11th sitting, p. 143.

[28] WHA42/1989/REC/2, p. 231 (1989). [29] *Ibid.* at p. 233.

[30] Rule 37 of the UNGA rules of procedure. Rule 23 of the UN Model Rules.

> and announce decisions. He shall rule on points of order and, subject to these rules, shall have complete control of the proceedings at any meeting and over the maintenance of order thereat. The President may, in the course of the discussion of an item, propose to the General Assembly the limitation of time to be allowed to speakers, the limitation of the number of times a representative may speak, the closure of the list of speakers or the closure of debate. He may also propose the suspension or the adjournment of the meeting or the adjournment of debate on the item under discussion.

The UN Model Rule's proposed definition is substantially the same.

Rule 8(1) of the rules of procedure of the League of Nations included among the general powers to be exercised by the President the power to open and close meetings, accord the right to speak, put questions to the vote, announce decisions and direct discussions. This list appears in the UNGA rules of procedure in substantially the same form.[31]

Bailey divides the formal powers of a presiding officer into three kinds: obligatory, discretionary and initiatory. As obligatory powers Bailey includes the following: opening and closing meetings; directing discussion; announcing decisions; according the right to speak; ruling on points of order; calling speakers to order when they exceed the allotted time; ensuring observance of rules of procedure; and controlling proceedings and maintaining order. Under discretionary powers Bailey includes calling a speaker to order if his remarks are not relevant; limiting time to be allowed speakers on motions for adjournment, closure or suspension; permitting explanation of vote; and permitting discussion and consideration of amendments not circulated in due time in advance. The initiatory powers that Bailey refers to include proposing limitations on time to be allocated to speakers and on the number of times each representative may speak; proposing suspension or adjournment; and proposing closing the list of speakers.[32]

5.1.3.1 Ensuring Observance of the Rules of Procedure

The phrase 'ensure observance of these rules' appears in the list of presidential functions in the rules of procedure of the Assemblies of the League of Nations and the UN. It also appeared in the rules of procedure of conferences until 1958. At the 1958 Law of the Sea Conference this phrase was omitted, and it then continued to be omitted in the rules of procedure of subsequent conferences. A clue to the reason for this omission may be

[31] Rule 35 of the UNGA rules of procedure.

[32] Bailey, *The General Assembly*, pp. 113, 114.

the addition, in 1949, to the rules of procedure of the UNGA of a rule stating, 'The President, in the exercise of his functions, remains under the authority of the General Assembly.'[33] This latter phrase appeared, apparently for the first time, in the conference rules of procedure of the 1958 Law of the Sea Conference,[34] at the same time as the phrase 'ensure the observance of the rules of procedure' was omitted. The replacement of the one phrase by the other appears to have been part of a process of transferring power from the presiding officer to the conference or assembly as a whole. Although the omission has not in practice affected the exercise of the powers of the presiding officer, the phrase is reintroduced in the UN Model Rules.

5.1.3.2 Ruling on Points of Order

The presiding officer has the authority and obligation to rule on points of order.[35]

5.1.3.3 Announcing Results of a Vote

At a meeting of the 1968 Non-Nuclear-Weapon State Conference, the President announced that a resolution had not obtained the required two-thirds majority. A dispute arose as to the number of votes that had been required, and the President announced that 'his interpretation of the results could be contested' by submitting an appeal against his ruling, although 'strictly speaking he had taken no decision'.[36]

5.1.3.4 Deciding Whether a Proposal Is an Amendment to Another Proposal

At conferences it is accepted practice that the presiding officer makes the decision about whether a proposal is an amendment to another proposal.[37] The rules of procedure of the ICAO General Assembly state explicitly:

[33] Rule 31(a) of the amendments and additions to the UNGA rules of procedure, UN GAOR, 4th Session, Plenary Meetings, Annex to the Summary Records of Meetings, Agenda Item 48, Annex I, UN Doc. A/937 (1949). Present Rule 36.

[34] Rule 8 of the rules of procedure of the 1958 Law of the Sea Conference: 'The President, in the exercise of his functions, remains under the authority of the Conference.' UN Doc. A/CONF.13/35 (1958).

[35] This issue is dealt with in Chapter 12.

[36] Summary Records of the 1968 Non-Nuclear-Weapon State Conference, pp. 221, 222, UN Doc. A/CONF.35/SR.18 (1968).

[37] See examples in Section 10.1.2 in Chapter 10.

Rule 50

> The presiding officer shall determine whether a proposed amendment is so related to the motion as to constitute a proper amendment thereto, or whether it must be considered as an alternative or substitute motion; this ruling may be reversed by a majority of votes cast.[38]

At a 1952 committee meeting of the UNGA, the Chairman made a ruling that an amendment, submitted by the United States, was an amendment and not a separate proposal. The representative of Poland argued that it was up to the Committee and not the Chair to make such a distinction. He, however, did not issue a formal challenge to the Chairman's ruling.[39] At the same session, when the Committee was discussing the report of the Trusteeship Council, it debated whether the Chairman or the Committee should make a decision about whether a proposal is an amendment to another proposal or a separate proposal. The Committee agreed to accept the Chairman's 'suggestion'.[40]

At a 2002 meeting of the World Health Assembly, the Legal Counsel gave his opinion that the Chairman 'could seek views before making a ruling' on whether an intervention was an amendment or a proposal, and '[t]he Rules of Procedure did not limit the number of speakers'.[41]

5.1.3.5 Determining Whether a Matter Is One of Substance or of Procedure

The UN Model Rules propose,

Rule 53

> 3. If the question arises whether a matter is one of procedure or of substance, it shall be decided by the Conference by a majority of the representatives present and voting.

The rules of procedure of UN-convened treaty-making conferences, in approximately the last seventy years, as well as of many other conferences, stipulate that matters of substance shall be determined by a two-thirds majority, and matters of procedure by a simple majority.[42] The rules of

38 Rule 50 of the rules of procedure of the ICAO General Assembly, ICAO Doc. 7600/5 (1990).

39 UN GAOR, 2nd Committee, 6th Session, 173rd Meeting, para. 10, UN Doc. A/C.2/6/SR.173 (1952).

40 UN GAOR, 4th Committee, 7th Session, 291st Meeting, paras. 41, 42, UN Doc. A/C.4/7/SR.291 (1952).

41 55th World Health Assembly, Committee 'B', Fifth Meeting, p. 203, WHA55/2002/REC/3 (2002).

42 The rules of procedure of the 1950 Conference on Missing Persons, UN Doc. A/CONF.1/3 (1950), and the 1951 Conference on Refugees, UN Doc. A/CONF.2/3/Rev.1 (1951), both stipulated that all decisions were to be taken by a simple majority.

procedure of the 1958 Law of the Sea Conference, which had such a stipulation, stated,

> *Rule 35*
>
> 3. If the question arises whether a matter is one of procedure or of substance, the President of the Conference shall rule on the question. An appeal against this ruling shall immediately be put to the vote and the President's ruling shall stand unless overruled by a majority of the representatives present and voting.

Most of the conferences where the rules of procedure distinguish, for the purposes of the majority required, between matters of substance and those of procedure follow the 1958 Law of the Sea precedent and grant such authority to the presiding officer. Such conferences include those convened by the IMCO, the ICAO and the Swiss Government. Amongst the latest conferences to adopt this rule are the 2002 IMO Conference on Oil Pollution Damage,[43] the 2004 World Conference on Disaster Reduction,[44] the 2004 Framework Convention on Tobacco Control,[45] the 2004 Review Conference of the Mine Ban Treaty,[46] the 2005 NPT Review Conference,[47] the 2009 Conference on the World Financial and Economic Crisis and Its Impact on Development,[48] and the 2010 Review Conference of the Rome Statute.[49]

The rules of procedure of other conferences, however, contain no reference as to how such a decision is made.[50] The logical inference in such a case is that the decision is to be made by the conference, being the repository of all residual rights. The rules of procedure of yet other conferences

[43] Rule 32(b) of the rules of procedure of the IMO International Conference on the Establishment of a Supplementary Fund for Compensation for Oil Pollution Damage, IMO Doc. LEG/CONF.14/2 (2002).

[44] Rule 35(1) of the rules of procedure of the World Conference on Disaster Reduction, UN Doc. A/CONF.206/PC(II)/2/Corr.1 (2004).

[45] Rule 49(3), Open Ended Intergovernmental Working Group on the WHO Framework Convention on Tobacco Control, WHO Doc. A/FCTC/IGWG/1/4 (2004).

[46] Rule 14(3) of the rules of procedure of the 2004 Review Conference of the Mine Ban Treaty APLC/CONF/2004/PM.2/L.3 (2004).

[47] Rule 28(5) of the rules of procedure of the 2005 NPT Review Conference, Doc. NPT/CONF.2005/1 (2004).

[48] Rule 35 (2) of the rules of procedure of the 2009 Conference on the World Financial and Economic Crisis and Its Impact on Development, A/CONF.214/2 (2009).

[49] Rule 54(2) of the rules of procedure of the 2010 Review Conference of the Rome Statute, International Criminal Court Document RC/3 (2010).

[50] See, for example, the rules of procedure of the 1974 Prescription in Sale of Goods Conference, UN Doc. A/CONF.63/8 (1974), and the various UN Conferences on the Prevention of Crime and the Treatment of Offenders.

stipulate explicitly that it is the conference that determines whether a matter is one of substance or procedure.[51]

The issue is not usually relevant to international organisations as no explicit distinction is normally made in the rules of procedure between matters of substance and those of procedure, as regards the majority required. The Assembly of the International Maritime Satellite Organization (INMARSAT), however, does make that distinction and its rules of procedure state,

> *Rule 23*
>
> (c) Decisions whether a question is procedural or substantive shall be made by the Chairman. His decisions may be overruled by a two-thirds majority.[52,53]

COMMENT

It is difficult to discern the criteria by which the rules of procedure of some conferences grant the authority to distinguish between matters of procedure and substance to the conference and others grant it to the presiding officer. It appears, however, that treaty-making conferences have adopted the option of granting such authority to the presiding officer.[54]

51 See, for example, the rules of procedure of the UN Conference on Technical Co-operation Operation among Developing Countries, UN Doc. A/CONF.79/2 (1978); UN Conference on Science and Technology for Development, UN Doc. A/CONF.81/2 (1979); UN Conference on the Least Developed Countries, UN Doc. A/CONF.104/16 (1981); UN Conference on New and Renewable Sources of Energy, UN Doc. A/CONF.100/2 (1981); UN Conference on the Exploration and Peaceful Uses of Outer Space, UN Doc. A/CONF.101/1 (1982); UN Conference for the Promotion of International Co-operation in the Peaceful Uses of Nuclear Energy, UN Doc. A/CONF.100/5 (1982); World Assembly on Ageing, UN Doc. A/CONF.113/2 (1982); International Conference on the Question of Palestine, UN Doc. A/CONF.114/18 (1982), A/CONF.114/12 (1983); World Conference to Review and Appraise the Achievements of the UN Decade for Women: Equality, Development and Peace, UN Doc. A/CONF.116/2 (1985); and Second UN Conference on the Least Developed Countries, UN Doc. A/CONF.147/3 (1990).

52 INMARSAT, Basic Documents, 3rd edn, 1986, p. 88.

53 Reference should be made to the procedure in the UN Security Council that is governed in this respect by the Statement of the four sponsoring Powers at San Francisco: 'the decision regarding the preliminary question as to whether or not such a matter is procedural, must be taken by a vote of seven [nine] members of the Security Council, including the concurring votes of the permanent members.' Statement by the delegations of the four sponsoring Governments on voting procedures in the Security Council, UN Doc. S/Procedure/79, reproduced in Repertory of Practice of UN Organs, vol. II, p. 104, Article 27, Annexes (1955), UN Sales No. 1955 V.2.

54 The rules of procedure of the Third Law of the Sea Conference granted the authority to the President (Rule 39(4)) (UN Doc. A/CONF.62/30/Rev.3 (1973)). A proposal by the

Granting the authority to the presiding officer, subject to appeal, appears to be preferable as it can obviate unnecessary voting. It might be useful to revise the UN Model Rules in this regard.

Unlike the situation in the UN Security Council,[55] surprisingly little debate appears to have occurred at other conferences about whether an issue is procedural or not.[56]

5.1.3.6 Deciding if an Amendment Necessarily Implies the Rejection of Another Amendment

The UNGA rules of procedure state, 'Where, however, the adoption of one amendment necessarily implies the rejection of another amendment, the latter amendment shall not be put to the vote.'[57] The UN Model Rules are substantially identical.[58] By implication the power to make such a ruling is part of the discretionary powers of the presiding officer, and the assembly or conference can overturn such a ruling by way of a successful challenge. This procedure has been followed in UN practice.

5.1.3.7 Determining What Are the Operative Parts of a Resolution

The UNGA rules of procedure state, 'If all operative parts of the proposal or of the amendment have been rejected, the proposal or the amendment shall be considered to have been rejected as a whole.'[59] The UN Model Rules are substantially the same.[60] The rule does not state who is to decide what the 'operative parts' are. By implication the power to make such a ruling is part of the discretionary powers of the presiding officer, and the assembly can overturn such a ruling by way of a successful challenge.

delegation of Spain to grant the authority to the Conference was not adopted (UN Doc. A/CONF.62/10 (1973)).

55 See, for example, Stephen Jacobs and Marc Poirier, 'The Right to Veto United Nations Membership Applications: The United States Veto of the Vietnams', 17 *Harvard International Law Journal* 581 (1976) and authorities quoted there.

56 See discussion of the issue in Chapter 12.

57 Rule 90 of the UNGA rules of procedure; Rule 59 of the UN Model Rules. This rule did not appear in the original UNGA rules of procedure and was adopted by the UNGA in 1949: UNGA Resolution 362 (IV) of 22 October 1949.

58 Rule 59(1) of the UN Model Rules.

59 Rule 89 of the UNGA rules of procedure. The rule is substantially the same in Rule 57 of the UN Model Rules. This rule did not appear in the original UNGA rules of procedure and was adopted by the UNGA in 1949: UNGA Resolution 362 (IV) of 22 October 1949.

60 Rule 57 of the UN Model Rules.

5.1.3.8 Deciding on Compatibility of Different Proposals

At a 1950 session of the UNGA, the Chairman ruled that two proposals that had been submitted were mutually exclusive and if one was adopted there would be no need to vote on the other.[61] At a 1992 meeting of the UNGA, when discussing the situation in Sudan, the Chairman ruled that, as one resolution had been passed, 'there was no reason to consider' another resolution that had been submitted.[62] It is not apparent what authority the Chairmen had to make these rulings. The correct procedure in these instances would seem to have been either a motion not to vote on the subsequent proposal or alternatively a Chairman's ruling that the subsequent proposal would be a reconsideration of the issue.

5.1.3.9 Deciding if a Motion Entails Reconsideration of a Previous Decision

It is the assembly or conference that will vote whether to allow a proposal to be reconsidered. However, it is the presiding officer who will make the initial decision about whether a proposal entails reconsideration of a previous decision or not: his decision can of course be appealed. Only when the presiding officer has made his decision can the assembly or conference proceed to decide if it wishes to allow reconsideration.[63]

5.1.3.10 Determining Which Amendment Is Furthest Removed from the Original Proposal

The UNGA rules of procedure state, 'When two or more amendments are moved to a proposal, the General Assembly shall vote first on the amendment furthest removed in substance from the original proposal.'[64] The UN Model Rules are substantially the same.[65] The rule does not state how a decision is to be made about which amendment is furthest removed. By implication the power to make such a ruling is part of the discretionary powers of the presiding officer, and the assembly or conference can

[61] UN GAOR, 1st Committee, 5th Session, 390th Meeting, para. 35, UN Doc. A/C.1/SR.390 (1950).

[62] UN GAOR, 3rd Committee, 47th Session, 58th Meeting, para. 99, UN Doc. A/C.3/47/SR.58 (1992).

[63] For examples of decisions by presiding officers on whether an issue entails reconsideration, see Section 11.2 in Chapter 11.

[64] Rule 90 of the UNGA rules of procedure. This rule has appeared substantially unchanged in all editions of the rules of procedure.

[65] Rule 59(1) of the UN Model Rules.

overturn such a ruling by way of a successful challenge. This procedure has been followed in UN practice.[66]

The rules of procedure of the World Health Assembly state explicitly that 'the Health Assembly shall first vote on the amendment *deemed by the President* to be furthest removed in substance from the original proposal'.[67] [emphasis added]

5.1.3.11 Deciding the Order of Voting on Proposals

The rules of procedure of assemblies and conferences reserve to the assembly or conference the right to decide the order of voting on proposals. Nevertheless, at a 1986 committee meeting of the IAEA General Conference, a delegation raised as a point of order the request that a certain proposal be voted on before another. The Chairman ruled on the request, and the Legal Adviser informed the Conference that '[a]s to the order in which the drafts submitted should be considered, the Committee was fully empowered to decide on that. However, in the given instance a point of order had been raised and the Chairman had given a ruling on it. It was now for the Committee to decide whether to accept that ruling or appeal against it.'[68]

5.1.3.12 Determining if a Proposal Is *Ultra Vires*

No rules of procedure explicitly authorise a presiding officer to decide if a proposal is *ultra vires* or not. At the 1961 Vienna Conference on Diplomatic Relations, the representative of Iran declared that it was 'a fundamental principle of a debate on amendments that the Chairman had full discretion to decide whether amendments were relevant or not. If the Conference rules of procedure did not contain that principle, he suggested that a new rule should be added'.[69] There was, however, no support for this view, and no formal proposal was introduced. At the 1958 Law of the Sea Conference, the Chairman of a committee ruled that an amendment was 'inadmissible',[70] but the ruling was not based on the proposal being *ultra vires* to the competence of the Conference.

66 See, for instance, UN GAOR, 4th Committee, 36th Session, 25th Meeting, paras. 1, 8, UN Doc. A/C.4/36/SR.25 (1981).

67 Rule 67 of the rules of procedure of the World Health Assembly, Geneva, 1985. See debate on this issue at the 34th World Health Assembly (WHA34/1981/REC/3, p. 312 (1981)).

68 GC(XXIX)/COM.5/OR.44, para. 12 (1986).

69 Official Records of the 1961 Vienna Conference on Diplomatic Relations, 11th Meeting of the Committee of the Whole, para. 10, p. 96, UN Doc. A/CONF.20/14 (1961).

70 Official Records of the 1958 Law of the Sea Conference, Committee I, vol. III, p. 99, UN Doc. A/CONF.13/39 (1958). The Chairman based his ruling on two grounds, first that the voting had commenced and second on the inadmissibility of a sub-amendment intended to negate the amendment and restore the original language of the ILC draft.

At a 1961 session of the ILO Conference, a delegation raised a point of order asking for a ruling as to whether a certain proposal was *intra vires* or not.[71] The President, although stating that it was for the Committee and Conference to look into these questions, nevertheless made a ruling that the proposal was *intra vires*.[72]

The rules of procedure of the ICAO Assembly and the ICAO Conferences do not contain a specific reference to decisions on competence. The issue, if raised, is treated as a question of a point of order to be dealt with by the presiding officer. For example, at a meeting of the 1971 Montreal Air Law Conference, the representative of France, on a point of order, pointed out that a proposal submitted by Ireland was 'not within the terms of reference of the Conference and outside its competence to discuss the matter'.[73] The President ruled the proposal to be 'out of order'.[74] At a 1986 meeting of the ICAO Assembly, the Chairman rejected a point of order raised by the United Kingdom, claiming that the issue of apartheid was *ultra vires* to the Assembly. The Chairman ruled that the inclusion of the item on the agenda 'was in order'.[75] The Chairman's ruling was upheld on a challenge.[76]

COMMENT

Despite these examples, it would appear that the decision whether a proposal is *ultra vires* or not is an issue to be decided by a conference, and not by the presiding officer. The presiding officer therefore should not attempt to give a ruling, but should put the issue directly to the conference for a decision.

5.1.3.13 Deciding if a Question Is Important

The rules of procedure of the UNGA list issues that are considered 'important questions' and provide that a decision on whether additional questions are 'important', and therefore requiring a two thirds majority, is a decision to be made by a vote of the Assembly.[77] The question of whether an issue comes within a category specified in the rules of procedure is thus

[71] ILO Conference, 45th Session, Geneva 1961, Record of Proceedings, 31st sitting, p. 529.

[72] *Ibid.*

[73] 1971 Montreal Air Law Conference, Commission of the Whole, 13th Meeting, vol. I, Minutes, p. 120, para. 44, ICAO Doc. 9081-LC/170–1.

[74] *Ibid.*, 14th Meeting, p. 121, para. 3.

[75] Minutes of the 10th Meeting of the Executive Committee of the 26th Assembly of ICAO, paras. 15.2, 16, ICAO Doc. 9489, A26-EX (1986).

[76] *Ibid.* at para. 18.

[77] Rule 85 of the UNGA rules of procedure, based on Article 18(3) of the UN Charter.

an issue to be decided by the presiding officer (subject of course to a possible challenge). If the presiding officer does not determine that an issue comes within one of the specified categories, then the Assembly may still decide, by a vote, to add it to the list of important questions requiring a two-thirds majority.

The rules of procedure of the World Health Assembly have a similar provision.[78] Nevertheless, at the 1993 World Health Assembly, where the Chairman of a committee put such an issue to the vote, a delegation complained at the 'Chairman's having put a procedural decision to the Committee', claiming that 'it was for the Chairman and the Legal Counsel to decide such matters'.[79] At a plenary meeting of the same session of the World Health Assembly, another decision about whether a question was important was put to the Assembly.[80]

The rules of procedure of the General Conference of the IAEA list, among issues requiring a two-thirds majority:

> *Rule 69*
>
> (c) A decision, upon recommendation of the Board of Governors, to suspend any Members from the exercise of the privileges and rights of membership.
>
> *Rule 70*
>
> Decisions of the General Conference on other questions, including the determination of additional questions or categories of questions to be decided by a two-thirds majority, shall be made by a majority of the Members present and voting.[81]

At the 1986 session of the General Conference of the IAEA, a debate took place on whether a draft resolution calling inter alia for 'withholding research contracts to Israel'[82] came within Rule 69(c) of the rules of procedure. The President, on the advice of the Legal Counsel, ruled that it came within the terms of Rule 69(c). The representative of Iraq then requested that the issue be decided by a vote of the Conference in accordance with Rule 70, and the Chairman interpreted this as a challenge to his ruling. The challenge was defeated on a vote.[83]

78 Rule 73 of the rules of procedure of the World Health Assembly.

79 WHA46/1993/REC/3, p. 268 (1993).

80 WHA46/1993/REC/2, p. 18 (1993).

81 IAEA Doc. GC(XXXI)/INF/245/Rev.1 (1992).

82 IAEA Doc. GC(XXIX)/764 (1986).

83 Official Records of the 280th Plenary Meeting, the 29th General Conference of the IAEA, p. 16, IAEA Doc. GC(XXIX)/OR.280 (1986).

COMMENT

The question whether an issue comes within a category specified in the rules of procedure is an issue to be decided by the presiding officer. Adding an additional category or issue requires a decision of the conference or assembly.

5.1.3.14 Approving a Request for a Separate Vote

All the rules of procedure examined provide that it is the conference or assembly that makes decisions on requests for a separate vote.

At a plenary meeting of the Third Law of the Sea Conference, the President ruled that 'the "package deal" should also apply to the Final Act . . . there was no reason to have separate votes on the various paragraphs of those texts'.[84] The President's ruling was upheld on a challenge.[85] It is submitted that the President should have put to the Conference the request for a separate vote and not have made the ruling himself.

At a 1973 meeting of the ICAO Assembly, a delegation claimed that a separate vote would be impossible and requested that 'perhaps the Chairman could rule on the matter'.[86] The Chairman replied that 'his personal opinion was that the Articles could not be divided, but he did not wish to rule on the question. He preferred the Assembly to decide it.'[87]

5.1.3.15 Proposing a Question of Principle

At a 1948 meeting of a UNGA committee, the Committee was faced with several conflicting resolutions on the question of the right of the UN to present a claim for reparations against a State. The Chairman ruled that the Committee should vote on a preliminary question that he had drafted. The Chairman's ruling was challenged inter alia on the grounds that it was out of order since a Chairman could not propose substantive proposals. The Chairman's ruling was upheld.[88] In treaty-making conferences it is a common procedure for presiding officers to draft and propose questions of principle.[89]

84 Official Records of the Resumed 11th Session of the Third Law of the Sea Conference, vol. XVIII, p. 10, para. 81, 184th Meeting, UN Doc. A/CONF.62 (1982).

85 *Ibid.* at paras. 82, 83.

86 Minutes of the 14th Executive Committee Meeting of the 20th Extraordinary Assembly of ICAO, para. 7, ICAO Doc. 9088, A20-Min.EX/14 (1973).

87 *Ibid.* at para. 8.

88 UN GAOR, 6th Committee, 3rd Session, 118th Meeting, p. 582, UN Doc. A/C.6/SR.118 (1948).

89 See examples in Section 14.6 in Chapter 14.

5.1.3.16 Making Substantive Proposals

At a 1993 meeting of a UNGA committee, the Chairman proposed an amendment to a resolution. A delegate pointed out to the Chairman 'that it was not appropriate for him to make formal proposals before the Committee, which was the prerogative of representatives'.[90] The representative of the Netherlands, while commending the initiative of the Chairman, adopted the proposal as a Netherlands proposal, thus avoiding a procedural debate on the issue.[91]

At the Third Law of the Sea Conference, it was the Chairmen of the Committees who prepared the various parts of the Single Informal Negotiating Text. Buzan comments on this that '[t]heir [the Chairmen's] most useful role[s] were as selectors, prompters, and legitimizing agents for compromises worked out by private groups of delegates'.[92]

5.1.3.17 Proposing Closure, Suspension or Adjournment of a Debate or Meeting

The rules of procedure of the UNGA state,

> *Rule 35*
>
> The President may, in the course of the discussion of an item, propose to the General Assembly . . . the closure of the list of speakers or the closure of the debate. He may also propose the suspension or the adjournment of the meeting or the adjournment of the debate on the item under discussion.

Rule 34 in the UN Model Rules is substantially the same.

There does not appear to have been any controversy as to the authority of presiding officers to make such proposals.

5.1.3.18 Authority of Presiding Officers Where Speakers Make Irrelevant or Offensive Statements

The UNGA rules of procedure and the UN Model Rules authorise the presiding officer to call a speaker to order if his speech is not relevant to the 'subject under discussion'[93] or, in the case of the UN Model Rules, not relevant to the 'question under discussion'.[94] The rules of procedure do not

[90] UN GAOR, 1st Committee, 48th Session, 30th Meeting, para. 46, UN Doc. A/C.1/48/SR.30 (1993).

[91] *Ibid.* at para. 48.

[92] Barry Buzan, 'Negotiating by Consensus: Developments in Technique at the United Nations Conference on the Law of the Sea', 75 AJIL 324 (1981) at 335.

[93] Rule 68 of the UNGA rules of procedure.

[94] Rule 36(2) of the UN Model Rules.

set out the result of a speaker being called to order.[95] The common practice is that presiding officers, usually at the initiative of another delegation, call upon speakers to confine their statements to the issue on the agenda.[96] Such calls do not normally result in any action or ruling from the Chair. Where such calls to order are unheeded, however, presiding officers have at times suspended meetings.[97]

There is no specific rule of procedure dealing with abusive language, and unlike the situation in national parliaments, presiding officers do not generally attempt to define certain phrases as 'out of order'. Hovey, writing in 1951, stated that 'the [UN] Assembly has never sought systematically to restrain "abusive" language or "imputations of falsehood"'.[98] On a number of occasions presiding officers have, however, called on speakers at the UNGA to address States members of the UN by their official names.[99]

A Chairman of a committee of the UNGA, at the 1981 session, ruled a speaker to be out of order where the speaker quoted a private

[95] *Robert's Rules* state, 'Calling a member to order.– [A]s when a member repeatedly questions the motives of other members whom he mentions by name, or persists in speaking on completely irrelevant matters in debate – the chair normally should first warn the member; but with or without such warning, the chair or any other member can "call the member to order". If the chair does this, he says, "The member is out of order and will be seated."' *Robert's Rules of Order, Newly Revised*, 11th edn (2011), p. 646. Sturgis defines 'Out of order' as 'Not correct from a parliamentary standpoint at the particular time'. Alice F. Sturgis, *Standard Code of Parliamentary Procedure* (1950), p. 246.

[96] For example, Official Records of the 1958 Law of the Sea Conference, Committee I, 4th Meeting, paras. 22–25, vol. III, p. 2, UN Doc. A/CONF.13/39 (1958); Official Records of the Third Law of the Sea Conference, Plenary, 55th Meeting, para. 43, vol. IV, p. 22, UN Doc. A/CONF.62 (1975); UN GAOR, 4th Committee, 20th Session, 1572nd Meeting, paras. 5–8, UN Doc. A/C.4/SR.1572 (1965); ILO Conference, 89th Session, 5th sitting (2001) p. 6; UN GAOR, 4th Committee, 20th Session, 1541st Meeting, paras. 75–77, UN Doc. A/C.4/SR.1541 (1965); UN GAOR, 3rd Committee, 20th Session, 1362nd Meeting, paras. 26, 29, 31, UN Doc. A/C.3/SR.1362 (1965); UN GAOR, Special Political Committee, 20th Session, 477th Meeting, paras. 14–16, UN Doc. A/SPC/SR.477 (1965); UN GAOR, Special Political Committee, 22nd Session, 558th Meeting, paras. 34–40, UN Doc. A/SPC/SR.558 (1968); UN GAOR, Plenary, 28th Session, 2148th Meeting, p. 452, UN Doc. A/PV.2148 (1973); UN GAOR, Special Political Committee, 45th Session, 7th Meeting, para. 23, UN Doc. A/SPC/45/SR.7 (1990); UN GAOR, 4th Committee, 46th Session, 11th Meeting, para. 54, UN Doc. A/C.4/46/SR.11 (1991).

[97] Although the rules of procedure of the UNGA only grant the presiding officer the right to propose suspension of meetings, in practice presiding officers tend to suspend meetings in such circumstances without consulting the forum. See UN GAOR, 1st Committee, 5th Session, 346th Meeting, para. 20, UN Doc. A/C.1/SR.346 (1950).

[98] Allan Hovey Jr, 'Obstructionism and the Rules of the General Assembly', 5 *UNESCO International Organization* 515 (1951 No. 3) at 519.

[99] See, for example, UN Doc. A/C.1/44/PV.52, p. 81 (1989); UN Doc. A/C.1/45/PV.23, p. 66 (1990); UN Doc. A/C.1/45/PV.49, p. 37 (1990).

conversation.[100] At a 1981 meeting of a committee of the UNGA, the Chairman ruled that the representative of Jordan was out of order in raising in the particular debate the issue of the extradition of Ziad Abu Ein from the United States to Israel. The Chairman's ruling was overruled on a challenge submitted by the representative of Jordan.[101]

At a 1988 meeting of the World Health Assembly, the representative of Iraq, on a point of order, repeatedly requested the President to direct the representative of Iran to 'confine himself to the items on the agenda'. The President refrained from doing so, commenting that the representative of Iraq would be allowed to exercise 'his right of reply' at the end of the meeting.[102] At a 1992 meeting of the World Health Assembly, where a point of order was raised objecting to a statement of a representative, the Legal Counsel gave his opinion that the President was not authorised to 'close a statement by a speaker', but could only grant a right of reply.[103]

The President of an ILO Conference ruled, however, that phrases such as 'a few madmen', 'treacherous and bloody', 'is it not criminal?' and 'is it not barbarous?' were unparliamentary language.[104]

COMMENT

The general practice is that chairmen do not intervene in regard to offensive statements made by delegations.

5.1.3.19 Authority of Presiding Officers to Remove a Speaker from the Rostrum

The rules of procedure of the Assembly of the League of Nations authorised the President, if necessary, to 'direct the speaker to resume his seat'.[105] Pastuhov, writing in 1945, stated that 'in extreme cases he [the President] may direct the speaker to resume his seat... it would create a sensation if the president of an intergovernmental conference were to resort' to this

[100] UN GAOR, 1st Committee, 3rd Session, 191st Meeting, p. 518, UN Doc. A/C.1/SR.191 (1948).

[101] UN GAOR, 3rd Committee, 36th Session, 33rd Meeting, paras. 4, 5, UN Doc. A/C.3/36/SR.33 (1981).

[102] Verbatim Records of the 4th Plenary Meeting of the 41st World Health Assembly, pp. 58, 59, WHA41/1988/REC/2 (1988).

[103] Verbatim Records of the 7th Plenary Meeting of the 45th World Health Assembly, p. 128, WHA45/1992/REC/2 (1992).

[104] ILO Conference, 49th Session, Geneva 1965, Record of Proceedings, 23rd sitting, p. 325.

[105] Rule 15(3) of the rules of procedure of the Assembly of the League of Nations.

measure.[106] Pastuhov adds that from his experience he 'has no recollection of a resort to the measure in question in the course of a conference held under the auspices of the League'.[107]

The rules of procedure of the UNGA do not contain such a provision.

The rules of procedure of the 1949 Geneva Conference stipulated,

> *Rule 28*
>
> The President may call to order any speaker whose remarks are not relevant to the question under discussion and, if necessary, withdraw his right to speak.

The draft rules of procedure of the 1974–1977 Geneva Humanitarian Law Conference contained a similar rule, stating,

> *Rule 19*
>
> The President may call a speaker to order if his remarks are not relevant to the subject under discussion and, should occasion arise, require him to stop speaking.[108]

At the initiative of the Syrian delegation, a second paragraph was added to the rule, stating,

> *Rule 19*
>
> 2. A representative may appeal against the ruling of the President. The appeal shall be immediately put to the vote and the President's ruling shall stand unless the appeal is approved by a majority of the representatives present and voting. A representative appealing against the President's ruling may not speak on the substance of the matter under discussion.[109]

Presumably the intention of the amendment was to emphasise that, on the issue of stopping a speaker from speaking, as on other issues, the exercise of authority by the President was subject to the control of the conference. Apparently, neither the rule in the 1949 Geneva Conference nor the rule in the 1974–1977 Humanitarian Law Conference was ever invoked. One of the rare occasions when a presiding officer attempted to withdraw a right to speak was at the 1968 Teheran Conference on Human Rights where the President 'asked the representative of the Republic of Viet-Nam to leave the rostrum'.[110] The President immediately pointed out that any representative could appeal against her decision;[111] no representative did so, however.

[106] Pastuhov, *Guide*, p. 122. [107] *Ibid.* at p. 122, n. 20. [108] CDDH/2.
[109] CDDH/2/Rev.3. [110] UN Doc. A/CONF.32/SR.24, p. 139. [111] *Ibid.*

Article 14(4) of the Standing Orders of the ILO Conference states, 'The President may require a speaker to resume his seat if his remarks are not relevant to the subject under discussion.'[112] Use has occasionally been made of this provision, and speakers have been asked to resume their seat.[113] At a 1965 session of the ILO Conference, the President summarised his policy as follows:

> I propose to appeal again to speakers to confine themselves to the subjects which we are discussing; but if there are speakers who choose to digress, I propose to exercise my discretion, as referred to in paragraph 4 of article 14, of the Standing Orders, only if I feel that they are using unparliamentary or abusive language. Apart from that, I do not propose to exercise the discretion merely if I do not agree with them or think that what they are saying is beyond the scope of this Conference.[114]

No delegate appears to have questioned this statement of policy.

5.1.3.20 Expunging Statements from the Record

The presiding officer apparently has no authority to order that statements be expunged from the record.[115]

5.1.3.21 Suspending a Meeting

All the rules of procedure studied provide that it is the conference or assembly that has the power to decide on suspension of a meeting. Nevertheless, presiding officers frequently decide on suspension of meetings without consulting the conference or assembly.[116]

[112] Standing Orders of the International Labour Conference, International Labour Office, Geneva, December 1992.

[113] See, for example, ILO Conference, 51st Session, Geneva 1967, 12th sitting, p. 171; ILO Conference, 55th (Maritime) Session, Geneva 1970, p. 116; ILO Conference, 57th Session, Geneva 1972, p. 99; ILO Conference, 82nd Session, Geneva 1995, 9th sitting, p. 10.

[114] ILO Conference, 49th Session, Geneva 1965, Record of Proceedings, 8th sitting, p. 82.

[115] See Chapter 19 on this issue.

[116] At the 2148th Plenary Meeting of the 28th Session of the UNGA, the President suspended the meeting without bringing the issue to a vote. Apparently, the representative of Cuba had tried to ascend the rostrum without obtaining permission from the President. UN Doc. A/PV.2148, para. 369 (1973).

> At the 88th Plenary Meeting of the 44th Session of the UNGA, the President decided to 'suspend the meeting for consultation' without requesting approval of the Assembly. UN Doc. A/44/PV.88, p. 62 (Provisional) (1989).
>
> At the 71st Plenary Meeting of the 47th Session of the UNGA, the President suspended the meeting without putting the motion to a vote. The President then explained, '[a]s presiding officer, I believed that it was in the best interests of these

5.1.3.22 Setting Limitations on the Time to Be Allowed to Speakers

5.1.3.22.1 Debates The presiding officer has the authority to propose to the conference,[117] assembly or committee the limitation of time to be allowed to speakers.[118] It is common practice for presiding officers to make such proposals.[119]

The early rules of procedure of the UNGA, until the changes introduced in the Fourth Session,[120] did not authorise presiding officers to propose any time limits for speeches.[121]

5.1.3.22.2 Procedural Motions On motions for adjournment of debate, closure of debate and suspension or adjournment of the meeting, the presiding officer in the UNGA has the authority to determine the time allotted for speeches.[122] In the UN Model Rules, the President is instructed to 'limit each intervention on a procedural question to a maximum of five minutes'.[123]

5.1.3.22.3 Right of Reply Regarding the right of reply, in the UNGA presiding officers may propose limitations on the time allotted to speakers but it is the Assembly or committee that has the authority to determine the time allotted.[124]

In the UN Model Rules, the presiding officer is given no discretion as to the time allotted for speakers exercising a right of reply; the time allotted is fixed in the rules of procedure.[125]

proceedings – to maintain order, and as it was unclear under which rule we were operating – to suspend the meeting briefly'. UN Doc. A/47/PV.71, p. 71 (1992). See also, for example, 1st Committee of the 1974–77 Geneva Humanitarian Law Conference, CDDH/I/SR.57, para. 80, vol. IX, p. 80.

117 Rule 34 of the UN Model Rules.

118 Rule 35 of the UNGA rules of procedure; Rule 50 of the rules of procedure of the General Conference of the IAEA.

119 For example, UN GAOR, 3rd Committee, 21st Session, 1434th Meeting, para. 2, UN Doc. A/C.3/21/SR.1434 (1966).

120 UNGA Resolution 362 (IV) of 22 October 1949.

121 In the UNGA, such limitations are often made by a plenary decision adopted on the recommendation of the Secretary-General.

122 Rules 74, 75, 76, 88 of the UNGA rules of procedure.

123 Rule 36(3) of the UN Model Rules.

124 Rule 72 of the UNGA rules of procedure. See discussion in UN GAOR, Ad Hoc Political Committee, 6th Session, 26th Meeting, where this issue arose. UN Doc. A/C.53/SR.26, paras. 9–12.

125 Rule 40(2)(b) of the UN Model Rules.

5.1.3.23 Proposing Limitation on Number of Interventions

The UNGA rules of procedure and the UN Model Rules authorise the presiding officer to propose to the Assembly or conference 'the limitation on the number of times each representative may speak'.[126] The power to make such a decision lies, however, with the respective bodies.[127] At one early meeting of the Plenary of the UNGA, the President ruled that only one speaker from each delegation could take the floor. This ruling was contested and does not appear to have served as a precedent.[128] The rules of procedure of the WHO do not grant the President authority to limit the number of interventions. Nevertheless, the President of the 1986 Assembly ruled, 'Only those delegates who had not already spoken, and who were not already sponsors of the resolution, would be given the floor.'[129] The ruling was not challenged.

5.1.3.24 Enforcing the Rule on Not Speaking to Substance on Procedural Motions

Rule 71 of the rules of procedure of the UNGA contains this ruling: 'A representative rising to a point of order may not speak on the substance of the matter under discussion.' The rule in the UN Model Rules is substantially the same.

This rule was enforced in the Third Law of the Sea Conference where the President warned two delegations that any further attempts to comment on matters of substance while speaking on a point of order 'would be ruled out of order'.[130] In the UNGA, the rule is not usually enforced, although the President has on at least one occasion called a delegate out of order for violating the rule.[131]

5.1.3.25 Setting Deadlines for Submission of Proposals and Amendments

It is common practice for presiding officers to propose deadlines for submitting proposals and amendments.[132] Nevertheless, there is usually no

[126] Rule 34(1) of the UN Model Rules; Rule 35 of the UNGA rules of procedure.
[127] Rule 36(3) of the UN Model Rules; Rule 72 of the UNGA rules of procedure.
[128] UN GAOR, Plenary, 2nd Session, 102nd Meeting, p. 530, UN Doc. A/PV.102 (1947).
[129] WHA39/1986/REC/3, p. 287.
[130] Third Law of the Sea Conference, Official Records, vol. XVI, 174th Meeting, para. 10, p. 127, UN Doc. A/CONF.62 (1982).
[131] UN GAOR, Plenary, 15th Session, Part II, 988th Meeting, para. 42, UN Doc. A/PV.988 (1961).
[132] For example, UN GAOR, Plenary, 21st Session, 1487th Meeting, paras. 94, 95, UN Doc. A/PV.1487 (1966); UN GAOR, Plenary, 21st Session, 1467th Meeting, para. 115, UN Doc. A/PV.1467 (1966).

mandate in rules of procedure for setting deadlines, and it is not clear therefore whether such a deadline, agreed to by the conference, can prevent a delegation from submitting a proposal after the deadline. It could be argued that preventing a delegation from submitting a proposal requires the authority of a specific rule of procedure.

5.1.3.26 Allowing Representatives to Speak

The assumption in all conferences and assemblies is that the president is obliged to call upon a speaker who has signified a desire to speak.[133] However, at the 1987 session of the IAEA General Conference, the President put a US proposal to an immediate vote, ignoring delegations who requested the floor. The President explained that 'certain delegates had asked to take the floor. However, he did not consider it desirable to engage in a long debate on procedural questions.' The delegations of the Syrian Arab Republic and Iraq subsequently protested, explaining that they had been requesting the floor in order to ask for a roll-call vote.[134]

Rule 68 of the UNGA rules of procedure states, 'No representative may address the General Assembly without having previously obtained the permission of the President.'[135] The Chairman of a UNGA committee, at its 1981 session, ruled that in the case of a representative of an organisation, it is the Assembly or conference that can authorise the right to speak. The Chairman's ruling was based on a legal opinion by the Legal Counsel.[136]

5.1.3.27 Clearing Visitors from the Hall

At a 1962 meeting of the UNGA, in response to interruptions from the public galleries, the President threatened to clear the galleries of visitors.[137] There is no specific reference to such authority in the rules of procedure, but presumably it is inherent in the presiding officer's authority to 'have complete control of the proceedings . . . and over the maintenance of order thereat'.[138]

[133] This is implied in Rule 68 of the UNGA rules of procedure and in Rule 36(1) of the UN Model Rules.

[134] IAEA General Conference, 30th Session, 291st Plenary Meeting, IAEA Doc. GC(XXX)/OR.291, paras. 78, 81, 82 (1987).

[135] Rule 36(1) of the UN Model Rules is substantially the same.

[136] UN GAOR, Special Political Committee, 36th Session, 41st Meeting, p. 1, UN Doc. A/SPC/36/SR.40 (1981).

[137] UN GAOR, Plenary, 17th Session, 1145th Meeting, para. 11, UN Doc. A/PV.1145 (1962).

[138] Rule 35 of the UNGA rules of procedure; Rule 34(1) of the UN Model Rules.

5.1.3.28 Issuing Invitations to Observers

The decision as to inviting organisations to attend conferences as observers is usually vested in the bureau of a conference subject to approval by the conference. However, at IMO Conferences this authority is vested in the president of the conference or chairman of the committee.[139]

5.1.3.29 Delegating Authority to the President

The ILO Conferences, in between sittings, delegate to the President together with the Vice-Presidents the 'authority to take any decisions or perform any functions within the competence of the Conference with respect to any matter that needs to be dealt with before the Conference resumes its plenary sittings'.[140]

5.1.3.30 Calling for Standing in Silence in Memory

One President of the UNGA reminded the Plenary that it was only the President who had authority to ask members to observe a minute of silence as an act of memory.[141]

5.1.4 Right of Presiding Officer to Change His Decisions

Unlike the 'law of the Medes and Persians',[142] a presiding officer is allowed to change his mind and alter a decision he has previously made. At the 1958 Law of the Sea Conference[143] and at the 1968 Vienna Conference on the Law of Treaties,[144] the Chairmen changed decisions they had made without this being challenged by the Conferences.

[139] For example, Rule 58 of the rules of procedure of the IMO International Conference on the Establishment of a Supplementary Fund for Compensation for Oil Pollution Damage, LEG/CONF.14/2 (2002).

[140] See, for example, delegation of authority by the ILO Conference, 91st Session, Geneva 2003, 1st sitting, pp. 6/7.

[141] UN GAOR, Plenary, 5th Session, 280th Meeting, para. 155, UN Doc. A/PV.280 (1950).

[142] 'Now, O king, establish the decree and sign the writing, that it be not changed, according to the law of the Medes and Persians, which altereth not.' Book of Daniel, VI, 8.

[143] 'The Chairman said that he would not wish to insist on his ruling, which had given rise to difficulties, and hoped that the Committee would be able to avoid similar predicaments in the future.' Official Records, 1958 Law of the Sea Conference, 37th Meeting of Committee I, vol. III, p. 109, para. 55, UN Doc. A/CONF.13/39 (1958).

[144] 'The Chairman said he had changed his decision in order to avoid difficulties in the Drafting Committee's work.' Official Records of the Vienna Conference on the Law of Treaties (First Session), Committee of the Whole, p. 59, para. 56, UN Doc. A/CONF.39/11 (1968).

At the 1952 session of the UNGA, the Chairman withdrew her decision after it caused controversy.[145] No objection was made to such withdrawal. At the 1961 session of the UNGA, in a debate in a committee, some delegations expressed doubt about whether a chairman could withdraw his ruling once it had been challenged. The Chairman nevertheless did withdraw his ruling, and no formal objection was raised to this procedure.[146]

5.2 Rapporteur

The UN Model Rules refer to the function of rapporteur, in stating,

> *Rule 25*
>
> *Officers*
>
> If necessary, the Rapporteur-General shall serve as Rapporteur of the General Committee.

It is rare for rules of procedure to specify the functions of the rapporteur.[147]

The rules of procedure of the Third Law of the Sea Conference stipulated, however,

> *Rule 13*
>
> The Rapporteur-General shall act in that capacity in respect of both the Conference and the General Committee. He shall prepare, for approval of the Conference, any reports to be submitted to the General Assembly of the United Nations.[148]

The function of a rapporteur has been defined as to 'give an account to the superior organ of the deliberations of the subordinate organ, either in the form of a written document or in an oral statement at one of the meetings of the superior organ'.[149] In practice, drafts are usually prepared by the secretariat of a conference. In a treaty-making conference an effective

[145] UN GAOR, 3rd Committee, 6th Session, 386th Meeting, para. 16, UN Doc. A/C.3/SR.386 (1952).

[146] UN GAOR, 1st Committee, 15th Session, 1148th Meeting, paras. 26, 39, 43, 48, UN Doc. A/C.1/SR.1148 (1961).

[147] Pastuhov writes, 'The rôle of the rapporteur is rarely defined in the regulations of an international conference.' Pastuhov, *Guide*, p. 105. Rule 103 of the UNGA rules of procedure instructs committees to elect a rapporteur, but does not refer to their tasks.

[148] Rules of procedure of the Third Law of the Sea Conference, UN Doc. A/CONF.62/30/Rev.3 (1975).

[149] S. E. Werners, *The Presiding Officers in the United Nations* (1967), p. 50.

rapporteur will often chair working groups and in effect act as the resident expert of a committee.

5.3 Secretariat

The UNGA rules of procedure state,

> *Duties of the Secretariat*
> *Rule 47*
> The Secretariat shall receive, translate, print and distribute documents, reports and resolutions of the General Assembly, its committees and its organs; interpret speeches made at meetings; prepare, print and circulate the records of the session; have the custody and proper preservation of the documents in the archives of the General Assembly; distribute all documents of the Assembly to the members of the United Nations, and, generally, perform all other work which the Assembly may require.

The UN Model Rules are substantially the same. The issues involved do not seem to have raised controversy at conferences; however, at the 2007 UN General Assembly a number of delegations vehemently criticized a decision by the Secretariat to return to sender as 'unreceivable' an application by Taiwan for membership in the UN.[150]

5.4 Vice-Presidents of a Conference or Assembly

It is usual for a conference to appoint a number of vice-presidents. The function of a vice-president is to substitute for the president. Vice-presidents are selected on the basis of regional representation, and such appointments are usually concluded in private consultations prior to the formal opening of a conference. The number of such vice-presidents is also an issue normally resolved prior to the opening of the conference. Vice-presidents are members of the general committee and thus preserve the principle of regional representation in that body.

[150] UN Doc.A/62/PV.2, pp. 3–7 (2007).

6

Meetings

6.1 Quorum

The UNGA rules of procedure, for the Plenary, state,

> *Rule 67*
>
> *Quorum*
>
> The President may declare a meeting open and permit the debate to proceed when at least one third of the members of the General Assembly are present. The presence of a majority of the members shall be required for any decision to be taken.

Regarding meetings of UNGA committees, the rule is

> *Rule 108*
>
> The Chairman may declare a meeting open and permit the debate to proceed when at least one quarter of the members of the committee are present. The presence of a majority of the members shall be required for any decision to be taken.

The UN Model Rules propose the following rule for the issue of a quorum:

> *Rule 33*
>
> *Quorum*
>
> The President may declare a meeting open and permit the debate to proceed when representatives of at least one third of the States participating in the current session of the Conference are present. The presence of representatives of a majority of such States shall be required for any decision to be taken.

The distinction between the quorum necessary for debates and that necessary for voting was introduced in 1949 by the Special Committee on Methods and Procedures of the General Assembly.[1] The proposal was

[1] Report of the Special Committee on Methods and Procedures of the General Assembly, para. 28, UN GAOR, 4th Session, Supplement No. 12, p. 9, UN Doc. A/937 (1949).

adopted,[2] despite the fact that, during the debate on the report in the Sixth Committee, several delegations argued that the proposal was undesirable as it would enable delegations to vote without their having been present during the debate.[3] The UNGA, in recent years, has waived the requirements of a quorum for the opening of meetings and holding of debates.[4] The waiver does not affect the requirement of a quorum for the taking of decisions.[5]

Randolph, writing on governmental organisations, states that the purposes of a quorum

> are to require the presence of a larger number of members than is necessary for decisions to be taken; to prevent decisions being taken by a minority of members, a possibility when the normal vote is based on a proportion of the votes cast . . . Accordingly, the quorum affects the voting outcomes by providing an allowance to reduce the possibility that abstentions will defeat the proposals.[6]

The rules of procedure of the League of Nations made no provisions as to the necessity for a quorum to conduct business. The provisional rules of procedure of the UNGA contained this clause: 'A majority of the Members of the General Assembly shall constitute a quorum.'[7] A requirement for a quorum has appeared in all successive revisions of the UNGA rules of procedure.

The rules of international conferences held since the Second World War at first closely followed the early General Assembly rule. Exceptions were the 1949 Geneva Conference and the 1954 Hague Conference, in neither of which cases was a quorum required. In 1971, the UNGA rule was amended by allowing the President to declare a meeting open for debate, as opposed to decision taking, if at least one-third of the members were present.[8] In the case of committees, an amendment in 1949 had already allowed a committee to discuss items if only one-third of the members

[2] UN GAOR, 6th Committee, 4th Session, 151st Meeting, para. 92, UN Doc. A/C.6/SR.151 (1949). UNGA Resolution 362 (IV) of 22 October 1949.

[3] UN GAOR, 6th Committee, 4th Session, 151st Meeting, pp. 53–56, paras. 53–92, UN Doc. A/C.6/SR.151 (1949).

[4] The PGA Handbook: A Practical Guide to the United Nations General Assembly (2011) para. 3.3., www.unitar.org/ny/sites/unitar.org.ny/files/UN_PGA_Handbook.pdf.

[5] See, for example, UN Doc. A/46/PV.3, pp. 3–4 (Provisional) (1991).

[6] Lillian Randolph, *The Fundamental Laws of Governmental Organizations* (1971) p. 49.

[7] Rule 56 of the provisional UNGA rules of procedure, UN Doc. A/4 (1946).

[8] Rule 67 of the UNGA rules of procedure.

were present, and by a further amendment in 1971 the quorum for committees was reduced to one-quarter.[9]

International conferences followed the change in the UNGA procedure only after a considerable time lag. The 1968 Vienna Conference on the Law of Treaties provided for a majority quorum in committees[10] despite the fact that the UNGA had reduced the quorum for committees to one-third nearly twenty years earlier. However, by 1974, international conferences began to adopt the UNGA changes, and the 1974–1977 Geneva Humanitarian Law Conference, while keeping the majority quorum for plenary sessions, allowed a one-third quorum for committee meetings.[11] The rules of the 1974 Prescription in Sale of Goods Conference stipulated a one-third quorum in all meetings, in plenary or committee.[12] The 1975 Vienna Conference on Representation of States followed the General Assembly precedent of requiring a quorum of one-third for plenary meetings and one-quarter for committee meetings.[13] Most UN-sponsored conferences now require a quorum of one-third of participating States for opening a meeting and conducting a debate, but a quorum of a majority for taking decisions.[14] The rules of procedure of the 1997 Mine Ban Treaty required a quorum only for 'decision making' and set it at the low figure of twenty-five.[15] However, the 2000 and 2005 NPT Review Conferences and IMO conferences continued to require, in

[9] Rule 108 of the UNGA rules of procedure, as amended by Resolution 362 (IV) of 22 October 1949 and Resolution 2837 (XXVI) of 17 December 1971. This requirement is routinely waived by the General Assembly.

[10] Official Records of the 1968 Vienna Conference on the Law of Treaties, p. xxvi. Rule 18 of the rules of procedure.

[11] Rule 17 of the rules of procedure of the 1974–1977 Geneva Humanitarian Law Conference, CDDH/2/Rev.3.

[12] Rule 18 of the rules of procedure of the 1974 Prescription in Sale of Goods Conference, UN Doc. A/CONF.63/8 (1974).

[13] Rules 18 and 50 of the rules of procedure of the 1975 Vienna Conference on Representation of States, UN Doc. A/CONF.67/8 (1975).

[14] See, for example, provisional rules of procedure of the Fourth World Conference on Women: Action for Equality, Development and Peace (1995), UN Doc. A/CONF.177/2 (1995); ICC Conference rules of procedure (1998), UN Doc. A/CONF. 183/13 (vol. II); rules of procedure of the World Summit on Sustainable Development (2002), UN Doc. A/CONF.199/2 (2002); rules of procedure of the Second World Assembly on Ageing (2002), UN Doc. A/CONF.197/2 (2002); rules of procedure of the World Conference on Disaster Reduction, UN Doc. A/CONF.206/PC(II)/2/Corr.1 (2004); rules of procedure of the International Meeting to Review the Implementation of the Programme of Action for the Sustainable Development of Small Island Developing States, UN Doc. A/CONF.207/2 (2004).

[15] Rule 17 of the rules of procedure of the 1997 Mine Ban Treaty, APL/CRP.2.

plenary,[16] a quorum of a majority of States for all purposes.[17] The 2004 Review Conference of the Mine Ban Treaty required a quorum of fifty of the participating States.[18] The annotation comments that the rule 'previously read "30" instead of "50". A quorum of 30 participating States Parties was set back when there were dramatically fewer States Parties to the Convention than there are today.'[19]

Where the European Commission participates fully in a conference, the following formulation has been used:

> For the purposes of determining a quorum for a decision to be taken on a matter within the competence of a regional economic integration organization, that organization shall be counted to the extent of the number of votes it is entitled to cast in accordance with [the relevant article of the Convention concerned].[20]

It is difficult to find an explanation on record for the changes in the quorum required. It is possible to surmise that the cause or reason may be the increased number of newly independent States. When the number of members of the UN was around forty, a quorum of one-quarter would have led to an international conference debating items with only ten members present. One-quarter, however, of a conference with 180 members provides a 'respectable' number of participants. A further cause of the change may be that many of the newly independent States were not capable of fielding large delegations to the numerous international conferences that they attended. Such delegations were not able to be present at all meetings and certainly not at all committee meetings, and therefore the

[16] However, Rule 34 of the IMO Rules of Procedure for Consultative Meetings and Special Meetings of Contracting Parties to the London Convention 1972 requires a quorum of 'two-fifths of the total number of Contracting Parties or twenty, whichever shall be less'. IMO Doc. LC 20/3 Annex (1998).

[17] Rule 13 of the rules of procedure of the 2000 NPT Review Conference, NPT/CONF.2000/1; Rule 13 of the draft rules of procedure of the 2005 NPT Review Conference, NPT/CONF.2005/1; Rule 43 of the rules of procedure of the IMO Assembly, IMO Basic Documents, vol. I. For examples of the rule at IMO conferences, see Rule 15 of the rules of procedure of the IMO Conference of Contracting States to the International Convention for the Safety of Life at Sea, 1974, IMO Doc. SOLAS/CONF.5/2 (2002); Rule 15 of the rules of procedure of the IMO International Conference on the Establishment of a Supplemental Fund for Compensation for Oil Pollution Damage (2002), IMO Doc. LEG/CONF.14/2 (2002).

[18] Rule 13 of the rules of procedure of the Second Preparatory Meeting for the 2004 Review Conference of the Mine Ban Treaty, APLC/CONF/2004/PM.2/L.3.

[19] APLC/CONF/2004/3 (2004).

[20] WHO, Draft rules of procedure for the Conference of the Parties, WHO Framework Convention on Tobacco Control, WHO Doc. A/FCTC/IGWG/1/4 (2004).

retention of the former majority quorum could have led to the paralysis of many conferences. Most of the committee meetings would not have been able to open on time if the former rigid quorum requirements had been maintained.

All conferences have, however, retained the rule requiring a quorum of a majority for decision taking. The usual quorum required for decision taking is that of a majority of States participating in a conference.[21] Some conferences, for purposes of decision taking, have required a quorum of two-thirds of the participating States.[22] The NPT Review conferences require a quorum of a majority of States Parties to the NPT participating in the Conference.[23]

There is an obvious corollary between the majority required for taking a decision and the quorum required. Where the majority required for decision taking is based on a proportion of the States participating in a conference, such a provision entails a built-in quorum provision for voting purposes. For example, requiring a quorum of two-thirds of the participating States, where the decisions are taken by a simple majority, would mean that a group of one-third plus one of the participating States can, by its absence from a vote, prevent decision taking.

The determination of the presence of a quorum is usually within the implicit powers of the presiding officer. The rules of procedure of the NPT Review Conferences stipulate the following, however:

> *Rule 13*
>
> 2. To determine whether the Conference is quorate, any State Party may call for a roll call at any time.[24]

If, during a meeting, the presence of a quorum is questioned, the presiding officer will usually request the secretariat to verify the presence of a quorum. If the issue is raised after the meeting, the question is usually settled by examining the report of the conference officer. Presumably the normal parliamentary rule applies that, once the Chairman determines that there

[21] For example, Rule 18 of the rules of procedure of the 1958 Law of the Sea Conference, UN Doc. A/CONF.13/35 (1958).

[22] For example, Rule 22 of the rules of procedure of the Third Law of the Sea Conference, UN Doc. A/CONF.62/30/Rev.3 (1975); Rule 17 of the rules of procedure of the 1986 Conference on Treaties between States and International Organisations, UN Doc. A/CONF.129/7 (1986).

[23] Rule 13 of the rules of procedure of the 1995 NPT Review Conference, Doc. NPT/CONF.1995/28 (1995); 2000 NPT Review Conference, Doc. NPT/CONF.2000/1 (2000); 2005 NPT Review Conference, Doc. NPT/CONF.2005/1 (2004).

[24] Rule 13 of the rules of procedure of the 2005 NPT Review Conference, Doc. NPT/CONF.2005/1 (2004).

is a quorum, the continued presence of a quorum is presumed, unless the Chairman subsequently rules that a quorum is no longer present.[25]

At a 2002 meeting of the World Health Assembly, the Legal Counsel gave his opinion that 'a Committee could not question the quorum after the vote, only before'.[26]

6.1.1 *Quorum for a Motion to Adjourn a Meeting*

Randolph has pointed out, 'The quorum may apply to all matters except motions to adjourn. Since the absence of a quorum means that decisions may not be taken, there must remain a means to recess meetings where the quorum requirement is not met.'[27]

6.1.2 *Is It Sufficient that There Be a Quorum at the Opening of a Meeting?*

At a 1949 meeting of the UNGA, a representative observed that there had not been a quorum present during two votes that had been held. The President ruled that the Assembly should decide whether to have another vote, and the Assembly decided, by a two-thirds majority, to conduct the voting again.[28]

At a 1973 meeting of the UNGA, the Chairman ruled that, since a quorum had been present at the opening of the meeting, the subsequent absence of a quorum did not render a representative's statement out of order.[29]

6.1.3 *Calculating a Quorum*

The UNGA rules of procedure refer to the 'presence of a majority of members' for the existence of a quorum. The World Health Assembly rules of procedure refer to '[a] majority of the Members represented at

[25] 'When the chair has called a meeting to order after finding that a quorum is present, the continued presence of a quorum is presumed unless the chair or a member notices that a quorum is no longer present.' *Robert's Rules of Order*, 11th edn (2011), p. 349.

[26] Opinion of the Legal Counsel to the WHO, 55th World Health Assembly, Committee 'B', Fifth Meeting, p. 207, WHA55/2002/REC/3 (2002).

[27] Randolph, *The Fundamental Laws*, p. 48 n. 26.

[28] UN GAOR, Plenary, 4th Session, 273rd Meeting, pp. 570–571, UN Doc. A/PV.273 (1949).

[29] UN GAOR, 2nd Committee, 28th Session, 1526th Meeting, para. 10, UN Doc. A/C.2/SR.1526 (1973).

the session'.[30] In committees of the WHO the rule is that '[o]ne third of the members of a committee shall constitute a quorum. The presence of a majority of a committee shall, however, be required for a question to be put to a vote.'[31] At a 1991 meeting of the World Health Assembly, a delegate raised a point of order claiming that a resolution had been approved without the presence of a quorum. The delegate pointed out that 139 States were present at the Conference, the presence of a majority was required to put a question to a vote, and only 65 States were recorded as voting or abstaining. The Legal Adviser replied that the 'quorum was determined not by the number of votes cast but by the number of delegates present in the room. Prior to the vote on the resolution . . . the Secretariat had counted the number of Committee members present and there had indeed been a quorum.'[32] At a 2002 World Health Assembly, delegations apparently left the meeting room deliberately so that the quorum would not be attained, and the Chairman, on the advice of the Legal Counsel, in the absence of a quorum, suspended and later adjourned the meeting.[33]

The issue arose at the 2001 Special Session of the UNGA where a group of States attempted to prevent voting on a Canadian amendment by claiming an absence of a quorum. The Egyptian representative argued that the basis for counting a quorum should be 'members present and voting'; hence, since States that abstain are not considered as voting they should not be considered for the purpose of counting a quorum. The President ruled – I believe correctly – that 'those delegations that are present compose the quorum, even those that are not voting if they are present'.[34]

6.1.4 *Voting again in the Absence of a Quorum*

The rules of procedure of the ILO provide,

> Where a quorum has not been obtained in a vote by a show of hands or in a record vote, the President may take a record vote on the same question at one of the two next sittings.[35]

[30] Rule 54 of the rules of procedure of the World Health Assembly. [31] *Ibid.*, Rule 85.

[32] WHA44/1991/REC/3, p. 198, para. 1 (1991).

[33] 55th World Health Assembly, Committee 'B', Fifth Meeting, p. 209, WHA55/2002/REC/3 (2002).

[34] UN GAOR, 26th Special Session, 1st Meeting, p. 47, UN Doc. A/S-26/PV.1 (2001).

[35] Article 20(3)(1) of the Standing Orders of the International Labour Conference, International Labour Office, Geneva, December 1992.

At a 1958 meeting of the International Labour Conference, the President ruled that, as there had not been a quorum present at a previous vote, he would put the issue to a record vote.[36] The Soviet delegate pointed out that a revote was unnecessary since there had been more votes against the proposal than votes in favour and therefore the question of quorum was irrelevant.[37] The President ruled that in the Standing Orders 'nothing is said as to whether the majority of votes were in favour or against. Therefore I think that I should order a second voting, in the way prescribed by the article.'[38,39]

6.2 Suspension or Adjournment of Meetings

The UNGA rule states,

> *Rule 76*
>
> *Suspension or Adjournment of the Meeting*
>
> During the discussion of any matter, a representative may move the suspension or the adjournment of the meeting. Such motions shall not be debated but shall be immediately put to the vote. The President may limit the time to be allowed to the speaker moving the suspension or adjournment of the meeting.

[36] ILO Conference, 42nd Session, Geneva 1958, Record of Proceedings, 27th sitting, p. 427.

[37] *Ibid.* [38] *Ibid.*

[39] The ILO has a unique method of calculating a quorum. The Chairman of the Credentials Committee at the 59th Session described it as follows:

> First of all, we take the number of government delegates accredited and registered. To this number, we add substitute delegates who are taking the place of titular Government delegates who are not at present registered. The number of Employer's delegates accredited and registered is now... To this number we add substitute delegates to be taken into account, replacing Employer's delegates who are not at present registered. The number of Worker's delegates accredited and registered is now... and in the same way, there is a substitute delegate to be taken into account because he replaces a non-registered titular delegate. The total of these six figures is the number of delegates and substitute delegates. From this figure must be deducted the members of the Conference who have notified their departure. Furthermore it is necessary to deduct from this figure the number of delegates of the Countries affected by article 13, paragraph 4, of the Constitution because of their being in arrears with the payment of their financial contribution. The quorum now is half the number of delegates present at this particular time.
>
> ILO Conference, 59th Session, Geneva 1974, p. 426.

The actual numbers at that particular session have been omitted from the quotation.

The UN Model Rules propose,

> *Rule 43*
>
> *Suspension or Adjournment of the Meeting*
>
> Subject to Rule 56 [conduct during voting], a representative may at any time move the suspension or the adjournment of the meeting. No discussion on such motions shall be permitted and they shall, subject to Rule 44 [priority of motions], be immediately put to the vote.

The rules of procedure of the League of Nations allowed for a representative to 'move the previous question' (the British parliamentary phrase for suspension) or to move to 'adjourn' or to 'close' the debate.[40] There was, however, no reference to suspending, adjourning or closing a 'meeting' as opposed to a 'debate'. The rules of procedure prepared for the UNGA by the Preparatory Commission distinguished between 'adjournment of the debate' and 'closure of the debate';[41] however, again no provision was made for suspension or adjournment of a meeting. The Report of the Committee on Procedures and Organisation set up in 1946 by the UNGA[42] recommended the inclusion of such a rule.[43]

6.2.1 *Suspension or Adjournment of a Meeting 'during the Discussion of Any Matter'*

The UNGA rules of procedure stipulate that a motion for adjournment or suspension of a meeting may be made 'during the discussion of any matter'.[44] The UN Model Rules propose that such a motion may be made 'at any time'.[45] The UN Model Rules could conceivably be understood as allowing motions for adjournment or suspension during voting and are therefore qualified by a reference to conduct during voting.

6.2.2 *Time Limit for Speaker Moving Suspension or Adjournment*

The UNGA rules of procedure provide that 'the President may limit the time to be allowed to the speaker moving the suspension or adjournment

[40] Rules 18(1), 18(3) of the rules of procedure of the Assembly of the League of Nations.
[41] Rules 60, 62, PC/20 Chap. 1, Sect. 3.
[42] UNGA Resolution 102 (I) of 15 December 1946.
[43] UN GAOR, 2nd Session, Plenary Meetings, vol. II, Annex 4, pp. 1455, 1471, UN Doc. A/388 (1947). Adopted by UNGA Resolution 173 (II) of 17 November 1947.
[44] Rule 76 of the UNGA rules of procedure.
[45] Rule 43 of the UN Model Rules.

of the meeting'. The UN Model Rules themselves stipulate that 'the President shall limit each intervention on a procedural question to a maximum of five minutes'.

6.3 Adjournment of a Meeting

If a meeting is adjourned and subsequently renewed, it requires a positive decision to renew the debate that was taking place at the time of the adjournment. The rules of procedure of the World Health Assembly define 'adjournment of the meeting' as 'termination of all business until another meeting is called',[46] 'usually on another day'.[47] At a 1958 meeting of the UNGA on the Cambodian question, after the representative of India had moved the adjournment of the meeting, the President refused to allow a representative of the USSR to raise a point of order. After the voting had been completed, and prior to adjournment, the President allowed the representative of the USSR to speak on an explanation of vote.[48]

6.3.1 When Can a Motion for Adjournment Be Proposed?

At a 1974 meeting of the UNGA, separate votes were held on two paragraphs of a draft resolution. One of the votes resulted in a tied vote, and the Assembly began discussing whether it should proceed to vote on the resolution as a whole. At this stage the representative of Iraq moved to adjourn the meeting, and the President ruled that the motion for adjournment was admissible as the Assembly was not yet in the process of voting.[49]

6.3.2 Adjournment of a Meeting to a Particular Date

At a 1957 meeting of the UNGA, during a debate on a motion to adjourn the debate, Syria moved the adjournment of the meeting until the next day.

[46] Rule 61 of the rules of procedure of the WHO General Assembly, Basic Documents, http://policy.who.int/cgi.

[47] The PGA Handbook: A Practical Guide to the United Nations General Assembly (2011) para. 3.3, www.unitar.org/ny/sites/unitar.org.ny/files/UN_PGA_Handbook.pdf.

[48] UN GAOR, Plenary, 13th Session, 753rd Meeting, paras. 279–284, UN Doc. A/PV.753 (1958).

[49] UN GAOR, Plenary, 29th Session, 2301st Meeting, para. 505, UN Doc. A/PV.2301 (1974).

The President ruled that, since the Syrian proposal was for an adjournment to a fixed day, it was not a proposal for adjournment under Rule 76, but a regular procedural motion with no priority. The Syrian representative then proposed a change to the motion to adjourn the debate, according to which the debate would be adjourned for a period not exceeding three days. The President thereupon put the proposed change and then the 'amended' proposal to adjourn the debate to an immediate vote.[50]

At a 1968 meeting of the UNGA, the representative of India moved the adjournment of the meeting until the middle of the following week. The representative of Ceylon pointed out that adjournment could not be moved to a particular date.[51] The representative of India then stated that he proposed leaving it to the Chairman to decide when the meeting was to be called; the motion was then put to the vote.[52] At a 2010 meeting of a committee of the World Health Assembly the Legal Counsel gave his opinion that a proposal to adjourn the meeting and establish a drafting group 'was not unqualified' and 'constituted a separate proposal and should be voted on after the original proposal'.[53]

COMMENT

A motion to adjourn a meeting to a specified date or a motion tied to some other proposed action is not entitled to special priority and is to be dealt with as any other procedural motion.

6.3.3 *Adjournment of a Meeting 'during the Discussion of Any Matter'*

At a 1962 meeting of the UNGA, a motion for adjournment on a point of order was made prior to any speaker being heard. The Chairman, ruling on a point of order, decided that the motion for adjournment was in order since the 'discussion' commenced when the Chairman opened the floor for debate.[54]

[50] UN GAOR, Plenary, 12th Session, 708th Meeting, paras. 256–258, 269, UN Doc. A/PV.708 (1957).

[51] UN GAOR, 1st Committee, 23rd Session, 1586th Meeting, paras. 159–171, UN Doc. A/C.1/PV.1586 (1968).

[52] *Robert's* writes, 'The *privileged* motion to *adjourn* (which is always moved in an unqualified form with no mention of a time either for adjourning or for meeting again) is a motion to close the meeting immediately.' *Robert's Rules of Order*, 11th edn (2011), p. 233. [emphasis in original]

[53] Committee B, Sixth Meeting, Sixty Third World Health Assembly, 20 May 2010.

[54] UN GAOR, Plenary, 16th Session, 1104th Meeting, para. 12, UN Doc. A/PV.1104 (1962).

6.3.4 *Interrupting a Speaker to Move Adjournment of a Meeting*

At a 1961 meeting of the UNGA, while the representative of Senegal was speaking, the representative of Morocco, on a point of order, moved the adjournment of the meeting. The President commented that he was sure the representative of Morocco would agree that it would be more appropriate and courteous to wait until the representative of Senegal finished his statement and then vote on the motion for adjournment.[55]

At a 1965 meeting of the UNGA, while the representative of Albania was speaking, the representative of the United States, on a point of order, moved the adjournment of the meeting. When the Chairman was about to put the motion for adjournment to an immediate vote, several representatives pointed out that it was customary to let speakers finish their statements before commencing voting. The United States concurred and the Chairman deferred the vote until the representative of Albania had completed his statement.[56]

The rules of procedure of the ILO Conference are unambiguous on this issue. They state, 'Motions as to procedure may be moved verbally and without previous notice. They may be moved at any time except after the President has called upon a speaker and before the speaker has terminated his speech.'[57]

6.3.5 *A Representative Who Had Requested the Floor prior to the Motion for Adjournment of the Meeting*

At the 1977 Conference on Territorial Asylum, a representative pointed out that he had asked for the floor prior to the motion for adjournment of the meeting. The President replied by informing the representative that he would be the first speaker at the next meeting.[58]

6.4 Suspension of a Meeting

A meeting that has been suspended and renewed, unless it decides otherwise, will continue the debate that was taking place at the time the

[55] UN GAOR, Plenary, 15th Session, 986th Meeting, para. 28, UN Doc. A/PV.986 (1961).
[56] UN GAOR, 1st Committee, 20th Session, 1405th Meeting, paras. 57–62, UN Doc. A/C.1/SR.1405 (1965).
[57] Article 15(2)(1) of the Standing Orders of the International Labour Conference, International Labour Office, Geneva, December 1992.
[58] Summary Records of the 1977 Conference on Territorial Asylum, UN Doc. A/CONF.78/C.1/SR.5, paras. 67, 68 (1977).

meeting was suspended. Bailey, writing on UN Security Council procedure, stated that suspension of a meeting means that 'the meeting is stopped for an agreed period of time'.[59] The rules of procedure of the World Health Assembly define 'suspension of the meeting' as 'the temporary postponement of the business of the meeting'.[60]

At a 1950 meeting of the UNGA, the Swedish representative proposed suspending the meeting until 'the Group of Cease Fire in Korea was in a position to give more definite information'. The Chairman ruled that, since the Swedish proposal involved a more general issue than simply suspending the meeting, he would not regard it as a motion for suspension under Rule 76.[61] At a 1958 meeting of the UNGA, the Chairman commented that in his view, a motion submitted by India for suspending a meeting until a day three days away was a motion for adjournment and not for suspension.[62]

At a 1973 meeting of the UNGA, after a representative had moved the suspension of the meeting, the President refused to give the floor to two representatives who wished to raise points of order. The President ruled that the Assembly must proceed immediately to voting on the motion for suspension.[63] The correct decision should have been to allow a point of order only if it related to the vote on the motion for suspension.

6.4.1 Suspension or Adjournment of a Meeting during Voting

The UN Model Rules state,

> *Rule 43*
>
> Subject to Rule 56 [conduct during voting], a representative may at any time move the suspension or the adjournment of the meeting.

At a 1958 meeting of the UNGA, the Chairman interrupted the voting on a resolution in order to allow the submission and immediate acceptance of a motion for suspension of the meeting.[64]

59 Sydney D. Bailey, *The Procedure of the UN Security Council*, 2nd edn (1988), p. 177.

60 Rule 61 of the rules of procedure of the WHO Assembly, Basic Documents, http://policy.who.int.

61 UN GAOR, 1st Committee, 5th Session, 418th Meeting, paras. 7, 24, UN Doc. A/C.1/SR.418 (1950).

62 UN GAOR, 1st Committee, 13th Session, 968th Meeting, paras. 4–26, UN Doc. A/C.1/PV.968 (1958).

63 UN GAOR, Plenary, 28th Session, 2140th Meeting, para. 85, UN Doc. A/PV.2140 (1973).

64 UN GAOR, 2nd Committee, 13th Session, 542nd Meeting, paras. 29–31, UN Doc. A/C.2/SR.542 (1958).

At a 1993 meeting of the UNGA, however, the Chairman, responding to a request for suspension of the meeting, stated that 'he could not suspend the meeting at the present stage'.[65] The Chairman did not explain the reason for his decision, but presumably it was because the Committee had commenced voting on resolutions.

COMMENT

It would appear that the correct ruling is that a motion for suspension of a meeting is not admissible during voting. One can deduce this from the language of the rule that states that motions for suspension of a meeting may be made 'during the discussion of any matter'.

A suspended meeting is usually resumed on the same day.[66]

6.5 Closed Meetings

The rules of procedure of conferences allow a meeting to be declared a private meeting. It is, however, extremely rare for plenary meetings of conferences to be closed to the public. The meetings of the Third Law of the Sea Conference were held in private when dealing with the status of the President of the Conference, Mr Amerasinghe, on his ceasing to represent his country, Sri Lanka. No records were published of those closed meetings. It is common for committee meetings to be held without public attendance, but reports of officially constituted committee meetings are published in records of the conference. An unofficial method of holding private meetings is to situate them in rooms inaccessible to the public.

The rules of procedure of the World Health Assembly provide, however, regarding the election of the Director-General,

Rule 110

> The Health Assembly shall consider the Board's nomination at a private meeting and shall come to a decision by secret ballot.[67]

[65] UN GAOR, 1st Committee, 48th Session, Part II, 30th Meeting, para. 8, UN Doc. A/C.1/48/SR.30/Add.1 (1993).

[66] The PGA Handbook: A Practical Guide to the United Nations General Assembly (2011) para. 3.3, www.unitar.org/ny/sites/unitar.org.ny/files/UN_PGA_Handbook.pdf.

[67] Rule 110 of the rules of procedure of the World Health Assembly, WHO Basic Documents, 35th edn, 1985. An example of application of the rule was the appointment of WHO Director-General Dr Nakajima, Verbatim Records of the 5th Plenary Meeting of the 41st World Health Assembly, p. 72, WHA41/1988/REC/2 (1988).

7

Statements by Delegations

7.1 Right of Representatives to Speak

The right of representatives to explain their position and attempt to convince other delegations is a fundamental right of all delegations participating in a conference. Together with the right to submit proposals and the right to participate in decision taking, it is one of the three basic rights that must appear in every set of rules of procedure.

Representatives are not, however, obliged to speak, and there does not appear to be any authority where a representative has been ordered to speak. At a 1973 meeting of the UNGA, the Libyan representative requested that the UK delegation immediately report to the Committee on the situation in Southern Rhodesia. The UK representative demurred, whereupon the Libyan representative proposed that the Committee call upon the UK representative to speak and the Committee approved the Libyan proposal. The UK representative said that it was not within the power of the Committee to insist on a particular delegation speaking at a particular time. The meeting was then adjourned without any further action being taken.[1]

The WHO has formalised the procedure whereby 'in order to save time, whenever one delegate is invited to come to the rostrum to make a statement, the next delegate on the list of speakers will also be called to the rostrum, where he or she will sit until the time to speak has come'.[2] This issue does not arise at conferences since statements at conferences are made by delegations from their seats and not from the rostrum. UN practice is also that, in committees, delegates and observers make all statements from their seats and not from the podium.[3]

1 UN GAOR, 4th Committee, 28th Session, 2038th Meeting, para. 23, UN Doc. A/C.4/SR.2038 (1973).

2 WHO, 55th World Health Assembly, 3rd Plenary Meeting, para. 1 (2002).

3 Statement by Legal Counsel, Mr. Corell, to 1st Committee, UNGA, 54th Session, 14th Meeting, UN Doc. A/C.1/54/PV.14, p. 1 (1999).

It is now common practice for a representative to speak on behalf of a number of States.[4] A representative can also speak on behalf of observers.[5] A chairman of a 2000 UNGA committee announced that since the speaker 'was speaking on behalf of the European Union and a number of other countries, he will be given ample time for his comprehensive statement'.[6] A chairman of the same committee in 2004 requested delegations to 'kindly limit their statements to five minutes for those speaking in their national capacities and to ten minutes for those speaking on behalf of a number of delegations'.[7]

7.1.1 Limiting the Number of Times a Representative May Speak

The UNGA rule is,

> *Time-Limit on Speeches*
> *Rule 72*
> The General Assembly may limit the time to be allowed to each speaker and the number of times each representative may speak on any question. Before a decision is taken, two representatives may speak in favour of, and two against, a proposal to set such limits. When the debate is limited and a representative exceeds his allotted time, the President shall call him to order without delay.[8,9]

The UN Model Rules propose,

> *Rule 36*
> *Speeches*
> 3. The Conference may limit . . . the number of times the representatives of each participant may speak on a question.

4 For example, El Salvador on behalf of the Central American countries, UN Doc. A/57/PV.43, p. 3; Samoa on behalf of the thirty-seven member countries of the Alliance of Small Island States, UN Doc. A/57/PV.72, p. 21.

5 Letter from the Office of Legal Affairs to the Secretary, UN World Food Council, 26 March 1992, 1992 UN Jur. Y.B. 430.

6 Chairman of the 1st Committee, UNGA, 55th Session, 3rd Meeting, UN Doc. A/C.1/55/PV.3 (2000).

7 Chairman of the 1st Committee, UNGA, 59th Session, 1st Meeting, UN Doc. A/C.1/59/PV.1, p. 3 (2004).

8 The Annex to UNGA Resolution 51/241 states,

> 21. There shall be no time limits or specified themes for the general debate but the General Assembly will indicate a voluntary guideline of up to twenty minutes for each statement.
> 22. Outside the general debate, there shall be a fifteen minute time limit in plenary meetings and in the Main Committees.

9 Report of the Special Committee on Methods and Procedures of the General Assembly, p. 10, para. 30, GAOR, 4th Session, Supplement No. 12, UN Doc. A/937 (1949).

At a 1951 meeting of the UNGA, the representative of Australia raised a point of order remonstrating that the Soviet representative was speaking for a second time in the debate. The President ruled that, although speakers usually spoke only once during a general debate, there was no rule in the rules of procedure prohibiting delegations from speaking more than once in the same debate.[10] A 1963 ad hoc UN committee on the methods of work of the General Assembly commented that 'the Assembly has almost never exercised its prerogative with regard to limiting the number of times representatives may speak'.[11] At a 1989 meeting of the UNGA, the representative of Jordan complained, on a point of order, that the Israel representative 'had made a second statement, and the Committee should not allow that to set a precedent'. The Chairman did not accept the complaint.[12] Conference practice and that of the UN is not to take such restricting decisions.

The rules of procedure of the International Labour Conference provide, however, that

> *Article 14*
>
> 3. No delegate shall speak more than once upon the same motion, resolution or amendment, without the special permission of the Conference, provided that the mover of a motion, resolution or amendment shall have the right to speak twice unless the closure has been adopted in accordance with article 16.[13]

At a1969 IMCO conference, the Chairman allowed delegations to speak for a second time only after ascertaining that 'no delegation which had not already spoken wished to do so'.[14]

7.1.2 Length of Statements

The Report of the Committee on Procedures and Organisation of the First Session of the UNGA called the attention of the General Assembly to 'the

[10] UN GAOR, Plenary, 6th Session, 348th Meeting, paras. 30–37, UN Doc. A/PV.348 (1951).

[11] Report of the Ad Hoc Committee on the Improvement of the Methods of Work of the General Assembly, GAOR, 18th Session, Annexes, Agenda Item 25, p. 8, para. 47, UN Doc. A/5423 (1963).

[12] UN GAOR, Special Political Committee, 44th Session, 25th Meeting, paras. 84, 85, UN Doc. A/SPC/44/SR.25 (1989).

[13] Article 14 of the Standing Orders of the International Labour Conference, International Labour Office, Geneva, December 1992.

[14] Summary Records of the 17th Meeting of Committee I of the 1969 IMCO Conference on Marine Pollution Damage, p. 392, IMCO Doc. LEG/CONF/C.1/SR.17 (1969).

serious difficulties attendant upon any general rule limiting the length of speeches, and it did not consider it advisable to recommend such a time limit'.[15] The UNGA rules of procedure, however, allow the Assembly to 'limit the time to be allowed to each speaker'.[16] The UN Model Rules propose a similar rule.

At the UN, this authority is applied in committees, although seldom enforced.[17] In a 2014 meeting of the Third Committee of the UNGA, a delegate requested extra time to respond to a report on his country, and the Secretary of the Committee commented that 'the rules of procedure were silent on that subject'.[18] At a 2008 meeting of the Third Committee of UNGA the delegate of the Russian Federation complained that the US delegate 'had exceeded the time limit'. When the Chairman refrained from interrupting the US delegate, the Russian delegate again raised a point of order that 'his delegation was officially requesting the Secretariat to consider whether the Chairman was competent to continue presiding over the meeting'. The Chairman responded by urging 'the United States representative to conclude his statement with a final sentence'.[19]

This authority to limit length of speeches is, however, rarely applied by Presidents of the plenary.[20] One US delegate commented,

> [T]here is practically no enforcement of the parliamentary rules in the United Nations. Rules governing the length of speeches or the subjects speakers are supposed to restrict themselves to are simply ignored. I asked the parliamentarian at USUN [US delegation to the UN] why this was so,

15 UN GAOR, 2nd Session, Plenary Meeting, vol. II, Annex 4, pp. 1455, 1459, para. 20, UN Doc. A/388 (1947).

16 Rule 72 of the UNGA rules of procedure.

17 For example, UN GAOR, 3rd Committee, 21st Session, 1434th Meeting, para. 2, UN Doc. A/C.3/SR.1434 (1966).

18 UN GAOR, Third Committee, 69th Session, 24th meeting, paras, 12,13, UN Doc. A/C.3/69/SR.24 (2014).

19 UN GAOR, Third Committee, 63rd Session, 30th meeting, paras. 16, 18, 19, UN Doc. A/C.3/63/SR.30 (2008).

20 The General Committee of the 48th UNGA in its First Report drew the attention of the Assembly to Rule 72 'in connection with the length of statements, with a view to streamlining the procedures of the General Assembly and as a cost saving measure'. UNGA, 48th Session, First Report of the General Committee, Organisation of the Forty-Eighth Regular Session of the General Assembly, Adoption of the Agenda and Allocation of Items, para. 18, UN Doc. A/48/250 (1993). The Plenary 'took note of the provisions regarding the length of statements contained in paragraph 18 [of the report]'. UN GAOR, 48th Session, 3rd Plenary Meeting, para. 59, UN Doc. A/48/PV.3 (1993).

> and he replied that the ruling of the President, if challenged, needs to be submitted to the Assembly, and the majority will not discipline one of their own.[21]

The 2011 Practical guide to the UNGA published by the Permanent Mission of Switzerland to the UN summarises the practice as

> There are 15 minute time limits for speeches in the Plenary and in the Main Committees. For the general debate the time limit (traditionally also 15 minutes) is agreed on at the beginning of each session. The President can call a speaker to order if he/she exceeds the agreed time limit.
>
> Some of the Main Committees agree on shorter time limits, with an implicit tolerance for longer group statements. Due to time constraints the speaking time during high-level meetings is often limited to five minutes. Experience shows that speakers in such meetings tend to take closer to nine minutes on average.[22]

Fitschen, however, comments, 'As a matter of practice, no time limit applies to statements delivered in the general debate, but delegations are encouraged to observe a voluntary guideline of up to fifteen minutes for their statements.'[23] The rules of procedure of all the conferences examined contain a similar rule, although in some the stipulation appears only in the article on the general powers of the presiding officer as an issue that the presiding officer can propose to the conference. The rules of procedure of the 1954 Hague Conference are unusual in that they authorised the President and not the Conference to 'limit the time to be allotted to each speaker'.[24]

At the 1980 Law of the Sea Conference, the President proposed to the Plenary that speeches be limited to ten minutes, and the proposal was adopted.[25] At the 1995 NPT Review Conference, closing statements were, by the decision of the Conference, limited to seven minutes.[26]

[21] William F. Buckley, *United Nations Journal, A Delegate's Odyssey* (1974), p. 43.

[22] The PGA Handbook: A Practical Guide to the United Nations General Assembly (2011), para. 3.4, www.unitar.org/ny/sites/unitar.org.ny/files/UN_PGA_Handbook.pdf

[23] Thomas Fitschen, 'Article 21', in *The Charter of the United Nations, A Commentary*, ed. Bruno Simma *et al*, 3rd edn (2012), p. 704.

[24] Rule 14 of the rules of procedure of the 1954 Hague Conference (CBC/2).

[25] Official Records of the Third Law of the Sea Conference, Plenary, 9th Resumed Session, 132nd Meeting, vol. XIV, p. 11, paras. 3, 4 UN Doc. A/CONF.62/SR.132 (1980).

[26] NPT/CONF.1995/PV.16, p. 5 (1995).

It is rare for limitations on the length of speeches to be applied at conferences, but it is common for such limitations to be applied at assemblies of international organisations.[27]

The Executive Board of the WHO recommended, in 1987, that speeches in main committees of the World Health Assembly be limited to five minutes and that the rules of procedure be amended accordingly.[28] The Assembly debated the recommendation and decided to monitor the work of the Assembly over a three-year period before taking a final decision on the recommendation.[29] In 1991, after the period of monitoring was over, the Executive Board reached the conclusion that the recommendation was not necessary and that the majority of speakers introducing draft resolutions spoke for less than five minutes.[30]

7.1.3 *Limiting the Number of Speakers*

Neither the UNGA rules of procedure nor the UN Model Rules refer to the possibility of limiting the number of speakers on substantive proposals.

At a 1978 IMCO Conference, the Conference, at the suggestion of the President, decided that 'the number of speakers on each proposal be restricted to one in favour and two against'.[31] This unusual procedure does not appear to have been applied in other conferences.

A restriction on the number of speakers was applied at the First Plenary Session of the UNGA.[32] At a meeting of the Third Committee of the UNGA, at its First Session, the Belgian delegation proposed limiting the number of speakers on the issue under discussion. Other delegates pointed out that this would be violating the rules of procedure. The Belgian proposal was rejected on a vote.[33]

[27] For example, speakers were limited to fifteen minutes in the general debate of the 34th General Conference of the IAEA. IAEA Doc. GC(XXXIV)/OR.323, para. 97 (1991). Speakers were limited to three minutes at the Executive Committee meetings of the 20th Extraordinary Session of the ICAO Assembly. ICAO Doc. 9088, A20-Min. EX/11, p. 107 (1973).

[28] Resolution EB79.R20, WHO Doc. EB79/1987/REC/Part I.

[29] Decision WHA40 (10), WHO Doc. WHA44/1991/REC/1, Annex 8.

[30] Report of the representative of the Executive Board to the Assembly, Summary Records of the 4th Meeting of Committee 'B' of the 44th World Health Assembly, p. 225, WHA44/1991/REC/3 (1991).

[31] IMCO Doc. CONF.2/SR.4, p. 674 (1978).

[32] UN GAOR, 1st Plenary Session, 1st Part, p. 458, UN Doc. A/PV.31 (1946).

[33] UN GAOR, 3rd Committee, 1st Session, 2nd Part, 35th Meeting, pp. 199, 202, UN Doc. A/C.3/SR.35 (1946).

It is common to have restrictions on the number of speakers on procedural issues. Conference practice, however, and that of the UN are not to restrict the number of speakers on issues of substance.

7.1.3.1 A Requirement of Two Speakers against a Procedural Motion

At a 2015 Session of the UNGA Plenary, the representative of Cuba claimed that since 'two delegations must speak in favour and two against' a proposal and he 'has heard only one delegation speak against' his proposal should be understood 'as accepted'. The President avoided the need to rule on this unusual claim by ruling that the Cuban 'proposal' was in fact an amendment.[34]

7.1.4 Statements by Observers

The UN Office of Legal Affairs gave its opinion, in 1982, that '[a]s a rule, in the practice of the General Assembly and its Main Committees, as well as that of other United Nations organs and conferences, observers are given the floor to make statements *after* representatives of Member States that have indicated a desire to speak have made their statements'.[35] According to a 1992 opinion of the UN Office of Legal Affairs, 'The key factor is not to give the floor to an observer when a member is prepared to speak. An observer should not usurp the place of a member on a speaker's list.'[36] At a 2006 meeting of a committee of the World Health Assembly, the Legal Counsel gave his opinion that 'intergovernmental organisations such as the European Commission were permitted to speak at the invitation of the Chairman. In the Health Assembly they normally spoke after Member States, but the Committee could allow them to speak earlier, at the Chairman's invitation.'[37] At a 2009 meeting of a committee of the World Health Assembly, the Legal Counsel gave his opinion that 'observers were not permitted to take the floor after a vote had taken place'.[38]

[34] UN GAOR, Plenary, 70th Session, 82nd Meeting, UN.Doc. A/70/PV.82 p. 18 (2015).

[35] Opinion, 9 December 1982, of the Office of Legal Affairs, prepared at the request of the Chairman of the Sixth Committee. 1982 UN Jur. Y.B. 160. [emphasis in original]

[36] Letter from the Office of Legal Affairs to the Secretary, UN World Food Council, 26 March 1992, 1992 UN Jur. Y.B. 429.

[37] Committee A, 5rd Meeting, Fifty-Ninth World Health Assembly, WHA 59/2006/REC/3 p. 145 (2006).

[38] Committee B, First Meeting, Sixty-Second World Health Assembly, p.145,WHA62/2009/REC/3 (2009).

7.1.5 *Statements on Behalf of Regional Groups*

It is common in modern assemblies for a delegate to speak on behalf of a regional group. At a 2013 meeting of UNGA one delegate, however, raised a point of order 'to ask you to request that representatives taking the floor on behalf of groups refrain from speaking in their national capacity'.[39]

7.1.6 *Speaking on Behalf of Other States*

It is common practice in the UNGA for a delegation to make statements on behalf of more than one State.[40]

7.1.7 *List of Speakers*

The UNGA rule is,

> *Rule 68*
>
> *Speeches*
>
> 1. [T]he President shall call upon speakers in the order in which they signify their desire to speak.

The UN Model Rules propose an identical rule.

The practical guide to the UNGA published by the Permanent Mission of Switzerland to the UN comments,

> Before the debate takes place, Member States and Observers register for the speakers list by contacting the secretaries of the Plenary or of a Main Committee, either in writing or by phone. During the debate the Member States approach a GA Affairs officer, sitting next to the podium, to add their names to the list. The speaking order in formal meetings is as follows: First, visiting Heads of State and Government or government Ministers speak, followed by the chairs of groups of Member States, speaking on behalf of the whole group (e.g. G-77, NAM), and the EU. Individual Member States follow on a first-come, first-served basis. Delegations can agree to switch speaking slots as long as they let the GA Affairs Officer know in advance. With the exception of the EU, Observers speak after the Member States. General debate follows a different order.[41]

[39] The representative of Algeria referring to a statement of the representative of Egypt on behalf of the Arab group. UNGA Plenary, 68th Session, 16th Meeting, UN Doc A/68/PV.46, p. 8 (2013).

[40] For example UNGA, Third Committee, 70th Session, 32nd Meeting, para. 28, UN Doc. A/C.3/70/SR. 32 (2015).

[41] Para 3.4, www.unitar.org/ny/sites/unitar.org.ny/files/UN_PGA_Handbook.pdf.

In the UN a list of speakers is usually drawn up for each agenda item and not for each meeting. 'In some bodies, a list of speakers is established for a debate lasting over several days ... In other contexts, lists of speakers are for a shorter period and may only be established one meeting at a time.'[42] In the UNGA Committees, use is also made of a 'rolling list' of speakers so that committee time is not wasted if a scheduled speaker does not take up his turn.[43] In conferences a list is usually drawn up for each issue or article in a draft treaty.

A 1963 ad hoc UN committee on the methods of work of the General Assembly recommended,

> The name of a representative who is not prepared to speak when his turn comes, should automatically be transferred to the bottom of the list of speakers unless, by agreement with the presiding officer, it can be arranged for that representative to speak earlier. However, it is the opinion of the Committee that the established practice whereby representatives are allowed to exchange places on the list of speakers should be maintained.[44]

The 1960 Law of the Sea Conference adopted a Mexican proposal to amend the draft rules of procedure by adding the sentence: 'The Secretariat shall be in charge of drawing up a list of such speakers.'[45] The representative of Mexico, in presenting his proposal, explained that its purpose 'was to make clear that the practice invariably followed by the General Assembly should be likewise applied at the Conference ... what was implicit in General Assembly procedure should now be made

[42] Letter from the Office of Legal Affairs to the Secretary, UN World Food Council, 26 March 1992, 1992 UN Jur. Y.B. 429.

[43] See for example, Chairman of the 1st Committee, UNGA, 59th Session, 1st Meeting, UN Doc. A/C.1/59/PV.1, p. 3 (2004). Chairman of the 1st Committee, UNGA 68th Session, 2nd Meeting, p. 5, UN Doc. A/C.1/68/PV.2 (2013).

[44] Report of the Ad Hoc Committee on the Improvement of the Methods of Work of the General Assembly, GAOR, 18th Session, Annexes, Agenda Item 25, p. 8, para. 48, UN Doc. A/5423 (1963). The recommendations of the Committee were endorsed by the General Assembly in its Resolution 1898 (XVIII) of 11 November 1963. The recommendation was repeated, in substance, in para. 204 of the Report of the Special Committee on the Rationalisation of the Procedures and Organisation of the General Assembly, GAOR, 26th Session, Supplement No. 26, UN Doc. A/8426 (1971).

[45] Mexican amendment to the draft rules of procedure, UN Doc. A/CONF.19/L.1 (1960), Summary Records of the 2nd Plenary Meeting of the 1960 Law of the Sea Conference, p. 4, para. 6, UN Doc. A/CONF.19/8 (1960).

explicit'.[46] The rules of procedure of conferences held after 1960 have not followed this precedent, and it would indeed appear to be an unnecessary addition since inevitably the technical preparation of a list of speakers is done by the secretariat of a conference.

The IAEA determines the order of speakers at the general debate by way of ballot among the States that apply to speak.[47]

At a 1988 meeting of the World Health Assembly, certain representatives on the list of speakers were not present when their names were called. The President utilised the procedure available to the World Health Assembly by which speeches may be added to the verbatim record even if they were not delivered.[48]

At a 1989 meeting of the World Health Assembly, the President gave the floor to the representative of Tonga, at the start of the meeting, explaining that the representative of Tonga had put his name down to speak at the previous meeting and had not been able to speak. The representative of Algeria complained, 'We are not in a cinema where seats can be reserved. There is a customary procedure for every meeting, and those wishing to speak put down their names.'[49]

Despite these examples, it is extremely rare for the issue of the list of speakers to arouse controversy. The UN Office of Legal Affairs opined that '[i]f a member wishes to have its place on the list [of speakers] taken by an observer, that may be done only with the unanimous consent of the body concerned'.[50] The legal opinion does not, however, quote any authority for demanding unanimity, and it would seem to be unjustified. During a 2013 meeting of the First Committee of the UNGA two delegations 'insisted on being the last speaker'. The Chairman commented that 'there is no stipulation under rule 68 of the rules of procedure where a specific request has been made by a delegation to speak in a certain order'. The Chairman, with the agreement of the two delegations, decided the issue by drawing lots.[51]

46 *Ibid.* at para. 5.

47 IAEA Docs. GC(XXXIII)/GEN/77, GC(XXXIII)/OR.320, paras. 12–15 (1989).

48 Verbatim Records of the 13th Plenary Meeting of the 41st World Health Assembly, p. 286, WHA41/1988/REC/2 (1988).

49 Verbatim Records of the 10th Plenary Meeting of the 42nd World Health Assembly, p. 228, WHA42/1989/REC/2 (1989).

50 Letter from the Office of Legal Affairs to the Secretary, UN World Food Council, 26 March 1992, 1992 UN Jur. Y.B. 430.

51 9th Meeting of the First Committee of the 68th session of the UNGA, p. 1. UN Doc. A/C.1/68/PV.9 (2013).

7.1.8 Closing the List of Speakers

The UNGA rules of procedure state,

> *Rule 73*
> *Closing of List of Speakers, Right of Reply*
> During the course of a debate, the President may announce the list of speakers and, with the consent of the General Assembly, declare the list closed. He may, however, accord the right of reply to any member if a speech delivered after he has declared the list closed makes this desirable.

The UN Model Rules propose:

> *Rule 39*
> *Closing the List of Speakers*
> In the course of a debate, the President may announce the list of speakers and, with the consent of the Conference, declare the list closed. When there are no more speakers, the President shall, with the consent of the Conference, declare the debate closed. Such closure shall have the same effect as closure pursuant to rule 42. [Rule 42 deals with closure of debate.]
>
> *Rule 40*
> *Right of Reply*
> 1. Notwithstanding rule 39, the President shall accord the right of reply to the delegation of any State participating in the Conference that requests it.

The rules of the Assembly of the League of Nations and of the Preparatory Commission of the United Nations contained no rule as to closing the list of speakers, and it was first introduced on the basis of the report of the 1947 Committee on Procedures and Organisation. This Committee proposed this rule: 'During the course of a debate the President may announce the list of speakers and, with the consent of the General Assembly, declare the list closed.' The report commented as follows on this proposal: 'The new rule confirms a procedure which has been followed during previous sessions of the General Assembly.'[52] The rule adopted by the General Assembly appears in the rules of all the conferences examined.

At the 1977 Vienna Conference on Succession of States in Respect of Treaties, the Norwegian representative stated that 'it was customary,

[52] Report of the Committee on Procedures and Organisation, UN GAOR, 2nd Session, vol. II, Annex 4, Part III, p. 1455, Rule 78, UN Doc. A/388 (1947).

before reading out the list of speakers and declaring it closed, to invite any delegations which so desired to be included in the list'.[53]

7.1.8.1 Objection to Closing the List of Speakers

It is rare for a delegation to object to closure of the list of speakers, although there are occasions on record. It is also rare for a vote to be held on the question of closing the list of speakers,[54] although rules of procedure allow for it.

At a 1966 meeting of the UNGA, the representative of the USSR objected to closing the list of speakers and the list remained open.[55]

The representative of India to the 1974–1977 Geneva Humanitarian Law Conference objected to a request for closure of the list of speakers and pointed out that 'the discussion did not relate to a procedural question and that all representatives who wished to speak should be permitted to do so'.[56] There was no follow-up to the remarks by the representative of India, and there do not appear to be any precedents for the attempt to distinguish between matters of procedure and those of substance on this issue.

7.1.8.2 Results of Closing the List of Speakers

At the UNGA the practice is mixed as to denying the right of speech because of a closed list of speakers. Some presiding officers are flexible in the application of the rule and add delegations to a list of speakers that had previously been closed[57]; others insist on the observance of the closure.[58] The Chairman of a 1990 UNGA meeting ruled that a representative 'who

[53] 1977 Vienna Conference on Succession of States in Respect of Treaties (First Session), Official Records, vol. I, Committee of the Whole, 11th Meeting, p. 81, para. 47, UN Doc. A/CONF.80 (1977).

[54] The Chairman of the 708th Meeting of the UN Commission on Narcotic Drugs put such an issue to the vote. UN Doc. E/CN.7/SR.708, p. 4 (1972).

[55] UN GAOR, 3rd Committee, 21st Session, 1438th Meeting, paras. 62–64, UN Doc. A/C.3/SR.1438 (1966).

[56] CDDH/I/SR.7, p. 51, para. 6.

[57] UN GAOR, Plenary, 22nd Session, 1664th Meeting, para. 2, UN Doc. A/PV.1664 (1968); UN GAOR, 4th Committee, 29th Session, 2104th Meeting, para. 71, UN Doc. A/C.4/29/SR.2104 (1974); UN GAOR, Special Political Committee, 29th Session, 921st Meeting, para. 1, UN Doc. A/SPC/29/SR.921 (1974); UN GAOR, Special Political Committee, 36th Session, 9th Meeting, para. 82, UN Doc. A/SPC/36/SR.9 (1981); UN GAOR, Plenary, 55th Session, UN Doc. A/55/PV.25, p. 9 (2000). UN GAOR, Third Committee, 61st session, 52nd meeting, paras. 5, 6, UN Doc. A/C.3/61/SR.52 (2006).

[58] UN GAOR, 3rd Committee, 36th Session, 33rd Meeting, paras. 45, 48, UN Doc. A/C.3/36/SR.33 (1981).

had not been present when the list of speakers had been closed, wished to speak on the item. If he heard no objection, he would take it that the Committee agreed to give him the floor.' No objection was made.[59] The President of the 1991 UNGA ruled that 'once the list is closed, no further names will be inscribed unless justified by special circumstances'.[60]

There appears no precedent on the record at conferences where the right of speech was denied because of the previous closure of the list of speakers. This of course could be because no delegate at any conference requested to speak after the closing of the list of speakers. However, based on the experience of this author, one can assume that the reason is that the rule of closure of the list of speakers has been applied flexibly.[61]

7.1.8.3 Who May Propose Closing the List of Speakers?

Both the UNGA rules of procedure and the UN Model Rules provide that the presiding officer has the authority to propose closure of the list of speakers. At a 1959 meeting of the UNGA, the Jordanian delegation proposed closing the list of speakers. The Australian representative pointed out that it was the prerogative of the Chairman to initiate such a process.[62]

7.1.8.4 Submitting an Amendment after the List of Speakers Has Been Closed

At a 1949 meeting of the UNGA, after the list of speakers had been closed, an amendment to a draft resolution was submitted by the Polish delegation. The Chairman, distinguishing this from a closure of debate, decided that the Polish amendment was in order and further decided, after some hesitation, that there could be a discussion of the amendment.[63] The UN Model Rules would lead to a different ruling since Rule 39 dealing with closure of the list of speakers states specifically, 'Such closure shall have the same effect as closure pursuant to rule 42.' (Rule 42 deals with closure of debate.)

59 UN GAOR, Special Political Committee, 45th Session, 4th Meeting, para. 33, UN Doc. A/SPC/45/SR.4 (1990).

60 UN GAOR, Plenary, 46th Session, 42nd Meeting, pp. 13, 64, UN Doc. A/46/PV.42 (Provisional) (1991).

61 Presiding officers usually 'assume' no objection by the conference.

62 UN GAOR, 4th Committee, 14th Session, 929th Meeting, paras. 45–48, UN Doc. A/C.4/14/SR.929 (1959).

63 UN GAOR, 2nd Committee, 4th Session, 103rd Meeting, paras. 1–8, UN Doc. A/C.2/4/SR.103 (1949).

7.2 Right of Reply

The UNGA rules of procedure recognise the right of reply by stating,

> *Rule 73*
>
> He [the President] may, however, accord the right of reply to any member if a speech delivered after he has declared the list closed makes this desirable.[64]

The UN Model Rules propose,

> *Rule 40*
> *Right of Reply*
>
> 1. Notwithstanding rule 39 [Rule 39 refers to closure of the list of speakers], the President shall accord the right of reply to the delegation of any State participating in the Conference that requests it. Other delegations may be granted the opportunity to make a reply.
> 2. Replies made pursuant to the present rule:
>   (a) Shall be made at the end of the last meeting of the day, or at the conclusion of the consideration of the relevant item if that is sooner;
>   (b) Shall be limited to two per item for any delegation at a given meeting, the first of which is not to exceed five minutes and the second three minutes.

The practical guide to the UNGA published by the Permanent Mission of Switzerland to the UN comments,

> The right of reply can also be requested in response to a statement made under the right of reply or an explanation of vote. A Member State cannot request the right of reply more than twice on the same agenda item on a given day. The first intervention is limited to 10 minutes, the second to 5 minutes. A statement under the right of reply is given from the floor at the end of the debate or at the end of the day.[65]

The right of reply is exercised by delegations to 'score' debating points. It is also used to negate any possible interpretation that a State tacitly accepts or acquiesces in a negative or critical statement made by another State.

[64] An equivalent rule has appeared in all the rules since they appeared in UN Doc. A/520 (1947). An equivalent rule also appears in all the rules of procedure of the conferences examined.

[65] Para 3.4, www.unitar.org/ny/sites/unitar.org.ny/files/UN_PGA_Handbook.pdf.

Bailey, writing in 1960, states, 'Few Rules of Procedure are abused as frequently as those relating to the right of reply.'[66] In a revised edition of his book, Bailey tempers the statement somewhat, writing instead that 'the practice is now carried to excess'.[67] The author however repeats this statement from the earlier book: 'It is, after all, a privilege and not a right to speak out of turn.'[68] A 1971 UN committee on the procedures and organisation of the General Assembly discussed the possibility of limiting the length or number of statements of reply.[69] The committee did not, however, recommend amending the rules of procedure in this respect.

In practice, every conference recognises the right of a representative to exercise the right of reply, which is the right to reply to criticism or abuse even if the delegation 'attacked' was not on the list of speakers. The authority in the rules of procedure for such a right is, however, scant. The reference to the right of reply as an exception to the closure of the list of speakers is usually the only reference to the right of reply in the rules of procedure examined, yet the right is universally recognised and routinely granted when requested. The examination of the records of the conferences does not disclose any case of a delegation being refused a right of reply. The practice has developed that the right of reply should be exercised at the end of meetings.[70]

7.2.1 *Discretion of President to Grant Right of Reply*

The UNGA rules of procedure allow the President discretion as to whether to allow a right of reply.[71] The UNGA rules use the word 'may'; however, the UN Model Rules use the word 'shall'. At a 2016 meeting of the Third Committee of the UNGA, the Secretary of the Committee stated that 'the right of reply was not an absolute right but rather was

66 Sydney D. Bailey, *The General Assembly of the United Nations, A Study of Procedure and Practice* (1960) p. 78.

67 Bailey, *The General Assembly*, rev. edn (1964), p. 124. 68 *Ibid.*

69 paras. 219–224 of the Report of the Special Committee on the Rationalisation of the Procedures and Organisation of the General Assembly, GAOR, 26th Session, Supplement No. 26, UN Doc. A/8426 (1971).

70 This principle was also adopted by the recommendation of the Special Committee on the Rationalisation of the Procedures and Organisation of the General Assembly, *ibid.*

71 *Rule 73*

He [the President] may, however, accord the right of reply to any member if a speech delivered after he has declared the list closed makes this desirable.

granted at the discretion of the Chair'.[72] Practice at the General Assembly and at conferences has, however, invariably been to grant a delegation that requests it a right to reply to criticism, perceived or otherwise.[73] The UN Office of Legal Affairs, in a 1983 opinion, concluded, 'Although rule 73 [of the UNGA rules of procedure] is formulated in a way that gives the President discretion to grant the right of reply or not to do so, in practice the right of reply is routinely granted to any Member State that requests it.'[74]

At the 1974–1977 Geneva Humanitarian Law Conference, although no provision in the rules of procedure referred to the right of reply, the President declared that the Conference would allow a right of reply and no delegation challenged the statement.[75]

Rule 57 of the rules of procedure of the WHO states explicitly that the right of reply 'shall be accorded by the President to any delegation or representative of an Associate Member who requests it'.[76] The rule of procedure referring to closing the list of speakers, however, follows the equivalent rule in the UNGA and states, 'He [the President] may, however, accord the right of reply to any member if in his opinion a speech delivered after he has declared the list closed makes this desirable.'[77] This rule apparently grants discretion to the President and appears to contradict Rule 57. In at least one case a president of a World Health Assembly denied a delegation the right of reply, stating that 'in the case at issue, he did not consider it desirable to prolong the debate'.[78]

The rules of procedure of the ILO Conference contain no provision as to the right of reply. At the 1973 session, the Legal Adviser of the Organisation was asked whether the President had authority to refuse a delegation

[72] UN GAOR 3rd Committee, 71st Session, 22nd Meeting, para. 69, UN Doc. A/C.3/71/SR.22 (2016).

[73] At an early session of the Third Committee, a chairman refused to grant a right of reply on the grounds that there was no attack on the country involved. UN GAOR, 3rd Committee, 3rd Session, 1st Part, 93rd Meeting, pp. 71, 72, UN Doc. A/C.3/3SR.93 (1948). Such rulings appear however to be rare. At a plenary meeting of the General Assembly, a President ruled that he would be 'extremely reluctant to establish any precedent which would tend to limit' the right of reply. UN GAOR, Plenary, 15th Session, 1st Part, 903rd Meeting, para. 51, UN Doc. A/PV.903 (1960).

[74] Cable (from UN Office of Legal Affairs) to the Legal Liaison Officer to the UN Environment Programme, 16 May 1983. 1983 UN Jur. Y.B. 170, UN Doc. ST/LEG/SER.C/21 (1983).

[75] CDDH/SR.12, para. 1, vol. V, p. 117.

[76] Rule 57 of the rules of procedure of the World Health Assembly, who.int/governance/rules_of_procedure_of_the_wha_en.pdf.

[77] *Ibid.*, Rule 58.

[78] 37th World Health Assembly, 7th Meeting of Committee 'B', WHA37/1984/REC/3, p. 216 (1984).

the right to reply. The Legal Adviser gave his opinion: 'The right to reply was granted by the President in the exercise of the functions vested to the President.' The President was entitled to take steps to prevent 'a reply to a speech and a reply to that reply and so on'. Since the issue was 'not in itself governed by the provisions governing the proceedings of the Conference ... we must therefore have regard essentially to the prerogatives entrusted to the President'.[79] At the 2003 session of the ILO Conference, the President stated, 'The right of reply will be at the discretion of the President.'[80] However, there appears to be no record of such a right being denied.

7.2.2 Right of Reply and Closure of Debate

During the1978 Hamburg Conference on Carriage by Sea, a representative moved the closure of debate.[81] The President of the Conference ruled that 'he must first give the representative of ... the right to reply'.[82]

At a 1960 meeting of the UNGA, the President ruled that the fact that the debate had been closed did not negate the right of a delegation to exercise its right of reply.[83]

7.2.3 At What Stage of a Debate Can the Right of Reply Be Exercised?

The UNGA rules of procedure do not specify at what stage of a debate the right of reply can be exercised. In the early years of the UNGA, a right of reply was at times exercised immediately,[84] but the practice has developed of exercising the right of reply after all scheduled speakers have spoken.[85] At a meeting of the UNGA, at its 1974 session, the Soviet delegate pointed out that the right of reply should be exercised only at the end of the meeting. The Chairman replied that in the First Committee the

[79] ILO Conference, 58th Session, Geneva 1973, p. 404.

[80] ILO Conference, 91st Session, Geneva 2003, 12th (special) sitting, p. 13/1.

[81] UN Doc. A/CONF.89/C.2/SR.6, p. 6, para. 29 (1978).

[82] *Ibid.* at p. 6, para. 30. The Summary Records do not state if in fact any action was taken on the motion for closure.

[83] UN GAOR, Plenary, 15th Session, Part I, 903rd Meeting, para. 51, UN Doc. A/PV.903 (1960).

[84] See UN GAOR, Plenary, 17th Session, 1128th Meeting, para. 139, UN Doc. A/PV.1128 (1962).

[85] See, for example, UN GAOR, 5th Committee, 31st Session, 18th Meeting, paras. 24, 25, UN Doc. A/C.5/31/SR.18 (1976).

practice was to allow the right of reply after every item on disarmament.[86] In 1979, the UNGA decided that '[d]elegations should exercise their right of reply at the end of the day whenever two meetings have been scheduled for that day and whenever such meetings are devoted to the same item.'[87] At a meeting of the UNGA in 1980, during a discussion relating to the status of national liberation movements, a delegation raised a point of order as to why the right of reply was being exercised during a meeting and not at the end of the day. The President ruled that 'rights of reply will be exercised after each item if several items are discussed in one session'.[88] At a 1980 meeting of the UNGA, the President made a 'technical point of clarification', stating 'when different items are considered during two different meetings on the same day, delegations may exercise their right of reply at the end of the morning's meeting on items that have been concluded during that morning's session'.[89] The UN Model Rules reflect this practice.

At a 1981 meeting of the UNGA, during a discussion on the report of ECOSOC, the representative of Syria pointed out that 'he needed to exercise the right of reply so that his reply would be included in the same record as the statement to which it referred: to postpone the exercise of the right of reply until the end of the discussions on an item would weaken the meaning of the reply'.[90] The representative did not, however, challenge the President's ruling that the right of reply was to be exercised only at the end of the day.

A 1982 opinion of the UN Office of Legal Affairs states that the practice of the UNGA is that 'when more than one item is considered by the Assembly in the course of a particular day, statements in the exercise of the right of reply have been made at the conclusion of the consideration of the relevant agenda item before the next agenda item is considered rather than at the end of the day'.[91] At a 2007 meeting of the First Committee of the UNGA a delegate complained that he had not been given the right

86 UN GAOR, 1st Committee, 29th Session, 2030th Meeting, pp. 58–60, UN Doc. A/C.1/PV.2030 (1974).

87 Resolution 'On the Rationalisation of the Procedures and Organisation of the General Assembly', para. 8, UNGA Resolution 34/401 of 12 December 1979.

88 UN GAOR, Plenary, 35th Session, 95th Meeting, para. 70, UN Doc. A/35/PV.95 (1980).

89 UN GAOR, Plenary, 7th Emergency Session, 8th Meeting, p. 2, UN Doc. A/ES.7/PV.8 (Provisional) (1980).

90 UN GAOR, 3rd Committee, 36th Session, 61st Meeting, para. 42, UN Doc. A/C.3/36/SR.61 (1981).

91 Opinion of the UN Office of Legal Affairs, 19 October 1982, prepared at the request of the Chairman of the Sixth Committee. 1982 UN Jur. Y.B. 161.

of reply the previous day, and therefore 'the point of the right of reply is simply lost'. The Chairman responded that on the previous day there had been only one meeting and that there had only been ninr minutes left at the end of it.[92]

At a 1989 meeting of the General Conference of the IAEA, the representative of Iran asked 'whether he could exercise his right of reply on the following day, as his statement was in the process of being typed'.[93] On the President agreeing to the request, the representative of Iraq asked 'whether it was permissible under the Rules of Procedure for Iran to defer the exercise of its right of reply until the following morning'.[94] The President confirmed that he abided by his decision.[95] After the representative of Iran exercised his right of reply, the representative of Iraq requested permission to reply. The President ruled that the right of reply 'could not be exercised indefinitely. He therefore requested the representative of Iraq to show understanding by forgoing his right of reply.'[96]

At a 2006 committee meeting of the World Health Assembly, the Legal Counsel gave his opinion that 'the right of reply was exercised during the course of debate on an agenda item. Since the debate on the item concerned had been closed and the Committee had already taken a vote, the right of reply could no longer be exercised.'[97] This legal opinion would not appear to reflect usual practice at conferences and at the UNGA.

7.2.4 *Right of Reply by Observers*

At a 1951 meeting of the UNGA, it was decided to grant the World Bank the right to reply.[98] At a 1962 meeting of the UNGA, a representative of South Korea, which was not a member of the Committee, was granted the floor to make a 'statement' in reply.[99] At a 1974 meeting of the UNGA, representatives of non-State communities who were invited to make

92 UN GAOR, 1st Committee, 62nd Session, 7th Meeting p. 20, UN Doc. A/C.1/62/PV.7 (2007).

93 IAEA Doc. GC(XXXIII)/OR.316, para. 95 (1989).

94 *Ibid.* at paras. 96, 97. 95 *Ibid.* at para. 98.

96 The representative of Iraq agreed to forgo his right of reply. IAEA Doc. GC(XXXIII)/OR.318, paras. 164, 165 (1989).

97 Committee B, First meeting, Fifty-Ninth World Health Assembly, p. 185. WHA 59/2006/REC/3 (2006).

98 UN GAOR, 2nd Committee, 6th Session, 167th Meeting, para. 75, UN Doc. A/C.2/SR.167 (1951).

99 UN GAOR, 1st Committee, 17th Session, 1301st Meeting, para. 25, UN Doc. A/C.1/SR.1301 (1962).

statements were also allowed to exercise a right of reply.[100] At a 1976 meeting of the UNGA, the President ruled that observers could exercise a right of reply.[101]

A 1983 opinion of the UN Office of Legal Affairs, in reference to the rules of procedure of ECOSOC, stated that although the relevant rule

> gives absolute right of reply only to Council members, it does not preclude the President from granting an opportunity to reply also to Observers. Traditionally this courtesy has been accorded by the Council to observer States and less frequently and consistently also to certain other entities, such as the Palestine Liberation Organization, authorised to participate in Council proceedings.[102]

The opinion continues by pointing out, 'As Observers have no absolute right of reply, opportunities to reply can be more readily restricted for them than for members. Presiding officers may completely deny Observers an opportunity to reply.'[103] The opinion adds that such a decision is subject to challenge.

In the UNGA, 'Palestine' has been granted an unconditional right of reply.[104] The European Commission has been granted such a right in UN-sponsored conferences.[105] The rules of procedure of the 2001 World Conference against Racism granted the President discretion as to whether to grant a right of reply to representatives other than those representing States.[106]

7.2.5 Right of Reply to Statements Made by Heads of State and Nondelegates

At a 1979 meeting of the UNGA, the President refused to allow the representative of Israel to exercise a right of reply to a speech by President

[100] UN GAOR, Special Political Committee, 29th Session, 923rd Meeting, paras. 204, 228, UN Doc. A/SPC/SR.923 (1974).

[101] UN GAOR, Plenary, 31st Session, 9th Meeting, para. 154, UN Doc. A/31/PV.9 (1976).

[102] Memorandum (by the UN Office of Legal Affairs) to the Assistant Secretary-General, Centre for Human Rights, 7 June 1983. 1983 UN Jur. Y.B. 188, UN Doc. ST/LEG/SER.C/21 (1983).

[103] *Ibid.* [104] UNGA Resolution 52/250 of 7 July 1998.

[105] UNGA Resolution 3208 (XXIX) of 11 October 1974. See comments on this issue in United Nations Treaty Collection, 'Summary of Practice of the Secretary General as Depositary of Multilateral Treaties' Prepared by the Treaty Section of the Office of Legal Affairs, UN Doc. ST/LEG/7/Rev.1, para. 98 (1999).

[106] Rule 25 of the rules of procedure of the 2001 World Conference against Racism, Racial Discrimination, Xenophobia and Related Intolerance, UN Doc. A/CONF.189/2 (2001).

Castro of Cuba. The Israel representative argued that Mr Castro had been speaking as the current Chairman of the Movement of Non-Aligned Countries and not as a head of State. The President of the Assembly ruled that Mr Castro 'continues to be the Head of State of Cuba', that 'the right of reply cannot be exercised in the Assembly hall in respect of a statement made by a Head of State' and that continuing the exercise of the right of reply 'is completely out of order and not in keeping with the established tradition'.[107]

At a 1983 meeting of the World Health Assembly, the President refused to grant a right of reply to Israel, 'because the statement has been made by the recipient of a prize, who was not speaking as a member of a delegation'. The President nevertheless permitted the representative of Israel 'to make a brief statement at the beginning of the next plenary meeting'.[108]

7.2.6 *Relevance of Right of Reply*

Neither the UNGA rules of procedure nor the UN Model Rules contain a stipulation as to the contents of a right of reply. On several occasions in the UNGA, delegates have asked the presiding officer to rule that a speaker exercising his right of reply was out of order. Most presiding officers have declined to intervene.[109] Several presiding officers have, however, called on speakers to confine themselves to reply 'to observations made during the debate' or similar language.[110] Some presiding officers have ruled speakers exercising their right of reply as being out of order,[111] but no consequences appear to have arisen from such ruling. At the 2002 ILO Conference, the President declared that a 'delegate must also present his reply in appropriate parliamentary language'.[112]

107 UN GAOR, Plenary, 34th Session, 32nd Meeting, paras. 149, 150, 152, 158, UN Doc. A/34/PV.32 (1979).

108 36th World Health Assembly, 11th Plenary Meeting, WHA36/1983/REC/2, p. 251 (1983).

109 See, for example, UN GAOR, 3rd Committee, 36th Session, 62nd Meeting, para. 75, UN Doc. A/C.3/36/SR.62 (1981); UN GAOR, 2nd Committee, 17th Session, 864th Meeting, para. 44, UN Doc. A/C.2/17/SR.864 (1962).

110 UN GAOR, Plenary, 3rd Session, Part II, 193rd Meeting, p. 72, UN Doc. A/PV.193 (1949); UN GAOR, 3rd Committee, 3rd Session, 120th Meeting, pp. 323, 324, UN Doc. A/C.3/3/SR.120 (1948).

111 UN GAOR, 3rd Committee, 20th Session, 1374th Meeting, paras. 5, 57, UN Doc. A/C.3/20/SR.1374 (1965).

112 ILO Conference, 90th Session, 3rd sitting, p. 9/8 (2002).

At a 1991 meeting of the UNGA, the representative of Syria requested the floor in exercise of his right of reply 'only to thank the representative of Czechoslovakia for his statement'.[113]

7.2.7 *Time Limit on Right of Reply*

The UN Model Rules propose a five-minute limit for the first use of a right of reply and three minutes for the second and final use. No such limit exists in the UNGA rules of procedure, although a limit of ten minutes, set by the President with the approval of the Assembly or committee, is common. At the 1980 session of the UNGA, the President proposed to the Assembly that each representative be limited to two exercises of the right of reply. The Assembly accepted the proposal, and it has since become accepted practice.[114] In 1979, the UNGA decided, 'The first intervention in the exercise of the right of reply for any delegation on any item at a given meeting should be limited to ten minutes and the second intervention should be limited to five minutes.'[115] During a General Assembly debate, a President ruled that a delegate had ten minutes in total and not ten minutes to reply to each attack on the delegate's country.[116] At a 2011 Committee meeting of the UNGA a delegate argued that he had not used his right of reply on the previous day; therefore he had the right to make two ten-minute statements. The Chairman ruled that

113 UN GAOR, Plenary, 46th Session, 49th Meeting, p. 61, UN Doc. A/46/PV.49 (Provisional) (1991).

114 UN GAOR, Plenary, 31st Session, 32nd Meeting, para. 279, UN Doc. A/31/PV.32 (1976).

115 Resolution 'On the Rationalisation of the Procedures and Organisation of the General Assembly', para. 9, UNGA Resolution 34/401 of 12 December 1979.

116 UN GAOR, Plenary, 36th Session, 62nd Meeting, para. 126, UN Doc. A/36/PV.62 (1981):

> At an earlier meeting of the Plenary of the UNGA, at its Twenty-Eighth Session, the representative of Egypt claimed that he was entitled to two allocations of ten minutes each since he had to reply to two delegations. There was no reaction to the Egyptian delegate's statement and he continued his speech. UN GAOR, Plenary, 28th Session, 2176th Meeting, para. 212, UN Doc. A/PV.2176 (1973).
>
> At a meeting of the Third Committee of the UNGA, at its Fortieth Session, the Soviet representative claimed he was entitled to more time as he was replying to a number of delegations. The Chairman stated that the ruling given by the General Assembly in decision 34/401 regarding the length of time allowed for the two statements permitted in exercise of the right of reply could be interpreted as referring either to one item or to one delegation's statement. He could ask the Legal Counsel for an opinion on the matter; however, he appealed to delegations to hear out the statements being made in exercise of that right, with a view to completing them during the meeting. UN GAOR, 3rd Committee, 40th Session, 68th Meeting, paras. 33, 34, UN Doc. A/C.3/40/SR.68 (1985).

nevertheless his second right of reply must be limited to five minutes.[117] On various procedural motions, the presiding officer in the UNGA has the authority to determine the time allotted for speeches.[118] Regarding the right of reply, it is the Assembly or committee that has the authority to determine the time allotted:[119] however, the presiding officers at times make rulings on allocation of time without consulting the Assembly or committee.[120]

7.2.8 *Under What Circumstances Does a Right of Reply Arise?*

At a 1981 meeting of a UNGA committee, during the debate on the report of ECOSOC, the Chairman of the Committee refused to rule that an exercise of the right of reply was out of order. The Chairman explained that 'it was impossible for the Chairman to decide what another delegation found offensive or not offensive in a statement or to what a representative was replying or not replying'.[121]

A 1963 ad hoc UN committee on the methods of work of the General Assembly gave its opinion that

> any delegation which has been attacked or criticised either by direct reference or by imputation is entitled, if it so desires, to exercise the 'right of reply'. The Committee also recognizes that there are other occasions when a representative may legitimately feel he should make a clarifying statement because of comments made with respect to the attitude or policy of his country before the closing of the list of speakers.[122]

The usual practice is for a representative to determine when his delegation feels that it wishes to exercise a right of reply.[123] Some presiding officers,

117 1st Committee of the 2011UNGA, 13th Meeting p. 4, UN Doc. A/C.1/66/PV.13, p. 4 (2011). Nevertheless the Chairman allowed the speaker to finish his statement.

118 Rules 74, 75, 76 and 88 of the UNGA rules of procedure.

119 Rule 72 of the UNGA rules of procedure. UN GAOR, Ad Hoc Committee, 6th Session, 26th Meeting, para. 11, UN Doc. A/C.53/SR.26 (1951).

120 UN GAOR, Plenary, 28th Session, 2148th Meeting, para. 375, UN Doc. A/PV.2148 (1973).

121 UN GAOR, 3rd Committee, 36th Session, 62nd Meeting, para. 75, UN Doc. A/C.3/36/SR.62 (1981).

122 Report of the Ad Hoc Committee on the Improvement of the Methods of Work of the General Assembly, GAOR, 18th Session, Annexes, Agenda Item 25, p. 8, para. 49, UN Doc. A/5423 (1963).

123 On one occasion at least, a delegation has exercised a right of reply on behalf of another delegation: Liberia on behalf of Tanzania and Ghana. UN GAOR, Plenary, 20th Session, 1390th Meeting, para. 237, UN Doc. A/PV.1390 (1965).

however, have refused to grant a right of reply where the State concerned was not referred to by name.[124]

At a meeting of the 1974–1977 Geneva Humanitarian Law Conference, the Ukrainian representative questioned the right of the representative of the Republic of Korea to exercise a right of reply. The Ukrainian representative pointed out that the speech of the representative of the Democratic People's Republic of Korea, to which the reply was being made, 'had not mentioned any country by name' and did not contain 'any element calling for a reply'.[125] The Chairman then 'asked whether the representative of the Republic of Korea would be willing to refrain from speaking'.[126] No decision, however, was made on the issue raised.

At a meeting of the 1977 Vienna Conference on Succession of States in Respect of Treaties, a representative claimed that there were no grounds for granting a right of reply to a speech he had made, since he had not mentioned a country by name. The Chairman ruled that 'the right of reply was recognized when one delegation mentioned another in such a way that it could be identified, even if it was not expressly named'.[127]

At the 2003 ILO Conference, the President, in an opening statement, declared that 'a delegate may only avail himself of a right of reply on a specific point in a speech in which his Government has been implicated'.[128]

COMMENT

The practice is that it is at the discretion of a delegation to determine if it feels a right of reply is called for.

7.2.9 Limit on Number of Interventions in Exercise of Right of Reply

At a 1987 meeting of a UNGA committee, the President refused to allow the representative of Iran to exercise a right of reply to a statement by a representative of Israel. The President ruled that the Iranian representative

[124] UN GAOR, 3rd Committee, 20th Session, 1372nd Meeting, para. 48, UN Doc. A/C.3/20/SR.1372 (1965).

[125] CDDH/I/SR.64, para. 107, vol. IX, p. 323. [126] *Ibid.* at para. 108.

[127] 1977 Vienna Conference on Succession of States in Respect of Treaties (First Session), Official Records, vol. I, p. 135, Committee of the Whole, 19th Meeting, paras. 58, 60, UN Doc. A/CONF.80 (1977).

[128] ILO Conference, 91st Session, Geneva 2003, 12th (special) sitting, p. 13/1.

had 'already spoken in exercise of right of reply twice. Under the rules of procedure, he is not entitled to anything more.'[129] At a 1998 meeting of a UNGA committee, the North Korean delegate complained that the Chairman had limited him to two rights of reply per meeting while the rules of procedure referred to 'two per item'.[130] The Chairman replied that since the committee dealt with all agenda items, 'It is extremely difficult to determine whether a reply is being exercised on one or several agenda items.'[131]

The UN Model Rules limit to two the number of times a delegation may exercise the right of reply per item at a given meeting. The UNGA rules of procedure contain no such limitation, but the General Assembly in 1979 decided that '[t]he number of interventions in the exercise of the right of reply for any delegation at a given meeting should be limited to two per item'.[132] This has become the accepted practice.

An ILO Conference ruling on this issue was that

> This right of reply will be granted once only, in each case at the end of the sitting. This means that the general limit of two minutes decided on at the beginning of the Conference for exercising the right of reply will not be multipliable by the number of statements to which the speaker wants to reply, it being understood that the President may, if time permits, allow this limit to be somewhat exceeded if the reply relates to a large number of statements.[133]

COMMENT

Practice is that representatives are limited to two replies per meeting and this right is exercised at the end of the meeting or at the beginning of the following meeting.

[129] UN GAOR, Plenary, 42nd Session, 59th Meeting, pp. 114–115, UN Doc. A/42/PV.59 (Provisional) (1987).

[130] UN GAOR, 1st Committee, 53rd Session, 12th Meeting, UN Doc. A/C.1/53/PV.12, p. 20 (1998). The delegate referred to the rules of procedure, but in fact the rule as to restriction to two statements appears as an annex to the rules: see note 113.

[131] UN GAOR, 1st Committee, 53rd Session, 13th Meeting, UN Doc. A/C.1/53/PV.13, p. 2 (1998).

[132] Resolution 'On the Rationalisation of the Procedures and Organisation of the General Assembly', para. 9, UNGA Resolution 34/401 of 12 December 1979.

[133] Statement by the President, ILO Conference, 89th Session, 11th (special) sitting, p. 10/1 (2001); ILO Conference, 91st Session, Geneva, 12th (special) sitting, p. 13/1 (2003).

7.2.10 Right of Reply to Explanation of Vote

At a 1993 meeting of the UNGA, the Chairman allowed a representative to exercise his right of reply to a statement made in explanation of vote. The Chairman added that this should not be regarded as a precedent.[134] At a 1993 meeting of the World Health Assembly, the President permitted the delegate of Cyprus to reply to an explanation of a vote given by the representative of Turkey.[135]

COMMENT

It would appear to be correct procedure to permit a right of reply to an explanation of vote.

7.2.11 Right of Reply to a Statement Made in Right of Reply

The UN Office of Legal Affairs, in a 1983 opinion, stated, 'If a statement in the exercise of a right of reply by one State gives rise to a request by another State for a statement in reply, this request is normally acceded to in the practice of the Assembly and the Economic and Social Council.'[136] This appears to be the only ground for granting a second right of reply at one meeting.

At the 2002 ILO Conference, the President ruled that 'there will be no right of reply to the reply itself, as this would create a vicious circle'.[137] Nevertheless, the practice is to allow one reply to a right of reply.

7.2.12 Closure of Debate on Right of Reply

At a 1952 meeting of the UNGA, it was decided to close the debate. It was then decided, by a further vote, to close the debate on the replies being exercised by virtue of the right of reply.[138] The Australian delegation

[134] UN GAOR, 1st Committee, 22nd Session, 1538th Meeting, para. 37, UN Doc. A/C.1/22/SR.1538 (1967).

[135] 46th World Health Assembly, 7th Meeting of Committee 'B', WHA46/1993/REC/3, p. 247 (1993).

[136] Cable (from UN Office of Legal Affairs) to the Legal Liaison Officer to the United Nations Environment Programme, 16 May 1983. 1983 UN Jur. Y.B. 170, UN Doc. ST/LEG/SER.C/21 (1983).

[137] ILO Conference, 90th Session, 3rd sitting, p. 9/8 (2002).

[138] UN GAOR, 3rd Committee, 6th Session, 379th Meeting, paras. 58–69, UN Doc. A/C.3/6/SR.379 (1952).

commented that this would establish an unfortunate precedent, which could be used by representatives wishing to prevent replies.[139]

7.3 Explanation of Vote

The UNGA rules of procedure state,

> *Rule 88*
>
> The President may permit members to explain their votes, either before or after the voting, except when the vote is taken by secret ballot. The President may limit the time to be allowed for such explanations. The President shall not permit the proposer of a proposal or of an amendment to explain his vote on his own proposal or amendment.

The UN Model Rules propose,

> *Rule 55*
>
> *Explanation of Vote or Position*
>
> 1. Representatives may make brief statements consisting solely of explanations of vote, before the voting has commenced or after the voting has been completed. The President may limit the time to be allowed for such explanations. The representatives of a State sponsoring a proposal or motion shall not speak in explanation of vote thereon, except if it has been amended.
> 2. When the same matter is considered successively in several organs of the Conference, the representatives of a State should, as far as possible, explain their votes only in one such organ unless those votes differ.
> 3. Similarly, explanatory statements of position may be made in connection with a decision taken without a vote.

A 1971 UN committee on procedures and organisation of the General Assembly commented that 'it was pointed out that explanations of vote frequently gave rise to abuses and were used to make statements of substance or reopen a debate'.[140] The committee, however, refrained from making any recommendation for changes in the rules of procedure of the Assembly. The usual criterion for distinguishing an explanation of vote

[139] *Ibid.* at para. 66.

[140] Para. 213 of the Report of the Special Committee on the Rationalisation of the Procedures and Organisation of the General Assembly, GAOR, 26th Session, Supplement No. 26, UN Doc. A/8426 (1971).

from a general statement is that an explanation of vote refers explicitly to a draft proposal.[141]

7.3.1 Discretion of President to Allow Explanation of Vote

The UNGA rule states, 'The President *may* permit members to explain their votes.'[142]

During the early years of the UNGA the right to explain a vote was not regarded as categorical or absolute.[143] A 1952 UNGA committee upheld a Chairman's ruling that the presiding officer had discretion as to whether to allow explanations of vote or not. The Committee did not accept the interpretation of the Soviet delegation that the discretion of the presiding officer referred only to the procedure of applying the right to explain a vote.[144] A right to explain a vote was denied in the Plenary where a motion, concerning an international regime for Jerusalem, had been defeated,[145] and in another case in the Plenary the right was denied to delegations that had participated in the debate.[146] However, recent UNGA practice and practice in conferences have invariably permitted explanations of vote, and there does not appear to be a recent example where such a right was denied. In a 1983 opinion, the UN Office of Legal Affairs stated that 'the right to explain a vote has become practically absolute'.[147]

The UN Model Rules avoid such possible ambiguity and state, 'Representatives may make brief statements consisting solely of explanations of vote.'[148]

141 See, for example, UN GAOR, 1st Committee, 54th Session, 24th Meeting, UN Doc. A/C.1/54/PV.24, p. 3 (1999).

142 Rule 88 of the UNGA rules of procedure. [emphasis added]

143 '[T]he Special Committee wishes to confirm the discretionary powers of the president to allow or disallow such explanations [of vote].' Report of the Special Committee on Methods and Procedures of the General Assembly, p. 10, para. 32, GAOR, 4th Session, Supplement No. 12, UN Doc. A/937 (1949).

144 UN GAOR, 3rd Committee, 6th Session, 405th Meeting, paras. 33–37, 46, UN Doc. A/C.3/6/SR.405 (1952).

145 UN GAOR, Plenary, 5th Session, 326th Meeting, para. 12, UN Doc. A/PV.326 (1950).

146 UN GAOR, Plenary, 5th Session, 312th Meeting, para. 113, UN Doc. A/PV.312 (1950).

147 Memorandum, 10 November 1983, from Office of Legal Affairs to the Under-Secretary-General for Political and General Assembly Affairs. 1983 UN Jur. Y.B. 174, 176, UN Doc. ST/LEG/SER.C/21 (1983).

148 Rule 55(1) of the UN Model Rules.

7.3.2 Explanation of Vote on Procedural Motions

A proposal was submitted to the 1949 Special Committee on UNGA Methods and Procedures to prohibit explanations of votes on procedural motions. The Committee did not accept the proposal.[149] The President of the 1952 session of the UNGA commented that generally there are no explanations of voting on procedural motions, but he permitted a delegation to do so.[150] The rules of procedure of the UNGA and the UN Model Rules, however, do not refer to the issue of explanations of votes on procedural motions.

At a meeting of the Third Committee of the 2007 UNGA an oral proposal was submitted that 'two reports should be deleted from the list of documents to be considered by the Committee'. When a number of delegates requested to give explanations of vote on the proposal, the Secretary of the Committee announced that 'the usual procedure was not being followed because the vote was not on a draft resolution'. The Secretary presumably was stating that it was procedural motion. The Committee voted on the proposal without any formal 'explanations of vote'.[151]

COMMENT

Since the relevant rules of procedure refer generally to voting, explanations of vote would appear to apply to all voting, including voting on procedural motions.

7.3.3 Explanation of Vote on Motions to Adjourn the Debate or Close the Debate

There can be no explanations of vote before voting on motions for adjournment of debate and closure of debate since the applicable rules[152] limit the number of speakers on these motions.[153] There do not appear to

[149] Report of the Special Committee on Methods and Procedures of the General Assembly, GAOR, 4th Session, Supplement No. 12, para. 32, UN Doc. A/937 (1949). The decision, which is not stated explicitly, is also referred to in UN Doc. A/AC.149/L.2, p. 26 (1971).

[150] UN GAOR, Plenary, 6th Session, 362nd Meeting, para. 59, UN Doc. A/PV.362 (1952).

[151] UN GAOR, Third Committee, 62nd Session, 1st Meeting, paras. 8, 29, 31, 45, 94, UN Doc. A/C.3/62/SR.1 (2007).

[152] Rules 74, 75 of the UNGA rules of procedure.

[153] This was the ruling of the Chairman of the 1st Committee of the UNGA at its 16th Session; the ruling was upheld in an appeal. UN GAOR, 1st Committee, 16th Session, 1176th Meeting, paras. 34, 35, 36, 41, UN Doc. A/C.1/16/SR.1176 (1961).

be any restrictions on explanations of vote after the vote on such motions, although the rules of procedure grant discretion to the presiding officer.

At a 1963 meeting of a UNGA committee, the representative of the United States gave an explanation of vote on a motion for closure of debate, after the motion had been passed. The US representative had requested the floor, however, on a point of order.[154]

At a 1974 meeting of a UNGA committee, the representative of the United Kingdom explained his vote on a motion of closure, and no objection was raised to his doing so.[155]

At a 1984 meeting of a UNGA committee, two delegations requested the floor to explain their vote after a motion for adjournment of debate had been approved. The Chairman commented that 'the adjournment of the debate means that the item is no longer under consideration' and agreed to allow explanations of vote only if there was no objection.[156]

At a 1986 meeting of the World Health Assembly, the Chairman permitted a delegation to explain its vote on a motion that had been adopted to adjourn the debate. One delegation protested the ruling but did not lodge an appeal against the decision.[157]

At a 2006 meeting of the IAEA General Conference, the Director of the Office of Legal Affairs at first denied a delegate the right to give an explanation of vote on a motion to adjourn the debate on the grounds that the delegate had already spoken on that motion. When challenged by the delegate, the Legal Advisor reversed his ruling and allowed the explanation of vote.[158]

7.3.4 Explanation of Vote on Motions to Adjourn or Suspend a Meeting

Motions for suspension or adjournment of a meeting must be put to the vote immediately.[159] Therefore, there cannot be explanations of vote before the voting on such motions. An explanation after the vote would

[154] UN GAOR, Special Political Committee, 18th Session, 381st Meeting, para. 41, UN Doc. A/SPC/SR.381 (1963).

[155] UN GAOR, 5th Committee, 29th Session, 1696th Meeting, para. 61, UN Doc. A/C.5/29/SR.1696 (1974).

[156] UN GAOR, 1st Committee, 39th Session, 49th Meeting, p. 86, UN Doc. A/C.1/39/SR.49 (1984).

[157] WHA/39/1986/REC/3, p. 268.

[158] IAEA 50th General Conference, Plenary Record of the 10th Meeting, p. 10, paras. 60–61, p. 12 paras. 70–78, GC(50)/OR.10 (2006).

[159] Rule 76 of the UNGA rules of procedure.

presumably have to take place at the next meeting if the motion for adjournment or suspension of the meeting was approved.

7.3.5 *Length of Explanations of Vote*

The phrase permitting the President to limit the time to be allowed for explanations of vote was proposed by the 1949 Special Committee on UNGA Methods and Procedures.[160] During the debate in the Sixth Committee, several delegations objected to the granting of this authority to the President. One delegation proposed that the authority to limit the length of explanations should be limited only to 'representatives who had spoken during the debate'.[161] The proposal, however, was adopted without being amended.[162] The usual practice in the UNGA is to limit explanations of vote to five,[163] seven or ten minutes.[164] They have even been limited to two minutes.[165]

The UNGA resolved in 1979 that explanations of vote should be limited to ten minutes.[166] The same resolution also stated, 'When the same draft resolution is considered in a Main Committee and in plenary meeting, a delegation should, as far as possible, explain its vote only once, i.e., either in the Committee or in plenary meeting, unless that delegation's vote in plenary meeting is different from its vote in the committee.'[167] This has become the accepted practice of the UNGA. At a 2008 meeting of the First Committee of the UNGA, the Chairman rebuked a delegate by stating that 'to make such a long statement in explanation of vote shows a lack of respect for other delegations', but nevertheless did not interrupt the

160 Report of the Special Committee on Methods and Procedures of the General Assembly, para. 32, GAOR, 4th Session, Supplement No. 12, p. 10, UN Doc. A/937 (1949).

161 UN GAOR, 6th Committee, 4th Session, 150th Meeting, para. 94, UN Doc. A/C.6/4/SR.150 (1949).

162 Adopted UN GAOR, 6th Committee, 4th Session, 150th Meeting, para. 96, UN Doc. A/C.6/4/SR.150 (1949). UNGA Resolution 362 (IV) of 22 October 1949.

163 UN GAOR, 1st Committee, 20th Session, 1416th Meeting, para. 37, UN Doc. A/C.1/20/SR.1416 (1965); UN GAOR, 1st Committee, 22nd Session, 1538th Meeting, para. 38, UN Doc. A/C.1/22/SR.1538 (1967) (by reference).

164 UN GAOR, Plenary, 11th Session, 632nd Meeting, para. 23, UN Doc. A/PV.632 (1956); UN GAOR, Plenary, 11th Session, 648th Meeting, para. 25, UN Doc. A/PV.648 (1957).

165 UN GAOR, 3rd Committee, 22nd Session, 1511th Meeting, paras. 53, 54, UN Doc. A/C.3/22/SR.1511 (1967).

166 UNGA Resolution 34/401, para. E.6, adopted 12 December 1979.

167 *Ibid.* at para. E.7.

speaker.[168] At a 2016 meeting of the First Committee of the UNGA, where resolutions are normally dealt with in clusters, a delegation representative argued that since he was 'making explanation of vote on several resolutions – 15 draft resolutions' he could not be limited to ten minutes.[169] The Chairman prohibited him from continuing beyond ten minutes, but later ruled that nevertheless 'on an exceptional basis. I will allow delegations that were not able to finish their explanations of vote to take the floor to do so.'[170]

7.3.6 Explanation of Vote by Proposer or Co-Sponsor

The UNGA rules of procedure and the UN Model Rules prohibit a proposer of a proposal or an amendment from explaining his own vote.[171] There was at least one case where the President of the General Assembly attempted to circumvent this rule by calling upon the proposer 'to make a statement'.[172] The UN Office of Legal Affairs gave its opinion that despite there being some occasions where the rule was not applied, 'when a proposer or co-sponsor has asked to explain his vote, the President would have no choice but to apply the rule by refusing the floor to the proposer or co-sponsor'.[173]

The First Committee of the UNGA votes on proposals in clusters, and the practice is that sponsors 'are permitted to make general statements at the beginning of consideration of the drafts under a given cluster'.[174]

168 UN GAOR 1st Committee, 63rd Session, 19th meeting, p. 31, UN Doc. A/C.1/63/PV.19 (2008).

169 UN GAOR, 1st Committee, 71st session 23rd meeting p. 8, UN Doc. A/C.1/PV.23 (2016).

170 *Ibid.*, p. 9, p. 20 UN Doc. A/C.1/PV.23 (2016).

171 Rule 88 of the UNGA Rules of Procedure (Rule 128 in committees). This has been enforced even by denying the right of a delegate to continue an explanation already commenced. See ruling in a meeting of the 1st Committee of the UNGA at its 55th Session, UN Doc. A/C.1/55/PV.28, p. 14 (2000).

172 UN Doc. A/ES-7/PV.11, p. 61 (Provisional) (1980). See Yehuda Z. Blum, *Eroding the United Nations Charter* (1993), p. 1. In fact the proposer in this case proceeded to submit an oral amendment.

173 *Memorandum to the Executive Office of the Secretary General*, 19 October 1966, Explanation of vote by the proposer of a proposal or of an amendment, Rule 90 of the rules of procedure of the General Assembly, http://legal.un.org/ola/media/GA_RoP/GA_RoP_EN.pdf.

174 UN GAOR 1st Committee, 62nd Session, 20th meeting, p. 20, UN Doc. A/C.1/62/PV.20 (2007). UN GAOR, 1st Committee. 69th Session, 20th meeting p. 33, UN Doc. A/C.1/69/PV.20 (2014).

The practice in the UNGA is that a sponsor is allowed to explain his vote where the proposal was amended or adopted by a committee.[175] The UN Model Rules explicitly allow a proposer to explain his vote on a proposal or an amendment where such proposal or amendment was itself amended.[176] This has been adopted by some conferences' rules of procedure.[177]

At a 1986 meeting of the World Health Assembly, the Chairman allowed the sponsors of a resolution to explain their vote after the Assembly had decided not to consider the draft resolution they had proposed. The explanation of vote was on the procedural motion that had been passed not to consider the proposal.[178]

7.3.7 Discretion of Conference or Assembly to Allow Proposer to Explain a Vote

The UNGA rules of procedure state, 'The President shall not permit the proposer of a proposal or of an amendment to explain his vote on his own proposal or amendment.'[179]

A logical inference from this language is that the General Assembly or the committee, as distinct from the president or the chairman, may allow such an explanation of vote. This was the inference of the President of the 1970 session of the UNGA, who requested authorisation from the Assembly to permit sponsors of a resolution to explain their vote.[180] There have been occasions when committees or chairmen with explicit or implicit approval of the committee have allowed co-sponsors to make 'explanations regarding their proposals' rather than explanations of votes.[181] At a 1996 meeting of a UNGA committee, the Chairman ruled that, although

175 See, for example, UN GAOR, 1st Committee, 35th Session, 47th Meeting, p. 72, UN Doc. A/C.1/35/SR.47 (1980); UN GAOR, Plenary, 36th Session, 100th Meeting, para. 85, UN Doc. A/36/PV.100 (1981).

176 Rule 55(1) of the UN Model Rules.

177 See Rule 39 of the rules of procedure of the Diplomatic Conference on an International Ban on Anti-Personnel Land Mines, APL/CRP.2 (1997); Rule 40 of the rules of procedure of the UN Diplomatic Conference of Plenipotentiaries on the Establishment of an International Criminal Court, UN Doc. A/CONF.183/13 (1998).

178 WHA39/1986/REC/3, pp. 267, 268.

179 Rule 88 of the UNGA rules of procedure.

180 UN GAOR, Plenary, 25th Session, 1897th Meeting, para. 64, UN Doc. A/PV.1897 (1970).

181 UN GAOR, 5th Committee, 31st Session, 58th Meeting, para. 67, UN Doc. A/C.5/31/SR.58 (1976); UN GAOR, 1st Committee, 29th Session, 2019th Meeting, p. 37, UN Doc. A/C.1/29/SR.2019 (1974); UN GAOR, 6th Committee, 46th Session, 42nd Meeting, paras. 9, 11, 12, UN Doc. A/C.6/46/SR.42 (1991).

delegates who were sponsors of a resolution were not allowed to explain their position, they would, however, be allowed 'to make general statements either prior to or after the action on the draft resolution in question'. From the Chairman's statement it appears that the ruling was given with the approval of the Office of Legal Affairs.[182]

The UN Model Rules use the language of a general prohibition, namely, 'The representative of a State sponsoring a proposal or motion shall not speak in explanation of vote.' Therefore, presumably, the conference has no discretion, unless it decides to amend or suspend its rules of procedure.[183]

7.3.8 *Explanation of Vote by Proposer Voting against the Resolution or Withdrawing Sponsorship*

At the 1974 session of the UNGA, the President permitted the delegation of Thailand to explain why it was voting against its own resolution. The delegation of Cuba protested that this was in violation of the rules of procedure, but did not challenge the ruling of the President.[184]

At the 1997 session of the UNGA, the Chairman permitted the UK and US representatives to utilise an explanation of vote, prior to a vote, in order to withdraw their sponsorship of the resolution.[185]

7.3.9 *Explanation of Vote on a Resolution Proposed by a Committee*

Sponsors of a resolution subsequently adopted by a committee are not considered sponsors of the resolution in that it is no longer their resolution, but the resolution of the committee. The original sponsors of the resolution may therefore explain their vote on the committee's resolution.[186]

182 UN GAOR, 1st Committee, 51st Session, 22nd Meeting, p. 2, UN Doc. A/C.1/51/PV.22 (1996).

183 Rule 55 of the UN Model Rules.

184 UN GAOR, Plenary, 29th Session, 2302nd Meeting, paras. 6, 20, 40, 41, UN Doc. A/PV.2302 (1974).

185 UN GAOR, 1st Committee, 52nd Session, 23rd Meeting, UN Doc. A/C.1/52/PV.23, p. 14 (1997).

186 UN GAOR, Plenary, 21st Session, 1484th Meeting, para. 59, UN Doc. A/PV.1484 (1966); UN GAOR, Plenary, 23rd Session, 1723rd Meeting, para. 16, UN Doc. A/PV.1723 (1968). UN GAOR, Plenary, 71st Session, 65th Meeting, p. 37, UN Doc. A/71/PV.65 (2016). See, however, the recommendation in UNGA Resolution 34/401 of 12 December 1979 that delegations 'as far as possible' should explain their vote only once.

7.3.10 *Explanation of Vote by Co-Sponsor*

The Chairman of a committee at the 1976 UNGA ruled that a delegation that became a co-sponsor of a resolution at a late stage and had not yet spoken on the issue could nevertheless not give an explanation of its vote.[187] This would appear to be an incorrect ruling.

COMMENT

The rationale of the prohibition against sponsors giving an explanation of vote is to avoid an explanation being given twice. Where there has been a change in the proposal or in the position of the sponsor, the rationale is no longer valid and the sponsor is allowed to give an explanation of vote.

7.3.11 *Explanation of Vote on a Consensus*

The UN Model Rules propose,

> *Rule 5*
>
> *Explanation of Vote or Position*
>
> 3. Similarly, explanatory statements of position may be made in connection with a decision taken without a vote.

Explanation of a vote, or rather of a position, on a consensus is usually done after the adoption of the consensus, but on at least one occasion the UNGA has permitted explanations before the adoption of the consensus.[188]

7.3.12 *Explanation of Vote on a Secret Ballot*

The rules of procedure of the World Health Assembly allow the Assembly to decide by a majority vote by show of hands whether to vote by secret ballot.[189] The President of the 1993 World Health Assembly refused to allow a delegation to explain its vote on the issue of whether to hold a secret ballot or not. The President explained that he 'would regard that as contrary to the idea of a secret ballot'.[190] This ruling does not, however,

[187] UN GAOR, 1st Committee, 31st Session, 44th Meeting, pp. 32–37, UN Doc. A/C.1/31/SR.44 (1976).

[188] UN GAOR, 1st Committee, 31st Session, 50th Meeting, pp. 2–5, UN Doc. A/C.1/31/SR.50 (1976).

[189] Rule 78 of the rules of procedure of the World Health Assembly.

[190] Verbatim Records, 46th World Health Assembly, 13th Plenary Meeting, p. 280, WHA46/1993/REC/2, A46/VR/13 (1993).

appear to be justified. At the same Assembly some delegations requested permission to explain how they had voted in the actual secret ballot. The President ruled that 'in principle' he would not allow it, but he gave permission to delegations 'to make a short statement declaring the principles that they adhere to, although not being allowed to mention how they voted'.[191]

7.3.13 Explanation of Vote on Nonparticipation in Voting

It is universal practice that an explanation of vote can also be made where a delegation abstained or refrained from participating in the voting.

7.3.14 Explanation of Vote Should Not Include Comments on Other Delegations

At a 1958 meeting of a UNGA committee, the Chairman stated that he interpreted the rule of procedure referring to explanations of vote as meaning that a delegation should only explain its own vote and not comment on the votes of other delegations.[192] During the 1991 World Health Assembly, the President repeatedly requested one delegation 'to speak only on the vote'.[193] There is, however, no bar to a delegation explaining the vote on behalf of a number of delegations. This is common practice, for example, for the member States of the European Union.

7.3.15 Explanation of Vote on Voting Taken Paragraph by Paragraph

At a 1968 meeting of a UNGA committee, the Chairman did not allow the representative of Bulgaria to give an explanation of his vote after separate voting had taken place on two paragraphs but before the vote had taken place on the resolution as a whole. The Chairman ruled that the representative must wait until the completion of the voting on the resolution as a whole.[194]

The practical guide to the UNGA published by the Permanent Mission of Switzerland to the UN comments, 'An explanation of vote concerning

[191] *Ibid.* at p. 282.

[192] UN GAOR, 4th Committee, 13th Session, 770th Meeting, para. 23, UN Doc. A/C.4/13/SR.770 (1958).

[193] Verbatim Records, 44th World Health Assembly, 12th Plenary Meeting, pp. 254, 255, WHA44/1991/REC/2 (1991).

[194] UN GAOR, 1st Committee, 23rd Session, 1642nd Meeting, paras. 96, 97, UN Doc. A/C.1/23/SR.1642 (1968).

a paragraph vote is made only after action is taken on the whole resolution/decision.'[195]

7.3.16 Explanation of Vote by a Representative of an Inter-Governmental Organisation

At the 1994 World Health Assembly, the Legal Adviser of the WHO stated that, 'according to a strict legal interpretation', a representative of an inter-governmental organisation did not have a right of explanation of vote. However, the Chairman could allow the representative to 'make a statement'.[196]

7.3.17 When to Explain a Vote?

There is a significant difference between an explanation of vote made before the vote and that made after the vote. Explanations made before the vote are in fact an extension of debate and part of a continued effort to persuade other delegations. Explanations made after the vote are usually intended to place on record a State's position or to give a legal interpretation to the results of the vote that took place. In a 1978 meeting of a committee of the General Assembly, this discretion was used by one President to rule that explanations of vote may be made only after the vote.[197] The UNGA rules of procedure, which theoretically grant discretion to the President as to whether to allow explanations of vote, also, by implication, grant discretion as to when such explanations should be made. The usual practice, however, is to allow explanations of vote either before or after the vote.[198] The UN Model Rules permit explanations of vote to be made either before or after the vote.

The rules of procedure of the World Health Assembly, however, explicitly state,

> *Rule 75*
>
> *After the voting has been completed*, a delegate may make a brief statement, consisting solely of an explanation of vote.[199] Where at a WHA

[195] Para. 3.5, www.unitar.org/ny/sites/unitar.org.ny/files/UN_PGA_Handbook.pdf.

[196] WHA47/1994/REC/3, p. 204 (1994).

[197] UN GAOR, 5th Committee, 33rd Session, 56th Meeting, paras. 57–63, 68, UN Doc. A/C.5/33/SR.56 (1978).

[198] Memorandum, 10 November 1983, from Office of Legal Affairs to the Under-Secretary-General for Political and General Assembly Affairs. 1983 UN Jur. Y.B. 174, 176, UN Doc. ST/LEG/SER.C/21 (1983).

[199] Emphasis added.

> Assembly, one delegate objected to another delegate giving an explanation of vote before the voting, the Chairman, after consulting the Legal Counsel, determined that explanations of vote would be only after the vote.[200]

7.3.18 Explanation of Vote after the List of Speakers Has Been Closed

At a meeting of the 1974–1977 Geneva Humanitarian Law Conference, the Chairman announced that 'he could entertain no further requests to speak in [explanation of vote in] respect of the amendments' since 'the list of speakers had been closed'.[201] The representatives of the Federal Republic of Germany, Pakistan, Iraq, France and Mexico pointed out that 'no delegation wishing to explain its vote could be denied its right to do so'.[202] The Chairman consequently reopened the list of speakers.[203]

7.4 Offensive or Irrelevant Statements

The UNGA rules of procedure state,

> *Rule 68*
>
> The President may call a speaker to order if his remarks are not relevant to the subject under discussion.

The UN Model Rule is identical except that it refers to the 'question under discussion'.

Jessup writes, 'Opprobrious epithets or offensive language may properly be considered by the chair to be "not relevant."'[204] Use, however, is rarely made of such authority. Hovey, writing in 1951, stated, 'Presidents have tended to slight their opportunities under this heading.'[205] This statement remains valid more than sixty years later.

It is fairly common in the UNGA and in other international organisations for delegations to make statements that are abusive of other States. Franck compares this with New York street language as 'a way of the poor and powerless to inflict psychic pain'.[206] The 'abused' delegations

[200] Sixty-Seventh World Health Assembly. Committee B, First meeting, p. 242, WHA67/2014/REC/3 (2014).

[201] CDDH/I/SR.68, para. 26, vol. IX, p. 374.

[202] *Ibid.* at para. 28, vol. IX, p. 375. [203] *Ibid.*

[204] Philip C. Jessup, 'Parliamentary Diplomacy, An Examination of the Legal Quality of the Rules of Procedure of Organs of the United Nations', 89 RCADI 181 (1956 I) at 268.

[205] Allan Hovey Jr, 'Obstructionism and the Rules of the General Assembly', 5 *UNESCO International Organization* 515 (1951 No. 3) at 525.

[206] Thomas M. Franck, *Nation against Nation* (1985), pp. 208, 209.

frequently raise points of order to complain about such language,[207] but neither the UNGA rules of procedure nor the UN Model Rules specifically authorise the chairman or president to declare a delegate's speech out of order for being offensive. It is, however, common for chairmen, usually at the request of a delegation, to call upon speakers to confine their statements to the issue on the agenda.[208] At a 2003 session of the UNGA, the President asked that 'appropriate use of language be observed; there is no place in our discussion for the word "stupid" or "stupefying"'.[209] Chairmen also frequently call upon delegations to use a country's official name.[210] The practice, however, is that such calls are not accompanied by any ruling from the chair.

The rules of procedure of the 1974–1977 Geneva Humanitarian Law Conference provided explicitly that the Chairman could require a speaker 'to stop speaking'.[211] At a meeting of the Conference, there was a sharp exchange of words between the delegations of the Democratic People's Republic of Korea and the Republic of Korea. The Chairman called upon the delegations

> to refrain from giving vent in their speeches to views that had nothing to do with the article under consideration . . . If they failed to comply, he would be forced to apply rule 19 of the Conference's rules of procedure, which empowered the Chairman to call a speaker to order if his remarks were not relevant to the subject under discussion and, should the occasion arise, to require him to stop speaking.[212]

207 See, for example, the point of order raised by the US delegate to the 3rd Committee of the 2011 UNGA, UN Doc. A/C.3/66/SR.24 para. 23. (2011).

208 UN GAOR, 4th Committee, 20th Session, 1572nd Meeting, paras. 5–8, UN Doc. A/C.4/20/SR.1572 (1965); UN GAOR, 4th Committee, 20th Session, 1541st Meeting, paras. 75–77, UN Doc. A/C.4/20/SR.1541 (1965); UN GAOR, 3rd Committee, 20th Session, 1362nd Meeting, para. 31, UN Doc. A/C.3/20/SR.1362 (1965); UN GAOR, Special Political Committee, 20th Session, 477th Meeting, paras. 14–16, UN Doc. A/SPC/SR.477 (1965); UN GAOR, Special Political Committee, 22nd Session, 558th Meeting, paras. 34–40, UN Doc. A/SPC/SR.558 (1967); UN GAOR, Plenary, 28th Session, 2148th Meeting, para. 452, UN Doc. A/PV.2148 (1973).

209 UN Doc. A/PV.58, p. 13 (2003).

210 See, for example, 24th Meeting of the 3rd Committee of the 2011 UNGA. UN Doc. A/C.3/66/SR.24, para. 42 (2011). 17th meeting of the 1st Committee of the 1987 UNGA pp.14–15, UN Doc. A/C.1/42/PV.17.

211 Rule 19 of the rules of procedure of the 1974–1977 Geneva Humanitarian Law Conference: 'The President may call a speaker to order if his remarks are not relevant to the subject under discussion and, should the occasion arise, require him to stop speaking' (CDDH/2).

212 Official Records of the 1974–1977 Geneva Humanitarian Law Conference, vol. XV, p. 54, CDDH/III/SR.44, para. 49.

At a 2009 Committee meeting of the World Health Assembly, a point of order was raised by the delegate from Sri Lanka requesting the Chairman to call on the delegate of Israel not to raise matters unrelated to the agenda item. The Chairman complied with the request, and the Legal Counsel gave his opinion that '[c]learly, if a delegate was speaking out of order, it was within the authority of the Chairman to call the delegate to order and, if necessary, terminate his or her statement. However such a step should be taken with caution, since all delegates had the right to take the floor.'[213]

At the 2009 Durban Review Conference a delegate on a point of order stated that 'no mention could be made of a specific country, let alone a Head of State whose dignity and status must be respected'. The President responded that 'a country could be mentioned' and delegations had a right of reply; however, '[s]peakers must show respect'.[214] At the same conference, in a later meeting, the President 'urged a representative "to use relevant and proper terminology"'[215] and on his own initiative 'reminded delegates to use respectful language when referring to a Head of State'.[216] No action, however, was taken by the President.

COMMENT

Although chairmen fairly frequently appeal to speakers not to use offensive language and not to stray from items on the agenda, it is extremely rare for a chairman to take any action in such matters.

7.5 Clarity of Speech

The rules of procedure of the ITU conferences stipulate that

> *Article 12(2) (2)*
>
> Any person speaking must express himself slowly and distinctly separating his words and pausing as necessary in order that everybody may understand his meaning.[217]

This highly practical injunction has apparently not been introduced in non-ITU conferences.

[213] Committee B, 1st Meeting, Sixty-Second World Health Assembly, WHA62/2009/REC/3 p.138 (2009).

[214] UN Doc. A/CONF.211/SR.9 paras. 66, 67 (2009).

[215] UN Doc. A/CONF.211/SR.9 para. 12 (2009).

[216] UN Doc. A/CONF.211/SR.10 para. 80 (2009).

[217] Article 32(12)(2)(2) of the Constitution of the International Telecommunication Union, Geneva 1993.

7.6 Personal Attacks

Neither the UNGA rules of procedure nor the UN Model Rules make any reference to the obligation to refrain from ad hominem attacks, but it is common procedure for chairmen to call upon speakers to refrain from such attacks.[218]

7.7 Speaking to Substance on Procedural Motions

The rule of procedure in the General Assembly is

> *Rule 71*
>
> A representative rising to a point of order may not speak on the substance of the matter under discussion.

The UN Model Rules state

> *Rule 35*
>
> A representative may not, in raising a point of order, speak on the substance of the question under discussion.

This rule has been enforced in the General Assembly by the President calling a delegate out of order for violating the rule.[219]

[218] See, for example, UN GAOR, Plenary, 15th Session, Part II, 968th Meeting, para. 198, UN Doc. A/PV.968 (1961).

[219] UN GAOR, Plenary, 15th Session, Part II, 988th Meeting, para. 42, UN Doc. A/PV.988 (1961).

8

Submission of Proposals

8.1 The Difference between Proposals and Motions

The term 'motion' denotes that the conference is being requested to take action; the action being requested could be either procedural or substantive.[1] The term 'proposal' usually refers to that part of the motion that contains the text proposed by a delegation in its motion.

The Legal Adviser to the UN has pointed out that 'the word "amendment" had a meaning distinct from that of the word "proposal"; only the word "motion" embraced both at one and the same time'.[2] A proposed amendment to an existing proposal is by definition a 'motion' on which the conference is being asked to take action.

A debate took place at the 1965 UNGA as to whether the word 'proposal' includes an amendment.[3] Those objecting to interpreting an amendment as being included pointed out that in Rule 78 reference is made to 'Proposals and amendments'; hence it can be deduced that they are separate terms. The results of the debate were inconclusive: however, a logical solution would dictate that the word 'proposal' includes an amendment. Otherwise, for example, the rule on reconsideration would not apply to amendments. The UN Model Rules avoid such possible ambiguity by

[1] A motion is defined by *Robert's Rules of Order*, 11th edn (2011) p. 27, as 'a formal proposal by a member, in a meeting, that the assembly take certain action'. Leigh states, 'Proposals requiring action by the meeting are called motions or principal motions.' Robert D. Leigh, *Modern Rules of Parliamentary Procedure* (1937), p. 21. *Black's Law Dictionary* states as regards a motion, 'In Parliamentary law; A proposal made in a meeting in a form suitable for its consideration and action, that the meeting . . . take certain action or view'. *Black's Law Dictionary*, 8th edn (2004).

[2] UN GAOR, 6th Committee, 4th Session, 165th Meeting, para. 75, UN Doc. A/C.6/4/SR.165 (1949).

[3] UN GAOR, 1st Committee, 20th Session, 1417th Meeting, paras. 1–41, UN Doc. A/C.1/20/SR.1417 (1965). Echoed in the Plenary Meeting, UN GAOR, Plenary, 20th Session, 1402nd Meeting, paras. 29–45, UN Doc. A/PV.1402 (1965).

stipulating in Rule 58(1) that a 'proposal is considered an amendment to another proposal' and '[u]nless specified otherwise, the word "proposal" in these rules shall be considered as including amendments'.

COMMENT

There tends to be a lack of consistency in the use of the terms 'motion' and 'proposal', and in practice the term 'motion' is often reserved for procedural motions.

8.2 Order of Discussion of Proposals

Proposals relevant to the same issue are usually discussed in the order in which they have been submitted. Rules of procedure contain detailed stipulations as to the *order of voting* on proposals, but do not contain such provisions as to the *order of discussion* of proposals. It is presumably accepted as axiomatic that proposals are discussed in the order in which they were submitted, although a chairman of a committee of the 1974–1977 Geneva Humanitarian Law Conference made a point of explicitly informing the participants that this would be the procedure.[4]

8.3 Sponsors

In conference procedure all proposals require sponsors, the only exception being basic proposals 'submitted to the Conference by the convening organ or the preparatory organ'.[5] Where observers are allowed to sponsor proposals, such sponsorship does not entitle them to submit the proposal to a vote. Only States can submit proposals to a vote. At the 1986 Conference on Treaties between States and International Organisations, the Chairman refused to submit to a vote a proposal submitted by the UN itself, as no State had requested such a vote.[6] The practical guide to the UNGA, published by the Permanent Mission of Switzerland to the UN,

[4] Official Records of the 1974–1977 Geneva Humanitarian Law Conference, Committee II, CDDH/II/SR.2, vol. XI, p. 17, para. 24.

[5] The description of a 'basic proposal' is taken from Rule 45 of the UN Model Rules.

[6] Official Records of the 1986 Conference on Treaties Between States and International Organisations, 29th Meeting, para. 6, UN Doc. A/CONF.129/16 (1986). The relevant rule of procedure was Rule 59*(d)* that observers could 'submit substantive proposals, which as such may only be put to the vote subject to rule 63 if a formal request is made by a State to that effect'.

explains, 'There are no co-sponsors of UNGA decisions and of draft resolutions/decisions tabled by the President of the UNGA.'[7]

8.3.1 *Limitation on Number of Sponsors*

None of the rules of procedure examined make any limitations on the number of sponsors of proposals.[8]

8.3.2 *Agreement to Join List of Sponsors*

It is accepted practice that the approval of the original sponsors is required for any additional sponsors to be added.[9] The practical guide to the UNGA, published by the Permanent Mission of Switzerland to the UN, explains, 'Upon invitation of the main sponsor; Member States can formally express their support for a draft resolution by "co-sponsoring it. Co-sponsoring is done by signing the official co-sponsor form."'[10]

[7] Para 3.5, www.unitar.org/ny/sites/unitar.org.ny/files/UN_PGA_Handbook.pdf.

[8] The suggestion had been made that '[a] maximum number of sponsors of draft resolutions should be agreed upon in order to lend greater flexibility to the proceedings and to facilitate the negotiations of compromise amendments'. UN Doc. A/AC.111/WP.1, p. 63. The Report of the Ad Hoc Committee on the Improvement of the Methods of Work of the General Assembly did not approve the suggestion, stating that it was for the authors of a proposal 'to decide whether other delegations should also become sponsors'. UN GAOR, 18th Session, Annexes, Agenda Item 25, para. 60, UN Doc. A/5423 (1963). The Report of the Special Committee on the Rationalisation of the Procedures and Organisation of the General Assembly, UN GAOR, 26th Session, Supplement No. 26, UN Doc. A/8426, p. 50, para. 260, commented, 'The Special Committee did not endorse the suggestion that the number of sponsors of a draft resolution should be limited.'

[9] Report of the Ad Hoc Committee on the Improvement of the Methods of Work of the General Assembly, UNGA, 18th Session, Annex, UN Doc. A/5423, 28 May 1963. 'It wishes, however, to make it clear that, in its view it is for *the authors of a proposal which has already been submitted to the Assembly or to a committee to decide whether other delegations should also become sponsors of it*. Delegations wishing to become co-sponsors ought therefore to approach the original sponsors if they wish their name to be added to the list already published.' [emphasis added]

At a meeting of the Sixth Committee of the UNGA, at its Twenty-Ninth Session, the Chairman asked prospective co-sponsors of a resolution whether they had consulted the original sponsors. UN GAOR, 6th Committee, 29th Session, 1502nd Meeting, paras. 17–18, UN Doc. A/C.6/29/SR.1502 (1974).

[10] Para 3.5, www.unitar.org/ny/sites/unitar.org.ny/files/UN_PGA_Handbook.pdf.

There is some authority for the practice that approval of all earlier sponsors is required;[11] however this practice has been questioned.[12] The Office of Legal Affairs of the UN, in a legal opinion, expressed disapproval of the procedure by which, where there is objection to sponsorship, the States involved are listed in reports of committees as 'having expressed the wish of their delegations to become co-sponsors'. The legal opinion states that where a UN committee decides nevertheless to include such a phrase in its report, the Secretariat must implement it, but only as regards objections made by the original sponsors of a resolution.[13]

8.3.3 *Withdrawal of Sponsorship*

At a 1974 meeting of the UNGA, during the debate on the report of ECOSOC, the Chairman ruled that the US delegation was not entitled to withdraw its sponsorship of a resolution once voting had commenced.[14] At a meeting of the 1993 UNGA, during a discussion on chemical warfare, the representative of the Netherlands listed thirty-seven delegations 'who would withdraw their sponsorship' of a draft resolution 'in the eventuality that the Iranian amendment was adopted by the Committee'.[15] The

11 'The Special Committee does, however, wish to draw attention to the practice whereby the sponsors of a proposal decide whether other delegations can become co-sponsors.' The Report of the Special Committee on the Rationalisation of the Procedures and Organisation of the General Assembly, UN GAOR, 26th Session, Supplement No. 26, UN Doc. A/8426, p. 50, para. 261. See also Statement by the Chairman of the Third Committee of the UNGA, 31st Session, 39th Meeting, para. 1, UN Doc. A/C.3/31/SR.39 (1976).

12 At a meeting of the Sixth Committee of the UNGA, at its Twenty-Ninth Session, the representative of Chile questioned the legality of allowing every sponsor to 'veto' subsequent sponsors. The representative did not, however, request a ruling on the issue. UN GAOR, 6th Committee, 29th Session, 1503rd Meeting, paras. 20–27, UN Doc. A/C.6/29/SR.1503 (1974).

At a meeting of the Second Committee of the UNGA, at its Twenty-Ninth Session, the name of Chile was omitted from a list of sponsors, although it had appeared on an earlier list. The representative of Chile requested an explanation from the Secretariat. One delegation explained that the decision to omit Chile's name was taken at the request of earlier sponsors. The representative of Chile apparently did not pursue the issue. UN GAOR, 2nd Committee, 29th Session, 1636th Meeting, paras. 30, 31, 36, 37, UN Doc. A/C.2/29/SR.1636 (1974).

13 Memorandum, 29 November 1976, by the Office of Legal Affairs to the Secretary of the Second Committee of the General Assembly, 1976 UN Jur. Y.B. 180.

14 UN GAOR, 2nd Committee, 29th Session, 1646th Meeting, para. 20, UN Doc. A/C.2/29/SR.1646 (1974).

15 UN GAOR, 1st Committee, 48th Session, 30th Meeting, para. 55, UN Doc. A/C.1/48/SR.30 (1993).

resolution itself was eventually withdrawn, prior to the Committee being given an opportunity to vote on the Iranian amendment.

At a 1988 meeting of the World Health Assembly, as a result of the adoption of a sharply contested amendment, and after a resolution had been adopted, several delegates requested that the names of their States be removed from the list of sponsors of the resolution. The Legal Counsel of the WHO pointed out that 'when the resolutions were printed, the names of the sponsors did not appear'.[16] When a delegate noted that 'the sponsors were withdrawing *en masse*',[17] the Chairman noted that 'at the time the vote had been taken, the draft resolution had had a large number of sponsors'.[18] A delegate queried that 'now that most of the sponsors had withdrawn, he wondered whether the resolution had indeed been legally approved'. The Legal Counsel responded by drawing the attention of the Committee to the fact that a motion can only be withdrawn by its proposers prior to voting and then only if it has not been amended.[19]

8.3.4 *Seconding of Motions*

Common law parliamentary systems often require that substantive motions be seconded.[20] As late as 1943, one author of a handbook on conferences wrote categorically, 'No resolution, amendment or motion shall be discussed unless it has been seconded.'[21]

The UN Model Rules and the rules of procedure of the UNGA do not contain any provision requiring that a motion be seconded. The provisional rules of procedure of the UN Security Council state explicitly that motions and draft resolutions do not need seconding.[22] Jessup writes, 'The reason why this rule requiring a second is not followed in the United

[16] Summary Records of the 10th Meeting of Committee 'B' of the 41st World Health Assembly, p. 241, WHA41/1988/REC/3 (1988).

[17] *Ibid.* [18] *Ibid.*

[19] *Ibid.* Rule 69 of the rules of procedure of the World Health Assembly is similar in substance to Rule 80 of the UNGA rules of procedure.

[20] Maurice W. Fox, *Parliamentary Usage* (1945), pp. 113, 118; *Robert's Rules of Order*, 11th edn (2011), pp. 35–37; However, Erskine May states that, except for election of the Speaker, seconding is no longer required in the House of Commons, *Erskine May's Treatise on the Law, Privileges, Proceedings and Usage of Parliament*, eds. Sir Donald Limon and W. R. McKay, 22nd edn (1997), p. 338.

[21] William O'Davoren, *Post-War Reconstruction Conferences, The Technical Organisation of International Conferences* (1943), p. 130.

[22] Rule 34 of the provisional rules of procedure of the UN Security Council, UN Doc. S/96/Rev.6 (1974).

Nations may perhaps be traced to the insistence upon the principle of "sovereign equality" of the members which is asserted in Article 2(1) of the Charter.'[23]

During the early years of the UNGA, representatives occasionally referred to seconding of motions, but such expressions have become rare in recent years.

The rules of procedure of the ICAO Assembly require motions and amendments to be seconded.[24] Some conferences convened by the ICAO, the IMO and the ITU also still maintain the necessity of having proposals seconded.[25] Presiding officers at such conferences have refused to accept proposals on matters of substance in the absence of a State willing to second the motion.[26]

The requirement of a seconder can prevent maverick representatives from abusing the process; however, it can also prevent the full participation in a conference of a State that is isolated politically.

COMMENT

The requirement of seconding proposals is nowadays clearly exceptional and does not reflect general practice.

8.4 Notice of Proposals

Rules of procedure require, in principle, that notice be given by delegations submitting proposals. Such notice is required to enable proper consideration of proposals and to protect delegations that may be temporarily absent from a meeting. It is usual, however, to provide exceptions to this requirement.

[23] Philip C. Jessup, 'Parliamentary Diplomacy, An Examination of the Legal Quality of the Rules of Procedure of Organs of the United Nations', 89 RCADI 181 (1956 I) at 221.

[24] Rule 39 of the standing rules of procedure of the Assembly of ICAO, ICAO Doc. 7600/5 (1990).

[25] See, for example, Rule 13, ICAO Doc. VIA, Doc. No. 2, 1 December 1987; Rule 28, IMCO Doc. LEG/CONF.5/1, 12 July 1976; Article 32(10)(1) of the Constitution of the International Telecommunication Union, Geneva 1993.

[26] See 1971 Montreal Air Law Conference, Commission of the Whole, 4th Meeting, vol. I, Minutes, p. 40, para. 9, ICAO Doc. 9081-LC/170–1; IMCO Doc. LEG/CONF./SR.5, p. 93; IMCO Doc. LEG/CONF./C.1/SR.22, p. 427; Official Records of the International Conference on the Limitation of Liability for Maritime Claims 1976, p. 309, IMCO Doc. CONF.5/C.1/SR.13 (1983).

8.4.1 Notice of Submission of Written Proposals

The UNGA rules of procedure state,

> *Rule 78*
> *Proposals and Amendments*
> Proposals and amendments shall normally be submitted in writing to the Secretary-General, who shall circulate copies to the delegations. As a general rule, no proposal shall be discussed or put to the vote at any meeting of the General Assembly unless copies of it have been circulated to all delegations not later than the day preceding the meeting. The President may, however, permit the discussion and consideration of amendments, or of motions as to procedure, even though such amendments and motions have not been circulated or have only been circulated the same day.[27]

The proposal in the UN Model Rules is similar, except discretion is granted to the Conference and not to the President.[28]

The principle underlying this rule appeared in the rules of procedure of the 1907 Peace Conference.[29] A similar text, as set out in the rules of procedure of the Assembly of the League of Nations, was reproduced practically without change in the rules of the[30] Preparatory Commission, in the various developments of the rules of the UNGA and in the rules of the international conferences examined. The rules of procedure of the Third Law of the Sea Conference were an exception, and they are referred to later. In the rules of procedure of the 1975 Vienna Conference on Representation of States, the rule was added that the circulation of proposals should 'be in the languages of the Conference'.[31]

[27] The UN Model Rules refer to 'languages of the Conference'. The UNGA rules of procedure make no reference to languages. The Legal Counsel of the UN has written, however, that the rule 'is understood to mean circulation in all the working languages'. Memorandum to the Officer-in-Charge, Department of Political Affairs, Trusteeship and Decolonization, 1983 UN Jur. Y.B. 171.

[28] Rule 46 of the UN Model Rules.

[29]

> *Article 9*
> Every proposition of a resolution or vœu to be discussed by the Conference must, as a general rule, be delivered in writing to the president in order to be printed and distributed before being brought to discussion.
>
> *The Proceedings of the Peace Conference, Translation of the Official Texts, Prepared in the Division of International Law of the Carnegie Endowment for International Peace, The Conference of 1907*, vol. I, Plenary Meetings of the Conference (1920), p. 53.

[30] Rule 17(2) of the rules of procedure of the Assembly of the League of Nations.

[31] UN Doc. A/CONF.67/8, Rule 30.

8.4.2 *Notice of Procedural Motions*

The first part of the UNGA rule of procedure 78 that, by implication, grants discretion to the Assembly[32], refers to 'proposals and amendments', which would appear to exclude procedural motions. The second part of the rule, however, grants discretion to the President and refers explicitly to motions as to procedure.

Pastuhov writes categorically that for 'questions of procedure such as those mentioned above [adjournment or closure], no previous notice of the motion need be given nor need a copy of it be handed in to the chair'.[33]

There is no exhaustive definition in the UNGA rules of procedure as to what is a 'procedural motion'.[34] The following motions are listed as procedural for purposes of being granted precedence: to suspend the meeting; to adjourn the meeting; to adjourn the debate on the item under discussion; and to close the debate on the item under discussion.[35] This list does not, however, exclude the possibility of a presiding officer deciding that a motion not on the list be considered procedural for the purposes of Rule 78 of the rules of procedure. At a 1997 meeting of the UNGA, a chairman allowed a committee to take action on a draft resolution of which insufficient notice had been given. The Chairman's reasoning was that '[w]hile he acknowledged that the proposed revisions were not procedural, he did not feel that they were substantive either, since they did not really alter the text of the draft resolution'.[36]

The Chairman of a UNGA committee, at its 1961 session, ruled that notice was required for the submission of procedural motions unless the requirement was waived by the presiding officer.[37]

The President of the UNGA, at its 1993 session, stated categorically, 'As members know, it is the established practice of the Assembly to consider oral procedural motions.'[38]

32 The phrases 'normally' and 'as a general rule' imply discretion.

33 Vladimir D. Pastuhov, *A Guide to the Practice of International Conferences* (1945), p. 133 n. 34.

34 See discussion in Chapter 12.

35 Rule 77 of the UNGA rules of procedure.

36 UN GAOR, 3rd Committee, 52nd Session, 49th Meeting, UN Doc. A/C.3/52/SR.49, p. 6 (1997). UN GAOR, 3rd Committee, 52nd Session, 49th Meeting, UN Doc. A/C.3/52/SR.49, p. 6 (1997).

37 UN GAOR, 6th Committee, 8th Session, 391st Meeting, para. 41, UN Doc. A/C.6/8/SR.391 (1953).

38 UN GAOR, Plenary, 47th Session, 94th Meeting, UN Doc. A/47/PV.94, pp. 13–15 (Provisional) (1993).

The UN Model Rules, by referring to 'Other [non-basic] proposals and substantive amendments', clearly exclude procedural motions from the rule as to notice, and therefore no notice need be given of procedural motions and they need not be in writing.

At a 1961 ILO Conference, a delegation moved, without due notice, a motion to place an item on the agenda for the next session. The President ruled that

> motions as to procedure which may be moved verbally and without previous notice have been defined to include the following: a motion to refer the matter back; a motion to postpone consideration of the question; a motion to adjourn the sitting; a motion to adjourn the debate on a particular question; a motion that the Conference proceed with the next item on the agenda for the sitting; a motion to ask for the opinion of the President, the Secretary-General or the Legal Adviser of the Conference.
>
> [T]his motion is not a motion of procedure, even though there may be precedents, because if we accept this as a motion of procedure it could lead to innumerable consequences.[39]

The Legal Adviser of the ILO, who was asked to give his opinion on the issue, wrote that he was not aware of a precedent and that the President was correct in using his discretion.[40] The President added that as far as he knew of parliamentary practice, 'a proposal to place any matter on the agenda is not treated as a procedural motion'.[41]

A reasonable interpretation of UNGA Rule 78 regarding procedural motions would be that the President has discretion to permit both discussion and voting on procedural motions submitted without due notice. The Assembly may also do so, as it inherently has whatever authority the President possesses.

COMMENT

There do not appear to be examples of procedural motions at conferences being disallowed in the absence of their not being submitted in writing a day before. It would therefore seem that practice is to allow the introduction of procedural motions submitted without prior notice.

[39] ILO Conference, 45th Session, Record of Proceedings, 34th sitting, pp. 587, 588 (1961).
[40] *Ibid.*, 35th sitting, p. 598. [41] *Ibid.*

8.4.3 *Notice of Substantive Proposals*

The UNGA rule states,

> *Rule 78*
>
> As a general rule, no proposal shall be discussed or put to the vote at any meeting of the General Assembly unless copies of it have been circulated to all delegations not later than the day preceding the meeting.

This UN Model Rule clearly stipulates that the conference, and not the presiding officer, has the discretion to waive the necessity of giving delegations a day's notice of substantive proposals. The requirement applies both to discussion and to voting on the proposal.[42]

At a 1997 session of the UNGA, the Egyptian representative argued that since a resolution in question, which had only been circulated that day, was dated 'the day before it had been circulated as an official document in all the languages of the Organisation, it was therefore perfectly in order for the Committee to take action on it'. The Russian delegate countered that 'his delegation had received the text in written form only that morning'.[43] The Egyptian delegate did not press his argument, and there was no ruling on the issue he raised.

COMMENT

The rule would appear to be that a delegation has the right to require that circulation of a document be in all official languages and that the time set for notice commence only when the proposal has been circulated in all languages.

8.4.4 *Discretion of Presiding Officer to Allow Discussion of Amendments Submitted without Due Notice*

The presiding officer in the UNGA has discretion regarding discussion of amendments submitted without due notice. This discretion may of course be overruled by a successful challenge to a ruling.

[42] Rule 46 of the UN Model Rules.

[43] UN GAOR, 3rd Committee, 52nd Session, 49th Meeting, UN Doc. A/C.3/52/SR.49, p. 6 (1997).

8.4.5 Discretion of Presiding Officer to Allow Voting on Amendments Submitted without Due Notice

Rule 78 of the rules of procedure of the UNGA refers to 'consideration' of amendments, and the question arises whether this includes voting on amendments.

At a 1953 meeting of the UNGA, the representative of Peru claimed that the Chairman had discretion to allow discussion, but had no discretion to allow voting on an Indian amendment submitted without due notice. The Committee voted on the question as to whether the Indian amendment should be put to the vote, and when the motion was approved, the Committee proceeded to vote on the Indian amendment.[44]

At a 1958 meeting of the UNGA Fourth Committee, the representative of Iraq argued that 'the third sentence of rule 121 [Rule 78 in the Plenary] referred to "the discussion and consideration of amendments". He felt that the word "consideration" must have been intended to include voting. Furthermore, the Fourth Committee has occasionally voted on proposals on the day of their submission.'[45] The Chairman, however, put to the vote the question whether the Committee should vote on the amendment submitted without notice.[46] The representative of Ireland commented later, 'Rule 121 of the rules of procedure provided that no proposal should be put to the vote unless copies of it had been circulated not later than the day preceding the meeting.' He did not agree with the interpretation given by the representative of Iraq.[47]

At a 1963 meeting of the UNGA, the representative of the Soviet Union objected to putting an Israel oral amendment to the vote. The Soviet representative argued that 'the last sentence of rule 122 [Rule 78] referred to the discussion and consideration of amendments or procedural motions, not to voting'. The Chairman put to the vote the question whether the Committee should vote on the oral amendment. The Committee decided not to put the amendment to the vote.[48]

A 1983 UN legal opinion on the issue was that 'frequent use is made of the exceptional authorization to act on uncirculated or only

[44] UN GAOR, 4th Committee, 8th Session, 330th Meeting, paras. 38, 42, UN Doc. A/C.4/8/SR.330 (1953).

[45] UN GAOR, 4th Committee, 13th Session, 840th Meeting, para. 63, UN Doc. A/C.4/13/SR.840 (1958).

[46] *Ibid.* at para. 67. [47] *Ibid.* at para. 2.

[48] UN GAOR, 3rd Committee, 18th Session, 1278th Meeting, para. 31, UN Doc. A/C.3/18/SR.1278 (1963).

recently circulated amendments, particularly towards the end of a session'.[49]

At a 2009 meeting of the UNGA, a representative, on a point of order, complained that 'we have not had an opportunity to discuss this proposed [oral] amendment'. The President subsequently allowed discussion, and no further objection was made to voting on the oral amendment.[50]

At a 2012 meeting of the First Committee of UNGA, the Secretary of the Committee gave his opinion regarding an oral amendment that 'it is prerogative of the presiding officer to put it to the Committee immediately or wait for the revised document to be published by the Secretariat'.[51]

The practical guide to the UNGA published by the Permanent Mission of Switzerland to the UN, in the item regarding voting on amendments, states that an amendment may be 'proposed orally from the floor, if no Member State objects'.[52] It might have been more correct to add that even if a Member State objects the president still has discretion, unless overruled by the meeting.

COMMENT

The UNGA Committees appear to have decided that they and not the Chairmen had the discretion to allow voting on amendments not submitted with due notice. It would appear, however, to this author that, since the word 'consideration' in Rule 78 applies both to amendments and to procedural motions, and since there is no doubt that voting may be permitted on procedural motions submitted without due notice, then the presiding officer in the UNGA also has discretion to allow voting on an *amendment* submitted without due notice.

At a 2009 meeting of the General Conference of the IAEA the question arose as to whether the President had discretion to allow voting on

[49] Legal opinion of UN Office of Legal Affairs PROCEDURAL QUESTIONS RAISED IN CONNECTION WITH THE ADOPTION OF A REPORT OF THE SUBCOMMITTEE ON PETITIONS. INFORMATION AND ASSISTANCE OF THE SPECIAL COMMITTEE ON THE SITUATION WITH REGARD TO THE IMPLEMENTATION OF THE DECLARATION ON THE GRANTING OF INDEPENDENCE TO COLONIAL COUNTRIES AND PEOPLES QUESTION WHETHER ACTION MAY VALIDLY BE TAKEN ON AN AMENDMENT NOT CIRCULATED IN ONE OF THE WORKING LANGUAGES *Memorandum to the Officer-in-Charge, Department of Political Affairs, Trusteeship and Decolonization* September 1983, http://legal.un.org/ola/media/GA_RoP/GA_RoP_EN.pdf.

[50] UN GAOR, Plenary, 62nd Session, 76th Meeting, p. 32, UN Doc. A/62/PV.76 (2009).

[51] UN GAOR, 1st Committee, 67th Session, 18th Meeting, p. 12, UN Doc.A/C.1/PV.18 (2012).

[52] Para 3.5, www.unitar.org/ny/sites/unitar.org.ny/files/UN_PGA_Handbook.pdf.

an amendment not submitted with sufficient notice. The rule of procedure in the IAEA used the same language on this issue as the rule in the UNGA, and the Legal Advisor gave his opinion that 'the term "consideration" should be interpreted to include voting'.[53] The President accepted the legal advice and allowed the voting to proceed; his ruling was not challenged.

8.4.6 *Substantive Proposals Submitted without Due Notice*

Since Rule 78 refers to 'discussion and consideration of amendments, or of motions as to procedure' and not to 'proposals', the presiding officer presumably has no discretion to permit discussion or voting regarding substantive proposals submitted without due notice. The Assembly or Committee of course has such discretion.

At the 1992 General Conference of the IAEA, two proposals to introduce changes in a draft resolution were submitted without due notice.[54] The President ruled that he had discretion regarding procedural motions or amendments and that one of the proposals 'was an amendment and was therefore covered by that rule [discretion of the President]: that was not the case with the other document'.[55]

The Assembly and Committee, as distinct from the presiding officer, have discretion, however, regarding proposals and amendments, since the UN rule and most conference rules state, 'Proposals and amendments shall *normally* be submitted in writing.' [emphasis added]

8.4.7 *Practice in Conferences Regarding Discussion and Voting on Substantive Proposals and Amendments Submitted without Due Notice*

At the 1954 Hague Conference, the USSR objected to putting an oral amendment to the vote, 'as the proposed amendment was on a point of substance and should be submitted in writing'.[56] The representative of the Netherlands replied that 'there had been no time to submit amendments

[53] 2009 IAEA General Conference, Plenary, 52nd Session, 8th Meeting, para. 173, IAEA Doc. GC(52)/OR.8 (2009).

[54] Rule 63 of the rules of procedure of the General Conference of the IAEA is substantially identical to Rule 78 of the UNGA rules of procedure.

[55] Official Records of the 352nd Plenary Meeting of the 36th General Conference of the IAEA, para. 48, GC(XXXVI)/OR.352 (1992).

[56] Records of the 1954 Hague Conference, p. 275, para. 1872.

in writing . . . and a vote had been taken on the principle underlying the amendment'.[57] The Chairman decided that it was for the Commission to decide whether voting should take place or not, and he put to the vote the USSR proposal that voting should not take place.[58] The USSR proposal was defeated, and the Chairman, in putting the oral amendment to the vote, stressed that 'the important phrase was "as a general rule" and that as a result of the vote on the USSR procedural motion a vote could be taken on the oral amendment'.[59]

At the 1958 Law of the Sea Conference, the delegation of Ghana requested that the Committee proceed to vote on a certain amendment and added, 'However in order that its validity might not be challenged, he hoped the Chairman would give a ruling as to whether the rules of procedure permitted a vote on a proposal circulated during a meeting.'[60] After the Chairman had stated that Rule 29 (the rule relating to notice as to motions)[61] made it impossible to proceed to the vote at once, the representative of the United States said that 'he thought the Committee was entirely master of its own procedure. Since the second sentence of rule 29 began with the words "as a general rule" it could very well decide to vote on the five power amendment at the present meeting.'[62] The Chairman then made the ruling that 'the words "as a general rule" appeared in rule 29 because the third sentence of the rule permitted exceptions'.[63] In other words, according to the Chairman's interpretation, the rule was obligatory, and the only exception related to a procedural motion as referred to in the third sentence of the rule. The representative of the United Kingdom objected to this interpretation, stating that 'the rule [the third

[57] *Ibid.* at para. 1877.

[58] The rules of procedure stipulated,

Rule 17

> As a general rule, no resolution or amendment shall be discussed or put to the vote unless it has been circulated sufficiently in advance to all delegations in the appropriate working languages. (CBC/2)

There was no clause, similar to the rules of procedure of the UNGA, that granted any discretion to the presiding officer.

[59] Records of the 1954 Hague Conference, p. 275, para. 1877.

[60] Official Records of the 1958 Law of the Sea Conference, 23rd Meeting of Committee V, vol. VII, p. 56, para. 19, UN Doc. A/CONF.13/43 (1958).

[61] Substantially identical to Rule 78 of the UNGA rules of procedure quoted above (p. 153).

[62] Official Records of the 1958 Law of the Sea Conference, 23rd Meeting of Committee V, vol. VII, p. 56, para. 27, UN Doc. A/CONF.13/43 (1958).

[63] *Ibid.* at para. 28.

sentence relating to procedural motions] authorised the Chairman on his own initiative to put to the vote motions as to procedure, but the Committee could decide that a vote should be taken even if a matter of substance was involved'.[64] The Chairman's ruling was thus challenged, and after a debate in which the only delegation to support the Chairman's ruling was that of Hungary, the Chairman's ruling was overruled. It was thus decided that the rule of procedure permitted the Committee to proceed to vote. It appears that the Chairman's interpretation was incorrect and was rightfully overruled by the Committee.

At the 1958 Law of the Sea Conference, the United States proposed that a motion previously voted down be reconsidered. The representative of the USSR objected and, speaking on a point of order, said,

> None of the delegations had come to the meeting prepared to discuss the important United States motion. He therefore invoked rule 29, which required that proposals should be introduced in writing and should not be discussed or put to the vote unless circulated not later than the day preceding the meeting. That rule had been applied to minor amendments and it was only proper to apply it to the United States motion.[65]

The Chairman ruled, 'The purpose of rule 29 was to enable the actual text of resolutions to be examined by delegations before the discussion in Committee. The text of the revised United States proposal had been before the Committee for several days. The United States motion for reconsideration was therefore in order.'[66] The Chairman's ruling was not challenged.

During the Vienna Conference on the Law of Treaties, practice seemed to show that where an oral sub-amendment was accepted by the original proposer of an amendment, no objection was made to an immediate vote on the oral sub-amendment.[67] Presumably if agreement of *all* the sponsors had been obtained, it would have been considered a revision of the proposal and there would have been no need to vote on the sub-amendment. Where an oral amendment did not involve any change of substance, no objection was made to an immediate vote.[68]

[64] *Ibid.* at para. 30.

[65] Official Records of the 1958 Law of the Sea Conference, 63rd Meeting of Committee I, vol. III, p. 196, para. 29, UN Doc. A/CONF.13/39 (1958).

[66] *Ibid.* at para. 31.

[67] Official Records of the Vienna Conference on the Law of Treaties – First Session, 44th Meeting of the Committee of the Whole, p. 248, para. 13, UN Doc. A/CONF.39/11 (1968).

[68] *Ibid.* at 81st Meeting, p. 481, paras. 66, 68.

At the Third Law of the Sea Conference, the draft rules of procedure followed the UNGA text by stating,

> *Rule 32*
>
> *As a general rule*, no proposal shall be discussed or put to the vote at any meeting of the Conference unless copies of it have been circulated to all delegations not later than the day preceding the meeting.[69] [emphasis added]

The delegations of Madagascar and the United Republic of Tanzania proposed deleting the phrase 'as a general rule' and adding a reference to 'working languages of the UN'.[70] The amendment was adopted, with a slight change, and the rules of procedure then read:

> *Rule 33*
>
> No proposal shall be discussed or put to the vote at any meeting of the Conference unless copies of it have been circulated to all delegations in all languages not later than the day preceding the meeting.[71]

Thus the rules of procedure of the Third Law of the Sea Conference granted the Conference no discretion and made the prior distribution of copies of proposals, in all languages, a condition sine qua non for discussion or voting.

At the 1974–1977 Geneva Humanitarian Law Conference, several delegations objected to voting on texts that had not been distributed in all languages twenty-four hours before they were to be considered. The President proposed 'that the meeting should be adjourned for half-an-hour, after which the non-controversial articles, which delegations would then have had time to read, would be considered'.[72] The President's proposal was adopted.[73]

During the 1975 Vienna Conference on Representation of States, the representative of the USSR objected to putting an oral amendment proposed by Israel to the vote. The Chairman said that 'the Committee had until now agreed to discuss oral amendments emerging from the discussion without observing the time limit set for the submission of written amendments. It would be for the Committee to decide whether it wished

[69] Third Law of the Sea Conference, draft rules of procedure, UN Doc. A/CONF.62/2 (1973).

[70] Third Law of the Sea Conference, Madagascar and the United Republic of Tanzania: amendments to the draft rules of procedure, UN Doc. A/CONF.62/12 (1973).

[71] UN Doc. A/CONF.62/30/Rev.3 (1975).

[72] Official Records of the 1974–1977 Geneva Humanitarian Law Conference, CDDH/SR.38, vol. VI, p. 84, para. 13.

[73] *Ibid.*

to discontinue that practice.'[74] No delegation expressed a wish to discontinue the previous practice, and the Israel amendment was put to the vote.

At a meeting of the 1976 IMCO Conference on Maritime Claims, the representative of Greece submitted, 'as a general principle, that the oral proposals might be discussed insofar as they were simple ones, but that it was essential for complicated proposals to be circulated in writing in advance'.[75] There was apparently no objection to the proposal.

At the 1978 Hamburg Conference on Carriage by Sea, the President ruled that 'the Conference should perhaps entertain oral amendments, in so far as they deal with essential points or were simple enough to be submitted verbally'.[76]

At the 1988 Vienna Conference on Narcotic Drugs, the representative of Turkey suggested that 'in future very detailed amendments . . . should be submitted in writing'.[77] The representative of the Netherlands commented that 'the Committee's work would be held up if it had to wait for a written text each time an amendment was proposed'.[78] The Chairman proposed that 'if an oral amendment consisted of more than a few words, it should be submitted in writing to the Secretary, who would read it out. The Committee could then decide whether it could be considered at once or whether it should be circulated as a document.'[79] There were no recorded objections to the Chairman's proposal.

One does find, however, conference decisions refusing to allow discussion of an amendment not submitted in writing.[80] At the 1974–1977 Geneva Humanitarian Law Conference, several delegations proposed that certain amendments not yet circulated be put to the vote. The representative of the United States objected, quoting the relevant rule of procedure and adding that it was particularly relevant as the proposed amendment

[74] Official Records of the 1975 Vienna Conference on Representation of States, vol. I, 42nd Meeting of the Committee of the Whole, p. 312, para. 9, UN Doc. A/CONF.67/18 (1975).

[75] Official Records of the International Conference on the Limitation of Liability for Maritime Claims, p. 219, IMCO Doc. CONF.5/C.1/SR.2 (1976).

[76] Summary Records of the 6th Plenary Meeting of the 1978 Hamburg Conference on Carriage by Sea, UN Doc. A/CONF.89/SR.6, para. 6 (1978).

[77] Official Records of the 1988 Vienna Conference on Narcotic Drugs, 20th Meeting of Committee II, vol. II, p. 277, para. 9, UN Doc. E/CONF.82/16/Add.1 (1988).

[78] *Ibid.* at para. 10. [79] *Ibid.* at para. 11.

[80] See, for instance, Official Records of the Vienna Conference on the Law of Treaties – First Session, 45th Meeting of the Committee of the Whole, p. 255, para. 37, UN Doc. A/CONF.39/11 (1968).

'seemed to entail a change in International Law'.[81] The US objection was sustained.[82]

At a 1988 meeting of the World Health Assembly, the Chairman informed the committee that since 'a number of delegates had requested full compliance with Rule 52 of the rules of procedure [the rule requiring two days' notice] ... those drafts, which had been circulated only on the morning of the day before, could not be considered at the present meeting'.[83]

At a 1991 meeting of the World Health Assembly, the representative of Ecuador submitted a draft resolution without due notice. In requesting the waiving of the necessary notice, the representative explained that the issue, an outbreak of cholera, should be given priority and 'the fact that over 60 delegations had sponsored it [the resolution] indicated that there was a substantial consensus'. The Chairman ruled that 'in the absence of any objection, he would take it that the Committee wished to discuss the draft resolution at once and to waive the 48-hour rule'.[84]

At the 1991 Conference on the Liability of Operators of Transport Terminals in International Trade, the representative of Japan requested permission to submit an oral proposal.[85] The Chairman responded that 'he preferred to adhere to the procedure of written proposals; the Japanese proposal would accordingly be discussed once it had been circulated in writing'.[86] In the same Committee, in response to a similar request from the Australian representative,[87] the Chairman, 'while pointing out that it was contrary to the rules of procedure to introduce an oral amendment, invited the representative of Australia to explain his proposal'.[88] After hearing the explanation by the representative of Australia, the Chairman then asked 'whether there were any objections to voting on the Australian proposal'.[89] Since there was an objection, the Chairman suggested that 'the representative of Australia should submit his proposal in writing'.[90]

[81] Official Records of the 1974–1977 Geneva Humanitarian Law Conference, CDDH/II/SR.3, vol. XI, p. 21, para. 6.
[82] *Ibid.* at para. 15.
[83] Summary Records of the 8th Meeting of Committee 'B' of the 41st World Health Assembly, p. 214, WHA41/1988/REC/3 (1988).
[84] Summary Records of the 3rd Meeting of Committee 'A' of the 44th World Health Assembly, p. 38, WHA44/1991/REC/3 (1991).
[85] Summary Records of the 1991 Conference on the Liability of Operators of Transport Terminals in International Trade, UN Doc. A/CONF.152/C.1/SR.1, para. 22 (1991).
[86] *Ibid.* at para. 24. [87] *Ibid.*, UN Doc. A/CONF.152/C.1/SR.16, para. 19.
[88] *Ibid.* at para. 20. [89] *Ibid.* at para. 23. [90] *Ibid.* at para. 27.

The rules of procedure of the ICAO Assembly are extremely rigid in this context as regards reports of commissions and committees. They stipulate,

> *Rule 33*
>
> Unless unanimously agreed by the Assembly, or the Executive Committee, items of the agenda referred to the Commissions or Committees shall not be discussed in plenary meetings of the Assembly until the expiration of twenty-four hours after the report of the Commission or Committee concerned has been presented and circulated.[91]

COMMENT

A review of conference practice shows that in multisession conferences there is a tendency to enforce strict observance of the need for due notice. Clearly in a one-session conference, particularly towards the end of it, there is more likelihood of flexibility on this issue.

8.4.8 Practice in UNGA Regarding Dispensing with the Need for Due Notice of Submission of Substantive Proposals and Amendments

As a matter of common practice, presiding officers in the UNGA have utilised their discretion under Rule 78 of the UNGA rules of procedure to dispense with the requirement of circulating amendments the day before they are discussed or voted on.[92] This is usually done without giving reasons and without objection being voiced by representatives.

The Chairman of the Sixth Committee of the UNGA, at its 1996 session, noted that requirement of a day's notice 'was usually waived when negotiations were prolonged and there was a deadline for the conclusion of the discussion'.[93]

At a 1957 meeting of the UNGA, where an oral proposal on the question of Algeria was adopted, the President, at the request of the Soviet representative, pointed out that this was being done as an exception.[94]

The inimitable representative of Saudi Arabia, Mr. Baroody, in a discussion on the Human Rights Covenants at the 1963 UNGA, attempted to summarise UN practice. Mr. Baroody stated,

[91] Rule 33 of the standing rules of procedure of the Assembly of ICAO, ICAO Doc. 7600/5, 5th edn, 1990.

[92] See, for example, UN GAOR, Plenary, 13th Session, 753rd Meeting, paras. 3–4, 48, UN Doc. A/PV.753 (1958).

[93] UN GAOR, 6th Committee, 51st Session, UN Doc. A/C.6/SR.62/Add.1, p. 2 (1997).

[94] UN GAOR, Plenary, 12th Session, 726th Meeting, paras. 109, 110, 112, UN Doc. A/PV.726 (1957).

> Oral amendments could be put to the vote if there was no objection, and there were many precedents for such action. The word 'normally' had been used in rule 121 of the rules of procedure in order to enable the organs of the General Assembly to bypass that rule in the case of very simple or purely drafting oral amendments. But as soon as the meaning or scope of a proposal was questioned, rule 121 should be applied to the letter.[95]

At a 1974 meeting of the UNGA, during a discussion on UN publications, the Philippine delegation requested that an oral amendment by Tanzania be circulated in accordance with the customary practice. The Chairman said that since the Tanzanian amendment was felt to be generally acceptable, it had been the intention to forgo circulation. The Philippine delegation agreed not to press his request.[96]

The Legal Counsel to the UN, writing in 1983, stated,

> The practice in implementing this rule has been that frequent use is made of the exceptional authorization to act on uncirculated or only recently circulated amendments, *particularly towards the end of a session*. In particular the procedure followed by the Chairman of the Sub-Committee, to read out the amendment at dictation speed to enable the interpreters to translate it carefully and the representatives to copy it down in their respective languages, is often followed.[97] [emphasis added]

At a 1991 meeting of the UNGA, on UN financing, the representative of the United Kingdom commented that 'the fact that his delegation had not insisted on the application of the provisions of rule 120 [Rule 78 in the Plenary] of the rules of procedure in the matter before the Committee did not imply that that rule should not normally be heeded'. The Chairman noted that 'the procedure followed by the Committee in its consideration of the draft resolution before it constituted an exception to rule 120'.[98]

At a 2007 meeting of the Third Committee of UNGA, the delegate of Benin submitted an oral proposal that 'two reports should be deleted from

[95] UN GAOR, 3rd Committee, 18th Session, 1278th Meeting, para. 32, UN Doc. A/C.3/18/SR.1278 (1963).

[96] UN GAOR, 5th Committee, 29th Session, 1651st Meeting, paras. 18–23, UN Doc. A/C.5/29/SR.1651 (1974).

[97] Memorandum, 1 September 1983, to the Officer-in-Charge, Department of Political Affairs, Trusteeship and Decolonisation, 1983 UN Jur. Y.B. 171, 172.

[98] UN GAOR, 5th Committee, 46th Session, 65th Meeting, paras. 40, 41, UN Doc. A/C.5/46/SR.65 (1991).

the list of documents to be considered by the Committee'. Another delegate invoked rule 120 [Rule 78 in the Plenary] and requested a twenty-four-hour delay. A lengthy debate ensued and the Chairman ruled that 'there was no consensus to withdraw the reports on the list, there was also no consensus to postpone the decision on the matter. The Chairman eventually put the proposal of Benin to a vote without making a formal ruling as to whether it was a procedural motion or not and without formally declaring that he was using his discretion to waive the requirement of notice.[99]

At the 2016 Session of UNGA a delegate orally requested a legal opinion from the Legal Counsel. The Chairman, on the advice of the Office of Legal Affairs, ruled that only the Assembly could make such a request and that the delegate should therefore 'put the request in writing so that it can be circulated to delegations for their review'.[100]

COMMENT

In seeking to find a common denominator in UNGA practice, one can discern that no objection is usually made to a vote on an oral amendment or on one not circulated in advance where it is of minor character or accepted by the proposer. However, in the case of substantial amendments, there is usually objection to voting on an amendment for which due notice has not been given in writing.

8.4.9 *Summary as to Requirement that Motions Be in Writing and Due Notice Be Given of their Submission*

8.4.9.1 UN General Assembly

In the UNGA, there is discretion of the presiding officer as to discussing and voting on procedural motions submitted orally or without due notice. In practice there are no restrictions. Discussion of substantive amendments submitted orally or without due notice is at the discretion of the presiding officer. Voting on amendments submitted without due notice is apparently also at the discretion of the presiding officer. Discussion and voting on substantive proposals are at the discretion of the Assembly or committee and not of the presiding officer.

[99] UN GAOR, Third Committee, 62nd Session, 1st Meeting, paras. 8, 29, 31, 45, 94, UN Doc. A/C.3/62/SR.1 (2007).

[100] UN GAOR, Plenary, 71st Session, 58th Meeting, p. 2, UN Doc. A/71/PV.57 (2016).

8.4.9.2 Conferences

At conferences, there are no restrictions on discussing and voting on *procedural* motions submitted orally or without due notice. However, discussion and voting on *substantive* proposals and amendments submitted orally or without due notice are at the discretion of the Conference.

8.4.10 Procedural Motions to Enforce the Rule on Due Notice

Where the rules of procedure specify that a proposal shall 'normally' be submitted with a stipulated period of notice, this implies that the assembly or conference may waive the requirement of the notice. This is the rule in the rules of procedure of the UNGA and of the conferences studied. A delegation wishing to waive the rule must submit a motion to do so. A delegation wishing to enforce the rule need not submit a motion, but can draw the attention of the presiding officer, by means of a point of order, to the rule.[101]

8.5 Time Limits for Submission of Amendments and Proposals

Rules of procedure do not normally refer to the setting of time limits for submission of amendments and proposals. Presiding officers at times propose or announce such limits, but it is not clear what the authority is for such limitation.

At a 1962 meeting of a UNGA committee, during a discussion on the issue of the permanent sovereignty over natural resources, the delegation of Afghanistan objected to the circulation by the Secretariat of a proposal that had been submitted after the deadline decided on by the Committee. The Secretary-General informed the Committee that, according to the rules of procedure, the Secretariat was obliged to circulate all proposals and it was up to the Committee to deal with the issue of the deadline.[102]

At a 1968 meeting of a UNGA committee, during a discussion on the 'World Social Situation', the Chairman ruled that the time limits for the

[101] At the Sixth Plenary Meeting of the Forty-Second World Health Assembly, a motion for adjournment was submitted in circumstances where, apparently, it would have been sufficient to have requested the President to enforce the due notice rule. WHA42/1989/REC/2, pp. 98–101 (1989).

[102] UN GAOR, 2nd Committee, 17th Session, 853rd Meeting, para. 17, UN Doc. A/C.2/17/SR.853 (1962); UN GAOR, 2nd Committee, 17th Session, 854th Meeting, para. 16, UN Doc. A/C.2/17/SR.854 (1962).

submission of amendments to a draft resolution did not apply to amendments submitted to those parts of the text that had been modified after the establishment of the time limit.[103]

8.6 Time Limit for Submission of Sub-Amendments

At a 1967 meeting of a UNGA committee on the issue of the elimination of racial discrimination,[104] the Chairman, by implication, ruled that a previously set time limit for the submission of amendments did not apply to the submission of sub-amendments.

8.7 Revision of Proposals by the Sponsors

There is no specific provision in the UNGA rules of procedure nor in the UN Model Rules allowing a delegation to revise its own proposal. The right of a delegation to do so does not seem, however, to have ever been questioned. The UN Model Rules deal with the question of the priority to be given to a revised proposal,[105] thus clearly enunciating the right of a delegation to revise its own proposal. Where a proposal has been amended by a plenary or committee decision, it is no longer considered the proposal of the original proposer, and since it cannot be withdrawn,[106] it presumably cannot be revised by the original proposer.

At the 1974–1977 Geneva Humanitarian Law Conference, the President refused to allow the Philippine delegation permission to adopt an oral amendment proposed by Cyprus and thus to revise its own proposal. The President explained that 'he could not take the suggestion made by the representative of Cyprus into consideration, the rules of procedure being framed as they were'.[107] The President stated later that 'he had not adopted the suggestion made by the representative of Cyprus, because the latter, when consulted on the matter, had stated that no formal proposal for an amendment was in question'.[108] The President's decision was criticized as

[103] UN GAOR, 3rd Committee, 23rd Session, 1618th Meeting, para. 40, UN Doc. A/C.3/23/SR.1618 (1968).

[104] UN GAOR, 3rd Committee, 22nd Session, 1510th Meeting, paras. 3–5, UN Doc. A/C.3/22/SR.1510 (1967).

[105] Rule 60(1) of the UN Model Rules.

[106] Rule 47 of the UN Model Rules; Rule 80 of the UNGA rules of procedure.

[107] Official Records of the 1974–1977 Geneva Humanitarian Law Conference, CDDH/SR.54, vol. VII, p. 169, para. 31.

[108] *Ibid.* at p. 170, para. 41.

being unnecessarily inflexible by most of the delegations who spoke in explanation of the vote.[109]

8.8 Submission of Proposals by the Secretariat

The Secretary-General of the UN has stated that in his opinion the Secretary-General may submit formal proposals to committees of the UNGA.[110]

8.9 Submission of Proposals by Observers

The rules of procedure of the 1974–1977 Geneva Humanitarian Law Conference provided that

> *Rule 61*
>
> Non-governmental organizations and groups of international nongovernmental organizations invited as observers may participate in the deliberations of the Conference and the Main Committees. They shall not have the right to vote. The Conference and its Main Committees shall decide as the case arises whether such observers shall be permitted to present written or oral statements on problems relating to their sphere of activity.[111]

The Chairman of the Second Committee of the Conference informed the Committee that the International Union of Police Trade Unions had submitted a proposal. The Danish representative stated that 'as a general principle the Committee should not consider proposals submitted by non-governmental organizations, whatever their merit, since a diplomatic conference should deal only with questions raised by the Governments taking part'.[112] Several delegations pointed out that if a delegation wished to support a proposal in the paper submitted by the Organisation, they could introduce it as an amendment. The proposal to allow the Organisation to submit its proposal was put to a vote and defeated.[113]

[109] *Ibid.* at pp. 169, 170, paras. 32, 33, 34, 35, 37, 38, 39.

[110] See statement by Mr Stavropoulos to the UNGA Sixth Committee at the Seventh Session of the UNGA. UN GAOR, 6th Committee, 7th Session, 346th Meeting, para. 40, UN Doc. A/C.6/7/SR.346 (1952).

[111] Rule 61 of the rules of procedure, CDDH/2.

[112] Official Records of the 1974–1977 Geneva Humanitarian Law Conference, CDDH/II/SR.72, vol. XII, p. 194, para. 62.

[113] *Ibid.* at p. 195, para. 70.

The rules of procedure of the 1986 Conference on Treaties between States and International Organisations listed in detail rights granted to observers, including the rights to 'submit substantive proposals, which as such may only be put to the vote ... if a formal request is made by a State to that effect', and 'to submit procedural motions ... which may not be put to the vote unless supported by a State'.[114] According to a 1995 legal opinion, observers do not have a right of 'introduction of substantive proposals or procedural motions, the raising of points of order, the circulation of communications as official documents of that organ and the exercise of the right of reply'.[115] The 1997 Mine Ban Treaty Conference formulated the 'general rights of observers' as follows: they 'May not participate in decision-making', 'May not make any procedural motion or request, raise points of order or appeal against a ruling of the Chairman', and 'May not introduce proposals or amendments to any proposal'.[116] The rules of procedure of the 2004 Review Conference of the Mine Ban Treaty omit the rule that observers may not 'introduce proposals or amendments to any proposal'.[117] The rules of procedure of some recent conferences make a

[114] Rule 60 of the rules of procedure, A/CONF.129/16 (vol. I) (1995):

(a) To participate in public and private meetings of the Conference, the Committee of the Whole, sub-committees and working groups, as well as in the process leading to general agreement;
(b) To submit documents for circulation;
(c) To intervene in the debates; – To exercise the right of reply in accordance with rule 22; – To explain their positions on any matter on which a decision has been or is to be taken;
(d) To submit substantive proposals, which as such may only be put to the vote subject to rule 63 if a formal request is made by a State to that effect. If the proposal has been circulated in writing, the formal request shall be circulated in the same manner;
(e) To submit procedural motions, including those referred to in rules 23, 24 and 25, which may not be put to the vote unless supported by a State.

2. Representatives of the organizations participating in the Conference in accordance with paragraph 1 of this rule may not:

(a) Object to any procedural motion put forward by a representative of a participating State;
(b) Prevent on their own the achievement of general agreement or participate in any vote.

[115] UN Office of Legal Affairs, 'Letter to the Director, Office of International Standards and Legal Affairs, UN ECOSOC', 29 September 1995, 1995 UN Jur. Y.B. 438, ST/LEG/SER.C/33.

[116] Rule 47 of the rules of procedure of the Diplomatic Conference on a Convention on the Prohibition of the Use, Stockpiling, Production and Transfer of Anti-Personnel Mines and on their Destruction, APL/CRP.2 (1997).

[117] Rule 24 of the rules of procedure of the First Review Conference of the States Parties to the Convention on the Prohibition of the Use, Stockpiling, Production and Transfer of

distinction between organisations that '*participate* as observers without the right to vote' and NGOs that '*sit* as observers'.[118] These rules state explicitly that procedural motions can only be submitted by representatives of States.[119] This could lead to the implication that organisations that 'participate', as opposed to those that only 'sit as observers', may submit substantive proposals.

COMMENT

There is inconsistency in recent rules of procedure as to the right of observers to submit proposals. However, none of the rules of procedure examined allow proposals to be submitted to a vote unless proposed by a State.

8.10 Decisions on Competence of a Conference to Deal with an Issue

The UNGA rule is,

> *Rule 79*
>
> Subject to rule 77 [Order of procedural motions] any motion calling for a decision on the competence of the General Assembly to adopt a proposal submitted to it shall be put to the vote before a vote is taken on the proposal in question.

The UN Model Rule is similar, except that it refers to the competence 'to discuss any matter' in addition to adopting proposals.[120]

The rules of procedure of the Assembly of the League of Nations and the rules proposed by the Preparatory Commission did not contain specific rulings as to decisions on competence, nor did the rules of the 1949 Geneva Conference or the 1954 Hague Conference. A rule on this matter was added in 1947 to the rules of the General Assembly, and since 1958 it has been included in the rules of every conference.

Anti-Personnel Mines and on their Destruction, APLC/CONF/2004/PM.2/L.3, 15 June 2004.

118 See Rules 60–65, International Meeting to Review the Implementation of the Programme of Action for the Sustainable Development of Small Island Developing States, A/CONF.207/2 (2004); Rules 25–27 of the rules of procedure of the World Conference on Disaster Relief, A/CONF.206/PC(II)/2/Corr.1 (2004). Emphasis added.

119 Rules 25–27 of the rules of procedure of the World Conference on Disaster Relief, A/CONF.206/PC(II)/2/Corr.1 (2004).

120 Rule 48 of the UN Model Rules.

During a committee meeting of the 1958 Law of the Sea Conference, the representative of Cuba commented on a Canadian proposal that had been adopted in part, and said 'it had nothing to do with the territorial sea or with any subject assigned to the First Committee'. The Cuban delegate proposed that it be referred to another committee.[121] The Canadian delegate objected to the Cuban proposal and stated that since it related to the question of competence, 'the point of order raised by the representative of Cuba should have been raised before the Canadian proposal was put to the vote. The proposal of the Cuban representative was therefore out of order.'[122] The Chairman, without giving his reason, ruled that the Cuban proposal was in order.

A request for a decision on competence is a procedural motion[123] that should be voted on and not a point of order to be decided by the presiding officer, although a delegate may take the floor on a point of order so as to move such a procedural motion. At a 1975 International Air Law Conference, a delegate claimed that 'whether a particular matter fell within the agenda or not was a question to be settled by a ruling from the President'. Nevertheless the President, I believe correctly, put it to the vote of the Conference.[124] Such a motion can be raised at any point in the proceedings prior to voting on the substance of a proposal and does not necessarily have to be raised as a preliminary objection.[125]

At a meeting of the 1974–1977 Geneva Humanitarian Law Conference, the representative of Israel,[126] on a point of order, requested a vote on whether the Conference was competent to allow national liberation movements to sign the Final Act of the Conference.[127] The President said that 'the proposal for a decision on the Conference's competence must be put to the vote immediately'.[128] The representative of Egypt commented that 'the proposal by Israel was seen to be nothing but a motion for a separate

[121] Official Records of the 1958 Law of the Sea Conference, 59th Meeting of Committee I, vol. III, p. 182, para. 1, UN Doc. A/CONF.13/39 (1958).

[122] *Ibid.* at paras. 2–3.

[123] Although Rule 30 of the rules of procedure of the 1974–77 Geneva Humanitarian Law Conference stipulated, 'Decisions on the competence of the Conference shall constitute matters of substance and be treated as such.' (CDDH/2/Rev.3). This stipulation presumably was intended to be relevant to the majority required.

[124] 1975 Montreal Air Law Conference, 5th Plenary Meeting, paras. 7,9, ICAO Doc. 9154-LC/174–1(1975).

[125] *Ibid.* at p. 184. [126] The present author.

[127] Official Records of the 1974–1977 Geneva Humanitarian Law Conference, CDDH/SR.57, vol. VII, p. 254, paras. 8, 10.

[128] *Ibid.* at para. 11.

vote'.[129] A number of other delegations supported the Egyptian position. The President then stated that 'the Conference was sovereign and that he himself was unable to give a ruling on whether the proposal was a motion of competence or a request for a separate vote. The question was a procedural one. He invited the Conference to take a decision on the nature of the motion.'[130]

At a meeting of the 1977 Conference on Territorial Asylum, the Chairman of the Committee of the Whole attempted to persuade the Mexican delegation not to press for a vote on a question of competence. The Chairman argued that 'by voting on the proposal, the Committee would in fact be voting on the question of competence'.[131] The Mexican representative replied that 'an affirmative vote on the question of the competence of the Committee would not necessarily signify a vote in favour of the article, since two entirely separate votes would be involved. He insisted that the Committee should vote on the question whether it was competent.'[132] The Committee subsequently voted on the question of whether it was competent.

8.10.1 *Can Legal Counsel Give an Opinion on Competence?*

The rule of procedure on competence in the World Health Assembly[133] is identical in substance to the rule of the UNGA. At a 1984 meeting of the World Health Assembly, the representative of Israel referred to the existence of phrases such as '[t]he PLO is the sole legitimate representative of the Palestinian people' that appeared in a draft resolution presented to the Committee. The representative of Israel requested the Legal Counsel to give his opinion as to whether such phrases were within the competence of the Assembly and its committee.[134] The Director-General intervened to state that the Legal Counsel 'could not deal with that kind of question without preempting the sovereignty of the World Health Assembly'. The

[129] *Ibid.* at para. 14.
[130] *Ibid.* at para. 17. The Conference decided by a vote that the Israel motion was not a motion on competence, and the President then ruled that it should be treated as a request for a separate vote. The request for a separate vote was rejected by the Conference.
[131] Summary Records of the 18th Meeting of the Committee of the Whole of the 1977 Conference on Territorial Asylum, para. 54, UN Doc. A/CONF.78/C.1/SR.18 (1977).
[132] *Ibid.* at para. 57.
[133] Rule 65 of the rules of procedure of the World Health Assembly.
[134] 37th World Health Assembly, Committee 'B', 7th Meeting, pp. 217–218, WHA37/1984/REC/3 (1984).

President then put to the vote the question of the competence of the Committee to deal with the draft resolution submitted to it.[135]

8.10.2 *Voting Procedure on a Question of Competence*

A lengthy acrimonious debate took place at the 1965 ITU Conference on the question of the competence of the Conference to expel South Africa. The United Kingdom had proposed a motion that the Conference was not competent to take a decision on expelling a member. The Chairman apparently put it to the vote as a question, rather than as a motion, by the United Kingdom; the result was a tied vote. The Chairman announced the result to be that the Conference was not competent. This was disputed and the matter was finally settled by putting to the vote again a clear motion, by the United States, that the Conference was not competent. This US motion was defeated and the Conference proceeded to expel South Africa.[136]

At a 1993 meeting of the World Health Assembly, the US representative moved a motion that a resolution 'was not within the competence of the WHO'.[137] The Legal Counsel explained that the United States 'had challenged the competence of the World Health Assembly on the issue . . . a "yes" vote would imply agreement that the Health Assembly did not have the competence to adopt the proposed resolution. A "no" vote would imply that the Health Assembly did have the competence to do so.'[138]

8.10.3 *A Vote on Competence Regarding Part of a Proposal*

At a 1984 meeting of the World Health Assembly, the President ruled that a decision on competence could only be made on an entire proposal and not on parts thereof.[139]

135 *Ibid.* The Committee decided it was competent.

136 Minutes of the 1965 Plenipotentiary Conference of the ITU, 5th and 6th Plenary Meetings, ITU Docs. Nos. 156-E, 157 (1965).

137 Summary Records of the 9th Meeting of Committee 'B' of the 46th World Health Assembly, p. 264, WHA46/1993/REC/3 (1993).

138 *Ibid.*

139 37th World Health Assembly, Committee 'B', 7th Meeting, pp. 217–218, WHA37/1984/REC/3 (1984).

8.10.4 *Priority as between a Motion on Competence and a Motion for Inclusion in the Agenda*

A question can arise as to the priority between a motion to include an item on the agenda of a conference and a motion to determine the competence of a conference to discuss the item. The 1952 UNGA decided that priority is to be given in such a case to a motion for including an item on the agenda.[140] Goodrich and Simons write, 'The majority of Members have taken the position that discussion of this point [the issue of competence] should take place after the inclusion of the item in the agenda.'[141]

8.10.5 *Debating a Motion on Competence in the UN General Assembly*

The rule adopted in the UNGA rules in 1947 stated that a motion on competence 'shall be put to the vote immediately'.[142]

At the 1949 session, a UNGA committee decided that a discussion on an issue, the treatment of Indians in South Africa, could take place, even though a delegate had requested a vote on the competence of the Committee to discuss the issue. The Committee interpreted Rule 110 of the UNGA rules of procedure – which in substance was identical to Rule 79 of the present rules – as meaning that a vote on competence must precede a vote on substance but that this rule applied to voting and not to the discussion.[143]

The UK delegation proposed to the 1949 session of the UNGA Sixth Committee the deletion of the word 'immediately' from the rule as to competence.[144] The UK representative explained that the word 'immediately' 'could be interpreted as meaning that the vote on the question of competence should be taken without discussion as soon as the question

[140] UN GAOR, Plenary, 7th Session, 381st Meeting, paras. 133–135, 150, 151, UN Doc. A/PV.381 (1952). It successfully challenged a ruling by the President (Lester B. Pearson of Canada).

[141] Leland M. Goodrich and Anne P. Simons, *The United Nations and the Maintenance of International Peace and Security* (1955), p. 162.

[142] Rule 72 of the rules of procedure, UN Doc. A/520 (1948).

[143] UN GAOR, 1st Committee, 3rd Session, Part II, 263rd Meeting, pp. 246–253, UN Doc. A/C.1/3/SR.263 (1949).

[144] UN Doc. A/C.6/4/L.8 (1949).

was raised'.[145] The Legal Adviser to the UN informed the Committee that the Secretariat in the past had given this opinion:

> The literal interpretation would be that the discussion on competence should take place jointly with the debate on the substance and that the vote on competence should be taken after that debate and immediately before the vote on the substance. The Secretariat's opinion, however, had not been accepted in all cases.[146]

The UK proposal was adopted and the word 'immediately' deleted.[147] The deletion of the word 'immediately', it is submitted, makes it clear that a motion on competence may be debated before being voted on. The Report of the Sixth Committee on this issue stated that 'motions of competence, as well as proposals on questions of substance, were to be discussed simultaneously, but that when it came to voting, the Assembly or the committee, as the case might be, had to decide first on the question of competence'.[148]

8.10.6 Competence of Conferences to Discuss an Issue as Opposed to Competence to Vote on an Issue

The rule of procedure as to competence, in all the conferences examined from 1958 onwards, refers to the competence of the conference '*to discuss* any matter' in addition to the '*adoption*' of a proposal. The UNGA rule of procedure refers only to competence to '*adopt*' a proposal. The UN Model Rules follow the practice of conferences and not that of the UNGA.

In the discussions on the issue of nuclear tests at the 1958 Law of the Sea Conference, the representative of Yugoslavia stated, 'In accordance with a General Assembly ruling, motions calling for a decision on competence were voted on first, but discussion on substance was not separated from discussion on competence. It was only the votes that were kept separate.'[149] The Chairman ruled that the problem as such was not one of competence, and therefore no ruling on the Yugoslavian submission was called for. The

[145] UN GAOR, 6th Committee, 4th Session, 157th Meeting, p. 93, para. 61, UN Doc. A/C.6/4/SR.157 (1949).

[146] *Ibid.* at p. 94, para. 68.

[147] *Ibid.* at p. 96, para. 100. UNGA Resolution 362 (IV) of 22 October 1949.

[148] Report of the 6th Committee, Agenda Item 48, p. 184, para. 33, GAOR, 4th Session, Plenary, Annex, UN Doc. A/1026 and Corr.1 (1949).

[149] Official Records of the 1958 Law of the Sea Conference, Committee II, vol. IV, p. 44, para. 19, UN Doc. A/CONF.13/39 (1958).

Chairman's reasoning was that the UK proposal calling on the Conference not to deal with the question of nuclear tests did not call for a decision that the Conference was not competent, but called for the Conference to declare that it did not wish to deal with the issue.[150]

The rule of procedure, as to competence, of the 1971 IMCO Oil Pollution Damage Fund Conference was substantially the same as that of the UN Model Rule.[151] At a meeting of the Committee of the Whole of the Conference, the Chairman ruled that, 'before considering the substance of the proposals before it, the Committee must decide the question of competence raised by the French delegation'.[152]

At a meeting of a Committee of the 1977 Conference on Territorial Asylum, the delegation of Mexico requested a vote on the competence of the Conference to vote on a certain text. The representative of the USSR argued that 'the issue had been discussed at a number of meetings so that the Committee of the Whole had inevitably settled the question of its competence in the matter. A decision of that kind did not always have to be explicit.'[153] The Chairman pointed out that the members of the Committee had agreed that the proposal be introduced, and he added that a motion on competence 'need not be put to the vote immediately'.[154] On the insistence of the Mexican delegation, the Chairman subsequently put the motion on competence to the vote, thus by implication not accepting the Soviet argument.

At a 1984 meeting of the World Health Assembly, the Legal Counsel gave his opinion:

> Since the Chairman had had the text circulated and submitted to the Committee, it appeared to have been the Chairman's ruling that the draft resolution was receivable . . . The Committee should decide, by a vote, whether to support the Chairman's ruling that the draft should be circulated and thus considered receivable, or whether to consider the draft resolution not receivable, as recommended by the delegate of Somalia.[155]

[150] *Ibid.* at para. 21.

[151] Rule 28 of the rules of procedure of the 1971 IMCO Oil Pollution Damage Fund Conference, IMCO Doc. CONF.2/2 (1971).

[152] Official Records of the 26th Meeting of the Committee of the Whole of the 1971 IMCO Oil Pollution Damage Fund Conference, p. 532, IMCO Doc. CONF.2/C.1/SR.26 (1971).

[153] Summary Records of the 17th Meeting of the Committee of the Whole of the 1977 Conference on Territorial Asylum, para. 51, UN Doc. A/CONF.78/C.1/SR.17 (1977).

[154] *Ibid.* at para. 54.

[155] Summary Records of the 5th Meeting of Committee 'B' of the 37th World Health Assembly, p. 190, WHA37/1984/REC/3 (1984).

COMMENT

Practice appears to be that where a vote is requested on competence, that vote precedes the vote on the substance of the issue. Requesting a vote on competence does not, however, act as a motion to close the debate, and therefore voting on motions on competence takes place only after the conclusion of the debate.

8.11 Basic Texts

The UN Model Rules propose,

Rule 45
Basic Proposals

1. Any draft texts submitted to the Conference by the convening organ or the preparatory organ shall, if such organ so recommends or the Conference so decides, constitute the basic proposals for consideration by the Conference.
2. Basic proposals shall have priority over all other proposals submitted to the Conference, unless it decides otherwise.
3. The preparatory organ may establish a target date, in advance of the date on which the Conference is to be convened, by which any amendments relating to the basic proposals should be submitted to the Executive Secretary of the Conference; amendments so submitted shall receive priority in their processing by the Secretariat and their consideration by the Conference.[156]

Treaty-making conferences as a rule base their work on a basic text. In conferences convened by the UN, this text has often been an ILC draft. The Third Law of the Sea Conference was a notable exception in that its work did not commence with a basic text.

At the 1973 Geneva IMCO Conference, the Executive Secretary of the Conference read out a list of documents that the Secretariat suggested be mentioned in the rules of procedure as 'basic' documents. The US representative commented that '[d]ocuments should not be described as "basic" merely because they had been submitted in advance of the

156 The UN Model Rules add in a footnote that this provision is '[b]ased on a standard provision of the rules of procedure of codification conferences (e.g. rule 27 of those of the Conference on Succession of States in Respect of Treaties (A/CONF.80/8))', A/40/611, p. 28, n. 27.

opening of the Conference'.[157] The US representative listed the two documents that he considered to be basic. The Executive Secretary replied that

> the use of the word 'basic' in Rule 29,[158] which had been taken from the rules of procedure of another international conference, might be unfortunate, but that rule had been included in the draft rules of procedure to avoid the need for the re-formulation of documents already before the Conference. To regard all documents circulated prior to the Conference as basic proposals would greatly complicate the work of the Conference.[159]

The representative of Sweden said that 'it was quite common for conferences of the present type to treat draft conventions as basic documents and to designate them as such in the rules of procedure'.[160] After further discussion, the Conference adopted a US proposal that stipulated that all documents 'submitted in advance of the Conference' would be considered as having been submitted to the Conference, but that only two, stipulated, documents that had been prepared by the preparatory body would be considered 'basic' documents.161[161]

157 Summary Records of the 2nd Plenary Meeting of the 1973 Geneva IMCO Conference, p. 13, UN Doc. E/CONF.59/PV.2 (1973).

158

> *Rule 29*
>
> Documents [E/CONF.59 . . . to E/CONF.59 . . .] shall constitute the basic proposals for discussion by the Conference.

Draft rules of procedure for the UN/IMCO Conference on International Container Traffic, UN Doc. E/CONF.59/18 (1973).

159 *Ibid.* at p. 14. 160 *Ibid.* 161 *Ibid.* at p. 15.

9

Adjournment and Closure of Debate

9.1 Adjournment of Debate

The UNGA rules of procedure state,

> *Rule 74*
>
> *Adjournment of Debate*
>
> During the discussion of any matter, a representative may move the adjournment of the debate on the item under discussion. In addition to the proposer of the motion, two representatives may speak in favour of, and two against, the motion, after which the motion shall be immediately put to the vote. The President may limit the time to be allowed to speakers under this rule.

The UN Model Rules has a similar rule.[1]

9.1.1 *Effect of Adjourning the Debate*

Motions to adjourn the debate are normally adopted *sine die*, that is without deciding on a time for renewal, and such motions result in the termination of discussion and the prevention of voting on the issue concerned.[2] A motion to adjourn the debate differs from a motion to close the debate in that a motion to 'close' terminates discussion and authorises the meeting to proceed immediately to a vote. A motion to adjourn prevents both debate and voting.

The practical guide to the UNGA published by the Permanent Mission of Switzerland to the UN defines a motion to adjourn debate:

1 UN Model Rule 41. UN Doc. A/37/163, Annex (1982).

2 *Robert's* definition is '*Postpone Indefinitely* is a motion that the assembly decline to take a position on the main question. Its adoption kills the main motion (for the duration of the session) and avoids a direct vote on the question.' *Robert's Rules of Order, Newly Revised*, 11th edn (2011), p. 126.

> Adjournment of debate ends parts or all of the consideration of the agenda item concerned. This can mean ending the debate, blocking action on a specific draft resolution/decision or ending the consideration of the item as a whole (i.e., closing the item for the remainder of the session). Member States requesting adjournment of debate specify which part of the consideration is to be ended. The motion to adjourn debate is put to an immediate vote, carried by a simple majority, after a maximum of two delegations have spoken in favor and two against.

The advantages of such a motion for a delegation that objects to a draft proposal, as compared to a vote on the substance, are twofold. It cuts short the discussion on that proposal, and the vote is held on a procedural issue and not on the substance of the proposal. Some delegations have gone on record stating that they are in principle against the use of such motions as they deprive States of the opportunity to state publicly their position on the issue concerned.[3] Nevertheless, they continue to be used as a procedural technique. The disadvantage of such a motion, for the delegation objecting to the draft proposal, is that a majority is required to adopt the motion, whereas in a vote on the substance, the proposer requires a majority to adopt the proposal.

At a 2007 meeting of the Plenary of the UNGA a delegate expressed 'regret that the motion to adjourn the debate is being moved for the second time on the same draft resolution after the first motion was rejected by the Third Committee'. The delegate, however, did not request a ruling on the issue, and the motion for adjournment was put to the vote.[4] An identical scenario took place at the 2008 Plenary of the UNGA.[5]

At a 2001 Special Session of the UNGA, Egypt proposed a motion to adjourn the debate on a Canadian amendment. The President decided that, notwithstanding the Egyptian procedural motion, he would allow Canada to introduce its amendment since 'the amendment on which a motion for no action had been made had not been introduced' and only then proceed to vote on the Egyptian motion.[6] The presidential ruling was criticised – I believe justifiably – but was not formally challenged.

[3] See, for example, the Japanese statement at the UNGA, 26th Special Session, UN Doc. A/S-26/PV.1, p. 46 (2001). The statement by Finland on behalf of the EU at a meeting of the Third Committee of the UNGA. UN Doc. A/C.3/61/SR.50, para. 101. Statements by delegates of France and the UK, UN Doc. A/63/PV.104, pp. 12, 13 (2009).

[4] UNGA, 62nd Session, 76th Meeting, p. 29, UN Doc. A/62/PV.76 (2007).

[5] UNGA, 63rd Session, 71st Meeting, p. 3, UN Doc. A/63/PV.71 (2008).

[6] UNGA, 26th Special Session, UN Doc. A/S-26/PV.1, p. 44 (2001).

A representative of the Office of the Legal Counsel to the WHO informed delegates to a 1993 World Health Assembly that 'votes cast for or against [a motion for adjournment of debate] should not be regarded as tantamount to a vote for or against the draft resolution itself'.[7,8]

A different interpretation of the term 'adjourn the debate' appears to have been given at a 1975 ICAO International Air Law Conference. The President ruled that 'adjournment of debate on an item assumed a return to that item later on in the session'[9] and that 'the Rules of Procedure did not provide any means through which a matter validly before the Conference would not be considered during the course of the Conference'.[10]

At a 2009 General Conference of IAEA, the President 'explained that if the motion [adjournment of debate] was carried, no further action would be taken by the Conference on the resolution *at the current session*'.[11] [emphasis added]

9.1.2 A Motion to 'Take No Action' or not to Take a Vote on a Proposal as a Motion for Adjournment of Debate

The only explicit provision in the UNGA rules of procedure allowing for a motion not to take a vote is the second sentence of Rule 91:

> The Conference may, after each vote on a proposal, decide whether to vote on the next proposal.

[7] Summary Records of the 7th Meeting of Committee 'B' of the 46th World Health Assembly, p. 243, WHA46/1993/REC/3 (1993).

[8] This tactic was adopted by Australia in the debate in the Twenty-Eighth IAEA General Conference on an Iranian proposal concerning the Israel attack on the Iraqi reactor. Official Records of the 268th Plenary Meeting of the IAEA General Conference, GC(XXVIII)/OR.268, para. 16 (1985). This tactic was also adopted against Iranian proposals to reject Israel's credentials at the Thirty-Seventh Session of the UNGA by a motion submitted by Denmark, Finland, Iceland, Norway and Sweden. UN GAOR, 37th Session, Annexes, Agenda Item 3, p. 6, UN Doc. A/37/L.11 (1982). At the Thirty-Eighth Session of the UNGA, it was done by raising a point of order. UN GAOR, Plenary, 38th Session, 34th Meeting, para. 43, UN Doc. A/38/PV.34 (1983). This procedure was followed at subsequent sessions, where such an amendment was proposed.

[9] ICAO Montreal International Conference on Air Law, ICAO Document 9154-LC/174–2, para. 18 (1975).

[10] 18th meeting of the Commission of the Whole, ICAO Montreal International Conference on Air Law, ICAO Document 9154-LC/174–1, p. 187. (1975).

[11] 53rd General Conference IAEA, Plenary, 10th Meeting, paras. 40, 41, IAEA Doc. GC953)/OR.10 (2009).

Nevertheless, the practice has developed of submitting motions not to take a vote on a proposal. The issue of not taking a vote arose at a plenary meeting of the UNGA debating an Iranian amendment to the report of the Credentials Committee on the issue of the credentials of the Israel delegation. The Norwegian representative, on a point of order, moved that no action be taken on the Iranian amendment.[12] A legal opinion was requested and the Legal Counsel of the UN gave his opinion: 'A review of the practice of the General Assembly shows that the Assembly has often, in the recent past, acted on motions to take no action on a proposal before it, based on rule 74.'[13]

The practical guide to the UNGA published by the Permanent Mission of Switzerland to the UN instructs that 'the term "no-action motion" is used when a motion for adjournment of debate is made to block action on a specific draft resolution or decision'.[14]

At a meeting of a committee of the 1975 ICAO Montreal Air Law Conference, the Norwegian delegate proposed that a vote on a proposal 'be deferred'. The president suggested that 'the Norwegian proposal should be understood as one of for suspension of debate', and it was treated as such.[15]

A motion not to take a decision has the same effect as a motion to adjourn the debate and in practice is submitted under Rule 74 as a motion to adjourn the debate.[16]

[12] UN GAOR, Plenary, 38th Session, 34th Meeting, para. 43, UN Doc. A/38/PV.34 (1983).

[13] Mr Fleischauer (Legal Counsel):

> A review of the practice of the General Assembly shows that the Assembly has on several occasions in the recent past acted on motions to take no action on a proposal before it on the basis of rule 74. Among the precedents which I have referred to, there are not only those which relate to the item as a whole, but also several which relate to a specific question or text under consideration and to adjournment *sine die*.
>
> UN GAOR, Plenary, 38th Session, 34th Meeting, para. 56, UN Doc. A/38/PV.34 (1983).

See also UN GAOR, 5th Committee, 29th Session, 1647th Meeting, para. 55, UN Doc. A/C.5/SR.1647 (1974).

[14] para. 3.3, www.unitar.org/ny/sites/unitar.org.ny/files/UN_PGA_Handbook.pd

[15] Commission of the Whole, Sixth Meeting, 1975 ICAO Montreal International Conference on Air Law, ICAO Document 9154-LC/174–1, p. 66 (1975).

[16] UN GAOR, 4th Committee, 11th Session, 582nd Meeting, para. 40, UN Doc. A/C.4/11/SR.582 (1956); UN GAOR, 4th Committee, 11th Session, 583rd Meeting, para. 2, UN Doc. A/C.4/11/SR.583 (1956); UN GAOR, Plenary, 46th Session, 45th Meeting, p. 8,

9.1.3 *Difference between a Motion not to Vote and a Motion to Adjourn the Debate*

At a 1986 meeting of the World Health Assembly, the representative of the United States proposed that 'the Committee take no decision on the draft resolution [concerning nuclear weapons]'. The Chairman invited the Committee to vote on the US proposal. The representative of Cuba appealed against the Chairman's decision to put the US proposal to the vote, and the appeal being accepted, the US proposal was not put to the vote.[17] Presumably, if the US representative had moved the 'adjournment of the debate'[18] rather than the motion to 'take no decision', the Committee, according to the rules of procedure, would have had to vote immediately, and there would have been no room for a ruling by the Chairman.

9.1.4 *A Motion to 'Refrain from Making a Decision' as a Motion for Adjournment of Debate*

At a 1962 meeting of the UNGA,[19] the Chairman ruled that an Indian proposal that the 'Committee should refrain from making an immediate decision on the relative priority' of items and that the Chairman should be left to 'continue his consultations' was a motion for the adjournment of debate.[20]

At a plenary meeting of the 1992 General Conference of the IAEA, a motion by the UK 'not to proceed to a vote' was treated as a motion for adjournment of the debate and put to the vote as such.[21]

UN Doc. A/46/PV.45 (Provisional) (1991); UN GAOR, 3rd Committee, 47th Session, 58th Meeting, paras. 85, 88, UN Doc. A/C.3/47/SR.58 (1992).

17 Summary Records of the 8th Meeting of Committee 'B' of the 39th World Health Assembly, pp. 312, 313, WHA/39/1986/REC/3 (1986).

18 Rule 62 of the rules of procedure of the World Health Assembly is substantially identical to Rule 74 of the rules of procedure of the UNGA.

19 UN GAOR, 1st Committee, 17th Session, 1245th Meeting, paras. 31, 41, UN Doc. A/C.1/17/SR.1245 (1962).

20 The rules of procedure of the UN Economic and Social Council (ECOSOC), unlike those of the UNGA, refer explicitly to a motion not to take a decision.

Rule 67

> 2. A motion requiring that no decision be taken on a proposal shall have priority over that proposal.

21 Official Records of the 352nd Plenary Meeting of the 36th General Conference of the IAEA, para. 76, IAEA Doc. GC(XXXVI)/OR.352 (1992).

9.1.5 A Motion for 'Postponement of Consideration' as a Motion for Adjournment of Debate

A motion for 'postponement of consideration' was submitted by the representative of Sierra Leone to a 1975 meeting of the UNGA dealing with the proposal, later rescinded, to brand Zionism as racism. One delegate pointed out that the rules of procedure did not grant priority to a motion 'to postpone consideration'. The delegate added that priority would be given if the motion was a procedural one to 'adjourn the debate'.[22] In the event, the motion was immediately put to the vote, so presumably the Chairman treated it as a procedural motion to 'adjourn the debate'.

9.1.6 Is a Motion for Postponement Synonymous with a Motion for Adjournment of Debate?

At a 1963 meeting of a UNGA committee, the Chairman ruled that a motion to postpone a decision was not a motion to adjourn the debate and therefore was not entitled to automatic priority, and it was up to the Committee to decide whether to grant priority to the motion.[23]

At a 1974 meeting of the UNGA, the Chairman ruled that a motion to postpone consideration of an item to the next session of the General Assembly was a 'proposal' and not a procedural motion and therefore was not, as such, entitled to priority over other proposals.[24] However, at the 1975 session of the UNGA, a proposal to postpone consideration was put immediately to the vote, it being considered therefore, by implication, as a motion for adjournment of the debate.[25]

At a 1974 meeting of the UNGA, the Chairman gave priority to a motion to 'close the debate' over a motion to 'postpone the debate'.[26] It may be that if the motion to 'postpone' had been couched in the procedural language of Rule 119, namely 'to adjourn', then the Chairman would have reached a different conclusion.

[22] UN GAOR, 3rd Committee, 30th Session, 2134th Meeting, para. 13, UN Doc. A/C.3/SR.2134 (1975).

[23] UN GAOR, 4th Committee, 18th Session, 1481st Meeting, paras. 59, 68, UN Doc. A/C.4/18/SR.1481 (1963).

[24] UN GAOR, 3rd Committee, 29th Session, 2102nd Meeting, paras. 23, 35, 36, 41, UN Doc. A/C.3/29/SR.2102 (1974).

[25] UN GAOR, 3rd Committee, 30th Session, 2134th Meeting, paras. 1, 13, UN Doc. A/C.3/30/SR.2134 (1975).

[26] UN GAOR, 5th Committee, 29th Session, 1668th Meeting, paras. 1–11, UN Doc. A/C.5/29/SR.1668 (1974).

At a 1981 meeting of a UNGA committee, the representative of Iraq proposed that the issue of a resolution on the respect of the privileges and immunities of UN officials be postponed until the next session of the General Assembly. The representative of the German Democratic Republic claimed that 'under the rules of procedure the proposal made by the representative of Iraq should be given priority'.[27] The Netherlands representative argued that 'Iraq's formal proposal was a substantive one, which, in accordance with the rules of procedure, should be taken up after a decision on [the] draft resolution'.[28] The Chairman decided, without objection being raised, to put to the vote a motion under Rule 131 that the Iraqi proposal be granted priority.[29] By putting the question of priority to the vote, the Chairman was clearly denying that the Iraqi proposal for postponement was entitled to any inherent priority, but rather it was treated as a regular proposal, the Committee being entitled to vote to grant it priority.

9.1.7 A Motion to Adjourn a Vote as a Motion for Adjournment of Debate

At a 1954 meeting of the UNGA, the President treated an Iraqi motion to adjourn the vote as a motion to adjourn the debate.[30]

9.1.8 A Motion for Referral as a Motion for Adjournment of Debate

At a 1983 meeting of the World Health Assembly, a delegation submitted a motion to refer a draft resolution to the Executive Committee of the Assembly. The Legal Counsel of the WHO gave his opinion that, 'despite the absence in the rules of procedure of any express provision concerning motions for referral, the same goal could have been obtained by using Rule 62, which provides for adjournment of the debate ... We should thus have arrived indirectly, by applying Rule 62, at a result identical to the one produced by tabling a motion for referral.'[31]

27 UN GAOR, 5th Committee, 36th Session, 71st Meeting, para. 34, UN Doc. A/C.5/36/SR.71 (1981).

28 *Ibid.* at para. 28.

29 UN GAOR, 5th Committee, 36th Session, 72nd Meeting, paras. 4, 5, UN Doc. A/C.5/36/SR.72 (1981). The Iraqi proposal was granted priority but subsequently rejected.

30 UN GAOR, Plenary, 9th Session, 477th Meeting, paras. 95–101, UN Doc. A/PV.477 (1954).

31 Verbatim Records of the 13th Plenary Meeting of the 36th World Health Assembly, pp. 270–273, WHA36/1983/REC/2 (1983).

9.1.9 A Motion to Adjourn the Debate after the Debate Is Completed and before Voting

During the 1953 meeting of the UNGA, the President ruled that a motion to postpone consideration of an item during that session was not a motion to 'adjourn the debate', since the debate had been completed and voting on it was about to begin.[32] However, at a committee meeting of the UNGA, at its 1985 session, a motion to adjourn the debate was moved by Syria after the Chairman had invited the members of the Committee to vote on a resolution. An objection was made to the motion, and the Legal Counsel of the UN gave his opinion to the Committee that the motion for adjournment had to relate to the item under discussion but at what time during the discussion the motion should be made was not specified. The Legal Counsel gave his opinion that, therefore, from the procedural standpoint, the motion of the delegation of Syria was admissible. The Chairman consequently ruled that the Syrian motion was admissible.[33]

9.1.10 A Motion to Adjourn the Debate on a Resolution until Completion of Discussion on Another Resolution

The Chairman of a committee of the UNGA, at its 1952 session, ruled that a motion was in order when it moved the adjournment of a debate on a resolution, 'until the completion of the debate on another resolution'.[34]

9.1.11 A Motion to Adjourn the Debate on a Procedural Motion

At a meeting of a committee of the 1974–1977 Geneva Humanitarian Law Conference, the representative of Italy moved the adjournment of the debate on the question of the competence of the Committee to deal with an issue.[35] The representative of Mexico reacted that 'it was the first time that he had heard of the postponement of a discussion on a point

32 UN GAOR, Plenary, 8th Session, 432nd Meeting, para. 96, UN Doc. A/PV.432 (1953).

33 UN GAOR, 3rd Committee, 40th Session, 70th Meeting, paras. 2, 9, 11, 15, UN Doc. A/C.3/40/SR.70 (1985). The delegation of France appealed against the ruling on the ground that the motion would adjourn the debate on two resolutions with one motion. The appeal was upheld on a vote. No appeal was made, however, to that part of the ruling that referred to when a motion for adjournment can be made.

34 UN GAOR, 2nd Committee, 6th Session, 186th Meeting, para. 28, UN Doc. A/C.2/6/SR.186 (1952).

35 CDDH/I/SR.68, vol. IX, p. 377, para. 38.

of procedure'.[36] The Chairman ruled that 'his intention was to adjourn the discussion on the question of competence in the light of the motion by the representative of Italy. He therefore suggested that the debate on that subject should be adjourned to [another] meeting.'[37] The Chairman's proposal was approved.

9.1.12 A Single Motion to Adjourn the Debate on Two Separate Resolutions

At a 1985 meeting of the UNGA, the Chairman, on the advice of the Legal Counsel, ruled as admissible a single motion, by Syria, to adjourn the debate on two draft resolutions.[38] The representative of France appealed against the ruling, claiming that

> it had never before been claimed that two draft resolutions submitted to an organ for consideration constituted only one issue. A decision whereby the debate on two draft resolutions could be adjourned under a single motion would establish an unusual precedent and would run counter to rule 116 of the rules of procedure.[39]

The appeal was upheld, and the Syrian proposal was held inadmissible.[40]

9.1.13 What Is 'an Item under Discussion' for Purposes of Adjournment of Debate?

At a 1960 meeting of the UNGA, the Assembly decided to adjourn a debate on the situation in Congo. The President ruled that the decision of the Assembly did not apply to discussion of the Report of the Credentials Committee on the Congolese credentials since that Report had not been before the Assembly when a decision on adjournment was made.[41]

At a 1989 meeting of the World Health Assembly, the Austrian delegation moved the adjournment of the debate on the admission of 'Palestine' to the Organisation. The representative of Libya claimed that the rule on adjournment 'is worded "during the discussion of any matter", but we

[36] *Ibid.* at p. 380, para. 60. [37] *Ibid.* at p. 380, para. 62
[38] UN GAOR, 3rd Committee, 40th Session, 70th Meeting, paras. 2, 9, 10, UN Doc. A/C.3/40/SR.70 (1985).
[39] *Ibid.* at para. 11. [40] *Ibid.* at paras. 15, 16.
[41] UN GAOR, Plenary, 15th Session, Part I, 918th Meeting, paras. 1–7, UN Doc. A/PV.918 (1960).

have not yet started our discussion'. The Legal Counsel, without giving a reasoned opinion, replied that the Austrian motion was in order.[42]

9.1.14 Adjournment of Debate on Specific Proposals or Amendments or on a Complete Agenda Item

Rule 67 of the rules of procedure of the ECOSOC explicitly allows for motions not to take a decision.[43] In the First Regular Session of the ECOSOC in 1981, the issue arose as to whether the Council could decide to apply Rule 67 to an amendment to a proposal. Although the President informed the Council that there was no such provision in the rules of procedure regarding amendments, the Council decided nevertheless to put to a vote a motion not to take a decision on certain amendments.[44]

At a 1958 meeting of the UNGA, the representative of France argued that a motion for adjournment of the debate on one specific amendment was out of order since adjournment had to apply to a complete item on the agenda. The issue was not resolved.[45]

42 Verbatim Records of the 6th Plenary Meeting of the 42nd World Health Assembly, p. 101, WHA42/1989/REC/2 (1989).

43 *Rule 67*

> 2. A motion requiring that no decision be taken on a proposal shall have priority over that proposal.
>
> UN Doc. E/5715/Rev.1 (1983).

At a meeting of the UN Commission on Human Rights, which has a similar provision in its rules of procedure, the representative of the Federal Republic of Germany complained that

> [t]o disagree with the contents of a draft resolution could not constitute a reason for refusing to decide upon the text itself. A motion requiring that no decision be taken was an attempt to weaken the Commission's decision making capacity.
>
> UN Doc. E/CN.4/1990/SR.52/Add.1, para. 62 (1990).

44 ECOSOC, Official Records of the First Regular Session, 1981, 15th Meeting, paras. 18, 19, UN Doc. E/1981/SR.15 (1981). The motion was moved under Rule 59 of the ECOCOC rules of procedure, which states:

> *Rule 59*
>
> *Request for a Vote*
>
> A proposal or motion before the Council for decision shall be voted upon if any member so requests. When no member requests a vote, the Council may adopt proposals or motions without a vote.

45 UN GAOR, 3rd Committee, 13th Session, 860th Meeting, para. 15, UN Doc. A/C.3/13/SR.860 (1958).

UNGA practice, however, is to allow motions for adjournment of debate on specific proposals.[46] Motions for adjournment of debate on amendments are also permitted; such motions leave the main proposal 'open for action'.[47] Such motions are submitted under Rule 74, which deals with adjournment of debate.

At a 1985 meeting of a committee of the UNGA, the representative of Morocco moved under Rule 116[48] of the rules of procedure that the Committee take no action on any of the amendments to a resolution that had been submitted by Morocco and others. The representative of Algeria questioned the legitimacy of a motion to prevent States presenting amendments to a draft resolution. The representative argued that the motion 'invoked rule 116 not for its proper function of adjourning discussion of the agenda item as a whole but as an expedient to prevent decision-making on a particular point'.[49] The representative of Algeria did not, however, submit a formal challenge.

At a 1986 meeting of the UNGA, Iraq submitted, under Rule 74, a motion that no amendments be introduced to a draft resolution (condemning Israel for the attack on the Iraqi nuclear reactor). The representative of Iran complained that 'there is no rule of procedure which prevents the introduction of amendments to draft resolutions'.[50]

[46] According to Suy (Legal Counsel), 'the terms of rule 116 of the rules of procedure of the General Assembly were interpreted to mean that discussion of a draft resolution which formed part of a broader item of the agenda could be deferred'. UN GAOR, 2nd Committee, 33rd Session, 60th Meeting, para. 77, UN Doc. A/C.2/33/SR.60 (1978).

[47] UN GAOR, 6th Committee, 8th Session, 391st Meeting, paras. 56, 57, UN Doc. A/C.6/8/SR.391 (1953). This motion referred to not taking a decision on a draft resolution and on the amendments thereto.

Mr Szasz (Office of the Legal Counsel) said,

> As I understand it, the question is this: whether a motion to adjourn the debate on some amendments means that, if adopted, no vote would be taken on those amendments but that action could be taken on the main proposal.
>
> ... [I]t could either be said that it is an accepted practice of the Assembly in interpreting rule 74 or that, as the President has just pointed out, the Assembly is master of its own procedure and there is no rule that is specifically contravened by this interpretation.
>
> UN GAOR, Plenary, 37th Session, 111th Meeting, paras. 82, 83, UN Doc. A/37/PV.111 (1982).

[48] Substantially identical to Rule 74 of the UNGA rules of procedure.

[49] UN GAOR, 4th Committee, 40th Session, 21st Meeting, para. 32, UN Doc. A/C.4/40/SR.21 (1985).

[50] UN GAOR, Plenary, 41st Session, 51st Meeting, p. 92, UN Doc. A/41/PV.51 (Provisional) (1986).

Nevertheless, the Iraqi motion was passed, as a motion to adjourn the debate, and no amendments were allowed.[51]

At a 1989 meeting of the UNGA, the representative of Chile argued strenuously against a motion to adjourn the debate on a Chilean amendment. The representative argued, 'What could be stronger than the right of a country to have its proposal considered?'[52] 'To deny, by a procedural maneuver, a country the right to raise such a vital issue as its own position in the Assembly would be incompatible with the atmosphere which should prevail in this body.'[53]

At a 1991 meeting of a committee of the UNGA, the representative of Luxembourg submitted a motion 'that the Committee should not take any decision on the last-minute amendments proposed by the Cuban delegation'.[54] The Chairman allowed the motion despite Cuban objection that it 'was, in fact, an attempt to gag one participant in the debate. To be fair, the Committee should postpone debate on the whole question.'[55] At a 1993 meeting of the UNGA, no procedural objection was raised to a proposal by the Netherlands that 'no action be taken' on an amendment.[56]

At a 2016 meeting of the Third Committee of UNGA a motion was submitted to adjourn the debate on a complete agenda item. The delegate explained that 'the motion was unprecedented in the history of the Third Committee'. The chairman put the motion to the vote and it was defeated.[57]

At a 1992 meeting of the General Conference of the IAEA, a decision was taken to adjourn the debate on a specific amendment.[58]

COMMENT

Despite criticism, practice is to allow motions to adjourn the debate on amendments.

[51] *Ibid.* at p. 96.

[52] UN GAOR, Plenary, 44th Session, 63rd Meeting, p. 83, UN Doc. A/44/PV.63 (Provisional) (1989).

[53] *Ibid.* The motion to adjourn the debate was adopted.

[54] UN GAOR, 3rd Committee, 46th Session, 59th Meeting, para. 39, UN Doc. A/C.3/46/SR.59 (1991).

[55] *Ibid.* at para. 41.

[56] UN GAOR, 1st Committee, 48th Session, 30th Meeting, para. 56, UN Doc. A/C.1/48/SR.30 (1993).

[57] UN GAOR, 3rd Committee, 71st Session, 48th meeting, paras. 13, 14, 20. UN Doc. A/C.3/71/SR.48 (2016).

[58] Official Records of the 352nd Plenary Meeting of the 36th General Conference of the IAEA, para. 76, IAEA Doc. GC(XXXVI)/OR.352 (1992).

9.1.15 Limits on Number of Speakers on a Motion to Adjourn the Debate

The rules of procedure of the UNGA state,

> *Rule 74*
>
> *Adjournment of Debate*
>
> During the discussion of any matter, a representative may move the adjournment of the debate on the item under discussion. In addition to the proposer of the motion, two representatives may speak in favour of, and two against, the motion, after which the motion shall be immediately put to the vote.

This rule thus allows three speakers in favour of the motion.

The UNGA rule allows the President to limit the time to be allowed to speakers. The UN Model Rules, in Rule 36, limit all speakers on procedural questions to a maximum of five minutes.

9.2 Closure of Debate

Closure of debate results in the debate being closed and the meeting proceeding immediately to voting on the issue.

The UNGA rules of procedure state,

> *Rule 75*
>
> A representative may at any time move the closure of the debate on the item under discussion, whether or not any other representative has signified his wish to speak. Permission to speak on the closure of the debate shall be accorded only to two speakers opposing the closure, after which the motion shall be immediately put to the vote. If the General Assembly is in favour of the closure, the President shall declare the closure of the debate. The President may limit the time to be allowed to speakers under this rule.[59]

The practical guide to the UNGA published by the Permanent Mission of Switzerland to the UN defines closure of debate as follows:

> A Member State may request closure of debate at any time, regardless of whether or not everyone on the list of speakers has spoken.

[59] The Draft of the Preparatory Commission did not call for a vote but stated, 'The President shall take the sense of the General Assembly on a motion for closure' (Rule 63). Report of the Preparatory Commission of the United Nations, p. 15, chap. I, sect. 3, PC/20 (1945). This wording was repeated in Rule 63 of the provisional rules of procedure of the General Assembly, UN Doc. A/4 (1946).

> The request is put to an immediate vote, carried by a simple majority, after a maximum of two delegations opposing the closure have spoken. If the motion passes, the President declares the debate closed. Otherwise, the President declares the debate closed after the last speaker has been given the floor. Usually, it is the main sponsor of a draft resolution/decision who requests the closure of debate to ensure that the adoption of the resolution/decision is not delayed.[60]

The UN Model Rule is similar.[61]

The right of a representative to move the closure of the debate has been recognised in all the rules of procedure since those of the League of Nations.

9.2.1 *Closure of Debate and Protection of the Minority*

It has been pointed out that a motion for closure of debate can be used by a majority to prevent the right of a minority to debate an issue.[62] *Robert's Rules of Order* comments,

> In ordinary bodies, the requirement of a two-thirds vote for ordering the *Previous Question* [closure of debate] is important in protecting the democratic process. If this rule were not observed, a temporary majority of only one vote could deny the remaining members all opportunity to discuss any measure that such a majority wished to adopt or kill.[63]

To attempt to prevent such abuse, the rules of procedure of the Third Law of the Sea Conference stipulated that

> *Rule 29*
>
> Adoption of the motion [for closure of debate] shall require a two-thirds majority of the representatives present and voting.[64,65]

The draft rules of procedure for the Conference further proposed, regarding committees, that

[60] para. 3.4, www.unitar.org/ny/sites/unitar.org.ny/files/UN_PGA_Handbook.pdf.

[61] UN Model Rule 42, UN Doc. A/37/163, Annex (1982).

[62] See UN GAOR, Plenary, 6th Session, 362nd Meeting, paras. 36–38, UN Doc. A/PV.362 (1952).

[63] *Robert's Rules of Order* 11th edn (2011), p. 200.

[64] Rule 29 of the rules of procedure of the Third Law of the Sea Conference, UN Doc. A/CONF.62/30/Rev.3 (1975).

[65] The US delegation proposed that such a vote be taken by 'a two-thirds majority of the representatives of States participating in that session of the Conference'. UN Doc. A/CONF.62/7/Rev.1 (1974). The proposal was not adopted.

Rule 54

(d) no Main Committee shall, if there is any objection, adopt a motion to close the debate on the question under discussion or proceed to a vote on a matter of substance, without the permission of the Conference.[66]

This draft rule as to committees was not adopted, and paradoxically, since all decisions of committees other than reconsideration of an issue were adopted by a simple majority, even the restriction applicable to motions for closure in the plenary meetings did not apply to committees.[67]

British parliamentary practice requires that at least 100 Members of Parliament support a motion for closure (out of a total of more than 600 Members).[68] Such restrictions on motions for closure are not common practice in conference rules of procedure and do not appear in the UN Model Rules.

At a 1952 meeting of the UNGA, the representative of Brazil moved the closure of debate on the report of the Fourth Committee regarding South West Africa. The representative of the United Kingdom, on a point of order, moved that no motion for closure be allowed in a situation where the Plenary had recently decided to discuss a report and only three speakers had spoken so far. The UK representative pointed out that the Assembly must protect the rights of the minority. The President decided nevertheless that the motion for closure was in order and put it to the vote.[69]

At a 1981 meeting of the World Health Assembly, the representative of Peru commented that, 'while conceding that any delegate had a right to propose closure of debate, he considered it undemocratic to do so when only seven or eight delegates had spoken on the item, out of 50 on the list of speakers'.[70]

At the 1993 World Health Assembly, a motion was proposed to terminate the membership of the Federal Republic of Yugoslavia, and a

[66] The Japanese delegation proposed that approval of closure in committees would require approval by two-thirds 'of the representatives of States participating in the Conference'. UN Doc. A/CONF.62/16 (1974).

[67] Rule 55(c) of the rules of procedure of the Third Law of the Sea Conference, UN Doc. A/CONF.62/30/Rev.3 (1975).

[68] S. C. Hawtrey and H. M. Barclay, *Abraham and Hawtrey's Parliamentary Dictionary*, 3rd edn (1970), p. 60.

[69] The motion for closure was defeated. UN GAOR, Plenary, 6th Session, 362nd Meeting, paras. 36–38, 39–41, UN Doc. A/PV.362 (1952).

[70] Summary Records of the 14th Meeting of Committee 'A' of the 34th World Health Assembly, p. 199, WHA34/1981/REC/3 (1981).

procedural motion was submitted to close the debate on the issue. The representative of Yugoslavia, although not speaking against the motion for closure, was allowed to make a statement on the substance of the motion. The Legal Counsel stated that 'the President decided to allow a short statement under these circumstances'.[71]

9.2.2 *Motion for Immediate Vote as Motion for Closure*

At a 1952 meeting of the UNGA, the Chairman ruled that he considered a motion for an immediate vote on a resolution as a motion for closure of the debate.[72] At a 1999 meeting of the UNGA, the Chairman ruled that an Iranian objection to postponement of consideration of a draft resolution, coupled with a request to 'take action' on the draft resolution, was a motion for closure. The Chairman made his ruling, even though the Iranian delegate had not explicitly invoked Rule 117 nor used the phrase 'closure of debate'.[73]

At a meeting of the 1975 ICAO Montreal International Conference on Air Law the President ruled that a proposal for 'an immediate vote' was a 'motion for closure of debate'.[74]

At a 1982 meeting of the World Health Assembly, a representative moved that 'the debate on the matter should be terminated and that the Committee should proceed to a vote'.[75] The Legal Counsel remarked that 'he assumed that the closure of the debate had been moved, since that was the only way in which draft resolutions could be voted on immediately'.[76]

9.2.3 *What Is an Item under Discussion for Purposes of Closure of Debate?*

The UN Office of Legal Affairs gave its opinion, in 1983, that the item under discussion to which a motion of closure applies 'need not be an entire agenda item, but can be a sub-item, a particular proposal or set of

[71] WHA46/1993/REC/2, A46/VR/1, p. 15 (1993).
[72] UN GAOR, 2nd Committee, 7th Session, 237th Meeting, paras. 25–26, UN Doc. A/C.2/7/SR.237 (1952).
[73] UN GAOR, 3rd Committee, 54th Session, 53rd Meeting, UN Doc. A/C.3/54/SR.53, p. 2 (1999). The Iranian delegation subsequently withdrew its motion.
[74] Fifth Plenary Meeting, 1975 ICAO Montreal International Conference on Air Law, ICAO Document 9154-LC/174–1, p. 212 (1975).
[75] Summary Records of the 10th Meeting of Committee 'B' of the 35th World Health Assembly, p. 245, WHA35/1982/REC/3 (1982).
[76] *Ibid.*

proposals, or even an amendment to a proposal'. The opinion continues by stating that 'it should usually be assumed that the motion is intended to have the broadest effect it can sensibly be given, i.e., to close debate on as much of the agenda item as possible; certainly it should never be presumed, without explicit confirmation, that debate was meant to be closed merely on an amendment or on one of a series of related proposals'.[77]

9.2.4 *Process of Voting on a Motion for Closure*

At a 1980 meeting of the World Health Assembly, the Chairman ruled that 'once the closure of debate has been moved, nobody – and accordingly neither the Director-General nor the Legal Adviser – could speak until after a vote had been taken on the motion, with the exception of two speakers against the motion for closure'.[78]

9.2.5 *Voting on Proposals after Adoption of a Motion for Closure*

The rules of procedure of the World Health Assembly stipulate that, after a motion for closure has been adopted, '[t]he Health Assembly shall thereafter vote only on the one or more proposals moved before the closure'.[79] The Legal Counsel to the WHO commented on this rule that it applies to 'texts [proposals and amendments] formally introduced before the motion for closure'.[80] On the basis of this rule, the chairman of a committee of the 1983 World Health Assembly refused to allow a delegation to introduce an amendment after a motion had been adopted to close the debate.[81] With regard to the procedure in the UNGA, the UN Office of Legal Affairs, however, gave its opinion, in 1983, that after the adoption of a motion for

77 Memorandum, 10 November 1983, from UN Office of Legal Affairs to the Under-Secretary-General for Political and General Assembly Affairs. 1983 UN Jur. Y.B. 174, 175, UN Doc. ST/LEG/SER.C/21 (1983).

78 Summary Records of the 7th Meeting of Committee 'B' of the 33rd World Health Assembly, p. 258, WHA33/1980/REC/3 (1980).

79 Rule 63 of the rules of procedure of the World Health Assembly. This rule is applied in practice. See, for example, Summary Records of the 9th Meeting of Committee 'B' of the 35th World Health Assembly, p. 234, WHA/35/1982/REC/3 (1982); Summary Records of the 12th Meeting of Committee 'B' of the 36th World Health Assembly, p. 367, WHA/36/1983/REC/3 (1983); Summary Records of the 6th Meeting of Committee 'B' of the 38th World Health Assembly, p. 259, WHA38/1985/REC/3 (1985).

80 Summary Records of the 10th Meeting of Committee 'B' of the 35th World Health Assembly, p. 254, WHA35/1982/REC/3 (1982).

81 Summary Records of the 12th Meeting of Committee 'B' of the 36th World Health Assembly, p. 367, WHA36/1983/REC/3 (1983).

closure, 'a proposal already submitted . . . but not yet formally introduced or even circulated should normally be dealt with'.[82] At times a conference or assembly debates at length the question of what is the issue or resolution that is to be voted on. Where, in such circumstances, a motion is passed to close the debate, the result is that it is the presiding officer who will have to make a ruling on what is to be voted on.[83] A delegation may submit an appeal against such a presidential ruling, although it will have to be the president who will decide whether to interrupt the voting procedure for such an appeal.

9.2.6 *Right of Reply after Closure of Debate*

At a 1952 meeting of the UNGA, after deciding to close the debate, it was decided by a further vote to close the debate on the replies being exercised by virtue of the right of reply.[84] The Australian delegation commented that this would establish an unfortunate precedent that could be used by representatives wishing to prevent replies.[85]

At a 1959 meeting of the UNGA, the Chairman put to vote a motion for closure, noting that closure of debate would not prevent the exercise of the right to reply by India and Ceylon, the two States that had requested it.[86]

During the 1978 Hamburg Conference on Carriage by Sea, a representative moved the closure of debate.[87] The President of the Conference ruled that 'he must first give the representative of . . . the right to reply'.[88]

At the 1975 Vienna Conference on Representation of States, the Chairman of the Committee of the Whole said 'that even if the motion for closure was carried, the sponsor of each amendment would, in accordance

[82] Memorandum, 10 November 1983, from Office of Legal Affairs to the Under-Secretary-General for Political and General Assembly Affairs. 1983 UN Jur. Y.B. 174, 175, UN Doc. ST/LEG/SER.C/21 (1983).

[83] See, for example, the lengthy procedural debate on the proposal to admit 'Palestine' to the WHO: WHA42/1989/REC/2, pp. 231–255 (1989).

[84] UN GAOR, 3rd Committee, 6th Session, 379th Meeting, paras. 58–69, UN Doc. A/C.3/6/SR.379 (1952).

[85] *Ibid.* at para. 66.

[86] UN GAOR, Special Political Committee, 14th Session, 138th Meeting, para. 28, UN Doc. A/SPC/SR.138 (1959).

[87] Summary Records of the 1978 Hamburg Conference on Carriage by Sea, UN Doc. A/CONF.89/C.2/SR.6, p. 6, para. 29 (1978).

[88] *Ibid.* at para. 30. The Summary Records do not state if in fact any action was taken on the motion for closure.

with the practice followed heretofore, be allowed to speak in order to withdraw or revise his amendment or in exercise of the right of reply'.[89] No objection was made to the Chairman's statement.

9.2.7 *Explanation of Vote after Closure of Debate*

As a general practice, presiding officers in the UNGA have allowed representatives to explain their vote notwithstanding the adoption of a motion to close the debate.[90] Allowing explanation of votes, after the adoption of a motion for closure, is the correct practice, since closure of debate does not prevent voting and explanation of vote is by now considered, for the most part, to be a stage in the voting process. In an opinion, written in 1983, the UN Office of Legal Affairs stated that 'it should be understood that explanations of vote are not part of the debate and that, therefore, the prior closure of debate does not affect the power of the President to permit explanations of vote'.[91]

It is submitted, however, that it is appropriate to restrict explanations to explanations after the vote and not before the vote. The Chairman of a committee of the UNGA, at its 1958 session, commented in this regard that explanations given before the vote would tend to be a reopening of the debate that had been closed.[92] According to Rule 88 of the UNGA rules of procedure, the President 'may permit members to explain their votes, either before or after the voting'. This rule would allow the President, where there has been a closure of debate, to confine explanations to after the vote. Rule 55 of the UN Model Rules, however, states, 'Representatives may make brief statements consisting solely of explanations of vote, before the voting has commenced or after the voting has been completed.' The UN Model Rules by implication grant the discretion to the representative and, unlike the situation in the UNGA, not to the presiding officer. It may

[89] Official Records of the 1975 Vienna Conference on Representation of States, 41st Meeting of the Committee of the Whole, para. 35, p. 313, UN Doc. A/CONF.67/C.1/SR.41 (1975).

[90] UN GAOR, Plenary, 5th Session, 303rd Meeting, para. 164, UN Doc. A/PV.303 (1950); UN GAOR, 2nd Committee, 23rd Session, 1240th Meeting, para. 93, UN Doc. A/C.2/23/SR.1240 (1968); UN GAOR, 4th Committee, 20th Session, 1544th Meeting, paras. 64–65, UN Doc. A/C.4/20/SR.1544 (1965); UN GAOR, 3rd Committee, 20th Session, 1312th Meeting, para. 28, UN Doc. A/C.3/20/SR.1312 (1965).

[91] Memorandum, 10 November 1983, from Office of Legal Affairs to the Under-Secretary-General for Political and General Assembly Affairs. 1983 UN Jur. Y.B. 174, 176, UN Doc. ST/LEG/SER.C/21 (1983).

[92] UN GAOR, 4th Committee, 13th Session, 781st Meeting, para. 38, UN Doc. A/C.4/13/SR.781 (1958).

be that this outcome is inadvertent since it would appear to be logical to grant this discretion to the presiding officer and not to representatives.

9.2.8 *Right to Complete a Statement after Closure of Debate*

At a 1981 meeting of a committee of the UNGA, a motion for closure of debate was moved during a statement being made by the representative of India. The Indian representative claimed that the wording of the rule of procedure (Rule 75) did not stipulate that a motion for closure prevented completion of a previously commenced statement. The Chairman ruled that the Indian representative could complete his statement only with the agreement of the mover of the motion for closure.[93]

At a 1980 meeting of the World Health Assembly, the representative of China moved the closure of debate. The representative of the USSR stated, 'I began speaking on behalf of my delegation and was interrupted. It strikes me that one should let the speaker finish his speech, and then reach a decision on the official motion to close the debate.'[94] The President ruled, 'When a point of order is raised, the President may stop the speaker and give the floor to the delegate raising the point of order. However, as this is a matter that is left to my judgement, I give the floor to the delegate of the USSR to continue his statement. After that, I will not permit anybody else to speak on this question.'[95]

At a 1988 meeting of the World Health Assembly, the representative of Jordan, on a point of order, moved the closure of the debate while the representative of Israel was speaking. The President allowed the Israel representative to conclude his statement, 'as the speaker is about to conclude and we shall then put the resolution to vote'.[96] When the President then gave the floor to another speaker, the representative of Jordan reminded the President that he had moved the closure of the debate and his proposal 'must take precedence over any other statement'.[97] The Legal Counsel then intervened to confirm that, in view of the motion for closure, 'if anyone

[93] UN GAOR, 3rd Committee, 36th Session, 55th Meeting, para. 122, UN Doc. A/C.3/36/SR.55 (1981).

[94] Verbatim Records of the 5th Plenary Meeting of the 33rd World Health Assembly, p. 102, WHA33/1980/REC/2 (1980).

[95] *Ibid.*

[96] Verbatim Records of the 14th Plenary Meeting of the 41st World Health Assembly, p. 307, WHA41/1988/REC/2 (1988).

[97] *Ibid.*

asks for the floor it can be given only to two speakers to speak against closure'.[98]

9.2.9 *Speakers Who Had Requested the Floor before the Closure of Debate*

Closure applies to speakers who were already inscribed on the list of speakers when the motion for closure was adopted. The UN Office of Legal Affairs stated its opinion, in 1983, that, after a motion for closure has been adopted, '[n]o exceptions may be made, even for representatives already on the list of speakers'.[99]

At a plenary meeting of the 1974–1977 Geneva Humanitarian Law Conference, a motion for closure was moved. The President stated that 'only one more speaker was on the list of speakers; he would call on him and then immediately deal with the motion'.[100]

At a 1963 meeting of the UNGA, a speaker took the floor on a point of order, stating that she had requested the floor before the closure of debate. The Chairman allowed the speaker to make her statement.[101]

These examples appear, however, to be the exception, rather than the rule.

The Standing Orders of the Conference of the ILO state,

> The President shall put a motion for the closure of the discussion if it is supported by at least 30 delegates. Before putting it to the vote, however, he shall call out the names of those delegates who had signified their wish to speak before the closure had been moved.[102]

At the 1955 Conference of the ILO, a motion for closure was approved.[103] The President subsequently gave the floor to a speaker who had been on the list and this decision was disputed. The President ruled that his 'interpretation of the Standing Orders, after having consulted the experts from

[98] *Ibid.*

[99] Memorandum, 10 November 1983, from Office of Legal Affairs to the Under-Secretary-General for Political and General Assembly Affairs. 1983 UN Jur. Y.B. 174, 175, UN Doc. ST/LEG/SER.C/21 (1983).

[100] Official Records of the 1974–1977 Geneva Humanitarian Law Conference, CDDH/SR.51, vol. VII, p. 116, para. 74.

[101] UN GAOR, 3rd Committee, 18th Session, 1278th Meeting, para. 28, UN Doc. A/C.3/18/SR.1278 (1963).

[102] Article 16(2) of the Standing Orders of the Conference of the International Labour Organisation, International Labour Office, Geneva, December 1992.

[103] ILO Conference, 38th Session, Geneva 1955, Record of Proceedings, 30th sitting, p. 492.

the office, is that when the list of speakers is read out it is to indicate to the Conference that these speakers will speak.'[104]

At the 1956 Conference of the ILO, a delegate claimed that those speakers who were on the list read out by the President were entitled to address the Conference even after the closure had been voted.[105] The President ruled, however, that nobody could speak, after closure, except on a point of order.[106] At the 1960 Conference of the ILO, the President ruled in a similar vein that 'once having moved the closure motion, no speaker, even though he may have been on the list of speakers before the motion was put, can speak.'[107]

At the 1975 Conference of the ILO, a motion for closure was moved. The President read out the names of the speakers who were on the list after which the motion for closure was approved. The President then proceeded immediately to a vote, no delegation claiming that the speakers who had already been inscribed on the list were entitled to speak after the closure motion had been passed.[108]

The rule in meetings of committees of the ILO Conference, as opposed to the rule in plenary meetings, is that the President 'shall read out the names of those persons who have already signified their wish to speak and they shall still have the right to speak after the closure has been voted.'[109]

9.2.10 Right of Proposer, after Closure of Debate, to Introduce a Previously Submitted Proposal

The UN Office of Legal Affairs gave an opinion, in 1983, in relation to proposals that had been submitted but not formally introduced prior to a motion for closure, that 'there are even precedents for permitting the principal sponsor to make a statement introducing such a proposal (particularly if the sponsors of other proposals had an opportunity to introduce these before the debate was closed).'[110]

[104] *Ibid.* at p. 493. [105] *Ibid.*, 39th Session, 1956, p. 429.

[106] *Ibid.* at pp. 429, 430. [107] *Ibid.*, 44th Session, 1960, 22nd sitting, p. 380.

[108] *Ibid.*, 60th Session, 1975, p. 252.

[109] Article 64(2) of the Standing Orders of the Organisation of the International Labour Organisation, International Labour Office, Geneva, December 1992.

[110] Memorandum, 10 November 1983, from Office of Legal Affairs to the Under-Secretary-General for Political and General Assembly Affairs. 1983 UN Jur. Y.B. 174, 175, UN Doc. ST/LEG/SER.C/21 (1983).

9.2.11 Right of Proposer to Reply to Questions after Closure of Debate

At a 1973 meeting of the ICAO Assembly, the representative of the Netherlands, 'pointing out that a number of delegations had asked questions, said that it would be unjust to close the debate before he had had an opportunity to reply'.[111] The Chairman replied that 'closure of the debate did not prevent a sponsor from clarifying his proposal'. After the motion for closure had been adopted, the Chairman 'invited the Delegate of the Kingdom of the Netherlands to reply to the questions on his proposal'.[112] This is a unique interpretation of the effect of a motion for closure. At the 1958 Law of the Sea Conference, after a motion for closure had been adopted, the Chairman refused to allow the Special Rapporteur of the ILC to give an explanation of a text, although the explanation had been requested prior to the motion for closure.[113]

9.2.12 Right to Propose Procedural Motions after Closure of Debate

At a 1949 meeting of the UNGA, after a motion to close the debate had been adopted, the Chairman refused to allow a motion for adjourning the vote, stating, inter alia, that there was no such procedural motion in the rules of procedure.[114]

This ruling appears to be incorrect in so far as it implies prohibition of all procedural motions after closure of debate. There does not appear to be any basis for a blanket prohibition of procedural motions and points of order once a debate is closed. The time period for such motions is, however, limited since, after closure of debate, 'the motion shall be immediately put to the vote'.[115] Once the presiding officer has announced the commencement of voting, only those points of order that are 'in connection with the actual conduct of voting'[116] are admissible. The UN Office of Legal Affairs gave its opinion, in 1983, that:

[111] Minutes of the 10th Meeting of the Executive Committee of the Extraordinary 20th Session of the ICAO Assembly, para. 18, ICAO Doc. 9088 A20-Min. EX/10 (1973).

[112] *Ibid.* at paras. 18, 22.

[113] Official Records of the 1958 Law of the Sea Conference, Committee I, vol. III, p. 192, paras. 39–42, UN Doc. A/CONF.13/39 (1958).

[114] UN GAOR, 6th Committee, 4th Session, 194th Meeting, paras. 87–88, UN Doc. A/C.6/4/SR.194 (1949).

[115] Rule 75 of the UNGA rules of procedure.

[116] Rule 88 of the UNGA rules of procedure.

> Normal procedural motions or manoeuvres . . . such as the withdrawal of a proposal as well as its immediate reintroduction; the division of a proposal; a motion that there be no vote on a proposal after another has been acted on; are permitted even after closure of debate. The same should be held of a motion to adjourn the debate (for the purpose of putting aside one or more proposals) or of one addressed to an issue of competence.[117]

9.2.13 Submission of Amendments after Closure of Debate

At a 1949 meeting of the UNGA, the question arose as to whether amendments to a resolution could be submitted after closure of debate. The Chairman ruled that he would put to the vote only those amendments that had been before the Committee when closure had been moved.[118]

It is not, however, readily apparent if closure of debate should also automatically mean closure of the possibility of submitting amendments. At a 1980 meeting of the UNGA, the Chairman ruled that, 'although the debate on the draft resolution was already closed, delegations were entitled to introduce amendments before it was announced that the process of voting had begun'.[119]

At a meeting of the 1974–1977 Geneva Humanitarian Law Conference, a motion for closure was moved. The representative of Saudi Arabia said that 'he would like the [oral] amendment he had suggested to be put to the vote before a vote was taken on the motion for closure of the debate'.[120] The President responded that 'he wished to deal first with the procedural motion; the point raised by Saudi Arabia would be considered after the vote on the motion'.[121] The motion for closure was adopted, and the President invited the Saudi Arabian representative to present his amendment. The US representative then pointed out 'that there was some confusion. In his opinion, the effect of the motion for closure of the debate was to stop the consideration of any amendment' and the Article 'should be put to the

[117] Memorandum, 10 November 1983, from Office of Legal Affairs to the Under-Secretary-General for Political and General Assembly Affairs. 1983 UN Jur. Y.B. 174, 175, UN Doc. ST/LEG/SER.C/21 (1983). (The numbers of the relevant UNGA rules of procedure have been omitted from the quotation.)

[118] UN GAOR, 1st Committee, 4th Session, 292nd Meeting, para. 33, UN Doc. A/C.1/4/SR.292 (1949).

[119] UN GAOR, 3rd Committee, 35th Session, 74th Meeting, para. 7, UN Doc. A/C.3/35/SR.74 (1980).

[120] Official Records of the 1974–1977 Geneva Humanitarian Law Conference, CDDH/SR.51, vol. VII, p. 117, para. 78.

[121] *Ibid.* at para. 79.

vote'.[122] After a discussion, the meeting was adjourned. By the next meeting the oral amendment had been submitted in writing, and the President ruled that the amendment could be put to the vote despite the closure of debate.[123]

9.2.14 *Submission of Sub-Amendments after Closure of Debate*

At a 1952 meeting of the UNGA, after the closure of the debate, the Chairman refused to allow the Soviet representative to submit an oral sub-amendment to a Saudi Arabian amendment.[124]

9.2.15 *Closure of Debate and Revision of Amendments*

At a 1962 meeting of the UNGA, the Chairman allowed representatives to revise amendments they had previously submitted, although a motion for closure of debate had been adopted.[125]

At a 1980 meeting of the UNGA, after a motion for closure of debate had been passed, the Chairman allowed the US delegation to revise amendments it had submitted.[126]

At the 1975 Vienna Conference on Representation of States, the Chairman said that 'even if the motion for closure was carried the sponsor of each amendment would, in accordance with the practice followed heretofore, be allowed to speak in order to withdraw or revise his amendment'.[127]

9.2.16 *Closure of Debate before Its Commencement*

At a 1948 meeting of the UNGA, the Chairman ruled that a motion of closure applied to discussion on an amendment previously submitted to

122 *Ibid.* at para. 84.

123 Official Records of the 1974–1977 Geneva Humanitarian Law Conference, CDDH/SR.52, vol. VII, p. 125, para. 1.

124 UN GAOR, 3rd Committee, 6th Session, 412th Meeting, para. 11, UN Doc. A/C.3/6/SR.412 (1952).

125 UN GAOR, 4th Committee, 16th Session, 1301st Meeting, paras. 10, 11, 13, UN Doc. A/C.4/16/SR.1301 (1962).

126 UN GAOR, 3rd Committee, 35th Session, 73rd Meeting, para. 40, UN Doc. A/C.3/35/SR.73 (1980).

127 Official Records of the 1975 Vienna Conference on Representation of States, 42nd Meeting of the Committee of the Whole, vol. I, p. 313, para. 35, UN Doc. A/CONF.67/18 (1975).

the resolution in question, although there had been no discussion at all of the amendment.[128]

At a 1961 meeting of the UNGA, a delegate requested closure of debate prior to the beginning of the debate. The delegate accepted the proposal of the Chairman that he postpone submitting the motion for closure until the Committee began to debate the resolution in question.[129]

9.2.17 *Closure of Debate on Points of Order*

At a committee meeting of the 1977 Conference on Territorial Asylum, when a representative moved the closure of debate, the Chairman ruled that 'the debate could not be closed as delegations were at present speaking on points of order'.[130]

[128] UN GAOR, 3rd Committee, 3rd Session, Part I, 160th Meeting, p. 713, UN Doc. A/C.3/3/SR.160 (1948).

[129] UN GAOR, 1st Committee, 16th Session, 1179th Meeting, para. 43, UN Doc. A/C.1/16/SR.1179 (1961).

[130] Summary Records of the 6th Meeting of Committee 1 of the UN Conference on Territorial Asylum, para. 24, UN Doc. A/CONF.78/C.1/SR.6 (1977).

10

Amendments

10.1 Distinguishing between Separate Proposals and Amendments

In view of the practical importance of the difference between separate proposals and amendments in determining the order of voting, at times lengthy procedural debates develop on the question whether a suggested action is a proposal or an amendment.

The rules of procedure of the UNGA define an amendment as follows:

> *Rule 90*
>
> *Voting on Amendments*
>
> A motion is considered an amendment to a proposal if it merely adds to, deletes from or revises part of the proposal.

The UN Model Rules definition is similar, but adds the phrase, 'Unless specified otherwise, the word "proposal" in these rules shall be considered as including amendments'.[1]

> *Rule 58*
>
> *Amendments*
>
> 1. A proposal is considered an amendment to another proposal if it merely adds to, deletes from or revises part of that proposal.

A similar phrase appears in the rules of procedure of all the conferences examined.

The rules of procedure of the Assembly of the ICAO state, regarding this issue:

[1] UN Model Rules of Procedure, Rule 48 UN Doc. A/37/163, Annex (1982).

Rule 50

> The presiding officer shall determine whether a proposed amendment is so related to the motion as to constitute a proper amendment thereto, or whether it must be considered as an alternative or substitute motion.[2]

Hovey, writing in 1950, stated,

> An amendment, however, which is too far removed in substance from the original, cannot properly be treated as an amendment at all. There is ample precedent for the view that a proposal – whether or not submitted as an amendment – will be treated as a separate proposition if it would either radically alter the original or eliminate for that session the possibility of voting on the original.[3]

The leading treatise on British parliamentary procedure defines an amendment as 'a subsidiary motion . . . upon another motion which interposes a new cycle of debate and decision between the proposal and decision of the main motion and question'.[4]

At the 1958 Law of the Sea Conference, the delegate of Ceylon stated that in his opinion an 'amendment' 'meant a positive suggestion for an interpolation or addition to, or for a deletion from, an original text' and not 'new texts which lay outside the Committee's terms of reference'.[5]

The Chairman of a committee of the 1958 Law of the Sea Conference (Bailey) defined the difference between an amendment and a proposal by stating that a proposal was 'a suggestion or idea relating to a subject matter not found in any of the [International Law] Commission's articles'; as to an amendment, 'it would not matter if [it] purported to replace the entire article or merely to add to, delete or revise individual words or phrases. Anything designed to effect an alteration in an anterior text would be regarded as an amendment.'[6] Bailey's allowing of an amendment to 'replace the entire article' ostensibly contradicts Rule 40 of the rules of procedure of that Conference, which referred to an amendment as deleting or revising

[2] The third sentence of Rule 50 of the standing rules of procedure of the Assembly of ICAO, ICAO Doc. 7600/5, 5th edn (1990). This rule also appears in the rules of procedure of International Air Conferences convened by ICAO.

[3] Allan Hovey Jr, 'Voting Procedure in the General Assembly', 4 *UNESCO International Organization* 412 (1950 No. 1) at 424.

[4] *Erskine May's Treatise on the Law, Privileges, Proceedings and Usage of Parliament*, eds. Sir Donald Limon and W. R. McKay, 22nd edn (1997) p. 343.

[5] Official Records of the 1958 Law of the Sea Conference, Committee IV, vol. VI, p. 39, para. 9, UN Doc. A/CONF.13/42 (1958).

[6] *Ibid.*, 25th Meeting of Committee I, vol. III, p. 74, UN Doc. A/CONF.13/39 (1958).

'a part' of a proposal. However, presumably Bailey treated the ILC text as the proposal and regarded any proposed correction as an amendment.

10.1.1 Definition by the Legal Counsel of the UN as to the Difference between Amendments and Separate Proposals

At a 1948 meeting of the UNGA, the Legal Counsel of the UN gave his opinion that a motion to delete or replace an article was a separate proposal and not an amendment.[7]

During a 1976 meeting of the UNGA, the Legal Counsel of the UN was requested to submit an opinion as to the difference between an amendment and a separate proposal. The opinion submitted stated,

> [R]ule 130 defined an amendment as something which added to, deleted from or revised part of an existing proposal. The definition set out in rule 130 was a technical one and there was no reason why an amendment might not have as its purpose to change completely part of the original proposal. There was no requirement that an amendment must be in agreement with the substance of the original proposal or that its purpose must be limited solely to adding details or specifications. If the changes proposed to a paragraph did not affect the substance of other paragraphs, it would seem that such changes constituted an amendment. However if a proposed change, although relating to a single paragraph, would deprive the other paragraphs of their meaning, it would not constitute an amendment.[8]

At a1986 meeting of the UNGA, the Legal Counsel was requested to give his opinion as to whether a proposal was an amendment or a separate proposal. The Legal Counsel stated that 'the heading under which a motion was submitted was not the deciding factor in categorising a motion as an amendment or a proposal. A motion submitted as an amendment could be a proposal and vice versa.'[9]

[7] UN GAOR, 6th Committee, 3rd Session, Part I, 105th Meeting, p. 451, UN Doc. A/C.6/3/SR.105 (1948).

[8] UN GAOR, 5th Committee, 31st Session, 41st Meeting, para. 108, UN Doc. A/C.5/31/SR.41 (1976). For an earlier definition by Mr Kerno, Assistant Secretary-General in charge of the legal department, quoting inter alia from his statement at A/C.6/SR.102 (1948), see UN GAOR, 6th Committee, 4th Session, 150th Meeting, paras. 17, 18, UN Doc. A/C.6/SR.150 (1949).

[9] UN GAOR, 2nd Committee, 41st Session, 33rd Meeting, para. 15, UN Doc. A/C.2/41/SR.33 (1986).

10.1.2 Practice Regarding Distinguishing between Amendments and Separate Proposals

It is difficult to ascertain any consistency in decisions as to the difference between amendments and separate proposals.

The UNGA, at its 1948 session, discussed the refusal of the Security Council to recommend the admission of Ceylon to the UN. Australia submitted a proposal for the admission of Ceylon, requesting that the Security Council reconsider its decision. Poland submitted an amendment omitting all the reasons Australia had submitted for Ceylon being admitted. The Chairman ruled that the Polish resolution was a separate proposal and not an amendment. The ruling was presumably based on the fact that the Polish amendment proposed making changes in the operative paragraph and every preambular paragraph of the Australian proposal.[10]

The UNGA, at its 1949 session, considered a Latin American proposal that the Interim Committee examine Soviet threats to China. The Philippines proposed an amendment repeating nearly all of the language of the Latin American proposal, but adding that the examination should also include Soviet 'violations'. The Chairman ruled that the Philippine amendment was an amendment and not a separate proposal.[11]

The issue arose at a meeting of the 1958 Law of the Sea Conference. During the debate on a US amendment, the delegate of Saudi Arabia stated that, under the terms of the rules of procedure, 'the revised United States proposal did not constitute an amendment; it did not merely add to, delete from, or revise part of the International Law Commission's text; it completely altered its structure; it therefore constituted a separate proposal'.[12] The Chairman ruled that 'the revised United States proposal constituted an amendment'.[13] One must assume that, since the Chairman did not attempt to refute the Saudi Arabian contention, the Chairman considered that an amendment may alter the structure of a proposal. The Chairman's ruling on the Saudi Arabian point of order was not challenged.

[10] UN GAOR, Ad Hoc Political Committee, 3rd Session, 22nd Meeting, pp. 261, 262, UN Doc. A/AC.24/SR.22 (1948).

[11] UN GAOR, 1st Committee, 4th Session, 343rd Meeting, paras. 40, 43, 45, 46, UN Doc. A/C.1/4/SR.343 (1949).

[12] Official Records of the 1958 Law of the Sea Conference, 31st Meeting of Committee I, vol. III, p. 92, para. 44, UN Doc. A/CONF.13/39 (1958).

[13] *Ibid.* at p. 92, para. 46.

In the Plenary of the same Conference, the reverse discussion took place. The Danish representative proposed a text to be adopted only 'in the event of the text proposed by the First Committee . . . not being adopted'.[14] The delegate of the Soviet Union 'speaking on a point of order said that the Danish proposal was in fact not a proposal but an amendment'.[15] The President drew attention to the fact that the Danish proposal was intended as an alternative text if the text approved by the First Committee were not adopted.[16] The Chairman later ruled that 'the Danish document had been submitted as a proposal and not as an amendment and that the text approved by the First Committee must therefore be voted on first according to the usual practice'.[17] This would appear to be a correct decision since the Danish text was an alternative to the Committee's text.

At the 1963 Tokyo Air Law Conference, the representative of Greece submitted a proposal that was identical to an earlier proposal made by Switzerland, except that it omitted a phrase referring to types of acts or offences committed on board an aircraft. The Greek representative requested that it be voted on as a separate proposal.[18] The Secretary-General of the Conference pointed out that, in substance, the proposal in question was an amendment to a previous proposal, and 'procedurally, the easiest way of proceeding would be for it to be moved and seconded'.[19] The President consequently ruled that the Greek proposal was 'a proposal for amending the Swiss proposal'[20] and should be voted on as such. No delegation challenged the ruling.

At the 1974–1977 Geneva Humanitarian Law Conference, the practice was that when a draft article was referred to a working group, all the amendments to that article were referred with it to the working group. The First Committee decided to refer draft Article 78, dealing with extradition, to a working group. A disagreement arose as to whether a Soviet proposal for an Article 78 *bis*, which dealt with the conditions of detainment of certain convicted prisoners, was an amendment to Article 78 and hence should also be referred to the working group. The Soviet representative argued that 'article 78 *bis* was simply an addition or a kind of appendix to article 78 and that it was therefore unnecessary to vote on whether

[14] Official Records of the 1958 Law of the Sea Conference, 20th Plenary Meeting, vol. II, p. 66, para. 18, UN Doc. A/CONF.13/18 (1958).

[15] *Ibid.* at para. 22. [16] *Ibid.* at para. [17] *Ibid.* at para. 25.

[18] ICAO International Conference on Air Law, Tokyo, 1963, vol. I, Minutes of 6th Plenary Meeting, ICAO Doc. 8565-LC/152–1, p. 65, para. 56.

[19] *Ibid.* at para. 57. [20] *Ibid.*

it should be referred to [a] working group'.[21] The Legal Secretary of the Conference, who was consulted, gave his opinion that Article 78 *bis* was 'a new article'.[22] After a lengthy debate, the Committee put to the vote the question whether the proposal for an Article 78 *bis* should be referred to a working group. The proposal for referral was rejected.[23]

A 1973 ICAO meeting discussed an Anglo-Swiss proposal on the issue of the ICAO Council taking action against States supporting air piracy. The Chairman ruled that a proposed amendment by Sudan, which required that such a decision be made by a two-thirds majority of the ICAO Assembly, differed in substance so much from the Anglo-Swiss proposal that it was in fact a separate proposal. The Chairman's decision was upheld on a challenge.[24]

The 1978 Vienna Conference on Succession of States in Respect of Treaties debated how many ratifications would be required to bring the draft convention into force. The Soviet delegate raised a point of order stating that 'the Conference did not have before it a basic proposal by the Drafting Committee and three amendments to that proposal, but rather four independent proposals concerning the number of ratifications'.[25] The President ruled that 'the proposals made during the discussion were amendments in that they sought to amend a figure established by the Drafting Committee. The Conference should therefore vote first on the amendment which was substantively farthest removed from the original proposal.'[26] The President went on to explain, 'For motions submitted during the discussion to be considered as independent proposals, they would have to be unrelated to other proposals; but the motions under discussion were concerned simply with figures which were meaningful only in relation to the Drafting Committee's proposal . . . What the Drafting Committee had submitted to the Conference was a proposal, and what had been submitted during the discussion were amendments to that proposal.'[27]

21 Official Records of the 1974–1977 Geneva Humanitarian Law Conference, CDDH/I/SR.55, vol. IX, p. 184, para. 38.

22 *Ibid.* at p. 185, para. 48. 23 *Ibid.* at p. 187, para. 67.

24 Minutes of the 6th Meeting of the Executive Committee of the 20th Extraordinary Session of the ICAO Assembly, p. 55, para. 3, ICAO Doc. A20-Min.EX/6 (1973).

25 Official Records of the 1978 Vienna Conference on Succession of States in Respect of Treaties (Resumed Session), vol. II, p. 16, Summary Records of the 13th Plenary Meeting, para. 46, UN Doc. A/CONF.80.

26 *Ibid.* at para. 47. 27 *Ibid.* at para. 49.

During the 1983 Vienna Conference on State Property (Succession), a representative proposed, orally, the deletion of a whole paragraph,[28] and the Chairman called for an immediate vote on the proposal. Several delegations explained that their position on the deletion would depend on decisions proposed for changes in the paragraph and requested prior voting on such changes. A delegate, speaking on a point of order, argued that 'the Chairman had given a ruling and that the only procedurally correct course of action was either to vote on the proposal [to delete the paragraph] or else to challenge the Chairman's ruling formally'.[29] No such challenge was made and a vote was taken, resulting in the proposal being adopted and the paragraph in question being deleted. The records do not elaborate the considerations of the Chairman, though presumably he chose to see the proposal for deletion as a separate proposal and then used his discretion, unchallenged, to give it precedence in voting.

At a 2013 meeting of the IMCO Marine Environment Protection Committee, the Legal Office gave its opinion that where documents referred to a previous document and suggested 'adding to, deleting from or revising the original proposal', they should be treated as amendments and not proposals.[30]

10.1.3 Can an Amendment Call for the Removal of the Substance of a Proposal?

The UNGA, at its 1952 session, debated a Polish proposal dealing with economic development. The Polish delegation argued that a US amendment calling for the omission of a paragraph relating to long-term trade agreements would remove the substance of the Polish proposal and was not an amendment, but a separate proposal. The Chairman ruled that nevertheless he considered it an amendment.[31]

At a 1957 meeting of the UNGA, Canada, Chile, Denmark and Norway submitted an amendment to a Greek draft resolution on the question of

[28] Summary Records of the 1983 Vienna Conference on State Property (Succession), 39th Meeting of the Committee of the Whole, p. 244, para. 4, UN Doc. A/CONF.117/C.1/SR.39 (1983).

[29] *Ibid.* at para. 13.

[30] Legal Opinion of the Legal Office of IMCO in reference to documents MEPC 66/6/3, MEPC66/6/6 and MEPC 66/6/10. On file with the author.

[31] UN GAOR, 2nd Committee, 6th Session, 173rd Meeting, paras. 2–7, 18, UN Doc. A/C.2/6/SR.173 (1952).

Cyprus. The amendment called for the replacement of the reference to self-determination[32] with a reference to reaching a solution in conformity with the UN Charter.[33] The Egyptian delegation argued that the 'amendments completely altered the Greek draft resolution [197] and were therefore contrary to the provisions of Rule 131 of the Rules of Procedure'.[34] The Syrian representative argued that 'the so-called amendments' were submitted as amendments 'in order to avoid application of Rule 132 and to obtain priority for it in the vote' (Rule 132 related to the order of voting on proposals).[35] The Chairman decided to put the four-Power amendment to the vote before voting on the Greek draft resolution, thus by implication accepting the four-Power amendment as a valid amendment.[36]

At a 1967 meeting of the UNGA, a proposal to delete the crucial provision from a resolution on Korea was nevertheless treated by the Committee as an amendment.[37]

At the 1989 World Health Assembly, Algeria and others submitted a proposal to admit the 'State of Palestine' to the WHO. Tonga and others submitted a resolution in effect calling for the deferment of the issue. Nicaragua then submitted an amendment to the Tongalese proposal adding several paragraphs, including one that read 'decides to admit the State of Palestine as a member of WHO'. The Nicaraguan text was thus diametrically opposed to the Tongalese proposal. A debate followed about whether the Nicaraguan text was an amendment or a separate proposal. The Assembly decided not to vote on 'any amendments' to the Tongalese proposal, by implication therefore accepting the Nicaraguan text as an amendment.[38]

[32] UN Doc. A/C.1/L.197 (1957). [33] UN Doc. A/C.1/L.199 (1957).

[34] UN GAOR, 1st Committee, 12th Session, 933rd Meeting, para. 19, UN Doc. A/C.1/SR.933 (1957).

[35] UN GAOR, 1st Committee, 12th Session, 934th Meeting, para. 24, UN Doc. A/C.1/SR.934 (1957).

[36] *Ibid.* at paras. 52–55. The Greek delegation submitted a sub-amendment to the four-Power amendment that in fact called for reinstalling its original proposal. The Chairman decided that the Committee should vote on the Greek sub-amendment before voting on the four-Power amendment. The Chairman's ruling thus negated the tactical advantage that, as the Syrian delegate pointed out, would have been obtained by the four-Power amendment.

[37] UN GAOR, 1st Committee, 22nd Session, 1511th Meeting, para. 115, UN Doc. A/C.1/22/SR.1511 (1967); UN GAOR, 1st Committee, 22nd Session, 1514th Meeting, para. 85, UN Doc. A/C.1/22/SR.1514 (1967).

[38] Verbatim Records of the 10th Plenary Meeting, WHA/42/1989/REC/2, pp. 231–255 (1989).

10.1.4 Can an Amendment Call for Deferment of Discussion?

At the 1974–1977 Geneva Humanitarian Law Conference, discussions were held concerning Article 1, which dealt, inter alia, with the scope of the proposed Protocol regarding wars of national liberation. The Canadian delegation submitted a proposal that the issue of wars of national liberation be deferred for discussion to an inter-sessional working group. The Chairman ruled that the Canadian document 'contained an entirely new proposal, which went beyond the scope of Article 1', and that the Committee should 'consider "amendments" to Article 1 instead of continuing to discuss the [Canadian] Resolution'.[39] The ruling was not challenged.

At a 1950 meeting of the UNGA, discussion took place on a joint resolution on the draft convention on freedom of information. The Chairman ruled that a US amendment that called for indefinite postponement of the issue was nevertheless an amendment and not a new proposal.[40]

At a 1972 meeting of the UNGA, the Democratic Yemen delegation submitted an amendment to the title of a resolution. The amendment proposed changing the title of the resolution to the effect that the issue involved should be deferred to the next session of the UNGA. The Legal Counsel to the UN gave his opinion that such an amendment was a new proposal and should be dealt with as such and not as an amendment. The delegation of Democratic Yemen accepted the Legal Counsel's opinion.[41]

10.1.5 Can an Amendment Call for Taking No Decision on a Committee Report?

At the 1959 session of the ILO Conference, the United Kingdom presented an amendment to the majority report of the Credentials Committee. The amendment read, inter alia: 'Decides to take no decision at its present session regarding the credentials of the Government of Hungary'.[42] The representative of the United Arab Republic, and others, pointed out that this was a resolution and was 'irreceivable' as an amendment.[43] The President ruled, 'I do not find that the text of article 26, paragraph 7 [of the standing

[39] Official Records of the 1974–1977 Geneva Humanitarian Law Conference, CDDH/I/SR.13, vol. VIII, p. 98, para. 10.

[40] UN GAOR, 3rd Committee, 5th Session, 320th Meeting, para. 41, UN Doc. A/C.3/5SR.320 (1950).

[41] UN GAOR, Plenary, 27th Session, 2037th Meeting, paras. 221–223, 227, UN Doc. A/PV.2037 (1972).

[42] ILO Conference, 43rd Session, Geneva 1959, Record of Proceedings, 30th sitting, p. 499.

[43] *Ibid.* at pp. 493, 497.

orders] . . . excludes the submission of an amendment as now submitted.' A declaration that 'an amendment [is] irreceivable must rest on a quite sure and incontestable basis and, in my opinion, this is not the case here'.[44]

10.1.6 Can an Amendment Call for Referring an Issue to a Different Committee?

At a 1947 meeting of the UNGA, Poland proposed acceding to a request by the Jewish Agency to appear before the Plenary. The Chairman ruled that an amendment to the Polish proposal submitted by the United States, proposing that the Jewish Agency's request should be referred to the First Committee for its decision, was not an amendment, but a separate proposal.[45] The US did not challenge the Chairman's ruling.

At a 1948 meeting of the General Committee of the UNGA, the Secretary-General proposed that the so-called Russian Wives case be referred to the Sixth Committee. Chile proposed that it be referred to the Third Committee. The Chilean proposal was treated as an amendment to the proposal of the Secretary-General.[46]

At a 1960 meeting of the UNGA, the Assembly had before it a report of the General Committee, which recommended that an issue of disarmament be considered by the First Committee of the UNGA.[47] The Soviet delegation submitted a proposal that the issue be dealt with by the Plenary of the General Assembly and claimed that its proposal was an amendment to the proposal of the General Committee. The President ruled that the Soviet proposal was a new proposal and not an amendment and that therefore the General Committee's proposal should be voted on first.[48] The President's ruling was not challenged.

10.1.7 Can an Amendment Call for Deleting Some Existing Paragraphs, Revising Others and Adding a New Paragraph?

During the 1963 Vienna Conference on Consular Relations, the delegate for France claimed that a joint proposal, by Brazil and others,[49] could not

44 *Ibid.* at p. 499.

45 UN GAOR, General Committee, 1st Special Session, p. 125, UN Doc. A/BUR/PV.33 (1947).

46 UN GAOR, General Committee, 3rd Session, 44th Meeting, p. 21, UN Doc. A/BUR/SR.44 (1948).

47 UN Doc. A/4520.

48 UN GAOR, Plenary, 15th Session, 900th Meeting, paras. 241, 247–248, UN Doc. A/PV.900 (1960).

49 UN Doc. A/CONF.25/16L./168 Rev.1.

be considered an amendment because 'it would replace the whole of the International Law Commission's draft'.[50] The Chairman ruled that since, in addition to replacing three original paragraphs of the ILC draft and revising two others, it also *added a paragraph*, the joint proposal was an amendment and should therefore be voted on as such.[51] The Chairman's ruling was challenged and upheld by a narrow majority.

10.1.8 Can a Separate Proposal Be Transformed into an Amendment?

During the 1963 Vienna Conference on Consular Relations, a debate took place about the jurisdiction clause. The question arose whether a motion could at one stage be a proposal and then transform itself into an amendment. The situation was that Switzerland had proposed a text 'as a subsidiary text to meet the situation that would arise if the United States proposal were not adopted'.[52] The US proposal was adopted and Switzerland then withdrew its proposal but Yugoslavia resubmitted it. The US representative pointed out that the Swiss proposal had been submitted as an alternative to his and 'was quite incompatible with his proposal'. The UK representative said 'that it would be out of order to take a vote. The Swiss proposal, as reintroduced by the Yugoslav delegation, could only be regarded as an amendment to the United States proposal. Consequently if it were to be voted on at all it should have been voted on *before* the United States proposal itself.' The Chairman, however, ruled that the Swiss proposal remained a proposal and that 'both the United States text and the Swiss text had been treated as proposals and not as amendments' and that it was not an amendment.[53]

10.1.9 How Are Decisions Made Whether a Proposal Is an Amendment to Another Proposal?

In most of the cases where debate arises about whether a motion is a proposal or an amendment, the issue is decided by the presiding officer without giving a reasoned opinion for his decision.[54] The taking of the

[50] Official Records of the 1963 Vienna Conference on Consular Relations, 24th Meeting of Committee II, vol. I, p. 368, para. 2, UN Doc. A/CONF.25/16 (1963).

[51] *Ibid.* at para. 4.

[52] Official Records of the 1963 Vienna Conference on Consular Relations, 30th Meeting of Committee I, vol. I, p. 250, para. 46, UN Doc. A/CONF.25/16 (1963).

[53] *Ibid.*, 31st Meeting, p. 259, para. 32.

[54] See, for example, Official Records of the 1963 Vienna Conference on Consular Relations, 7th Meeting of Committee I, Vol. I, p. 124, para. 51, UN Doc. A/CONF.25 (1963); *Ibid.*, 11th Meeting, p. 153, para. 57.

decision by the presiding officer and not by the conference is the correct procedure, for there is no procedural motion before the conference. The issue is implicitly raised by the sponsors in their characterisation of the motion as either a proposal or an amendment. Should the issue be raised by another delegate, it can normally be only as a point of order requiring a presidential ruling.

The Chairman of the Sixth Committee of the UNGA, at its1948 session, decided to let the Committee decide by a vote whether a proposal was an amendment to another proposal.[55]

However, at the 1974–1977 Geneva Humanitarian Law Conference, the President, explaining that the Conference did not yet have rules of procedure, took the unusual step of referring the question as to whether a motion was a proposal or an amendment directly to the Conference, without first giving a ruling.[56]

10.1.10 Adoption of an Amendment by the Proposer

Most rules of procedure do not contain any specific reference to a situation where the proposer of the main proposal agrees to accept an amendment. If the agreement is reached before presentation, it can be incorporated in the original proposal and no procedural issue arises. Where the agreement by the proposer is made after presenting the proposal, the practice is for the chairman normally to treat it as an oral amendment by the proposer, and usually such an oral proposal is allowed. The World Health Assembly rules and those of WHO conferences, however, state explicitly:

> If an amendment to a proposal has been accepted by the original proposer, such an amendment shall be deemed to be an integral part of the original proposal and no separate vote shall be required thereon.[57]

10.1.11 Presenting an Amendment before Presenting the Resolution Itself

At a meeting of the 2002 World Health Assembly, the Chairman asked the proposers of amendments to present their amendments. When it was

[55] UN GAOR, 6th Committee, 3rd Session, 77th Meeting, p. 129, UN Doc. A/C.6/3/SR.77 (1948).

[56] Official Records of the 1974–1977 Geneva Humanitarian Law Conference, CDDH/SR.3, vol. V, p. 30, para. 47.

[57] Rule 67 of the rules of procedure of the World Health Assembly.

pointed out to him that the resolution itself had not yet been presented, he corrected himself and ruled that the draft resolution should be presented 'by the sponsors before the introduction of proposed amendments'.[58]

10.1.12 A Series of Amendments as a Package

At a meeting of the 2000 ILO Conference, the President proposed the unusual step of voting as a package on all amendments presented by one delegation. Since the delegation concerned agreed to the procedure, the value of the incident as a precedent is doubtful.[59]

10.2 An Inadvertent Oral Amendment

At the 1974–1977 Geneva Humanitarian Law Conference, the representative of the United Kingdom remarked, in a statement concerning neutral ships rescuing the shipwrecked, that 'he was therefore not sure that an article on the subject was really needed'.[60] The Chairman immediately ruled 'that he regarded the statement which the United Kingdom representative had just made as an oral amendment . . . the Committee would first vote on the United Kingdom oral amendment, which was furthest removed from the Article'.[61] Since the UK delegate did not demur, the Chairman may well have been correctly interpreting a British understatement.

10.3 Amendments to Procedural Motions

The UNGA rules of procedure and the UN Model Rules define an amendment as an amendment to a 'proposal',[62] therefore, by implication, not applying the rule on amendments to procedural motions. Nevertheless, some procedural motions are clearly amendable.

There is no clear pattern of precedents on this issue. At a 1957 meeting of the UNGA, Paraguay moved the adjournment of the debate to a date to be determined at the discretion of the President. The Syrian representative proposed an amendment to this motion by which the debate would be

[58] 55th World Health Assembly, Committee 'B', WHA55/2002/REC/3, p. 200 (2002).
[59] ILO Conference, 88th Session, 4th Report of the Selection Committee (2000).
[60] Official Records of the 1974–1977 Geneva Humanitarian Law Conference, CDDH/II/SR.59, vol. XII, p. 49, para. 72.
[61] *Ibid.* at para. 73.
[62] Rule 90 of the UNGA rules of procedure; Rule 58 of the UN Model Rules.

adjourned for a period not exceeding three days. The Syrian amendment was adopted by a vote, and then the amended Paraguayan motion was adopted.[63]

The Chairman of a committee of the UNGA, at its 1961 session, refused to allow an amendment of a procedural motion.[64]

COMMENT

It would appear that there are certain procedural motions that are not amenable to being amended. Among the procedural motions that cannot be amended are a motion to adjourn a meeting and a motion to close the debate. Other motions that apparently cannot be amended include a motion for a separate vote and a motion to reconsider a vote.

Motions to suspend a meeting or adjourn the debate are granted priority and debate is limited. Nevertheless, such motions can stipulate, explicitly or implicitly, the length of time of suspension or adjournment. It would appear that in such motions references to the length of time can be amended, although it is rare for this to be done.

There is no reason to prevent the submission of amendments to other motions that are procedural in character, such as motions referring issues to a committee or deferring discussion to a specified date.

10.4 Revising Amendments by Proposer

The UNGA rules of procedure and other rules of procedure do not explicitly provide for the revision of an amendment by the proposer. The Secretary of the First Committee at the 2012 UNGA stated, 'A revision normally comes from the sponsor of a draft resolution, while amendments normally are introduced by delegations that are not sponsors.'[65] Nevertheless, there does not appear to have been an objection raised to a delegation revising its amendment either at its own volition or by accepting a sub-amendment proposed by another delegation.[66]

[63] UN GAOR, Plenary, 12th Session, 708th Meeting, paras. 256–258, 268, 270, UN Doc. A/PV.708 (1957).

[64] UN GAOR, 1st Committee, 16th Session, 1176th Meeting, paras. 24–26, UN Doc. A/C.1/16/SR.1176 (1961).

[65] UN GAOR 1st Committee, 67th Session, 18th meeting, p. 13, UN Doc. A/C.1/67/PV.18 (2012).

[66] At the First Plenary Session of the UNGA, Thirtieth Meeting, the President commented that such a procedure was an exception. UN GAOR, Plenary, 1st Session, Part I, p. 439, UN Doc. A/PV.30 (1946).

At a 1988 meeting of the World Health Assembly, sponsors of a resolution concerning the Israel Occupied Territories submitted, without due notice, an amendment revising their proposal. The Legal Counsel of the WHO gave his opinion that it was a revision of the original proposal and that it was therefore 'not necessary to vote on the amendment submitted by the sponsors of the resolution and it might be considered that the Committee had a single revised text before it'.[67]

At the 1973 Assembly of the ICAO, the Israel representative expressed his hope that the sponsors of a proposal would accept an amendment suggested by Israel. The Chairman pointed out that 'it was not for the sponsors of the proposal . . . to accept or reject suggestions' since the article in question came from the Drafting Committee and thus the sponsors could no longer revise it.[68]

COMMENT

Conferences vote first on the amendment that is furthest removed from the original proposal. A substantive revision to an amendment, by its proposers, might therefore legitimately enable a delegation to question a previous decision as to the order of voting. This would, it is submitted, not be considered a reconsideration requiring a special majority.

10.5 Voting on an Amended Proposal

All rules of procedure require that where an amendment has been adopted, the amended proposal itself shall be put to the vote. The UNGA rules of procedure stipulate:

Rule 90[69]

> . . .
>
> If one or more amendments are adopted, the amended proposal shall be voted upon.

The UN Model Rule[70] is identical.

This rule has generated little controversy. However, at a 2003 meeting of the UNGA, a delegation argued that 'under rule 130 of the rules of

67 Summary Records of the 4th Meeting of Committee 'B' of the 41st World Health Assembly, p. 183, WHA41/1988/REC/3 (1988).

68 Minutes of the 14th Meeting of the 20th Extraordinary Assembly of ICAO, paras. 23, 24, ICAO Doc. 9088, A20-Min.EX/14 (1973).

69 Rule 130 in committees.

70 Model UN Rule 59, UN Doc. A/37/163, Annex (1982).

procedure, if the proposed amendments were adopted by a recorded vote, the draft resolution could not be adopted by consensus'.[71] No ruling was made on this issue but it would appear to be an incorrect contention, and the use of the phrase 'be voted on' in the Rule does not prohibit adoption by consensus.

At a meeting of the First Committee of the 2009 UNGA, a delegation argued that 'if an amendment is not adopted, one need not necessarily have a vote on a proposal'. The Chairman responded that 'a delegation has requested a vote on the draft resolution as a whole, so we have no other option than to proceed with a vote'.[72]

10.6. Submitting an Amendment after a Vote

At a 2008 UNGA Plenary Meeting two delegations objected to an oral amendment on the grounds that '[p]roposing an amendment when concerns have not been previously raised at any point in the Third Committee .... is highly irregular', and '[d]elegations then had an opportunity to express their views and present amendments, which they did not do'. The President did not respond to the objection and subsequently put the amendment to the vote.[73]

At another 2008 Plenary meeting of the UNGA, a delegate requested permission to propose an oral amendment after a vote had been taken on the proposal itself. The delegate explained that his delegation had informed the Secretariat that it had 'an oral amendment to propose' and 'we wanted to present it prior to the adoption of the decision', but his delegation 'was not seen'. The President ruled that 'the moment had passed', and the intervention 'can be considered to be an explanation of vote for the record of the meeting'.[74]

The rules of procedure of the 1995 NPT Review Conference stipulated,

> *Rule 28*
>
> (3)(h) A proposal [dealing with the extension of the NPT] may not be amended in accordance with Rule 24 [the rule dealing with amendments],

[71] UN GAOR, 3rd Committee, 58th Session, 59th Meeting, UN Doc. A/C.3/58/SR.59, p. 6 (2003).

[72] UN GAOR, 1st Committee, 64th Session, 23rd Meeting, p. 8, UN Doc. A/C.1/64/PV.23 (2009).

[73] UN GAOR, Plenary 63rd Session, 71st Meeting, p. 6, UN Doc. A/63/PV.71 (2008).

[74] UN GAOR, Plenary, 63rd Session, 104th Meeting, p. 2, UN Doc. A/63/PV.104 (2008).

> but may be revised or withdrawn by its sponsor(s) at any time except when a vote is in progress.[75]

This unusual rule was relevant in the context of the particular conference, which was a one-issue conference on the question of extending the duration of the NPT.

10.7 Sub-Amendments

The rules of procedure of the UNGA and of the conferences studied do not refer to sub-amendments. The practice, however, is that the rules applicable to amendments are also applied to sub-amendments.

The UN Model Rules proposes explicitly,

> *Rule 58*
> *Amendments*
> 2. Unless the Conference decides otherwise, amendments may be subject to sub-amendments, but the latter may not be subject to further amendment.[76]

During the 1958 Law of the Sea Conference, the representative of Chile stated that as a result of a sub-amendment 'the Committee had considered the Turkish amendment which was nearer to the original text before the US proposal which was the one further removed'.[77]

At the same 1958 conference, the representative of Saudi Arabia proposed that a Greek sub-amendment 'should not be incorporated in the Mexican text, because an obvious inconsistency would result if it were', and it should be treated as an independent proposal. The Chairman ruled the Saudi proposal to be 'out of order', explaining that 'he could not regard as an independent proposal a text which he had already ruled to be an amendment'.[78] The Chairman's ruling was challenged, but upheld on a vote.

At the 1975 Vienna Conference on Representation of States, the representative of Byelorussia stated that he objected to treating a Canadian amendment as a sub-amendment to the amendment of which he was

[75] Rule 28 of the rules of procedure of the 1995 NPT Review Conference, Doc. NPT/CONF.1995/28 (1995).

[76] UN Doc. A/37/163, Annex (1982).

[77] Official Records of the 1958 Law of the Sea Conference, 34th Meeting of Committee I, vol. III, p. 99, paras. 1–5, UN Doc. A/CONF.13/39 (1958).

[78] *Ibid.*, 35th Meeting, p. 102, paras. 2–13.

co-sponsor (the five-Power amendment).[79] The Byelorussian representative pointed out that 'the purpose of a sub-amendment to an amendment was always to clarify or supplement the text of an amendment whereas the Canadian proposal ran counter to the five-power amendment'.[80] The Chairman, however, refusing to accept the objection, put the Canadian sub-amendment to the vote first and his ruling was not challenged. It can happen, of course, because of this procedure, that the text of an amendment is radically changed, and a delegation is obliged to vote against its own amendment; this, however, is equally true of amendments to proposals.[81]

At the 1975 Montreal International Conference on Air Law the President ruled that a proposal that would limit the scope of an amendment 'must be considered as an amendment to that amendment and would therefore have to be voted on first'.[82]

10.7.1 Adoption of a Sub-Amendment and Subsequent Rejection of the Amendment Itself

A situation can arise by which a sub-amendment is adopted, but the amendment itself is subsequently rejected. In such a situation the sub-amendment becomes irrelevant by virtue of the subsequent rejection of the amendment.[83]

At the 1952 ILO Conference, the Conference adopted a Norwegian sub-amendment to an amendment submitted by Mexico and Colombia regarding a proposed Convention Concerning Minimum Standards of Social Security. The Mexican–Colombian amendment, as amended by Norway, was subsequently rejected.[84] The representative of India then argued, 'The correct procedure should have been first to put the

[79] Official Records of the 1975 Vienna Conference on Representation of States, vol. I, p. 283, Summary Records of the 36th Meeting of the Committee of the Whole, para. 58, UN Doc. A/CONF.67/18 (1975).

[80] *Ibid.*, p. 284, Summary Records of the 37th Meeting of the Committee of the Whole, para. 2.

[81] See, for example, UK statement, Official Records of the 1975 Vienna Conference on Representation of States, 38th Meeting of the Committee of the Whole, paras. 7, 8, UN Doc. A/CONF.67/C.1/SR.38 (1975).

[82] 1975 Montreal International Conference on Air Law, Commission of the Whole, Seventh Meeting, para. 55, ICAO Document 9154-LC/174 (1975).

[83] This situation occurred, for example, in UN GAOR, 3rd Committee, 22nd Session, 1511th Meeting, paras. 20, 30, UN Doc. A/C.3/22/SR.1511 (1967); UN GAOR, 3rd Committee, 29th Session, 2110th Meeting, para. 21, UN Doc. A/C.3/29/SR.2110 (1974).

[84] ILO Conference, 35th Session, Geneva 1952, Record of Proceedings, 22nd sitting, p. 329.

Norwegian sub-amendment to the vote, then the amendment submitted by the Mexican and Colombian Government delegates, and then, if this were rejected, to put the original draft [Mexican–Colombian amendment again] to the vote.' The President ruled, however, as follows: 'The position is that the Norwegian sub-amendment was adopted and the Colombian and Mexican amendment as amended by the sub-amendment submitted by the Norwegian Government delegate, was rejected; and the original text of Article 2 in the report is maintained.'[85] The President's ruling, it is submitted, was correct.

10.7.2 Adoption of a Sub-Amendment Implying Rejection of Another Sub-Amendment that Had Been Accepted by the Sponsors of the Original Amendment

At a 1974 meeting of the UNGA, separate sub-amendments were submitted by Pakistan and Bulgaria to an amendment that had been submitted by the Netherlands and Sweden. The Netherlands and Sweden accepted the Pakistani sub-amendment, but not the Bulgarian one. The Bulgarian sub-amendment was voted on first, and after being accepted in part, the Chairman ruled that adopting the Bulgarian sub-amendment had implied rejection of the Pakistani sub-amendment. The Chairman made his ruling notwithstanding that the Pakistani sub-amendment had been accepted by the sponsors of the amendment. The Netherlands–Sweden amendment was subsequently adopted with the Bulgarian sub-amendment, but without the Pakistani sub-amendment.[86]

[85] *Ibid.*

[86] UN GAOR, 3rd Committee, 29th Session, 2095th Meeting, para. 49, UN Doc. A/C.3/29/SR.2095 (1974); UN GAOR, 3rd Committee, 29th Session, 2096th Meeting, paras. 1–14, UN Doc. A/C.3/29/SR.2096 (1974).

11

Withdrawal and Reconsideration of Motions and Proposals

11.1 Withdrawal of Motions

The UNGA rules of procedure state,

> *Rule 80*
>
> A motion may be withdrawn by its proposer at any time before voting on it has commenced, provided that the motion has not been amended. A motion thus withdrawn may be reintroduced by any member.

The UN Model Rules propose,

> *Rule 47*
>
> *Withdrawal of Proposals and Motions*
>
> A proposal or a motion may be withdrawn by its sponsor at any time before voting on it has commenced, provided that it has not been amended by decision of the Conference. A proposal or a motion thus withdrawn may be reintroduced by any representative with its original priority, provided he does so promptly and it has not been substantially changed.

Neither the rules of procedure of the Assembly of the League of Nations nor those prepared by the Preparatory Commission of the United Nations contain any rule as to the withdrawal of motions. However, subsequent conferences follow the rules of the UNGA in allowing for withdrawal of motions provided that the motion has not been amended. A motion thus withdrawn may be reintroduced by any delegation.

11.1.1 Withdrawal of a Motion Adopted by a Committee

If a proposal has been adopted by a committee, then it can no longer be withdrawn by its original sponsors.[1]

[1] See, for example, UN GAOR, Plenary, 13th Session, 792nd Meeting, para. 199, UN Doc. A/PV.792 (1958).

11.1.2. Withdrawal of a Motion Submitted by the Chairman

At a 2008 meeting of the Third Committee of the UNGA, a delegate objected to a draft decision on programme planning submitted by the Chairman, whereupon the Chairman declared 'that he was compelled to withdraw the text'. The text was subsequently resubmitted by a number of delegations. It is not clear from the record why the Chairman felt he was 'compelled' to withdraw the draft.[2]

11.1.3 Withdrawal of Part of a Motion

The UNGA rule refers to withdrawal of a 'motion'. At a 1981 meeting of the UNGA, after the defeat of a motion for a separate vote on parts of an amendment, the sponsor of the amendment proposed withdrawing parts of the amendment. A point of order was raised that the wording of Rule 80 does not allow for the withdrawal of part of an amendment. The speaker continued by stating that the only choice open to the proposer was to withdraw the motion as a whole.[3] The Chairman ruled that the amendment be voted on as a whole. Although the ruling of the Chairman would appear to be correct in accordance with the wording of Rule 80, a delegation nevertheless may *revise* its proposal and thus achieve the identical intended result.

11.1.4 Resubmitting a Proposal Previously Withdrawn

At the 1974 Prescription in Sale of Goods Conference, the representative of Iraq claimed that 'a delegation could withdraw an amendment but not propose it again during the same meeting'.[4] The President ruled that he 'could allow an amendment to be proposed a second time in the course of the same meeting'.[5]

At a meeting of the 1974–1977 Geneva Humanitarian Law Conference, the representative of Israel informed the Committee that the 'Israeli delegation would not press for its amendment to be put to the vote at the

[2] UN GAOR, 3rd Committee, 63rd Session, 49th Meeting, para. 4, UN Doc. A/C.3/63/SR.49 (2008).

[3] UN GAOR, 2nd Committee, 36th Session, 48th Meeting, para. 72, UN Doc. A/C.2/36/SR.48 (1981).

[4] Official Records of the 1974 Prescription in Sale of Goods Conference, Plenary, p. 117, paras. 51–56, UN Doc. A/CONF.63/16 (1974).

[5] *Ibid.*

present stage of the work, but it reserved the right to submit it to the plenary Conference'.[6] The representative of Syria argued that this Israel withdrawal 'was conditional' and that 'it was hard to agree that the Israel proposal should be resubmitted subsequently'. He therefore requested 'that unless the Israeli representative withdrew his proposal once and for all, the matter should be put to the vote'.[7] The Chairman ruled that, as regarded Committee I, the Israel proposal had been withdrawn, and it was not up to Committee I to decide if the proposal could be resubmitted to the Plenary: 'If the Committee decided that a vote was necessary, a vote would be taken, but whatever its results the final decision would be taken in the plenary Conference.'[8] The Committee subsequently decided to 'terminate the discussion without voting'.[9]

11.1.5 Time Limits for Withdrawal

During the 1967 Special Session of the UNGA, the President ruled that previously agreed time limits for the submission of proposals did not apply to their withdrawal by the sponsors.[10]

11.1.6 Agreement by All Sponsors for Withdrawal

During a 1965 meeting of the UNGA, the Chairman ruled that the agreement of all the sponsors of a proposal to withdraw their proposal was needed to effect such withdrawal.[11]

At a 2014 meeting of the Third Committee of the UNGA, one of the sponsors of a resolution withdrew its sponsorship, and the Secretary of the Committee gave his opinion that 'because the main sponsor, Italy, had clearly indicated its readiness to take action on the draft resolution, the Committee was bound to do so'.[12]

[6] Official Records of the 1974–1977 Geneva Humanitarian Law Conference, CDDH/I/SR.74, vol. IX, p. 465, para. 25. The amendment referred to the use of the emblem of the Red Shield of David.

[7] *Ibid.* at p. 466, paras. 32, 33.

[8] *Ibid.* at pp. 466, 467, paras. 34, 36, 39.

[9] *Ibid.* at p. 467, paras. 40, 42.

[10] UN GAOR, Plenary, 5th Emergency Special Session, 1545th Meeting, paras. 5, 19, UN Doc. A/PV.1545 (1967).

[11] UN GAOR, Special Political Committee, 20th Session, 459th Meeting, para. 25, UN Doc. A/SR.792 (1965).

[12] UN GAOR, Third Committee, 69th Session, 54th Meeting, para. 81, UN Doc. A/C.3/69/SR.54 (2014).

11.1.7 Meaning of the Qualification that the Motion 'Has Not Been Amended'

O'Davoren, writing in 1943,[13] formulated this general rule for conferences: 'Any amendment may be withdrawn by the person who moved it unless an amendment to it is under discussion or has been adopted.'

The UNGA Rule of Procedure 80 stipulates that withdrawal is possible 'provided that the motion has not been amended'. An earlier version of the UN Model Rules also stated the qualification for permitting withdrawal as being that the motion 'has not been amended'.[14] The present UN Model Rules formulate the qualification as being that the motion 'has not been amended *by decision of the conference*'. [emphasis added] Thus the fact that an amendment had been proposed but not yet voted on would not negate the right of the sponsors to withdraw their motion. Presumably, even if an amendment had been accepted by the sponsors but not yet adopted by the conference, it could still be withdrawn.[15] The Rules of Procedure of the 2005 Conference of the Parties to the UN Convention against Transnational Organized Crime adopted the Model Rules formula of 'provided it has not been amended *by decision of the Conference*.'[16] [emphasis added] However, the practical guide to the UNGA published by the Permanent Mission of Switzerland to the UN states categorically that 'the main sponsors can withdraw the draft resolution/decision anytime, as long as no amendments have been *proposed* [emphasis added] by another Member State.[17]

At a 1946 meeting of the UNGA, the President commented that 'so long as no vote has been taken on a sub-amendment, any delegation certainly has the right to withdraw its amendment'.[18] At a 1993 meeting of the UNGA, during a discussion on biological and chemical warfare, a draft resolution was withdrawn by the sponsors although an amendment had

[13] William O'Davoren, *Post-War Reconstruction Conferences, The Technical Organisation of International Conferences* (1943) p. 130.

[14] UN Doc. A/37/163 of 28 April 1982.

[15] Rule 35 of the provisional rules of procedure of the UN Security Council states,

> A motion or draft resolution can at any time be withdrawn so long as no vote has been taken with respect to it. UN Doc. S/96/Rev.6 (1974).

[16] Rule 54, The Rules of Procedure of the 2005 Conference of the Parties to the UN Convention against Transnational Organized Crime, Published by the UN Office on Drugs and Crime, Vienna, Sales number V.05-85142-July 2005–2,350 (2005).

[17] Practical Guide to the UNGA published by the Permanent Mission of Switzerland to the UN, para. 3.5, www.unitar.org/ny/sites/unitar.org.ny/files/UN_PGA_Handbook.pdf.

[18] UN GAOR, Plenary, 1st Session, 30th Meeting, p. 431, UN Doc. A/PV30 (1946).

been submitted to the resolution and a motion had been moved to take no action on the amendment. Neither the amendment nor the motion to take no action was, however, voted on prior to the withdrawal of the resolution.[19]

The rules of procedure of the ICAO Assembly adopt a different policy in this respect by stipulating

> *Rule 40*
>
> No motion may be withdrawn if an amendment to it is under discussion or has been adopted.[20]

At a committee meeting of the Montreal 1975 International Air Law Conference the Chairman stated, 'It could be argued that it [withdrawal] was possible' because the rules of procedure stipulated 'a motion could not be withdrawn when an amendment to it was under discussion or had been adopted, and this was not the case here'.[21] In the particular case, withdrawal of the motion was not allowed because there had been a closure of debate.

The IMO conferences use a formula substantially the same as that of the ICAO.[22] The rules of procedure of the World Health Assembly use this formula:

> *Rule 69*
>
> A motion may be withdrawn by its proposer at any time before voting on it has commenced, provided that the motion has not been amended, or if amended, that the proposer of the amendment agrees to the withdrawal.

At a meeting of the 1963 Vienna Conference on Consular Relations,[23] the chairman of a committee ruled that 'the Australian amendment could be withdrawn only if the Netherlands delegation did not maintain its sub-amendment'.

[19] UN GAOR, 1st Committee, 48th Session, 30th Meeting, para. 1, UN Doc. A/C.1/48/SR.30/Add.1 (1993).

[20] Rule 40 of the standing rules of procedure of the Assembly of the ICAO, ICAO Doc. 7600/5, 5th edn, 1990.

[21] Montreal 1975 International Air Law Conference. Commission of the Whole, 31st Meeting, para. 69, ICAO Doc. 9154-LC/174–1 (1975).

[22] Rule 54 of the rules of procedure of the IMO Assembly.

[23] Official Records of the 1963 Vienna Conference on Consular Relations, 13th Meeting of Committee II, vol. I, p. 318, para. 52, UN Doc. A/CONF.25 (1963).

At a meeting of a 1971 IMCO Conference,[24] the Chairman refused to allow the Norwegian delegation to withdraw its amendment as it had been 'the subject of an [sub-] amendment',[25] even though the sub-amendment had not been voted on. When the sub-amendment was defeated, the Chairman allowed the Norwegian amendment to be withdrawn.

At a meeting of the 1974–1977 Geneva Humanitarian Law Conference, Sri Lanka submitted an oral amendment to a US amendment dealing with the issue of a fact-finding commission. The US representative stated, 'If the sub-amendment was retained, he would prefer to withdraw the amendment submitted by his delegation.'[26] The Pakistani representative then submitted the US amendment on behalf of Pakistan. The Mexican representative pointed out that, according to the Conference rules of procedure, a motion could only be withdrawn if it 'has not been amended'.[27] The President did not attempt to settle this issue, but ruled that 'the Conference had before it an amendment by the United States, taken up by the Pakistan delegation and a sub-amendment by the Sri Lanka delegation to that text, both of which he would put to the vote'.[28]

COMMENT

Although practice is not always consistent, it would appear that the sponsors of a proposal should be able to withdraw a motion unless the conference has adopted an amendment to the proposal. An amendment that has been proposed but not yet adopted should not be a bar to withdrawal.

11.1.8 A Motion Not to Vote on a Proposal as an Alternative to Withdrawal

Where a proposal cannot be withdrawn because it has been amended, an alternative procedure would be for the sponsors to propose a procedural motion that the conference not vote on the amended proposal.

[24] Official Records of the 25th Meeting of the Committee of the Whole, 1971 IMCO Oil Pollution Damage Fund Conference, p. 516, IMCO Doc. 2/C.1/SR.25 (1971).

[25] *Ibid.*

[26] Official Records of the 1974–1977 Geneva Humanitarian Law Conference, CDDH/SR.45, vol. VI, p. 323, para. 71.

[27] Rule 31 of the rules of procedure of the 1974–1977 Geneva Humanitarian Law Conference, CDDH/2.

[28] Official Records of the 1974–1977 Geneva Humanitarian Law Conference, CDDH/SR.45, vol. VI, p. 323, para. 77.

Such a motion, unlike withdrawal, of course requires a decision by the conference.

11.1.9. Withdrawal of a Proposal after Closure of Debate

At a 1975 committee meeting of the Montreal 1975 International Air Law Conference, the Chairman refused to allow withdrawal of a proposal 'as a motion for closure of debate on it had been carried'.[29]

11.1.10. Withdrawal of a Proposal after Voting Has Commenced

At a 1975 committee meeting of the Montreal 1975 International Air Law Conference, the Chairman refused to allow withdrawal of a proposal as the 'committee was in the process of voting on the proposal'.[30]

11.2 Reconsideration of Proposals

11.2.1 Majority Required for Reconsideration

The rules of procedure of the UNGA state,

> *Rule 81*
>
> When a proposal has been adopted or rejected it may not be reconsidered at the same session unless the General Assembly, by a two-thirds majority of the members present and voting, so decides. Permission to speak on a motion to reconsider shall be accorded only to two speakers opposing the motion, after which it shall be immediately put to the vote.

The UN Model Rules is identical, except that it adds a sentence, 'The Conference may decide to limit this rule to the reconsideration of proposals at the same session.'[31]

The rules of procedure of the Assembly of the League of Nations were silent on this question, as were the rules of procedure of the 1949 Geneva Conference and the 1954 Hague Conference. The rule appears, however, *mutatis mutandis*, in the rules of procedure of all the conferences since 1958.

[29] Montreal 1975 International Air Law Conference, Commission of the Whole, 31st Meeting, para. 69, ICAO Doc. 9154-LC/174–1 (1975).

[30] Montreal 1975 International Air Law Conference, Commission of the Whole, 4th Meeting, para. 36, ICAO Doc. 9154-LC/174–1 (1975).

[31] Rule 50 (2) UN Model Rule, UN Doc. A/37/163, Annex (1982).

Some of the UN Specialised Agencies however allow reconsideration of an issue by a decision of a simple majority; this is the rule in the ICAO Assembly.[32] The ICAO standing rules of procedure for Meetings in the Air Transport Field (World-Wide Conferences and Division Sessions) follow the ICAO Assembly rules and allow reconsideration by a majority of votes cast.[33] However, many major ICAO Air Conferences have adopted the requirement of a two-thirds majority for reconsideration of an issue.[34] Both the Assembly and Council of the IMO[35] also allow for reconsideration by a simple majority. Earlier IMO Conferences followed the IMO Assembly practice.[36] However, more recent IMO conferences have adopted the requirement of a two-thirds majority for reconsideration of an issue.[37] The ECOSOC rules of procedure also allow reconsideration by a simple majority, presumably because of the wording of Article 67(2) of the UN Charter, which states,

> Decisions of the Economic and Social Council shall be made by a majority of the members present and voting.

The NPT Review conferences use this formula:

> Proposals adopted by consensus may not be reconsidered unless the Conference reaches a consensus on such reconsideration. A proposal that has been adopted or rejected by a majority or two-thirds vote may be reconsidered if the Conference, by a two-thirds majority, so decides.[38]

At a committee meeting of the 1988 UN Conference for the Adoption of a Convention against Illicit Traffic in Narcotic Drugs and Psychotropic

[32] Rule 43 of the rules of procedure of the Assembly of the ICAO, ICAO Doc. 7600/5, 5th edn, 1990.

[33] The ICAO standing rules of procedure for Meetings in the Air Transport Field (World-wide Conferences and Division Sessions), ICAO Doc. 8683-AT/721 (1967).

[34] For example, 1971 Montreal Air Law Conference; 1973 Rome Air Law Conference.

[35] Rule 55 of the rules of assembly of the IMO Assembly; Rule 51 of the rules of procedure of the IMO Council.

[36] See, for example, Rule 46 of the rules of procedure for the Consultative and Special Meetings of Contracting Parties to the London Convention 1972, IMO Doc. LC 20/3 (1998).

[37] See, for example, Rule 28 of the rules of procedure of the IMO Conference of Contracting Governments to the International Convention for the Safety of Life at Sea, 1974, IMO Doc. SOLAS/CONF.5/2 (2002); Rule 29 of the rules of procedure of the IMO International Conference on the Establishment of a Supplementary Fund for Compensation for Oil Pollution Damage, IMO Doc. LEG/CONF.14/2 (2002).

[38] Rule 27, NPT/CONF.2000/1; NPT/CONF.2005/1.

Substances the Chairman permitted reconsideration of an item without recourse to a vote as 'there was no objection to a reopening of the discussion'.[39]

COMMENT

Allowing reconsideration by a simple majority is clearly an unsatisfactory procedure, and the majority of conferences have adopted the requirement of a two-thirds majority. The NPT stipulation that a consensus decision can only be reconsidered by consensus is not self-evident. Since even a unanimous decision can be reconsidered by a two-thirds majority, it could well be argued that two-thirds of an assembly should be able to reconsider a decision that was taken without a vote.

11.2.2 Reconsideration in Committees

The rule in committees of the UNGA is the same rule as in the Plenary:

> *Rule 123*
>
> When a proposal has been adopted or rejected, it may not be reconsidered at the same session unless the committee, by a two-thirds majority of the members present and voting, so decides.

The UN Model Rules propose,

> *Rule 67*
>
> (c) . . . except at a treaty-making conference, the reconsideration of a proposal shall require the majority established by paragraph 1 of rule 50 [Paragraph 1 of Rule 50 refers to a two-thirds majority].

The 1958 Law of the Sea Conference revealed a lacuna in its rules of procedure in this respect. Rule 53 stated that the rules of conduct of business apply *mutatis mutandis* to the proceedings of committees, except that decisions shall be taken by a simple majority. During the discussions in the First Committee, the representative of India proposed that a motion be reconsidered and claimed that a simple majority would suffice in accordance with Rule 53.[40] The representative of France claimed that a committee had no right at all to reconsider proposals and that that privilege

[39] UN Conference for the Adoption of a Convention against Illicit Traffic in Narcotic Drugs and Psychotropic Substances, 1st Committee, 21st Meeting, para. 72, UN Doc. E/CONF.82/C.1/SR.21 (1988).

[40] Official Records of the 1958 Law of the Sea Conference, 57th Meeting of Committee I, vol. III, p. 180, para. 13, UN Doc. A/CONF.13/39 (1958).

belonged only to the Plenary.[41] The Indian motion did not obtain a simple majority, and the Chairman was therefore not called upon to make a decision as to the majority required.

During a debate in the Second Committee of the same conference, the representative of the United Kingdom requested reconsideration of the definitions article of the Draft Convention (Article 33A). The Chairman decided that the rule stipulating that committees adopt decisions by simple majority did not apply in this case. It is not clear what was the reasoning of the Chairman; his ruling, however, was overturned on a challenge, and the Committee decided that 'the decision to reconsider the adoption of article 33A be taken by a simple majority'.[42]

The draft rules of procedure of the 1960 Law of the Sea Conference followed the wording of the 1958 rules.[43] The Conference, however, adopted a Mexican proposal to add to the relevant draft rule of procedure the phrase 'but not in the case of a reconsideration of proposals or amendments in which the majority required shall be that established by rule 32' (a two-thirds majority).[44] The amendment thus clarified that reconsideration in committees, as in plenary meetings, required a two-thirds majority.

The draftsman of the provisional rules of procedure of UN conferences (the Legal Secretariat of the UN) apparently took note of the problem. Rules of procedure of conferences convened since then include, after the rule that committees decide by a simple majority, the following phrase: 'but not in the case of a reconsideration of proposals or amendments in which the majority required shall be that established by rule' (the rule relating to reconsideration, stipulating a two-thirds majority). With that amendment to the rules of procedure, it was made clear that committees are entitled to reconsider proposals and amendments provided a two-thirds majority is obtained.

The ITU rules for conferences are unusual in that they categorically stipulate that there cannot be reconsideration of a vote in committees.[45]

41 *Ibid.* at para. 14.

42 Official Records of the 1958 Law of the Sea Conference, 32nd Meeting of Committee II, vol. IV, p. 98, paras. 38–41, UN Doc. A/CONF.13/40 (1958).

43 Rule 49 of the draft rules of procedure of the 1960 Law of the Sea Conference, UN Doc. A/CONF.19/2 (1960).

44 1960 Law of the Sea Conference, amendment by Mexico to the draft rules of procedure, UN Doc. A/CONF.19/L.1 (1960), adopted at the 2nd Plenary Meeting of the Conference, para. 21, Official Records of the Conference, p. 5, UN Doc. A/CONF.19/8 (1960).

45 Rule 32 (14)(12)(1) of the Constitution of the International Telecommunication Union, Geneva 1993.

The UN Model Rules propose that committees of *treaty-making conferences* be entitled to reconsider decisions by a simple majority. The exception as regards treaty-making conferences did not appear in the original draft, but was added in a subsequent draft,[46] without any explanation being given for the change.

COMMENT

It appears advisable to allow every organ of a conference, including committees, to be able to reconsider decisions. In order to prevent interminable debates, it is also advisable to require a special majority for reconsideration. The UN Model Rules, in regard to law-making treaties, appear, in this case, to be unsatisfactory.

11.2.3 Reconsideration in Regard to Proposals in Different Committees

During a debate in the Third Committee of the 1949 session of the UNGA, the Legal Department of the UN Secretariat submitted its opinion that a decision in one committee of the UNGA (the Third Committee) would not bind an ad hoc committee set up by the General Assembly. The legal opinion continued by stating that therefore it would not be considered a reconsideration if the ad hoc committee dealt with an issue that had already been dealt with by the Third Committee.[47]

11.2.4 Reconsideration in Plenary of Decisions of Committees

The Legal Counsel of the WHO gave his opinion at the 1983 World Health Assembly: 'It is perfectly possible in plenary session to reopen a question that was the subject of a resolution adopted in committee. The purpose of the plenary session is precisely to allow the Assembly to consider a problem that has been considered by a lower echelon.'[48]

At a 2006 meeting of Committee "A" of the World Health Assembly, the Committee was in the process of approving its report to the Plenary. The

[46] Draft standard rules of procedure for United Nations conferences, Report of the Secretary-General, Revisions to the draft proposals, UN Doc. A/C.6/37/5 (1982).

[47] UN GAOR, 3rd Committee, 3rd Session, Part II, 218th Meeting, p. 354, UN Doc. A/C.3/3/SR.218 (1949).

[48] Verbatim Records of the 13th Plenary Meeting of the 36th World Health Assembly, p. 273, WHA36/1983/REC/2 (1983).

Office of the Legal Counsel stated, 'The debate on its substantive content could not be reopened. Once the Committee had adopted the draft report, it would be referred to the plenary, where delegates would have a further opportunity to express their views on the substance'.[49]

COMMENT

Any proposal voted on in a committee can be resubmitted at a plenary meeting of a conference and such resubmission is not considered a reopening of the issue. This is not set out in any rule of procedure, but is part of the inherent powers of the 'parent' body[50] and apparently has never been disputed.

11.2.5 Is It a Reconsideration When There Is a Request for a Separate Vote on Part of a Text on Which There Had Been a Previous Request for a Separate Vote?

During the 1963 Vienna Conference on Consular Relations, the US delegation requested a separate vote on the last two sentences of the draft article dealing with the liability of consuls to give evidence. The request was put to the vote and defeated. The delegation of Tunisia then requested a separate vote on the latter of the two sentences involved. Several delegations objected to the Tunisian request. They claimed it would be a reconsideration of the decision made on the US request to have a separate vote on both the sentences, a motion that had been defeated. The Tunisian delegation replied that 'to vote separately on two sentences regarded as a whole and on one of them alone were two quite different operations'.[51] The President then ruled that the Tunisian motion was admissible and did not constitute a reopening of the issue. The President's ruling was not challenged. The ruling would appear to be correct.

[49] Committee "A" of the 59th World Health Assembly, 5th Meeting, p. 60, WHO Doc.WHA 59/2006/REC/3 (2006).

[50] UN Doc. A/CONF.29/11/Add.1, p. 23, para. 50. The President (Mr Ago of Italy) said that 'any delegation was free to resubmit a rejected amendment to the Plenary'.

The Netherlands delegate to the 1969 IMCO Conference on Marine Pollution Damage stated that his delegation was submitting an amendment 'which had not been accepted in the Committee, but which it wished to submit to the plenary meeting'. IMCO Doc. LEG/CONF/SR.5, p. 101 (1969).

[51] Official Records of the 1963 Vienna Conference on Consular Relations, 16th Plenary Meeting, p. 58. para. 13, UN Doc. A/CONF.25/16 (1963).

11.2.6 Is it a Reconsideration to Request a Separate Vote on a Text When an Amendment for Deletion of the Text Has Been Defeated?

At a 1966 meeting of the UNGA, a delegate objected to a request from Cameroon for a separate vote on a part of a resolution. The objection was based on the grounds that the request was tantamount to the resubmission of a Cameroonian amendment that had previously been withdrawn. The Cameroonian representative withdrew his request.[52]

During the 1963 Vienna Conference on Consular Relations, the Austrian delegation requested a separate vote on a phrase referring to employees of an honorary consulate. The representative of Morocco objected, stating that 'the motion for division of the text was the same as the Swiss proposal for the deletion of the words concerned, which had already been rejected. The Conference could not revert to a matter with which it had already dealt.'[53] Other delegations drew attention to the rule that accorded representatives the unconditional right to move that parts of a proposal should be voted on separately, irrespective of the result of any previous vote. The President ruled that the Austrian motion for division of the vote was in accordance with the rules of procedure and hence not a reopening of the issue. The ruling was challenged but the President proceeded to put to the vote the Austrian motion for a separate vote, and not his ruling. The Legal Counsel of the UN, in an opinion given immediately after the vote, did not dispute the President's ruling, namely that in the circumstances described above, it was not a reconsideration of the issue.[54]

COMMENT

It would appear to be a correct ruling to allow a separate vote on a text notwithstanding that an amendment calling for rejection of the text has previously been rejected.

11.2.7 Is a Request to Vote again, due to Misunderstandings during the Vote, a Request for Reconsideration?

There have been a number of occasions when delegations have requested holding a vote again, claiming that in the circumstances it would not be a reopening of the issue.

52 UN GAOR, 1st Committee, 21st Session, 1449th Meeting, para. 51, UN Doc. A/C.1/21/SR.1449 (1966); UN GAOR, 1st Committee, 21st Session, 1450th Meeting, para. 25, UN Doc. A/C.1/21/SR.1450 (1966).

53 UN GAOR, 18th Plenary Meeting at p. 72, para. 37.

54 *Ibid.* at p. 73, para. 53.

At the 1949 session of the UNGA, there was an interruption in the simultaneous translation that, it was claimed, had caused a delegation to misunderstand the vote. The Chairman ruled that nevertheless voting again would be considered a reconsideration requiring a two-thirds majority.[55]

At the 1963 Vienna Conference on Consular Relations, the representative of Congo asked for a recount, 'as he thought there might have been a mistake'.[56] The Chairman ruled that 'a recount was not possible because it would involve another vote on the same proposal which would be contrary to rule 33 of the rules of procedure'. The Chairman added that 'the representative of the Congo (Leopoldville) could ask for the reconsideration of his proposal but that would require a two-thirds majority'.[57] After a discussion, the Chairman put the Congolese proposal to the vote under Rule 33 (the rule referring to reconsideration and requiring a two-thirds majority); in the event the proposal did not obtain a simple majority.

At the Vienna Conference on the Law of Treaties, after a complicated vote with an unclear result, the representative of Ghana stated that 'he knew of at least one delegation which had not taken part in the voting because it had not known exactly what was being put to the vote. He would therefore like a second vote.'[58] A number of delegations spoke on a point of order that such a vote would be a motion to reconsider and would require a two-thirds majority. The representative of India countered that, as many delegations had not known what they were voting on, 'for all practical purposes there had been no vote'.[59] The President ruled that 'a second vote would undoubtedly be a motion to reconsider'.[60] The meeting was then, however, suspended, and it was later agreed to take the vote again without taking any decision as to the legal situation.

At the 1968 Teheran Conference on Human Rights, the representative of India proposed that, 'as many representatives might not have had the amendment before them at the time of voting, a second vote should be taken'.[61] The Chairman asked the Conference to 'vote on whether a new

[55] UN GAOR, 3rd Committee, 4th Session, 238th Meeting, para. 50, UN Doc. A/C.3/4/SR.238 (1949).

[56] Official Records of the 1963 Vienna Conference on Consular Relations, 13th Meeting of Committee I, vol. I, p. 163, para. 58, UN Doc. A/CONF.25/16 (1963).

[57] *Ibid.* at para. 59.

[58] Official Records of the Vienna Conference on the Law of Treaties – Second Session, 16th Plenary Meeting, p. 76, para. 46, UN Doc. A/CONF. 9/11/Add.1 (1969).

[59] *Ibid.* at para. 49. [60] *Ibid.* at para. 52.

[61] Summary Records of the 25th Plenary Meeting of the 1968 Teheran Conference on Human Rights, p. 144, UN Doc. A/CONF.32/PV.25 (1968).

vote should be taken on the amendment'.[62] The Conference decided to take a new vote, but no reference was made to the question of whether this was considered a reconsideration or not.[63]

11.2.8 *Is Voting again due to a Discrepancy in Language Versions to Be Considered a Reconsideration?*

At the 1950 session of the UNGA, after a vote a number of delegations stated that it had not been clear what they had previously been voting on. The Chairman decided that the Committee should vote again, without considering it to be a reconsideration.[64]

At a 1952 meeting of the UNGA, after voting had commenced, a substantial discrepancy was discovered between the Spanish and English versions of an amendment. The Chairman allowed a subsequent second vote on the amendment without raising the issue of reconsideration.[65]

A 1966 meeting of the UNGA decided to ignore a previous decision that had 'clearly been taken by mistake'. It did so, however, by a vote for reconsideration.[66]

At a 1992 meeting of the UNGA, during elections to ECOSOC, the representative of the Group of Western European and Other States failed, due to a misunderstanding, to announce the candidates of his group and no representative of the group was elected. After voting had taken place, a number of delegations requested a revote. The President announced that, if there was no objection, there would be a 'new vote on the Group of Western European and Other States'. No objection was raised.[67]

At a meeting of a committee of the 1977 Conference on Territorial Asylum, the representative of Ecuador informed the meeting that 'according to the Spanish interpretation, the text proposed by the Group of Experts had been put to the vote without the Jordanian amendment. That error

[62] *Ibid.*

[63] The decision was that a new vote should be taken on the amendment. The result of the vote was thirty-nine votes to five, with six abstentions; thus a two-thirds majority was achieved even if not required.

[64] UN GAOR, 4th Committee, 5th Session, 155th Meeting, paras. 27–30, UN Doc. A/C.4/5/SR.155 (1950).

[65] UN GAOR, 6th Committee, 7th Session, 311th Meeting, para. 28, UN Doc. A/C.6/7/SR.311 (1952).

[66] UN GAOR, Plenary, 21st Session, 1499th Meeting, paras. 113, 114, UN Doc. A/PV.1499 (1966).

[67] UN GAOR, Plenary, 47th Session, 50th Meeting, pp. 26–40, UN Doc. A/47/PV.50 (Provisional) (1992).

of interpretation might have vitiated the vote.'[68] After a discussion, the Chairman stated that 'he was convinced that the Spanish-speaking delegations had voted in full knowledge of the question at issue. He urged them not to press for a second vote on the text adopted, as that would give rise to serious procedural difficulties.'[69] No delegation requested holding the vote again.

11.2.9 Is a Motion to Vote on an Amendment Inadvertently Not Voted on to Be Considered a Motion to Reconsider?

At a 1952 meeting of a committee of the UNGA, a delegation requested that the Committee vote on an oral amendment. The delegation claimed that the oral amendment had been submitted prior to the vote on a proposal, but inadvertently had not been voted on prior to the proposal itself being adopted. The Chairman ruled that voting on the amendment at this stage would constitute reconsideration and would require a two-thirds majority.[70]

COMMENT

Where there was a genuine misunderstanding during a vote, for instance in the case of different language versions, it is important and reasonable that the vote be taken again. Nevertheless, taking the vote again is a reconsideration requiring a two-thirds majority. If no delegation objects to taking the vote again, then the existence of a two-thirds majority can be inferred from the absence of objection.

11.2.10 Recounting the Vote as Reconsideration

At a meeting of the 1977 Conference on Territorial Asylum, a tied vote led to a resolution not being adopted. The representative of the USSR proposed consequently that 'the vote should be recounted in order to dispel any doubts about the results'.[71] The Chairman ruled that 'if the Soviet

[68] Summary Records of the 6th Meeting of Committee I of the 1977 Conference on Territorial Asylum, para. 50, UN Doc. A/CONF.78/C.1/SR.6 (1977).

[69] *Ibid.* at para. 51.

[70] UN GAOR, 3rd Committee, 6th Session, 386th Meeting, paras. 17–37, UN Doc. A/C.3/6/SR.386 (1952).

[71] Summary Records of the 21st Meeting of the Committee of the Whole of the 1977 Conference on Territorial Asylum, para. 45, UN Doc. A/CONF.78/C.1/SR.21 (1977).

delegation insisted on maintaining its proposal, it would have to be put to a vote'.[72] The Soviet delegation did not request a vote.

COMMENT

Recounting a vote, except in the case of a ballot, normally entails voting again and should, it is submitted, therefore be treated as a reconsideration of the issue.

11.2.11 Is a Motion Not to Discuss an Item Inscribed on the Agenda a Motion for Reconsideration?

At a 1954 meeting of a committee of the UNGA, a delegation proposed that the Committee not consider an item that was on the agenda. The question arose as to whether that would be a reconsideration of the decision to inscribe the item on the agenda. The Chairman ruled that a motion not to consider the item, prior to the general debate on the item, would be a motion for reconsideration requiring a two-thirds majority.[73]

11.2.12 Where a Decision Has Been Taken Not to Inscribe an Item on the Agenda, Is a Draft Resolution on that Item a Motion for Reconsideration?

At a meeting of the 1984 World Health Assembly, it was decided, on the advice of the Legal Counsel, that a draft resolution was 'not receivable' as it dealt with an issue that the Assembly had decided to exclude from the agenda.[74]

At a 1987 meeting of a World Health Assembly committee, the Legal Counsel recalled that the Plenary had decided not to inscribe on the agenda the issue of 'Embargo of medical supplies and its effect on people's health'. He gave his opinion that presenting an 'almost identical' proposal to the Committee would be contrary to the decision of the Plenary. He added that for the Plenary to change its decision would require a motion

[72] *Ibid.* at para. 46.
[73] UN GAOR, 1st Committee, 9th Session, 749th Meeting, para. 17, UN Doc. A/C.1/9/SR.749 (1954).
[74] Summary Records of the 2nd Meeting of the General Committee of the 37th World Health Assembly, pp. 8–11, WHA37/1984/REC/3 (1984).

for reconsideration. The Chairman adopted the Legal Counsel's opinion, and a challenge to his ruling was defeated.[75]

11.2.13 Is a Motion to Change the Order of Items in an Agenda a Reconsideration of the Adoption of the Agenda?

At a 1989 meeting of a committee of the World Health Assembly, the Legal Counsel gave his opinion that 'once the agenda of the Health Assembly was adopted, the order in which items were to be considered could be changed without the adopted agenda having to be renumbered or amended'.[76] A logical inference from this opinion would be that changing the order of items in an agreed agenda does not constitute a reconsideration of the agenda.

11.2.14 Is a Motion for Adjournment of Debate a Motion for Reconsideration of the Decision to Hold the Debate?

The Fourth Committee of the UNGA at its 1949 session decided to invite a representative of the indigenous population of South West Africa to attend hearings.[77] One delegation moved the adjournment of the discussion on the credentials of the representative until the issue was considered by the Plenary of the UNGA. Some delegations argued that this was an artificial use of the procedure for adjournment, and the Chairman ruled that the motion for adjournment was a motion for reconsideration and required a two-thirds majority.[78]

This decision by the Chairman would seem questionable since every motion for adjournment of debate is inherently a reconsideration of the decision to hold the discussion.

11.2.15 Reconsideration of Invitations to Multisession Conferences

During the 1974–1977 Geneva Humanitarian Law Conference, a discussion arose as to the invitation of the Viet Cong. There had been a previous amendment to the rules of procedure (Rule 35(4)), whereby it had been

[75] Summary Records of the 9th Meeting of Committee 'B' of the 40th World Health Assembly, pp. 314, 315, WHA40/1987/REC/3 (1987).
[76] Summary Records of the 1st Meeting of the General Committee of the 42nd World Health Assembly, p. 1, WHA42/1989/REC/3 (1989).
[77] UN Doc. A/C.4/L.60.
[78] UN GAOR, 4th Committee, 4th Session, 136th Meeting, para. 61, UN Doc. A/C.4/4/SR.136 (1949).

decided that matters of invitation would be decided by a simple majority. During the First Session of the Conference, there had been a vote on whether or not to invite the Viet Cong and it had been decided not to invite them. At the Second Session of the Conference, a proposal was again submitted to invite the Viet Cong. The US representative objected to the proposal, arguing that it would be a reconsideration and would therefore require a two-thirds majority in accordance with the relevant rule (Rule 32). The supporters of the proposal to invite the Viet Cong countered by arguing that on matters of invitations the rule stipulating a simple majority, as opposed to the usual two-thirds majority, was a *lex specialis* and therefore not subject to the reconsideration rule. It was further argued, by Hans Blix of Sweden, that 'it would be unreasonable to apply the reconsideration rule from one session to another with respect to invitation issues'.[79] The representative of the United States, George Aldrich, argued,

> Rule 32 applied to reconsideration during subsequent sessions of the Conference as well as during the same session . . . that was supported by contrast with the comparable rule (rule 81) of the rules of procedure of the United Nations General Assembly that added the phrase 'at the same session' after the words 'it may not be reconsidered'. The only way in which rule 32 and rule 35(2)(4) could be reconciled was to interpret them in their normal way – that decisions on procedure and decisions on invitations were taken by simple majority vote in the first instance, but that once taken they could be reconsidered only if the Conference decided by a two-thirds vote to do so . . . in order to prevent situations in which questions of invitation and questions of procedure could continually be reopened many times during a session and during later sessions whenever the presence or absence of various representatives seemed to offer opportunities for different results.[80]

After a lengthy debate and several votes, the Conference decided that a two-thirds majority was required.

11.2.16 Can a Conference Decide to Reserve the Right to Reconsider an Item in the Future?

During the 1955 session of a UNGA committee, a delegation proposed that the Committee should, while approving a proposal, decide to reserve its right to reconsider the proposal at a later stage. The Chairman was

[79] Official Records of the 1974–1977 Geneva Humanitarian Law Conference, CDDH/SR.24, vol. V, p. 284, para. 44.

[80] Official Records of the 1974–1977 Geneva Humanitarian Law Conference, CDDH/SR.23, vol. V, p. 273, paras. 21, 22.

requested to rule whether such a reservation could be made in accordance with the rules of procedure, and he ruled that such a proposal was in order.[81] Presumably, therefore, a later reconsideration of an issue in accordance with such a reservation would not require a two-thirds majority.

At a meeting of the 1951 Conference on Refugees, the records recall that '[t]he President put to the vote paragraph 11, as amended by the United Kingdom delegation, it being understood that the matter could be reopened if some other delegation or delegations found a more satisfactory wording'.[82]

At a meeting of a 1971 IMCO Conference, the representative of Norway proposed that 'any vote taken with regard to Article 1 should be subject to reconsideration'.[83] The US representative asked 'whether, in the case of a subsequent amendment to an Article that had already been voted upon, a two-thirds majority vote would be required'. The Executive Secretary of the Conference suggested that 'the Committee should agree to reconsider any Article on which a decision had already been taken on the basis of a vote by a simple majority only and not of a vote by a two-thirds majority'.[84] The Executive Secretary's suggestion was apparently adopted.

At a meeting of a 1976 IMCO Conference, the Chairman ruled that a 'preliminary indication of preferences' would take place and that '[r]epresentatives would be free to revert to the question of . . . and the provisions of the rules of procedure governing the reconsideration of issues would not apply'.[85]

11.2.17 Where There Has Been a Vote on a Proposal, Is It a Reconsideration to Then Convene a Discussion Group?

At a meeting of a 1971 IMCO Conference, the US representative pointed out that 'the votes gave a general indication that the delegations were not satisfied'. The representative suggested that the Committee 'establish a

81 UN GAOR, 3rd Committee, 10th Session, 640th Meeting, paras. 48–58, UN Doc. A/C.3/10/SR.640 (1955).
82 Summary Records of the 32nd Plenary Meeting of the 1951 Conference on Refugees, p. 11, UN Doc. A/CONF.2/PV.32 (1951).
83 Official Records of the 3rd Meeting of the Committee of the Whole of the 1971 IMCO Oil Pollution Damage Fund Conference, p. 323, IMCO Doc. CONF.2/C.1/SR.3 (1971).
84 *Ibid.*
85 Official Records of the 4th Meeting of the Committee of the Whole of the 1976 IMCO Conference on Maritime Claims, p. 232, IMCO Doc. CONF.5/C.1/SR.4 (1976).

discussion group and endeavour to find a compromise formula'.[86] The Chairman ruled that 'as a vote had already been taken, he could only agree to a discussion group meeting in an informal capacity. A two-thirds majority would be required in order to reopen the debate on the sub-stance.'[87]

11.2.18 *Relocation of Part of a Paragraph as a Reconsideration*

At a meeting of the 1971 Montreal Air Law Conference, the US representative proposed the relocation of two lines of a paragraph. The President ruled that the 'repositioning' of the paragraph 'would constitute a reopening of the debate'.[88] The US representative informed the Commission that he would not appeal against the ruling of the Chair.

11.2.19 *An Interpretive Vote as a Reconsideration*

At a committee meeting of a 1969 IMCO Conference, a discussion took place on the meaning of a vote that had been taken by the Committee. The Chairman suggested that the Committee 'should not attempt to reverse its previous vote – which in any case would require a decision by a two-thirds majority – but should take an interpretive vote'.[89] The Committee adopted the Chairman's proposal. This would appear to be a correct procedure provided that the interpretive vote does not negate any part of the previous vote.

11.2.20 *After a Motion Not to Vote on a Resolution Has Been Defeated, Is It a Reconsideration to Move that the Conference Is Not Competent to Discuss the Issue?*

At a 1986 meeting of a committee of the World Health Assembly, the Committee decided not to vote on a US proposal 'not to take a decision' on a resolution by the Non-Aligned Movement.[90] At a subsequent meeting, the

[86] Official Records of the 19th Meeting of the Committee of the Whole of the 1971 IMCO Oil Pollution Damage Fund Conference, p. 459, IMCO Doc. CONF.2/C.1/SR.19 (1971).

[87] *Ibid.*

[88] 1971 Montreal Air Law Conference, Commission of the Whole, 17th Meeting, vol. I, Minutes, p. 154, para. 41, ICAO Doc. 9081-LC/170–1.

[89] Summary Records of the 10th Meeting of Committee II of the 1969 IMCO Conference on Marine Pollution Damage, p. 676, IMCO Doc. LEG/CONF/C.2/SR.10 (1969).

[90] Summary Records of the 8th Meeting of Committee 'B' of the 39th World Health Assembly, pp. 312, 313, WHA/39/1986/REC/3 (1986). The decision was taken by the Committee to allow an appeal against the Chairman's decision to put the US proposal to the vote.

representative of the United Kingdom called for a vote on the 'receivability' of the motion submitted by the Non-Aligned Movement. The representative of Cuba claimed that the UK motion entailed reconsideration of the previous decision on the US motion. The Legal Counsel submitted his opinion that 'the proposal just made by the delegate of the United Kingdom differed from that of the United States. The question was no longer one of considering or not considering the draft resolution but of declaring it not receivable.'[91] A debate followed on the Legal Counsel's opinion. After a motion for closure was adopted, the Chairman put the Non-Aligned motion to the vote while ignoring the UK motion on irreceivability. Although no decision appears to have been taken on the opinion of the Legal Counsel, it is submitted that the opinion was correct.

11.2.21 Inserting a New Paragraph as a Reconsideration

At a 2008 meeting of the Plenary of the IAEA the President decided that a request to add a new paragraph to a resolution that had already been adopted would constitute 'reconsideration' of the resolution.[92]

11.2.22 Is It a Reconsideration after a Proposal Was Referred without Vote to a Drafting Committee?

At a meeting of a 1955 International Air Law Conference an issue arose as to whether it would be a reconsideration of a proposal if an amendment was made to a text that had been referred, without a vote, to a drafting committee. The amendment was put to the vote and defeated, apparently without a clear presidential decision on the issue.[93]

11.3 Reconsideration of Amendments

The UNGA has debated whether the rule as to reconsideration applies to amendments, the debate being based on the issue as to whether an

[91] Summary Records of the 9th Meeting of Committee 'B' of the 39th World Health Assembly, p. 315, WHA/39/1986/REC/3 (1986).

[92] Plenary meeting, 52nd Session of the IAEA General Conference, 10th Meeting, paras. 1–33, IAEA Doc. GC(52)/OR.10 (2008).

[93] The Hague, International Air Law Conference, 30th Plenary Meeting, pp. 267–269. ICAO Doc. 3801-LC/149–1 (1955).

amendment was a 'proposal'.[94] At a 1948 meeting of the Third Committee of the UNGA, a sub-amendment submitted by the USSR was defeated. When the USSR subsequently submitted the same text as an amendment, the Chairman ruled it out of order as it had previously been defeated when submitted as a sub-amendment.[95] The Chairman's ruling was upheld on a challenge.

At a 1948 meeting of the Sixth Committee of the UNGA, the Chairman refused to allow the Soviet Union to introduce an amendment on the grounds that the issue had already been decided by the rejection of a previous Soviet amendment to a different paragraph employing the same language.[96] However, at the meeting of the Fourth Committee of the UNGA, at the same 1948 session, the Soviet delegation introduced an amendment to a proposal of the Special Committee, even though the amendment was a repetition of a separate proposal that had been rejected earlier. The Chairman allowed the Soviet delegation to introduce the amendment. Furthermore, the earlier, rejected proposal had in itself been treated by implication as an amendment in that it had been given priority as being furthest removed from the Special Committee's proposal.

At a 1965 committee meeting of the UNGA, the Committee was discussing the question of Cyprus. Some delegations argued on the basis of a distinction between proposals and amendments that the rule on reconsideration does not apply to amendments.[97] Other delegations argued that every amendment is a proposal, and therefore the rule of reconsideration should apply if an amendment is resubmitted.[98] The Chairman ruled that the amendment submitted was not identical to the earlier amendment, and therefore the issue of reconsideration did not arise.[99] The Chairman refrained from making a ruling on the question of principle as to whether the rule of reconsideration applies to amendments, and attempts by the Saudi Arabian delegate to obtain a legal opinion on the issue were unsuccessful.[100]

[94] See discussion on the difference between a motion and a proposal in Sections 10.1 and 10.1.1 in Chapter 10.

[95] UN GAOR, 3rd Committee, 3rd Session, 126th Meeting, p. 389, UN Doc. A/C.3/3/SR.126 (1948).

[96] UN GAOR, 6th Committee, 3rd Session, 93rd Meeting, p. 322, UN Doc. A/C.6/3/SR.93 (1948).

[97] UN GAOR, 1st Committee, 20th Session, 1417th Meeting, paras. 2, 7, UN Doc. A/C.1/20/SR.1417 (1965).

[98] *Ibid.* at paras. 4, 5, 6, 12. [99] *Ibid.* at para. 11. [100] *Ibid.* at para. 18.

Where an earlier amendment has been adopted that is incompatible with a later amendment, the issue would be covered by Rule 90 of the UNGA rules of procedure, which states,

> *Voting on Amendments*
> *Rule 90*
> Where, however, the adoption of one amendment necessarily implies the rejection of another amendment, the latter amendment shall not be put to the vote.

In other words, where the presiding officer makes a decision that Rule 90 applies, then, unless the ruling is successfully challenged, a delegation would have to request reconsideration in order to bring the 'latter' amendment to a vote.

Rule 90 of the UNGA rules of procedure does not, however, state what procedure is to be applied if a previous amendment that was *rejected* necessarily implies the rejection of a 'latter' amendment. If an amendment is considered a proposal, then the presiding officer may declare that the latter amendment is a reconsideration. If amendments are not considered proposals, then the conference or assembly must put the 'latter' amendment to the vote.

It is submitted that the correct interpretation is that amendments are subject to the rule as to reconsideration. This issue is resolved as regards the UN Model Rules:

> *Rule 58*
> *Amendments*
> ... Unless specified otherwise, the word 'proposal' in these rules shall be considered as including amendments.

At a 2008 meeting of the Committee of the Whole of the General Conference of the IAEA, the Committee decided to allow a proposed amendment to a resolution that had already been adopted on the basis that the proposed amendment had been included in a document previously adopted by the committee.[101]

Reconsideration of an amendment is obviously not possible if the text to which it relates has been rejected.

[101] Committee of the Whole, IAEA General Conference, 52nd Session, 4th Meeting, p. 1, IAEA Doc. GC(52)/COM.5/OR.4 (2008).

11.3.1 Where an Amended Basic Text Is Defeated, Is It a Reconsideration to Revert to the Original Basic Text?

At the 1958 Law of the Sea Conference, two amendments to an ILC draft article were adopted; the amended article as a whole was, however, not adopted. When a delegation then proposed voting on the original ILC draft, without the amendments, the Chairman at first ruled that it would entail reconsideration. The Chairman subsequently withdrew his ruling and the Committee proceeded to vote on the ILC draft on the understanding, as one delegate phrased it, that it was not reconsideration as the article was still open for consideration.[102]

11.4 Reconsideration of Procedural Decisions

In the UNGA rules of procedure[103] and in the UN Model Rules,[104] the rules as to reconsideration both refer to 'proposals'. Therefore, presumably, there is no rule requiring a two-thirds majority for reconsideration of procedural motions.

The chairman of a committee of the UNGA, at its1948 session, however, ruled that a motion to explain a vote, after a decision had been taken to close the debate, would be a motion to reconsider the closure and would thus require a two-thirds majority.[105]

At a meeting of the Third Committee of the 1975 UNGA a debate took place as to whether a two-thirds majority was required to reconsider a procedural decision. This question was put to a vote, and the Committee decided that a simple majority was sufficient.[106]

The UNGA, at its 1966 session, held a lengthy but inconclusive discussion about whether a proposal to reconsider the order of priority of items on the agenda was a reconsideration of a 'proposal' requiring a two-thirds majority.[107]

[102] Official Records of the 1958 Law of the Sea Conference, 34th Meeting of Committee I, vol. III, p. 101, para. 39; *ibid.*, 35th Meeting at p. 102, paras. 7, 8; *ibid.*, 36th Meeting at p. 109, paras. 49–57, UN Doc. A/CONF. 13/39 (1958).

[103] Rule 81. [104] Rule 50.

[105] UN GAOR, 2nd Committee, 3rd Session, 85th Meeting, p. 364, UN Doc. A/C.2/3/SR.85 (1948).

[106] UN GAOR, 3rd Committee, 30th Session, 2130th Meeting, paras. 7–18, UN Doc. A/C.3/SR.2130 (1975). It is of interest to note that, in accordance with *Robert's Rules of Order*, a point of order can never be reconsidered. *Robert's Rules of Order, Newly Revised*, 11th edn (2011), p. 249.

[107] UN GAOR, 1st Committee, 21st Session, 1470th Meeting, paras. 36–145, UN Doc. A/C.1/21/SR.1470 (1966); *ibid.*, 1471st Meeting, paras. 36–40, UN Doc. A/C.1/21/SR.1471

At a 1985 meeting of the UNGA, the US delegation proposed an amendment to a proposal by Nicaragua and others. The representative of Nicaragua proposed that 'no action' be taken on the US amendment and that the proposal of Nicaragua and others be immediately put to the vote.[108] The Nicaraguan procedural motion was adopted. The representative of St Lucia then moved a procedural motion that no action be taken on the substantive proposal by Nicaragua and others. The Chairman, after consulting with the representatives of the Legal Department of the UN, ruled that the St Lucia procedural motion was in order.[109] Arguably the Chairman regarded the St Lucia motion as a new proposal and not a reconsideration.

At a meeting of the 1992 UNGA,[110] Belarus, under Rule 74 of the rules of procedure, proposed to adjourn the debate on the subject of the scale of assessment 'until the resumed 47th Session of the UNGA'. The motion was defeated. Later, at the same meeting, the United States requested the Assembly to reconsider the Belarus motion under Rule 81 (the rule on reconsideration). The US delegation therefore assumed that, despite the procedural character of the Belarus motion, its reconsideration would require a two-thirds majority. The President indeed stated that its reconsideration would require a two-thirds majority.[111] It could be that the President regarded the motion as substantive rather than purely procedural.

At a meeting of a committee of a 1969 IMCO conference, it was decided to hold a vote on three questions of principle. When, at the next meeting, a delegate proposed to defer the vote on the third question, the President ruled that 'according to the rules of procedure, a decision to defer the third vote could be taken only on a point of order and by a two-thirds majority'.[112]

(1966); *ibid.*, 1472nd Meeting, paras. 1–3, UN Doc. A/C.1/21/SR.1472 (1966); *ibid.*, 1473rd Meeting, paras. 1–24, UN Doc. A/C.1/21/SR.1473 (1966).

108 The proposal was submitted under Rule 116 of the rules of procedure of the General Assembly, which refers to adjournment of debate.

109 UN GAOR, 2nd Committee, 40th Session, 48th Meeting, paras. 44, 45, UN Doc. A/C.2/40/SR.48 (1985).

110 UN GAOR, Plenary, 47th Session, 94th Meeting, p. 12, UN Doc. A/47/PV.94 (Provisional) (1993).

111 *Ibid.* at p. 41. The motion for reconsideration failed to obtain a simple majority.

112 Official Records of the 1969 IMCO Conference on Marine Pollution Damage, Summary Records of the 9th Meeting of the 2nd Committee, p. 664, IMCO Doc. LEG/CONF/C.2/SR.9 (1969).

11.4.1 Does the Rule on Reconsideration Apply to Motions for Adjournment or Suspension?

During the 1958 Law of the Sea Conference, the representative of Mexico moved the adjournment of the meeting, and the motion was rejected.[113] The representative of Egypt moved the adjournment of the debate, and this was also defeated. The representative of Morocco again moved the adjournment of the meeting, and the Chairman stated that 'the rules of procedure did not preclude a second motion on the adjournment of the meeting at that stage'.[114]

At a 1947 meeting of the UNGA, two motions for adjournment, in quick succession, were allowed. No issue as to reconsideration arose.[115] At a 1953 meeting of the UNGA, the Chairman allowed two motions for adjournment of debate in quick succession, and no issue as to reconsideration arose.[116]

British parliamentary procedure is that if a motion for the adjournment of the debate is defeated, a second motion to the same effect cannot be moved unless some other motion or an amendment has in the meantime been moved.[117]

COMMENT

There is inconsistency in reported decisions, but it appears that where there has been some passage of time between motions, then the rule as to reconsideration does not apply to motions for suspension of a meeting, adjournment of a meeting, adjournment of debate and closure of debate. This rule is logical in that a later motion applies to a different stage of a meeting or a debate. It would appear that other procedural motions are subject to the normal rule as to reconsideration.

113 Official Records of the 1958 Law of the Sea Conference, 62nd Meeting of Committee I, vol. III, p. 196, para. 28, UN Doc. A/CONF.13/39 (1958).

114 *Ibid.* at para. 37.

115 UN GAOR, Plenary, 2nd Session, 93rd Meeting, pp. 325–327, UN Doc. A/PV.93 (1947).

116 UN GAOR, 6th Committee, 8th Session, 391st Meeting, paras. 20, 33, 47, 48, UN Doc. A/C.6/8/SR.391 (1953).

117 S. C. Hawtrey and H. M. Barclay, *Abraham and Hawtrey's Parliamentary Dictionary*, 3rd edn (1970), p. 6; *Erskine May's Treatise on the Law, Privileges, Proceedings and Usage of Parliament*, eds. Sir Donald Limon and W. R. McKay, 22nd edn (1997), p. 340.

11.4.2 Does the Rule on Reconsideration Apply to Motions to Suspend the Rules of Procedure?

At a meeting of the 1973 Rome Air Law Conference, the USSR proposed suspension of a rule of procedure after a similar proposal had been defeated at an earlier meeting.[118] The representative of the United Kingdom 'requested a ruling by the President on whether the Soviet proposal came under Rule 16 (Reconsideration of Proposals)'.[119] The President ruled,

> [T]he proposal did not fall under Rule 16. If any provision of the Rules of Procedure was clear, it was Rule 29 which said that the Rules might be amended or any portion of them suspended 'at any time' by decision of the Conference, taken by a majority vote of the Representatives present and voting.[120]

The reasoning of the President was based on the phrase 'at any time'.

118 Minutes of the 8th Meeting of the Plenary of the 1973 Rome Air Law Conference, p. 299, para. 19, ICAO Doc. 9225-LC/178 (1973).

119 Minutes of the 9th Meeting of the Plenary of the 1973 Rome Air Law Conference, p. 302, para. 8, ICAO Doc. 9225-LC/178 (1973).

120 *Ibid.* at para. 9.

12

Procedural Motions and Points of Order

12.1 Procedural Motions

12.1.1 Definition of a Procedural Motion

A definition, necessarily circular, of a procedural motion is that it is a request by a delegation for the conference or assembly to decide on an issue of procedure. There is no exhaustive list of what issues constitute issues of procedure.

Examples of procedural motions are motions to

1. Suspend a meeting
2. Adjourn a meeting
3. Adjourn a debate
4. Close a debate
5. Reconsider a proposal
6. Divide a proposal for purposes of voting
7. Refrain from taking a decision
8. Decide the order of voting on proposals
9. Decide whether to vote on the next proposal where a previous proposal related to the same question
10. Challenge the ruling of a presiding officer on a point of order
11. Ask for an opinion of the President, the Secretary-General or the Legal Adviser of the Conference[1]
12. Suspend the rules of procedure.

At a 1966 meeting of the UNGA, a discussion took place about whether the rule as to reconsideration applied to procedural proposals. The US representative argued, 'The rules of procedure did not make a distinction between substantive and non-substantive proposals. They did distinguish

[1] Included in the definition of a motion as to procedure in Article 15(2)(2)(f) of the Standing Orders of the ILO Conference, ILO, Geneva 1992.

between proposals, on the one hand, and motions of a particular character, such as those mentioned in rules, 117, 120 and 122, on the other.'[2]

The statement of the US representative was correct regarding the UNGA. There are, however, rules of procedure of conferences and organisations that explicitly distinguish, for purposes of the majority required, between substantive and procedural issues.

12.1.2 *Examples of Decisions as to What Is a Procedural Motion*

At a meeting of the 1974–1977 Geneva Humanitarian Law Conference, the Chairman ruled that a Swiss proposal to hold a vote on the principle of an issue before voting on texts was a 'point of substance and not a point of order [*sic*]'.[3]

At the 1951 session of the UNGA, there was an oral proposal by Iraq that the Committee resolve that it was empowered to discuss political matters and political aspects in regard to non-self-governing territories. The question arose as to whether that proposal was procedural, in which case it could be moved without giving due prior notice. By allowing it, the Chairman, by implication, regarded it as a procedural proposal.[4]

At a 1981 meeting of a UNGA committee, a representative of the UN Office of Legal Affairs referred to the distinction between procedural and substantive motions. The representative gave the Committee his opinion that a draft decision that called for procedural action by the General Assembly was a substantive motion since 'it did not relate to a matter on which the Committee could make a final decision'.[5]

Rule 19 of the rules of procedure of the Assembly of the League of Nations stated:

> 2. All matters of procedure at a meeting of the Assembly, *including the appointment of Committees to investigate particular matters*, shall be decided by a majority of the Members.[6] [emphasis added]

[2] UN GAOR, 1st Committee, 21st Session, 1471st Meeting, para. 40, UN Doc. A/C.1/21/SR.1471 (1966).

[3] Official Records of the 1974–1977 Geneva Humanitarian Law Conference, CDDH/II/SR.62, vol. XII, p. 87, Summary Records of the 62nd Meeting of the 2nd Committee, para. 14.

[4] UN GAOR, 4th Committee, 6th Session, 210th Meeting, paras. 24, 25, 44, UN Doc. A/C.4/6/SR.210 (1951).

[5] UN GAOR, 2nd Committee, 36th Session, 48th Meeting, para. 50, UN Doc. A/C.2/36/SR.48 (1981).

[6] League of Nations Doc. C.472.M.204.1934.V.

Presumably, without such a rule, appointment of committees of investigation would not have been considered a procedural issue.[7] It is submitted that current practice would not deem such a proposal to be a procedural issue.

12.2 Points of Order

The rules of procedure of the UNGA stipulate,

> *Points of Order*
> *Rule 71*
> During the discussion of any matter, a representative may rise to a point of order, and the point of order shall be immediately decided by the President in accordance with the rules of procedure. A representative may appeal against the ruling of the President. The appeal shall immediately be put to the vote, and the President's ruling shall stand unless overruled by a majority of the members present and voting. A representative rising to a point of order may not speak on the substance of the matter under discussion.

The UN Model Rules proposal is substantially the same except that it adds that the rule is subject to the rule as to conduct during voting.[8]

The Secretary-General of the UN, in a report submitted in 1952, proposed adding the phrase, 'A point of order may relate only to such questions as lie within the competence of the President (Chairman).'[9] The Soviet representative argued against the proposal, stating that

> it would distort the true meaning of a point of order, and would, by an unduly restrictive definition, prevent the settlement of a great number of matters which were now regarded as points of order despite the fact that in some cases those matters could not be decided by the President or Chairman but required a vote.[10]

The phrase proposed by the Secretary-General was not adopted.[11]

7 Substantive decisions of the Council of the League of Nations required unanimity.

8 Rule 35 of the UN Model Rules.

9 Measures to limit the duration of regular sessions of the General Assembly: Memorandum by the Secretary-General, UN GAOR, Plenary, 7th Session, Annex VII, p. 7, para. 5, UN Doc. A/2206 (1952).

10 UN GAOR, 6th Committee, 7th Session, 347th Meeting, p. 236, para. 11, UN Doc. A/C.6/7/SR.347 (1952).

11 The Seventh Session of the UNGA set up a Special Committee on Measures to Limit the Duration of Regular Sessions of the General Assembly to 'consider the Secretary-General's

A detailed description of a point of order in UN practice is given in a report of a 1971 UN Special Committee on the Rationalisation of the Procedures and Organisation of the General Assembly. The definition – with present numbering of the UNGA rules of procedure in square brackets – is worth quoting in full. It states:

(a) A point of order is basically an intervention directed to the presiding officer, requesting him to make use of some power inherent in his office or specifically given him under the rules of procedure. It may, for example, relate to the manner in which the debate is conducted, to the maintenance of order, to the observance of the rules of procedure or to the way in which presiding officers exercise the powers conferred upon them by the rules. Under a point of order, a representative may request the presiding officer to apply a certain rule of procedure or he may question the way in which the officer applies the rule. Thus, within the scope of the rules of procedure, representatives are enabled to direct the attention of the presiding officer to violations or misapplications of the rules by other representatives or by the presiding officer himself. A point of order has precedence over any other matter including procedural motions (rules 73 and 79) [71 and 77].
(b) Points of order raised under rule 73 [71] involve questions necessitating a ruling by the presiding officer, subject to possible appeal. They are therefore distinct from the procedural motions provided for in rules 76 to 79 [74 to 77] which can be decided only by a vote and on which more than one motion may be entertained at the same time, rule 79 [77] laying down the precedence of such motions. They are also distinct from requests for information or clarification, or from remarks relating to material arrangements (seating, interpretation system, temperature of the room), documents, and translations etc. which – while they may have to be dealt with by the presiding officer – do not require rulings from him. However, in established United Nations practice, a representative intending to submit a procedural

memorandum' (UNGA Resolution 689 (VII) of 21 December 1952). The Special Committee concluded that 'the difficulties which have arisen [on points of order] have been due primarily to the manner in which these rules have been applied rather than to the text of their provisions'. UN GAOR, Plenary, 8th Session, Annexes, Agenda Item 54, para. 40, UN Doc. A/2402 (1953). The Committee did not recommend amending the rules of procedure in this respect.

motion or to seek information or clarification often rises 'to a point of order' as a means of obtaining the floor. The latter usage, which is based on practical grounds, should not be confused with the raising of points of order under rule 73 [71].

(c) Under rule 73 [71], a point of order must be immediately decided by the presiding officer in accordance with the rules of procedure, any appeal arising there from must also be put immediately to the vote. It follows that as a general rule:
  (i) A point of order and any appeal arising from a ruling thereon is not debatable;
  (ii) No point of order on the same or a different subject can be permitted until the initial point of order and any appeal arising there from have been disposed of.

Nevertheless, both the presiding officer and delegations may request information or clarification regarding a point of order. In addition, the presiding officer may, if he considers it necessary, request an expression of views from delegations on a point of order before giving his ruling; in the exceptional cases in which this practice is resorted to, the presiding officer should terminate the exchange of views and give his ruling as soon as he is ready to announce that ruling.

(d) Rule 73 [71] provides that a representative rising to a point of order may not speak on the substance of the matter under discussion. Consequently, the purely procedural nature of points of order calls for brevity. The presiding officer is responsible for ensuring that statements made on a point of order are in conformity with the present description.[12]

The practical guide to the UNGA published by the Permanent Mission of Switzerland to the UN explains,

[12] Report of the Special Committee on the Rationalisation of the Procedures and Organisation of the General Assembly, para. 229, UN GAOR, 26th Session, Supp. No. 26, UN Doc. A/8426 (1971). The Committee was established by UNGA Resolution 2632 (XXV) of 9 November 1970. The Report, including this definition, was approved by UNGA Resolution 2837 (XXVI) of 17 December 1971, and the General Assembly decided that the Report should be annexed to the UNGA rules of procedure.

Earlier and shorter definitions of a point of order appeared in the Report of the Special Committee on Methods and Procedures of the General Assembly, p. 11, para. 37, UN GAOR, 4th Session, Supp. No. 12, UN Doc. A/937 (1949); Memorandum of the Secretary-General on Measures to Limit the Duration of Regular Sessions of the General Assembly, UN GAOR, 7th Session, Annexes, Agenda Item 50, para. 38, UN Doc. A/2206 (1952).

> If a Member State raises a point of order, the proceedings of the meeting are interrupted and the point of order is addressed immediately as follows; the president or chairman rules on the point of order and the meeting continues. A. Member State can challenge the ruling. The Office of Legal Affairs may be requested to provide clarification on the specific provision in the GA Rules of Procedure. In rare cases, the challenge is put to a vote, carried by a simple majority; there is no debate on the point of order and there are no explanations of vote. The meeting continues based on the' outcome of that vote. The delegate of the Member State who raised the point of order cannot speak on the substance of the item under discussion.[13]

12.2.1 Distinction between a Point of Order and a Procedural Motion

Points of order are decided by the presiding officer while a procedural motion is decided by vote. The difference between a point of order and a procedural motion was illustrated during the 1975 Vienna Conference on Representation of States.

The delegate of Cameroon at the 1975 Vienna Conference on Representation of States requested that on a certain issue the text of the International Law Commission be voted on before the vote on amendments to the text. The delegate of Canada pointed out that it would be against the rules of procedure to do so and requested the Chairman to rule the Cameroonian proposal out of order. The delegate of Belarus then stated that 'two procedural proposals had been made [that of Cameroon and that of Canada] ... it was now therefore a matter of putting the two proposals to the vote in the order in which they had been submitted'. The Chairman immediately ruled that 'while the Cameroonian proposal was in fact a proposal, the same was not true of the Canadian one which was in reality a motion on a point of order'.[14]

On the difference between a point of order and a procedural proposal, the representative of Australia to the Sixth Committee of the 1952 UNGA pointed out that while 'procedural motions required the Assembly's or the Committee's decision, points of order came within the competence of the President or the Chairman'.[15] The representative of the UK explained that

[13] The Practical Guide to the UNGA published by the Permanent Mission of Switzerland to the UN, para. 3.3, www.unitar.org/ny/sites/unitar.org.ny/files/UN_PGA_Handbook.pdf.

[14] Summary Records of the 1975 Vienna Conference on Representation of States, 41st Meeting of the Committee of the Whole, pp. 308, 309, paras. 15, 22, 23, UN Doc. A/CONF.67/C.1/SR.41 (1975).

[15] UN GAOR, 6th Committee, 7th Session, 349th Meeting, para. 30, UN Doc. A/C.6/7/SR.349 (1952).

> the request for permission to speak could properly be called a point of order even though the statement itself could not. He believed that it was within the President's or Chairman's competence to allow a representative to make a procedural motion. If the motion came within any specific rule of procedure which gave it priority, the President or Chairman was entitled to so rule.[16]

At a 1982 meeting of the World Health Assembly, the Legal Counsel of the WHO stated that a description of a point of order 'was applicable only to points of order to be decided by the Chair and not to procedural motions which had to be voted on'.[17]

12.3 Categories of Points of Order

There are five basic categories of points of order.

12.3.1 A Point of Order Requesting a Decision by the Presiding Officer

A common type of point of order is where a delegation requests the presiding officer to make a decision that, in accordance with the relevant rules of procedure, is within the competence of the presiding officer. Examples of this type of point of order would be:

1. A request for the application of a rule of procedure
2. A request to rule that an action or a statement is out of order[18]
3. A request to exercise a right of reply. The right of reply is, however, usually automatically granted by the presiding officer after such a request is registered with the Secretariat, thus obviating the need to raise a point of order.[19]

12.3.2 A Point of Order Raised in Order to Submit a Procedural Motion

Although the procedural motion is not in itself a point of order, a delegation wishing to submit a procedural motion needs to obtain the floor in

[16] *Ibid.* at para. 55.
[17] Summary Records of the 8th Meeting of Committee 'B' of the 35th World Health Assembly, p. 233, WHA35/1982/REC/3 (1982).
[18] See discussion on this issue in Chapter 5.
[19] See, for example, Official Records of the 253rd Meeting of the 27th General Conference of the IAEA, paras. 73–75, IAEA Doc. GC(XXVII)/OR.253 (1984).

order to submit the motion. Unless the delegation is scheduled to speak, obtaining the floor is done by way of a point of order. It is common practice to bring a procedural motion to the attention of a conference or assembly by way of raising a point of order.

At the 1982 session of the UNGA, Iran submitted an amendment to the Report of the Credentials Committee calling for the rejection of the credentials of the Israel delegation.[20] The Nordic countries submitted a written motion 'not to take any action' on the Iranian amendment.[21] Norway, on a point of order, introduced the motion on behalf of the Nordic countries, explaining that the motion was 'within the terms of rule 74 of the rules of procedure of the General Assembly'.[22] In the next session of the General Assembly, the Iranian delegation again submitted an amendment calling for the rejection of Israel's credentials.[23] This time Norway, on behalf of the Nordic countries, dispensed with the submission of a written motion and moved, on a point of order, that 'no action be taken' on the Iranian amendment and that this motion was 'made within the terms of rule 74 of the rules of procedure of the General Assembly'.[24] In both cases a point of order was used to introduce the procedural motion; in one case the motion was written and in the other it was an oral motion.

At a 1982 meeting of the World Health Assembly, the representative of Algeria called for a closure of debate, whereupon the representative of Botswana, speaking on a point of order, moved the suspension of the meeting. The representative of Saudi Arabia said that 'in his delegation's view, a new proposal could not be made by a member speaking on a point of order'.[25] The Legal Counsel gave his opinion that 'in fact, the customary way to move a suspension when the closure of a debate had already been moved was to rise to a point of order; to do so was in conformity with the practice observed in the WHO and elsewhere in the United Nations System'.[26]

At the 1960 Conference of the ILO, a delegation requested the floor on a point of order in order to move a motion for closure of debate. The motion for closure was adopted. The Government delegate from the USSR objected, claiming that this had prevented another Government

[20] UN Doc. A/37/L.9 (1982). [21] UN Doc. A/37/L.11 (1982).

[22] UN GAOR, Plenary, 37th Session, 45th Meeting, paras. 2–5, UN Doc. A/37/PV.45 (1982).

[23] UN Doc. A/38/L.4 (1983).

[24] UN GAOR, Plenary, 38th Session, 34th Meeting, para. 43, UN Doc. A/38/PV.34 (1983).

[25] Summary Records of the 8th Meeting of Committee 'B' of the 35th World Health Assembly, p. 232, WHA35/1982/REC/3 (1982).

[26] *Ibid.*

delegate from the USSR, Mr Goroshkin, from speaking. The Soviet delegate argued,

> Now in accordance with article 15 of our Standing Orders, motions of closure are not points of order and therefore Mr Rossetti [the delegate who moved the closure] did not speak to the point to which he had risen. He could have asked for closure but then he would have had to ask for the floor separately and not state that he was going to raise a point of order. You would then, Mr President, have given the floor to Mr Goroshkin, who would have been asked to say what he had in mind on the matter.[27]

The President ruled, 'Article 15 includes, among motions as to procedure, nothing referring specifically to closure, which is dealt with separately in Article 16.' The President accepted the Soviet intervention and permitted the Government delegate from the USSR to speak, notwithstanding the motion for closure that had been passed.[28]

12.3.3 A Point of Order Requiring Neither a Vote nor a Presidential Decision

There are some points of order that require neither a vote nor a decision by the presiding officer. Examples are a request for a roll-call vote, withdrawal of a proposal that has not been amended, and reintroduction of a proposal. A delegation moving one of these procedural motions does so by way of a point of order. The presiding officer has no discretion and must comply with such a request without referring it to the assembly or conference.[29]

12.3.4 A Point of Order on a Matter of Clarification

A delegation wishing the presiding officer to provide clarification requests such clarification by way of a point of order. The presiding officer is requested to provide information and not necessarily to make a ruling. An example is where the presiding officer is asked to clarify, during a voting process, exactly what proposals or amendments are being voted on.

[27] ILO Conference, 44th Session, Geneva 1960, 22nd sitting, p. 380.

[28] *Ibid.* at p. 381. The omission of a reference to closure in Article 15(2)(2) was apparently inadvertent, and the article was subsequently amended to include a specific reference to closure.

[29] Rule 54(1) of the UN Model Rules; Rule 87(a) of the UNGA rules of procedure.

12.3.5 A Point of Order on Technical Arrangements

A presiding officer is frequently asked to make arrangements of a technical matter such as:

1. Interpretation
2. Seating and arrangement of rooms for meetings
3. Information on times of meetings
4. Distribution of documents

The presiding officer in such cases is being requested to make arrangements not requiring a ruling. The request for the action is, however, in the form of a point of order.

12.4 Decisions by Presiding Officers on Points of Order

The UNGA rules of procedure state,

> *Rule 71*
>
> During the discussion of any matter, a representative may rise to a point of order, and the point of order shall be immediately decided by the President in accordance with the rules of procedure.[30]

The UN Model Rules is similar, except that it adds 'at any time' and excludes the voting process.[31]

12.5 Discretion of Presiding Officer to Allow a Delegation to Raise a Point of Order

The presiding officer must allow a delegate to raise a point of order.

During the 1973 ILO Conference, the President refused to allow a delegation to raise a point of order during a speech by another delegation. The Legal Adviser was asked for his opinion as to whether there 'is a clause in the Standing Orders permitting the President to refuse to allow a point of order to be raised or a motion as to procedure to be moved without knowing what it is'. The Legal Adviser replied, 'On the point of order it is clear, under article 14(5), that "a delegate may at any time rise to a point of order, which shall be decided forthwith by the President" . . . The President

[30] The first sentence of Rule 71 of the UNGA rules of procedure.

[31] UN Model Rule 35. UN Doc. A/37/163, Annex (1982).

should have taken a decision forthwith if it had been clear that a point of order was involved.'[32]

12.6 Can a Conference or Assembly Decide a Point of Order?

The question has arisen as to whether the presiding officer must make a decision or whether he can request that the assembly or conference take the decision.

A 1952 memorandum by the Secretary-General of the UN to the Seventh Session of the UNGA stated,

> Rules 72 and 112 properly require the President or Chairman immediately to decide on points of order. The clear implication of this provision it [*sic*] that a point of order must relate to a question which is within the competence of the Chairman either by means of his own ruling *or, at his discretion, by referring the question at issue to the judgement of the body as a whole.*[33] [emphasis added]

This comment is in contradiction to the plain text of the rule.

The 1963 Ad Hoc Committee on the Improvement of the Methods of Work of the General Assembly commented on this question: 'The responsibility for deciding is his [the presiding officer's] alone and the rules do not provide that he may request the Assembly or committee to make a ruling for him; a representative who is not satisfied with the presiding officer's decision is entirely free to appeal to the Assembly or the committee.'[34]

The Report of the 1971 Special Committee on the Rationalisation of the Procedures and Organisation of the General Assembly categorically states that

> a point of order must be immediately decided by the presiding officer in accordance with the rules of procedure . . . It follows that as a general rule:
>
> (1) A point of order and any appeal arising from a ruling thereon is not debatable;
>
> . . .
>
> In addition, the presiding officer may, if he considers it necessary, request an expression of views from delegations on a point of order before giving

32 ILO Conference, 58th Session, Geneva 1973, p. 404.

33 UN GAOR, Memorandum by the Secretary-General, 7th Session, Annex, Agenda Item 50, para. 39, UN Doc. A/2206 (1952).

34 Report of the Ad Hoc Committee on the Improvement of the Methods of Work of the General Assembly, UN GAOR, 18th Session, Annexes, Agenda Item 25, para. 52, UN Doc. A/5423 (1963).

> his ruling; in the exceptional cases in which this practice is resorted to, the presiding officer should terminate the exchange of views and give his ruling as soon as he is ready to announce that ruling.[35]

The issue of who should decide on a point of order arose at the 1974–1977 Geneva Humanitarian Law Conference when the President replied to a delegate who raised a point of order that if a ruling was requested he would submit the question to the Conference.[36] Later at the same Conference when a decision of the President was challenged, the President referred the original question on which the decision had been made, and not the challenge, to the Conference.[37] The delegate from Romania commented that 'it was customary for votes in connexion with presidential rulings in international conferences to be taken on challenges to those rulings, not on the rulings themselves'.[38] It is submitted that the Romanian delegate was correct on this issue.

At a 1980 committee meeting of the UNGA, the Committee decided to vote on two resolutions together. After the vote on the first resolution, the meeting was adjourned, and at the next meeting the Algerian representative requested permission to submit an amendment to the second resolution. The Chairman stated that the voting had already begun on the second resolution, and therefore the Committee would have to decide whether to allow amendments to be submitted at this stage.[39] Several representatives pointed out that the Algerian proposal was in fact a challenge to the Chairman's ruling that voting had commenced and therefore should be treated as a challenge to a ruling and not as a proposal to be put to the vote of the Committee. The Chairman apparently accepted the argument since he reiterated his ruling that voting had commenced and stated that 'a vote should now be taken to determine whether the Committee endorsed Algeria's appeal against his ruling'.[40]

[35] Report of the Special Committee on the Rationalisation of the Procedures and Organisation of the General Assembly, UN GAOR, 26th Session, Supp. No. 26, para. 229, UN Doc. A/8426 (1971).

[36] Official Records of the 1974–1977 Geneva Humanitarian Law Conference, CDDH/SR.24, vol. V, p. 277, para. 2.

[37] *Ibid.*, CDDH/SR.25, vol. V, p. 298, para. 64.

[38] *Ibid.*, CDDH/SR.26, vol. V, p. 304, para. 25.

[39] UN GAOR, 4th Committee, 35th Session, 22nd Meeting, para. 3, UN Doc. A/C.4/35/SR.22 (1980).

[40] UN GAOR, 4th Committee, 35th Session, 22nd Meeting, para. 13, UN Doc. A/C.4/35/SR.22 (1980).

The rule in the UN Model Rules on the order of voting on proposals, Rule 60, illustrates the issue of the difference between issues to be decided by the presiding officer and those to be decided by the conference.

Rule 60

1. If two or more proposals, other than amendments, relate to the same question, they shall, unless the Conference decides otherwise, be voted on in the order in which they were submitted. The Conference may, after each vote on a proposal, decide whether to vote on the next proposal.[41]

In such a case the issue of whether a proposal 'relates to the same question' is an issue to be decided by the presiding officer. His decision can, of course, be challenged. The issue, however, of the order of voting and whether to vote on the 'next' proposal is an issue to be decided by the conference and not by the presiding officer.

12.7 Raising a Point of Order while a Representative Is Speaking on an Earlier Point of Order

The 1963 UN Ad Hoc Committee on the Improvement of the Methods of Work of the General Assembly commented, 'No other point of order should be discussed before the presiding officer has decided upon the previous one.'[42]

The UNGA rule states, 'During the discussion of any matter, a representative may rise to a point of order.'[43] The UN Model Rules state that 'a representative may at any time raise a point of order'. A Canadian working paper submitted to a UN committee stated, 'A point of order cannot be raised on a point of order' and that 'confusion results' when a presiding officer fails to rule immediately on a point of order. The Canadian paper reaches the conclusion that 'no additional point of order may be raised until the presiding officer's ruling has been made and any consequent appeal disposed of.'[44] Bailey, writing on UN Security Council procedure,

[41] Rule 91 of the UNGA rules of procedure is substantially identical, although it does not include the specific exception as to amendments referred to in the UN Model Rules.

[42] Report of the Ad Hoc Committee on the Improvement of the Methods of Work of the General Assembly, UN GAOR, 18th Session, Annexes, Agenda Item 25, p. 8, para. 52, UN Doc. A/5423 (1963).

[43] Rule 71 of the UNGA rules of procedure.

[44] Working Paper submitted by Canada, Special Committee on the Rationalisation of the Procedures and Organisation of the General Assembly, p. 3, UN Doc. A/AC.149/DG.II/5 (1971).

states that 'no point of order on the same or a different subject may be entertained until the initial point of order and any challenge thereto have been disposed of'. Bailey adds that 'the only circumstance in which the President may refuse to entertain a point of order . . . is if an earlier point of order has not been resolved'.[45] Nevertheless, the practice of the UNGA is at times to allow points of order to be raised while a representative is speaking on an earlier point of order. If this procedure were not followed, there would be no way, for instance, for a delegate to point out that a point of order was being misused.

An accumulation of points of order can, however, in the experience of the present author, lead to procedural chaos, and I would unhesitatingly support the opinion of Lang, who suggests that a presiding officer 'will also be well advised to dispose quickly of points of order, even at the risk that his ruling is challenged and overruled by a majority'.[46]

12.8 Limiting the Duration of Statements on Points of Order

The General Committee of the 1993 UNGA recommended that statements on points of order should be limited to five minutes. The General Assembly adopted the recommendation.[47]

12.9 Limiting the Number of Points of Order

At a meeting of the 1968 Teheran Conference on Human Rights, the Chairman of a committee proposed that the Israel representative, who was being continuously interrupted by points of order, be given 'seven minutes without interruption'. The representative of the Ukrainian Soviet Socialist Republic said that 'he had doubts about the Chairman's ruling that the Israel representative should speak without interruption. According to Rule 22 of the rules of procedure, a representative might rise to a point of order during the discussion of any matter. Surely the Committee would not wish to violate that rule.' The Chairman replied that 'he could propose the limitation of time to be allowed to speakers and the limitation

[45] Sydney D. Bailey, *The Procedure of the UN Security Council*, 2nd edn (1988), p. 168.

[46] Winfred Lang, 'Multilateral Negotiations: The Role of Presiding Officers', in *Processes of International Negotiations*, ed. Frances Mautner-Markhof (1989), p. 35.

[47] UNGA, 48th Session, First Report of the General Committee, Organisation of the Forty-Eighth Regular Session of the General Assembly, Adoption of the Agenda and Allocation of Items, UN Doc. A/48/250, para. 17 (1993). Adopted by the Plenary, UN GAOR, 48th Session, 3rd Meeting, para. 58, UN Doc. A/48/PV.3 (1993).

of the number of times each representative might speak on any question. Under that rule he would limit the number of times a representative might rise to speak while another member was speaking.'[48] The Chairman's ruling would appear to be understandable but incorrect.

12.10 Challenging a Decision of a Presiding Officer

Rule 71 of the rules of procedure of the UNGA stipulates that, as regards a decision of the President on a point of order,

> A representative may appeal against the ruling of the President. The appeal shall immediately be put to the vote, and the President's ruling shall stand unless overruled by a majority of the members present and voting.

The proposal in the UN Model Rules is identical.

The report of the Sixth Committee to the UNGA, at its 1949 session, stated that there was general agreement that '[t]he General Assembly and its Committees should remain the final masters of the conduct of their proceedings and that therefore it was not desirable to confer upon the President or the Chairman any powers of decision which would be without appeal to the organ over which they preside'.[49] This is a reflection of the general rule that presiding officers remain under the control of the assembly or conference.

12.10.1 The Process of Voting on a Challenge to a Decision by a Presiding Officer

During the 1974 session of the UNGA, the President of the Assembly, at the request of some delegations, decided to put to the vote his ruling and not the challenge that had been submitted. The President explained that in his opinion this would be more courteous to those delegations challenging his ruling.[50]

At a 1965 committee meeting of the UNGA, during a debate on the question of Cyprus, the Chairman, after lengthy discussions, accepted the contention of some delegates that the voting on a challenge is held on the appeal and not on the ruling of the Chairman. This was important

[48] Summary Records of the 1968 Teheran Conference on Human Rights, UN Doc. A/CONF.32/C.2/SR.10, pp. 114, 115 (1968).

[49] Report of the 6th Committee, Agenda Item 48, UN GAOR, 4th Session, Plenary Meetings, Annex, p. 182, para. 15, UN Doc. A/1026 and Corr.1 (1949).

[50] UN GAOR, Plenary, 29th Session, 2281st Meeting, para. 182, UN Doc. A/PV.2281 (1974).

in the particular case since the appeal concerned only a part of the Chairman's ruling.[51]

At a 1981 meeting of a UNGA committee, there was a challenge to the Chairman's ruling as to which amendment was furthest removed from the original. The representative of the United Kingdom said that 'the interests of clarity would be served if the Chairman requested the Committee to vote on the Chairman's ruling rather than on the appeal against it'.[52] The Chairman nevertheless proceeded to put to the vote the appeal against his ruling and not the ruling itself.[53]

COMMENT

The prevalent practice is to put to the vote the appeal and not the presiding officer's ruling. This practice conforms to the language of the rule that states that '[t]he appeal shall be immediately put to the vote'[54] and is a logical practice since a majority is needed to reverse a ruling. A tied vote means the presiding officer's ruling stands.[55]

12.10.2 Can a Challenge to a Ruling Be Debated?

At a 1948 meeting of a committee of the UNGA, the Chairman ruled that a Soviet amendment was admissible as an amendment. The ruling was challenged by the representative of the Netherlands who then requested permission to explain his reasons for the challenge. The Chairman ruled that it was his duty to put the challenge to an immediate vote without debate. The representative of Belgium then submitted a motion to allow the Netherlands to explain its challenge. The Belgian proposal was adopted. The Soviet delegation explained that the reason it had voted in

[51] UN GAOR, 1st Committee, 20th Session, 1418th Meeting, para. 14, UN Doc. A/C.1/20/SR.1418 (1965).

[52] UN GAOR, 4th Committee, 36th Session, 25th Meeting, para. 7, UN Doc. A/C.4/36/SR.25 (1981).

[53] *Ibid.* at para. 8.

[54] The equivalent UN Security Council rule, Rule 30, states that 'the President shall submit his ruling to the Security Council for immediate decision'. The ambiguity led, in the early years of the Council, to uncertainty as to whether the challenge or ruling should be put to the vote.

[55] *Robert's Rules of Order* states categorically that the correct procedure is to put the ruling to the vote and not the challenge: 'The vote is taken so that the affirmative will be in favor of sustaining the chair's decision.' *Robert's Rules of Order, Newly Revised*, 11th edn (2011), p. 260.

Leigh, in 1937, however, wrote, 'The vote is on reversing his [the Chairman's] ruling', Robert D. Leigh, *Modern Rules of Parliamentary Procedure* (1937), p. 48.

favour of the Belgian motion to allow a debate on a challenge was because there was no explicit rule in the rules of procedure that excluded debating a challenge to a chairman's ruling. The Soviet delegation pointed out that the rule as regards suspension or adjournment of a meeting states explicitly, 'Such motions shall not be debated', and that there was no such language regarding a challenge to the ruling of a presiding officer.[56]

At a 1949 meeting of the UNGA, the President ruled that a challenge to his ruling could not be debated and must be put immediately to the vote.[57]

At the Preparatory Conference to the 1979 Weapons Conference, the draft rules of procedure, in referring to points of order, stated that 'the President will, if he deems it necessary, either upon his own initiative or upon request from a representative or several representatives, give the floor alternately to speakers in favour and against each point raised'.[58] However the President later informed the Conference that this phrase 'had been included by mistake and should be deleted'.[59]

COMMENT

The prevalent practice is that if a ruling is challenged, it is put to the vote without debate. The phrase that the challenge should be put to the vote 'immediately' would appear to justify this practice.[60]

12.10.3 Can There Be Separate Votes on Parts of a Challenge to a Ruling by the Presiding Officer?

At a 1965 meeting of a committee of the UNGA, the Chairman refused to allow a request that the 'ruling should be put to the vote in two parts'.[61] Later, however, in the discussion on the same issue, the Chairman conceded that, since the vote would be on the appeal and not on the ruling,

56 UN GAOR, 6th Committee, 3rd Session, 111th Meeting, pp. 515, 516, UN Doc. A/C.6/3/SR.111 (1948).

57 UN GAOR, Plenary, 3rd Session, Part II, 219th Meeting, p. 611, UN Doc. A/PV.219 (1949).

58 Rule 20 of the draft rules of procedure of the Preparatory Conference for the 1979 Weapons Conference, UN Doc. A/CONF.95/PREP.CONF./2/Rev.1 (1978).

59 UN Doc. A/CONF.95/PREP.CONF./1/SR.16, para. 2 (1978).

60 American textbooks on parliamentary procedure state, however, that appeals against rulings are debatable. See *Robert's Rules of Order*, p. 257; Keesey, *Modern Parliamentary Procedure*, p. 66; Sturgis, *Standard Code*, p. 206; Leigh, *Modern Rules*, p. 47.

61 UN GAOR, 1st Committee, 20th Session, 1417th Meeting, paras. 33, 37, UN Doc. A/C.1/20/SR.1417 (1965).

it was up to the challenger to formulate his appeal. The challenger could thus obtain the formulation that he wished the Committee to vote on.[62]

12.11 Speaking to the Substance during a Statement on a Point of Order

Rule 71 of the rules of procedure of the UNGA stipulates,

> A representative rising to a point of order may not speak on the substance of the matter under discussion.

The proposal in the UN Model Rules is substantially the same.

Hovey writes, 'It is clear that Members tend to regard the point of order as a means of getting the floor when other means appear less promising.'[63] Speakers have been known to try to utilise a point of order as a substitute for a right of reply. An effective presiding officer will, if necessary, rule such a speaker to be out of order.[64]

At a 2010 meeting of the UNGA Plenary a delegate utilised a point of order to make a clearly political statement. The President settled for remarking after the statement that 'we are not currently discussing the substance of the agenda item'.[65]

12.12 Who Can Raise a Point of Order?

A 1988 opinion by the UN Office of Legal Affairs states UN practice to be 'reserving procedural motions, which concern conduct of business, for full members of the body'.[66] A 2007 opinion reiterates the UN policy that

[62] UN GAOR, 1st Committee, 20th Session, 1418th Meeting, paras. 1, 14, UN Doc. A/C.1/20/SR.1418 (1965).

[63] Allan Hovey Jr, 'Obstructionism and the Rules of the General Assembly', 5 *UNESCO International Organization* 515 (1951 No. 3) at 528.

[64] See, for example, UN GAOR, Plenary, 28th Session, 2138th Meeting, para. 201, UN Doc. A/PV.2138 (1973); UN GAOR, 1st Committee, 21st Session, 1484th Meeting, paras. 40–43, UN Doc. A/C.1/21/SR.1484 (1966); UN GAOR, 3rd Committee, 20th Session, 1372nd Meeting, paras. 44–50, UN Doc. A/C.3/20/SR.1372 (1965); UN GAOR 3rd Committee, 61st Session, 43rd Meeting, para. 29, UN Doc. A/C.3/61/SR.43 (2006).

[65] UN GAOR, Plenary, 65th session, 2nd Meeting, p. 6, UN Doc. A/65/PV.2 (2010).

[66] UN Office of Legal Affairs, *Cable to the Director-General, United Nations Office at Geneva* QUESTION OF WHETHER A STATE NOT A MEMBER OF AN ECONOMIC AND SOCIAL COUNCIL FUNCTIONAL COMMISSION PARTICIPATING IN ITS DELIBERATIONS MAY RAISE POINTS OF ORDER OR MAKE PROPOSALS OF A PROCEDURAL NATURE RULE 69, PARAGRAPH 3, OF THE RULES OF PROCEDURE OF FUNCTIONAL COMMISSIONS

'procedural motions which concern conduct of business are reserved for full members of the organ'. The opinion also states that the Holy See and Palestine can raise points of order but 'are not permitted to challenge the decision of the presiding officer or to raise points of order in connection with the actual conduct of voting'.[67]

'POINTS OF ORDER', PARAGRAPH 79 OF ANNEX V TO GENERAL ASSEMBLY RULES OF PROCEDURE *29 January 1988*, http://legal.un.org/ola/media/GA_RoP/GA_RoP_EN.pdf.

67 UN Office of Legal Affairs, REQUEST FOR LEGAL ADVICE FROM THE ASSISTANT SECRETARY-GENERAL FOR LEGAL AFFAIRS TO THE SECRETARY OF THE HUMAN RIGHTS COUNCIL 19 November 2007.

13

Priorities between Different Proposals

13.1 Order of Voting on Proposals

A study of records of international conferences reveals that more time is devoted to debating the order of voting on proposals and amendments than to any other single procedural issue. Delegations will attempt to achieve priority for their proposal as there are obvious advantages to the proposers if a proposal is voted on before an opposing one. This is particularly true when there are similarities between two different proposals and either one of them is likely to attract floating or neutral votes. In such a case, either proposal is likely to get a majority, or once the one proposal is accepted, the other alternative is likely to fall. It is therefore often the order in which proposals are put to the vote that determines which proposal will be adopted.

The rules of procedure of the UNGA stipulate,

Voting on Proposals
Rule 91

> If two or more proposals relate to the same question, the General Assembly shall, unless it decides otherwise, vote on the proposals in the order in which they have been submitted. The General Assembly may, after each vote on a proposal, decide whether to vote on the next proposal.

The UN Model Rules propose,

Rule 60
Order of Voting on Proposals

1. If two or more proposals, other than amendments, relate to the same question, they shall, unless the Conference decides otherwise, be voted on in the order in which they were submitted. The Conference may, after each vote on a proposal, decide whether to vote on the next proposal.
2. Revised proposals shall be voted on in the order in which the original proposals were submitted, unless the revision substantially departs

from the original proposal. In that case, the original proposal shall be considered as withdrawn and the revised proposal shall be treated as a new proposal. If it does substantially depart from the original proposal then it will no longer enjoy priority.

3. A motion requiring that no decision be taken on a proposal shall have priority over that proposal.

This rule of the UNGA is followed in all the rules of procedure of the conferences examined.[1]

The President of the First Session of the UNGA addressed a letter to the Chairman of the Sixth Committee requesting the Sixth Committee 'to state a view with regard to the order in which, under the provisional rules of procedure for the General Assembly, votes should be taken in the Assembly or its Committees on various proposals relating to one and the same question'.[2] A subcommittee of the Sixth Committee reported,

> It was its opinion that there could be only one resolution relating to one and the same question. All other proposals must be in the nature of amendments to the main resolution. Therefore Rule 75 [dealing with the order of voting on amendments] can be given effect in all cases where there are more proposals than one relating to one and the same question. The President of the Assembly, or the Chairman of the Committee, shall determine which proposal is to be taken as the basic draft resolution to which the other proposals will be considered as amendments.[3]

The Committee on Procedures and Organisation of the UNGA, at its Second Session, recommended the adoption of a rule stating,

> *Rule 84*
>
> If two or more proposals are moved relating to the same question, the General Assembly shall first vote on the most far-reaching proposal and then on the next most far-reaching proposal, and so on. The most far-reaching

[1] The equivalent rule in the rules of procedure of the Assembly of the League of Nations stated,

> *Rule 18*
>
> 5. When a number of proposals are before the Assembly, the proposal furthest removed in substance from the principal one shall be voted on first.

This formulation raised obvious problems as to the making of such a decision, and the UN formula appears to be preferable.

[2] UN GAOR, 6th Committee, 1st Session, p. 240, Annex 14, UN Doc. A/C.6/1/70 (1946).

[3] *Ibid.*, p. 241, Annex 14a, UN Doc. A/C.6/1/87 (1946).

> proposal means the proposal the adoption of which would result in the greatest change from the existing situation.[4]

This text was discussed in a subcommittee of the Sixth Committee, the report of the subcommittee stating that the majority of members were 'of the opinion that the test of "most far-reaching" contained in the rule proposed by the Committee on Procedures may cause practical difficulties'.[5] The subcommittee adopted a US proposal that provided that 'if two or more proposals relate to the same question, they should be voted on in the order in which they have been submitted, unless the General Assembly decides otherwise'.[6] The proposal of the subcommittee was discussed at a meeting of the Sixth Committee. Speaking against the proposed rule, the Norwegian representative argued,

> It might result in the adoption of a proposal which was not in accordance with the wish of the majority, as a representative might vote in favour of a proposal which was not their first choice, because they anticipated the rejection of the one they really preferred. Moreover, such a method might result in the failure to adopt any proposal at all.[7]

The Soviet representative on the Sixth Committee argued that the phrase 'unless the General Assembly decides otherwise' in the subcommittee draft

> might allow a proposal to be accepted without discussion of further proposals. This procedure of accepting one proposal and of refusing to consider others had been called a 'guillotine' procedure since it made it possible to avoid disagreeable proposals presented by the minority.[8]

The representative of the United Kingdom commented that 'in any general rule it helped to solve procedural difficulties if there was an escape clause'.[9] The text proposed by the subcommittee was adopted.[10]

At a meeting of a committee of the UNGA, at its 1981 session, the Chairman called for the vote to proceed on resolutions, in the order in

4 UN GAOR, 2nd Session, Plenary Meetings, vol. II, Annex 4, pp. 1455, 1473, UN Doc. A/388 (1947).

5 UN GAOR, 6th Committee, 2nd Session, p. 266, Procedures and Organisation of the General Assembly, Report of Sub-Committee 3 on Part III of the Report of the Committee, Annex 4c, Rule 84, UN Doc. A/C.6/2/182/Corr.1/Corr.2 (1947).

6 *Ibid.*

7 UN GAOR, 6th Committee, 2nd Session, 56th Meeting, p. 133, UN Doc. A/C.6/2/SR.56 (1947).

8 *Ibid.* at p. 135. 9 *Ibid.* 10 *Ibid.* at p. 136.

which they had been submitted. The USSR representative requested that priority be given to a certain resolution. The representative of Pakistan then stated that the Committee must vote on the resolutions in the order in which they were submitted and that '[i]f any delegation wished to appeal against the Chairman's ruling, that appeal would have to be put to the vote'.[11] The representative of the UN Office of Legal Affairs explained that 'the request that a vote should be taken first on draft decisions ... was not equivalent to an appeal against the Chairman's ruling under rule 113 of the rules of procedure. That request was solely equivalent to utilising the possibility provided for in rule 131 [order of voting on proposals].'[12]

During the 1958 Law of the Sea Conference, the representative of Viet Nam proposed that a United States proposal, although not submitted first, should, for various reasons, be put to the vote first. The representative of the United Arab Republic objected, holding that 'the rules of procedure should be strictly adhered to when there were several proposals on the same subject'. The US representative observed that 'rule 41 of the rules of procedure allowed the Committee to adopt any order of voting it saw fit'. The representative of the USSR (Professor Tunkin) stated, 'Every proposal had equal standing and when there were several on the same subject, the only reasonable criterion must be the order of submission.' The Viet Nam motion was put to the vote (and rejected).[13]

During the 1961 Vienna Conference on Diplomatic Relations, the UK representative pointed out, 'Since the ... texts were not amendments, the Committee could decide to vote on them out of the order of submission.'[14] In the 1963 Vienna Conference on Consular Relations, a similar problem arose when the representative of India proposed that an Indian proposal submitted as a later proposal should be voted on first. Here the representative of Switzerland objected, saying that 'the Conference should approach legal issues dispassionately ... the rules of procedure should be applied in the normal way'. The representative of the USSR stated that the Indian proposal 'was fully in accordance with rule 42 of the rules of procedure', while the representative of Sweden 'opposed the Indian motion which might create a somewhat dangerous precedent. If such motions were

[11] UN GAOR, 2nd Committee, 36th Session, 48th Meeting, para. 47, UN Doc. A/C.2/36/SR.48 (1981).

[12] *Ibid.* at para. 48.

[13] Official Records of the 1958 Law of the Sea Conference, 56th meeting of Committee I, vol. III, p. 175, paras. 5, 6, 7, 9, 11, UN Doc. A/CONF.13/39 (1958).

[14] Official Records of the 1961 Vienna Conference on Diplomatic Relations, 41st Meeting of the Committee of the Whole, p. 238, para. 35, UN Doc. A/CONF.20/14 (1961).

carried, it would be possible to prevent a relevant proposal from being put to the vote.' It was the representative of Ceylon who pointed out that 'such motions were quite normal and very common at UN meetings'. The Indian motion was put to the vote (and defeated).[15]

13.1.1 When Is a Proposal Considered to Have Been Submitted?

A 1976 legal opinion of the UN Office of Legal Affairs stated, 'It is now clearly established that the order referred to [in Rule 91 of the UNGA rules of procedure] is the order of submission of a draft to the Secretariat, not the date of circulation of the document or its formal introduction in the organ concerned.'[16]

13.1.2 Decision Not to Vote on Subsequent Proposals

Rule 91 of the rules of procedure of the UNGA states,

> The General Assembly may, after each vote on a proposal, decide whether to vote on the next proposal.

The UN Model Rules use the same formula.

This phrase appears in the rules of procedure of the 1958 Law of the Sea Conference. It was omitted from the rules of procedure of the 1960 Law of the Sea Conference, at the initiative of the Mexican delegation.[17] The representative of the United States explained his support for the Mexican amendment by stating that it 'would give the members of the Conference an opportunity to express their views on all the proposals and provide for the flexibility essential in a conference of that kind'.[18] The rule was then omitted in the rules of subsequent conferences until it reappeared in those conferences convened from 1975.

The rule allowing a conference to decide whether to vote on the next proposal apparently reflects the rule as to reopening of an issue and would appear to be superfluous, for if a succeeding proposal relates to an issue

[15] Official Records of the 1963 Vienna Conference on Consular Relations, 31st Meeting of Committee I, p. 257, paras. 2–16, UN Doc. A/CONF.25/16 (1963).

[16] Memorandum (by the UN Office of Legal Affairs) to the Deputy Executive Assistant to the Secretary-General, 19 November 1976. 1976 UN Jur. Y.B. 181.

[17] 1960 Law of the Sea Conference, Mexican amendment to the draft rules of procedure, UN Doc. A/CONF.19/L. 1 (1960).

[18] Summary Records of the 2nd Plenary Meeting of the 1960 Law of the Sea Conference, p. 4, para. 8, UN Doc. A/CONF.19/8 (1960).

that has already been decided by an earlier proposal, then a vote on that subsequent proposal would in any event come within the reconsideration rule. If the succeeding proposal does not relate to an issue decided by an earlier vote, it is difficult to find any circumstance in which the rule would apply.

At a 1976 meeting of a committee of the UNGA, the representative of Uruguay argued that the rule allowing a committee not to vote on a proposal should only be applied if, as a result of a vote on a proposal, the subsequent proposal is contradictory or superfluous. Other delegates argued that the Committee had complete discretion to apply Rule 91[19] and to decide, for whatever reason, not to vote on the 'next proposal'. In the event the Committee decided not to vote on the 'next proposal'.[20] The UN Model Rules do not deal with the circumstances under which this rule is to be applied.

13.1.3 How Is a Decision Made about Whether to Vote on a Subsequent Proposal?

A question arises about how to make a decision whether to vote on a subsequent proposal after voting on a previous proposal. There appear to be three possibilities.

13.1.3.1 Decision by Presiding Officer

It would appear that the logic behind the rule is the prevention of reopening of an issue resolved by the previous proposal. If this is true, it follows that it can be the presiding officer who makes the decision about whether the next proposal does reopen the issue. A presiding officer's decision can of course be challenged.

13.1.3.2 A Delegation that Objects to Voting on the Next Proposal Is Obliged to Submit a Motion to that Effect

Since the conference or assembly has all the authority that its presiding officer possesses, a delegation is presumably entitled to propose that the conference or assembly take the decision not to vote on the next proposal.

[19] Rule 131 in committees.

[20] UN GAOR, 3rd Committee, 31st Session, 58th Meeting, para. 69, UN Doc. A/C.3/31/SR.58 (1976).

13.1.3.3 A Delegation that Wishes that a Vote Take Place on the Next Proposal Has to Submit a Motion to that Effect

The general rule is that all proposals are voted on unless a decision is taken to the contrary. That being so, there would appear to be no reason for a delegation to submit a proposal to vote on the next proposal. Nevertheless, this procedure was followed at a 1992 meeting of a UNGA committee, and a motion to vote on the next proposal was put to the vote.[21]

13.1.4 Is a Decision Granting Priority to a Proposal Affected by a Subsequent Revision of the Proposal?

During the 1974 session of the UNGA, it was decided to give priority to a certain motion (on Cambodia).[22] This motion was subsequently amended, with the agreement of the original sponsors. The question was raised as to whether the decision on priority still applied. The President of the session ruled that since a separate vote had been requested on the paragraph containing the amendment, he would continue to grant priority to the motion as a whole.[23] His ruling was not challenged.

13.1.5 Do Subsequent Revisions of Proposals Affect the Rule as to Voting on Proposals in the Order in Which They Were Submitted?

At the 1975 session of the UNGA, the Chairman decided that voting on proposals would be in accordance with their original date of submission, notwithstanding the fact that one of the proposals had been subsequently revised.[24]

The UN Model Rules deal with this issue in Rule 60:

> *Rule 60*
>
> *Order of Voting on Proposals*
>
> 2. Revised proposals shall be voted on in the order in which the original proposals were submitted, unless the revision substantially departs from the original proposal. In that case, the original proposal shall be considered as withdrawn and the revised proposal shall be treated as a new proposal. If it does substantially depart from the original proposal then it will no longer enjoy priority.

[21] UN GAOR, 3rd Committee, 47th Session, 58th Meeting, para. 58, UN Doc. A/C.3/47/SR.58 (1992).

[22] UN Doc. A/L./737/Rev.1 (1974).

[23] UN GAOR, Plenary, 29th Session, 2301st Meeting, paras. 447–450, UN Doc. A/PV.2301 (1974).

[24] UN GAOR, 1st Committee, 13th Session, 970th Meeting, para. 57, UN Doc. A/C.1/13/SR.970 (1958).

13.1.6 Order of Priority of Reintroduced Proposals

The UN Model Rules propose,

> *Rule 47*
>
> *Withdrawal of Proposals and Motions*
>
> A proposal or a motion may be withdrawn by its sponsor at any time before voting on it has commenced, provided that it has not been amended by decision of the Conference. A proposal or a motion thus withdrawn may be reintroduced by any representative *with its original priority*, provided he does so promptly and it has not been substantially changed. [emphasis added]

13.2 Priority of Procedural Motions over Substantive Motions

Although priority for voting on procedural motions over voting on draft resolutions has been claimed in the UNGA and sometimes granted,[25] there is no general rule in the UNGA rules of procedure or in the UN Model Rules that grants such priority.[26] It could be argued that the fact that certain procedural rules have been granted priority[27] provides proof *au contraire* that no blanket right of priority for procedural motions was intended. Nevertheless, usually it is logical to vote on a procedural motion concerning an issue before voting on the substance of an issue. It is submitted that this could be done, based on the right of a conference to decide the order of voting on proposals.[28]

13.2.1 Does a Motion Not to Take a Vote on a Proposal Have Priority over the Substantive Proposal?

The UN Model Rules propose,

> *Rule 60*
>
> *Order of Voting on Proposals*
>
> (3) A motion requiring that no decision be taken on a proposal shall have priority over that proposal.

25 See UN GAOR, 3rd Committee, 6th Session, 385th Meeting, para. 67, UN Doc. A/C.3/6/SR.385 (1951); UN GAOR, Plenary, 13th Session, 789th Meeting, para. 237, UN Doc. A/PV.789 (1958); UN GAOR, 3rd Committee, 3rd Session, Part I, 110th Meeting, p. 220, UN Doc. A/C.3/3/SR.110 (1948).

26 The President of the General Assembly at its Second Session made the point that only those procedural motions specifically enumerated in the rules of procedure as such were entitled to priority. UN GAOR, Plenary, 2nd Session, Part I, 128th Meeting, p. 1423, UN Doc. A/PV.128 (1947).

27 Rules 44, 60(3) of the UN Model Rules; Rule 77 of the UNGA rules of procedure.

28 Rule 60 of the UN Model Rules; Rule 91 of the UNGA rules of procedure.

Logic would dictate that a motion not to take a decision must have priority over the proposal it wishes to postpone.[29] There is no reference to such a rule in the UNGA rules of procedure, where, nevertheless, such motions have always been voted on before voting on the substantive proposal.[30] A 1971 UN Committee on the Procedures and Organisation of the General Assembly considered this issue. It was proposed to the Committee that the General Assembly adopt the ECOSOC rule that, at the time, stated,

> *Rule 66*
>
> Any motion requiring that no decision be taken on the subject of such proposal shall, however, be considered as previous questions and shall be put to the vote before them.[31]

The Committee did not adopt the suggestion.[32]

13.3 Priority between Procedural Motions

The UNGA rules of procedure stipulate,

> *Order of Procedural Motions*
>
> *Rule 77*
>
> Subject to rule 71,[33] the motions indicated below shall have precedence in the following order over all other proposals or motions before the meeting:
>
> (a) To suspend the meeting;
> (b) To adjourn the meeting;
> (c) To adjourn the debate on the item under discussion;
> (d) To close the debate on the item under discussion.

The UN Model Rules proposal[34] is identical in substance; however, the *chapeau* of the UNGA rule refers to 'precedence', whereas the UN Model Rules refer to 'priority'. It is submitted that in this context the word

[29] See UN GAOR, General Committee, 17th Session, 149th Meeting, paras. 18, 22, UN Doc. A/BUR/SR.149 (1962).

[30] See discussion and examples, in Chapter 9.

[31] UN Doc. E/3063/Rev.1 (1967), UN Sales No. E.67.I.32. The rule now reads,

> *Rule 67*
>
> 2. A motion requiring that no decision be taken on a proposal shall have priority over that proposal.
>
> UN Doc. E/5715/Rev.1 (1983), UN Sales No. E.83.I.a.

[32] para. 352 of the Report of the Special Committee on the Rationalisation of the Procedures and Organisation of the General Assembly, UN GAOR, 26th Session, Supp. No. 26, UN Doc. A/8426 (1971).

[33] Article 71 refers to points of order.

[34] Rule 44 of the UN Model Rules.

'priority' is the more felicitous of the two words since the word 'precedence' also has the connotation of 'right of preceding others in ceremonies and social formalities',[35] a connotation that the word 'priority' does not normally have.

The listing of order of priority of procedural motions recommended in the Report of the Committee on Procedures and Organisation set up in 1946 by the UNGA[36] has remained substantially the same since 1947.[37]

13.3.1 Priority of Motion for Suspension of Meeting

This motion has priority over all other motions and cannot be debated, but must be put immediately to the vote.[38]

At a 1960 meeting of the UNGA, when the Assembly was considering a motion to adjourn the debate, the President refused to grant priority to a subsequent motion for suspension of the meeting. The President explained his ruling by stating that suspension can apply only to a discussion on substance and not to one on procedure.[39] It would appear, however, that this is an incorrect interpretation since it would render meaningless the list of precedence of procedural motions.

At a 1973 meeting of the UNGA, after a representative had moved the suspension of the meeting, the Chairman refused to give the floor to two representatives who wished to raise points of order. The Chairman ruled that the Assembly must proceed immediately to voting on the motion for suspension.[40]

13.3.2 Priority of Motion for Adjournment of Meeting

A motion to adjourn a meeting ranks in priority immediately below a motion to suspend the meeting. The motion cannot be debated, but must be put immediately to the vote.[41]

35 *The Shorter Oxford English Dictionary on Historical Principles*, 3rd edn (1972).

36 UNGA Resolution 102 (I) of 15 December 1946.

37 UN GAOR, 2nd Session, Plenary Meetings, vol. II, Annex IV, p. 1455, UN Doc. A/388. Adopted by UNGA Resolution 173 (II) of 17 November 1947.

38 Rule 76 of the UNGA rules of procedure; Rule 43 of the UN Model Rules.

39 UN GAOR, Plenary, 15th Session, 913th Meeting, paras. 93, 144, UN Doc. A/PV.913 (1960).

40 UN GAOR, Plenary, 28th Session, 2140th Meeting, para. 85, UN Doc. A/PV.2140 (1973).

41 Rule 76 of the UNGA rules of procedure; Rule 43 of the UN Model Rules.

At a 1952 meeting of the UNGA, the representative of Denmark moved the adjournment of the debate on a draft resolution. The Saudi Arabian representative subsequently moved adjournment of the meeting, and the Saudi Arabian motion was granted priority.[42]

At a 1974 meeting of the UNGA, the representative of Paraguay submitted a motion to adjourn the debate. When Syria subsequently submitted a motion to adjourn the meeting, the President granted priority to the Syrian motion for adjournment of the meeting.[43]

At a 1958 meeting of the UNGA, after the representative of India had moved the adjournment of the meeting, the President refused to allow a representative of the USSR to raise a point of order. After the voting had been completed, the President allowed the representative of the USSR to speak on an explanation of vote.[44]

13.3.3 Priority of Motion for Adjournment of Debate

A motion for adjournment of debate ranks in priority immediately below a motion to adjourn the meeting. At a 1974 session of the UNGA, the Chairman gave a motion to 'close the debate' priority over a motion to 'postpone the debate' to the next session of the UNGA.[45] It may be that if the motion to 'postpone' had been couched in the procedural language of Rule 119, namely 'to adjourn', then the Chairman would have reached a different conclusion. At the same session of the UNGA, the Chairman ruled that a motion to postpone consideration of an item to the next session of the General Assembly was a 'proposal' and not a procedural motion. The Chairman said that therefore the 'proposal' was not entitled to priority over other proposals.[46]

At a 1967 meeting of the UNGA, a motion for closure of the debate had been proposed. Two speakers opposing it had spoken, and the Chairman ordered that the motion for closure be put to the vote. A representative then proposed adjournment of the debate, claiming that a motion to adjourn the debate takes priority over a motion to close the debate. The

[42] UN GAOR, 2nd Committee, 7th Session, 236th Meeting, paras. 6, 12, 14, UN Doc. A/C.2/7/SR.236 (1952).

[43] UN GAOR, Plenary, 12th Session, 708th Meeting, para. 258, UN Doc. A/PV.708 (1957).

[44] UN GAOR, Plenary, 13th Session, 753rd Meeting, para. 283, UN Doc. A/PV.753 (1958).

[45] UN GAOR, 5th Committee, 29th Session, 1668th Meeting, paras. 1–11, UN Doc. A/C.5/29/SR.1668 (1974).

[46] UN GAOR, 3rd Committee, 29th Session, 2102nd Meeting, paras. 23, 35, 36, 41, UN Doc. A/C.3/29/SR.2102 (1974).

Chairman refused to grant priority to the motion for adjournment and proceeded with the vote to close the debate.[47] It is submitted that the outcome in this case was correct, although it should have been arrived at by refusing to consider the motion for adjournment once voting had commenced (on the motion for closure).

At a 2009 meeting of the General Conference of the IAEA, the Director of the Office of Legal Affairs succinctly stated that a motion to adjourn the debate 'must take precedence over any motion to close the debate'.[48]

13.3.4 *Priority of Motion for Adjournment of Debate Coupled with a Substantive Motion*

The relevance of the wording of a procedural motion was vividly illustrated during the UNGA debate of 1947 on the Partition of Palestine. The representative of Iran proposed a resolution that called for the adjournment of the debate and provided for further studies by the Ad Hoc Committee. The Iranian representative requested priority for his motion. The President ruled that because one of the provisions in the Iranian resolution called for 'further study by the Ad Hoc Committee', the proposal was no longer a procedural one, but a substantive one and therefore had no right of priority.[49] The President then put to the vote the Palestine Partition Plan, with the result well known to history.

13.3.5 *Priority as between Different Motions for Adjournment of Debate*

At a 1986 meeting of the UNGA, the representative of the United States moved that no action be taken (adjournment of the debate) on a Soviet amendment to a draft resolution on human rights. The representative of Belarus then moved that no action be taken (adjournment of the debate) on the resolution as a whole, including the proposed amendments. A debate then followed about which motion should be voted on first, and the decision was that the US motion should be first.[50]

47 UN GAOR, 3rd Committee, 22nd Session, 1480th Meeting, paras. 17–22, UN Doc. A/C.3/22/SR.1480 (1967).

48 53rd General Conference, IAEA, Plenary, 10th Meeting, para. 48, IAEA, Doc. GC(53)/OR.10 (2009).

49 UN GAOR, Plenary, 2nd Session, 128th Meeting, p. 1423, UN Doc. A/PV.128 (1947).

50 UN GAOR, 3rd Committee, 41st Session, 60th Meeting, paras. 48, 53–63, UN Doc. A/C.3/41/SR.60 (1986).

At a 1986 meeting of a committee of the World Health Assembly, the representative of Jordan, on a point of order, proposed that the Committee 'decide not to consider' an Iranian draft proposal.[51] Such a motion is usually considered a motion for adjournment of debate *sine die*. The representative of Iran then moved that the discussion 'be adjourned until the next meeting'.[52] The Legal Counsel gave his opinion that the Iranian proposal had priority over the Jordanian proposal.[53]

13.3.6 Order of Priority between Different Procedural Motions Not Entitled to Special Priority under the Rules of Procedure

During the Vienna Conference on the Law of Treaties, the question arose as to whether the rules of priority of proposals also applied to procedural motions. The United States had proposed that a vote on a certain article be deferred and referred to the Drafting Committee, and the representative of Ghana had proposed an immediate vote. The Chairman ruled that the Committee should take a decision on the motion submitted first. The representative of the USSR objected, arguing that 'rule 42 dealt only with proposals relating to the item under discussion'. The Chairman nevertheless decided to put the proposals to the vote in the order in which they had been submitted.[54]

13.3.7 Order of Priority between Different Motions to Grant Priority

Where a conference is faced with several motions each requesting that priority be granted to a different proposal or motion, the question arises as to the order of voting regarding such motions for priority. It is submitted that in such a case, the only logical solution is to vote on such motions in the order in which they were submitted. This was the system adopted in the 1961 UNGA.[55]

[51] Summary Records of Committee 'B' of the 39th World Health Assembly, p. 262, WHA39/1986/REC.3 (1986).

[52] *Ibid.* [53] *Ibid.*

[54] Official Records of the Vienna Conference on the Law of Treaties – First Session, 57th Meeting of the Committee of the Whole, pp. 330–334, paras. 29–75, UN Doc. A/CONF.39/11 (1968). This was one of the issues in a lengthy and involved procedural debate.

[55] UN GAOR, 1st Committee, 15th Session, 1159th Meeting, para. 50, UN Doc. A/C.1/15/SR.1159 (1961).

13.4 Voting on Amendments prior to Voting on the Proposal Itself

The rules of procedure of the UNGA stipulate:

> *Rule 90*
>
> *Voting on Amendments*
>
> When an amendment is moved to a proposal, the amendment shall be voted on first.

The rule that an amendment is put to the vote before the proposal to which it refers is apparently universally accepted. Sturgis, writing on parliamentary procedure, states that 'if a main motion is being considered, a motion to amend is in order and takes precedence over the main motion. This is the proper sequence because it is necessary to correct or perfect the motion before it is voted on.'[56]

The rules of procedure of the Assembly of the League of Nations stated, 'When an amendment adds to a proposal it shall be voted on first'[57] and that '[i]f an amendment striking out part of a proposal is moved, the Assembly shall first vote on whether the words in the amendment shall stand as part of the proposal'.[58] The same rule appears in the rules of all conferences.

Dunn, in commenting on the Congress of Berlin of 1878, writes, 'Even the ordinary rules of parliamentary practice were not observed. Where a proposal and an amendment thereof were up for consideration, it was not unusual for the main proposal to be acted on first and then the amendment.'[59] From Dunn's comment, one can assume that the rule itself must have been well established by 1878.

The well-established distinction between a proposal and an amendment was illustrated at the beginning of the 1974–1977 Geneva Humanitarian Law Conference. Prior to the adoption of rules of procedure for the Conference, the President stated that 'since the Conference did not yet have any rules of procedure . . . it should first determine the procedure to be used in voting on these two documents',[60] and he 'invited the Conference to decide whether document No . . . . was an amendment to Draft Resolution No . . . . or was a separate draft resolution'.[61]

[56] Alice F. Sturgis, *Standard Code of Parliamentary Procedure* (1950), p. 6.

[57] Rule 18(7) of the rules of procedure of the Assembly of the League of Nations.

[58] *Ibid.*, Rule 18(6).

[59] F. S. Dunn, *The Practice and Procedure of International Conferences* (1929), p. 96.

[60] Official Records of the 1974–1977 Geneva Humanitarian Law Conference, CDDH/SR.3, vol. V, p. 29, para. 38.

[61] *Ibid.* at p. 30, para. 47.

Despite the unequivocal rule applicable to all conferences, there are occasions when the rule has been queried. Where many amendments are submitted to a contentious proposal, it at times prompts a delegation to propose that a vote be held on the proposal itself, before entering the lengthy process of voting on the various amendments.

A request to vote on the proposal itself, prior to voting on an amendment, was submitted at the 1963 Vienna Conference on Consular Relations. The Chairman curtly replied 'that it was not possible'.[62]

During the Vienna Conference on the Law of Treaties, such procedure was proposed by the delegate of Venezuela. The President (Mr Ago of Italy) ruled that 'the Conference was bound by rule 41 of its rules of procedure which provided that amendments must be voted on before the proposal to which they related'.[63]

At a meeting of the 1971 Montreal Air Law Conference, a representative argued that 'it was up to the Commission to vote on the text presented by the Drafting Committee. Then, if the Delegate of Spain had an amendment to propose to the text it could be taken up immediately following.'[64] The President ruled that 'according to the Rules of Procedure a vote must be taken first on an amendment to a motion'.[65]

At the 1975 Vienna Conference on Representation of States, the representative of Cameroon said that since it would be difficult to reconcile the various amendments, the International Law Commission text should be voted on first.[66] The Chairman ruled that 'when an amendment was moved to a proposal, the amendment should be voted on first. There was no rule which authorised the Committee to vote on a proposal before voting on the amendments. The proposal . . . was therefore irreceivable.'[67]

At the 1977 Vienna Conference on Succession of States in Respect of Treaties, there was a proposal to delete a draft article. The US delegate commented that 'it would be preferable to vote on the article itself first and

[62] Official Records of the 1963 Vienna Conference on Consular Relations, 32nd Meeting of Committee I, vol. I, p. 265, paras. 29, 31, UN Doc. A/CONF.25/16 (1963).

[63] Official Records of the Vienna Conference on the Law of Treaties – Second Session, 15th Plenary Meeting, p. 71, paras. 56, 57, UN Doc. A/CONF.39/11 Add.1 (1969).

[64] 1971 Montreal Air Law Conference, Commission of the Whole, 16th Meeting, vol. I, Minutes, p. 148, para. 54, ICAO Doc. 9081-LC/170–1.

[65] *Ibid.* at para. 55.

[66] Official Records of the 1975 Vienna Conference on Representation of States, 39th Meeting of the Committee of the Whole, p. 299, para. 25, UN Doc. A/CONF.67/18 (1975).

[67] *Ibid.* at 41st Meeting, p. 309, para. 16.

then on the amendment relative to it'.[68] The Chairman ruled that 'unless the sponsors of the draft withdrew their proposal, the Commission had to vote on the draft amendment first'.[69] The Chairman's ruling was not challenged.

However, during a committee meeting of the 1961 Vienna Conference on Diplomatic Relations, the delegate of Ghana stated that he considered a Mexican amendment as only 'complicating matters' and proposed to vote first on the original ILC draft. The delegate of Venezuela objected, quoting the relevant rule of procedure. The Chairman replied that 'the Committee was master of its own procedure'. The delegate of France pointed out that the rules of procedure could only be changed by the Conference as a whole and not by a committee. The Chairman replied that a two-thirds majority could change the rule, and on putting the Ghanaian proposal to the vote, a two-thirds majority was obtained. The Chairman then pointed out that, as a result of the adoption of the Ghanaian motion, no amendment to the ILC draft could now be proposed unless it was by a two-thirds majority. The delegates of Yugoslavia, France and Italy strenuously objected to the procedure adopted, calling it 'extremely dangerous'.[70] The delegate of Ghana summed up by reassuring the delegations that the Conference 'would have recourse to the procedure followed in voting . . . only when it was absolutely necessary'.[71] It is submitted that the Chairman was clearly wrong in his ruling.

The UNGA, during the early years, also resorted to ignoring all amendments and proceeding to vote directly on a proposal.[72]

13.5 Voting on the Main Proposal When the Voting on an Amendment Is Tied

At a 1974 meeting of the UNGA, the result of the voting was a tied vote on one paragraph, and, in accordance with Rule 95 of the rules of procedure, it was decided to hold a second vote on the paragraph within forty-eight

[68] Official Records of the 1977 Vienna Conference on Succession of States in Respect of Treaties – First Session, vol. I, Summary Records of the 27th Meeting of the Committee of the Whole, p. 190, para. 55, UN Doc. A/CONF.80/16 (1977).

[69] *Ibid.* at para. 56.

[70] Official Records of the 1961 Vienna Conference on Diplomatic Relations, 12th Meeting of the Committee of the Whole, vol. I, p. 97, paras. 7–19, UN Doc. A/CONF.20/14 (1961).

[71] *Ibid.* at para. 25.

[72] UN GAOR, 1st Committee, 5th Session, 425th Meeting, para. 6, UN Doc. A/C.1/5/SR.425 (1951); UN GAOR, 6th Committee, 4th Session, 201st Meeting, paras. 70–72, UN Doc. A/C.6/4/SR.201 (1949).

hours. The President, without waiting for the revote on the paragraph, put to the vote the draft resolution as a whole without the paragraph in question. At its following meeting, the Assembly voted again on the outstanding paragraph.[73]

13.6 Priority between Amendments

The rules of procedure of the UNGA stipulate,

> *Rule 90*
>
> *Voting on Amendments*
>
> When two or more amendments are moved to a proposal, the General Assembly shall first vote on the amendment furthest removed in substance from the original proposal and then on the amendment next furthest removed therefrom and so on until all the amendments have been put to the vote. Where, however, the adoption of one amendment necessarily implies the rejection of another amendment, the latter shall not be put to the vote. If one or more amendments are adopted, the amended proposal shall then be voted upon.

The UN Model Rules are the same but add,

> When the Conference decides, in accordance with rule 57, to consider an extensive text in convenient portions (such as paragraphs or articles), each of these shall be treated as a separate proposal for the purpose of paragraph 1.[74]

The rules of procedure of the League of Nations stated that 'when a number of proposals are before the Assembly, the proposal furthest removed from the principal one shall be voted on first'.[75] The rules of procedure of the UNGA, in all the revisions, have applied this language to amendments only and not to proposals as such. The UNGA, at its Fourth Session, on the initiative of the United Kingdom, added the phrase: 'Where, however, the adoption of one amendment necessarily implies the rejection of another amendment, the latter amendment shall not be put to the vote.'[76]

[73] UN GAOR, Plenary, 29th Session, 2301st Meeting, para. 508, UN Doc. A/PV.2301 (1974); UN GAOR, Plenary, 29th Session, 2302nd Meeting, para. 22, UN Doc. A/PV.2302 (1974).

[74] Rule 59 of the UN Model Rules.

[75] Rule 18(5) of the rules of procedure of the Assembly of the League of Nations.

[76] Adopted UN GAOR, 6th Committee, 4th Session, 158th Meeting, p. 98, para. 10, UN Doc. A/C.6/4/SR.158 (1949), UNGA Resolution 362 (IV) of 22 October 1949.

The 1949 Geneva Conference rules of procedure left the order of voting on amendments to the discretion of the Chairman, subject to challenge from the floor.[77,78] With that exception, however, all the conferences examined have followed the League/UNGA example and use the criterion of examining which amendment is substantively furthest removed from the original proposal.

There have nevertheless been exceptions in application of the rule. During the 1974–1977 Geneva Humanitarian Law Conference, the Chairman proposed that amendments be voted on in the order of submission. There was, however, no follow up to the suggestion and it was not adopted.[79]

In the 1958 Law of the Sea Conference, the Chairman, after stating that 'it was impossible to establish which [amendment] was furthest removed from the original text',[80] decided to put to the vote the amendments in the order of their submission. The ruling was challenged and upheld by a vote.

Five years later, the representative of France at the 1963 Vienna Conference on Consular Relations challenged the Chairman's ruling as to order of voting, and claimed that as 'there was little to choose' between the amendments they should be voted on in the order in which they were submitted. The French challenge to the Chairman was defeated by a large majority.[81]

At a 1983 meeting of the World Health Assembly, the Chairman ruled that the order of voting on amendments to a proposal be based on their remoteness from the original proposal. The representative of Belgium, on a point of order, argued that

> the amendments were concerned with different paragraphs of the draft resolution. There was thus no problem as to whether one amendment was further removed than another from the original. Voting should proceed in the order of the amendments, paragraph by paragraph.
>
> . . .

[77] Rule 29 of the rules of procedure of the 1949 Geneva Conference.

[78] This is the ILO procedure. Rule 63 of the Standing Orders of the International Labour Conference reads,

> 7(2). If there are several amendments to a motion or resolution the Chairman shall determine the order in which they shall be discussed and put to the vote.

[79] Official Records of the 1974–1977 Geneva Humanitarian Law Conference, CDDH/II/SR.2, vol. XI, p. 17, para. 24.

[80] Official Records of the 1958 Law of the Sea Conference, 22nd Meeting of Committee II, vol. IV, p. 55, paras. 11, 12, UN Doc. A/CONF.13/40 (1958).

[81] Official Records of the 1963 Vienna Conference on Consular Relations, 9th Meeting of Committee II, vol. I, p. 303, paras. 10–14, UN Doc. A/CONF.25/16 (1963).

> In the present case there were four amendments, each of which affected a different part of the resolution. There could thus be no competition between them.[82]

The Legal Counsel 'acknowledged that that might be a possible interpretation. The question, however, was whether the Committee was considering the resolution as a whole or the separate paragraphs.' The Legal Counsel continued by stating that the Chairman was correct in deciding that voting be based on which amendment would lead to the new resolution being furthest removed from the original resolution.[83] Kaufmann writes,

> If a delegation wants priority for its amendment, it will then consider submitting a rather drastic proposal, hoping thus to be 'furthest removed'. However, in so doing a delegation risks that . . . the chairman will rule (or the meeting decide on a procedural motion) that the amendment does not 'merely adds to, deletes from or revises part of the proposal' and is therefore not an amendment.[84]

In practice, maybe for the reason Kaufmann states, delegations do not appear to have frequently utilised such tactics.

The rule as to voting on *amendments* does not allow for motions calling for precedence for one amendment over another. The rules of procedure of the UNGA as to voting on *proposals* include the phrase 'unless it decides otherwise', thus allowing the Assembly to vary the order of voting.[85] The UN Model Rules adopt the same formula.[86] This phrase, however, is omitted in the parallel rule concerning voting on amendments in the UNGA and in the rules of procedure of the various conferences. The logical conclusion is that a conference cannot change the order of voting on amendments except by a presidential or conference ruling that one amendment is further removed than another. Vallat, the UK delegate to the 1961 Vienna Conference on Diplomatic Relations, enunciated this

[82] Summary Records of the 12th Meeting of Committee 'B' of the 36th World Health Assembly, p. 367, WHA36/1983/REC/3 (1983).

[83] *Ibid.* [84] Johan Kaufmann, *United Nations Decision Making* (1980), p. 123.

[85] Rule 91 of the UNGA rules of procedure, with the exception of the exclusion of amendments.

[86]
Rule 60
Order of Voting on Proposals

1. If two or more proposals, other than amendments, relate to the same question, they shall, unless the Conference decides otherwise, be voted on in the order in which they were submitted. The Conference may, after each vote on a proposal, decide whether to vote on the next proposal.

distinction when he said, in relation to two proposals, 'Since the two texts were not amendments, the Committee could decide, under Rule 42 of the rules of procedure, to vote on them out of their order of submission.'[87]

In practice, the distinction between the rule applying to proposals and that applying to amendments is not always observed. For example, during the 1974–1977 Geneva Humanitarian Law Conference, the Chairman ruled that a certain amendment was furthest removed from the original proposal. A delegation expressed its objection to the ruling, but did not submit an appeal. The Indian delegation requested that a different amendment be granted priority. The Chairman put the Indian request to the vote.[88]

A chairman's ruling in deciding which amendment is furthest removed from the original proposal is of course subject to challenge by the conference.

COMMENT

Formally, the only way a conference can grant priority to an amendment is by appealing a presiding officer's decision as to which amendment is furthest removed from the original. This is not a happy solution, and it might well be advisable for the rules of procedure of future conferences to include a rule enabling the conference to grant priority to an amendment.

13.6.1 Decisions as to Which Amendment Is 'Furthest Removed in Substance from the Original Proposal'

Hovey, writing in the early years of the UN, stated,

> This rule poses practical problems in specific cases with regard to which amendments are 'furthest removed in substance', but there does not seem to be any convenient rule-of-thumb to lessen the difficulties. In general it might be true that an amendment that would delete a paragraph is further 'removed in substance' than one that would change or delete a word – but even this principle would fail where deletion of the word reverses the sense of the proposal, for example, the word 'not' in the proposition 'Thou shall not covet.' The reason for taking up amendments to a proposal in their order of 'radicalness' is simply to save time: approval of an amendment

[87] Official Records of the 1961 Vienna Conference on Diplomatic Relations, 41st Meeting of the Committee of the Whole, vol. I, p. 238, para. 35, UN Doc. A/CONF.20 (1961).

[88] Official Records of the 1974–77 Geneva Humanitarian Law Conference, CDDH/I/SR.13, vol. VIII, pp. 101, 102, paras. 33–38.

furthest removed in substance may obviate the need to vote on those less removed in substance.[89]

At a 1946 meeting of the UNGA, there was a proposal by the General Committee that members of Councils should hold office for twenty months. One amendment proposed a period of twelve months and another proposed eight months. The President ruled that the proposal for eight months was the amendment 'furthest removed' from the original.[90]

At a 1950 meeting of the UNGA, the Report of the General Committee recommended that consideration of a draft resolution on the rights and duties of States be postponed to a future session. Yugoslavia proposed that it be dealt with at that session and Cuba proposed that it be dealt with at the next session. The President ruled that the Yugoslav amendment was furthest removed from the original and should be voted on first.[91]

At another 1950 meeting of the UNGA, the Chairman ruled that an amendment submitted by Lebanon would, if adopted, eliminate an amendment by Afghanistan and Saudi Arabia. Since, he ruled, the same was not true vice versa, then voting should take place on the Afghanistan–Saudi Arabia amendment first.[92]

At the 1983 Vienna Conference on State Property (Succession), it was decided that an amendment calling for deletion of the whole of a paragraph should be voted on before an amendment calling for the deletion of part of that paragraph.[93]

13.7 Can a Conference Decide not to Vote on an Amendment?

As regards *proposals*, the UNGA rule states,

Rule 91

The General Assembly may, after each vote on a proposal, decide whether to vote on the next proposal.

[89] Allan Hovey Jr, 'Voting Procedure in the General Assembly', 4 *UNESCO International Organization* 412 (1950 No. 1) at 424.

[90] UN GAOR, Plenary, 1st Session, Part I, 32nd Meeting, pp. 466, 467, UN Doc. A/PV.32 (1946).

[91] UN GAOR, Plenary, 5th Session, 284th Meeting, para. 56, UN Doc. A/PV.284 (1950).

[92] UN GAOR, 3rd Committee, 5th Session, 311th Meeting, paras. 50–51, UN Doc. A/C.3/5/SR.311 (1950).

[93] Official Records of the 1983 Vienna Conference on State Property (Succession), 39th Meeting of the Committee of the Whole, vol. I, p. 244, para. 14, UN Doc. A/CONF.117/16 (1995).

At a 1965 meeting of the UNGA, the United States and Brazil proposed an amendment to a Draft Human Rights Convention that would have included a reference to anti-Semitism. Hungary and Greece submitted a proposal to omit any reference in the Convention to specific forms of racial discrimination. The Hungarian–Greek proposal was given priority and adopted. The Chairman then announced that, as a result, the US–Brazil and other amendments were redundant and would not be voted on.[94] The same result would have been achieved by a presidential ruling invoking Rule 90 of the UNGA rules of procedure, which states that 'the adoption of one amendment necessarily implies the rejection of another amendment' or a ruling that the issue involved reconsideration. Nevertheless, the application of UNGA Rule 91, which refers to proposals and not to amendments, was, it is submitted, incorrect.

13.8 Order of Voting on Sub-Amendments

The UN Model Rules propose,

> *Rule 58*
>
> 2. Unless the Conference decides otherwise, amendments may be subject to sub-amendments, but the latter may not be subject to further amendment.

None of the rules of procedure refer specifically to the question of order of voting on sub-amendments. On several occasions, delegations have raised the question of what they consider to be illogical results emanating from the application to sub-amendments of rules drafted to deal with amendments to proposals.

During the 1958 Law of the Sea Conference, the representative of Chile proposed that 'if a sub-amendment moved to an amendment had the effect of bringing the latter closer to the ILC draft, the Committee would vote first on the amendment without the sub-amendment'. The Chairman 'regretted that he could not accept the Chilean representative's suggestion'.[95]

At the 1975 Vienna Conference on Representation of States, the representative of Belarus stated that 'he doubted whether the Canadian amendment could be treated as a sub-amendment to the amendment of which

[94] UN GAOR, 3rd Committee, 20th Session, 1312th Meeting, para. 33, UN Doc. A/C.3/20/SR.1312 (1965).

[95] Official Records of the 1958 Law of the Sea Conference, 34th Meeting of Committee I, vol. III, p. 99, paras. 1–5, UN Doc. A/CONF.13/39 (1958).

he was co-sponsor [the five-Power amendment]'. He pointed out that 'the purpose of a sub-amendment to an amendment was always to clarify or supplement the text of an amendment whereas the Canadian proposal ran counter to the five-power amendment'.[96] The Chairman, refusing to accept the objection, put the Canadian sub-amendment to the vote first and his ruling was not challenged. It can happen, of course, that because of this procedure the text of an amendment is radically changed and a delegation is obliged to vote against its own amendment.[97] This can be true for any proposal that has been amended.

13.8.1 Voting First on the Sub-Amendment Furthest Removed from the Amendment

The issue of sub-amendments was at the centre of a very tortuous procedural debate in the 1952 UNGA. From the Chairman's ruling it can be inferred that the order of voting on sub-amendments is to vote first on the sub-amendment furthest removed from the amendment to which it applies and not on the sub-amendment furthest removed from the original proposal.[98]

[96] Official Records of the 1975 Vienna Conference on Representation of States, 37th Meeting of the Committee of the Whole, p. 284, para. 2, UN Doc. A/CONF.67/18 (1975).

[97] See, for example, UK statement, *ibid.* at 38th Meeting, p. 289, para. 9.

[98] UN GAOR, 3rd Committee, 6th Session, 402nd Meeting, paras. 47, 48, 50, UN Doc. A/C.3/6/SR.402 (1952).

14

Decision Taking and Method of Voting

14.1 Determining the Issue to be Voted On

14.1.1 Reading out Proposals or Amendments prior to the Vote

At the 1974–1977 Geneva Humanitarian Law Conference, the representative of Libya requested that 'each article be read out before a vote was taken, in order to identify clearly the article on which representatives were voting'.[1] The representative of Canada commented that 'it was true that at certain conferences where perhaps there were not so many articles to be considered articles were read out before the vote . . . As a rule, an article should not be read out before the vote unless a representative specially asked for it.'[2] The President accepted the Canadian proposal, and the Conference acted accordingly.[3]

14.1.2 Declarations as Part of a Decision

At a 2002 meeting of the Council of the IMO, a representative requested that 'comments made expressing discontent with the [issue decided] should also be reflected in the summary of decisions'.[4] In support of this request it was argued that 'a proposal made by one delegation and supported by another delegation, and which had not been opposed, should constitute a decision of the Council'. The Secretary-General of the IMO responded that 'those comments did not constitute a decision and would be covered in the summary record'. The Chairman adopted the position of the Secretary-General and proposed to the Council that it 'note' the comments 'as reflected in the summary records'.[5]

1 Official Records of the 1974–1977 Geneva Humanitarian Law Conference, CDDH/SR.36, vol. VI, p. 35, para. 14.
2 *Ibid.* at para. 17. 3 *Ibid.* at p. 36, para. 18.
4 Summary Records of the 89th IMO Council Meeting, C 89/SR.7, p. 6 (2002).
5 *Ibid.*

14.2 Method of voting

The rules of procedure of the UNGA state,

Method of Voting
Rule 87

(a) The General Assembly shall normally vote by show of hands or by standing, but any representative may request a roll-call. The roll-call shall be taken in the English alphabetical order of the names of the members, beginning with the member whose name is drawn by lot by the President. The name of each member shall be called in any roll-call, and one of its representatives shall reply 'yes', 'no' or 'abstention'. The result of the voting shall be inserted in the record in the English alphabetical order of the names of the members.
(b) When the General Assembly votes by mechanical means, a non-recorded vote shall replace a vote by show of hands or by standing and a recorded vote shall replace a roll-call vote. Any representative may request a recorded vote. In the case of a recorded vote, the General Assembly shall, unless a representative requests otherwise, dispense with the procedure of calling out the names of the members; nevertheless, the result of the voting shall be inserted in the record in the same manner as that of a roll-call vote.

The proposal in the UN Model Rules is substantially the same.[6]

Wellington Koo, in referring generally to voting in international organisations, writes that 'voting procedures in an international organization are the rules according to which the member states can operate the machinery they have set up'.[7] The UNGA method of voting allows for voting by a show of hands, by standing or by roll call.[8] The method of voting by standing is apparently not applied in practice.[9] Since the introduction of electronic voting, a fourth system has been introduced, that of electronically recorded votes. However, even where the electronic system used allows for recorded votes, a roll-call vote may still be called for. Rules of procedure for the conferences examined follow General Assembly practice and allow for electronic voting where the facilities are available.

6 Rule 54 of the UN Model Rules.
7 Wellington Koo Jr, *Voting Procedures in International Political Organizations* (1947), p. 7.
8 Rule 87 of the UNGA rules of procedure.
9 See Johan Kaufmann, *Conference Diplomacy, An Introductory Analysis*, 2nd rev. edn (1988), p. 22.

14.2.1 Voting by the European Union

It is rare for the European Union to be given voting rights at conferences but where such rights have been granted, the following rule has been applied:

> A regional economic integration organization, on matters within its competence, shall exercise its right to vote with a number of votes equal to the number of its Member States that are Parties to this Convention. Such an organization shall not exercise its right to vote if any of its Member States exercise its right, and vice versa.[10]

Nevertheless, conference rules of procedure usually contain a phrase 'Save where otherwise specifically provided with respect to the European Union'[11] which envisages the possibility that voting rights might be granted to the European Union.

14.2.2 Voting by Show of Hands

Voting by show of hands is used nowadays for taking a sense of the meeting or where the exact counting of votes is not required. Where votes are to be counted, electronic voting has effectively superseded voting by show of hands, except where a conference is held in facilities where there is no electronic system.

14.2.3 A Recorded Vote

The accepted practice is that every State has the right to request a recorded or roll-call vote,[12] and the assembly or conference must comply with such a request. Hovey, writing in 1951, lists 'demanding unnecessarily the time consuming vote by roll-call' as among the avenues open to those wishing to obstruct the work of the UNGA.[13] A subcommittee of the Sixth

[10] Article 23, UNEP Stockholm Convention on Persistent Organic Pollutants, 2001; WHO, Draft Rules of Procedure for the Conference of the Parties, WHO Framework Convention on Tobacco Control, WHO Doc. A/FCTC/IGWG/1/4 (2004); Article 57, Rules of Procedure for the Conference of the Parties to the UN Convention against Transnational Organized Crime UNITED NATIONS OFFICE ON DRUGS AND CRIME, Vienna 2005.

[11] For example, Article 63 Rules of Procedure, UN Conference to Support the Implementation of Sustainable Development Goal 14: Conserve and sustainable use the oceans, seas and marine resources for sustainable development, UN Doc. A/CONF.230/2 (2017).

[12] Since votes are recorded electronically, it is rare for a vote to be held by roll call, but the terms are used synonymously.

[13] Allan Hovey Jr, 'Obstructionism and the Rules of the General Assembly', 5 *UNESCO International Organization* 515 (1951 No. 3) at 517.

Committee of the UNGA in 1947 discussed this issue and proposed that a two-thirds majority should be able to deny the right of a delegation to have a roll-call vote.[14] At the meeting of the Sixth Committee, discussing the report, the Soviet representative objected to this proposal, arguing that 'world opinion was entitled to know how States had voted'.[15] On the initiative of the USSR, the Sixth Committee rejected the proposal of the subcommittee.[16]

The issue was discussed again at a 1971 UN Committee on the Procedures and Organisation of the General Assembly. The Committee reported the proposal that the 'agreement of the majority, or of one third of the members, would be required before a roll-call vote could be taken'. This was suggested since 'a roll-call vote took a considerable amount of time and that, thanks to the electronic system, a recorded vote made it possible to determine, with the same precision, how each delegation had voted'.[17] The report continues, however, by stating that the majority of members of the Committee opposed any change in the rules of procedure on this question, emphasising that 'a roll-call vote was taken in a solemn atmosphere and had political and psychological advantages which a recorded vote did not have'.[18] A 1990 UN Special Committee on Procedure recommended that 'when an electronic voting system is available for recording how votes were cast, a roll-call vote should as far as possible not be requested'.[19]

The practice in the First Committee of the UNGA is that delegations advise the Secretariat in advance if they intend to request a recorded vote.[20]

At the 1974–1977 Geneva Humanitarian Law Conference, a representative requested a roll-call vote. The representative of Cuba stated that,

[14] UN GAOR, 6th Committee, 2nd Session, p. 267, Procedures and Organisation of the General Assembly, Report of Sub-Committee 3 on Part III of the Report of the Committee, Annex 4c, Rule 91, UN Doc. A/C.6/2/182/Corr.1/Corr.2 (1947).

[15] UN GAOR, 6th Committee, 2nd Session, 56th Meeting, p. 139 (1947).

[16] *Ibid.*

[17] Paras. 244–245 of the Report of the Special Committee on the Rationalisation of the Procedures and Organisation of the General Assembly, GAOR, 26th Session, Supp. No. 26, UN Doc. A/8426 (1971).

[18] *Ibid.* at para. 246.

[19] para. 86(2) of the Report of the Special Committee on the Charter of the United Nations and on the Strengthening of the Role of the Organisation, UN GAOR, 45th Session, Supp. No. 33, UN Doc. A/45/33 (1990). Adopted by the General Assembly in its Resolution 45/45, of 28 November 1990, Annex, para. 2.

[20] See, for example, UN Doc. A/C.1/52/PV.17, p. 23 (1997).

although 'any representative might request a roll-call, that rule gave no indication that such a request would automatically be granted in cases where other representatives were not in favour of that form of vote. The Cuban representative therefore requested that a vote should be taken first on the request for a roll-call vote.'[21] After the meeting was suspended and reconvened, the Chairman informed the Committee that, 'as well as the Legal Adviser of the United Nations, the Legal Adviser of the Conference had confirmed that it was established United Nations practice (on which also the rules of procedure of the Conference had been based) to grant a roll-call vote if any delegation so requested. No vote was ever taken on that request.'[22]

In 1987, the Executive Board of the WHO proposed that the rules of procedure of the organisation be amended so that, inter alia, a request for a roll call be itself subject to a vote and not be granted automatically.[23] The proposed amendment was discussed at the 1987 World Health Assembly. In support of the proposed amendment, it was argued that 'roll-call votes could be asked for on any trivial matter';[24] that it was 'eminently logical to make the requirements for such a vote the same as for a vote by secret ballot';[25] that 'a delegate calling for a roll-call vote would have to abide by the decision of the majority on whether such a vote should be taken';[26] that 'the existing system had been abused';[27] and that it 'prolonged the debate unnecessarily'.[28] In opposition to the proposed change it was argued that 'it would be doing away with a sovereign right of Member States';[29] 'delegates had not abused their right to ask for a roll-call vote';[30] the proposed amendment 'would lead to duplication of voting';[31] and that 'all delegations should be able to have their votes recorded when they considered that to be warranted by the importance of a given matter'.[32]

[21] Official Records of the 1974–1977 Geneva Humanitarian Law Conference, CDDH/II/SR.89, vol. XII, p. 360, para. 35.

[22] *Ibid.* at p. 361, para. 38.

[23] WHO Executive Board Resolution EB79.R20 (1987).

[24] The representative of Australia, Summary Records of the 7th Meeting of Committee 'B' of the 40th World Health Assembly, p. 296, WHA40/1987/REC/3 (1987).

[25] The representative of Canada, *ibid.*

[26] The representative of the United Kingdom, *ibid.* at p. 297.

[27] The representative of the United States, *ibid.* at p. 300.

[28] The representative of the Federal Republic of Germany, *ibid.* at p. 301.

[29] The representative of Cuba, *ibid.* at p. 296.

[30] The representative of the USSR, *ibid.* at p. 298.

[31] The representative of Argentina, *ibid.* at p. 302.

[32] The representative of Ireland, *ibid.*

The proposed amendment was not adopted, and it was agreed to monitor the work of the Assembly over a three-year period.[33]

At a 2012 meeting of the Plenary of the IAEA General Conference, a delegate argued that the rule of procedure that stated that '[a]ny Member may request a vote by roll-call' 'did not oblige the Conference to accede to a Member State's request'. The President did not explicitly respond to this argument but since the Conference proceeded to a roll-call vote, by inference, the argument was, correctly, rejected.[34]

After three years' monitoring, the issue was discussed at the 1991 World Health Assembly, the previous arguments for and against being raised again.[35] The Legal Counsel was asked as to the situation in other international organisations. He reported that

> not only in WHO but also in the United Nations, FAO, UNESCO, and ITU a roll-call vote was held if requested. In some international organizations such as ILO, UNESCO, WIPO, and ITU a roll-call vote could be held if there was doubt as to the result of a previous vote, as was proposed in the draft resolution. It was left to a decision of the presiding officer to ask the meeting whether a roll-call vote should be held. In ILO and FAO a vote by roll-call was also necessary when a two-thirds majority was required.[36]

The proposed amendment to the rules of procedure was defeated by a vote in a committee of the 1991 World Health Assembly.[37]

At the 1999 International Labour Conference, the Legal Adviser of the ILO confirmed that once a record vote has been requested, 'The request does not have to be adopted; there has to be a record vote.'[38] At a 2002 Meeting of the World Health Assembly, a delegate pointed out that the records of a previous meeting did not record the results of a roll-call vote. The Legal Counsel to the WHO responded that the records should be corrected.[39]

[33] Second Report of World Health Assembly Committee 'B', WHO Doc. A/40/32 of 15 May 1987. Approved by World Health Assembly Decision WHA/40/1987/REC/2, p. 255 (1987).

[34] IAEA General Conference, Plenary, 56th Session, 9th Meeting, p. 5, IAEA Doc. GC(56)/OR.9 (2012).

[35] Summary Records of the 4th and 5th Meetings of Committee 'B' of the 44th World Health Assembly, pp. 225–232, WHA/44/1991/REC/3 (1991).

[36] Summary Records of the 4th Meeting of Committee 'B' of the 44th World Health Assembly, p. 227, WHA44/1991/REC/3 (1991).

[37] Summary Records of the 6th Meeting of Committee 'B' of the 44th World Health Assembly, p. 247, WHA44/1991/REC/3 (1991).

[38] ILO, Provisional Records of the International Labour Conference, 87th Session, 21st sitting, p. 27/12 (1999).

[39] WHO, 55th World Health Assembly, 2nd Meeting, WHA55/2002/REC/3, p. 151. (2002).

At a 2006 meeting of the General Conference of the IAEA, the Director of the Office of Legal Affairs gave his opinion that the word 'against' expressed by a delegate in a roll-call vote 'was clearly equivalent to "no"'.[40]

14.2.4 Disclosing Who Requested a Recorded Vote

At a 1996 meeting of the UNGA, the Chairman informed a committee that there had been a request for a recorded vote. A delegation wanted to know from the Chairman which delegation had requested the recorded vote, and the Chairman provided the requested information, adding that 'if the sponsors of a draft resolution make that request, we must disclose the information'.[41] A similar ruling was made at 2003, 2004 and 2006 meetings of UNGA and UNGA committees.[42] However, at the same 2003 UNGA session, in a different committee, a chairman gave an opposite response, stating 'in conformity with established practice, the Chair is not in a position to divulge information as to which delegation it was',[43] and at a 2009 Session of the Third Committee of the UNGA, the Secretary of the Committee ignored a request to declare who had requested a recorded vote.[44] At a 2011 meeting of the First Committee of the UNGA, the Secretary of the Committee stated, 'It has been a long-held tradition and custom of the First Committee not to ask from the floor . . . which delegation requested the vote. It has never been done. But the practice is that when it is done from the floor, we have to divulge the name.'[45]

COMMENT

It would appear that, if requested, a chairman should disclose which delegation requested a recorded vote. As a matter of transparency, there is no reason why a delegation has to rely on the word of a chairman as to the

[40] 2006 IAEA General Conference, Plenary, 50th session, 10th Meeting, para. 26, IAEA Doc. GC(50)/OR. 10 (2006).

[41] UN GAOR, 1st Committee, 51st Session, 23rd Meeting, p. 10, UN Doc. A/C.1/51/PV.23 (1996).

[42] UN GAOR, 3rd Committee, 58th Session, 59th Meeting, p. 5, UN Doc. A/C.3/58/SR.59 (2004), UN Doc. A/C.3/58/Sr.334.para. 28 (2003), UNGA, Plenary, 61st session, 107th Meeting, p. 18, UN Doc. A/61/PV.107 (2006).

[43] UN GAOR, 1st Committee, 58th Session, 21st Meeting, p. 6, UN Doc. A/C.1/58/PV.21 (2003).

[44] UN GAOR, 3rd Committee, 64th Session, 42nd Meeting, paras. 2,3, UN Doc. A/C.3/SR.42 (2009).

[45] UNGA, First Committee, 66th Session, 23rd Meeting, p. 38, UN Doc. A/C.1/66/PV.23 (2009).

fact that a recorded vote has been requested. Furthermore, a chairman has no inherent right to suppress information from the body that appointed him.

14.2.5 A Recorded Indicative Vote

There does not appear to be any reason why an indicative vote cannot be held by roll call, and there is at least one precedent where such a vote took place.[46]

14.2.6 When Can a Recorded Vote Be Requested?

At a 1989 meeting of the World Health Assembly, a delegation claimed that the rules of procedure allowed that 'the votes of Member States by roll-call be inserted in the record of the meeting', even though the vote had not been taken by roll call. The Legal Counsel gave his opinion that 'the result of the voting had already been announced and it is too late to request a roll-call'.[47]

At the 1991 session of the UNGA, the President ruled that 'the request for a recorded vote must be made before the beginning of the voting'.[48]

14.2.7 Recording Delegations Present and Not Voting

There have been occasions in the UNGA where, in addition to listing 'yes', 'no' or 'abstention', the results of roll calls list delegations as 'present and not voting'.[49] This is done even though there is no provision for it in the

[46] Official Records, 1986 Conference on Treaties Between States and International Organisations, 29th Meeting, para. 6, UN Doc. A/CONF.129/16 (1986).

[47] Verbatim Records of the 6th Plenary Meeting of the 42nd World Health Assembly, p. 102, WHA42/1989/REC/2 (1989).

[48] UN GAOR, Plenary, 46th Session, 78th Meeting, p. 31, UN Doc. A/46/PV.78 (Provisional) (1992).

[49] For example: UN GAOR, Plenary, 15th Session, 924th Meeting, para. 200, UN Doc. A/PV.924 (1960); UN GAOR, Plenary, 16th Session, 1121st Meeting, paras. 15–17, UN Doc. A/PV.1121 (1961); UN GAOR, Plenary, 17th Session, 1129th Meeting, para. 315, UN Doc. A/PV.1129 (1962).

At a meeting of the 4th Committee of the UNGA at its 13th Session, the Rapporteur commented on a request by a delegation to be recorded as not participating in a vote that 'the question involved a moot point which had never been clarified in the United Nations. Some delegations felt that declared non-participation in the vote should be recorded. In drawing up the report he had been guided by that principle, which he felt to be correct.' UN GAOR, 4th Committee, 13th Session, 840th Meeting, para. 15, UN Doc. A/C.4/13/SR.840 (1958).

UNGA rules of procedure. On one occasion the President of the UNGA refused a request to register a delegation as 'not participating',[50] although at a later meeting of the same session of the UNGA, delegations were noted as 'not participating'.[51]

At a 1963 meeting of the UNGA, an agreed formula was announced whereby the recorded results of the vote would not contain a reference to States present and not voting. States would, however, be entitled to state in explanations of vote that they were not participating in the vote.[52] At a subsequent plenary meeting of the same session, the President repeated the formula, adding that 'the statement of any delegation which has expressly requested that its non-participation in the voting should be recorded will appear in a note to that effect in the verbatim record of the relevant meeting'.[53] The formula announced at the 1963 session of the UNGA is implemented in practice. For example, the records of a plenary meeting of the UNGA at its 1992 session record, in a footnote, the list of States that 'announced that they were not participating' in a roll-call vote.[54]

A 1986 opinion of the UN Office of Legal Affairs states that 'non-participation in the vote is not indicated in the official results of the vote announced by the President and reflected in the official record of the meeting. From a legal standpoint, a Member that declares its non-participation in the voting process is in the same situation as a Member State that was absent during the voting.'[55]

14.2.8 *Recording Abstentions*

The rules of procedure of the 1963 Tokyo Air Law Conference stipulated,

> *Rule 21*
>
> The vote or *abstention* of each State participating in a roll call shall be recorded in the minutes.[56] [emphasis added]

[50] UN GAOR, Plenary, 5th Session, 327th Meeting, para. 91, UN Doc. A/PV.327 (1950).

[51] UN GAOR, Plenary, 5th Session, 330th Meeting, para. 137, UN Doc. A/PV.330 (1951).

[52] UN GAOR, 4th Committee, 18th Session, 1457th Meeting, para. 2, UN Doc. A/C.4/18/SR.1457 (1963).

[53] UN GAOR, Plenary, 18th Session, 1255th Meeting, para. 20, UN Doc. A/PV.1255 (1963).

[54] UN GAOR, Plenary, 47th Session, 81st Meeting, p. 66, UN Doc. A/47/PV.81 (Provisional) (1992).

[55] Letter (from the UN Office of Legal Affairs) to the Permanent Observer of an intergovernmental organisation to the United Nations, 9 May 1986. 1986 UN Jur. Y.B. 275, 276 (ST/LEG/SER.C/24) (1994).

[56] Documents of the 1963 Tokyo Air Law Conference, vol. II, Doc. No. 3, ICAO Doc. 8565-LC/152-2 (1963).

The Conference decided that Rule 21, which calls for the recording of abstentions on the occasion of a roll-call vote, applied only to roll-call votes and that there should be no recording of the number of abstentions in non-roll-call votes.[57]

The issue of announcing the number of abstentions arose at a meeting of the 1991 Conference on the Liability of Operators of Transport Terminals in International Trade. In a reply to a question by the representative of Yugoslavia, the Chairman said 'that in accordance with rule 36 of the rules of procedure,[58] States which abstained from voting were to be considered as not voting. For that reason, he had not called on those abstaining to declare themselves.'[59] The representative of the Philippines commented that he 'felt that a count should be taken of the number of abstainers, since that seemed to be the intention of the rules of procedure'.[60]

COMMENT

The usual procedure in the UNGA and in conferences is to call for abstentions and for the record to show the number of abstentions.[61]

14.2.9 *Order of Voting in a Roll-Call Vote*

Rule 87 of the UNGA rules of procedure states:

(a) The roll-call shall be taken in the English alphabetical order of the names of the members, beginning with the member whose name is drawn by lot by the President.
(b) When the General Assembly votes by mechanical means . . . a recorded vote shall replace a roll-call vote.

[57] Minutes of the 1963 Tokyo Air Law Conference, vol. I, 11th Meeting, para. 29, ICAO Doc. 8565-LC/152–1 (1963) (published 1966).

[58] *Rule 36*

For the purpose of these rules, the phrase 'participating States present and voting' means participating States present and casting an affirmative or negative vote. Participating States that abstain from voting shall be considered as not voting.

UN Doc. A/CONF.152/3.

The rule is identical in substance to the rule in the UNGA rules of procedure.

[59] UN Doc. A/CONF.152/C.1/SR.2, para. 15. [60] *Ibid.* at para. 16.

[61] Rule 87(a) of the UNGA rules of procedure states that the 'result of the voting' shall be recorded.

The UN Model Rules have a similar stipulation.[62] In 1974, the ICAO Assembly amended its rules of procedure to include a similar stipulation. This was done on the basis of an ICAO Council recommendation that it was 'the practice of most other international organizations'.[63] Where the language of the host State is French or Spanish, the order will normally be of the names of the States in the language of the host State.

14.2.10 Voting by Mechanical or Electronic Means

As a result of the introduction of mechanical voting in 1967, the rules of procedure of the UNGA were changed so as to allow a vote by mechanical – or electronic – means.[64] The vote can be either nonrecorded, recorded or recorded with a calling out of the names of the States.

All recent conferences have employed electronic voting systems. Most assembly halls are equipped with such facilities, and where there are no such permanent facilities, temporary systems, unattached to desks or tables, have been employed. The ILO Conferences enable electronic voting even for secret ballots.[65]

14.2.11 Voting on Behalf of More than One State

Although delegates frequently make statements on behalf of more than one State, there is no provision in the UN for a delegate to vote on behalf of more than one State. A 1965 letter from the UN Office of Legal Affairs states that 'representation by one delegate of more than one country is improper and undesirable... It would be undesirable and open to objections.'[66]

At a 2007 meeting of the Plenary of the UNGA, a delegation complained that 'a representative from the delegation of Andorra is sitting in the seat of Israel and exercising the vote on behalf of Israel'. The President explained,

[62] Rule 54 of the UN Model Rules.

[63] ICAO Docs. A/21-WP/27, EX/4; Doc. 9113, A/21-EX, p. 26 (1974).

[64] UNGA Resolution 2323 (XXII) of 16 December 1967.

[65] Article 19 of the Standing Orders of the International Labour Conference.

[66] Letter of the Office of Legal Affairs to a resident representative of the Technical Assistance Board, 1 September 1965, concerning 'QUESTION OF VOTING OR REPRESENTATION BY PROXY IN THE UN AND ITS SPECIALIZED AGENCIES', http://legal.un.org/ola/media/GA_RoP/GA_RoP_EN.pdf

'The necessary document was already submitted to the Credentials Committee of the Secretariat.' The delegate further complained that he was 'not aware of any notification to the General Committee or the Credentials Committee'. The President responded 'that it has been submitted to the Office of Legal affairs'.[67] The explanation for this unusual procedure presumably was that the voting was taking place on Saturday, the Jewish day of rest.

14.3 Secret Ballot

The rules of procedure of the UNGA state:

> *Rule 92*
>
> All elections shall be held by secret ballot. There shall be no nominations.

The UN Model Rules propose,

> *Rule 61*
>
> 1. All elections shall be held by secret ballot unless, in the absence of any objection, the Conference decides to proceed without taking a ballot on an agreed candidate or slate.

The rules of procedure of the UNGA allow for secret ballots only in the case of elections. At a 1966 meeting of a committee of the UNGA, the Committee decided that the selection of the site for the headquarters of UNIDO should be chosen by secret ballot.[68] When a number of delegations pointed out that this was in violation of the rules of procedure, the Legal Counsel to the UN gave his opinion that rules of procedure could be suspended by 'common accord' or 'general agreement'.[69] This opinion of the Legal Counsel is vehemently criticised by Blum.[70] The Office of Legal Affairs was asked in 1971 to give an opinion on holding a secret ballot as to holding a session away from Headquarters. The opinion was that '[t]he rules of procedure of the Assembly thus do not provide for a secret ballot other than for elections'. However, 'it does not exclude the authority of the General Assembly itself to decide by a majority vote to

[67] UN GAOR, Plenary, 62nd Session, 79th Meeting, p. 11, UN Doc. A/62/PV.79 (2007).

[68] UN GAOR, 2nd Committee, 21st Session, 1101st Meeting, para. 13, UN Doc. A/C.2/21/SR.1101 (1966).

[69] *Ibid.*, para. 24, UN Doc. A/C.2/21/SR.1102 (1966).

[70] See quotation at footnote 19 in Section 21.1.2 in Chapter 21.

resort to secret ballot, since even if this is considered as amounting to a suspension or amendment of the rules of procedure, such power is vested in the Assembly by Article 21of the Charter'.[71]

An additional case of the use of secret ballot is by the UN ECOSOC, Commission on Human Rights, Sub-Commission on Prevention of Discrimination and Protection of Minorities, when it votes on allegations of violations of human rights.[72] There were lengthy discussions as to whether to allow such secret ballots, and at one stage the UN Office of Legal Affairs was requested to submit its opinion. The opinion stated that 'a secret ballot could only be taken if two conditions were met: the decision to take a secret ballot was reached by general agreement; and the question was akin to an election (e.g. the selection of a site among several proposals)'.[73] Nevertheless, the Office of Legal Affairs proceeded to outline a possible draft amendment to the rules of procedure that would permit the holding of a secret ballot.

The rules of procedure of the conferences examined allow for secret ballot only in cases of elections. The only exception appears to have been the 1949 Geneva Conference, which allowed for a secret ballot by a conference or committee decision,[74] and voting by secret ballot in fact took place at this Conference.[75]

The draft rules of procedure of the 1974–1977 Geneva Humanitarian Law Conference allowed for a secret ballot at the request of

[71] *Memorandum by the Office of Legal Affairs to the Under-Secretary-General for Political and General Assembly Affairs* 2 December 1971, regarding COMMENTS ON SOME PROCEDURAL QUESTIONS IN CONNEXION WITH THE PROPOSAL THAT THE THIRTY-THIRD SESSION OF THE GENERAL ASSEMBLY BE HELD A WAY FROM UNITED NATIONS HEADQUARTERS, http://legal.un.org/ola/media/GA_RoP/GA_RoP_EN.pdf

[72] Resolution 1990/4 of UN ECOSOC, Commission on Human Rights, Sub-Commission on Prevention of Discrimination and Protection of Minorities, adopted 23 August 1990. The text of the Resolution appears in UN Doc. E/CN.4/Sub.2/1990/L.11/Add.1 (1990). The report of the debate on the draft of the Resolution appears in UN ECOSOC, Commission on Human Rights, Sub-Commission on Prevention of Discrimination and Protection of Minorities, 1990, Summary Records of the 24th Session, paras. 1–64, UN Doc. E/CN.4/Sub.2/1990/SR.24 (1990).

[73] Memorandum (from the Office of Legal Affairs) to the Assistant Secretary-General for Human Rights, Centre for Human Rights, 16 February 1984. 1984 UN Jur. Y.B. 170 (ST/LEG/SER.C/22) (1991).

[74] Rule 36 of the rules of procedure of the 1949 Geneva Conference. A proposal to introduce a secret ballot in the 1995 NPT Review Conference was not adopted.

[75] Records of the Geneva Conference 1949 L-B, p. 232.

ten representatives.[76] Egypt proposed the deletion of the secret ballot provision,[77] and at the recommendation of the drafting committee, the Egyptian amendment was adopted by consensus. There was no explanation given by the drafters of the rules of procedure as to why they had included the unusual procedure of a secret ballot. A surmise may be that the intention was to emphasise continuity from the 1949 Geneva Conference.

At the 1977 Conference on Territorial Asylum, the representative of Bolivia proposed that 'as the Conference was to deal with humanitarian questions affecting the international community as a whole' there should be no secret ballots for elections.[78] The proposal was not adopted.

The older established international organisations allow for secret ballot, under certain conditions, for issues other than elections. The rules of procedure of the ICAO Assembly state,

> *Rule 48*
>
> The vote on any question shall be by secret ballot if the Delegations of two or more Contracting States so request and the request is not opposed. In case of opposition the question whether there shall be a secret ballot shall be decided by a majority of votes cast in secret ballot. The provisions of this Rule shall prevail over those of Rule 47 [dealing with method of voting].[79]

The rules of procedure of the ILO Conference state,

> *Article 19*
>
> 11. A vote by secret ballot shall also be taken on any question not covered by paragraph 5 [a record vote], if the request is made by show of hands of not less than 90 delegates present at the sitting or by the Chairman of a group acting on behalf of his group.
>
> 13. If, on the same question, requests are made both for a record vote in pursuance of paragraph 6 of this article and for a vote by secret ballot in pursuance of paragraph 11 of this article, the vote shall be taken by secret ballot if the Conference so decides by a simple majority vote by secret ballot.[80]

The rules of procedure of the World Health Assembly state,

[76] CDDH/2 Rule 37(2). [77] CDDH/8.

[78] Summary Records of the 2nd Meeting of the 1977 Conference on Territorial Asylum, para. 14, UN Doc. A/CONF.78/SR.2 (1977).

[79] Standing rules of procedure of the Assembly of the ICAO, ICAO Doc. 7600/5, 5th edn, 1990.

[80] Standing Orders of the International Labour Conference, ILO Office, Geneva, December 1992.

Rule 78

> In addition to the cases provided for elsewhere by these Rules, the Health Assembly may vote on any matter by secret ballot if it has previously so decided by a majority of Members present and voting, provided that no secret ballot may be taken on budgetary questions.

A decision under this Rule by the Health Assembly whether or not to vote by secret ballot may only be taken by a show of hands; if the Assembly has decided to vote on a particular question by secret ballot, no other mode of voting may be requested or decided upon.[81]

At a 2000 meeting of a committee of the WHO, a delegation demanded that ballot papers in a secret ballot be in all official languages. However, the Legal Counsel responded that 'ballot papers in English and French had been used within the Organization for decades', but that 'votes could be recorded in any of the official languages used by the Health Assembly'.[82]

At a Committee meeting of the 2010 World Health Assembly, the Legal Counsel gave his opinion that '"a show of hands was only necessary in the event of objection to taking the vote by secret ballot'.[83]

The Constitution of the ITU states,

Article 32(14)(5)

> 1. The voting procedures are as follows:
>
> . . .
>
> (c) by a secret ballot, if at least five of the delegations present and entitled to vote so request before the beginning of the vote.[84]

At a 1993 meeting of the World Health Assembly, one delegation requested a vote by secret ballot, and this was followed by another delegation that requested a vote by roll call. The Chairman ruled that 'a request for a vote by secret ballot under Rule 78 should be given priority'.[85]

81 Rules of procedure of the World Health Assembly, WHO Basic Documents, 35th edn, 1985. 64th World Health Assembly, Committee 'A', 11th Meeting, p. 201, WHO Doc. WHA64/2011/REC/3 (2011).

82 Summary Records of the 7th Meeting of Committee 'B' of the 52nd World Health Assembly, p. 178 (2000), WHA52/1999/REC/3 (1999).

83 Summary Records of the 7th Meeting of Committee "B" of the 63rd World Health Assembly, WHA/63/2010/REC/3, p. 285 (2010).

84 Article 32(14) (5)(1)(c) of the Constitution of the International Telecommunication Union, Geneva 1993.

85 Summary Records of the 9th Meeting of Committee 'B' of the 46th World Health Assembly, p. 263, WHA46/1993/REC/3 (1993).

There was an unsuccessful attempt at the 1995 NPT Review Conference to introduce voting by secret ballot. The proposal was intended presumably as a measure to counter US pressure for unlimited extension of the Treaty.

COMMENT

It would appear that on nonpersonnel issues, as a matter of accountability, delegations of States should be obliged to be on record as to their voting. The stance adopted by the UN Model Rules is, in the opinion of this author, in keeping therefore with the accepted practice of conferences to restrict secret ballots to matters of elections.

14.3.1 Representatives Absent When Their Names Are Called in a Secret Ballot

A 1963 UN Ad Hoc Committee on the Methods of Work of the General Assembly considered the case where a secret ballot takes place and 'all representatives are not in their places when the conference officer collects the ballot papers. The Committee recommends that in such cases, committees should follow the practice of the General Assembly and that the balloting should be done by roll-call, representatives being allowed to vote up to the moment when the Chairman declares the voting closed.'[86]

14.4 Voting by Proxy and by Correspondence

The draft rules of the 1907 Hague Conference proposed a rule whereby '[t]he delegation of one Power may have itself represented by that of another'.[87] This draft rule was not adopted in the final text.

The rules of procedure of the ITU Plenipotentiary Conferences allow proxy voting.[88] Apparently, however, ITU conferences are the only modern international inter-governmental conferences to follow such procedure.

The Commission on Narcotic Drugs has allowed voting by proxy, but the UN Office of Legal affairs commented, 'We do not believe that any

[86] Report of the Ad Hoc Committee on the Improvement of the Methods of Work of the General Assembly, GAOR, 18th Session, Annexes, Agenda Item 25, p. 10, para. 61, UN Doc. A/5423 (1963). The UNGA, in Resolution 1898 (XVIII) of 11 November 1963, inter alia 'approved the recommendations submitted by the committee'.

[87] Deuxième Confèrence Internationale de la Paix, Tome Premier, La Haye, Imprimerie Nationale 1907, vol. I, Deuxième Sèance Plènière de la Confèrence.

[88] Article 31(6) of the Constitution of the International Telecommunication Union, Geneva 1993.

other UN organ has adopted a similar form of procedure for taking decisions by correspondence.' It is, however, allowed for in approving reports and in a decision to hold a regular session of the UNGA away from Headquarters.[89]

14.5 Voting on Principles

At a 1947 meeting of a committee of the UNGA, the Soviet representative commented that 'the United Kingdom representative was suggesting a vote on principles; this was not possible since a proposal must have a sponsor before a vote could be taken'. The Chairman agreed.[90]

At a 1948 meeting of a committee of the UNGA, the Committee was faced with a number of conflicting resolutions on the question of the right of the UN to present a claim for reparations against a State. The Chairman ruled that the Committee should vote on a preliminary question that he had drafted. The Chairman's ruling was challenged inter alia on the grounds that it was out of order since a Chairman could not propose substantive proposals. The Chairman's ruling was upheld.[91]

At the 1958 Law of the Sea Conference, a representative suggested that a vote be held on the principle of an issue before voting on a text. The Chairman commented, 'If the committee wished to ascertain before proceeding further whether the Commission's draft were [*sic*] acceptable, in the hope that they would automatically eliminate a series of amendments, it would be departing from the rules of procedure.'[92] At the 1961 Vienna Conference on Diplomatic Relations, the delegate of

[89] Letter to the Deputy Secretary-General, World Meteorological Organization. 7 April 1970, "QUESTION OF VOTE BY CORRESPONDENCE, PROCEDURE APPLIED BY THE COMMISSION ON NARCOTIC DRUG, http://legal.un.org/ola/media/GA_RoP/GA_RoP_EN.pdf.

[90] UN GAOR, 6th Committee, 2nd Session, 56th Meeting, p. 136, UN Doc. A/C.6/2/SR.56 (1947).

[91] UN GAOR, 6th Committee, 3rd Session, 118th Meeting, pp. 579–584, UN Doc. A/C.6/3/SR.118 (1948).

[92] The Chairman (Mr Bailey of Australia):

> 26. With regard to the order of voting, he must state emphatically that the rules of procedure stipulate that amendments be put to the vote first. Hence, if the Committee wishes to ascertain, before proceeding further, whether the Commission's draft were [*sic*] acceptable, in the hope that that would automatically eliminate a series of amendments, it would be departing from the rules of procedure which would itself require a separate decision.
>
> Official Records of the 1958 Law of the Sea Conference, 30th Meeting of Committee I, vol. III, p. 88, para. 24, UN Doc. A/CONF.13/39.

Switzerland proposed that before voting on amendments, a vote be held on the principle of the clause (compulsory jurisdiction of the International Court). Some delegations objected, demanding strict application of the rules of procedure, and in view of the objections, the Chairman announced that the Committee would proceed to vote on the amendments themselves.[93]

The ICAO Air Law Conferences use the device of votes on principles, with considerable effect, as a means of narrowing the issues prior to developing actual texts.[94] At a meeting of the 1971 Montreal Air Law Conference, the President called for a vote on a question of principle. The US delegate, on a point of order, argued that the Commission did not have before it a proposal on the question the President wished to propose. As a result of the ensuing discussion, the Commission decided to convene a working group to prepare a text for a proposal.[95]

At a meeting of a 1971 IMCO Conference, the Chairman ruled that 'the Committee could only vote on motions which had been tabled. It could not vote on interpretations.'[96] The Chairman, however, later permitted a vote on the principle of a proposal that had been submitted.[97]

At a meeting of a committee of the 1974–1977 Geneva Humanitarian Law Conference, the representative of Denmark objected to the Chairman's proposal that the Committee vote on a list of principles. The Danish representative stated that he hoped 'that when the time came, the Committee would vote on the basis of written texts'.[98] The Chairman replied that 'international conferences often voted on principles, leaving details of drafting to be attended to later'.[99]

At a meeting of the 1974 Prescription in Sale of Goods Conference, a vote on principle was held without any delegation raising objection.[100]

93 UN Doc. A/CONF.20/14, p. 244 (1961).

94 For example, ICAO International Conference on Air Law, Tokyo, 1963, vol. I, Minutes, p. 340, paras. 24–28, Doc. 8565-LC/152–1.

95 1971 Montreal Air Law Conference, vol. I, Minutes, Commission of the Whole, 4th Meeting, p. 48, para. 50, ICAO Doc. 9081-LC/170–1.

96 Official Records of the 1971 IMCO Oil Pollution Damage Fund Conference, Summary Records of the 9th Meeting of Committee 1, p. 370, IMCO Doc. CONF.2/C.1/SR.9 (1971).

97 Official Records of the 1971 IMCO Oil Pollution Damage Fund Conference, Summary Records of the 17th Meeting of Committee 1, p. 440, IMCO Doc. CONF.2/C.1/SR.17 (1971).

98 Official Records of the 1974–1977 Geneva Humanitarian Law Conference, CDDH/II/SR.69, vol. XII, p. 160, para. 6.

99 *Ibid.* at p. 161, para. 7.

100 Official Records of the 1974 Prescription in Sale of Goods Conference, Committee I, p. 212, UN Doc. A/CONF.63 (1974).

14.5.1 *What Is the Effect of Having a Vote on Principle?*

At a meeting of the 1971 Montreal Air Law Conference, the President ruled that 'decisions in principle had already been taken. These decisions were binding to the effect that if contrary proposals were made it would constitute a reopening of the debate requiring a two-thirds majority vote.'[101]

At a 1973 committee meeting of the ICAO Assembly, the Chairman ruled that, after a vote on principle had taken place, 'the Committee now had to consider the proposals for the amendment of the Chicago Convention that *were consonant with the principles* accepted in the vote at the Sixth meeting'.[102] [emphasis added] At a later meeting of the Committee, the delegate of Norway stated that he 'had understood that any decisions of principle taken by the Committee would not preclude consideration of any formal proposal made by a delegation'.[103] The Chairman replied, 'Logically the rejection of certain principles ruled out consideration of proposals embodying them.'[104]

The Chairman at the 1973 ICAO Rome Air Law Conference, held concurrently with the ICAO Assembly, also acted on the assumption that, in the absence of a due decision to reconsider an issue, a vote on principle precluded reconsideration.[105]

In the 1978 Hamburg Conference on Carriage by Sea, the Chairman of a committee ruled that since a decision had been taken 'on the Principle ... a decision of the Committee could not be reconsidered unless a two-thirds majority of the members present and voting so wished'.[106] A similar ruling was made in the 1991 Conference on the Liability of Operators of Transport Terminals in International Trade: the Chairman proposed voting on a question of principle and a vote was taken.[107] When a delegate then requested a vote on an amendment that had been proposed previously, the Chairman ruled that it would 'mean

[101] 1971 Montreal Air Law Conference, vol. I, Minutes, Commission of the Whole, 9th Meeting, p. 77, para. 1, ICAO Doc. 9081-LC/170–1.

[102] Minutes of the 7th Meeting of the Executive Committee of the 20th Extraordinary Session of the ICAO Assembly, p. 65, ICAO Doc. 9088, A20-Min. EX/7 (1973).

[103] Minutes of the 9th Meeting of the Executive Committee of the 20th Extraordinary Session of the ICAO Assembly, p. 83, ICAO Doc. 9088, A20-Min. EX/9 (1973).

[104] *Ibid.* at p. 84.

[105] Minutes of the 14th Meeting of the Commission of the Whole of the 1973 Rome Air Law Conference, paras. 37, 40, 41, 42, ICAO Doc. 9225-LC/178 (1973).

[106] UN Doc. A/CONF.89/C.1/SR.32, paras. 61, 63 (1978).

[107] UN Doc. A/CONF.152/C.1/SR.15, p. 9 (1991).

reopening the debate' since, he implied, it was contrary to the principle voted on.[108]

14.5.2 *Decision Making as to Whether to Hold a Vote on Principle*

At a committee meeting of a 1969 IMCO conference committee, the Chairman decided to put to the vote the question as to whether the Committee should vote on a question of principle.[109]

COMMENT

Voting on a principle circumvents the well-established rule that amendments to a proposal are always voted on before voting on the proposal itself. It appears that when there has been a vote on the principle of a proposal, this has been done only when no delegation has raised the objection that amendments must be voted on first. Once such objection has been raised, the only way to overcome it would be by change of the rules of procedure. In committee meetings this option is not available, as the right to change the rules of procedure is reserved, by nearly all rules of procedure, to the plenary of the conference and not to committees.

The potential deficiency of voting on questions of principle, as opposed to voting on specific texts, was illustrated in a debate during the 1978 Hamburg Conference on Carriage by Sea. At this conference a decision had been taken on a question of principle, but subsequently all drafts based on the principle were rejected by the Conference.[110]

It is usually the presiding officer who formulates the principles to be voted on, and the formulation can lead to disagreement. For example, at a 1973 meeting of the ICAO Assembly, a delegation complained that the question put to the vote by the Chairman 'did not correctly represent the underlying principle of their proposal'.[111]

[108] *Ibid.* at p. 10. In this particular case the motion to reopen the debate was carried by a two-thirds majority.

[109] Summary Records of the 20th Meeting of Committee 1 of the 1969 IMCO Conference on Marine Pollution Damage, p. 414, IMCO Doc. LEG/CONF/C.1/SR.20 (1969).

[110] UN Doc. A/CONF.89/C.1/SR.32, paras. 61–72, SR.33, paras. 1–32 (1978).

[111] Minutes of the 10th Meeting of the Executive Committee of the 20th Extraordinary Session of the ICAO Assembly, p. 102, ICAO Doc. 9088, A20-Min. EX/10 (1973).

Nevertheless, the advantages of the system of voting on principles, when coupled with an indicative vote, appear to outweigh any disadvantages.

14.6 Indicative Vote

Some of the deficiencies of voting on principles can be overcome, it is suggested, by increased reliance on the nonbinding method of asking for 'an indicative'[112] or straw vote.

At a 1948 meeting of a UNGA committee, the Chairman put to the vote a question of principle raised by several amendments that had been submitted. The Chairman, however, assured the delegations that whatever the results, he would nevertheless put to the vote all amendments that had been submitted.[113]

An indicative vote was used at a 1969 IMCO conference, for the purpose of ascertaining the preferences of delegations on a number of possibilities.[114]

At the 1973 Rome Air Law Conference, the Chairman explained that an indicative vote 'was not, however, to be considered as a deciding vote. It was an indication of preference only.'[115] This ruling led to a discussion in which one delegation moved the adjournment of the meeting, but agreed to withdraw the motion 'on condition that from now on the Commission would be told, before it voted, what the significance of the vote would be. The fact that this had not been done before what was now described as an indicative vote . . . was responsible for the last half hour's discussion on procedure.'[116]

The draft rules of procedure for the Third Law of the Sea Conference proposed:

> *Rule 36*
>
> The President may at any time ascertain the sense of the meeting on any matter. This procedure shall not have the effect of a vote.[117]

112 See, for instance, UN Doc. A/CONF.152/C.1/SR.9, p. 7 (1991).

113 UN GAOR, 6th Committee, 3rd Session, 86th Meeting, p. 243, UN Doc. A/C.6/3/SR.86 (1948).

114 Summary Records of the 8th Meeting of Committee 2 of the 1969 IMCO Conference on Marine Pollution Damage, pp. 656, 657, IMCO Doc. LEG/CONF/C.2/SR.8 (1969).

115 Minutes of the 15th Meeting of the Commission of the Whole of the 1973 Rome Air Law Conference, p. 262, para. 6, ICAO Doc. 9225-LC/178 (1973).

116 *Ibid.* at para. 16.

117 Third UN Conference on the Law of the Sea, draft rules of procedure, UN Doc. A/CONF.62/2 (1973).

A number of delegations proposed omitting this article.[118] The Australian delegation, in explaining its proposal to omit the article, stated that 'the President is always able to take the sense of the meeting in a general way and it is therefore unnecessary to make special provisions for this procedure. Any provision with respect to voting should appear elsewhere in the Rules.'[119] The article was omitted from the final text of the rules of procedure.

At a 1976 IMCO conference, the Chairman explained that a 'preliminary' vote would allow representatives to revert to the issue and that 'the provisions of the rules of procedure governing the reconsideration of issues would not apply'.[120]

At the 1980 Vienna Conference on International Sale of Goods, the Chairman of a committee explained the nature of an indicative vote as being based 'on the understanding that the vote would not affect the proposals themselves'.[121] When an indicative vote was requested on another issue, the Chairman told the Committee that 'some representatives had objected to the taking of an indicative vote on the grounds that no provision was made for it in the Rules of Procedure. He would therefore prefer to avoid the taking of such a vote.'[122] One delegate commented that 'although the Rules of Procedure made no provision for indicative voting, neither did they prohibit it. An indicative vote on the question at issue would be useful in giving the working group guidance on how to go about its work.'[123]

An indicative vote was used at the 1988 Vienna Conference on Narcotic Drugs, on the question of the inclusion of a paragraph in a convention, prior to a detailed discussion of its wording.[124]

[118] See, for example, Cameroon, Chile, Colombia, Mexico, United Republic of Tanzania, UN Doc. A/CONF.62/4 (1973).

[119] Third UN Conference on the Law of the Sea, Australia: amendment to the draft rules of procedure, UN Doc. A/CONF.62/9 (1973).

[120] Official Records of the 1976 IMCO Conference on Maritime Claims, Summary Records of the 4th Meeting of the Committee of the Whole, p. 232, IMCO Doc. CONF.5/C.1/SR.4 (1976).

[121] Official Records of the 1980 Vienna Conference on International Sale of Goods, Summary Records of the 20th Meeting of Committee 1, p. 343, para. 65, UN Doc. A/CONF.97/C.1/SR.20 (1980).

[122] *Ibid.* at 29th Meeting, p. 391, para. 34

[123] *Ibid.* at para. 35.

[124] Summary Records of the 26th Meeting of Committee 1 of the 1988 Vienna Conference on Narcotic Drugs, para. 72, UN Doc. E/CONF.82/C.1/SR.26 (1988).

The UK delegate to the 1991 Conference on the Liability of Operators of Transport Terminals in International Trade pointed out, 'The practice of taking indicative votes was a useful means of sounding a committee's general feeling.'[125]

The results of such an indicative vote do not necessarily appear in a detailed form in the summary records. They may be reflected in a phrase such as appears in the records of the 1988 Vienna Conference on Narcotic Drugs: 'The Chairman having called for an indicative vote on the inclusion of… noted that there appeared to be a majority in favour.'[126]

At the World Health Assembly, trial votes are held on elections to the Executive Board. The records, however, do not give the results of such votes but state that 'the Chairman informed the Committee of the results of the trial vote'.[127]

At a 1971 IMCO conference, a representative asked 'exactly what was meant by an indicative vote, since nothing of the kind was provided for in the Rules of Procedure'.[128] An unusual interpretation of the significance of an indicative vote was given by the Chairman in his reply. The Chairman ruled that 'the only difference between that type of voting [indicative voting] and final voting was that a simple majority instead of a two-thirds majority was all that was needed to reverse a decision'.[129]

At a 2004 meeting of the International Labour Conference, the Chairperson proposed to hold 'a straw vote as a quick way to solicit the views of the Government members'.[130]

An indicative vote was used at a 2012 committee meeting of the IAEA General Conference.[131]

125 UN Doc. A/CONF.152/C.1/SR.3, para. 43 (1991). For examples of where an indicative vote was taken at this Conference, see A/CONF.152/C.1/SR.9, para. 44 (1991); A/CONF. 152/C.1/SR.15, para. 47 (1991).

126 E/CONF.82/C.1/SR.26, p. 9, para. 72 (1988).

127 See, for instance, Summary Records of the 3rd Meeting of the General Committee of the 33rd World Health Assembly, p. 10, WHA33/1980/REC/3 (1980).

128 Official Records of the 1971 IMCO Oil Pollution Damage Fund Conference, Summary Records of the 6th Meeting of Committee 1, p. 346, IMCO Doc. CONF.2/C.1/SR.6 (1971).

129 *Ibid.* at p. 347.

130 Provisional Records, ILO Conference, 92nd Session, 20th Meeting, section 480, p. 20/46 (2004).

131 IAEA 2012 General Conference, Committee of the Whole, 55th Session, 7th Meeting, para. 64, IAEA Doc. GC(55)/COM.5/OR.7 (2012).

14.6.1 Indicative Vote by Roll Call

There does not appear to be any reason why an indicative vote cannot be held by roll call, and there is at least one precedent where such a vote took place.[132]

14.7 Voting on Preferences

Treaty-making conferences at times employ a method of voting on preferences. Under the usual procedure, once a proposal is adopted, all other incompatible proposals are eliminated without voting, even though they might have received, on a vote, a larger majority than the first proposal that was approved. In accordance with the method of voting on preferences, the presiding officer requests the conference to express preferences between a number of mutually exclusive proposals. The debate and drafting then continue only as regards the proposal that received the most votes. The advantage of this system is that, to a large extent, it eliminates the procedural advantage that normally accrues to the proposal being voted on first.

The draft rules of procedure of the Third Law of the Sea Conference proposed the following article:

> *Rule 45*
>
> 2. Whenever a text to be voted on by the Conference embodies optional or alternative passages, the Conference shall, unless it decides otherwise, vote on them in an order determined by the following procedure:
>
> (a) whenever multiple brackets or other devices are used to indicate that the Conference is to consider the inclusion or exclusion of optional passages, votes shall first be taken on the parts enclosed within the innermost brackets, including on any amendments proposed thereto;
> (b) a choice between alternative passages shall only be made after all decisions required to determine the precise formulation of each such passage have been taken, including decisions on any amendments proposed thereto;
> (c) to determine the sequence of voting on alternative passages each representative shall be called upon to indicate, by any method proposed by the President, the one alternative on which he wishes to vote first; the order of voting shall be determined according to the number of

132 Official Records, 1986 Conference on Treaties between States and International Organisations, 29th Meeting, para. 6, UN Doc. A/CONF.129/16 (1986).

> representatives indicating their preference for each alternative, provided that if the number is tied with respect to two or more alternatives, the President shall determine the order between them by drawing lots.[133]

The Secretary-General added an explanatory note stating,

> It is likely that the Conference, and in particular the Main Committees, will frequently be required to consider complex texts which summarize and present numerous alternative approaches and formulations. Since the usual rules as to priority of proposals would not be applicable, paragraph 2 of rule 45 presents a special procedure for dealing with such situations.[134]

Draft Rule 45 (2) was omitted from the final text of the rules of procedure of the Third Law of the Sea Conference.[135] One can assume that, although ingenious, the proposed text was far too detailed and elaborate for a conference.

In a meeting of the 1973 Rome Air Law Conference, a debate took place on the method of holding a vote on preferences. Some delegations maintained that 'as the Commission was being asked to express a preference among three alternatives, only the number in favour of each should be ascertained'.[136] Other delegations thought 'that delegations should be given an opportunity to vote for or against, or abstain on, each alternative'.[137] One delegation suggested that there should be 'a fourth alternative to permit those who wanted none of the three to express their position clearly'.[138] The Director of the Legal Bureau of the ICAO explained 'that it was normal to vote on amendments in the order of their remoteness from the original proposal and, by analogy', the same rule should apply in a vote on preferences.[139] The Chairman ruled as to the order of voting (without giving his reasons) and added that 'each delegation would be given an opportunity to record their position, by vote, on each of the alternatives'.[140] The Chairman's ruling was challenged on the ground that 'only the number in favour of each alternative should be ascertained'.[141] Following a motion for closure of debate, the vote took

[133] Third UN Conference on the Law of the Sea, draft rules of procedure, UN Doc. A/CONF.62/2 (1973).

[134] *Ibid.*, Note by the Secretary-General, para. 5.

[135] See Adoption of the rules of procedure, Amendments to the draft rules of procedure, Proposals by the President, UN Doc. A/CONF.62/WP.4/Add.1 (1974).

[136] Minutes of the 10th Meeting of the Commission of the Whole of the 1973 Rome Air Law Conference, para. 23, ICAO Doc. 9225-LC/178 (1973).

[137] *Ibid.* [138] *Ibid.* [139] *Ibid.* [140] *Ibid.* at para. 24. [141] *Ibid.* at para. 26.

place in accordance with the Chairman's ruling, delegations voting for, against or abstaining on each of the three alternatives.[142]

At a meeting of a 1976 IMCO conference, the Chairman proposed having an indicative vote on three proposals and 'after the three indicative votes, a definitive vote would be taken on the proposal that had received the widest support'.[143] Some delegations objected, claiming that it would be preferable to vote first on the principle; however the Committee, by a vote, decided to adopt the Chairman's proposal concerning voting procedure.[144]

The method of voting on preferences is employed for both indicative votes[145] and decisive votes.[146]

The 1995 NPT Review Conference employed a version of voting by preferences that eliminated completely the element of advantage embodied in consecutive voting. The relevant rule stated,

> *Rule 28*
>
> 3(f). All proposals shall be voted on simultaneously by written ballot. Each State Party shall have one vote, to be cast in favour of one of the proposals.[147]

The system, however, would not be practicable for a conference that had to draft a complex document with a large number of proposals and amendments.

[142] *Ibid.*

[143] Official Records of the 1976 IMCO Conference on Maritime Claims, Summary Records of the 22nd Meeting of the Committee of the Whole, p. 381, IMCO Doc. CONF.5/C.1/SR.22 (1976).

[144] *Ibid.* at p. 382.

[145] Minutes of the 10th Meeting of the Commission of the Whole of the 1973 Rome Air Law Conference, para. 2, ICAO Doc. 9225-LC/178 (1973). The Chairman, referring to a vote on preferences, emphasised, however, that 'the results of the vote would be merely an indication for guidance in the Commission's future work'.

[146] Voting on preferences can theoretically have its own pitfalls.

The 'voter's paradox' examines a situation where three voters have to choose between possibilities A, B and C.

The order of preference of voter No. 1 is A, B, C.
The order of preference of voter No. 2 is B, C, A.
The order of preference of voter No. 3 is C, A, B.

If the three voters are first asked to choose between A and B, then A will be chosen; as between A and the remaining choice, C, the final choice will be C. If, however, the voters are first asked to choose between B and C, then B will eventually be chosen. Kenneth J. Arrow, *Social Choices and Individual Values*, 2nd edn (1963), p. 2.

[147] Rule 28(3)(f) of the rules of procedure of the 1995 NPT Review Conference, Doc. NPT/CONF.1995/28 (1995).

14.8 Voting in Elections

The UNGA rules of procedure stipulate,

Elections
Rule 92

All elections shall be held by secret ballot. There shall be no nominations.

Rule 93

When only one person or Member is to be elected and no candidate obtains in the first ballot the majority required, a second ballot shall be taken, which shall be restricted to the two candidates obtaining the largest number of votes. If in the second ballot the votes are equally divided, and a majority is required, the President shall decide between the candidates by drawing lots. If a two-thirds majority is required, the balloting shall be continued until one candidate secures two thirds of the votes cast; provided that, after the third inconclusive ballot, votes may be cast for any eligible person or Member. If three such unrestricted ballots are inconclusive, the next three ballots shall be restricted to the two candidates who obtained the greatest number of votes in the third of the unrestricted ballots, and the following three ballots thereafter shall be unrestricted, and so on until a person or Member is elected.

Rule 94

When two or more elective places are to be filled at one time under the same conditions, those candidates obtaining in the first ballot the majority required shall be elected. If the number of candidates obtaining such majority is less than the number of persons or Members to be elected, there shall be additional ballots to fill the remaining places, the voting being restricted to the candidates obtaining the greatest number of votes in the previous ballot to a number not more than twice the places remaining to be filled; provided that, after the third inconclusive ballot, votes may be cast for any eligible person or Member. If three such unrestricted ballots are inconclusive, the next three ballots shall be restricted to the candidates who obtained the greatest number of votes in the third of the unrestricted ballots, to a number not more than twice the places remaining to be filled and the following three ballots thereafter shall be unrestricted, and so on until all the places have been filled.

The UN Model Rules proposal is less convoluted:

Rule 61
Elections

1. All elections shall be held by secret ballot unless, in the absence of any objection, the Conference decides to proceed without taking a ballot on an agreed candidate or slate.

Rule 62
Balloting

1. When one or more elective places are to be filled at one time under the same conditions, each delegation entitled to vote may cast a vote for as many candidates as there are places to be filled, and those candidates, in a number not exceeding the number of such places, obtaining in the first ballot a majority of the votes cast and the largest number of votes shall be elected.
2. If the number of candidates so elected is less than the number of places to be filled, additional ballots shall be held to fill the remaining places. From such ballots the candidates obtaining the least number of votes in the previous ballot may be eliminated on the proposal of the President.

The rule whereby a conference elects its officers by secret ballot is common to the rules of procedure of all conferences. In practice however, conferences usually elect officers by acclamation, without recourse to voting.

Where candidates do not obtain the required majority, most rules of procedure, since 1958, contain provisions for further rounds of voting while eliminating from the elections the candidates obtaining the least number of votes. In case of a tied vote, the decision is usually made by the presiding officer drawing lots. The practice in the UNGA is to dispense with the need for a secret ballot 'when the number of candidates corresponds to the number of seats to be filled'.[148]

Notwithstanding the complexity of some of the systems employed for voting in elections, it is extremely rare to find procedural debates or decisions in conferences on this issue. The reason is that elections to posts in conferences are usually arranged as part of interregional negotiations, the results being approved by acclamation rather than by employing a system of voting.[149]

14.9 Request Not to Vote

Sponsors of a proposal at times have informed a conference that they are not requesting a vote or not requesting a vote at the present time.[150] Such

[148] Letter from the Office of Legal Affairs to the Permanent Representative of a Member State to the UN, 12 May 1995, "Meaning of the words 'Agreed Candidate', rule 68 of the rules of procedure of ECOSOC, paragraph 16 of Annex VI the rules of procedure of the UNGA, http://legal.un.org/ola/media/GA_RoP/GA_RoP_EN.pdf.

[149] An examination of the UNGA system of elections for such bodies as the UN Security Council, ECOSOC, the ICJ and the ILC is beyond the scope of this study.

[150] See, for example, UN GAOR, General Committee, 1st Special Session, 31st Meeting, p. 79, UN Doc. A/BUR/PV.31 (1947); Official Records of the 1974–1977 Geneva Humanitarian Law Conference, CDDH/I/SR.74, vol. IX, p. 465, para. 25.

procedure is not covered by rules of procedure since, strictly speaking, only the conference and not the sponsors can decide whether to vote on a proposal and when to do so. When a delegation requests not to vote on a proposal, the proposal remains on the agenda, whereas this is not so for a proposal that is withdrawn.

At a meeting of a committee of the 1974–1977 Geneva Humanitarian Law Conference, a proposal concerning the protective emblem was submitted by Canada, the Federal Republic of Germany, Nicaragua and the Philippines. After the discussion had commenced, Canada proposed that discussion should continue in the working group.[151] The representatives of Iraq and India requested that the Committee vote on the proposal. The representative of Canada then proposed that the vote be deferred to the next meeting and the Chairman agreed to the Canadian proposal.[152] The representatives of India and Iraq insisted, however, on the proposal being put to the vote immediately: this was done and the proposal was rejected.[153]

14.10 Invalid Vote

At a 2003 session of the UNGA involving elections to the International Criminal Tribunal for Rwanda, it transpired that a member State had, unwittingly, voted, notwithstanding that, since it was in arrears, it was denied voting rights under the UN Charter.[154] The President, on the advice of the Legal Counsel, ruled that the voting was invalid and should be held again.[155] The President referred to the fact that the one invalid vote cast could have influenced the results of the elections, hence this ruling cannot necessarily serve as guidance to a situation where an invalid vote could not have influenced the outcome.

151 Official Records of the 1974–1977 Geneva Humanitarian Law Conference, CDDH/I/SR.49, para. 47 vol. IX, p. 106.

152 *Ibid.* at paras. 50, 51. 153 *Ibid.* at paras. 52, 57. 154 Article 19 of the UN Charter.

155 UN GAOR, Plenary, 57th Session, UN Doc. A/57/PV.80, pp. 7–13 (2003).

15

Majority Required

15.1 Unanimity

In the nineteenth and the early twentieth centuries, conference decisions, on issues of substance, were taken by unanimity. Scelle writes that the 'establishment of the theoretical principle of the "sovereign equality" of States led to the proclamation of the sacrosanct rule of unanimity'.[1] The only formal exceptions to this were the technical unions such as the International Telegraph Union, which, in the middle of the nineteenth century, introduced majority voting.

Sohn points out that the 1899 First Hague Conference used a procedure of 'unanimity less two votes' and that the 1907 Hague Conference 'seems to have invented the principle of near unanimity or quasi-unanimity'.[2] The latter conference, however, adopted its final decisions unanimously 'with various delegations recording their reservations or abstaining',[3] so that ostensibly the unanimity principle was not breached. Hill, writing in 1928, stated, 'The conventions of nearly every nineteenth-century conference that has included representatives from a considerable number of states have been dependent upon the signature of all diplomats present.'[4] After listing some exceptions, Hill continues by stating that, apart from procedural issues, '[i]nternational gatherings since the World War have tended in the main to do homage to the earlier practice'.[5] Riches, writing in 1940, stated that 'those responsible for the determination of state policy

[1] Georges Scelle, 'The Evolution of International Conferences', 5 *UNESCO International Social Science Bulletin* 241 (1953 No. 2) at 251.

[2] Louis B. Sohn, 'Voting Procedure in International Conferences for the Codification of International Law, 1864–1930', in *Jus et Societas, Essays in Tribute to Wolfgang Friedmann*, ed. Gabriel M. Wilner (1979), p. 278 at pp. 280, 281.

[3] *Ibid.* at p. 282.

[4] Norman L. Hill, 'Unanimous Consent in International Organizations', 22 AJIL 319 (1928) at 320.

[5] *Ibid.*

have been singularly unwilling to commit the state to acceptance of a rule of law whereby the state is bound to accept the will of the majority'.[6] Pastuhov, in 1945, wrote, 'Equality of voting power and unanimous consent have been throughout the centuries, the two pillars on which international conferences have rested.'[7]

The Covenant and rules of procedure of the Assembly of the League of Nations adopted the unanimity rule on issues of substance.[8] The Permanent Court of International Justice commented on this provision that it was 'in accordance with the unvarying tradition of all diplomatic meetings or conferences'.[9] Pastuhov relates that most 'of the ad hoc conferences held under the auspices of the League of Nations followed the practice of the Assembly concerning the unanimity rule even if their rules of procedure were silent on this subject'.[10] In practice, however, the Assembly of the League mitigated the unanimity rule both by adopting *vœux* instead of resolutions and through decision taking by majority in committees.[11]

The rules of procedure of the 1930 Conference for the Codification of International Law provided that the Plenary of the Conference adopt 'conventions, protocols, recommendations and *vœux*' by majority voting.[12] The Conference decided to do so notwithstanding the admonition of the President that 'we should maintain the principle that we must adopt unanimous resolutions. Unless we do so, we cannot have any codification of international law.'[13]

At the 1946 Paris Peace Conference, Molotov, the Soviet delegate, declared that the USSR 'will always be proud to defend the necessity of achieving unanimity in the settlement of international problems and

[6] Cromwell A. Riches, *Majority Rule in International Organizations: A Study of the Trend from Unanimity to Majority Decision* (1940), p. 8.

[7] Vladimir D. Pastuhov, *A Guide to the Practice of International Conferences* (1945), p. 135.

[8] The rule as to unanimity did not apply to procedural issues. Procedure was defined in Article 5 of the Covenant of the League of Nations as including 'the appointment of Committees to investigate particular matters'.

[9] *Advisory Opinion concerning Article 3, Paragraph 2, of the Treaty of Lausanne (Frontier between Turkey and Iraq)* [1925] PCIJ, Series B, No. 12, p. 29.

[10] Pastuhov, *Guide*, p. 137.

[11] See in general on this issue, Riches, *Majority Rule*.

[12] Rules 20, 23 of the rules of procedure of the 1930 League of Nations Conference for the Codification of International Law. Acts of the Conference for the Codification of International Law, vol. I, Plenary Meetings, p. 64, League of Nations Official No. C.351.M.145.1930. V. Series of League of Nations Publications V. Legal 1930.V.14 (1930).

[13] *Ibid.* at p. 21.

considers it inadmissible to abandon this principle'.[14] The representative of Yugoslavia, Mr Kardelj, argued that 'the principle of unanimity was the rule at international congresses and conferences. According to this rule, which is one of the basic principles of international relations, at no international conference, and still less at a peace conference, consisting of independent and sovereign states, may a majority impose its will on the minority, or even on a single state.'[15] Notwithstanding these declarations, the Paris Peace Conference adopted the following rule: 'Decisions of the Conference on questions of procedure will be adopted by a majority vote. Decisions on all other questions will be adopted by a two-thirds majority.'[16] The Soviet Bloc members acquiesced in this formula, restricting their action to proposing that the rule apply to 'recommendations' as well as to 'decisions'.[17]

The UN has no rule of unanimity, and Wilcox writes in this regard, 'With respect to the principle of unanimity, the [UN] Charter turns its back upon the past.'[18]

Although delegations would nowadays not put the issue in such blunt language as did the representative of Yugoslavia to the Paris Peace Conference, nevertheless it is submitted that the disappearance of the requirement of unanimity is intrinsically linked to the nonbinding nature of decisions of international conferences. It can be assumed that States would require a return to the tradition of unanimity in any international organisation whose decisions, outside issues of internal procedure and organisation, would be binding on States. With the exception of internal procedure and organisational matters,[19] and decisions of some technical committees,[20] decisions of universal international organisations do not bind States; hence the abandonment of the unanimity rule in such organisations. Bennet writes in this regard,

> As long as international agencies are more administrative than prescriptive, more cooperative than coercive, as long as they are lacking in true legislative and enforcement powers and are limited to discussion

[14] Paris Conference to Consider the Draft Treaties of Peace with Italy, Rumania, Bulgaria, Hungary and Finland, 1946, Collection of Documents of the Paris Conference, Verbatim Records of the 7th Plenary Meeting, C.P./Plen./7, p. 110 (1946).

[15] *Ibid.* at p. 117. [16] Rule 6(a), *ibid.* at p. 151. [17] *Ibid.* at p. 129.

[18] Francis O. Wilcox, 'Representation and Voting in the UN General Assembly', in *The Strategy of World Order, The UN*, eds. Richard A. Falk and Saul H. Mendlovitz (1966), p. 274.

[19] Including decisions on budget. [20] Notably the ICAO.

> and to recommendations that are unenforceable on individual states, the members of such organizations see no great threat to their sovereignty if they agree to modify the requirements of unanimity.[21]

Decisions and resolutions of conferences do not bind States attending such conferences, and the text of conventions adopted by a conference does not bind the States attending the conference unless ratified.[22] States are free to abstain from signing or ratifying conventions of which they do not approve, or to adhere to them with reservations. Hence the phenomenon of the disappearance of the unanimity rule from the rules of procedure of conferences. It was the binding nature of the extension of the NPT that contributed to the unusually intensive negotiations on the voting system of the 1995 NPT Review Conference and the eventual adoption there of a consensus system.[23]

Waldock, in the First Report on the Law of Treaties, writes as regards the demise of the rule of unanimity,

> The general feeling in the Commission, however, was that in recent times the practice at large international conferences of adopting texts by some kind of majority had become so invariable that it would now be unrealistic to postulate any other system.[24]

The unanimity rule is nowadays associated with the procedure of those international organisations that have the power to pass decisions binding on their member States.[25] The procedure and authority of the UN Security Council are both a reflection of this rule as regards permanent members and a notable exception with regard to other member States of the UN.

[21] A. LeRoy Bennet, *International Organizations, Principles and Issues*, 5th edn (1991), p. 83.
[22] Amendments adopted into the UN Charter come into force for all States members of the UN. The source of this obligation is, however, the Charter, which itself is a treaty that required ratification by each member State of the UN. This is true for other international organisations.
[23] Discussed in Chapter 16.
[24] First Report on the Law of Treaties, by Sir Humphrey Waldock, Special Rapporteur, [1962] 2 YBILC 40, UN Doc. A/CN.4/144 (1962).
[25] Feld, Jordan and Hurwitz list 'the Committee of Ministers in the Council of Europe, the Council of the OECD, the Council of the Arab League, COMECON, the Political Consultative Committee of the Warsaw Treaty (WTO) and the NATO Council' as organisations that apply the rule of unanimity. Werner J. Feld and Robert S. Jordan with Leon Hurwitz, *International Organizations, A Comparative Approach* (1983), p. 134.

15.1.1 *Unanimity and Consensus*

To a certain extent the emergence of decision making by consensus is a muted return to the idea of unanimity. Sohn writes that 'the pendulum has swung around the circle, from unanimity to consensus',[26] and that 'a new rule of consensus emerged, quite similar to the 1907 rule of quasi-unanimity. *Plus ça change, plus c'est la même chose.*'[27] Szasz comments that 'a consensus requirement constitutes something of a reversion to the classical unanimity principle that was the typical rule for international organs and conferences until the First World War and largely even until the Second'.[28] All writers are aware, however, of the differences between the two. Cassese points out, 'Consensus is different from *unanimity*, for in the latter case there exists full agreement on a given text and in addition the general consent is underscored by a vote.'[29]

An interesting situation occurred at the 1979 Weapons Conference, which was unable to agree on a decision-taking process, some States wanting a consensus process and others demanding the adoption of the UNGA voting procedure. The outcome was that the rules of procedure[30] contained no reference to decision taking, and by default, all decisions were taken without a vote.

15.1.2 *Unanimity in the UN*

Although there is no reference in the UNGA rules of procedure or UN Model Rules to the word 'unanimity', it is sometimes used by presiding officers to denote a vote where there were no negative votes cast. References to *unanimous* decisions appear in some UN conference reports,[31] but the phrase is not used in the official UN booklet on resolutions and decisions of the General Assembly.

15.1.3 *Do Abstentions Negate Unanimity?*

Abstentions are not usually considered as negating a unanimous vote.

[26] Louis B. Sohn, 'Voting Procedures in United Nations Conferences for the Codification of International Law', 69 AJIL 310 (1975) at 352.
[27] Sohn, 'Voting Procedure 1864–1930', p. 296.
[28] Paul C. Szasz, 'Improving the International Legislative Process', 9 *Georgia Journal of International and Comparative Law* 519 (1979) at 529.
[29] Antonio Cassese, *International Law* (2001), p. 43. [emphasis in original]
[30] UN Doc. A/CONF.95/2 (1979).
[31] For example, NPT/CONF.1995/32 (Part I), para. 10 (1995).

At the 1950 Special Session of the UNGA, the President announced that 'the Norwegian proposal was practically unanimously approved, because those who abstained practically do not vote'.[32]

However, at a 1951 meeting of a committee of the UNGA, the representative of Guatemala objected to the use of the word 'unanimous' since his delegation had abstained. The Chairman, with the approval of the Committee, agreed to correct the Committee's Report by deleting the word 'unanimous'.[33]

At a 1958 meeting of the UNGA, the representative of Australia wished it to be recorded 'that his understanding of the words "adopted without objection" . . . did not imply that the vote approving the draft resolution had been unanimous'.[34]

Schermers writes categorically that '[a]bstention does not bar unanimity. This rule is so strong that even when "concurring votes" are required, such as those of the permanent members of the Security Council, abstentions will not block adoption.'[35]

15.2 Majority Voting

The background to the development of majority rule in national societies has been described as the realisation that 'the greater number is also the more powerful physically', and 'the advantages of a device for submitting peacefully to this superior force became increasingly apparent in various primitive groups and ancient states'.[36] This reasoning is not, however, valid in international relations where counting votes does not normally produce a reflection of the balance of power. In multilateral international conferences, majority voting is accepted by States not because of the normative authority of the majority but rather as a convenience to enable the orderly functioning of an international organisation.

32 UN GAOR, Plenary, 1st Special Session, 79th Meeting, p. 174, UN Doc. A/PV.79 (1947); UN GAOR, Plenary, 5th Session, 298th Meeting, para. 143, UN Doc. A/PV.298 (1950).

33 UN GAOR, 4th Committee, 6th Session, 247th Meeting, para. 38, UN Doc. A/C.4/6/SR.247 (1951).

34 UN GAOR, 4th Committee, 13th Session, 840th Meeting, para. 19, UN Doc. A/C.4/13/SR.840 (1958).

35 Henry G. Schermers, 'Voting Rules in International Conferences and Organizations', in *Encyclopedia of Public International Law*, ed. Rudolph Bernhardt, vol. V (1983), p. 397.

36 Ladislas Konopczyski, 'Majority Rule', in *Encyclopaedia of the Social Sciences*, vol. X (1953), p. 55.

The principle of deciding issues at conferences by one State, one vote on the basis of the 'sovereign equality' of all States[37] may seem well nigh immutable, but it has in fact been subject to much criticism. The US representative to the UNGA's Sixth Committee at the Forty-Fifth Session, Mr Rosenstock, stated,

> It could also be hoped that by that time [in the future] there would no longer be any support for the idea that there was something democratic in the principle of 'one nation one vote'. Giving one vote to both Liechtenstein and the People's Republic of China might be reasonable or unreasonable, logical or illogical, workable or unworkable, but it was certainly not democratic – nor was it undemocratic.[38]

Eban writes, 'The voting habit is the greatest enemy of the United Nations system . . . The absurdity of the UN voting system is aggravated by the almost grotesque inequalities of power between states having equal votes. China, Russia and the United States equal Fiji, Papua and the Maldive islands.'[39]

In a memorandum prepared for the 1958 Law of the Sea Conference, the Secretary-General of the UN referred to four different voting systems adopted in international conferences:

(a) Simple majority for questions of procedure and two-thirds majority for other questions;
(b) The UNGA procedure of two-thirds majority for important questions and simple majority for other questions;
(c) Simple majority for all questions; and
(d) Two-thirds majority for decisions to amend the basic draft submitted to the Conference and simple majority for other decisions.[40]

To such a list should be added the possibilities of requiring majorities of States represented at conferences (and not only those present and voting) and consensus.

[37] Article 2(1) of the UN Charter.
[38] UN GAOR, 6th Committee, 45th Session, 16th Meeting, p. 13, para. 55, UN Doc. A/C.6/45/SR.16 (1990).
[39] Abba Eban, *The New Diplomacy, International Affairs in the Modern Age* (1983), p. 280.
[40] 1958 Law of the Sea Conference, Methods of Work and Procedures of the Conference; Report of the Secretary-General, para. 28, footnote 7, UN Doc. A/CONF.13/11 (1957), in Official Records of the 1958 Law of the Sea Conference, vol. I, p. 175, UN Doc. A/CONF.13/37 (1958).

15.3 Simple Majority

The UNGA rules of procedure state,

Rule 85

> Decisions of the General Assembly on questions other than those provided for in rule 83,[41] including the determination of additional categories of questions to be decided by a two-thirds majority, shall be made by a majority of the members present and voting.[42]

The UN Model Rules propose,

Rule 53

> 2. Unless the Conference decides otherwise and except as otherwise provided in these rules, decisions on all matters of procedure shall be taken by a simple majority of the representatives present and voting.
>
> 3. If the question arises whether a matter is one of procedure or of substance, it shall be decided by the Conference by a majority of the representatives present and voting.

There does not appear to have been an exception to the rule that conferences vote on matters of procedure by a simple majority. Waldock, in his First Report on the Law of Treaties, writes, 'The rule of the simple majority vote for *procedural* decisions is universally admitted.'[43]

Although the usual rule is that conferences vote on matters of substance by a two-thirds majority, there have been exceptions. Conferences that adopted substantive proposals by a simple majority include the early UN-convened conferences,[44] the 1963 Tokyo Air Law Conference,[45] ECOSOC technical conferences on geographical names and mapping,[46] pledging conferences and some political conferences.[47]

Other UN-convened conferences have adopted the UNGA rules on voting, by implication adopting thereby the distinction between important

41 Rule 83 refers to decisions taken by a two-thirds majority.

42 The rule is based on Article 18(3) of the UN Charter.

43 First Report on the Law of Treaties, by Sir Humphrey Waldock, Special Rapporteur, [1962] 2 YBILC 40, n. 30, UN Doc. A/CN.4/144 (1962). See the discussion in Chapter 11, concerning reconsideration of procedural decisions.

44 For example, Rule 10 of the rules of procedure of the 1950 Conference on Missing Persons, UN Doc. A/CONF.1/3 (1950).

45 Rule 20 of the rules of procedure of the 1963 Tokyo Air Law Conference, ICAO Doc. 8565-LC/152-2 (published 1963).

46 For example, Rule 24, UN Doc. E/CONF.74/3 (Annex IV) (1982).

47 Second World Conference to Combat Racism and Racial Discrimination, Rule 32, UN Doc. A/CONF.119/2 (1983).

questions and other issues.[48] In view of the problems that have arisen in the UNGA on defining 'important questions', this does not appear to be an advisable procedure.

COMMENT

Despite some exceptions, the accepted rule is the necessity of a two-thirds majority for votes on issues of substance.

15.4 Two-Thirds Majority

The UNGA rules of procedure state,

> *Rule 83*
>
> Decisions of the General Assembly on important questions shall be made by a two-thirds majority of the members present and voting.[49]
>
> *Rule 85*
>
> Decisions of the General Assembly on questions other than those provided for in rule 83, including the determination of additional categories of questions to be decided by a two-thirds majority, shall be made by a majority of the members present and voting.[50]

A decision whether an issue is 'important' within the meaning of Rule 83 is made by the President of the General Assembly. His ruling is subject, of course, to appeal. In practice, where objection was made to a ruling, Presidents have put the question itself to a vote and not dealt with it as an appeal against their ruling.

A decision to define an additional category of issues or a specific issue as 'important' is decided by a majority vote of the Assembly. The Assembly has decided in the past, by a majority vote, that, among others, the issues of Algeria, Cyprus, Morocco, Palestine Conciliation Commission, Representation of China, South Africa, South West Africa and West Irian were

[48] For example, Rule 35 of the rules of procedure of the UN Conference on Environment and Development, UN Doc. A/CONF.151/2 (1992); Rule 35 of the rules of procedure of the World Summit on Sustainable Development, UN Doc. A/CONF.199/2 (2002).

[49] The rule is based on Article 18(2) of the UN Charter, which states that 'important questions' include 'recommendations with respect to the maintenance of international peace and security, the election of the non-permanent members of the Security Council, the election of the members of ECOSOC… the admission of new members to the UN, the suspension of the rights and privileges of membership, the expulsion of members, questions relating to the operation of the trusteeship system, and budgetary questions'.

[50] Based on Article 18(3) of the UN Charter.

'important issues'. However, many similar resolutions were decided by a simple majority. There is little consistency in Assembly decisions, and the process of requesting that an issue be treated as an important question is often used where a delegation believes that it can garner more support on such a procedural motion than it could on the substantive issue.[51] The ad hoc political nature of such decisions is emphasised by a 1984 opinion of the UN Legal Adviser that such decisions are valid only for that specific session.[52] In that particular case, a resolution on the Middle East, Legal Counsel was of the opinion that 'a finding would be appropriate' that the draft resolution came within the category of Article 18(2) of the Charter. Nevertheless, the Assembly voted that the draft resolution did not come within that category and did not require a two-thirds majority.[53]

The UN Model Rules propose,

Rule 53
Majority Required

1. Unless the Conference decides otherwise and subject to paragraph 1 of rule 51 [the need to attempt to achieve consensus], decisions on all matters of substance shall be taken by a two-thirds majority of the representatives present and voting.
2. Unless the Conference decides otherwise and except as otherwise provided in these rules, decisions on all matters of procedure shall be taken by a simple majority of the representatives present and voting.
3. If the question arises whether a matter is one of procedure or of substance, it shall be decided by the Conference by a majority of the representatives present and voting.

The UN Model Rule proposed for voting in committees is

Rule 67

(c) Decisions of committees and working groups shall be taken by a majority of the representatives present and voting, but, except at a treaty-making conference, the reconsideration of a proposal shall require the majority established by paragraph 1 of rule 50 [a two-thirds majority].

The Vienna Convention on the Law of Treaties states,

[51] For a study of the issues involved, see Benedetto Conforti, *The Law and Practice of the United Nations*, 4th rev. edn. (2010), pp. 106–114; Rüdiger Wolfrum, 'Article 18', in *The Charter of the United Nations, A Commentary*, ed. Bruno Simma, 2nd edn (2002), p. 351.

[52] Opinion of the Legal Counsel. UN GAOR, Plenary, 39th Session, 101st Meeting, para. 238, UN Doc. A/39/PV.101, (1984).

[53] *Ibid.* at para. 239.

Article 9

1. The adoption of the text of a treaty takes place by the consent of all the States participating in its drawing up except as provided in paragraph 2.
2. The adoption of the text of a treaty of an international conference takes place by the vote of two-thirds of the States present and voting, unless by the same majority they shall decide to apply a different rule.[54]

Szasz writes that 'the general formula rule that has emerged in the post-World War II period is adoption [of treaties] by a two-thirds majority of those voting for or against'.[55]

International law-making conferences usually require that the texts be approved in plenary meetings by a two-thirds majority of States present and voting and there are few exceptions.

The rules of procedure of the 1963 Tokyo Air Law Conference stipulated,

Rule 20

Except as otherwise provided in these Rules, decisions shall be by a majority of votes cast. An abstention shall not be considered a vote.[56]

During the consideration of the Report of the Committee on Rules of Procedure of the 1963 Tokyo Air Law Conference, a number of delegations recommended that decisions on matters of substance be taken by a two-thirds majority. The Conference consequently added to the record the observation that 'the Conference refers to the [ICAO] Council a proposal that in future conferences a two-thirds majority of the votes cast in matters of substance should be required to carry a motion'.[57]

At the 1969 IMCO Conference on Marine Pollution Damage, the Chairman of a committee reminded members that

[54] Done at Vienna on 23 May 1969, came into force on 27 January 1980. The background to this article is dealt with in detail in Sohn, 'Voting Procedures in UN Conferences'.

[55] Szasz, 'Improving', p. 528. Rule 20 of the rules of procedure of the 1930 League of Nations Conference for the Codification of International Law used the formula, as regards voting in committees, of 'two-thirds of the delegations present at the meeting at which the vote takes place'. Acts of the Conference for the Codification of International Law, vol. I, Plenary Meetings, p. 64, League of Nations Official No. C.351.M.145.1930.V. The ambiguity of the phrase 'present at the meeting' would appear to be an invitation for disputes.

[56] Volume II, Documents of the 1963 Tokyo Air Law Conference, Doc. No. 3, ICAO Doc. 8565-LC/152–2 (1963).

[57] Volume I, Minutes of the 13th Meeting of the 1963 Tokyo Air Law Conference, para. 13, ICAO Doc. 8565-LC/152–1 (1963) (published 1966).

> decisions of committees were taken by a simple majority whereas decisions at plenary meetings were taken by a two-thirds majority. It would therefore serve no purpose for the Committee to adopt rules by a small majority, which would stand no chance of being adopted in plenary.[58]

15.4.1 Majority Required for Amendments to Proposals Requiring a Two-Thirds Majority

The UNGA rule states,

> *Rule 84*
>
> Decisions of the General Assembly on amendments to proposals relating to important questions, and on parts of such proposals put to the vote separately, shall be made by a two-thirds majority of the members present and voting.[59]

The issue of the majority required for amendments to proposals that require a two-thirds majority was raised by the 1949 Special Committee on Methods and Procedures of the General Assembly, without it proposing any rule.[60] During the debate on the Report, in the Sixth Committee of the UNGA, the Legal Counsel of the UN stated, 'The practice followed hitherto had not been uniform. The parts of important proposals voted on in parts were subject to a two-thirds majority, while the amendments to those proposals were adopted by a simple majority.'[61] The Legal Counsel pointed out that this led to 'illogical results'.

Hovey, writing in 1950, advocated that amendments to important questions should not require a two-thirds majority since a simple majority permitted 'the extension to plenary meetings of the more flexible sort of negotiation possible in the committees'.[62] Hovey attempts to meet the

58 Official Records of the 1969 IMCO Conference on Marine Pollution Damage, Summary Records of the 1st Meeting of Committee 2, p. 612, IMCO Doc. LEG/CONF/C.2/SR.1 (1969).

59 The 1949 Committee adopted a Belgian proposal identical to the present wording of Rule 84 (UN Doc. A/C.6/L.22 (1949). Adopted UN GAOR, 6th Committee, 4th Session, 157th Meeting, p. 93, para. 58, UN Doc. A/C.6/4/SR.157 (1949). UNGA Resolution 362 (IV) of 22 October 1949). This proposal was, however, defeated in the 1949 Plenary (UN GAOR, Plenary, 4th Session, 236th Meeting, p. 166, para. 153, UN Doc. A/PV.236 (1949)), only to be adopted by the Plenary in 1950 (UNGA Resolution 475 (V) of 1 November 1950).

60 UN Doc. A/937 (1949).

61 UN GAOR, 6th Committee, 4th Session, 157th Meeting, p. 91, para. 20, UN Doc. A/C.6/4/SR. 157 (1949).

62 Allan Hovey Jr, 'Voting Procedure in the General Assembly', 4 *UNESCO International Organization* 412 (1950 No. 1) at 423.

argument that 'deletion of a part can be accomplished by amendment' by pointing out that 'a Member who desires the deletion of a part would be well advised to call for a vote on the part rather than on a motion to delete. The reason is, of course, that in the former case a deletion could be effectively secured by one-third plus one of those voting, whereas in the latter case it could be obtained only with the concurrence of some majority.'[63] Hovey's argument does not, however, appear to answer the point he himself raised against his proposal.

Amendments to the 1944 Chicago Convention on International Civil Aviation required a two-thirds majority. The 1974 Assembly of the ICAO debated a number of proposals to amend the rules of procedure, with the aim of clarifying whether a sub-amendment to an amendment to the Convention also requires a two-thirds majority. There was no agreement among the representatives, and the existing rules of procedure, with their ambiguity, were not changed.[64]

The question of the majority required for amendments to proposals requiring a special majority does not appear to have been raised at conferences. Where the rules of procedure of conferences require different majorities, the rule is usually that issues of substance require a two-thirds majority but for issues of procedure a simple majority suffices. Thus where proposals of substance require a two-thirds majority, it appears to have been assumed automatically, without it being articulated, that an amendment to a substantive proposal also requires the same two-thirds majority.

15.5 'Representatives Present and Voting'

The UNGA rules of procedure state,

> *Rule 86*
>
> *Meaning of the Phrase 'Members Present and Voting'*
>
> For the purpose of these rules, the phrase 'members present and voting' means members casting an affirmative or negative vote. Members which abstain from voting shall be regarded as not voting.

The UN Model Rules are substantially the same.[65]

[63] *Ibid.* at 426.

[64] Report and Minutes of the Legal Commission, ICAO Doc. 9116 A21-LE, pp. 16–19 (1974); Report of the Executive Committee, paras. 143–145, ICAO Doc. 9113 A21-EX (1974). The terminology may be misleading since an amendment to an existing treaty is in fact a proposal, and only a sub-amendment to such an amendment has the nature of the amendments discussed in this chapter.

[65] Rule 53 of the UN Model Rules.

In the provisional rules of procedure of the UNGA,[66] such a provision did not exist, and the Plenary at times took into account invalid votes cast in voting by ballot, when calculating the majority required.[67] Since the early days, UNGA practice has been not to take invalid votes into account in calculating the majority.[68]

There were also instances where the issue arose as to whether abstentions should be taken into account.[69] The 1947 Committee on Procedures and Organisation proposed an amendment to the rule on voting, stating explicitly that abstentions would not be taken into account. The proposal of the Committee was adopted.[70] The amendment has been criticised on the ground that it enables resolutions to be passed by a small fraction of the membership of the UN.[71] A 1971 UN Committee on the Procedures and Organisation of the General Assembly discussed the issue of abstentions. There was a suggestion that 'either abstentions and non-participation should be counted in deciding whether the required majority had been obtained... or the number of affirmative votes required to adopt a draft resolution should be greater than a majority of the total of the affirmative and negative votes and abstentions'.[72] The report continues by stating that the majority of the members of the Committee objected to the proposal, since, inter alia, 'the act of abstention had political significance and was sometimes the only way in which a delegation could indicate its position'.[73]

66 UN Doc. A/71/Rev. 1.

67 UN GAOR, Plenary, 1st Session, 65th Meeting, p. 1391, UN Doc. A/PV.65 (1946); UN GAOR, Plenary, 1st Session, 66th Meeting, pp. 1418–1420, UN Doc. A/PV.66 (1946).

68 Hovey, 'Voting Procedure', p. 422.

69 UN GAOR, 1st Committee, 1st Session, Part II, 13th Meeting, pp. 43–46, UN Doc. A/C.1/1/SR.13 (1946); UN GAOR, 1st Committee, 1st Special Session, 57th Meeting, pp. 346, 347 (1947); UN GAOR, 2nd Session, 118th Plenary Meeting, vol. II, pp. 1098–1100 (1947). On abstentions in the UNGA, see Conforti, *Law and Practice of the UN*, 4th edn. (2010) pp. 76–79.

70 Report of the Committee on Procedures and Organisation, UN GAOR, Plenary, 2nd Session, vol. II, Annex 4, pp. 1474, 1480, Rules 99, 140 (1947). The Soviet Bloc countries proposed a contrary rule whereby abstentions would be taken into account, but the proposal was not adopted. *Ibid.*, Report of Sub-Committee 3, 6th Committee, Annex 4c, pp. 266, 267.

71 Hovey, 'Voting Procedure', p. 420.

72 para. 278 of the Report of the Special Committee on the Rationalisation of the Procedures and Organisation of the General Assembly, UN GAOR, 26th Session, Supp. No. 26, UN Doc. A/8426 (1971).

73 *Ibid.* at para. 281.

With the exception of the issue of a quorum in the ILO, abstentions are apparently not taken into account in calculating a majority in voting. At a meeting of the First Committee of the 1974–1977 Geneva Humanitarian Law Conference, a proposal, to which Syria objected, was adopted by a vote of thirty-four votes to nine, with thirty-five abstentions.[74] The Syrian representative contested the result, stating that 'according to the rules of procedure, the decision should have been adopted by a simple majority of the "representatives" present, i.e. at least 40'. The Chairman confirmed his previous announcement that the proposal had been adopted.[75]

At the 1983 Vienna Conference on State Property (Succession), the Executive Secretary of the Conference explained, in regard to a vote where there had been no negative votes, that 'representatives who abstained from voting should be considered as not voting. The number of those representatives present and voting was therefore the same as the number of those who had voted in favour of the article.'[76]

The rules of procedure of the International Labour Conference provided, 'In order to determine the majorities by record vote all votes cast, for and against, shall be counted.'[77] At the 1952 session of the ILO Conference, a representative claimed that 'there is required a majority of two-thirds of those who were present at the voting, and I think that those who abstained were present and that the interpretation which is given to the voting system by the fact that the votes declared as abstentions are not counted in the basis of the two-thirds majority is therefore wrong'.[78] The President, however, quoted Article 21 of the Standing Orders and added, 'The statement made of abstention is not a vote for or against, and it could not therefore be counted under the provisions of Article 21 as a vote. The Standing Orders are precise and clear, and say that a vote is only to be counted if it is "yes" or "no."'[79]

The rules of procedure of ICAO International Conferences on Air Law stipulate that decisions on matters of substance require a two-thirds majority of the Representatives present and voting, while decisions on

[74] Official Records of the 1974–1977 Geneva Humanitarian Law Conference, CDDH/I/SR.69, vol. IX, p. 387, para. 38.

[75] *Ibid.* at p. 388, para. 43.

[76] Official Records of the 7th Plenary Meeting of the 1983 Vienna Conference on State Property (Succession), vol. I, p. 15, para. 10, UN Doc. A/CONF.117 (1995).

[77] Article 21 of the Standing Orders of the Conference of the International Labour Organisation, International Labour Office, Geneva 1992.

[78] ILO Conference, 35th Session, Geneva 1952, Record of Proceedings, 30th sitting, p. 196.

[79] *Ibid.*

procedure require only a majority. At a Plenary meeting of the 1975 Montreal Conference the Legal Advisor gave his opinion that an amendment to the agenda was a procedural matter requiring only a regular majority.[80]

15.6 Calculating Fractions of Votes

At a meeting of the 1968 Non-Nuclear-Weapon State Conference, the results of a vote on a resolution were '39 in favour and 20 against, with 25 abstentions'. The President announced that the resolution (which required a two-thirds majority) was not adopted.[81] The representative of Costa Rica argued that 'if the number of representatives present and voting, which was 59, was divided by three and the resultant figure multiplied by 2, the two-thirds majority was 38, not 39'.[82] The representative of Kenya countered that 'the two-thirds majority could be calculated either on the principle that a fraction of a vote corresponds to one vote, in which case the majority would be 40 votes, or on the principle that the fraction should be disregarded, in which case the majority would be 38'.[83] After further discussion and two suspensions of the meeting, the Chairman announced that he was maintaining his ruling. No delegation challenged the ruling, but the representative of Uruguay, on behalf of the Latin American Group, informed the Conference that 'the results of the voting which had been announced did not, [in] its opinion, reflect the true situation'. The Group, however, 'would abstain from contesting those results'.[84]

15.7 Absolute Majority of All States Represented

At a committee meeting of the 1966 UNGA, the Committee decided to select the headquarters site of UNIDO on the basis of an absolute majority[85] and not on the basis of 'a majority of the members present and voting'.[86] It was, presumably, because of the UN Charter rules regarding amendments to the Charter[87] that in 1998 the UNGA resolved 'not

[80] ICAO 1975 Montreal International Conference on Air Law, Plenary, 6th Meeting, para. 22, ICAO Doc.9154-LC/174–1 (1975).

[81] Summary Records of the 18th Plenary Meeting of the 1968 Non-Nuclear-Weapon State Conference, p. 219, UN Doc. A/CONF.35/SR.18 (1968).

[82] *Ibid.* at p. 220. [83] *Ibid.* [84] *Ibid.* at p. 222.

[85] UN GAOR, 2nd Committee, 21st Session, 1102nd Meeting, paras. 27, 28, UN Doc. A/C.2/21/SR.1102 (1966).

[86] Rule 85 of the UNGA rules of procedure, reproducing Article 18 of the UN Charter.

[87] Article108 of the Charter requires a majority of 'two thirds of the member of the General Assembly'.

to adopt any resolution or decision on the question of equitable representation on and increase in the membership of the Security Council and related matters, without the affirmative vote of at least two-thirds of the Members of the General Assembly'.[88]

A 1984 Internal Memorandum of the UN Office of Legal Affairs, on elections to the ICJ, quotes the definition of absolute majority as 'one half of the whole membership plus one' and states that the relevant rule of the Statute of the ICJ 'does not provide for any reduction in calculating the absolute majority required by reason of inability to vote'.[89] A 1986 legal opinion by the Office of Legal Affairs refers to two cases in UNGA procedure where

> the majority required is an absolute or a qualified majority based on a definite number of States which is not affected by abstentions, absences or announcements by States that they are not participating in the vote. In these two special cases, abstentions, absences and non-participation in the vote do not have the effect of reducing [the] majority required (which would be the case if the present and voting requirement applied) and therefore have a negative impact.[90]

The usual basis for calculating a majority is the number of representatives present and voting. Nevertheless, there are precedents for requiring a majority of States represented at a conference, namely an absolute majority.

The rules of procedure of the Third Law of the Sea Conference stipulated,

> *Rule 39*
>
> 1. Decisions of the Conference on all matters of substance, including the adoption of the text of the Convention on the Law of the Sea as a whole, shall be taken by a two-thirds majority of the representatives present and voting, *provided that such majority shall include at least a majority of the States participating in that session of the Conference.*[91] [emphasis added]

The rule is a departure from the usual rule prevailing. The representative of Trinidad and Tobago commented that

88 UN Doc. A/RES/53/30 (1998).

89 Internal Memorandum (of the Office of Legal Affairs), 6 November 1984. 1984 UN Jur. Y.B. 173, 174. Where the number of the whole membership is an odd number, then of course the total of half has to be rounded out.

90 Letter (from the UN Office of Legal Affairs) to the Permanent Observer of an intergovernmental organisation to the United Nations, 9 May 1986. 1986 UN Jur. Y.B. 274.

91 Rules of procedure of the Third Law of the Sea Conference, UN Doc. A/CONF.62/30/Rev.3.

> his delegation had always supported classical rules of procedure and still do so. Those rules made no reference to a majority in terms of the number of participants. However, his delegation was prepared in a spirit of compromise, to depart from its position and to accept the quorum and qualified majority in terms of the number of participants.[92]

The text of Rule 39 was a compromise between the draft rules of procedure that called for decisions to be taken by a 'two-thirds majority of the representatives present and voting',[93] and a US proposal that referred to a 'two-thirds majority of the representatives of States participating in that session of the Conference'.[94]

The rules of procedure of the Third Law of the Sea Conference define the phrase 'States participating':

> *Rule 40*
>
> 2. Subject to the provisions of rules 1 to 5 [credentials of delegations] and without prejudice to the powers and functions of the Credentials Committee, the term 'States participating' in relation to any particular session of the Conference means any State whose representatives have registered with the Secretariat of the Conference as participating in that session and which has not subsequently notified the Secretariat of its withdrawal from that session or a part of it. The Secretariat shall keep a Register for this purpose.[95]

The original proposal submitted by the Chairman of the General Committee of the Third Law of the Sea Conference was as follows:

> The term 'States participating' in relation to any particular session of the Conference means those States which inform the Secretariat of the Conference that they will be participating in that session.[96]

The representative of Trinidad and Tobago commented on this rule that it referred to 'intent only'.[97] After a discussion in which a number of

92 Official Records of the Third Law of the Sea Conference, vol. I, p. 50, Summary Records of the 18th Plenary Meeting, para. 36, UN Doc. A/CONF.62 (1973).

93 Third Law of the Sea Conference, draft rules of procedure, Rule 39(1), UN Doc. A/CONF.62/2 (1973).

94 Third Law of the Sea Conference, US revised amendments to the draft rules of procedure, para. 2, UN Doc. A/CONF.62/7/Rev.1 (1974).

95 Rules of procedure of the Third Law of the Sea Conference, UN Doc. A/CONF.62/30/Rev.3 (1975).

96 Official Records of the Third Law of the Sea Conference, vol. I, p. 222, Summary Records of the 2nd Meeting of the General Committee, para. 3, UN Doc. A/CONF.62 (1973).

97 *Ibid.* at para. 6.

alternative wordings were proposed, the Committee adopted the wording that appears in Rule 40.[98]

15.8 Two-Thirds Majority of All States Represented

The rules of procedure of the 1973 Rome Air Law Conference stated,

> *Rule 20* bis
>
> Any draft convention shall be adopted by a two-thirds majority of the *total number of States represented at the Conference*. The provisions of this Rule shall prevail over those of Rule 20 [Rule 20 deals with the majority required].[99] [emphasis added]

The rule was proposed by the delegations of France, Switzerland and the United Kingdom. The delegate of France explained that it was necessary in order to have the rules of procedure of the Conference correspond to those of the Assembly of the ICAO, which was dealing with the same issues concurrently.[100] The representative of France added that 'the sponsors did not believe the adoption of such a rule should be regarded [as] a precedent for future air-law conferences dealing with the normal kind of subject'.[101]

The rule in question, moreover, was suspended when the Conference came to vote on the Draft Convention.[102]

At the Third Law of the Sea Conference, the US delegation proposed amending the draft rules of procedure so that decisions on substance would be taken by a 'two-thirds majority of the representatives of States participating in that session of the Conference'.[103] The proposal was not adopted.

15.9 Weighted Majority

The World Bank, the International Monetary Fund, the International Bank for Reconstruction and Development, the International Finance

[98] *Ibid.* at para. 58. [99] ICAO Doc. 9225-LC/178, CAS Doc. No. 3 (1973).

[100] The issue of sanctions against States acquiescing in air piracy. Minutes of the 1st Meeting of the 1973 Rome Air Law Conference, p. 18, para. 10, ICAO Doc. 9225-LC/178 (1973).

[101] *Ibid.*

[102] Minutes of the 9th Meeting of the Plenary of the 1973 Rome Air Law Conference, para. 10, ICAO Doc. 9225-LC/178 (1973).

[103] Official Records of the Third Law of the Sea Conference, UN Doc. A/CONF.62/7/Rev.1 (1974).

Corporation, the International Fund for Agricultural Development, International Commodity Boards[104] and other financial and trade organisations[105] have systems of weighted voting that take into account the financial weight or contribution of a State. The weighted voting system has been criticised in that it 'is contrary to the generally accepted principle of the sovereign equality of States and does not make it possible for all the members to participate fully and effectively in the decision making process'.[106] Although there is increased use of decision taking by consensus in these organisations,[107] there does not appear to have been a determined effort to change the weighted voting system, a system that has proved to work effectively.

No modern international conference has, however, attempted to introduce such a system, and it is difficult to conceive of a successful application of this method. Goodrich, Hambro and Simons write, in regard to the UN, that

> no consideration was given at San Francisco to introducing a system of weighted voting and though these inequalities have become even more manifest in recent years as a result of the large number of small states admitted to membership, no proposals have been made in the United Nations for changing the rule of Article 18(1) [of the Charter] that each member has one vote.[108]

Clark and Sohn, in 1953, studied the possibility of introducing in the UN a voting system based on population.[109] McIntyre, in her article on the subject in 1954, reached the conclusion that such proposals were not feasible.[110] One study, in 1966, advocated introducing weighted voting

[104] See William N. Gianaris, 'Weighted Voting in the International Monetary Fund and the World Bank', 14 *Fordham Int'l L.J.* 910 (1990–91); Kurt Hendl, 'Reflections on the Role, Functions and Procedures of the Security Council of the United Nations', 206 RCADI 319 (1987 VI); Elizabeth McIntyre, 'Weighted Voting in International Organizations', 8 *UNESCO International Organization* 484 (1954 No. 1).

[105] Inter alia the European Bank for Reconstruction and Development, Asian Development Bank and OPEC Special Fund.

[106] Ebere Osieke, 'Majority Voting Systems in the International Labour Organisation and the International Monetary Fund', 33 *ICLQ* 381 (1974) at 403.

[107] *Ibid.* at 404–408.

[108] Leland M. Goodrich, Edvard Hambro and Anne P. Simons, *Charter of the United Nations*, 3rd rev. edn (1969), p. 169.

[109] Grenville Clark and Louis B. Sohn, *Peace through Disarmament and Charter Revision* (1953).

[110] McIntyre, 'Weighted Voting', p. 484.

into the UNGA.[111] More recently, however, Anand studied the issue of introducing weighted voting and reached the conclusion that 'it has not been possible to find any satisfactory solution to the problem. Indeed, it would be impossible to reach any satisfactory agreement since in the search for any formula "the subjective aspect of the problem would overshadow the objective aspect" and bitterness and discord would be unavoidable accompaniments.'[112] Szasz, writing in 1979, reaches what, it is submitted, is a correct conclusion in regard to weighted voting at conferences: 'no serious consideration has yet been or in the foreseeable future is likely to be given to a solution along this line'.[113] Writing fourteen years later, Szasz points out that there is no legal reason to maintain the one-State-one-vote rule but that 'the likely opposition of the great majority of states makes the introduction of weighted voting unfeasible in most international organizations, unless the expected benefits of the organization are irresistible'.[114]

15.10 Equally Divided Votes

The UNGA rule for plenary meetings is

> *Rule 95*
>
> If a vote is equally divided on matters other than elections, a second vote shall be taken at a subsequent meeting which shall be held within forty-eight hours of the first vote; and it shall be expressly mentioned in the agenda that a second vote will be taken on the matter in question. If this vote also results in equality, the proposal shall be regarded as rejected.

The UNGA rule for committee meetings is

> *Rule 133*
>
> If a vote is equally divided on matters other than elections, the proposal shall be regarded as rejected.

[111] Catherine Senf Manno, 'Selective Weighted Voting in the UN General Assembly: Rationale and Methods', 20 *UNESCO International Organization* 37 (1966).

[112] R. P. Anand, 'Sovereign Equality of States in International Law', 197 RCADI 141 (1986 II).

[113] Szasz, 'Improving', p. 529. See, however, Szasz's draft for a 'Binding Triad Concept' quoted in Richard Hudson, 'Quick Calculator for Estimating Outcomes of Votes in the UN General Assembly under the Binding Triad System for Global Decision-Making', *Center for War/Peace Studies, Special Study No. 8*, Summer 1995.

[114] Paul C. Szasz, 'Remarks by Paul Szasz', in *The American Society of International Law, The Nederlandse Vereniging voor Internationaal Recht, Contemporary International Law Issues: Opportunities at a Time of Momentous Change, Proceedings of the Second Joint Conference held in the Hague, the Netherlands, July 22–24, 1993* (1993), p. 304.

The UN Model Rules propose,

> *Rule 53*
>
> 4. If a vote is equally divided on a decision requiring a simple majority, the proposal or motion shall be regarded as rejected.

There does not appear to have been any dispute as to the rule that an equally divided vote serves to reject a proposal. Although this rule was not set out in some of the early UN-convened conferences, it was nevertheless applied. It has been set out explicitly in conferences in the last half-century.

The rules of the League of Nations Assembly provided that, where unanimity was not required, in the case of an equally divided vote a second vote should be taken in the course of the next meeting, and if it again resulted in an equally divided vote, only then would the proposal be regarded as rejected.[115] The UNGA, in its plenary meetings, applies a similar rule.

The rules of procedure of the 1949 Geneva Conference provided that a tied vote in a committee should be considered as a rejection of the proposal. In the case of a tie in a plenary meeting, a delegation could request that the proposal be submitted again for a vote, after a delay of twenty-four hours.[116]

The rules of procedure of the ICAO Assembly and the ICAO-convened conferences provide that

> in the event of a tie vote, a second vote on the motion concerned shall be taken at the next meeting, unless the body concerned decides that such a second vote be taken during the meeting at which the tie vote took place.[117]

The rules of procedure of the IMO Assembly also provide that '[i]f a vote is equally divided, a second vote shall be taken at the next meeting'.[118]

Other than those conferences convened by the ICAO and the IMO, no conference appears to have adopted a rule requiring a second vote in cases of a tie. The problem is of course usually academic, since decisions on substance are as a general rule taken by a two-thirds majority, a tie thus being automatically a rejection of a proposal. The issue has arisen, however, as regards a procedural motion. At the 1965 ITU Conference,

115 Rule 22 of the rules of procedure of the Assembly of the League of Nations.
116 Rule 35 of the rules of procedure of the 1949 Geneva Conference.
117 Rule 53 of the rules of procedure of the ICAO Assembly, ICAO Doc. No. 7600/4 (1980).
118 Rule 36 of the rules of procedure of the IMO Assembly, Basic Documents, vol. I, IMO Sales No. 001.86.17.E (1986).

the United Kingdom proposed a motion that the Conference was not competent to take a decision on a proposal to expel South Africa. The Chairman apparently put it to the vote as a question rather than as a motion by the United Kingdom, stating that 'those who considered that the Conference was competent should vote "yes" and those who considered that it was not should vote "no."' The result was a tied vote. The Chairman then announced that the proposal 'was rejected'[119] and subsequently explained that the Conference was not competent.[120] This ruling was disputed but not formally challenged, and the matter was finally settled by putting to the vote again a clear motion, by the United States, that the Conference was not competent. This US motion was defeated, and the Conference proceeded to expel South Africa.[121]

15.11 A Situation Where Two Alternative Proposals Each Receive Equally Divided Votes

A lengthy procedural debate arose at the 1974–1977 Geneva Humanitarian Law Conference regarding a situation where two alternative proposals received equally divided votes. The Plenary of the Conference had to decide whether a decision to invite the Provisional Government of South Viet Nam to attend the Conference came under the 'invitation' clause of the rules of procedure. This 'invitation' clause allowed for a simple majority. If, however, it was a 'reconsideration' of a proposal voted on at the previous session, it required a two-thirds majority. The United States proposed that each representative be asked in turn which of the two rules it supported. The President said 'that such a procedure would depart somewhat from standard voting practice at international conferences; if there were no objections he was prepared to adopt it because it seemed practical', and the method was in fact adopted.[122] The result, however, was a drawn vote, and the President had to announce that 'the method of voting had not produced any result'. The President then announced, 'There was no alternative in the present instance... to returning to the first more traditional voting method', and he put the proposal submitted first to the vote. The result was again a drawn vote, and the President

[119] Minutes of the 1965 Plenipotentiary Conference of the ITU, 4th Plenary Meeting, ITU Doc. No. 155-E, p. 10 (1965).

[120] *Ibid.*, 5th Plenary Meeting, ITU Doc. No. 156-E, p. 11 (1965).

[121] *Ibid.*, 5th and 6th Plenary Meetings, ITU Docs. Nos. 156-E, 157, 157-E (1965).

[122] CDDH/SR.25, p. 29, paras. 30–32.

announced that the first proposal (to enable the invitation to be extended under a simple majority) was rejected and a two-thirds majority was required. The delegate of the Soviet Union, however, challenged the presidential ruling, stating that the rejection of the first proposal did not mean the adoption of the second proposal. He added that, unless a vote was held on the second proposal, it should be regarded as rejected since it, along with the first proposal, had not obtained a majority in the first vote. The President reiterated his ruling that, despite the first drawn vote, the fact that the first proposal had not obtained a majority on the second vote meant the adoption ipso facto of the second proposal. The President's ruling was upheld by a majority vote.[123]

[123] CDDH/SR.25–26, pp. 34–41.

16

Consensus

16.1 Defining Consensus

The UNGA rules of procedure do not refer to consensus. The UN Model Rules propose,

Rule 51
Consensus

1. The Conference shall make every effort to ensure that its decisions on all matters of substance are taken by consensus or general agreement, or otherwise without a vote.[1]
2. Notwithstanding any measures that may be taken in compliance with paragraph 1, a proposal or motion before the Conference shall be voted on if a representative so requests.[2]

Decision making by consensus is a fairly recent innovation in the procedure of international conferences, and there is, as yet, no clear agreement as to its significance.

Skubiszewski refers to three meanings of consensus:

(a) Means of adopting a resolution;
(b) A kind of agreement, often loosely formulated, which concludes the deliberations, usually conducted in an organ or by a conference;
(c) Consensus is said to perform the role of a law formative agency other than custom or treaty.[3]

[1] The UN Model Rules add a footnote that this provision is based on 'provisions appearing in several recent conference rules (e.g. draft rule 30 prepared for the Second United Nations Conference on the Exploration and Peaceful Uses of Outer Space (A/CONF.101/PC/L.12))'.

[2] The UN Model Rules add a footnote that this provision is based on 'rule 59 of the rules of procedure of the Economic and Social Council (E/5715)'.

[3] Krzysztof Skubiszewski, 'The Elaboration of General Multilateral Conventions and of Non-Contractual Instruments Having a Normative Function or Objective, Resolutions of the General Assembly of the United Nations', 'Provisional Report', 61 *Yearbook of the Institute of International Law* 154–158 (1985 I).

The present analysis centers on the first meaning, namely 'means of adopting a resolution'.

In order to avoid voting, and thus raising the issue of States that were in arrears, the UNGA, at its Nineteenth Session, adopted a 'no objection' system[4] described by Plant as being 'tantamount to unanimity'.[5] The system was in reality decision making by consensus, and the President of the session explicitly referred to the fact that 'decisions were taken on the basis of a non-voting consensus'.[6] A resolution of the Population Commission of the ECOSOC in 1974 defined consensus as 'general agreement without vote but not necessarily unanimity'.[7] A UN legal opinion stated in this connection that 'in UN organs the term consensus was used to describe a practice under which every effort is made to achieve unanimous agreement; but that if it could not be done, those dissenting from the general trend were prepared simply to make their position or reservations known and placed on the record'.[8]

A UN Secretariat paper states, 'No consensus may be obtained if even a single representative objects explicitly to a consensus being recorded: in such cases, the only possibility is to proceed to a vote.' 'Decisions made by consensus have the same legally binding status as decisions adopted by other methods.'[9]

The rules of procedure of the 'Helsinki Process' define consensus as 'the absence of any objection expressed by a Representative and submitted by him as constituting an obstacle to the taking of the decision in question'.[10]

The representative of El Salvador to the Third Law of the Sea Conference referred to consensus as 'an agreement to which there was no formal opposition even if some delegations made reservations or comments'.[11] The Law of the Sea Convention itself defines consensus as 'the absence

4 See Leland M. Goodrich, Edvard Hambro and Anne P. Simons, *Charter of the United Nations*, 3rd rev. edn (1969), p. 170.

5 G. Plant, 'The Third United Nations Conference on the Law of the Sea and the Preparatory Commission: Models for United Nations Law-Making?' 36 ICLQ 525 (1987) at 526.

6 UN GAOR, Plenary, 19th Session, 1330th Meeting, para. 20, UN Doc. A/PV.1330 (1965).

7 ECOSOC Resolution 1835 (LVI) of 14 May 1974.

8 1974 UN Jur. Y.B. 163 (ST/LEG/SER.C/12 (1976)), summarising a statement by the Director of the General Legal Division, UN Office of Legal Affairs, Official Records of ECOSOC, 56th Session, Supp. No. 3A, UN Doc. E.5462, para. 64 (1974).

9 'Consensus in UN practice General', paras. 10, 17, (undated) Paper prepared by the UN Secretariat. http://legal.un.org/ola/media/GA_RoP/GA_RoP_EN.pdf.

10 Rule 69 of the rules of procedure of the Conference on Security and Co-operation in Europe, taken from Jan Sizoo and Rudolph Jurrjens, *The Madrid Experience* (1984), p. 285.

11 Official Records of the Third Law of the Sea Conference, vol. I, p. 44, Summary Records of the 17th Meeting of the Plenary, para. 2, UN Doc. A/CONF.62 (1973).

of any formal objection'.[12] Lateef refers to adopting a resolution where 'no one opposes the contents strongly enough to insist upon the right to vote against the text'.[13] Skubiszewski's definition is 'the absence of voting linked to the absence of opposition to the adoption of the resolution. The absence of opposition means there is general agreement on the contents of the resolution, but no more than that.'[14] At a 1998 session of the IAEA General Conference, there was no opposition to the statement by a delegation that 'for a proposal to be adopted by acclamation, there had to be a consensus'.[15] Adoption by acclamation would appear, in fact, to be synonymous with adoption by consensus.

During a meeting of the 1988 Vienna Conference on Narcotic Drugs, the representative of Argentina stated that in his view 'delegations which did not indicate their opposition to the consensus should be deemed to accept it'.[16] Vignes points out that from 'a formal point of view consensus is often considered not as being a decision of the body in which it emerged, but rather as coming from the Chairman of that body'.[17] Vignes also writes as regards consensus that 'it sometimes appears that delegations, without opposing or abstaining, nevertheless regard themselves as less closely committed to its detailed wording than if there had been a formal decision for which they had expressly voted'.[18] Feltham, in a handbook for diplomats, writes that consensus is 'based on an assumption by the presiding officer of what is sufficiently self-evident not to warrant taking up the time of the meeting on preparing a resolution' or can be used 'for those items to which a minority of representatives object, but would rather not be seen to object through the publicity of a vote'.[19]

Evensen comments, '"Consensus" is not a clearly defined concept . . . a consensus approach does not seem reconcilable with the taking of votes.

[12] Article 161(7) (e) of the UN Convention on the Law of the Sea, 1982.

[13] Noel Lateef, 'Parliamentary Diplomacy and the North–South Dialogue', 11 *Georgia Journal of International and Comparative Law*. 1 (1981) at 41 n. 94.

[14] Krzysztof Skubiszewski, 'The 'Elaboration of General Multilateral Conventions and of Non-Contractual Instruments Having a Normative Function or Objective, Resolutions of the General Assembly of the United Nations, Definitive Report and Draft Resolution', 61 *Yearbook of the Institute of International Law* 325 (1984 I).

[15] Delegate of Morocco, Official Records of the 42nd IAEA General Conference, GC(42)/OR.9, para. 60, p. 11 (1998).

[16] Summary Records of the 23rd Meeting of Committee 1 of the 1988 Vienna Conference on Narcotic Drugs, para. 58, UN Doc. E/CONF.82/C.1/SR.23 (1988).

[17] Daniel Vignes, 'Will the Third Conference on the Law of the Sea Work According to the Consensus Rule?' 69 AJIL 119 (1975) at 120.

[18] *Ibid.* [19] R. G. Feltham, *Diplomatic Handbook*, 7th edn (1998), p. 146.

Consensus is a state of the art emerging from the negotiations.'[20] Szasz defines it as 'taking a decision only when no participant opposes it so strongly as to insist on blocking it'.[21] Peterson makes this interesting comment: 'In the late 1990s "consensus" came to be viewed as the stronger endorsement and delegations no longer requested formal votes to demonstrate unanimity. Now requests for votes typically come from delegations desiring to register opposition by abstaining or voting "no."'[22]

A problem that can arise with the use of consensus was illustrated at the 1988 Vienna Conference on Narcotic Drugs. There was disagreement as to whether there had been in fact a consensus, and the Chairman's statement was that 'it had been his impression that no objection had been voiced'.[23] Such misunderstandings do not normally arise after a formal vote. Another problem with consensus as described by the UN Secretariat is that '[d]ecisions made by consensus will tend to result in a text that is the least common denominator... which may make the text "practically meaningless."'[24]

16.1.1 *Taking Decisions by 'General Agreement' or 'without a Vote'*

A common procedure in the UNGA and in conferences is for a presiding officer to ask if the conference or assembly agrees to a decision. If no objection is made, the presiding officer announces the decision.[25] The UN Secretariat describes the phrase "Without a Vote" as a 'weak form of consensus,... in cases where delegations do not wish to be closely associated with the decision, yet have no formal objection to the adoption. Such decisions have less of a positive connotation than those made by consensus and do not represent "consensus" in its truest form'.[26] Notwithstanding

[20] Jens Evensen, 'Working Methods and Procedures in the Third United Nations Conference on the Law of the Sea', 199 RCADI 485 (1986 IV) at 486.

[21] Paul C. Szasz, 'Improving the International Legislative Process', 9 *Georgia Journal of International and Comparative Law* 519 (1979) at 529.

[22] M. J. Peterson, 'General Assembly', in *The Oxford Handbook on the United Nations*, eds Thomas G Weiss and Sam Daws, p. 102 (2007).

[23] Summary Records of the 21st Meeting of Committee 1 of the 1988 Vienna Conference on Narcotic Drugs, para. 30, UN Doc. E/CONF.82/C.1/SR.21 (1988).

[24] "Consensus in UN practice General", para. 21, (undated) Paper prepared by the UN Secretariat. http://legal.un.org/ola/media/GA_RoP/GA_RoP_EN.pdf.

[25] See, for example: UN GAOR, 4th Committee, 16th Session, 1189th Meeting, para. 38, UN Doc. A/C.4/16/SR.1189 (1961); UN GAOR, Special Political Committee, 29th Session, 925th Meeting, para. 27, UN Doc. A/SPC/29/SR.925 (1974).

[26] 'Consensus in UN practice General', para. 12, (undated) Paper prepared by the UN Secretariat, http://legal.un.org/ola/media/GA_RoP/GA_RoP_EN.pdf.

this opinion I believe that in modern practice the terms 'consensus', 'general agreement' or 'without a vote' are used interchangeably.

At the 1991 Conference on the Liability of Operators of Transport Terminals in International Trade, the Executive Secretary of the Conference explained to the delegates of one of the committees that if the Chairman of one of the Committees saw that there was general agreement on a text discussed by the Committee, there was no reason to put it to the vote. Voting was only necessary if there was obvious disagreement among delegations.[27]

The phrase 'acclamation' is usually used where such decision taking is on an election. There is no provision in the rules of procedure for such decision making, and presumably it is to be seen as an informal method of consensus and should be treated as such.[28] States can be considered as being parties to a consensus but no such phrase exists as regards a decision taken without a vote. Terminology aside, there appears to be no difference between such decision making and consensus. Schaefer, however, is of the opinion that resolutions adopted without a vote are 'even less binding than traditional consensus'.[29]

The term 'consensus' is at times erroneously used as a synonym for 'agreement' or 'decision', as in the statement by a delegation to the 2004 International Labour Conference that 'a consensus had been reached on the sub-amendment through the vote'.[30]

COMMENT

Whatever the subjective feelings of delegations may be as to the subtle differences between 'consensus', taking decisions by 'general agreement' or taking decisions 'without a vote', this author's experience is that States regard the three terms as synonymous.

16.2 Background to the Increased Use of Consensus

Rosenstock, in 1985, pointed out that more than 60 per cent of issues that come before the UNGA are adopted by consensus.[31] This percentage is

[27] UN Doc. A/CONF.152/C.1/SR.1, para. 25 (1991).

[28] The issue of consensus is dealt with in chapter 16.

[29] Michael Schaefer, 'Article 21', in *The Charter of the United Nations, A Commentary*, ed. Bruno Simma (1994), p. 361 at p. 372.

[30] ILO International Labour Conference, 92nd session, Committee on Human Resources, Official Records 20/47, para. 489 (2004).

[31] Robert Rosenstock,' The United Nations at Forty: The US Policy Perspective', 79 *Proceedings of the American Society of International Law* 150 (1985).

now considerably higher.[32] The background to the increased use of consensus is examined by Buzan, who states,

> The key problem in contemporary international decision making is the divorce of power from voting majorities resulting from the expansion of membership in the international system. This renders majority voting increasingly useless for lawmaking decisions because of the danger of powerful alienated minorities. The need is for a technique that will ensure very broadly based support for decisions in a highly divided system, and it is on this ground that consensus exercises its appeal.[33]

Abi-Saab is of the opinion that the Great Powers, when they did not command a majority in the UNGA, 'insisted' on the use of the mechanism of consensus 'with the intent of introducing a qualitative difference between resolutions adopted by consensus and those which, failing consensus, are finally adopted by majority; a distinction which has no basis in the letter or the spirit of the Charter'.[34]

Evensen explains that the background to the adoption of the consensus principle in the Third Law of the Sea Conference was that

> it would be an exercise in futility to work on the assumption that one or more major groupings of the Conference should be occasionally or consistently outvoted with regard to main aspects of the Law of the Sea Convention. Such an approach would result in a situation where the necessary universal adherence to the Convention was made impossible.[35]

Although the UN Sea-Bed Committee had from 1971 to 1973 operated on the consensus method, the first formalisation of consensus appears to have been in the Third Law of the Sea Conference. Buzan notes, 'Nearly all prior use of consensus had been conducted informally, and has been based simply on the consent of the actors involved.'[36] The Conference was conducted on the premise that every effort should be made to reach consensus and voting should be used only as a measure of last resort. The Chairman of the Drafting Committee characterised the role of consensus:

[32] See Rüdiger Wolfrum, 'Article 18', in *The Charter of the United Nations, A Commentary*, ed. Bruno Simma, 2nd edn (2002), p. 362.

[33] Barry Buzan, 'Negotiating by Consensus: Developments in Technique at the United Nations Conference on the Law of the Sea', 75 AJIL 324 (1981) at 326.

[34] Georges Abi-Saab, 'Membership and Voting in the United Nations', in *The Changing Constitution of the United Nations*, eds. Georges Abi-Saab and Hazel Fox (1997), p. 31.

[35] Evensen, 'Working Methods', p. 483.

[36] Buzan, 'Negotiating by Consensus', p. 328.

> While the role of consensus must be maintained, it must not be so misused as to become either the tyranny of the majority or a veto by the minority. Furthermore, if a consensus could not be reached in the time available, that should not mean that the Conference was prevented from applying its ordinary rules of procedure and proceeding to vote in the committees in order to arrive at a solution.[37]

The representative of Norway, Mr. Vindenes, commented,

> Delegations taking part in substantive negotiations on matters of great national interest would be more inclined to seek mutual accommodation of interests if they were aware that the alternative to general agreement was a Conference decision by way of a vote.[38]

Buzan comments, 'It was necessary to have voting rules in order both to give the weak some leverage and to guard against the tendency of consensus procedures to drift into paralysis because of a lack of pressure to come to decisions.'[39,40] A large part of the procedural discussions during the Third Law of the Sea Conference was devoted to what Vignes refers to as the 'preliminary question',[41] namely at what stage and by what procedure does the Conference abandon attempts to reach consensus and move to voting. The compromise reached is reflected in Rule 37 of the rules of procedure:

> *Rule 37*
>
> 1. Before a matter of substance is put to the vote, a determination that all efforts at reaching general agreement have been exhausted shall be made by the majority specified in paragraph 1 of rule 39 [two-thirds of the representatives present and voting, provided that such majority shall include at least a majority of the States participating in that session of the Conference].[42]

[37] Official Records of the Third Law of the Sea Conference, vol. VI, p. 39, Summary Records of the 24th Meeting of the General Committee, para. 40, UN Doc. A/CONF.62 (1976).

[38] Official Records of the Third Law of the Sea Conference, vol. I, p. 21, Summary Records of the 8th Meeting of the Plenary, para. 11, UN Doc. A/CONF.62 (1973).

[39] Buzan, 'Negotiating by Consensus', p. 331.

[40] McWhinney, writing in 1975, was pessimistic that the consensus system could produce anything but 'another exercise in "soft law"'. Edward McWhinney, 'The Codifying Conference as an Instrument of International Law-Making: From the "Old" Law of the Sea to the "New"', 3 *Syracuse Journal of International Law and Commerce* 301 (1975) at 304.

[41] Vignes, 'Will the Third Conference', p. 126.

[42] Rules of procedure of the Third Law of the Sea Conference, UN Doc. A/CONF.62/30/Rev.3, UN Publication Sales No. E.76.I.4 (1981).

The term 'consensus' was not used in the text of the rules of procedure of the Conference.[43] Amerasinghe stated during the debate in the First Committee of the UNGA that 'a consensus is beyond definition'.[44] As President of the Conference, he later commented that the 'word "consensus" had not been used as it did not seem appropriate to use a term that defied definition'.[45] The representative of El Salvador stated that his delegation would have preferred an explicit reference to consensus.[46]

The term 'consensus' appears, however, in the 'Gentleman's Agreement' attached as an appendix to the rules of procedure:

> Declaration incorporating the 'Gentleman's Agreement' made by the President and endorsed by the Conference at its 19th meeting on 27 June 1974. Bearing in mind...
>
> The Conference should make every effort to reach agreement on substantive matters by way of consensus and there should be no voting on such matters until all efforts at consensus have been exhausted.[47]

The President of the Conference was able to state, 'In the eight long years in which the Conference had been working on the draft convention, it had never taken a vote on a matter of substance.'[48] In the Final Session of the Conference, the Chairman proposed that the Final Act reflect that 'except for the voting at the 38th meeting and during the adoption of the Convention as a whole and the amendments thereto, the Conference had always proceeded on the basis of consensus'.[49] The Chairman's proposed language was adopted. The use of 'consensus' in the Third Law of the Sea Conference has been termed 'active consensus'[50] in that it involved informal negotiating texts 'which effectively obliged interested States to take

43 Although the USSR submitted an amendment referring to consensus, UN Doc. A/CONF.62/6 (1973).

44 UN GAOR, 1st Committee, 28th Session, 1924th Meeting, para. 51, UN Doc. A/C.1/28/SR.1924 (1973).

45 Official Records of the Third Law of the Sea Conference, vol. I, p. 43, Summary Records of the 16th Meeting of the Plenary, para. 32, UN Doc. A/CONF.62 (1974).

46 Official Records of the Third Law of the Sea Conference, vol. I, p. 44, Summary Records of the 17th Meeting of the Plenary, para. 2, UN Doc. A/CONF.62 (1974). The definition of consensus proposed by the delegate is quoted above.

47 Appendix to rules of procedure of the Third Law of the Sea Conference, UN Doc. A/CONF.62/30/Rev.3, UN Publication Sales No. E.76.I.4 (1981).

48 Third Law of the Sea Conference, Summary Records of the 175th Plenary Meeting, vol. XVI, p. 131, para. 2, UN Doc. A/CONF.62 (1984).

49 Third Law of the Sea Conference, Summary Records of the 184th Plenary Meeting, vol. XVII, p. 10, para. 80, UN Doc. A/CONF.62 (1984).

50 Among others, see Plant, 'The Third UN Conference', pp. 527, 528.

positions to encourage or discourage the formation of consensus around them'.[51] The University of Virginia Commentary on the Law of the Sea Convention remarks that the consensus rule 'accounted for the very long duration of the Conference', but enabled the adoption of 'a Convention which would enjoy the widest possible support'.[52]

Koh and Jayakumar write,

> The underlying philosophy appears to have been the achievement of a Convention commanding the widest possible support. Hence, it was felt necessary to work into the Rules safeguards against hasty voting, for cooling-off periods and to provide for special majorities. Another underlying rationale was that important interest groups, e.g., the major powers, who were numerically in the minority, did not want to be railroaded into voting where they might not have the votes to win.[53]

Buzan also points to the possible negative consequences that can arise from the use of consensus. 'Consensus rules, with their opportunities for delay and defense, offer maximum scope for the law of disproportionate emphasis to come into play.'[54] 'But given the large amount of negative power implicit in consensus procedures, it is reasonable to fear that their product might contain more than the usual amount of vague and ambiguous drafting.'[55] Righter graphically describes the weakness of the consensus system as being 'an enormously elaborate mating ritual that ends with the pretence of a consummation that has not taken place'.[56]

The apprehension that the use of consensus is liable to undermine the majority enjoyed by developing States may underlie statements such as those made at the 1986 Conference on Treaties between States and International Organisations, where the Mexican delegate stated that his delegation's agreement to adopting the rules of procedure 'did not, however, mean that the agreement reflected in rule 63 [consensus] constitutes a binding precedent for the adoption of resolutions and decisions of

[51] *Ibid.* at p. 527.

[52] Myron H. Nordquist, ed., *United Nations Convention on the Law of the Sea 1982, A Commentary*, vol. I (1985), p. 104.

[53] Tommy T. B. Koh and Shanmugam Jayakumar, 'The Negotiating Process of the Third United Nations Conference on the Law of the Sea', in *United Nations Convention on the Law of the Sea 1982, A Commentary*, ed. Myron H. Nordquist, vol. I (1985), p. 29 at p. 101.

[54] Buzan, 'Negotiating by Consensus', p. 344.

[55] *Ibid.* at p. 345. See also Daniel Bodansky, 'The Legitimacy of International Governance: A Coming Challenge for International Environmental Law?' 39 AJIL 596 (1999) at 607.

[56] Rosemary Righter, *Utopia Lost, The United Nations and World Order* (1995), p. 138.

the United Nations and its organs, commissions and committees'.[57] The Egyptian delegate to the same conference stated that 'while his delegation was able to accept the rules of procedure, including rule 63, for the special purposes of the Conference, it considered that they should not be deemed to constitute a precedent for all international meetings'.[58]

16.3 Use of the Word 'Consensus' in the Rules of Procedure of the UN General Assembly

Increasing use is made in the UNGA of decision making by consensus. Writing in 1994, Kaufmann stated, 'It can be noted that methods of consensus are increasingly replacing or at least complementing more automatic majority vote related procedures. The UN has become an experimental laboratory for new decision making procedures.'[59] The practical guide to the UNGA published by the Permanent Mission of Switzerland to the UN even states, 'It is assumed that all tabled draft resolutions/decisions will be adopted without a vote. A vote must be requested.'[60]

UNGA rules of procedure do not, however, reflect this development. The 1984 Report of the Special Committee on the Charter of the United Nations and on Strengthening of the Role of the Organisation discussed a working paper that included the following sentence: 'The concept of seeking consensus should be incorporated into the rules of procedure of the Assembly.'[61] The 1984 Report noted this sentence among the items 'which were viewed as deserving further consideration'.[62] The 1986 Report of the Committee states, in relation to this proposal, that several delegations were of the opinion that 'consensus was a vague concept' and that 'consensus was not a procedural matter and therefore had no place in the rules of procedure'.[63] The phrase on inclusion of consensus in the rules of procedure was omitted from subsequent drafts of the Committee, but the drafts continued to state that 'consensus' was desirable where possible. The 1988

[57] Official Records of the 1986 Conference on Treaties between States and International Organisations, 1st Plenary Meeting, UN Doc. A/CONF.129/16, para. 30 (1986).

[58] *Ibid.* at para. 33.

[59] Johan Kaufmann, 'The Evolving United Nations; Principles and Realities', *ACUNS Reports and Papers 1994 No. 4, The Academic Council on the United Nations System* (1994), p. 27.

[60] The Practical Guide to the UNGA published by the Permanent Mission of Switzerland to the UN, para 3.5, www.unitar.org/ny/sites/unitar.org.ny/files/UN_PGA_Handbook.pdf

[61] UN GAOR, 39th Session, Supp. No. 33, para. 160, UN Doc. A/39/33 (1984); Working Paper submitted by France and the UK, UN Doc. A/AC.182/L.43/Rev.1 (1986).

[62] UN GAOR, 39th Session, Supp. No. 33, para. 160, UN Doc. A/39/33 (1984).

[63] UN GAOR, 41st Session, Supp. No. 33, para. 39, UN Doc. A/41/33 (1986).

Report of the Committee reflects the fact that some delegations objected to any reference at all to consensus.[64] In the draft contained in the 1989 Report of the Committee, the word 'consensus' is replaced with the phrase 'without a vote'.[65] At a 1990 meeting of the Sixth Committee of the UNGA, a debate took place on the Report of the Committee. During the debate, the representative of Mexico expressed this caveat: 'As far as the possible binding force of consensus was concerned, it was not appropriate for the Sixth Committee to recommend the use of legal or political mechanisms which it had not yet defined.'[66]

The text of the draft was finally agreed in 1990 and refers to the desirability of the 'adoption by the General Assembly of agreed texts of resolutions and decisions'.[67] The text is reproduced as an amendment to the annexes of the rules of procedure.[68] No reference is made in the text either to 'consensus' or to decision making 'without voting'. The background to the objection to having an explicit reference to consensus appears to be the apprehension of developing States that it is an attempt 'to create a *de facto* veto for the minority countries'.[69]

16.4 Consensus without Possibility of Voting

Rules of procedure can specify that a conference is obliged to take decisions by consensus, leaving no option for voting; such a rule is rarely adopted.[70] Since there is little incentive to compromise, the outcome of such a conference is very likely to be 'the least common denominator of agreement'.[71] No treaty-making conference has adopted such a pure form of consensus, and it appears unlikely that it will be adopted in the future.

[64] UN GAOR, 43rd Session, Supp. No. 33, para. 70, UN Doc. A/43/33 (1988).

[65] UN GAOR, 44th Session, Supp. No. 33, paras. 84(1), 87, UN Doc. A/44/33 (1989).

[66] UN GAOR, 6th Committee, 45th Session, 16th Meeting, para. 17, UN Doc. A/C.6/45/SR.16 (1990).

[67] Report of the Special Committee on the Charter of the United Nations and on the Strengthening of the Role of the Organisation, UN GAOR, 45th Session, Supp. No. 33, para. 86, UN Doc. A/45/33 (1990). Adopted by the UNGA in its Resolution 45/45 of 28 November 1990.

[68] UN Doc. A/520/Rev.15/Amend. (1991).

[69] Michael Schaefer, 'Article 21', in *The Charter of the United Nations, A Commentary*, ed. Bruno Simma (1994), p. 361.

[70] Rules of procedure of the International Conference on the Relationship between Disarmament and Development, UN Doc. A/CONF.130/1 (1987); Rule 30 of the rules of procedure of the Conference on Facilitating the Entry into Force of the Comprehensive Nuclear-Test-Ban Treaty, CTBT-Art. XIV/2001/2 (2001).

[71] Szasz, 'Improving', p. 530.

16.5 Consensus with Possibility of Voting

The approach adopted by the Third Law of the Sea Conference was that a strenuous effort should be made to reach consensus, but if consensus was not obtained the Conference would proceed to a vote. This approach of 'qualified consensus'[72] with different variants has been adopted by most rules of procedure of subsequent conferences.

The different variants include the 1990 Second UN Conference on the Least Developed Countries, one of the rules of which stated,

> *Rule 36*
>
> 1. The Conference shall make every effort to ensure that all its substantive decisions are taken by consensus.
> 2. Notwithstanding any measures that may be taken in compliance with paragraph 1, a proposal before the Conference shall be voted on if a representative so requests.[73]

At the 1993 UN Conference on Straddling Fish Stocks and Highly Migratory Fish Stocks, the rule, clearly influenced by the Third Law of the Sea Conference, stated,

> *Rule 33*
>
> The Conference should conduct its work on the basis of general agreement. It may proceed to vote in accordance with rule 35 only after all efforts at achieving general agreement have been exhausted. Before doing so, the Chairman shall inform the Conference that all efforts at achieving general agreement have been exhausted.[74]

At the 1994 International Conference on Population and Development, the relevant rule was

> *Rule 33*
>
> The Conference should make best endeavours to ensure that its work and the adoption of its report are accomplished by general agreement.[75]

The most efficacious approach, it is submitted, is as described by Szasz, whereby

[72] *Ibid.* at p. 529.

[73] Rule 36 of the rules of procedure of the Second UN Conference on the Least Developed Countries, UN Doc. A/CONF.147/3 (1990).

[74] Rules of procedure of the UN Conference on Straddling Fish Stocks and Highly Migratory Fish Stocks, UN Doc. A/CONF.164/6 (1993).

[75] Rules of procedure of the International Conference on Population and Development, UN Doc. A/CONF.171/2 (1994). This rule is the most common variant in recent conferences.

> if a representative is generally perceived as acting unreasonably in preventing the taking of decisions, and cannot be moved by other appeals, then a resort to voting under the standard rules can always be threatened and, if necessary, carried out.[76]

In view of the uncertainty surrounding the word 'consensus', it is likely that use in the future will be made of the phrase 'general agreement' rather than consensus.

16.6 Reservations to a Consensus

Suy writes that if a 'text is adopted by consensus, statements expressing fundamental reservations would be contrary to the very idea of the non-objection procedure which implies a positive attitude of the participants towards the substance'.[77] Skubiszewski states in a similar vein that '[o]bjections which do not concern the fundamentals of the resolution are admissible'.[78] These statements do not, however, appear to reflect State practice, where it is common procedure for a State to 'participate' in a consensus, but to make a statement that if there had been a vote the State in question would have voted against the motion or abstained.[79] Cassese states, 'Often "reservations" and objections are expressed either before or after it is declared that a consensus decision has been taken.'[80]

A 1982 legal opinion by the UN Office of Legal Affairs dealt with a "reservation" made to a consensus after the close of the session where it was adopted. The opinion points out that 'even a reservation made formally at the time of adoption of the text, while indicative of a qualified assent, does not prevent the adoption of the consensus text in question'. If the reservation is made after the session 'it must be regarded as reflecting the position of the State concerned with regard to the consensus resolution at the time the statement was made'.[81]

[76] Paul Szasz, 'General Law Making Process', in *United Nations Legal Order*, eds. Oscar Schachter and Christopher C. Joyner, vol. I (1995), p. 35 at p. 85.

[77] Eric Suy, 'Consensus', in *Encyclopedia of Public International Law*, ed. R. Bernhardt, vol. I (1992), p. 759 at p. 760.

[78] Skubiszewski, 'Definitive Report', p. 325.

[79] One of the early examples was in the Sixth Committee of the UNGA at its Thirty-First Session. UN GAOR, 6th Committee, 31st Session, 19th Meeting, UN Doc. A/C.6/31/SR.19 paras. 53–69 (1976).

[80] Antonio Cassese, *International Law in a Divided World* (1986), p. 196.

[81] *Memorandum of the UN Office of Legal Affairs, 4 May 1982, to the Senior Legal Liaison Officer, United Nations Conference on Trade and Development QUESTION WHETHER*

An example of a 'reservation' is the US statement at the 2001 UNGA on the issue of disarmament and development that 'the record of today's proceedings reflect that the United States did not participate in the consensus'.[82]

At a 2008 plenary meeting of the UNGA, a delegation complained that 'the consensus approach can work only if negotiations are undertaken in a transparent and inclusive manner'.[83] This plaint, however, has remained a wish and not a command.

WITHIN THE TRADE AND DEVELOPMENT BOARD A DELEGATION CAN INTRODUCE RESERVATIONS TO A CONSENSUS RESOLUTION AFTER THE CLOSURE OF THE SESSION DURING WHICH THAT RESOLUTION WAS ADOPTED, http://legal.un.org/ola/media/GA_RoP/GA_RoP_EN.pdf.

[82] UN GAOR, 56th Plenary Session, UN Doc. A/56/PV.68, p. 21 (2001).

[83] UN GAOR, 63rd Plenary Session, 68th Meeting, UN Doc. A/63/PV.68, p. 9 (2008).

17

Separate Votes

17.1 Separate Votes on Parts of Proposals and Amendments

It is accepted practice that rules of procedure contain provisions for dividing proposals and the holding of separate votes on parts of a proposal. The only exception appears to have been the 1995 NPT Review Conference, which prohibited division of proposals for the extension of the NPT.[1]

The various rules of procedure do not stipulate restrictions on motions for separate votes, but it would be logical to assume that the 'provisions may be related, but to be divided each must be free-standing so that should one pass and the other fail, the part of the question that passed would still make sense and be a whole proposition'.[2]

The rules of procedure of the UNGA state,

> *Division of Proposals and Amendments*
>
> *Rule 89*
>
> A representative may move that parts of a proposal or of an amendment should be voted on separately. If objection is made to the request for division, the motion for division shall be voted upon. Permission to speak on the motion for division shall be given only to two speakers in favour and two speakers against. If the motion for division is carried, those parts of the proposal or of the amendment which are approved shall then be put to the vote as a whole. If all operative parts of the proposal or of the amendment have been rejected, the proposal or the amendment shall be considered to have been rejected as a whole.

The UN Model Rule is similar.[3]

At a 2008 meeting of the Third Committee of the UNGA, the Committee rejected a proposal to have a separate vote on the first preambular

[1] Rule 28(3)(i) of the rules of procedure of the 1995 NPT Review Conference:

> No Parties may move that part of a proposal [on the duration of the NPT] be voted on separately. Doc. NPT/CONF.1995/28 (1995).

[2] Hugh Cannon, *Cannon's Concise Guide to Rules of Order* (1992), p. 125.

[3] UN Model Rule 57. UN Doc. A/37/163, Annex (1982).

paragraph of a draft resolution. When a request was then made to have a separate vote on paragraph 1 of the draft resolution, several delegations objected, claiming that the principle of a separate vote had already been rejected. The Secretary of the Committee, correctly, pointed out that the second proposal 'concerned another part of the draft resolution' and that 'rule 129 should be implemented on an individual basis'.[4]

17.2 Consequence of Holding a Separate Vote

Delegations may disapprove of one or more elements in a proposal and would vote against them if a separate vote were held on those elements. If, however, all elements of a proposal are voted on as a 'package deal', then delegations often will vote in favour or abstain on the 'package' despite their reservations on one or more of its constituent elements. Therefore the decision as to holding, or not holding, a separate vote may well decide the fate of an issue.

Rosenne points out that, in the 1958 Law of the Sea Conference, an article on passage through straits, which contained a clause important to Israel, was adopted only as a result of the (narrow) defeat of an Egyptian proposal to hold a separate vote on that clause.[5]

17.3 The Right of a Delegation to Have a Separate Vote on Parts of a Proposal

The UNGA text has undergone several changes. The provisional rules of procedure of the UNGA stated,

> *Rule 65*
>
> Parts of a proposal may be voted on separately if a representative requests that the proposal be divided.[6]

[4] UN GAOR, 3rd Committee, 63rd Session, 42nd Meeting, UN Doc. A/C.3/63/SR.42 paras. 37–41 (2008).

[5] Shabtai Rosenne, 'Israel and the First United Nations Conference on the Law of the Sea: The Straits of Tiran', in *An International Law Miscellany* (1993), p. 723 at pp. 757–759.

[6] Rule 65 of the provisional rules of procedure of the General Assembly, UN Doc. A/4. This rule was following the practice of the rules of procedure of the Assembly of the League of Nations:

> *Rule 18*
>
> 2. Parts of a proposal shall be voted on separately, if a representative requests that the proposal be divided.

This language was regarded by some delegations as unsatisfactory since the use of the word 'may' left discretion as to whether to accede to a request. The 1947 UNGA Committee on Procedures and Organisation[7] proposed replacing the word 'may' with 'shall', commenting, 'The right of representatives to ask that proposals should be divided for the purpose of voting has been clarified.'[8]

A subcommittee of the Sixth Committee of the UNGA, convened in 1947, recommended that a majority of two-thirds of the General Assembly should be able to deny a representative the right to have a separate vote.[9] In the discussions in the Sixth Committee, the representative of the USSR proposed omitting this restriction, explaining that 'a proposal might be rejected although only a part of it was unacceptable to the majority'.[10] The representative of the United Kingdom, who supported the proposed restriction, argued that 'he could envisage a situation wherein a member, for obstructive reasons, would insist upon divisional voting'.[11] The Soviet proposal, to omit the recommendation of the subcommittee, was accepted, and consequently the following text was adopted:

> *Rule 82*
>
> Parts of a proposal *shall* be voted on separately if a representative requests that the proposal be divided. The resulting proposal shall then be put to a final vote. [emphasis added]

The Special Committee on Methods and Procedures of the General Assembly, of 1949, discussed the issue and proposed no change in the absolute right of a representative to demand a division.[12] During the debate in the Sixth Committee of the UNGA, the Netherlands delegation, however, proposed that a majority decision should be able to deny a request for a division.[13] The Netherlands representative explained that

[7] Established by UN Resolution 102 (I) of 15 December 1946. The Report of the Committee appears in UN GAOR, 2nd Session, Plenary Meetings, vol. II, p. 1455, Annex 4, UN Doc. A/388 (1947).

[8] The Report of the Committee appears in UN GAOR, 2nd Session, Plenary Meetings, vol. II p. 1472, Annex 4, UN Doc. A/388, (1947).

[9] UN GAOR, 6th Committee, 2nd Session, Annexes, p. 265, Procedures and Organisation of the General Assembly, Report of Sub-Committee 3 on Part III of the Report of the Committee, Annex 4c, Rule 82, UN Doc. A/C.6/182/Corr.1/Corr.2 (1947).

[10] UN GAOR, 6th Committee, 2nd Session, 56th Meeting, p. 132, UN Doc. A/C.6/2/SR.56 (1947).

[11] *Ibid.* [12] UN Doc. A/937 (1949). [13] UN Doc. A/C.6/L.17 (1949).

his amendment would 'obviate, at least in part, the drawbacks and loss of time involved by frequent requests for a vote in parts'.[14] The representative of the USSR argued against the Netherlands amendment that 'it would derogate from the fundamental right of a delegation to express its opinion with regard to the various parts of a proposal'.[15] The representative of France, who also objected to the Netherlands proposal, argued that 'representatives would be obliged to adopt a rigid position'.[16] The text incorporating the Netherlands proposal was, however, adopted[17] and has been emulated in the various rules of procedure of subsequent conferences.

The present rules of procedure of the UNGA,[18] and those of all the conferences examined, permit any representative to request that parts of a proposal or amendment be voted on separately. The rules of procedure, however, provide that if objection is made, then the motion requesting a separate vote is itself voted on by the conference, assembly or committee. The 1949 Geneva Conference was an exception in this respect in that it did not make any stipulation as to denying a request for a separate vote.[19]

The rules of procedure of the Security Council for a separate vote on parts of a proposal ostensibly require the approval of the original mover, thus giving the original mover of a proposal the power to block such a request.[20] The Egyptian delegation to the Sixth Committee of the 1949 UNGA proposed that the sponsor of a resolution in the General Assembly would, as in the Security Council, have a right to veto a request for a separate vote on a proposal.[21] When the proposal received little support, the Egyptian delegation withdrew it.[22]

14 UN GAOR, 6th Committee, 4th Session, 152nd Meeting, para. 3, UN Doc. A/C.6/4/SR.152 (1949).

15 *Ibid.* at para. 54.

16 UN GAOR, 6th Committee, 4th Session, 153rd Meeting, para. 9, UN Doc. A/C.6/4/SR.153 (1949).

17 *Ibid.* at para. 23. UNGA Resolution 362 (IV) of 22 October 1949.

18 Rule 89 of the UNGA rules of procedure.

19 Rule 29 of the rules of procedure of the 1949 Geneva Conference.

20 Rule 32(2) of the provisional rules of procedure of the Security Council. This rule was adopted on the basis of a proposal by the Netherlands amended by Poland, 41st Meeting of the Security Council, 16 May 1946.

21 UN Doc. A/C.6/L.18 (1949).

22 UN GAOR, 6th Committee, 4th Session, 152nd Meeting, para. 76, UN Doc. A/C.6/4/SR.152 (1949).

17.4 The IMO Formula for Authorising Requests for Separate Votes

The IMO Conferences use an unusual formula, which states that a motion for division will only be voted on if the original proposer objects to the motion for division:

> *Rule 50*
>
> Parts of a proposal or amendment thereto shall be voted on separately if the President, with the consent of the proposer, so decides, or if any representative of a Member requests that the proposal or amendment thereto be divided and the proposer raises no objection. If objection is raised, permission to speak on the point shall be given first to the mover of the motion to divide the proposal or amendment, and then to the mover of the original proposal or amendment under discussion, after which the motion to divide the proposal or amendment shall be put immediately to the vote.[23]

IMO convened conferences use the same formula, *mutatis mutandis*.[24]

At a meeting of the Plenary of a 1969 IMCO conference, the President decided, in accordance with Rule 37 of the rules of procedure, to allow a separate vote, without putting the issue to a vote.[25] At a meeting of a 1971 IMCO conference, the sponsors of a resolution proposed separate votes on two parts of their resolution. The French delegation objected and the Chairman said he would put the issue to a vote. The Rapporteur took the unusual step of declaring that the Chairman had not adhered to the rules of procedure. The Chairman replied that 'according to his interpretation of Rule 37 he had no option in face of the objection raised by France but to put the question to the Committee for decision'.[26] The representative of India commented, 'Irrespective of the Rules of Procedure, the most authoritative decision on any point of procedure was that arrived at by majority vote. The procedure adopted had therefore been perfectly correct.'[27]

The IMO formula has not been imitated by other organisations.

[23] Rule 50 of the rules of procedure of the IMO Assembly.

[24] See, for example, Rule 37(1) of the rules of procedure of the 1971 IMCO Oil Pollution Damage Fund Conference, IMCO Doc. LEG/CONF.2/2 (1971); Rule 37(1) of the rules of procedure of the 1969 IMCO Conference on Marine Pollution Damage, IMCO Doc. LEG/CONF.2 (1969).

[25] Official Records of the 5th Plenary Meeting of the 1969 IMCO Conference on Marine Pollution Damage, p. 108, IMCO Doc. LEG/CONF/SR.5 (1969).

[26] Official Records of the 24th Meeting of the Committee of the Whole of the 1971 IMCO Oil Pollution Damage Fund Conference, pp. 510, 511, IMCO Doc. CONF.2/C.1/SR.24 (1971).

[27] *Ibid.*

17.5 Does a Delegation Requesting a Separate Vote Need to Submit a Motion?

At a 1981 meeting of the UNGA, the Chairman put to the vote the proposal 'to vote on the amendments as a whole'.[28] This ruling was not in accordance with the rules of procedure nor with usual practice, both of which determine that the vote should be on the proposal to have a separate vote. The established procedure is that all proposals are voted on as a whole unless a delegation requests a separate vote and that request is acceded to.

During the 1978 Hamburg Conference on Carriage by Sea, the representative of the Netherlands requested that an article be voted on paragraph by paragraph. The representative claimed that it 'was the practice in United Nations plenipotentiary conferences not to consider articles as a whole unless the members of the Conference had unanimously agreed to do so'.[29] The President ruled, however, that he would put the article as a whole to a vote unless the delegation 'wished to press its motion for division'. The representative then requested a vote on the motion for division.[30] The accepted practice, however, is that proposals are voted on as a whole unless a motion for division is approved. At the 1999 International Labour Conference, the Legal Adviser to the ILO confirmed that any delegate can request a separate vote, but that such request is a 'procedural motion' and 'has to have a majority in its favour'.[31]

17.6 Voting on a Request for a Separate Vote

At a 1989 meeting of the UNGA, the President ruled, 'The representative of the Federal Republic of Germany has asked for a division. If your vote is "yes" it will be in favour [of division].'[32]

The accepted practice is that those voting for division should vote 'yes'.

The usual rule is that a motion for a separate vote has to obtain a majority to be carried. The ICAO Assembly rule, however, is

[28] UN GAOR, 2nd Committee, 36th Session, 48th Meeting, paras. 61, 65, UN Doc. A/C.2/36/SR.48 (1981).

[29] Summary Records of the 6th Plenary Meeting of the 1978 Hamburg Conference on Carriage by Sea, UN Doc. A/CONF.89/PV.6, para. 47 (1978).

[30] *Ibid.*

[31] ILO, Provisional Records of the International Labour Conference, 87th Session, 21st sitting, p. 27/12 (1999).

[32] UN GAOR, Plenary, 44th Session, 63rd Meeting, p. 92, UN Doc. A/44/PV.63 (Provisional) (1989).

Rule 49

On request of the Delegation of any Contracting State and *unless opposed by a majority of those voting*, parts of a motion shall be voted on separately. The resulting motion shall then be put to a final vote in its entirety.[33]

17.7 Form of Voting on the Separate Vote

The universal practice is that delegations supporting the part of a proposal subject to a separate vote cast an affirmative vote.[34] Delegations objecting to that part of the proposal vote in the negative. At a 1980 meeting of a UNGA committee, a debate arose as to the form of the separate vote. The representative of the USSR had requested a separate vote on two phrases.[35] Some delegations argued that those wishing to delete the phrases should vote in the affirmative.[36] The Chairman ruled that 'those in favour of retaining the words should vote in the affirmative'.[37] At a 2009 meeting of a UNGA committee, the Secretary of the Committee explained that voting on the proposal for a separate vote would be 'a vote for or against the current wording'.[38]

COMMENT

The accepted practice is that those wishing to retain the part of the proposal in question vote 'yes'.

17.8 Number of Speakers on a Motion for a Separate Vote on Part of a Proposal

The UNGA rules of procedure limit the number of speakers on a motion for division of a proposal. This rule was followed by all UN conferences up to 1963. Conferences after 1963 dropped this provision. However, it was reintroduced in the UN Model Rules, where the proposal was to limit

[33] Rule 49, Standing Rules of Procedure of the Assembly of ICAO, ICAO Doc. 7600/5 (1990). Emphasis added.

[34] See, for example, UN GAOR, 1st Committee, 53rd Session, 23rd Meeting, UN Doc. A/C.1/53/PV.23, p. 8 (1998).

[35] UN GAOR, 6th Committee, 35th Session, 68th Meeting, para. 44, UN Doc. A/C.6/35/SR.68 (1980).

[36] *Ibid.* at paras. 54, 56.

[37] *Ibid.* at para. 60.

[38] UN GAOR, 3rd Committee, 64th session, 46th meeting, UN Doc. A/C.3/64/SR.46 para. 38 (2009).

the number of speakers to two in favour and two opposing the motion.[39] Most recent conferences have adopted the UN Model Rules formula.[40]

At a 1965 meeting of the UNGA, the President ruled that an appeal by a representative to the proposer to withdraw his request for a separate vote did not constitute one of the two speeches permitted to representatives opposing the motion for division.[41]

At a 1985 meeting of the UNGA, the Chairman allowed several speakers to explain their vote before voting on a motion for a separate vote.[42] It is submitted that this was an incorrect ruling since such explanations of vote should be made after the vote and not before it.

17.9 Right to Object to a Motion for a Separate Vote on Part of a Proposal

The rules of procedure of the 1949 Geneva Conference made no provision for objection to a request for a separate vote. On several occasions representatives have claimed that no objection should be made to a request for division of a vote. During the 1958 Law of the Sea Conference, the representative of Yugoslavia remarked that 'it was extremely rare for a proposal for such a procedure [division of a vote on a proposal] to be rejected'.[43]

During the 1963 Vienna Conference on Consular Relations, the representative of Saudi Arabia stated that 'delegations are entitled to request separate votes on different paragraphs of the same article without being subject to Rule 40. [The rule allowed a delegation to object to a motion for division.] Rule 40 applied to requests for division of a paragraph, a sentence or an amendment but certainly not to an article containing several

39 Rule 57 of the UN Model Rules.

40 See Rule 41 of the rules of procedure of the World Summit against Racism, Racial Discrimination, Xenophobia and Related Intolerance, UN Doc. A/CONF.189/2 (2001); Rule 40 of the rules of procedure of the World Summit on Sustainable Development, UN Doc. A/CONF.199/2 (2002); Rule 40 of the rules of procedure of the International Meeting to Review the Implementation of the Programme of Action for the Sustainable Development of Small Island Developing States, UN Doc. A/58/567 (2003); Rule 40 of the rules of procedure of the World Conference on Disaster Reduction, UN Doc. A.CONF/206/PC(I)/2 (2004); Rule 43 of the WHO draft rules of procedure for the Conference of the Parties to the Framework Convention on Tobacco Control, WHO Doc. A/FCTC/IGWG/1/4 (2004).

41 UN GAOR, Plenary, 20th Session, 1400th Meeting, para. 18, UN Doc. A/PV.1400 (1965).

42 UN GAOR, 6th Committee, 40th Session, 55th Meeting, paras. 24–30, UN Doc. A/C.6/40/SR.55 (1985).

43 Official Records of the 1958 Law of the Sea Conference, 20th Meeting of Committee II, vol. IV, p. 52, para. 4, UN Doc. A/CONF.13/40 (1958).

independent ideas in separate paragraphs.'[44] The Legal Counsel of the UN replied by stating that the article in question was a proposal and therefore 'any delegation might request that there should be a separate vote on parts of that proposal'. The Legal Counsel added that such a request came within Rule 40 and was therefore subject to a vote, if there was objection to the motion.[45]

During the Vienna Conference on the Law of Treaties, when a delegation objected to a division of a vote on a proposal, the Canadian representative stated that 'he wishe[d] to call attention to the fact that, for the first time during the nine weeks of the Conference, a request for a separate vote had been opposed'.[46] At the Second Session of the same conference two delegations objected to a Venezuelan request for a separate vote. The representative of Venezuela declared that 'the request for a separate vote represented the right of every State to express its views as part of a proposal. The Conference has never yet denied any such request[47] and he appealed to it not to set a precedent in that regard.'[48] The representative of Costa Rica wished 'to place on record its protest against that antidemocratic gesture'.[49] The representative of El Salvador declared that 'El Salvador had always upheld the view that it was inadvisable to deny delegations the opportunity of expressing their opinion by means of a separate vote ... He would request that in the future every effort be made to meet requests for separate votes.'[50] At a 1981 meeting of the UNGA, the Chairman remarked that it was unprecedented in the Committee to deny a request by a delegation for a separate vote. He added that it would be a serious precedent for the work of the Committee if the request was denied.[51] At a 1989 meeting of the UNGA, an objection was made to a request for a division of the vote. The representative of France declared on behalf of the European Community that 'the Twelve would recall that it is not the

[44] Official Records of the 1963 Conference on Consular Relations, vol. I, 6th Plenary Meeting, p. 14, para. 30, UN Doc. A/CONF.25/16 (1963).

[45] *Ibid.* at para. 31.

[46] Official Records of the Vienna Conference on the Law of Treaties – First Session, 83rd Meeting of the Committee of the Whole, p. 492, para. 52, UN Doc. A/CONF.39/11 (1968).

[47] Not strictly accurate.

[48] Official Records of the Vienna Conference on the Law of Treaties – Second Session, 17th Plenary Meeting, p. 83, para. 54, UN Doc. A/CONF.39/11/Add.1 (1969).

[49] *Ibid.* at para. 57.

[50] *Ibid.* at para. 64.

[51] UN GAOR, 5th Committee, 36th Session, 26th Meeting, para. 49, UN Doc. A/C.5/36/SR.26 (1981).

practice to object to a separate vote when a Member State requests such a vote'.[52]

COMMENT

Despite statements made to the contrary, the records of conferences show that where a delegation objected to holding a separate vote on part of a proposal, the issue of holding a separate vote was itself always put to the vote.[53]

17.10 Can a Motion be Submitted for a Separate Vote on a Particular Sub-Paragraph after Defeat of a Previous Motion for a Separate Vote on Every Sub-Paragraph?

An issue that has arisen concerning the division of proposals and amendments is this: if a delegation proposes that a separate vote be held on every sub-paragraph of a proposal and that proposal is defeated, does the defeat of the motion preclude motions for voting on a particular sub-paragraph or phrase? At the 1963 Vienna Conference on Consular Relations, the President ruled that it would not preclude separate voting on particular paragraphs and that delegations were free to propose such separate votes.[54] A number of delegations disagreed with the presidential ruling, others agreed, but the ruling as such was not challenged as apparently no delegation requested a separate vote on a particular sub-paragraph. The ruling of the President would appear to be correct.

17.11 What Are 'Parts of a Proposal' for Purposes of a Separate Vote?

The UNGA rules of procedure and the UN Model Rules[55] allow a request for a separate vote to be made regarding 'parts of a proposal'. Practice is to permit representatives to choose which parts of a proposal they wish to propose voting on separately. However, a request for a separate vote that

52 UN GAOR, Plenary, 44th Session, 63rd Meeting, p. 87, UN Doc. A/44/PV.63 (Provisional) (1989).

53 See, for example, Official Records of the 1974–77 Geneva Humanitarian Law Conference, CDDH/SR.36, vol. VI, p. 40, para. 51.

54 Official Records of the 1963 Vienna Conference on Consular Relations, 12th Plenary Meeting, vol. I, p. 41, paras. 24–31, UN Doc. A/CONF.25/16 (1963).

55 Rule 57 of the UN Model Rules; Rule 89 of the UNGA rules of procedure.

would render a proposal meaningless would be unacceptable. The President of the 1949 UNGA refused to allow a motion that, in his opinion, split a sentence. He suggested that the representative submit an amendment rather than a request for a separate vote.[56]

At the 1998 session of a UNGA committee, a delegation requested a separate vote on three words in a resolution. The Chairman at first responded that 'there is no very clear rule on this subject in the rules of procedure'. One delegation commented that allowing such a vote could lead to a 'surrealistic situation in which someone who does not like a definite article in a given paragraph can ask for a separate vote – on the word "the"'.[57] The Chairman allowed the separate vote to take place.

COMMENT

If a delegation objects to a request for a separate vote, then the request is subject to a vote. This requirement can serve to prevent frivolous or meaningless separate votes.

17.12 A Motion for a Separate Vote on a Paragraph after Such a Motion Had Been Defeated Regarding Other Paragraphs of the Resolution

The President of a 1961 session of the UNGA ruled that the fact that a motion had been defeated for separate votes on some paragraphs of a draft resolution did not preclude a new motion for a separate vote on another paragraph of that resolution.[58] The ruling of the President would appear to be correct.

17.13 A Motion for a Separate Vote on a Phrase after the Failure of a Motion for Deletion of the Phrase

During the 1963 Vienna Conference on Consular Relations, Switzerland had proposed that a certain phrase be deleted. The Swiss proposal was defeated. Austria then proposed a separate vote on the same phrase, and the question arose, as put by the delegate of Saudi Arabia, 'whether it was appropriate to move that a part of a proposal which the Conference had

[56] UN GAOR, Plenary, 3rd Session, Part II, 212th Meeting, p. 454, UN Doc. A/PV.212 (1949).
[57] UN GAOR, 1st Committee, 53rd Session, 23rd Meeting, UN Doc. A/C.1/53/PV/23, p. 6 (1998).
[58] UN GAOR, Plenary, 15th Session, 994th Meeting, paras. 65–68, UN Doc. A/PV.994 (1961).

already decided should not be deleted, should again be voted on separately in order to effect its deletion'.[59] The President ruled that 'the Austrian motion for division of the vote was in accordance with the rules of procedure'.[60] The ruling was challenged, but rather than putting the ruling to the vote, the President put the Austrian motion for a separate vote on the phrase to the vote and the Conference rejected this motion. From the vote it is therefore impossible to know whether the ruling itself was upheld or not. One delegation (the Czechoslovakian) made the point that it had voted against the Austrian motion for a separate vote, but supported the President's ruling that the Austrian motion, as such, was in accordance with the rules of procedure.[61]

At a plenary meeting of the 1974–1977 Geneva Humanitarian Law Conference, the Conference rejected a Soviet amendment to delete a certain paragraph 3 from a draft article. When a separate vote was requested on the paragraph, the Swiss delegation objected. The argument put forward by the Swiss delegation was that 'a separate vote on paragraph 3 would deal with the same subject matter as the vote on the amendment which had just been rejected'.[62] The Syrian representative retorted, 'The first vote had been on the acceptance or rejection of an amendment. The Conference now had to vote on whether it should retain paragraph 3. It would be illogical to claim that paragraph 3 had been adopted because the amendment to delete it had not obtained the necessary two-thirds majority.'[63] The President ruled that the Conference should proceed with the separate vote and commented that 'it would seem that a delegation wishing to delete a paragraph would be better advised to ask for a vote on the paragraph in question rather than to submit an amendment proposing its deletion'.[64]

At a later meeting of the Plenary of the 1974–1977 Geneva Humanitarian Law Conference, the Conference rejected an amendment to delete from a draft article the reference to the 1954 Hague Convention. A separate vote was then requested on the reference to the 1954 Hague Convention. The representative of the United Kingdom objected, claiming that 'a separate vote would amount to a reconsideration of the decision which

[59] Official Records of the 1963 Vienna Conference on Consular Relations, 18th Plenary Meeting, vol. I, p. 72, para. 42, UN Doc. A/CONF.25/16 (1963).

[60] *Ibid.* at para. 43. [61] *Ibid.* at para. 49.

[62] Official Records of the 1974–1977 Geneva Humanitarian Law Conference, CDDH/SR.43, vol. VI, p. 259, para. 113.

[63] *Ibid.* at para. 116. [64] *Ibid.* at p. 260, para. 119.

the Conference had just taken'.[65] The representative of Pakistan drew the attention of the Conference to the ruling of the President at the earlier meeting of the Plenary.[66] The representative of Sri Lanka remarked,

> [A] separate vote on [the reference to the 1954 Hague Convention] would not amount to a reconsideration of the proposal to delete it; the present request for such a vote merely reflected the fact that a simple majority of delegations did not agree with the phrase in question. To avoid a procedural debate, however, he would withdraw his proposal for a separate vote and simply request that a vote be taken on the article as a whole.[67]

At a meeting of the Commission of the Whole of the 1975 Montreal International Conference on Air Law, a delegate claimed that the Commission had earlier decided to add a certain phrase to the text and that therefore a proposal to have a separate vote on that text 'amounted to a reopening of the debate'. The President rejected the claim ruling that 'any delegation had the right to request a separate vote on a motion'.[68]

COMMENT

It would seem that the correct ruling is that a delegation may request a separate vote on a paragraph, notwithstanding the defeat of a previous motion to delete the paragraph.

17.14 Status of Preambular Parts of an Amendment When Operative Parts Have Been Rejected

At a 1980 meeting of a committee of the UNGA, a separate vote was held on parts of a series of amendments. The preambular parts were adopted and the operative parts were rejected. The delegate of France then claimed that the Committee should apply the rule in Rule 129(89) of the rules of procedure that states, 'If all operative parts of the proposal or of the amendment have been rejected, the proposal or the amendment shall be considered to have been rejected as a whole.' The Legal Counsel of the UN

65 Official Records of the 1974–1977 Geneva Humanitarian Law Conference, CDDH/SR.53, vol. VII, p. 142, para. 8.

66 *Ibid.* at p. 143, para. 10. (The earlier ruling of the President had been in CDDH/SR.43, para. 119.)

67 Official Records of the 1974–1977 Geneva Humanitarian Law Conference, CDDH/SR.53, vol. VII, p. 143, para. 11.

68 Commission of the Whole, 1975 Montreal International Conference on Air Law, 24th Meeting, ICAO. Doc. 9154-LC/174–1, paras. 84, 85 (1975).

was consulted and he gave his opinion that, although grouped together, the amendments were not one amendment but a series of amendments, and therefore the amendments to the preambular parts of the resolution should be considered as having been adopted.[69] The Chairman, who accepted the opinion of the Legal Counsel, also gave his interpretation as to Rule 129. The Chairman stated that when 'the operative part of a particular amendment is rejected, then whatever remains is also automatically rejected'.[70] According to the Chairman's ruling, Rule 129 does not differentiate between the preamble and other parts of a proposal being amended. The rule applies to the operative part of the amendment itself. The Chairman illustrated his ruling by quoting the amendment, which read,

> Urging all States to refrain from the development, production and deployment of new types of chemical munitions, in particular binary and multi-component munitions.

The Chairman pointed out that in this amendment, the operative part is 'to refrain from'. If that were to be defeated, then necessarily the whole amendment would automatically be rejected.[71] Rule 129 refers to a situation where 'all operative parts of the proposal or of the amendment have been rejected'. One delegate questioned the meaning of the addition of the word 'amendment'.[72] The Legal Counsel of the UN replied, 'At the end of the discussions in the Sixth Committee, the words "or of an amendment" were added [to Rule 129] out of the blue, and we could not find any explanation except that the addition may have been made mainly for editorial reasons'.[73] Rule 57 of the UN Model Rules omits the phrase 'or of an amendment' as the word 'proposal' in the UN Model Rules explicitly includes amendments.

17.15 Can a Motion for a Separate Vote Be Amended?

At a 1958 session of the UNGA, one delegate requested a separate vote on a particular paragraph, and another delegate requested a separate vote only on a part of the paragraph. The President observed that the second

[69] UN GAOR, 1st Committee, 35th Session, 47th Meeting, pp. 73–75, 48th Meeting, pp. 3–4, UN Docs. A/C.1/35/PV.47 (1980), A/C.1/35/PV.48 (1980).

[70] UN GAOR, 1st Committee, 35th Session, 47th Meeting, p. 87, UN Doc. A/C.1/35/PV.47 (1980).

[71] *Ibid.* [72] *Ibid.* at p. 96.

[73] UN GAOR, 1st Committee, 35th Session, 48th Meeting, p. 3, UN Doc. A/C.1/35/PV.48 (1980).

proposal was an amendment to the first. The question was not resolved because the Assembly decided to have no separate votes at all.[74]

COMMENT

It is submitted that the President was incorrect in allowing an amendment to a motion for a separate vote since such a motion is not amenable to being amended. The correct procedure should have been to have treated them as two separate motions to be voted on in the order of their submission or in any other order the Assembly might have decided.

17.16 Voting on the Proposal as a Whole Following a Separate Vote

17.16.1 If All Parts of the Proposal Were Rejected

If all parts of proposal are rejected, the rules of procedure of the UNGA are unequivocal. They state,

> *Rule 89*
>
> ... If all operative parts of the proposal or of the amendment have been rejected, the proposal or the amendment shall be considered to have been rejected as a whole.

The earlier UNGA rule[75] stated that 'the resulting proposal shall be put to a final vote in its entirety'. This phrasing led to claims that every resolution must be voted on even if its constituent elements had been rejected.

At the early sessions of the UNGA there was conflicting practice, with some presiding officers putting resolutions to the vote even when all their constitutive paragraphs had been rejected[76] and other presiding officers refraining from putting such resolutions to the vote.[77]

During a 1953 meeting of the UNGA, the Assembly adopted several paragraphs of the preamble of a draft resolution, but rejected the sole operative paragraph. The President ruled that no vote should be taken on the resolution as a whole. The President's ruling was upheld.[78]

[74] UN GAOR, Plenary, 13th Session, 792nd Meeting, paras. 215, 250–254, UN Doc. A/PV.792 (1958).

[75] Rule 118 of the UNGA rules of procedure.

[76] UN GAOR, 1st Committee, 3rd Session, Part I, 171st Meeting, p. 258 (1948); UN GAOR, Plenary, 3rd Session, Part II, 215th Meeting, pp. 526–527 (1949).

[77] See UN GAOR, Plenary, 3rd Session, Part II, 218th Meeting, p. 596 (1949); UN GAOR, 1st Committee, 3rd Session, Part I, 192nd Meeting, pp. 536–538 (1948).

[78] UN GAOR, Plenary, 8th Session, 455th Meeting, paras. 70–74, UN Doc. A/PV.455 (1953).

17.16.2 If Parts of a Proposal Are Accepted or Rejected

17.16.2.1 Practice in the UN

The rules of procedure of the UNGA state,

> *Rule 89*
>
> *Division of Proposals and Amendments*
>
> ... If the motion for division is carried, those parts of the proposal or of the amendment that are approved shall then be put to the vote as a whole.

In 1983, the UN Office of Legal Affairs gave its opinion that

> a final vote must be taken on the proposal as a whole (i.e., on the sum of all the parts adopted separately). This is so whether the division was a formal one ... or is merely done informally. It is also immaterial whether the separate parts were adopted by votes or by consensus. The body as a whole must be given an opportunity of acting on (i.e., adopting or rejecting) the sum of all the separate parts.[79]

At a 2002 session of the UNGA, the delegate of Egypt informed the Assembly,

> My reading of this sentence is that if a part of a resolution is voted on, be it one paragraph or two paragraphs, then the whole resolution should be automatically put to a vote without the need for any delegation to request a vote. I understand that that has not been common practice in the Committee or in other Committees of the General Assembly, but I am afraid that that must change.[80]

At a 2003 meeting of the UNGA, separate votes were held on a number of paragraphs. The Chairman then ruled that there must be a vote on the draft resolution as a whole even though there had been no objection to holding the separate vote and that 'there was no need for a vote to be requested' as the rules of procedure required such a vote. An appeal against the Chairman's ruling was rejected.[81] A 2007 opinion of the Secretary of the Third Committee of UNGA also seems to support the

[79] Memorandum, 1 September 1983, UN Office of Legal Affairs to the Officer-in-Charge, Department of Political Affairs, Trusteeship and Decolonisation. 1983 UN Jur. Y.B. 171, 172.

[80] UN GAOR, Plenary, 57th Session, 77th Meeting, UN Doc. A/57/PV.77 (2002).

[81] UN GAOR, 3rd Committee, 58th Session, 61st Meeting, UN Doc. A/C.3/58/SR.61, p. 7 (2003).

automatic requirement for a vote if there had been a separate vote on part of a resolution.[82]

At a 2008 meeting of the Third Committee of the UNGA a delegate stated that 'it had been the past practice of the Committee, in case of a separate vote under rule 129 of the rules of procedure, to put the entire draft resolution to a vote'. The Secretary of the Committee responded that the rule only applied if objection had been expressed to the motion for a separate vote, and the Chairman ruled accordingly. A delegate insisted on having a vote on the Resolution as a whole; the Chairman before putting the issue to a vote stated that 'the request for a vote was was not linked either to his ruling or to rule 129'.[83]

At a 2009 meeting of the UNGA Third Committee a delegation stated that 'by taking a vote under rule 129' [Division of proposals], the result of the vote being that the paragraph in question was retained, 'the Committee had adopted the resolution as a whole'. The Secretary of the Committee responded that 'voting in favour of one part of a draft resolution was not the same as adopting the entire resolution'.[84]

At the same 2009 meeting of the UNGA Third Committee a delegation requested a separate vote on a paragraph; there was no objection to holding this separate vote, but the result of the vote was that the paragraph in question was retained. The Secretary explained that when a vote taken under rule 129 'resulted in the retention of the part of the draft voted upon, the text as a whole could be adopted without a vote' unless a delegation specifically requested a vote. According to the Secretary, a vote is mandatory only if there had been an objection to the request for a separate vote.[85]

The practical guide to the UNGA published by the Permanent Mission of Switzerland to the UN also apparently does not call for an automatic vote. It reads, 'A paragraph vote will be immediately followed by the consideration of the whole draft resolution/decision. Adoption without a vote remains the assumption.'[86]

[82] UN GAOR, 3rd Committee, 62nd Session, 51st Meeting, UN Doc. A/C.3/62/SR.51, para. 111 (2007).

[83] UN GAOR, 3rd Committee, 63rd Session, 45th meeting, UN Doc. A/C.3/63/SR.45, paras. 75.

[84] UN GAOR, 3rd Committee, 64th Session, 46th Meeting, UN Doc. A/C.3/64/SR.46, paras. 42, 43, (2009).

[85] UN GAOR, 3rd Committee, 64th Session, 46th Meeting, UN Doc. A/C.3/64/SR.46, paras. 45, 47, (2009).

[86] The Practical Guide to the UNGA published by the Permanent Mission of Switzerland, para. 3.5, www.unitar.org/ny/sites/unitar.org.ny/files/UN_PGA_Handbook.pdf.

COMMENT

Although the wording of rule 129 (89 in Plenary) is not unambiguous, it seems to reflect common sense that if the UNGA or a UNGA Committee is willing to adopt a resolution by consensus, the rules of procedure should not be interpreted as requiring a vote.

17.16.2.2 Practice in Conferences

During the 1958 Law of the Sea Conference, a certain amendment consisted of two phrases. The first was adopted and the second rejected. The Mexican representative said that 'the amendment should be put to the vote as a whole'.[87] The Chairman ruled 'that it was unnecessary to put the amendment to the vote as a whole since it consisted of two phrases which were mutually independent'.[88] This ruling was not challenged, although it appears to have been an erroneous decision. During the same conference, on a different amendment, the representative of the United Kingdom submitted 'that as the only part of the Canadian proposal with any direct bearing on the article had been rejected, the Chairman should declare under rule 39 that the proposal had been defeated in its entirety'.[89] The Chairman 'overruled the United Kingdom representative's submission'.[90] The Chairman's ruling was not challenged.

During the 1978 Hamburg Conference on Carriage by Sea, the Chairman put to vote a proposal that consisted of two separate elements.[91] After the vote, several delegates stated that they were under the impression that only a part of the proposal was being voted on. After a procedural discussion, the Chairman put to the vote again, this time separately, the two parts of the proposal.[92] Although one delegate expressed 'reservations concerning the voting procedure',[93] no delegate made any procedural proposal on the issue.

At a committee meeting of the 1980 Vienna Conference on International Sale of Goods, two amendments submitted to the basic document

[87] Official Records of the 1958 Law of the Sea Conference, 34th Meeting of Committee I, vol. III, p. 101, paras. 34–38, UN Doc. A/CONF.13/39 (1958).

[88] *Ibid.* at para. 37.

[89] Official Records of the 1958 Law of the Sea Conference, 56th Meeting of Committee I, vol. III, p. 177, para. 29, UN Doc. A/CONF.13/39 (1958).

[90] *Ibid.* at para. 30.

[91] Official Records of the 1978 Hamburg Conference on Carriage by Sea, p. 5, para. 29, UN Doc. A/CONF.89/C.2/SR.11 (1978).

[92] *Ibid.* at p. 6, para. 40. [93] *Ibid.* at para. 44.

(a UNCITRAL text) were rejected. The representative of Sweden then proposed that the Committee vote on the basic document. The representative of Norway suggested, however, that 'any delegation that felt that an affirmative vote was needed on a particular article could ask for a vote to be taken. Otherwise the article could be regarded as tacitly adopted.'[94] The Chairman stated that 'to require a vote to be taken on each article was tantamount to a proposal to delete them all'.[95] After an unrecorded procedural discussion, the Chairman ruled that 'as there appeared to be a majority against both the Swedish proposal and the Norwegian proposal, he would, if there was no objection, consider them rejected'.[96]

17.17 Voting on Parts of a Resolution Rejected in a Separate Vote

The UNGA rules of procedure stipulate,

> *Rule 89*
>
> *Division of Proposals and Amendments*
>
> ... If the motion for division is carried, those parts of the proposal or of the amendment that are approved shall then be put to the vote as a whole.

A similar phrase appears in the UN Model Rules.[97] Prior to the inclusion of this phrase in the UNGA rules of procedure,[98] there had been occasions when parts of a resolution that had been rejected on a separate vote were nevertheless put to the vote with the resolution as a whole.

At a 1952 meeting of the UNGA, a separate vote was held on the two paragraphs of a Pakistani proposal. One paragraph was accepted, the other rejected. The Chairman then proposed putting the resolution as a whole to the vote. As a result of the intervention of several delegates, the Chairman changed his ruling and put to the vote only that paragraph of the resolution that had been approved.[99]

94 Official Records of the 1980 Vienna Conference on International Sale of Goods, Summary Records of the 13th Meeting of Committee I, p. 304, para. 38, UN Doc. A/CONF.97/C.1/SR.13 (1980).

95 *Ibid.* at para. 37.

96 *Ibid.* at para. 39.

97 Rule 57 of the UN Model Rules.

98 UNGA Resolution 362 (IV) of 22 October 1949.

99 UN GAOR, 1st Committee, 7th Session, 542nd Meeting, paras. 59–62, 64, 65, UN Doc. A/C.1/7/SR.542 (1952). The resolution as a whole was rejected.

17.18 A Motion to Vote on the Text as a Whole, Paragraph by Paragraph, after Each Paragraph Had Been Earlier Voted on Separately

At a 1952 meeting of the UNGA, a UK draft resolution was voted on paragraph by paragraph. After the Chairman called for a vote on the resolution as a whole, the US delegate requested that it be voted on paragraph by paragraph since it had been impossible to anticipate, during the debate, the ultimate form that the draft resolution would take. A number of delegations pointed out that this would be tantamount to a reconsideration. The US motion for division was rejected.[100]

17.19 Voting on the Remainder of a Proposal after Voting on Separate Paragraphs

At a 1951 meeting of the UNGA, a separate vote was held on two paragraphs of a draft resolution on admission of new members. After the vote, the Chairman put the remainder of the resolution to a vote and then put the resolution as a whole to a vote.[101] It is submitted that the vote on the remainder of the resolution, prior to the vote on the resolution as a whole, was an unnecessary vote.

COMMENT

The correct procedure would appear to be that, after a separate vote, all parts of a proposal that have been approved, or not subjected to a separate vote, shall be put to the vote as a whole. If all the operative parts have been rejected, the proposal as a whole is deemed to have been rejected.

17.20 Priority as between Voting on Amendments and Voting on a Separate Part of a Proposal

The UN Model Rules stipulate,

> *Rule 59*
>
> 2. When the Conference decides, in accordance with rule 57, to consider an extensive text in convenient portions (such as paragraphs or articles),

[100] UN GAOR, 6th Committee, 7th Session, 312th Meeting, paras. 3–6, UN Doc. A/C.6/7/SR.312 (1952).

[101] UN GAOR, 1st Committee, 6th Session, 506th Meeting, paras. 71–73, UN Doc. A/C.1/6/SR.506 (1951).

> each of these shall be treated as a separate proposal for the purpose of paragraph 1.[102]

Where a decision has been taken to conduct separate voting on parts of a proposal, the question arises as to whether, before commencing voting on the separate parts of the proposal, voting has to be conducted first on all amendments to the whole proposal.

At a 1954 meeting of the UNGA, a decision had been made to vote on a draft resolution, paragraph by paragraph. Since there were amendments to some paragraphs, it was decided by the President to vote paragraph by paragraph until reaching the paragraphs to which there were amendments and then vote on the amendments to those paragraphs before voting on the paragraph itself.[103]

In a situation where amendments were proposed for some paragraphs of a draft resolution while a separate vote had been requested for other paragraphs, the 1971 session of the UNGA decided that the amendments should be voted on prior to the separate vote being held. The Legal Adviser stated that, in his opinion, it would be 'peculiar', but the French and Tunisian representatives pointed out that this was regular UN practice.[104]

At a meeting of the 1977 Conference on Territorial Asylum, the Chairman ruled that 'he intended to proceed by division, putting to the vote in turn, the amendments relating to each paragraph or subparagraph'.[105]

There are some examples in the early sessions of the UNGA where voting was completed on all amendments prior to the voting on separate parts of a proposal.[106] This does not, however, appear to have been a common practice.

COMMENT

The common practice is that where a motion has been passed for separate votes, each portion subject to a separate vote is to be treated as a separate proposal. Amendments to that separate portion, and to that portion

[102] Paragraph 1 deals with order of voting on amendments.

[103] UN GAOR, Plenary, 9th Session, 503rd Meeting, para. 105, UN Doc. A/PV.503 (1954).

[104] UN GAOR, Plenary, 26th Session, 2017th Meeting, paras. 147, 150, 152, 154, 155, UN Doc. A/PV.2017 (1971).

[105] Summary Records of the 16th Meeting of the Committee of the Whole of the 1977 Conference on Territorial Asylum, para. 2, UN Doc. A/CONF.78/C.1/SR.16 (1977).

[106] UN GAOR, Plenary, 1st Session, 54th Meeting, pp. 1099–1102, UN Doc. A/PV.54 (1946); UN GAOR, 3rd Committee, 6th Session, 402nd Meeting, para. 42, UN Doc. A/C.3/6/SR.402 (1952).

only, are voted on prior to the voting on the portion.[107] According to this practice, if there are no amendments submitted to a separate portion of a proposal, that portion may be voted on prior to the voting on amendments submitted to other portions of the proposal.

17.21 Combining the Vote on Several Proposals

At the Third Law of the Sea Conference, the delegation of Peru proposed amending the draft rules of procedure to allow that '[a]ny representative may move that two or more proposals be considered as related questions and voted on jointly'.[108] The proposal was not adopted.

At the 1975 Conference of the ILO, a delegation requested combining the vote on several related proposals concerning the invitation of national liberation movements to participate in the work of the Conference. The Legal Adviser was asked whether this was legal and gave his opinion:

> Each of those proposals is separate and the proposals do not necessarily follow on from one another in their details: they are separate proposals submitted to you, although they have some mutual relationship in substance, but one is no way necessarily subordinated to another; each contains distinct elements. I believe, since any amendment to an existing text – and these are amendments to the Standing Orders of the Conference – should be voted on separately, that a separate vote on each of these proposals ought to be taken by the Conference.[109]

When it was suggested that the vote be held twice, once on each group of amendments, the Legal Adviser responded that he did not hold that

> a decision in which you would group in a first vote the changes to be made to the Standing Orders of the General Conference, and [in] a second vote, the modifications to be made in the Rules for regional conferences would be necessarily unlawful. The problem is that some delegates may wish to vote on a provision in the one group and in another way on the other provisions. Thus as I said in my first opinion, there should be a separate vote on each of the proposals before you.[110]

[107] See UN GAOR, 1st Committee, 2nd Special Session, 141st Meeting, pp. 261, 262, UN Doc. A/C.1/2/SR.141 (1948).

[108] Third Law of the Sea Conference, Peru: amendment to the draft rules of procedure, UN Doc. A/CONF.62/13 (1973).

[109] ILO Conference, 60th Session, Geneva 1975, Record of Proceedings, pp. 252, 253.

[110] *Ibid.* at p. 253.

The President consequently decided to have a separate vote on each amendment, stating,

> I would like to propose that we take the path of stronger traction rather than the path of least resistance to meet with the exacting standards that the Legal Adviser has put forward concerning the legality of the acts of this Conference in accordance with its own Standing Orders.[111]

17.22 Separate Votes on Two Amendments Submitted Together

At a 1993 General Conference of the IAEA, the Chairman announced that 'the delegate of Iraq had proposed two amendments to the draft resolution' and that the delegate of Iraq had 'also requested that separate roll-call votes be taken on each of these two amendments and on the text as a whole'.[112] The US delegate, based on the right to object to a separate vote, objected to the request of Iraq. The Iraqi delegate pointed out that the objection was not in order 'since he was not asking for a separate vote on each part of the draft resolution but for separate votes on two amendments'.[113] The President, by implication, accepted the Iraqi position.

Szasz points out that the question whether or not a number of amendments proposed by the same delegation(s) are one amendment or more (for the purpose of voting) has come up with some frequency. Szasz quotes the UN Legal Counsel as suggesting that this question should be decided by the form of the submission. Thus if the submission refers to one amendment, even though it is to separate provisions, it should be treated as such, and vice versa.[114]

17.23 Does a Decision to Have Separate Discussions on Parts of a Proposal Also Imply Holding Separate Votes?

The 1981 World Health Assembly was considering a number of resolutions on the periodicity and duration of World Health Assemblies. Delegations pointed out that if it were to be decided to hold assemblies at less frequent intervals, this would necessarily influence the position of States as to the duration of such assemblies. It was decided therefore to discuss first the issue of periodicity, and later the issue of duration. When the time

[111] *Ibid.*

[112] Official Records of the 362nd Plenary Meeting of the 37th Session of the General Conference of the IAEA, p. 13, para. 51, IAEA Doc. GC(XXXVII)/OR.362 (1993).

[113] *Ibid.* at para. 53.

[114] Paul Szasz in a note to the author, April 1996.

came to vote on the issues, the Soviet delegation argued that 'the Committee's decision to divide discussion of the topic into two parts did not necessarily affect the order of voting... [S]ince the two parts of the discussion formed a single item, the draft resolution furthest from the original should be put to the vote first.'[115] Other delegations supported the Soviet position. The Chairman ruled that the vote be taken first on those parts of the resolutions and amendments referring to periodicity, and then on the remaining parts of the resolutions and amendments thereto. The ruling was not challenged.[116]

17.24 A Separate Vote on Parts of a Procedural Motion

There is no logical reason why a delegation should not be able to request a separate vote on parts of a procedural motion. Rules of procedure refer in general to division of 'a proposal', a phrase that applies both to procedural motions and to substantive proposals.

At the Vienna Conference on the Law of Treaties, a procedural proposal was submitted to defer the vote on an amendment and to transfer the amendment to the Drafting Committee. A motion was then proposed to hold separate votes on the two parts of the procedural motion. There was objection to the motion, but no State appears to have raised a claim that a procedural motion, as such, cannot be subject to division, and the motion for division was adopted.[117]

[115] Summary Records of the 9th Meeting of Committee 'B' of the 34th World Health Assembly, pp. 304, 305, WHA34/1981/REC/3 (1981).

[116] *Ibid* at p. 307.

[117] Official Records of the Vienna Conference on the Law of Treaties – First Session, 57th Meeting of the Committee of the Whole, p. 333, para. 75, UN Doc. A/CONF.39/11 (1968).

18

Conduct of Voting: Interruption of Voting and Correction of Vote

18.1 Interruption of Voting

All rules of procedure recognise the principle that voting should not be interrupted except on a point of order concerning the actual conduct of voting. At the UNGA the rule has also been interpreted as prohibiting campaigning or distribution of campaign material once voting on elections has begun.[1]

18.2 Interruption When Voting on Individual Proposals

The 1960 Law of the Sea Conference adopted the Secretariat's proposal for the inclusion, in the article on conduct during voting, of the following definition:

> *Rule 38*
> *Conduct during Voting*
> 2. For the purpose of this rule 'voting' refers to the voting on each individual proposal or amendment.[2]

A discussion took place on a Mexican amendment to omit this definition from the rules applicable to committees. During the discussion, the representative of the Secretariat explained the background to the definition, stating,

> [A]lthough the substance of the new paragraph 2 of rule 38 was not explicitly stated in rules 90 and 129 of the General Assembly's rules of procedure – on conduct during voting – the Secretariat's intention had been to stress the importance of completing the voting on individual proposals and amendments. At the General Assembly and at international conferences held under United Nations auspices, delegations often submit documents

[1] UN GAOR, Plenary, 57th Session, UN Doc. A/57/PV.35, p. 2 (2002).
[2] Rules of procedure of the 1960 Law of the Sea Conference, UN Doc. A/CONF.19/7 (1960).

> described as a proposal, consisting of a series of proposals or amendments. Such composite proposals had sometimes been regarded as a single proposal for the purpose of voting, and difficulties had arisen when a number of separate amendments or proposals were not intimately linked and the process of voting could not be finished until the series had been exhausted.[3]

The definition was adopted in the rules of procedure of the 1961 Vienna Conference on Diplomatic Relations,[4] but has apparently not been included in the rules of procedure of subsequent conferences. To this author, it seems a useful addition to rules of procedure.

18.3 When Does Voting Commence?

For purposes of 'interruption of vote', the UNGA rules of procedure use the phrase: 'After the President has announced the beginning of voting.'[5] The UN Model Rules define the commencement of voting as follows: 'After the President has announced the commencement of a vote.'[6] The UN Office of Legal Affairs, in a 1983 opinion, stated that the period commences when 'the presiding officer actually initiates the voting process by calling for the casting of votes or ballots on a particular question'.[7]

At a 1974 meeting of the UNGA, during a discussion on budgets, the Chairman called upon representatives to explain their vote before the voting. At that stage the representative of the USSR proposed an oral amendment and the US delegate, speaking on a point of order, objected, claiming voting had begun. The representative of Algeria argued that no representative had yet spoken in explanation of vote; therefore voting had not yet begun. The Chairman ruled that he would allow the Soviet oral amendment.[8]

At a 1976 meeting of the UNGA, the Chairman announced the beginning of voting on a draft resolution. The representative of Canada,

[3] Official Records of the 1960 Law of the Sea Conference, Amendment by Mexico to the rules of procedure, UN Doc. A/CONF.19/L.1 (1960), adopted by the Conference, Summary Records of the 2nd Plenary Meeting, p. 5, para. 21, UN Doc. A/CONF.19/8 (1960).

[4] Rule 39(2) of the rules of procedure of the 1961 Conference on Diplomatic Relations, UN Doc. A/CONF.20/14 (1961).

[5] Rule 88 of the UNGA rules of procedure.

[6] Rule 56 of the UN Model Rules.

[7] Memorandum, 10 November 1983, from Office of Legal Affairs to the Under-Secretary-General for Political and General Assembly Affairs. 1983 UN Jur. Y.B. 174, 176, UN Doc. ST/LEG/SER.C/21 (1983).

[8] UN GAOR, 5th Committee, 29th Session, 1658th Meeting, paras. 37–42, UN Doc. A/C.5/29/SR.1658 (1974).

speaking on a point of order, requested a postponement of the voting, stating that he had asked for the floor before the Chairman announced the beginning of voting. The Chairman ruled that in view of the special circumstances he would allow the motion.[9] The Chairman did not specify if 'special circumstances' referred to the fact that the floor had been requested prior to his announcement of the beginning of the voting.

At a 1976 meeting of a UNGA committee, the Chairman announced that the Committee was 'proceeding to vote'. He then allowed a revision of a proposal and a subsequent motion to adjourn the debate. When his ruling was questioned, the Chairman replied that 'we have not yet started the voting procedure'.[10]

At a 1980 meeting of a UNGA committee, during a discussion on arms control, the Chairman made the following announcement before proceeding with the voting process:

> May I also draw the attention of the Committee to the fact that it is a long-standing practice to consider that voting in the sense used in rule 128 consists of and encompasses explanation of vote before the vote and after the vote. Therefore, it should be understood that a vote on a draft resolution begins when the Chairman calls on the first speaker wishing to explain his vote before the vote.[11]

At a 1980 meeting of a UNGA committee, during a discussion on the 'good offices' role of the UN Secretary-General, the Chairman allowed a motion not to vote on a proposal, notwithstanding that the voting process had commenced. The representative of Ireland, who had proposed the motion, commented subsequently 'that, as his delegation interpreted the rules of procedure of the General Assembly, the Committee could decide to interrupt the voting process at any time as long as the results of the vote were not known'.[12] No delegation commented on this unusual interpretation by the representative of Ireland.

At a 1984 meeting of a UNGA committee, during a discussion on the Conference on Disarmament, the Chairman announced, 'We now turn to

[9] UN GAOR, 2nd Committee, 31st Session, 65th Meeting, paras. 33, 35, 36, UN Doc. A/C.2/31/SR.65 (1976).

[10] UN GAOR, 1st Committee, 31st Session, 49th Meeting, pp. 11, 16, 18–21, UN Doc. A/C.1/31/SR.49 (1976).

[11] UN GAOR, 1st Committee, 35th Session, 37th Meeting, pp. 13–15, UN Doc. A/C.1/35/SR.37 (1980).

[12] UN GAOR, 3rd Committee, 35th Session, 82nd Meeting, para. 66, UN Doc. A/C.3/35/SR.82 (1980).

draft resolution . . . .'[13] The Chairman then gave the floor to a delegate to explain his vote. A representative, on a point of order, objected to granting a right of explanation of vote, claiming that voting had commenced. The Chairman ruled that 'the voting procedure proper had not started'.[14]

At a 1986 meeting of a UNGA committee, during a discussion on the trade embargo against Nicaragua, the Chairman announced that 'he would ask the Committee to take a decision' on a question raised by the representative of Nicaragua as to whether a proposal was an independent proposal or an amendment.[15] At the request of a representative, the Chairman subsequently asked the Legal Counsel for an opinion on the question. Two representatives objected to referring the matter to the Legal Counsel, claiming this could not be done 'at that stage' (as voting was in progress).[16] The Chairman ruled that 'he had not announced that the voting had commenced. He had ruled that the Committee should take a decision on the Nicaraguan motion, but that did not prevent it from hearing the Legal Counsel first.'[17]

At a 1990 meeting of the UNGA, at the stage where the Assembly was voting on resolutions adopted by committees, the President had read out the title of a draft resolution concerning Kuwait, but had not yet referred to the issue of voting on it. The representative of Iraq, on a point of order, submitted that the Assembly had no competence to deal with the draft resolution as it was in violation of the UN Charter. The representative of Kuwait, on a point of order, interrupted the delegate of Iraq and claimed that 'we are already in the process of voting, and if a matter is to be raised it must concern the conduct of the voting'.[18] The President allowed the representative of Iraq to continue with his statement.

At a 2008 meeting of the Third Committee of the UNGA, the Secretary of the Committee gave his opinion that 'the voting procedure itself had not yet begun' as 'the Chairman had not yet announced that a recorded vote had been requested'.[19]

[13] UN GAOR, 1st Committee, 39th Session, 47th Meeting, p. 41, UN Doc. A/C.1/39/SR.47 (1984).

[14] *Ibid.*

[15] UN GAOR, 2nd Committee, 41st Session, 33rd Meeting, para. 7, UN Doc. A/C.2/41/SR.33 (1986).

[16] *Ibid.* at para. 12. [17] *Ibid.* at para. 14.

[18] UN GAOR, Plenary, 45th Session, 69th Meeting, p. 49, UN Doc. A/45/PV.69 (Provisional) (1991).

[19] UN GAOR, 3rd Committee, 63rd Session, 44th Meeting, UN Doc A/C.3/63/SR.44 para. 108 (2008).

At a meeting of the 1973 Rome Air Law Conference, when the President announced his intention of putting Article 1 to a vote, a delegate proposed amendment of the rules of procedure to permit the vote to be taken by secret ballot.[20] After an objection was submitted by a delegate on the ground that the voting process had already started, the President ruled that 'the preamble having been approved, the voting stage on Article 1 had begun and no change in voting methods could be made until it had been completed'.[21]

18.3.1 When Does Voting Commence during a Connected Series of Voting?

At a 1980 meeting of a UNGA committee, it was decided to vote on two resolutions together. After the vote on the first resolution, the Algerian delegation requested permission to submit an amendment to the second resolution. The issue arose as to when the voting had commenced on the second resolution. The Chairman ruled that the proposed amendment was inadmissible as voting had commenced.[22] The Legal Counsel of the UN was requested to submit an opinion. The opinion of Counsel was that 'the Chairman had given the floor to the representative of Mozambique to explain his vote before the vote on [the second resolution]. The voting process had begun at that moment, and that voting could not now be interrupted except for points of order in connexion with the actual conduct of the voting.'[23]

In a 1983 opinion, the UN Office of Legal Affairs wrote, 'In respect of a connected series of votes, it follows from the above that the first sentence of Rule 88 [of the UNGA rules of procedure] is not intended to cover the entire period during which several votes are taken including the intervals between such votes (i.e., between two amendments to the same proposal or even between two ballots for the same post).'[24] The opinion continues by stating that other restrictions may apply in the period between

[20] Minutes of the 9th Meeting of the Plenary of the 1973 Rome Air Law Conference, para. 12, ICAO Doc. 9225-LC/178 (1973).

[21] *Ibid.* at para. 13.

[22] UN GAOR, 4th Committee, 35th Session, 22nd Meeting, para. 20, UN Doc. A/C.4/35/SR.22 (1980).

[23] *Ibid.* at para. 24.

[24] Memorandum, 10 November 1983, from Office of Legal Affairs to the Under-Secretary-General for Political and General Assembly Affairs. 1983 UN Jur. Y.B. 174, 176, UN Doc. ST/LEG/SER.C/21 (1983).

connected votes, these restrictions emanating from the closure of debate or from specific voting instructions of the presiding officer.

18.3.2 When Does Voting Commence in Elections?

At a 1955 meeting of the UNGA, during elections to the Security Council, the President allowed a motion for suspension of the meeting after he had called the tellers to come forward to the ballot box but before votes had been cast. The Chairman ruled that the motion was in order as voting had not yet commenced.[25]

18.3.3 When Does Voting Commence in a Vote Paragraph by Paragraph?

At a 1949 meeting of a UNGA committee, the Chairman denied the right of a delegation to submit an oral amendment to a paragraph on which voting had not yet commenced. The Chairman based his ruling on the reasoning that, although voting was being done paragraph by paragraph, voting on the resolution as a whole had commenced.[26]

At a 1974 meeting of the UNGA, the President allowed a motion by Iraq for adjournment of the meeting in a situation where he had announced the commencement of voting, there had been a separate vote on two paragraphs of a draft resolution and the Assembly was discussing whether to proceed with a vote on the resolution as a whole.[27]

18.3.4 When Does Voting End?

The rules of procedure of the UNGA and of earlier conferences do not define when the process of voting ends. The UN Model Rules[28] and a number of rules of procedure of recent conferences refer to restrictions on conduct during voting 'until the results of the vote have been announced'.[29] This phrase has not aroused controversy and apparently

[25] UN GAOR, Plenary, 10th Session, 534th Meeting, para. 18, UN Doc. A/PV.534 (1955).

[26] UN GAOR, 4th Committee, 4th Session, 98th Meeting, para. 54, UN Doc. A/C.4/4/SR.98 (1949).

[27] UN GAOR, Plenary, 29th Session, 2301st Meeting, paras. 496, 497, 504, 505, 507, UN Doc. A/PV.2301 (1974).

[28] Rule 56.

[29] See Rule 38 of the rules of procedure of the Diplomatic Conference on an International Ban on Anti-Personnel Land Mines, APL/CRP.2 (1997); Rule 39 of the rules of procedure

reflects conference practice even where it is not explicitly stated in the rules of procedure.

18.4 Interruption of Voting

The relevant part of the UNGA rule of procedure states,

> *Rule 88*
> *Conduct during Voting*
> After the President has announced the beginning of voting, no representative shall interrupt the voting, except on a point of order in connection with the actual conduct of the voting.

The UN Model Rule is substantially the same.[30]

No such rule appeared in the rules of procedure of the League of Nations nor in the rules prepared by the Preparatory Commission. The 1947 Report on the Procedures and Organisation of the UNGA, in its comment when introducing this rule, stated, 'It was considered important that the procedure for conducting votes should be defined with precision in this rule.'[31]

18.4.1 Is an Adjournment of a Meeting an Interruption of the Voting Procedure?

At a 1952 meeting of a UNGA committee, the Chairman refused to allow a motion to adjourn the meeting, since, as he explained, voting had begun.[32]

of the UN Diplomatic Conference of Plenipotentiaries on the Establishment of an International Criminal Court, UN Doc. A/CONF.183/13 (1998); Rule 38 of the rules of procedure of the IMO Diplomatic Conference on Arrest of Ships, UN Doc. A/CONF.188/2 (1998); Rule 41 of the rules of procedure of the Third UN Conference on the Least Developed Countries, UN Doc. A/CONF.191/4 (2001); Rule 33 of the rules of procedure of the Conference on Facilitating the Entry into Force of the Comprehensive Test Ban Treaty, CTBT-Art. XIV/2001/2 (2001); Rule18 of the rules of procedure of the Meeting of the States Parties to the Convention on the Prohibition of the Use, Stockpiling, Production and Transfer of Anti-Personnel Mines and on their Destruction, APLC/MSP.4/L.3 (2002).

30 Rule 56 of the UN Model Rules.

31 Report of the Committee on Procedures and Organisation, UN GAOR, 2nd Session, Annex 4, Part III, p. 1474, Comment on Rule 92 (present Rule 88 of the UNGA rules of procedure), UN Doc. A/388 (1947).

32 UN GAOR, 1st Committee, 7th Session, 510th Meeting, para. 81, UN Doc. A/C.1/7/SR.510 (1952).

At a 1974 meeting of the UNGA, during the process of voting, a delegation moved to adjourn the meeting. The delegate of Saudi Arabia, Mr Baroody, in his inimitable style, commented,

> Has rule 88[33] been forgotten? Anyone who felt that things were going against him during the voting could say, 'Let us adjourn.' The raison d'être of rule 88 is precisely to avoid such a situation. If the rule did not exist, there would be nothing to prevent anyone from saying, during the course of the voting, 'Let us adjourn; let us not continue voting.' We have been told that a motion for adjournment cannot be debated. I am not debating the motion for adjournment. The point is: Was the motion for adjournment in order, since the voting was in progress?[34]

The Chairman ruled that since there was a discussion on whether to vote on the resolution as a whole, the Committee was 'not in the process of voting' and the motion for adjournment was allowed.[35]

At a 1980 meeting of a UNGA committee, a decision was made to 'vote together' on two resolutions. The meeting was adjourned after the vote on the first resolution. At the subsequent meeting, the representative of Algeria requested permission to submit an amendment to the second resolution, arguing,

> Once the voting procedure had been initiated in accordance with rule 128, it should have been completed at the same meeting. The decision to adjourn the 21st meeting without the voting procedure having been completed had created a new legal situation. Firstly, it placed the continuation of the work outside the scope of rule 128 and, secondly, it opened up the possibility of making amendments.[36]

The Chairman ruled that 'the adjournment of the previous meeting did not constitute an interruption in the voting procedure, which continued to be subject to rule 128 of the rules of procedure'.[37]

At a 2010 meeting of a committee of the World Health Assembly, the Legal Counsel gave this opinion: "with regard to adjourning the meeting

[33] Rule 88 of the UNGA rules of procedure: 'After the President has announced the beginning of voting, no representative shall interrupt the voting except on a point of order in connection with the actual conduct of the voting.'

[34] UN GAOR, Plenary, 29th Session, 2301st Meeting, paras. 496–502, UN Doc. A/PV.2301 (1974).

[35] *Ibid.* at paras. 503–507.

[36] UN GAOR, 4th Committee, 35th Session, 22nd Meeting, para. 2, UN Doc. A/C.4/35/SR.22 (1980).

[37] *Ibid.* at para. 3.

during a vote, previous practice had been to consider such adjournments compatible with the Rules of Procedure if voting had reached a stage where it could be interrupted without disruption, as in the present instance. The final decision must rest with the Committee'.[38]

18.4.2 Is a Suspension of a Meeting an Interruption of the Voting Procedure?

At a 1998 UNGA meeting, a chairman refused to accept a motion to suspend a meeting for ten minutes as the committee was 'in the midst of voting process'.[39]

At a 1988 meeting of the World Health Assembly, after the President had announced the beginning of voting, the representative of the Federal Republic of Germany, on a point of order, moved the 'postponement of the vote' for a few minutes for consultations.[40] A representative objected, claiming that this would be an interruption of voting. The Legal Counsel gave his opinion that the German request was a motion for suspension of the debate and was not therefore 'a point of order in connection with the vote'.[41] The President consequently refused to allow the German motion.

At the 1963 Vienna Conference on Consular Relations, the UK representative requested a short suspension of the meeting in between the vote on two paragraphs of an amendment, in order for the sponsors to consider 'what should be done' in regard to the text.[42] The representative of Czechoslovakia pointed out that 'there was nothing in rule 27 of the rules of procedure on the suspension or adjournment of meetings, to imply that a representative could move the suspension of a meeting during voting'.[43] The representative of the United Kingdom then gave details of a possible oral amendment that he was considering. The Chairman ruled that the voting must proceed immediately. There was further discussion, which the Chairman said he felt was a challenge to his ruling. The ruling was put to the vote and upheld.[44]

[38] Committee 'B', 63rd World Health Assembly, 6th Meeting, WHO Doc. WHA63/2010/REC3 p. 282 (2010).

[39] UN GAOR, 1st Committee, 53rd Session, 23rd Meeting, UN Doc. A/C.1/53/PV.23, p. 8 (1998).

[40] Verbatim Records of the 15th Plenary Meeting of the 41st World Health Assembly, p. 316, WHA41/1988/REC/2 (1988).

[41] *Ibid.*

[42] Official Records of the 1963 Vienna Conference on Consular Relations, 24th Meeting, Committee II, vol. I, pp. 370, 371, para. 27, UN Doc. A/CONF.25/16 (1963).

[43] *Ibid.* at para. 28. [44] *Ibid.* at para. 36.

18.4.3 Interruption of Voting between Votes on a Series of Amendments

The issue arose during the debate on the credentials of the Israel delegation to the 1982 session of the UNGA. The representative of Singapore claimed that

> once the process of voting has begun it cannot be interrupted. In other words, the Assembly cannot vote on one amendment and then suspend or adjourn the meeting and resume the voting at the next meeting. Once the Assembly has started voting on one amendment, it has to carry on until it has completed the process of voting.[45]

The Office of Legal Affairs was requested to submit an opinion on this issue. The opinion of the Legal Office was that

> in the normal practice of the General Assembly when the Assembly has commenced voting on a draft resolution, it completes action on it at the same meeting. However, this is not an invariable practice. As long as the Assembly completes a particular voting process, that has in the past been deemed sufficient. For example, if there were an amendment with sub-amendments, it would be necessary to dispose of the sub-amendments and the amendment in one particular voting process. However it would then be possible to adjourn a meeting and hold another meeting to complete the voting. I believe that has happened in quite a number of cases in the past where there have been a number of amendments to a draft resolution.[46]

The President then ruled, on the basis of the legal opinion, that the Assembly could proceed with the voting on the next amendment at a subsequent meeting.[47]

At the 1961 Vienna Conference on Diplomatic Relations, the delegate of Senegal submitted an oral sub-amendment to a ten-nation amendment. This was objected to on a point of order, it being argued that the President had announced the commencement of voting. The President consequently ruled the Senegalese sub-amendment as out of order. The French delegate appealed against the ruling, arguing that 'the term voting referred to the voting on each individual proposal or amendment, in the particular case, that meant the ten-year [*sic*] amendment on which the

[45] UN GAOR, Plenary, 37th Session, 43rd Meeting, para. 195, UN Doc. A/37/PV.43 (1982).
[46] *Ibid.* at para. 204. [47] *Ibid.* at p. 88.

Conference had not yet begun to vote'.[48] The appeal was sustained and the President's ruling overturned.

During the 1974 Prescription in Sale of Goods Conference, there arose an issue as to whether a discussion on the substance of an amendment was in order once the beginning of voting had been announced. The Chief of the International Trade Law Branch of the United Nations stated, 'It was the understanding of the Secretariat officials whom he had consulted on the matter that rule 38 (the relevant rule) forbade the interruption of a vote on an individual amendment, but did not preclude discussion between votes on a series of amendments.'[49]

18.4.4 Interruption of Voting for Points of Order

At a 1955 meeting of the Conference of the ILO, the President stated that, according to the opinion of the legal advisers, as the vote had begun he could not 'accept a point of order until the vote is terminated'.[50] The correct ruling should have been to add 'except in connection with the actual conduct of the voting'.

18.4.5 Interruption of Voting for Proposal Not to Vote

At a 1952 meeting of a UNGA committee, after the first part of a proposal had been rejected, the Chairman ruled that since voting had commenced, it was inadmissible to propose not to vote on the remainder of the proposal.[51]

At a 1980 meeting of a UNGA committee, during the discussion on chemical and bacteriological weapons, a number of amendments had been adopted. The representative of India then moved that the Committee should decide to take no vote on the amended resolution. The Legal Counsel of the UN, who was consulted, gave his opinion that, as the voting had commenced, such a motion was out of order. The

[48] Official Records of the 1961 Vienna Conference on Diplomatic Relations, 12th Plenary Meeting, vol. I, p. 48, paras. 11–18, UN Doc. A/CONF.20/14 (1961).

[49] Official Records of the 1974 Prescription in Sale of Goods Conference, Committee I, p. 166, para. 73, UN Doc. A/CONF.63/16 (1974). (There appears to have been only one amendment being voted on at the time.)

[50] International Labour Conference, 38th Session, Geneva 1955, Record of Proceedings, 4th sitting, p. 18. Article 5 of the Standing Orders of the Conference stipulates however, that, '[a] delegate may at any time rise to a point of order'.

[51] UN GAOR, 2nd Committee, 6th Session, 180th Meeting, para. 38, UN Doc. A/C.2/6/SR.180 (1952).

Chairman ruled in accordance with the Counsel's opinion.[52] At the same, 1980, session of the UNGA, in another committee, a different ruling was made, apparently without consulting the Legal Counsel. The Chairman allowed a motion by the representative of Ireland 'not to vote' on an amendment and on a resolution, even though voting had commenced on the amendments to the resolution.[53] The Chairman ruled that the motion 'could not be considered a point of order in connexion with the conduct of the voting',[54] but he nevertheless allowed the motion. The representative of Guinea-Bissau subsequently commented that 'the Committee, by voting on the Irish proposal, had contravened the rules of procedure. The Chairman had already announced that a vote would be taken on the Brazilian amendment, and it had not been possible for him to reverse his decision.'[55] The Chairman replied 'that he took notice of the comment of the representative of Guinea-Bissau but considered that his decision had been entirely in order'.[56]

At another 1980 meeting of a UNGA committee, a decision had been taken to 'vote together' on two resolutions. A vote was held on the first resolution. A discussion then arose as to whether a motion could be submitted in regard to the second resolution under Rule 131 (to decide whether to vote on the next proposal). The Chairman refused to accept such a motion. The Legal Counsel to the UN submitted his opinion that he

> confirmed the interpretation which the Chairman had given regarding rule 131. After each vote, that rule could be invoked. However, since the previous day, when the vote on the [first resolution] had taken place, rule 131 had not been invoked. When the Chairman had stated, at the outset of the current meeting, that there were no speakers wishing to explain their vote after the vote on [the first resolution] and that the Committee would next hear those representatives wishing to explain their vote before the vote on the [second resolution], that had been the time when rule 131 could have been invoked, if it had been so intended. As no such motion had been made, the Chairman had given the floor to the representative of Mozambique to explain his vote before the vote on the [second resolution]. The voting process had begun at that moment, and that voting could not now be interrupted except for points of order in connexion with the actual conduct of the voting.[57]

[52] UN GAOR, 1st Committee, 35th Session, 48th Meeting, pp. 16, 31, 32, UN Doc. A/C.1/35/SR.48 (1980).

[53] UN GAOR, 3rd Committee, 35th Session, 82nd Meeting, paras. 42, 47, UN Doc. A/C.3/35/SR.82 (1980).

[54] *Ibid.* at para. 43. [55] *Ibid.* at para. 51. [56] *Ibid.* at para. 52.

[57] UN GAOR, 4th Committee, 35th Session, 22nd Meeting, para. 24, UN Doc. A/C.4/35/SR.22 (1980).

18.4.6 *Interruption of Voting for Proposal to Defer the Vote*

At a 1981 meeting of a UNGA committee, the Chairman refused to allow a motion to defer the vote after the voting process had begun and several delegations had already explained their votes before the vote.[58]

18.4.7 *Interruption of Voting to Make Comments*

During the 1969 Vienna Conference on the Law of Treaties, the President interpreted the rule of procedure to mean that, once voting had commenced, he had to refuse a Netherlands request 'to make a few comments before a vote was taken'.[59]

18.4.8 *Interruption of Voting with a Request for Explanation*

At a 1952 meeting of a UNGA committee, after announcing the commencement of voting, the Chairman refused a request by the Netherlands for an explanation of the text being voted on.[60] At a 1980 meeting of a UNGA committee, after the Chairman had announced the commencement of the voting process, he refused to allow a request by the delegation of Bulgaria for an explanation of a proposal by the sponsors.[61]

18.4.9 *Interruption of Voting due to Discrepancy in Language Versions*

At a 1952 meeting of a UNGA committee, after the Chairman had announced the commencement of voting, he refused to allow a proposal that would have clarified a substantial difference between the English and Spanish versions of an amendment. The Chairman, however, did allow a subsequent second vote on the amendment.[62]

[58] UN GAOR, 5th Committee, 36th Session, 58th Meeting, para. 28, UN Doc. A/C.5/36/SR.58 (1981).

[59] Official Records of the Vienna Conference on the Law of Treaties – Second Session, 28th Plenary Meeting, p. 153, para. 30, UN Doc. A/CONF.39/11/Add.1 (1969).

[60] UN GAOR, 6th Committee, 7th Session, 345th Meeting, paras. 40, 48, UN Doc. A/C.6/7/SR.345 (1952).

[61] UN GAOR, 3rd Committee, 35th Session, 82nd Meeting, paras. 155, 156, UN Doc. A/C.3/35/SR.82 (1980). The sponsors subsequently provided the requested explanation without being challenged on their right to do so.

[62] UN GAOR, 6th Committee, 7th Session, 311th Meeting, paras. 11, 19, 28, UN Doc. A/C.6/7/SR.311 (1952).

At a 1981 meeting of a UNGA committee, after an announcement that voting was commencing, the Chairman, after ascertaining that the proposer objected to an amendment intended to correct a discrepancy between the English and French versions of the text, refused to allow the submission of the amendment.[63]

18.4.10 Interruption of Voting in Order to Submit an Amendment

Several delegations at conferences have, at times, requested permission to submit amendments and sub-amendments after the announcement that voting had commenced.

At a 1980 meeting of a UNGA committee, the sponsors of a resolution wished to accept a comment by a representative and amend their proposal. The Chairman ruled 'that under the rules of procedure the sponsors of the amendment could not revise it when it was being put to the vote'.[64] The ruling was not challenged.

At the 1958 Law of the Sea Conference, the Chairman of a committee ruled that 'no amendment could be made to a proposal during the conduct of voting'.[65] His ruling was challenged but upheld. At the 1961 Vienna Conference on Diplomatic Relations, when the same ruling was made by the Chairman, it was not challenged.[66]

At the 1963 Vienna Conference on Consular Relations, the representative of the UK submitted an amendment during voting. The representative of Norway, who supported the UK amendment, proposed that the Committee 'suspend the rules of procedure so that the UK representative's request could be granted'.[67] The representative of France stated that 'he approved of the UK representative's improvised amendment, although it was in open violation of the rules of procedure'.[68] The Chairman refused

63 UN GAOR, 1st Committee, 36th Session, 51st Meeting, p. 21, UN Doc. A/C.1/36/SR.51 (1981).

64 UN GAOR, 3rd Committee, 35th Session, 82nd Meeting, paras. 167, 168, UN Doc. A/C.3/35/SR.82 (1980).

65 Official Records of the 1958 Law of the Sea Conference, 57th Meeting of Committee I, vol. III, p. 178, para. 3, UN Doc. A/CONF.13/39 (1958).

66 'It would not be in order to introduce a sub-amendment since voting on the article was in progress.' Official Records of the 1961 Vienna Conference on Diplomatic Relations, 34th Meeting of the Committee of the Whole, p. 204, paras. 36, 37, UN Doc. A/CONF.20/14 (1961).

67 Official Records of the 1963 Vienna Conference on Consular Relations, 24th Meeting of Committee 2, p. 370, para. 32, UN Doc. A/CONF.25/16 (1963).

68 *Ibid.* at para. 34.

to allow the submission of the amendment, and his ruling was upheld on a challenge.

18.4.11 Interruption of Voting to Submit an Oral Amendment

At a 1950 meeting of a UNGA committee, the Chairman ruled that the rules of procedure did not allow submission of amendments once voting had begun.[69] At a 1974 meeting of the UNGA, the President asked the Assembly if there would be any objection to allowing Australia to submit a slight oral amendment to a resolution although voting had begun. The President added that strictly according to the rules of procedure, such a procedure is out of order. There was no objection by the Assembly.[70]

At the 1961 Vienna Conference on Diplomatic Relations, a delegation submitted an oral amendment after the President had 'invited the Conference to vote'.[71] The submission of the amendment was objected to on the grounds that voting was already in progress. The representatives of Senegal and France argued that the amendment could be submitted as 'voting referred to the voting on each individual proposal or amendment' and the Conference had not actually begun to vote. The President ruled that the proposed oral amendment was out of order. The President's ruling was challenged and overruled. The representative of the United Kingdom stated after the vote that 'he regretted that the President's decision had been overruled on appeal for it had been fully in conformity with the rules of procedure'.[72]

18.4.12 Interruption of Voting to Submit an Amendment Where the Right to do so Had Been Previously Reserved

At a 1949 meeting of a UNGA committee, the Chairman refused to allow Australia to submit an amendment to a paragraph of a resolution being voted on paragraph by paragraph, although Australia had earlier 'reserved the right' to submit the amendment at a later stage.[73]

[69] UN GAOR, Ad Hoc Political Committee, 5th Session, 56th Meeting, paras. 43, 52, 53, UN Doc. A/AC.38/5/SR.56 (1950).

[70] UN GAOR, Plenary, 29th Session, 2316th Meeting, para. 210, UN Doc. A/PV.2316 (1974).

[71] Official Records of the 1961 Vienna Conference on Diplomatic Relations, 12th Plenary Meeting, p. 48, para. 11, UN Doc. A/CONF.20/14 (1961).

[72] *Ibid.* at para. 18.

[73] UN GAOR, 4th Committee, 4th Session, 98th Meeting, para. 54, UN Doc. A/C.4/4/SR.98 (1949).

18.4.13 *Interruption of Voting to Submit Sub-Amendments*

At a 1986 meeting of a UNGA committee, a lengthy procedural debate took place on the question of whether a US proposal was an amendment or a separate proposal. After the Chairman decided that it was an amendment, he declared that 'the voting would now begin' on the US amendment.[74] At this stage several delegations requested permission to submit sub-amendments. The Chairman at first refused to allow the submission of the sub-amendments, ruling that they were inadmissible as voting had commenced.[75] The Chairman, however, then reversed his ruling and allowed the submission of sub-amendments. The Chairman explained his change of ruling by stating that 'the United States had had an opportunity to submit an amendment. It would therefore be unfair to deny other delegations the same right.'[76]

This unusual ruling illustrates that the rule against interruption of voting can become unenforceable and irrelevant where lengthy procedural discussions take place after the announcement of the commencement of voting.

18.4.14 *Interruption of Voting to Ascertain What Majority Is Required*

At a 1966 meeting of a UNGA committee, the Chairman refused to entertain a point of order requesting information as to whether a simple or two-thirds majority was required for the resolution being voted on. The Chairman's reply was that this issue could be taken up after the vote and there was no reason to interrupt the vote.[77]

18.4.15 *Interruption of Voting to Withdraw Sponsorship of a Resolution*

At a 1974 meeting of a UNGA committee, the Chairman ruled that a delegation was not entitled to withdraw its sponsorship of a resolution once voting had commenced.[78]

[74] UNGAOR, 2nd Committee, 41st Session, 33rd Meeting, para. 19, UN Doc. A/C.2/41/SR.33 (1986).

[75] *Ibid.* at para. 21.

[76] *Ibid.* at para. 27.

[77] UN GAOR, 1st Committee, 21st Session, 1470th Meeting, paras. 103–105, 118, UN Doc. A/C.1/21/SR.1470 (1966).

[78] UN GAOR, 2nd Committee, 29th Session, 1646th Meeting, para. 20, UN Doc. A/C.2/29/SR.1646 (1974).

18.4.16 Interruption of Voting to Allow Explanation of Vote on a Separate Paragraph

At a 1968 meeting of a UNGA committee, the Chairman did not allow the representative of Bulgaria to give an explanation of his vote after separate voting had taken place on two paragraphs, but before the vote had taken place on the resolution as a whole. The Chairman ruled that the representative must wait until the completion of the voting on the resolution as a whole.[79] At a meeting of the same Committee, at the 1996 session of the Assembly, the representative of the Netherlands, on a point of order, argued that 'once we have voted on the amendment, we should immediately continue with the vote on the draft resolution as a whole. After that, of course, delegations can make statements in explanation of vote.'[80] The representative of the United Kingdom replied that 'even though it may be a departure from the rules of procedure, those of us who wish to explain our vote . . . before the voting, should be allowed to do so'.[81] The Chairman allowed the delegate of the United Kingdom to make an explanation of vote before voting on the resolution as a whole, explaining, rather enigmatically, that the 'committee was following the established procedure'.[82]

At a 1997 meeting of a UNGA committee, a delegation requested permission to explain its vote before the voting on a separate paragraph. The delegate argued that the 'Committee was not aware that a separate vote would be taken', and hence his delegation should be allowed to explain its vote on the separate paragraph. The Chairman responded that he appreciated the point but that 'we cannot go back to explanations of vote once we have started the voting process'.[83]

COMMENT

Even after a decision has been made to take a separate vote, the text to be voted on remains as it was, and there would therefore appear to be no justification in allowing delegations to make explanations of vote once the voting process has commenced.

[79] UN GAOR, 1st Committee, 23rd Session, 1642nd Meeting, paras. 96–97, UN Doc. A/C.1/23/SR.1642 (1968). (In fact the Bulgarian delegate utilised a point of order to give what was in reality an explanation of vote.)

[80] UN GAOR, 1st Committee, 51st Session, 21st Meeting, UN Doc. A/C.1/51/PV.21, p. 17 (1996).

[81] *Ibid.* at p. 18. [82] *Ibid.*

[83] UN GAOR, 1st Committee, 52nd Session, 23rd Meeting, UN Doc. A/C.1/PV.23, p. 16 (1997).

18.4.17 *Interruption of Voting to Revise a Proposal*

At a 1950 meeting of a UNGA committee, the Chairman allowed the Mexican delegation to make a change in an amendment it had submitted to a proposal, although voting had taken place on other amendments to the proposal.[84]

At a 1952 meeting of a UNGA committee, after the commencement of voting had been announced, the Chairman refused to allow Peru to revise its proposal by accepting an Argentine amendment.[85]

At a 1976 meeting of a UNGA committee, the Chairman allowed the sponsor of a proposal to revise his proposal even though the Chairman had previously announced that the Committee was proceeding to vote. The decision was not challenged.[86]

18.4.18 *Interruption of Voting to Request a Reconsideration*

During the 1958 Law of the Sea Conference, the Chairman of a committee ruled that a motion for reconsideration of voting on an amendment could not be put to the vote before the Committee had concluded voting on all the other amendments to the article in question.[87]

The President of the 1963 Vienna Conference on Consular Relations made a similar ruling on a motion of reconsideration.[88] The President's ruling was upheld on a challenge.

18.4.19 *Interruption of Voting for Withdrawal of Candidatures*

At a 1997 session of the UNGA, during elections to ECOSOC, the President refused to allow the representative of Guatemala to withdraw its candidacy since 'it was made during a vote, and in accordance with the rules of procedure, it is only points of order in connection with the actual conduct

[84] UN GAOR, 3rd Committee, 5th Session, 309th Meeting, paras. 3, 14, UN Doc. A/C.3/5/SR.309 (1950).

[85] UN GAOR, 1st Committee, 6th Session, 501st Meeting, paras. 28–30, UN Doc. A/C.1/6/SR.501 (1952). The Chairman's ruling was upheld on a challenge.

[86] UN GAOR, 1st Committee, 31st Session, 49th Meeting, UN Doc. A/C.1/31/SR.49 pp. 11–16 (1976).

[87] Official Records of the 1958 Law of the Sea Conference, 56th Meeting of Committee I, vol. III, p. 177, paras. 37–41, UN Doc. A/CONF.13/39 (1958).

[88] Official Records of the 1963 Vienna Conference on Consular Relations, 12th Plenary Meeting, p. 42, paras. 49–52, UN Doc. A/CONF.25/16 (1963).

of the voting that are allowed'.[89] At a 2003 session of the UNGA involving elections to the International Criminal Tribunal for Rwanda, the President ruled that 'any announcement such as those concerning withdrawals of candidatures should be made prior to the commencement of the voting process, that is to say before the announcement of the beginning of the voting process'.[90]

COMMENT

Although the precedents are not consistent, it is apparent that the rule against interruption of voting cannot be strictly enforced in a process of voting on a number of proposals or where a procedural dispute arises during explanation of votes.

It would appear that the rule against interruption of voting should be strictly applied only during the actual physical conduct of voting and counting of votes. In those circumstances, it is reasonable to enforce the prohibition against raising any point of order other than one concerned with the actual voting process.

18.5 Correction of Vote

The rules of procedure of the UNGA do not contain any provision as to correction of votes, nor do the rules of the conferences examined contain such a rule.

18.5.1 The Report of the UN Secretary-General on Correction of Vote

The delegation of France proposed, during the 1954 session of the General Assembly, that the Assembly debate the question of correcting of votes 'with the view of filling an obvious gap in the General Assembly's rules of procedure which did not stipulate in what manner the Chair should announce the results of a vote and also did not offer delegations an opportunity to correct their votes during or after the voting'.[91] The Secretary-General was asked to submit a report on the subject.[92] The

[89] UN GAOR, Plenary, 52nd Session, 43rd Meeting, UN Doc. A/52/PV.43, p. 2 (1997).
[90] UN GAOR, Plenary, 57th Session, 80th Meeting, UN Doc. A/57/PV.80, p. 4 (2003).
[91] UN GAOR, 6th Committee, 9th Session, 438th Meeting, para. 20, UN Doc. A/C.6/9/SR.438 (1954). The request for inclusion of the item on the agenda was in a letter, UN Doc. A/2700 and A/2700/Rev.1 (1954).
[92] UNGA Resolution 901 (IX) of 14 December 1954.

report[93] examined the procedure of various international organisations and national legislative assemblies and said that in the General Assembly and committees 'the practice is that, until the result of the voting is announced by the presiding officer, corrections of votes are normally accepted and the result is modified accordingly'.[94] The report went on to say that 'in a limited number of cases, when the decision was not affected thereby, corrections have been accepted after the announcement of the result. Only once does it appear that a correction was permitted to affect the outcome of a vote as announced.'[95]

The report was submitted to the Sixth Committee during the 1955 session of the UNGA, which conducted a desultory debate on the subject; many delegations expressed the view that a set method of correcting votes might be open to misuse as delegations might choose to abstain from voting, then ascertain how other delegations voted and 'correct' their abstention. Other delegations, and the Legal Counsel, pointed out that the whole problem very seldom arose in practice, and it was not advisable to attempt to legislate for every possible eventuality.

On the recommendation of the Sixth Committee, the UNGA adopted a resolution by which it was decided to take no further action on the subject 'for the present'.[96]

18.5.2 Practice as to Correction of Votes before Announcement of Results

Robert's Rules of Order notes, 'At the conclusion of the roll call, the names of those who failed to answer can be called again, or the chair can ask if anyone entered the room after his or her name was called . . . Changes of vote are also permitted at this time before the results are announced.'[97] As regards electronic voting, '[c'hanges of votes after the results have been announced by the chair on allegation of machine error are not entertained'.[98] This appears to be the practice at international conferences.

At a 1961 meeting of the UNGA, the President allowed a correction of vote, explaining that the results of the vote had not yet been declared.[99]

[93] UN GAOR, Annexes, 10th Session, Agenda Item 51, UN Doc. A/2977 (1955).
[94] *Ibid.* at para. 85. [95] *Ibid.* at para. 93.
[96] UNGA Resolution 983 (X) of 29 November 1955.
[97] *Robert's Rules of Order, Newly Revised*, 11th edn, (2011), p. 421. [98] *Ibid.* at p. 423.
[99] UN GAOR, Plenary, 15th Session, 993rd Meeting, para. 133, UN Doc. A/PV.993 (1961).

A 1997 report of a UNGA committee stated, 'Before the voting machine was locked, the Chairman in response to a point of order by the delegation of Cuba, announced that Cuba had voted in favour and would be so counted, in spite of a mechanized failure of the voting buttons at the Cuban seat.'[100]

At a 2014 meetings of the First Committee of the UNGA the Chairman informed delegates that

> [i]n the case of a voting error, delegations wishing to register their original voting intention should not disrupt the voting process to request the correction by taking the floor. They should instead approach the Secretariat to clarify the original voting intention, which will be reflected in the official records.[101]

The question of correction of votes has arisen several times at international conferences. During a 1958 conference, after the voting had been completed but before the results were announced, the representative of Ecuador asked to change his vote. The Chairman of the committee ruled 'that under the rules of procedure, representatives were not entitled to change their votes after those had been cast and duly recorded'.[102] The representative of the USSR appealed against the Chairman's ruling but the ruling was upheld. At the same conference, before the results had been announced, the representative of Hungary said 'that he had been absent when the name of Hungary had been called. He wished his affirmative vote to be recorded.'[103] The Chairman again ruled 'that it was not possible to record the vote of the Hungarian representative because, at the time of his request, the voting had ended . . . The opinion of the Hungarian delegation on the motion would however be placed on record.'[104]

At the 1974–1977 Geneva Humanitarian Law Conference, after a roll-call vote, but before the announcement of the results, two delegations announced that they wished to correct their vote.[105] The representative of El Salvador wished his abstention to be recorded as a vote against. The representative of Haiti announced that he had been absent when his name

[100] UN GAOR, Sixth Committee, 52nd Session, para. 11, UN Doc. A/52/650 (1997).

[101] UN GAOR, 1st Committee, 69th Session, 20th Meeting, UN Doc. A/C.1/PV.20 p.1 (2014).

[102] Official Records of the 1958 Law of the Sea Conference, 56th Meeting of Committee I, vol. III, p. 177, paras. 32–36, UN Doc. A/CONF.13/39 (1958).

[103] Official Records of the 1958 Law of the Sea Conference, 62nd Meeting of Committee I, vol. III, p. 197, para. 38, UN Doc. A/CONF.13/39 (1958).

[104] *Ibid.* at para. 39.

[105] Official Records of the 1974–1977 Geneva Humanitarian Law Conference, CDDH/SR.25, vol. V, p. 294, paras. 32–34.

was called and requested that his country's vote (against) be recorded. The President ruled as to Haiti that 'if a delegation was absent when called upon to vote it could not vote later'.[106] As to El Salvador, the correction was allowed as a delegation was entitled 'before the result of the voting was known, to do what El Salvador had done and correct its vote'.[107] The US representative questioned the President's ruling in not allowing the Haitian representative to vote, and the representative of Mali questioned the President's ruling as to the vote of the El Salvador delegation, but no formal challenge was issued to either of the President's rulings. There do not appear to be logical grounds for the distinction the President made between adding a vote and changing a vote.

COMMENT

Correct practice is to allow correction of votes at any time until the announcement that voting has been completed or the announcement of the results. In electronic voting, a correction must be done before the voting mechanism is 'frozen' and votes areshown on the electronic board[108]: 'belated requests to change a vote after the voting machine has been locked are no longer granted.'[109]

18.5.3 *Correction of Votes after Announcement of Results*

At a 1954 meeting of the UNGA, the Chairman stated that the only circumstance in which a correction of vote could be made after the announcement of results would be where a vote had been miscounted.[110] However, at the same session of the UNGA, the President allowed a correction of vote in the Plenary, after the results had been announced. The President explained his ruling by pointing out that the correction would not change the results of the vote.[111] This appears clearly to be an incorrect ruling.

106 *Ibid.* at p. 295, para. 42. 107 *Ibid.*

108 Michael Schaefer, 'Article 21', in *The Charter of the United Nations, A Commentary*, ed. Bruno Simma (1994), p. 361 at p. 373.

109 Thomas Fitschen, 'Article 21', in *The Charter of the United Nations, A Commentary*, ed. Bruno Simma *et al*, 3rd edn (2012), p. 708.

110 UN GAOR, 1st Committee, 9th Session, 726th Meeting, paras. 109–111, UN Doc. A/C.1/9/SR.726 (1954).

111 UN GAOR, Plenary, 9th Session, 509th Meeting, paras. 304, 306, UN Doc. A/PV.509 (1954). See discussion on this issue in UN GAOR, 6th Committee, 9th Session, 438th, 439th Meetings, UN Doc. A/C.6/9/SR.438, 439 (1954); UN GAOR, 6th Committee, 10th Session, 455–458th Meetings, UN Doc. A/C.6/10/SR.455–458 (1955).

A 1984 opinion by the UN Office of Legal Affairs states that 'under no condition should the Secretariat agree to change the result of a roll-call vote. United Nations practice is clear that the results of a vote are never altered after the results are announced.'[112] This opinion appears to leave open the question as to whether a correction can be made to a non-roll-call vote prior to announcement of results.

At a 2008 meeting of the Plenary of the UNGA, a delegation raised a point of order that 'at least two delegations that were indicated on the board as having voted in favour had in fact abstained in the voting. Therefore, the results declared at the outcome of the voting are not fully valid.' The Chairman responded that the printout of the voting reflected one correction '[s]o I do not think that this impinges in any way on the validity of the voting or on the results as announced. At any rate, any delegation can place its intended vote on record, if it is not that which appeared on the panel.'[113]

At the 1969 Vienna Conference on the Law of Treaties, the delegate of India stated that he wished to correct a vote cast in error at a previous meeting.[114] The Chairman made no reference to the Indian request; however, the report of the Committee to the Plenary of the Conference notes the Indian statement.[115]

At the 1974–1977 Geneva Humanitarian Law Conference, after announcing the results of a vote, several delegations complained to the President that, although they were not present when their names were called, they had arrived in the hall while the voting was still taking place but had failed to catch the President's attention. The President took no action on the complaints and commented that 'he took note of that remark. But if representatives were absent when their names were called, it was difficult to return to them later.'[116]

At a 1983 meeting of the General Conference of the IAEA, Iraq submitted a proposal denying recognition of the credentials of the Israel

[112] Cable (from the UN Office of Legal Affairs) to the Chief, Treaty Implementation and Commission Secretariat Section, Division on Narcotic Drugs, 9 February 1984. 1984 UN Jur. Y.B. 159.

[113] UN GAOR, Plenary 63rdSession, 104th Meeting, p. 817, UN Doc. A/63/PV.104 (2008).

[114] Official Records of the Vienna Conference on the Law of Treaties – First Session, 82nd Meeting of the Committee of the Whole, p. 484, para. 20, UN Doc. A/CONF.39/11 (1969).

[115] Official Records of the UN Conference on the Law of Treaties – First and Second Sessions, Documents, Report of the Committee of the Whole, p. 164, para. 386, UN Doc. A/CONF.39/11/Add.2 (1971).

[116] Official Records of the 1974–1977 Geneva Humanitarian Law Conference, CDDH/SR.44, vol. VI, p. 291, para. 70.

delegation. The results of the vote on the proposal were announced as forty in favour and forty against, and consequently the proposal was not adopted.[117] The representative of Madagascar explained that 'he had been present at the time of the vote[118] and that he wished his vote to be recorded. His delegation voted "yes,"' The Director of the Legal Division referred to an earlier opinion of his at the Board of Governors where a Governor had returned to the room before the end of the ballot. His advice on that occasion had been that the Governor's vote should be regarded as valid. The advice of the Legal Counsel, on that occasion, had been that the vote of the Governor who had been temporarily absent was a valid vote

> in accordance with the principle of international law whereby a defect of form – in that case the late recording of a representative's vote – should not invalidate substance, in other words the vote of the representative in question. In the United Nations Organisation, the practice was also based on the desire not to deprive a delegation of its right to vote. The vote of the Malagasy delegate should, therefore, be counted in the result.[119]

The representative of the United States, on a point of order, argued that 'the present situation was different because the results of the vote had already been announced. In the present case, the recording of an additional vote amounted to a reconsideration of the ballot which had already taken place.'[120]

The President ruled that

> in the General Assembly of the United Nations, a delegation could still take part in a vote before the results were announced. In the present case the decision was a difficult one. Whichever way the decision went, the rights of one State would be affected. However, basing himself on the opinion of the Director of the Legal Division, he considered that the vote of the Malagasy delegation was valid.[121]

An appeal against the ruling of the President was not approved. Commenting on the opinion of the Legal Counsel and the President's ruling, the UK representative said he was 'disquieted', the US delegate 'was appalled', the

[117] Official Records of the 246th Plenary Meeting of the 26th Session of the General Conference of the IAEA, para. 28, IAEA Doc. GC(XXVI)/OR.246 (1983).

[118] *Ibid.* at para. 30. The representative of Iraq, later in the debate, reported that 'the Malagasy representative had been in the hall', *ibid.* at para. 56. See Leo Gross, *Selected Essays on International Law and Organization* (1992), p. 377.

[119] Official Records of the 246th Plenary Meeting of the 26th Session of the General Conference of the IAEA, paras. 27, 30, 31, IAEA Doc. GC(XXVI)/OR.246 (1983).

[120] *Ibid.* at para. 32.

[121] *Ibid.* at para. 35.

Canadian delegate referred to 'recourse to devious means', the Italian delegate was 'surprised' and the representative of France said that 'the acceptance of an additional vote after the results had been officially announced was without precedent'.[122]

Sir Francis Vallat, writing in the *British Year Book of International Law* for 1954, stated that 'it is believed that as a general rule the results of voting cannot properly be altered by the wish of a representative to change his vote after it has been announced'.[123]

COMMENT

In no voting system is correction of vote allowed after the announcement of results.

18.5.4 Correction of Votes in a Roll-Call Vote

There is no clear pattern of precedents as to correction of votes in a roll-call vote before the announcement of the results. Theoretically there are no grounds for denying a delegation the right to correct its vote during a roll-call vote or to add a vote if absent when the State's name was called, provided that the correction is done before the results are announced. In practice, this is sometimes difficult to implement as it requires drawing the attention of the presiding officer, by a point of order, to a delegation's wish to change its vote.

18.5.5 Correction of Votes: Indication in the Records

Where no correction of vote is allowed, it is accepted practice that a statement by a delegation as to how it intended to vote is recorded in the records of the conference.[124] A 1984 opinion of the UN Office of Legal Affairs states that 'usually a footnote to the tabulation of votes is used, reading along [the] following lines: "Subsequent to the vote, the representative of... announced that he had been unable to participate in the vote but that, if present, his delegation would have cast an [affirmative] [negative]

122 *Ibid.* at paras. 48, 49, 51, 52, 53.

123 F. A. Vallat, 'Voting in the General Assembly of the United Nations', 31 BYIL 273 (1954) at 297.

124 See, for example, UN GAOR, 2nd Committee, 22nd Session, 1171st Meeting, para. 13, UN Doc. A/C.2/22/SR.1171 (1967).

vote."'[125] Such a statement does not affect the results of the vote. The legal opinion points out that a delegation that is not satisfied with such a note in the record can always propose a reconsideration of the vote.

At a meeting of the 1974–1977 Geneva Humanitarian Law Conference, the representative of Jordan informed the Conference that he 'apologized for his delegation's absence for reasons beyond his control, and said that had it been present it would have cast an affirmative vote'.[126] The President observed 'that the results of the vote at the morning meeting would not be affected by the statement of the representative of Jordan'.[127] The Jordanian statement appears in the records of the Conference.

At a 1998 meeting of the IAEA General Conference, a delegation asked 'whether it would be in accordance with the Rules of Procedure of the General Conference for delegations of countries which had not been present in the room during the vote to write to the Secretariat expressing their support for the draft resolution'. The President responded that 'there would be no objection to that procedure'.[128]

COMMENT

A State is always at liberty to state for the record a correction of vote. However, such statements do not affect the results of the vote.

18.6 Irregularity in Voting

At a very contentious 2010 session of a committee of the World Health Assembly a State that was not entitled to participate in the voting, because of financial arrears, nevertheless participated in a vote. The Legal Counsel gave an opinion that 'the vote would have to be repeated'. He added that, however, 'when a vote had been concluded and no objection had been raised during the voting procedure, the vote was considered to have been regular'. A procedural discussion then ensued as to whether a formal complaint of irregularity had in fact been made during the voting process.

[125] Cable (from the UN Office of Legal Affairs) to the Chief, Treaty Implementation and Commission Secretariat Section, Division on Narcotic Drugs, 9 February 1984. 1984 UN Jur. Y.B. 159.

[126] Official Records of the 1974–1977 Geneva Humanitarian Law Conference, CDDH/SR.58, vol. VII, p. 281, para. 1.

[127] *Ibid.* at para. 2.

[128] Official Records of the 42nd IAEA General Conference, IAEA Doc. GC(42)/OR.9 paras. 28, 29, p. 6 (1998).

The Chairman ruled that 'it was a moot point' whether in fact a formal complaint had been made, and therefore 'he had decided to declare the results of the vote'.[129]

[129] 63rd World Health Assembly, Committee "B" 7th Meeting, WHA/63/2010/REC/3 pp. 286–290 (2010).

19

Languages, Records and Documents

19.1 Languages of the Conference

19.1.1 Official Languages

The UN Model Rules propose,

Rule 69
Languages of the Conference

Arabic, Chinese, English, French, Russian and Spanish shall be the languages of the Conference, unless the convening organ decides that not all these languages are required.

Rule 70
Interpretation

1. Speeches made in a language of the Conference shall be interpreted into the other such languages, unless such interpretation has not been requested by the representative of any State participating in the Conference.
2. A representative may speak in a language other than a language of the Conference if the delegation concerned provides for interpretation into one such language.

Rule 71
Languages of Documents

1. Any reports submitted by the General Committee, a Main Committee or a Drafting Committee, as well as any report or final act of the Conference, shall be published in the languages of the Conference.
2. All resolutions and other formal decisions of the Conference shall be published in the languages of the Conference.
3. Treaty instruments adopted by a treaty-making conference shall be published in the languages in which they are authentic.

The UN Model Rules generally follow UNGA practice.

The number of official languages of conferences has been steadily increasing from the original French-only of nineteenth- and early twentieth-century conferences. Both French and English were official languages of the 1919 Paris Peace Conference and the League of Nations, and then English, French and Russian were recognised at the 1946 Paris Peace Conference. The UN, in its early days, had English and French as working languages. Over the years, Spanish,[1] Russian,[2] Chinese[3] and Arabic[4] were added. The present six official languages of the UN are also the official languages of most conferences.[5] The ILO Conference still preserves English and French as the only official languages,[6] but the ILO is apparently an exception in this regard.

A 1985 memorandum by the UN Office of Legal Affairs states that

> although use of a language other than an official language is not expressly prohibited, it is essential that business be conducted in an official language of the Congress... bearing in mind that the rules of procedure and all the documentation for the Congress are only available in its official languages, and that any rulings relating to the conduct of business should properly be made only in one of the official languages of the Congress.[7]
>
> On those occasions in the UNGA when no translations are available into all languages, delegations usually make a point of expressing regret but allow the proceedings to continue, in English.[8]

At a 1965 ITU Conference there was a dispute as to the record of what had been said at a meeting. The Secretary-General of the Organisation was asked to distribute a transcript of the tape recording made of the proceedings. The Secretary-General, however, explained that he was distributing it in the original language since any subsequent translation might differ

[1] UNGA Resolution 262 (III) of 11 December 1948.

[2] UNGA Resolution 2479 (XXIII) of 21 December 1968.

[3] UNGA Resolutions 3189, 3190 (XXVIII) of 18 December 1973.

[4] UNGA Resolutions 35/219A and B of 17 December 1980.

[5] Arabic, Chinese, English, French, Russian and Spanish. See Mala Tabory, *Multilingualism in International Law and Institutions* (1980).

[6] Article 24 of the Standing Orders of the International Labour Conference, www.ilo.org.

[7] Memorandum (by the UN Office of Legal Affairs) to the Special Assistant to the Under Secretary-General, Department of Administration and Management, 5 June 1985. 1985 UN Jur. Y.B. 133.

[8] For example, the Russian delegate's statement, UNGAOR 69th Session, Plenary, 77th Meeting, UN Doc. A/69/PV.77, p. 10 (2014); Chairman's statement, UNGAOR, 3rd Committee, 68th Session, 54th Meeting, UN Doc. A/C.3/68/SR.54 para. 144 (2013).

from the simultaneous translation provided when the statements were made.[9]

The practice has developed that delegations, usually heads of State, can address a conference in a language other than an official language provided they provide the secretariat, in advance, with a written translation into an official language. This translation is regarded by the conference as the official text that was delivered.

19.1.2 Working Languages

In practice, English and to a lesser extent French are the working languages of the UN, and the practical guide to the UNGA published by the Permanent Mission of Switzerland to the UN states unequivocally, 'English and French are the two working languages of the UN Secretariat.'[10] Nevertheless, formally the UN has no 'working languages'. No reference is made in the UN Model Rules to a distinction between official and working languages. The Legal Counsel to the WHO explained the difference as '[t]he concept of official languages was for the purpose of simultaneous interpretation, while that of working languages was for document translation'.[11] This definition may, however, be valid only for the WHO.

In the early years of UN-convened conferences, English and French were termed working languages.[12] Later Spanish and then Russian were added,[13] and recent practice has been to omit reference to working languages, since all the official languages in effect became working languages.

19.1.3 Voting on One Language Version of a Text

At a 1949 committee meeting of the UNGA, the Chairman stated, in reply to a question, that the Committee had voted on the English-language text of a resolution. In reply to a point of order by the representative of

[9] Minutes of the 1965 Plenipotentiary Conference of the ITU, 6th Plenary Meeting, ITU Doc. No. 157-E, p. 7 (1965).

[10] The Practical Guide to the UNGA published by the Permanent Mission of Switzerland to the UN, para. 3.4, www.unitar.org/ny/sites/unitar.org.ny/files/UN_PGA_Handbook.pdf.

[11] 52nd World Health Assembly, Committee 'B', 7th Meeting, p. 199 (2000).

[12] See, for example, Rule 16 of the rules of procedure of the 1951 Conference on Refugees, UN Doc. A/CONF.2/3/Rev.1 (1951).

[13] See, for example, Rule 52 of the rules of procedure of the 1968 Non-Nuclear-Weapon State Conference, UN Doc. A/CONF.35/1 (1968).

Belgium, the Chairman corrected himself by stating that the working languages, English and French, were on an equal footing.[14]

19.1.4 Authentic Language

At a meeting of the 1977 Conference on Territorial Asylum, a problem arose as to the translation of proposed amendments. The Chairman stated that 'in all cases, the text in which an amendment had been submitted was the authentic text. The Drafting Committee would be entitled to modify the translation into all other languages of the Conference.'[15] The Chairman continued by stating, 'He invited the Committee to vote on the amendments on the understanding that the text in the language in which each amendment had been submitted was the only authentic text and that the Drafting Committee would be responsible for bringing the other language versions into line with it.'[16] When this ruling was queried, the Chairman summarised by saying 'all languages of the Conference were of equal status; but, for every proposal submitted, there was one basic text, which was the original language text. The procedure he proposed had been followed by the General Assembly since 1945.'

COMMENT

Although the Chairman's ruling appears logical, it is not apparently legally correct since the texts in all the official languages are equally authentic.

19.1.5 Voting again because of a Discrepancy between Different Language Versions

At a 1952 meeting of a committee of the UNGA, the Chairman ruled that, as there was a discrepancy between different language versions of a resolution, the Committee should vote again on the resolution. The Chairman ruled furthermore that, in the circumstances, such a revote was not to be considered a reconsideration of the issue.[17]

[14] N GAOR, 6th Committee, 3rd Session, 81st Meeting, p. 179, UN Doc. A/C.6/3/SR.81 (1949).

[15] Summary Records of the 1977 Conference on Territorial Asylum, UN Doc. A/CONF.78/C.1/SR.16, paras. 25, 27 (1977).

[16] *Ibid.* at paras. 29, 34.

[17] UN GAOR, 6th Committee, 7th Session, 311th Meeting, paras. 19, 28, UN Doc. A/C.6/7/SR.311 (1952).

19.2 Records and Documents of the Conference

19.2.1 Summary and Verbatim Records

The rules of procedure of the UNGA state that verbatim records are to be kept of the meetings of the Plenary and the First Committee. The General Assembly is to decide on the form of records of other committees.[18] The UNGA has authorised summary records for all other committee meetings.

In the past, most conferences also published summary or verbatim records of proceedings. The modern trend is that only lawmaking conferences publish such records.[19] This would seem to be logical, as in the case of lawmaking conferences the records can play an important part of the *travaux préparatoires* of the treaty that was drafted. The NPT Review conferences, however, keep summary records.[20] Most general assemblies of international organisations continue to publish records of their meetings.

The UN Model Rules propose,

Rule 72
Verbatim Records

1. No conference shall have verbatim records.
2. Statements made at the Conference shall not be reproduced *in extenso* either as separate documents or in or attached to any summary record or report of a subsidiary organ or of the Conference unless, in exceptional cases, they are of a technical nature and served or are to serve as bases for discussion, and a decision to reproduce them has been taken by the Conference or the organ concerned.

Rule 73
Summary Records

1. No conference shall have summary records, except that the convening organ may authorize such records for a treaty-making conference.
2. If the Conference is authorized to have summary records, these shall only be provided for plenary meetings of the Conference and for meetings of those main Committees specified by the convening organ, or by the preparatory organ consistently with the statement of financial

[18] Rule 58 of the UNGA rules of procedure. UNGA Resolution 2837 (XXVI) of 17 December 1971.

[19] See for example the Rules of Procedure of the 3rd UN Conference on the Least Developed Countries, Rule 55(1) 'There shall be neither verbatim nor summary records of meetings.' UN Doc. A/CONF.191/4 (2001).

[20] See Rule 42 of the rules of procedure of the 2005 NPT Review Conference, NPT/CONF/.2005/1(2004).

> implications previously considered by the convening organ, and the bodies concerned shall dispense with such records whenever possible.

At a 1948 meeting of the First Committee of the UNGA, it transpired that there was a discrepancy between the Summary Records and the Verbatim Records. The Chairman informed the Committee that the Verbatim Records were not official and that only the Summary Records were the official records.[21] In recent years, UN bodies have used either verbatim or summary records but not both. Unedited transcripts have been used on an experimental basis as a substitute for verbatim records, but the practice appears to have been discontinued.[22]

Modern international conferences, other than lawmaking conferences, usually dispense even with summary records and publish only reports and resolutions of the conferences. At its 2002 meeting, the IMO Council debated whether to reinstate summary records for conferences. It was pointed out that there had been no summary records of diplomatic conferences since 1985, and the Council decided, 'for budgetary reasons', not to reinstate the publication of such records.[23]

The rules of procedure of the IAEA, as amended in 1989, provide that, although the records shall be in the form of summary records, 'delegates may on special occasions, request that their remarks made at a plenary meeting of the General Conference be set forth verbatim in the record'.[24] Conferences at times decide to include full statements in summary records. For example, a committee of the Third Law of the Sea Conference decided, at one stage, that 'all the statements at the current meeting should be included *in extenso* in the summary record in view of the importance of the issues involved and of the statements themselves'.[25] Since records of treaty-making conferences serve as part of the *travaux preparatoires* of the treaties that have been drafted, there is some justification in providing verbatim records, but the expense involved is usually prohibitive.

[21] UN GAOR, 1st Committee, 3rd Session, 229th Meeting, p. 937, UN Doc. A/C.1/3/SR.229 (1948).

[22] See Report of the Secretary of the 1st Committee, UNGA, 52nd Session, 2nd Meeting, UN Doc. A/C.1/52/PV.2, p. 7 (1997).

[23] IMO C 89/SR.3, p. 10 (2002).

[24] Rule 89(b) of the rules of procedure of the General Conference of the IAEA as amended by GC(XXXIII)/DEC/14 (1989) 29/9/89, GC(XXXIII)/OR.321, paras. 108, 109 (1989).

[25] Official Records, Third Law of the Sea Conference, vol. II, p. 75, Summary Records of the 14th Meeting of Committee 1, para. 62, UN Doc. A/CONF.62 (1975).

During an acrimonious session of a 1965 ITU conference, there was a dispute as to the veracity of the record, and the Conference took the unusual step of requesting the Secretary-General of the Organisation to read out, and later distribute, the transcript taken from a tape recording of the proceedings.[26]

COMMENT

At the UNGA, the Plenary and the First Committee publish verbatim records. All other UNGA Committees publish only summary records. Treaty-making conferences usually publish records, and other UN-convened conferences usually record only resolutions and keep neither verbatim nor summary records. Sound records are kept but not distributed.[27] Most assemblies of international organisations continue to keep records, usually summary ones.

19.2.2 Distribution of Documentation Submitted by Observers

The Chairman of a committee of the 1953 UNGA ruled that the Secretariat should distribute only those documents published by the Secretariat and not unofficial documents.[28] However, the more recent conference practice is to allow observers to distribute documents, at their expense, but such documents do not receive the status of official conference documents.

At the 2000 NPT Review Conference, the rules of procedure stated that observers 'shall also be entitled to submit documents to the participants in the Conference'.[29] The President of the Conference commented on this that 'the rules of procedure were not clear' but that 'since, at the 1990 Review Conference several States non-parties to the Treaty had been allowed to circulate their documents as official documents', he

[26] Minutes of the 1965 Plenipotentiary Conference of the ITU, 5th and 6th Plenary Meetings, ITU Docs. Nos. 156-E, 157 (1965).

[27] See, for example, Rule 38 of the rules of procedure of the Conference on Facilitating the Entry into Force of the Comprehensive Nuclear-Test-Ban Treaty, CTBT-Art. XIV/2001/2 (2001); RULES OF PROCEDURE, UN CONFERENCE TO REVIEW PROGRESS MADE IN THE IMPLEMENTATION OF THE PROGRAMME OF ACTION TO PREVENT, COMBAT AND ERADICATE THE ILLICIT TRADE IN SMALL ARMS AND LIGHT WEAPONS IN ALL ITS ASPECTS, UN DOC A/CONF.192/2006/RC/5 RULE 56 (2006).

[28] UN GAOR, 1st Committee, 7th Session, 585th Meeting, para. 30, UN Doc. A/C.1/7/SR.585 (1953).

[29] Rule 44 of the rules of procedure of the 2000 NPT Review Conference, NPT/CONF/2000/1 (2000). The draft rules for the 2005 NPT Review Conference used the identical phrase, NPT/CONF.2005/1.

'took it' that the Conference would continue to allow such distribution. The Conference agreed.[30] The rules of procedure of the 2001 CTBT Conference allowed observers to 'submit written contributions'.[31] Earlier IMO conferences allowed observers to 'submit relevant documents' 'with the approval of the Contracting Parties at the Meeting'.[32] Later IMO conferences stipulate, 'Written statements submitted by observers or experts may be distributed by the Secretariat to the delegations at the Conference.'[33] The rules of procedure of recent UN conferences state that written statements by observers 'shall be distributed by the secretariat to all delegations in the quantities and in the languages in which the statements are made available' by the observer.[34] Some UN conference rules of procedure add explicitly, 'Written statements shall not be made at United Nations expense and shall not be issued as official documents.'[35]

19.2.4 Adding Written Statements to the Record

The procedure of adding written statements to the record was proposed, but not adopted at the 1981 meeting of the UNGA. The representative of Israel objected, stating that this would be 'most irregular' and could prevent the exercise of the right of reply.[36] At a 1989 meeting of the UNGA,

[30] 2000 NPT Review Conference, 6th Plenary Meeting, NPT/CONF.2000/28 (Part IV), p. 68 (2000).

[31] Rules 40–43 of the rules of procedure of the 2001 CTBT Conference, CTBT-Art.XIV/2001/2 (2001).

[32] See, for example, Rule 4, IMO Doc. LC 20/3 (1998).

[33] See, for example, Rule IX (f) of the rules of procedure of the IMO International Conference on the Establishment of a Supplementary Fund for Compensation for Oil Pollution, LEG/CONF.14/2 (2002); Rule 58 of the rules of procedure of the IMO Conference of Contracting Governments to the International Convention for the Safety at Life at Sea, SOLAS/CONF.5/2 (2002).

[34] Rule 66 of the rules of procedure of the 2002 World Summit on Sustainable Development, A/CONF.199/2 (2002); 2004 World Conference on Disaster Reduction, Preparatory Commission, 2nd Session, A/CONF.206/PC(II)/2/Corr.1 (2004).

[35] Rule 66 of the rules of procedure of the International Conference on Population and Development, A/CONF.171/2 (1994); Rule 67 of the rules of procedure of the World Conference on Natural Disaster Reduction, A/CONF.172/2 (1994); Rule 64 of the rules of procedure of the 1998 ICC Conference, A/CONF.183/13 (vol. II) (1998); Rule 62 of the rules of procedure of the Second World Assembly on Ageing, A/CONF.197/2 (2002); Rule 66 of the rules of procedure of the 2005 International Meeting to Review the Implementation of the Programme of Action for the Sustainable Development of Small Island Developing States, A/CONF.207/2 (2004).

[36] UN GAOR, 6th Committee, 36th Session, 64th Meeting, para. 97, UN Doc. A/C.6/36/SR.64 (1981).

the Chairman ruled that 'it is not in keeping with the rules and procedures of the Assembly to include in the verbatim record statements that are not made orally in meetings. The verbatim reporters can only include material that is actually spoken.'[37]

A 1963 Ad Hoc Committee on the Methods of Work of the UNGA discussed the issue of adding written statements to the record. The Committee's conclusion was as follows:

> The delegations which advocated this method pointed out that it would be particularly appropriate for explanations of votes, lengthy or technical statements and statements made in exercise of right of reply. The majority of the committee, however, did not support these suggestions, the effect of which would be to alter the nature of the Assembly's debate considerably and to raise a certain number of practical problems which would be difficult to solve.[38]

The 1974–1977 Geneva Humanitarian Law Conference made extensive use of the procedure by which written statements, usually in explanation of vote, although not delivered, are nevertheless attached to the records of the conference.[39]

The Third Law of the Sea Conference also permitted delegations to submit written statements to be added to the records. The President informed the Conference that 'delegations would be permitted to present written statements whose contents would appear as part of the official records of the Conference'.[40] The Third Law of the Sea Conference also permitted – in fact obliged – delegations to exercise their right of reply in writing.[41]

The World Health Assembly allows written statements, which were not delivered orally, to be included in the verbatim records of the Assembly.[42]

37 UN GAOR, Special Political Committee, 44th Session, 14th Meeting, UN Doc. A/SPC/44/SR.14, pp. 9–10 (1989).

38 Report of the Ad Hoc Committee on the Improvement of the Methods of Work of the General Assembly, GAOR, 18th Session, Annexes, Agenda Item 25, p. 10, para. 64, UN Doc. A/5423 (1963). The UNGA, in Resolution 1898 (XVIII) of 11 November 1963, inter alia 'approved the recommendations submitted by the committee'.

39 See, for example, Official Records of the 1974–1977 Geneva Humanitarian Law Conference, CDDH/I/SR.77, vol. IX, p. 488, para. 49.

40 Official Records, Third Law of the Sea Conference, vol. XIII, p. 4, para. 15, 9th Session, 121st Plenary Meeting, UN Doc. A/CONF.62 (1981); vol. XIV, p. 11, para. 3, Resumed 9th Session, 132nd Plenary Meeting, UN Doc. A/CONF.62 (1982); vol. XVII, p. 14, para. 57, Resumed 11th Session, 185th Plenary Meeting, UN Doc. A/CONF.62 (1984).

41 Official Records, Third Law of the Sea Conference, vol. XVII, p. 14, para. 58, 185th Plenary Meeting, UN Doc. A/CONF.62 (1984).

42 WHO Resolution WHA20.2.

This arrangement does not appear to have engendered any procedural problems.

19.2.5 Correcting the Record

It is accepted practice that delegations submit to the secretariat of a conference proposed corrections to their statements as they appear in the records. Pastuhov wrote this in 1945 of this practice: 'It rarely happened that a delegate tried to change his speech to the extent that the meaning was altered. When this did occur, the Secretariat had to act with firmness and, if necessary, to resort to the authority of the President.'[43] The present author must add that he is not aware of any such confrontation between the secretariat of a conference and a delegation; however, this may be because such confrontations occurred in the privacy of secretariat offices. In earlier years, conferences used to produce provisional records and then incorporate corrections into the final version. In recent years, the provisional version has been omitted for budgetary reasons, and corrections are issued as a separate 'corrections' document.

19.2.6 Adding to the Record

At a meeting of the Third Law of the Sea Conference, the Australian delegation circulated in a private, nonconference paper a proposal that it described during the meeting as not constituting 'a formal draft amendment or a revision to the single negotiating text, but . . . simply a suggestion'.[44] At the next meeting, the Mexican delegation proposed that the Australian proposal be 'included in the record of the last meeting'.[45] Several delegations objected to such inclusion in the records, claiming that other informal proposals had not been so included.[46] The Chairman ruled that he could not include it in the records of the last meeting since the representative of Australia had stated at the meeting that his text was not a formal amendment to or a revision of the single negotiating text. It could,

[43] Vladimir D. Pastuhov, *A Guide to the Practice of International Conferences* (1945) p. 154.

[44] Official Records, Third Law of the Sea Conference, 3rd Committee, 5th Session, 29th Meeting, vol. VI, p. 92, UN Doc. A/CONF.62/SR.29, paras. 17, 18 (1977).

[45] Official Records, Third Law of the Sea Conference, 3rd Committee, 5th Session, 30th Meeting, vol. VI, p. 97, UN Doc. A/CONF.62/SR.30, para. 24 (1977).

[46] See, for example, the statement of the representative of Brazil, Official Records, Third Law of the Sea Conference, 3rd Committee, 5th Session, 31st Meeting, vol. VI, p. 100, UN Doc. A/CONF.62/SR.31, para. 3 (1977).

however, appear in the summary record of the current meeting if the representative of Australia wished to submit it formally. The proposal would then be reproduced in the summary record of the current meeting, but it could certainly not be inserted retroactively in the summary record of the previous meeting. In any event, he thought that that would be an unfortunate procedure, and he urged the representative of Australia to reconsider his position.[47]

Some delegations commented that if the Australian proposal were to be included in the records, then all informal proposals should be included. The Australian representative, at the Chairman's suggestion, withdrew his proposal.[48]

19.2.7 Deleting from the Records

Neither the rules of procedure of the UNGA nor the UN Model Rules provide for the presiding officer or the meeting to be able to expunge statements from the record. In 1969 the UN Office of Legal Affairs gave its opinion that 'it is not proper for a Committee to direct that statements made be excluded'.[49] Again, in 1991, the UN Office of Legal Affairs gave its opinion in regard to the records of the UN Commission on Human Rights that 'it is not the practice of the United Nations to expunge from official records statements duly entered into such records'. The 'request for deletion of the statement from the records of the Commission cannot, in accordance with established United Nations practice, be acceded to'.[50]

When proposals to delete statements from the record of UNGA debates have been made, presiding officers have usually ruled that there is no authority in the rules of procedure for such action.[51] At a 1961 meeting of the UNGA, the representative of Liberia moved that 'the whole speech of the representative of South Africa be deleted from the official records of the Assembly'.[52] The representative of Australia, on a point of order, stated

[47] *Ibid.* at p. 102, paras. 31, 33. [48] *Ibid.* at p. 103, para. 42.

[49] Office of Legal Affairs, *Note to the Chairman of the Third Committee*, 26 November 1969, QUESTION WHETHER IT IS PROPER FOR THE GENERAL ASSEMBLY OR ITS MAIN COMMITTEES TO DIRECT THAT STATEMENTS MADE BE DELETED FROM THE RECORDS, http://legal.un.org/ola/media/GA_RoP/GA_RoP_EN.pdf.

[50] Cable (from UN Office of Legal Affairs) to the Chief of Protocol, Office of the Director General, United Nations Office at Geneva, 26 February 1991, 1991 UN Jur. Y.B. 296.

[51] UN GAOR, 3rd Committee, 6th Session, 398th Meeting, paras. 18, 21, UN Doc. A/C.3/6/SR.398 (1951); UN GAOR, 2nd Committee, 17th Session, 864th Meeting, para. 49, UN Doc. A/C.2/17/SR.864 (1962).

[52] UN GAOR, Plenary, 16th Session, 1033rd Meeting, para. 151, UN Doc. A/PV.1033 (1961).

that 'except where the President calls people to order these [statements] have not been expunged. Now if we adopt the present motion, which I think is unprecedented in the plenary meeting, we will have expunged something because we disagree with it. We will have expunged a statement by a sovereign Government.'[53] The representative of Uruguay argued that 'the official records should be an exact account of our proceedings'.[54] Liberia withdrew its motion.[55]

Nevertheless, there appear to have been at least two occasions when statements have been expunged from the records. At the 1961 meeting of the UNGA, the President ruled that the speaker, Nikita Khrushchev, Chairman of the Council of Ministers of the USSR, was out of order for making personal offensive remarks[56] and ordered the offensive remarks to be deleted from the record.[57] The chairman of a UNGA committee at a 1965 meeting ordered deletion of a statement, by the representative of South Africa, from the records.[58] Prevailing practice clearly, however, is that presiding officers have no such authority.

At the 1958 Law of the Sea Conference, the representative of Israel objected to a statement by the representative of Saudi Arabia and requested that 'it should not appear in the records'. The Chairman ruled that the statement was 'out of order', but that 'it should appear in the records'.[59]

At a meeting of the 1974–1977 Geneva Humanitarian Law Conference, the representative of Sri Lanka, speaking on a point of order, said that 'what had been said was a regrettable attack on a delegation and should not be included in the record'.[60] The President replied that 'it was the rule to include in the record all statements made during the course of a meeting'.[61]

[53] *Ibid.* at para. 172. [54] *Ibid.* at para. 182.

[55] UN GAOR, Plenary, 16th Session, 1034th Meeting, para. 35, UN Doc. A/PV.1034 (1961).

[56] Mr Khrushchev described General Franco as 'that butcher of the Spanish people'. *Keesing's Contemporary Archives*, vol. XIII (1961–62), p. 17927.

[57] UN GAOR, Plenary, 15th Session, 881st Meeting, para. 108, UN Doc. A/PV.881 (1960).

[58] UN GAOR, 5th Committee, 20th Session, 1087th Meeting, paras. 1–4, UN Doc. A/C.5/20/SR.1087 (1965).

[59] Official Records of the 1958 Law of the Sea Conference, Committee I, vol. III, p. 3, paras. 23–25, UN Doc. A/CONF.13/39 (1958).

[60] Official Records of the 1974–1977 Geneva Humanitarian Law Conference, CDDH/SR.57, vol. VII, p. 256, para. 25, referring to a statement by the present author, on behalf of Israel, in reference to the PLO signing the Final Act of the Conference.

[61] Official Records of the 1974–1977 Geneva Humanitarian Law Conference, CDDH/SR.57, vol. VII, p. 256, para. 26.

At a meeting of the Third Law of the Sea Conference, a delegation complained about the contents of a statement by the representative of the International Ocean Institute, who had been invited to speak as a representative of a nongovernmental organisation. The Chairman ruled that 'parts of that statement which were not connected with the item under discussion would be omitted from the record'.[62] This ruling may perhaps be explained by the very limited right to speak that conferences grant to representatives of nongovernmental organisations.

At the 1967 ILO Conference, the President announced, 'If he [a speaker] persists in the use of such language he will be requested to resume his seat. Any such language will be expunged from the record before it is published.'[63] Several delegations expressed objection to such procedure, and the government representative from Poland asked the President 'in which paragraph of the Standing Orders of the Constitution is it stated that you can expunge from the records a statement criticising imperialist aggression?'[64] No answer was given from the Chair.

The President of the 1972 session of the ILO Conference ordered that parts of various statements be deleted from the records of the Conference.[65] The decision was subject to criticism as being beyond the authority of the presiding officer.[66] The President claimed that he possessed such authority in accordance with the rule of procedure that stipulated that the President 'shall direct the debates, maintain order, ensure the observance of the Standing Orders by such means as circumstances may demand'.[67] When several delegates insisted on restoring the words deleted from their speeches, the President reluctantly agreed to do so.[68] A footnote was added in the records in each instance, noting, 'The President decided that the preceding words from ... should be expunged. These words were subsequently restored at the request of the delegate.'[69]

At a 2006 meeting of a committee of the World Health Assembly, a delegation asked that a 'reference be removed from the record'. The Legal Counsel gave his opinion that '[t]he Secretariat could not censor such

[62] Official Records, Third Law of the Sea Conference, vol. II, p. 63, Summary Records of the 12th Meeting of Committee I, para. 35, UN Doc. A/CONF.62 (1974).
[63] ILO Conference, 51st Session, Geneva 1967, Record of Proceedings, 12th sitting, p. 171.
[64] *Ibid.* at p. 209.
[65] ILO Conference, 57th Session, Geneva 1972, Record of Proceedings, pp. 183, 293, 351, 362.
[66] See, for example, *ibid.* at pp. 99, 293, 366.
[67] Article 13(2) of the Standing Orders of the ILO Conference, Geneva 1992.
[68] See, for example, ILO Conference, 57th Session, Geneva 1972, Record of Proceedings, preambular 'Note by the President of the Conference'.
[69] For example, *ibid.* at p. 351, n 1.

records in any way, nor could it delete parts of statements at the request of a Member State'.[70]

COMMENT

Despite the exceptions referred to, it would appear to be established practice that there is no authority to expunge statements from the records of the UNGA or a conference.

19.2.8 Final Act

Treaty-making conferences complete their work by adopting a document known as the Final Act. The Final Act includes the text of the treaty drafted, texts of resolutions adopted and organisational details of the conference. Rosenne describes a Final Act as

> a highly concentrated summary of the principal events in the history of the Conference itself, from the decision to convene it to its termination, incorporating by reference all the relevant documentation and records, and its mandate. Very occasionally it may include statements made specifically for inclusion in the Final Act.[71]

[70] Committee 'A', World Health Assembly, 59th Session, 1st Meeting, WHA 59/2006/REC/3 p. 20 (2006).

[71] Shabtai Rosenne, *Practice and Methods of International Law* (1984), p. 39.

20

Committees

20.1 Committees

Each conference determines its own needs for committees, although in treaty-making conferences, a credentials committee, a drafting committee and a general or steering committee are always among the committees appointed. The large size of international conferences requires that the conference set up main committees to carry out the task of preparing texts or resolutions. The practice of conferences appointing a committee of the whole, composed of the plenary, has become less common.

Pastuhov commented in 1945 that, according to custom, 'all delegations are entitled to be represented on each main committee of an international conference',[1] and this custom remains valid.

20.2 Procedure of Committees

Most rules of procedure stipulate that, with some exceptions, the rules applicable to the plenary apply to committees *mutatis mutandis*. The exceptions are usually that the quorum for opening a meeting is smaller than that required in plenary meetings; all decisions are taken by majority vote and a two-thirds majority is required only for reconsideration of an issue; and the chairmen can participate in the voting.

20.3 Relations between Committees and Plenary

At a 1989 meeting of the General Conference of the IAEA, the Legal Adviser was asked whether a proposal not approved by the Committee of the Whole could nevertheless be subject to a vote in the Plenary. The Legal Adviser gave his opinion that the 'plenary, as master of its own procedure,

[1] Vladimir D. Pastuhov, *A Guide to the Practice of International Conferences* (1945), p. 154.

could consider any proposal' subject to the rules of procedure concerning notice of submission of proposals.[2]

At a 2000 meeting of the Plenary of the World Health Assembly, the Legal Counsel was asked whether a committee could decide not to discuss an issue even though it had been inscribed on the agenda by the plenary. The Legal Counsel ruled that 'a committee often decides to take no action on an agenda item. This flows from the natural authority of any parliamentary body when confronted with a particular question'[3] and 'the Committee came to a conclusion, which it had the authority to come to'.[4]

20.4 The Different Committees

Most conferences will usually appoint the following committees: general committee; credentials committee,[5] main committees and drafting committee.

20.4.1 General Committee

The UNGA rules of procedure state,

> *Rule 41*
>
> The General Committee shall make recommendations to the General Assembly concerning the closing date of the session. It shall assist the President and the General Assembly in drawing up the agenda for each plenary meeting, in determining the priority of its items and in coordinating the proceedings of all committees of the Assembly. It shall also assist the President in the general conduct of the work of the General Assembly which falls within the competence of the President. It shall not, however, decide any political question.[6]

The UN Model Rules propose,

> *Rule 26*
>
> *Functions*
>
> In addition to performing other functions specified in these rules, the General Committee shall assist the President in the general conduct of the

[2] Official Records of the 67th Meeting of the Committee of the Whole of the 33rd General Conference of the IAEA, IAEA Doc. GC(XXXIII)/COM.5/OR.67, para. 93 (1989).

[3] WHO, Verbatim Records of the 53rd World Health Assembly, 8th Plenary Meeting, p. 137, WHA/53/2000/REC/2 (2000).

[4] *Ibid.* at p. 135.

[5] The role of the credentials committee is discussed in Chapter 4.

[6] Rule 40 of the UNGA rules of procedure refers to the functions of the Committee in relation to the agenda.

business of the Conference and, subject to the decisions of the Conference, shall ensure the co-ordination of its work.

Pastuhov defined the role of a general committee of a conference as

> to assist the president in the general direction of the conference, in regulating the composition of all such committees as the gathering may decide to create, in deciding on the communications to be made to the conference, in the framing of the agenda for each meeting, in determining the order of priority for its various items, etc.[7]

20.4.1.1 Composition of the General Committee

The UNGA rules of procedure state,

> *Rule 38*
>
> The General Committee shall comprise the President of the General Assembly, who shall preside, the twenty-one Vice-Presidents and the Chairmen of the seven Main Committees. No two members of the General Committee shall be members of the same delegation, and it shall be so constituted as to ensure its representative character. Chairmen of other committees upon which all members have the right to be represented and which are established by the General Assembly to meet during the session shall be entitled to attend meetings of the General Committee and may participate without vote in the discussions.
>
> *Rule 43*
>
> A member of the General Assembly which has no representative on the General Committee and which has requested the inclusion of an item in the agenda shall be entitled to attend any meeting of the General Committee at which its request is discussed and may participate, without vote, in the discussion of that item.[8]

The UN Model Rules propose,

> *Rule 24*
>
> *Composition*
>
> 1. The officers elected pursuant to rule 20 [the president, a vice-president in charge of coordination, a rapporteur-general, and chairmen of main committees and of drafting committees] shall constitute the General Committee. The chairman or another designated representative of any subsidiary organ not represented on the Committee may participate in its proceedings, without the right to vote.

[7] Pastuhov, *Guide*, p. 94.

[8] Rule 39 of the UNGA rules of procedure deals with substitute members.

2. If any member of the General Committee is to be absent from one of its meetings, he may designate another member of his delegation to participate and vote in his place. The chairman of any subsidiary organ represented on the Committee may also designate a vice-chairman to participate in the proceedings of the Committee, without the right to vote.

Rule 25

Officers

The President, or in his absence one of the Vice-Presidents designated by him, shall serve as Chairman and, if necessary, the Rapporteur-General shall serve as Rapporteur of the General Committee.

At the 1968 Teheran Conference on Human Rights, the representative of Israel asked to take part in the discussions in the General Committee.[9] The Executive Secretary of the Conference replied that 'the rules of procedure did not contain any provision on the point. It was therefore for the General Committee itself to decide how to deal with the request.'[10]

Rosenne points out that it is usual to appoint a representative from the host State to membership in the general committee of a conference.[11] This is clearly achieved if the president of the conference is a representative of the host State.

20.4.2 Main Committees

In a treaty-drafting conference each of the main committees will be allocated different sections of the basic text. The usual procedure is for proposals to be submitted to one of the main committees and for committees to submit reports to the plenary. Such reports include the texts of resolutions and proposals approved by the committee. Main committees are identified by number.

20.4.2.1 Submission of Proposals to Main Committees

At the Third Law of the Sea Conference, a delegation objected to the submission of a Canadian proposal directly to the Plenary and argued that it should have been submitted to a committee. The President ruled,

[9] Concerning the inclusion in the agenda of a draft resolution on 'Human Rights in the Occupied Territories'.

[10] A/CONF.32/BUR/SR.2, p. 6 (1968). As a result of a vote, the request by Israel was rejected.

[11] From a discussion by the author with Shabtai Rosenne, Jerusalem, July 1995.

> [A]ny delegation had the right to choose the forum in which it introduced a proposal. Proposals, in strict constitutional terms, should be made to the Conference, despite the fact that subjects and issues were assigned to the Main Committees. That was an act of delegation by the Conference: it indicated the precise subsidiary organ of the Conference to which proposals should be referred but did not extinguish the right to which he had referred. If a proposal was introduced in the Conference, the Conference took the decision to refer it to the appropriate subsidiary organ. If a delegation chose, for reasons of convenience or other reasons, to introduce a proposal in the first instance in a Committee, it was free to do so.[12]

A challenge to the President's ruling was defeated.[13]

20.5 Drafting Committee

The UNGA rules of procedure do not refer to drafting committees, and such committees are not a feature of UN procedural practice. However, the 1994 UNGA Resolution calling for a study of the Non-Navigational Uses of International Watercourses proposed that the UNGA Sixth Committee, acting as a committee of the whole, should set up a drafting committee when examining the ILC draft on the subject, and a drafting committee was accordingly set up.[14]

20.5.1 Drafting Committees at Conferences

Treaty-drafting conferences invariably appoint a drafting committee as one of the committees of the conference.

20.5.1.1 Mandate of a Drafting Committee

The UN Model Rules propose,

> *Rule 64*
>
> *Drafting Committee*
>
> 2. The Drafting Committee shall prepare drafts and give advice on drafting as requested by the Conference or any Main Committee. Subject to any

[12] Official Records of the Third Law of the Sea Conference, vol. I, p. 201, Summary Records of the 46th Plenary Meeting, para. 50, UN Doc. A/CONF.62 (1974).

[13] *Ibid.* at p. 202, para. 52.

[14] Annex to UNGA Resolution 49/52 of 9 December 1994; UN Doc. A/C.6/51/NUW/DC (1996) (1997).

> general instructions of the Conference, it shall co-ordinate and review the drafting of all texts referred to it and shall report, as appropriate, either to the Conference or the Main Committee concerned.

It was only after debating the issue for some time that the 1926 League of Nations Committee included drafting committees as an item in its list of rules of procedure.[15] Nowadays however, although many recent conferences have no reference in their rules of procedure to drafting committees, 'the use of drafting committees is almost universal'.[16]

Drafting committees are at times a problematic issue in conferences since they have limited membership, and thus not all States can participate. Yet, drafting committees often possess, in practice, powers beyond the language of their mandate.

The increasingly active role of drafting committees is reflected, to a certain extent, in the differing mandates granted to them in rules of procedure over the years. The rules of procedure of the 1949 Geneva Conference stipulated that the Drafting Committee should 'report to the Conference on the final wording of the Conventions drawn up by Committees'.[17] The rules of procedure of the 1954 Hague Conference stated that the Drafting Committee 'is responsible for drawing up the final text of the Convention and the annexed instruments in the three working languages of the Conference'.[18] The rules of procedure of the 1958 Law of the Sea Conference stated that the Drafting Committee 'shall be entrusted with the final drafting and co-ordination of the instruments approved by the Committees'.[19] The rules of the 1968 Non-Nuclear-Weapon State Conference stated that the Drafting Committee 'shall give advice on drafting as requested by other committees and by the Conference and shall

[15] Committee of Experts for the Progressive Codification of International Law, Report to the Council of the League of Nations on the Questions Which Appear Ripe for International Regulation, Questionnaire No. 5, Procedure of International Conferences and Procedure for the Conclusion and Drafting of Treaties, 18th Session of the Committee, 22 January 1926, reproduced in Shabtai Rosenne, ed., *League of Nations Committee of Experts for the Progressive Codification of International Law (1925–1928)*, vol. I (1972), p. 141.

[16] UNGA, 35th Session, Item 105 of the provisional agenda, Review of the Multilateral Treaty-Making Process, Report of the Secretary-General, para. 39, UN Doc. A/35/312 (1980).

[17] Rule 19 of the rules of procedure of the 1949 Geneva Conference.

[18] Rule 11 of the rules of procedure of the 1954 Hague Conference.

[19] Rule 49 of the rules of procedure of the 1958 Law of the Sea Conference, UN Doc. A/CONF.13/38 (1958). The rules of procedure of the 1960 Law of the Sea Conference contained no reference to a drafting committee.

coordinate and review the drafting of all texts adopted'.[20] The rules of the 1974–1977 Geneva Humanitarian Law Conference provided that the Drafting Committee should 'prepare drafts and give advice on drafting as requested by the Conference or by the main Committees. It shall co-ordinate and review the drafting of all texts adopted.'[21] These phrases, in different combinations, appear in most rules of procedure that have a reference to drafting committees.

The ITU rules of procedure for conferences are more demanding of drafting committees. The rules state that texts should be submitted to an 'Editorial Committee charged with perfecting their form without altering the sense and, where appropriate, with combining them with those parts of former texts which have not been altered'.[22] The Standing Orders of the International Labour Conference stipulate, 'Amendments to a text submitted to a committee by its drafting committee may be admitted by the Chairman after consultation with the Vice Chairmen.'[23]

Unease by States at the increasingly active role played by drafting committees led to the restrictive drafting of the rule in the Third Law of the Sea Conference. The rules of the Third Law of the Sea Conference explicitly limited the functions of the drafting committee. The rules state that the drafting committee

Rule 53

1 . . . . shall, without reopening substantive discussion on any matter, formulate drafts and give advice on drafting as requested by the Conference or by a Main Committee, co-ordinate and refine the drafting of all texts referred to it, without altering their substance, and report to the Conference or to the Main Committee as appropriate. It shall have no power of or responsibility for initiating texts.[24]

The restrictions on the drafting committee, as set out in the rules of procedure of the Third Law of the Sea Conference, have been replicated in

[20] Rule 47 of the rules of procedure of the 1968 Non-Nuclear-Weapon State Conference, UN Doc. A/CONF.35/1 (1968). The 1968 Teheran Conference on Human Rights used the same language in Rule 47 of its rules of procedure, UN Doc. A/CONF.32/2 (1968).

[21] Rule 47(1) of the rules of procedure of the 1974–77 Geneva Humanitarian Law Conference, CDDH/2/Rev.3.

[22] Rule 32(4)(3)(a) of the Constitution of the International Telecommunication Union, Geneva 1993.

[23] Rule 67 of the Standing Orders of the International Labour Conference.

[24] Rule 53(1) of the rules of procedure of the Third Law of the Sea Conference, UN Doc. A/62/30/Rev.3 (1975).

recent conferences, including the 1995, 2000 and 2005 NPT Review Conferences and the Conference on Establishing the ICC.[25] The last sentence of the Third Law of the Sea Conference rule, referring to not initiating texts, has, however, not been included in subsequent rules.

At the 1998 ICC Conference, the Chairman of the Drafting Committee explained that the committee 'did not deal with matters of substance but was responsible for ensuring that the text as a whole was a homogenous [*sic*] and cohesive one which avoided ambiguities and matters which were not clear'.[26] A member of the same drafting committee commented that 'it was not the task of that committee to divine the intention underlying the articles of the Statute, but rather to clarify the language in which they were expressed'.[27]

Irrespective of the exact formulation of the mandate of drafting committees, the reality is that such committees play an important part in the work of conferences, particularly treaty-making conferences. An early example of the use of a drafting committee was at the 1950 Conference on Missing Persons where the Conference approved a proposal by a representative that 'the problems could be easily solved if the Conference agreed to differentiate between the articles of the draft convention itself, amendments of substance, and drafting amendments. All drafting amendments should be submitted direct to the drafting committee.'[28]

At the Vienna Conference on the Law of Treaties, the Chairman ruled on the significance of transferring an article to a drafting committee. He stated that the principle involved 'had been adopted and that the Drafting Committee was now being called upon, in view of the suggested changes, to have another look at the text and see whether it could be made clearer'.[29]

At the 1963 Tokyo Air Law Conference, it was proposed that a UK draft proposal be referred to the Drafting Committee. A representative stated his understanding that 'neither the wording nor the substance of the text to be prepared by the Drafting Committee on the basis of the UK

[25] Rule 36(1) of the rules of procedure of the 1995, 2000, 2005 NPT Review Conferences, Docs. NPT/CONF.1995/28 (1995), NPT/CONF.2000/1 (2000), NPT/CONF.2005/1 (2004); Rule 49 of the rules of procedure of the UN Diplomatic Conference of Plenipotentiaries on the Establishment of an International Criminal Court, UN Doc. A/CONF.183/13 (1998).

[26] 1998 ICC Conference, Mr. Bassiouni, Chairman of the Drafting Committee, Summary Records of the 37th Meeting of the Committee of the Whole, para. 19 (1998).

[27] *Ibid.* at para. 30.

[28] Summary Records of the 1950 Conference on Missing Persons, 3rd Plenary Meeting, para. 24, UN Doc. A/CONF.1/SR.3 (1950).

[29] Official Records of the Vienna Conference on the Law of Treaties, 1st Session, 57th Meeting of the Committee of the Whole, p. 334, para. 96, UN Doc. A/CONF.39/11 (1969).

resolution would be final'. The President commented that the contents of the UK proposal as adopted by the Conference could not be changed by the Drafting Committee, and that only if some new principle were brought in by the Drafting Committee could there be a discussion in the Conference.[30]

At the 1974–1977 Geneva Humanitarian Law Conference, the US representative 'urged the Conference not to turn itself into a drafting committee but to leave it to the official Drafting Committee to make drafting amendments'.[31]

At a meeting of the 1986 Conference on Treaties between States and International Organisations, the delegate of Brazil commented that the drafting committee 'could send articles back to the Committee of the Whole for further consideration'.[32] The Chairman confirmed this opinion, stating that 'if discussions which had already taken place in the Committee of the Whole were repeated in the Drafting Committee, the latter should send the articles back to the former for further consideration'.[33]

20.5.2 Drafting Committee as a Body for Informal Negotiations

Use is often made of a drafting committee as an unofficial working group to solve problems of substance. At the 1957 Brussels Conference on Maritime Law, one delegate pointed out that 'every time a tricky question arose we were able to say that we would refer it to the Drafting Committee . . . [S]everal questions on a material difference were referred to the Drafting Committee in the hope that they would sort out the difficulties.'[34] Scelle, writing in 1953, pointed out that a drafting committee 'does much more than deal with questions of form and of wording. It is in the drafting committee that the opposition makes its last – and frequently best camouflaged – stand.'[35]

At a 1976 IMCO conference, the Chairman noted that 'the amendment had been approved; but in view of the large number of abstentions, it

[30] Minutes of the 9th Meeting of the 1963 Tokyo Air Law Conference, paras. 48, 50, ICAO Doc. 8565-LC/152–1 (1963) (published 1966).

[31] Official Records of the 1974–1977 Geneva Humanitarian Law Conference, CDDH/SR.39, vol. VI, p. 98, para. 41.

[32] Official Records of the 1986 Conference on Treaties between States and International Organisations, 22nd Meeting, para. 48, UN Doc. A/CONF.129/16 (1986).

[33] *Ibid.* 23rd Meeting, para. 50.

[34] Records of the 1957 Brussels Conference on Maritime Law, 2nd Session, p. 254.

[35] Georges Scelle, 'The Evolution of International Conferences', 5 *UNESCO International Social Science Bulletin* 241 (1953 No. 2) at 249.

would be submitted to the Drafting Committee to see if the text could be made more precise'.[36]

At the 1977 Vienna Conference on Succession of States in Respect of Treaties, the Chairman gave one delegation the unusual assurance that '[t]he Drafting Committee would naturally take account in its discussion of any article, however adopted, of the range of views expressed in the Committee'.[37]

At a meeting of the 1978 Vienna Conference on Succession of States in Respect of Treaties, a lengthy debate took place on a proposal to transfer to the Drafting Committee, without a vote, a proposed amendment with instructions to the Committee 'to find an appropriate solution'.[38] The representative of Venezuela stated that he felt that 'the reference of the amendment to the Drafting Committee implied that the Committee of the Whole had agreed in principle that it should be incorporated somewhere in the text, or that it had been approved *a priori* by the Committee'.[39] The representative of Hungary stated that 'the mandate intended for the Drafting Committee went beyond its actual competence. If the amendment were to be referred anywhere, it would be more appropriately referred to the informal consultation group.'[40] The representative of Cyprus gave his opinion that, by referring the amendment to the Drafting Committee without a decision, the Committee of the Whole would be 'asking the Drafting Committee to function as its legal adviser'.[41] The representative of Italy pointed out that the Committee

> should not allow itself to be bemused by titles. Drafting committees had historically had different functions, and one of the roles which it was now customary for them to play was that of adviser to the larger bodies of which they were organs in matters such as that which was now before the Committee of the Whole. It should be noted that the Drafting Committee would be asked to do no more than to say whether, in the light of the present text of the draft articles . . . an amendment such as the one proposed was

[36] Official Records of the International Conference on the Limitation of Liability for Maritime Claims, London 1976, Summary Records of the 17th Meeting of Committee I, IMCO Doc. CONF.5/C.1/SR.17, p. 340.

[37] 1977 Vienna Conference on Succession of States in Respect of Treaties, 1st Session, Official Records, vol. I, Committee of the Whole, 5th Meeting, para. 70, UN Doc. A/CONF.80/C.1/SR.5 (1977).

[38] 1977 Vienna Conference on Succession of States in Respect of Treaties, Resumed Session, Official records, vol. II, p. 45, para. 24, Summary Records of the 39th Meeting of the Committee of the Whole, UN Doc. A/CONF.80/C.1/SR.39 (1978).

[39] *Ibid.* at p. 46, para. 32. [40] *Ibid.* at p. 46, para. 36. [41] *Ibid.* at p. 47, para. 46.

> necessary. The decision whether to accept the substance of such an amendment would, of course, lie with the Committee of the Whole.[42]

The Chairman of the Drafting Committee commented that as an 'organ of the Conference, the Drafting Committee could study only such matters as were referred to it by the Conference or by the Committee of the Whole'.[43] After further discussion, and on the advice of the Chairman of the Drafting Committee, the issue of transferring the amendment to the Drafting Committee was put to the vote.[44]

At a meeting of the 1983 Vienna Conference on State Property (Succession), the Chairman pointed out, 'A decision to refer the text to the Drafting Committee could be taken only after due consideration of all formal amendments.'[45] The Chairman, however, later proposed that an amendment that had not been voted on be transferred to the Drafting Committee 'for possible use in the final formulation of the text'.[46] When this ruling was queried, the Chairman amended his ruling, stating that the amendment would go forward to the Drafting Committee 'as material for discussion without any formal status'.[47] The Chairman again reminded the Committee that '[t]he Committee of the Whole would first have to adopt any texts it wished to refer to the Drafting Committee'.[48] The representative of the United Kingdom commented later in the debate that 'his delegation was unable to accept any suggestion that the role of the Drafting Committee was confined to examining texts which had been adopted by the Committee of the Whole. Such an interpretation would make the opening phrase of rule 47, paragraph 2, of the rules of procedure totally meaningless.'[49] The Committee nevertheless put the amendments to the vote before transferring them to the Drafting Committee.[50]

[42] *Ibid.* at p. 47, para. 50. [43] *Ibid.* at p. 48, para. 56. [44] *Ibid.* at p. 48, paras. 56, 57.

[45] Official Records of the 1983 Vienna Conference on State Property (Succession), 3rd Meeting of the Committee of the Whole, para. 41, vol. I, p. 54, UN Doc. A/CONF/117 (1995).

[46] Official Records of the 1983 Vienna Conference on State Property (Succession), 6th Meeting of the Committee of the Whole, para. 27, vol. I, p. 64, UN Doc. A/CONF/117 (1995).

[47] *Ibid.* at p. 6.

[48] Official Records of the 1983 Vienna Conference on State Property (Succession), 7th Meeting of the Committee of the Whole, para. 33, vol. I, p. 70, UN Doc. A/CONF/117 (1995).

[49] The text of Rule 47, para. 2 reads: 'The Drafting Committee shall prepare drafts and give advice on drafting as requested by the Conference or by the Committee of the Whole.' UN Doc. A/CONF/117/2 (1983). This text is substantively identical to the text of the UN Model Rules. Official Records of the 1983 Vienna Conference on State Property (Succession), 12th Meeting of the Committee of the Whole, para. 18, vol. I, p. 91, UN Doc. A/CONF/117 (1995).

[50] UN Doc. A/CONF/117/2 (1983).

Writing in 1995, Szasz stated that a drafting committee, at the minimum, examines the texts that emerge from the general representative organ(s); coordinates them with each other; sees that their formulation is clear, consistent and reflects the decisions of the organ accurately – and does so in all the languages in which the text is to be authentic. Often additional functions are assigned, such as the complete drafting of the final or formal provisions of the treaty and possibly also of the primary legal ones.[51]

20.5.3 Deciding to Transfer a Proposal to a Drafting Committee

Conferences at times engage in procedural debates as to whether an issue should be transferred to a drafting committee. Clearly delegations that are unable to obtain a majority in a vote on a proposal or amendment can attempt to infiltrate the desired principle into the final text via a drafting committee.

At the 1977 Vienna Conference on Succession of States in Respect of Treaties, a dispute arose about whether a proposed amendment was merely one of drafting or not. The Chairman proposed that the amendment 'be transmitted to the Drafting Committee as a mere suggestion that would in no way be binding, so that it could only be examined from the point of view of form and not of substance'. The Chairman's proposal was accepted.[52] At a later meeting at the same conference, a dispute again arose about whether an amendment was one of drafting or not. After a discussion, the Chairman asked the Committee to vote on the issue.[53]

At the 1977 Conference on Territorial Asylum, the Chairman of the Committee of the Whole requested the Chairman of the Drafting Committee 'to indicate to the Committee of the Whole, at his convenience, which of those proposals related to substantive matters and which were concerned solely with questions of drafting'.[54] One delegate commented, on a point of order, that 'he had been both surprised and disappointed that

[51] Paul Szasz, 'General Law Making Process', in *United Nations Legal Order*, eds. Oscar Schachter and Christopher C. Joyner, vol. I (1995), p. 35 at p. 78.

[52] 1977 Vienna Conference on Succession of States in Respect of Treaties (First Session), Official Records, 4th Meeting of the Committee of the Whole, para. 33, vol. I, p. 37, UN Doc. A/CONF.80 (1978).

[53] *Ibid.* at paras. 26, 27.

[54] 1977 Conference on Territorial Asylum, Committee of the Whole, 10th Meeting, para. 59, UN Doc. A/CONF.78/C.1/SR.10 (1977).

the Chairman of the Drafting Committee had been asked for his opinion on the various amendments'.[55] The Chairman responded that 'if there was the slightest doubt as to whether an amendment was or was not substantive, he would seek the view of the Committee by putting the question to the vote'.[56] At a later meeting of the same committee, the Chairman declared that 'if any delegation took the view that an amendment was substantive and should not therefore be referred to the Drafting Committee, it had only to say so – without making a statement – and the amendment in question would be put to the vote'.[57]

At a 1978 IMCO conference, a dispute arose about whether a proposal was a matter of substance or a matter of drafting that could be referred to a drafting committee. The Chairman decided that the question as to whether the issue was one of drafting or not should be decided by a vote.[58]

At a meeting of the 1978 Vienna Conference on Succession of States in Respect of Treaties, the delegate of the United Kingdom submitted that since 'what the delegation of Switzerland was seeking was simply an opinion as to whether or not the current text of the draft Convention covered the concern it had sought to express in its draft amendment, he believed that the Committee of the Whole could ask the Drafting Committee to look into the matter'.[59] The Chairman ruled that 'when any article has [been] referred to the Drafting Committee, it was subject to the understanding that that body could not take up any references in the article to other provisions of the draft until those provisions had themselves been approved by the Committee of the Whole'.[60]

At a meeting of a committee of the Third Law of the Sea Conference, the representative of India proposed that 'the editorial changes should be referred to the Drafting Committee in the first instance. If difficult issues then emerged, they might be referred back to the Committee at

55 1977 Conference on Territorial Asylum, Committee of the Whole, 11th Meeting, para. 51, UN Doc. A/CONF.78/C.1/SR.11 (1977).

56 *Ibid.* at para. 54.

57 1977 Conference on Territorial Asylum, Committee of the Whole, 16th Meeting, para. 13, UN Doc. A/CONF.78/C.1/SR.16 (1977).

58 IMCO Doc. CONF.2/C.2/SR.3, p. 571 (1978).

59 Sir Ian Sinclair at the 1978 Vienna Conference on Succession of States in Respect of Treaties, Resumed Session, Official Records, vol. II, p. 47, para. 48, Summary Records of the 39th Meeting of the Committee of the Whole, UN Doc. A/CONF.80/C.1/SR.39 (1979).

60 1978 Vienna Conference on Succession of States in Respect of Treaties, Resumed Session, Official Records, vol. II, p. 72, para. 8, Summary Records of the 43rd Meeting of the Committee of the Whole, UN Doc. A/CONF.80/C.1/SR.43 (1979).

a later stage.'[61] The representative of Czechoslovakia pointed out that it 'was sometimes impossible to draw a dividing line between drafting changes and substantive changes. All delegates should have an opportunity to express their views on the proposed amendment.'[62] The representative of the United States commented that 'the Drafting Committee had followed the rule that if any delegation viewed a particular change as substantive, that change should not be accepted'.[63] This particular issue was apparently solved by informal discussions.[64]

At a meeting of the 1986 Conference on Treaties between States and International Organisations, the delegate of France stated that

> his delegation could not agree to the transmission of the . . . text to the Drafting Committee together with two amendments which partly contradicted each other. The Drafting Committee was not a negotiating body; it could adapt a text but it could not be expected to combine two amendments with opposing points of view. If amendments which involved substantive differences were referred to the Drafting Committee, his delegation might well be obliged to refuse to examine them there. Articles on which there was disagreement should be regarded as pending and negotiated elsewhere than in the Drafting Committee.[65]

The same 1986 conference had a rule of procedure whereby '[t]he Conference shall decide which of the draft articles of the basic proposal . . . require substantive consideration. These draft articles shall be referred to the Committee of the Whole and all other draft articles shall be referred directly to the Drafting Committee.'[66] The Egyptian delegate presented, to the Committee of the Whole, an amendment to an article that had been submitted by the Plenary directly to the Drafting Committee. The delegate from the United Kingdom, on a point of order, stated that 'he was somewhat perplexed by the situation which had arisen, inasmuch as it was now seemingly proposed to reopen substantive discussion of an article in respect of which the Drafting Committee had already

[61] Official Records of the Third Law of the Sea Conference, Resumed 9th Session, 45th Meeting of Committee III, vol. XIV, p. 102, para. 20, UN Doc. A/CONF.62 (1980).

[62] *Ibid.* at para. 23 [63] *Ibid.* at para. 24.

[64] See Official Records of the Third Law of the Sea Conference, Resumed 9th Session, 46th Meeting of Committee III, vol. XIV, p. 103, para. 14, UN Doc. A/CONF.62 (1980).

[65] Official Records of the 1986 Conference on Treaties between States and International Organisations, 22nd Meeting, para. 47, UN Doc. A/CONF.129/16 (1986).

[66] Rule 28 of the rules of procedure of the 1986 Conference on Treaties between States and International Organisations, UN Doc. A/CONF.129/7 (1986).

completed its deliberations'.[67] The Egyptian delegation subsequently withdrew its amendment so no ruling was made on the issue.

COMMENT

The practice of conferences shows clearly that where objection is made to transferring an issue to a drafting committee, the conference (committee or plenary) must take a decision as to whether the issue concerned is one of drafting that it wishes to transfer to the drafting committee.

20.5.4 *Drafting Committees Acting beyond their Mandate*

There are instances where delegations complain that drafting committees are acting beyond their competence by dealing with issues of substance.[68]

At the 1973 ICAO Extraordinary Assembly, the Chairman of the Executive Committee ruled that a drafting committee 'must confine itself strictly to the matters referred to it by the Committee and be guided by the Committee's decisions on them'.[69] The Chairman ruled later that the Drafting Committee 'had gone beyond its terms of reference' and the draft they presented could not be discussed 'without a reopening of debate'.[70]

At the Committee of the Whole of the 1977 Vienna Conference on Succession of States in Respect of Treaties, several schools of thought became apparent as to the task of the drafting committee. The Algerian representative argued that 'it would be a dangerous precedent for the Committee of the Whole to entrust the Drafting Committee with the task of solving its problems'.[71] The Swedish representative cautioned, 'Reference to that [Drafting] Committee of amendments which clearly related to the substance of a draft article should be avoided at all costs.'[72] The representative of France argued, however, that 'amendments should be referred to

[67] Official Records of the 1986 Conference on Treaties between States and International Organisations, 29th Meeting, para. 14, UN Doc. A/CONF.129/16 (1986).

[68] See, for example, the complaint by the representative of the People's Republic of the Congo at the 1971 Montreal Air Law Conference, 8th Plenary Meeting, Vol. I, Minutes, p. 175, para. 53, ICAO Doc. 9081-LC/170–1.

[69] Minutes of the 11th Meeting of the Executive Committee of the 20th Extraordinary ICAO Assembly, para. 26, ICAO Doc. 9088, A20-Min.EX/11, p. 112, (1973).

[70] Minutes of the 12th Meeting of the Executive Committee of the 20th Extraordinary ICAO Assembly, para. 2, ICAO Doc. 9088, A20-Min.EX/12, p. 121 (1973).

[71] 1977 Vienna Conference on Succession of States in Respect of Treaties (First Session), Official Records, vol. I, Committee of the Whole, 14th Meeting, p. 98, para. 8, UN Doc. A/CONF.80 (1978).

[72] *Ibid.* at para. 11.

the Drafting Committee, which had so far succeeded in finding satisfactory solutions in most cases, including those raising substantive points. Frequent recourse to voting would produce a worthless convention.'[73]

At a later meeting of the same committee of the Conference, a dispute again arose as to the functions of a drafting committee. Two delegations complained that by going into a question of interpretation of an article, the Drafting Committee had gone beyond its mandate.[74] The Chairman of the Drafting Committee explained that 'it did have a mandate to draft a clear text, and it was incumbent on it to point out to the Committee of the Whole cases in which the rule adopted by that body was not sufficiently clear from the proposed wording and could perhaps be better expressed'.[75] The representative of Sri Lanka commented that 'the report by the Chairman of the Drafting Committee ... amounted to a suggestion that the Committee of the Whole should reconsider one of its own decisions; in making such a suggestion, the Drafting Committee had clearly exceeded its mandate'.[76] The representative of the United Kingdom stated that 'his delegation wished to defend the approach of the Drafting Committee'.[77] No ruling was made on the issue.

At a plenary meeting of the 1988 Conference for the Adoption of a Convention against Illicit Traffic in Narcotic Drugs and Psychotropic Substances, a delegate complained, 'The final text of the Convention had now been adopted in the form in which it had emerged from the Drafting Committee, without consideration of its separate articles by the Committee or the Conference.' The Chairman responded that 'the procedure which has been followed was valid'.[78]

20.5.5 Composition of a Drafting Committee

The UN Model Rules propose,

> *Rule 64*
>
> *Drafting Committee*
>
> 1. A treaty-making conference shall and any other conference may establish a Drafting Committee which, unless the Conference decides otherwise,

73 *Ibid.* at para. 13.

74 1977 Vienna Conference on Succession of States in Respect of Treaties (First Session), Official Records, vol. I, Committee of the Whole, 35th Meeting, p. 240, paras. 61, 62, UN Doc. A/CONF.80 (1978).

75 *Ibid.* at para. 63. 76 *Ibid.* at para. 68. 77 *Ibid.* at para. 71.

78 1988 Conference for the Adoption of a Convention against Illicit Traffic in Narcotic Drugs and Psychotropic Substances, UN Doc. E/CONF/.82/SR.6, paras. 38, 39 (1988).

> shall consist of a Chairman, elected by the Conference pursuant to sub-paragraph (a) of rule 20, and of eighteen other members, selected so that each language in which any instrument to be adopted by the Conference is to be authentic will be adequately represented, and with due regard to equitable geographical distribution. The Rapporteur-General shall be an *ex-officio* member of the Committee, without the right to vote.

Traditionally drafting committees were small. O'Davoren, writing in 1943, stated that a drafting committee should consist 'of a small number of persons, not necessarily delegates or advisers'.[79] The present author is not aware of a practice of appointing to a drafting committee persons from outside the conference.

Over the years, the number of members of drafting committees appears to have been increasing. The Third Law of the Sea Conference had twenty-three members in its drafting committee,[80] and the 1977 Conference on Territorial Asylum had a membership of thirty-one.[81]

The UN Model Rules make no provision as to participation in the Drafting Committee of States that have a special interest, such as States that presented the proposals transferred to the drafting committee. The rules of procedure of the 1977 Conference on Territorial Asylum had a very liberal policy concerning participation in the Drafting Committee:[82]

> *Rule 47*
>
> 2. All delegations may attend the meetings of the Drafting Committee. The sponsors of proposed amendments which are referred to the Drafting Committee may, at their own request or at the request of the Chairman of the Drafting Committee, participate in the discussions held by the Committee on their proposals. In addition, its Chairman may, if he sees fit, permit other delegations present to take the floor in the Committee on specific questions under discussion.[83]

[79] William O'Davoren, *Post-War Reconstruction Conferences, The Technical Organisation of International Conferences* (1943) p. 95.

[80] Rule 53(1) of the rules of procedure of the Third Law of the Sea Conference, UN Doc. A/CONF.62/30/Rev.3 (1975).

[81] UN Doc. A/CONF.78/12, para. 12 (1977).

[82] The debate on the proposals to open the Drafting Committee to a wide membership took place at the 4th Plenary Meeting of the 1977 Conference on Territorial Asylum, UN Doc. A/CONF.78/PV.4, paras. 1–34 (1977).

[83] UN Doc. A/CONF.78/9, Rule 47 (1977).

The Chairman of the Committee of the Whole of the Conference ruled, however, that 'only delegations submitting written amendments could be invited to participate in the Drafting Committee's discussions'.[84]

At a meeting of a committee of the 1974–1977 Geneva Humanitarian Law Conference, the Chairman pointed out,

> The rules of procedure laid down that any delegation might attend the meetings of the Drafting Committee.[85] That rule, however, applied only to the Drafting Committee of the Conference itself; adopted by a small majority at the first session of the Conference, it was an exception to the rule observed in almost all international conferences, namely, that membership of drafting committees was limited . . . Participation in any of the Committee's subsidiary bodies, including the Drafting Committee, should therefore be limited to persons appointed by the Chairman.[86]

The Drafting Committee of the Third Law of the Sea Conference had separate language groups representing each of the six languages of the Conference, the groups being open to all delegations. One writer comments that in practice therefore this served a 'political function', as the Drafting Committee 'was not a small group making decisions affecting the majority of delegations without their participation'.[87] The rules of procedure of the Third Law of the Sea Conference had a provision whereby

> *Rule 53*
>
> 2. . . . the sponsor or a representative of the group of sponsors of a proposal shall be invited to the appropriate meetings of the Drafting Committee and may participate, without the right to vote, in the discussion at the discretion of the Chairman, in case the Conference or a Main Committee decides to refer that proposal to the Drafting Committee without taking a decision thereon.[88]

[84] 1977 Conference on Territorial Asylum, Committee of the Whole, 1st Meeting, para. 22, UN Doc. A/CONF.78/C.1/SR.1 (1977).

[85] CDDH/2/Rev.3, Rule 47(2). The rule is substantially the same as the rule in the 1977 Conference on Territorial Asylum quoted earlier.

[86] Official Records of the 1974–1977 Geneva Humanitarian Law Conference, CDDH/II/SR.57, vol. XII, p. 19, para. 3, Summary Records of the 57th Meeting of Committee II.

[87] L. D. M. Nelson, 'The Work of the Drafting Committee', in *United Nations Convention on the Law of the Sea 1982, A Commentary*, ed. Myron H. Nordquist, vol. I (1985), p. 135 at p. 141.

[88] UN Doc. A/CONF.62/30/Rev.3 (1981).

At the initiative of the UK delegation, the 1979 Weapons Conference adopted the same formula.[89]

The rules of procedure of the NPT Review Conferences stipulate that

Rule 36

2. Representatives of other delegations may also attend the meetings of the Drafting Committee and may participate in its deliberations when matters of particular concern to them are under discussion.[90]

At the 2002 World Health Assembly, the question arose whether a committee could instruct a drafting group that it 'should not meet when the Committee was deliberating so as to avoid the simultaneous occurrence' of meetings. The Legal Counsel advised 'that as far as he was aware there were no rules concerning the number of meetings that could be held concurrently... [I]f the timetable so required, meetings of informal working groups had been held simultaneously.'[91] The Chairman at first ruled, incorrectly, that 'the suspension of the drafting group's meeting was a matter for that body to decide', but later a pragmatic solution was found.[92]

COMMENT

It would indeed seem desirable to allow interested delegations to attend meetings of drafting committees, and the experience of this author is that, despite their being open ended, such meetings usually attract only a limited number of delegations.

[89] UN Doc. A/CONF.95/PREP.CONF./II/SR.27, para. 45 (1978); A/CONF.95/2, Rule 34(3) (1979).

[90] Rule 36(2) of the rules of procedure of the 1995, 2000, 2005 NPT Review Conferences, Docs. NPT/CONF.1995/28 (1995), NPT/CONF.2000/1 (2000), NPT/CONF.2005/1 (2004).

[91] 55th World Health Assembly, Committee 'A', 5th Meeting, p. 69, WHA55/2002/REC/3 (2002).

[92] *Ibid.* at p. 67. The Secretary of the Committee later announced that most of the drafting groups would not be meeting simultaneously with committee meetings.

21

Suspension and Amendment of Rules of Procedure

21.1 Suspension of Rules of Procedure

There is no provision in the rules of procedure of the UNGA concerning their suspension. The Canadian representative to the Sixth Committee of the 1949 session of the UNGA raised the issue, but did not press for any action.[1]

The UN Model Rules propose,

> *Rule 84*
>
> *Suspension*
>
> Any of these rules or any of its supplementary rules may be suspended by the Conference, provided that twenty-four hours' notice of the proposal for the suspension has been given, which may be waived if no representative objects; subsidiary organs may by unanimous consent waive rules pertaining to them. Any such suspension shall be limited to a specified and stated purpose and to a period required to achieve that purpose, and shall not be inconsistent with the decisions of the General Assembly taken to achieve administrative simplification and budgetary savings in the conduct of conferences, with any decisions of the convening organ, or with the rights of States participating in the Conference but temporarily absent from a given meeting.[2]

[1] In 1949, the Canadian delegation recommended introducing a rule whereby 'a rule of procedure shall not be suspended, nor shall the President put a vote for the suspension of any rule unless: (a) the motion has been submitted in writing to the Secretary-General; and (b) copies of the motion have been distributed to all the delegations' with forty-eight hours' notice. UN Doc. A/AC.30/7 attached to the Report of the Special Committee on Methods and Procedures of the General Assembly, Annex 1, p. 19, para. 5, UN GAOR, 4th Session, Supp. No. 12, UN Doc. A/937 (1949). UN GAOR, 6th Committee, 4th Session, 158th Meeting, para. 104, UN Doc. A/C.6/4/SR.158 (1949).

[2] This rule follows, in the main, Rule 64 of the rules of procedure of the 1979 Weapons Conference, UN Doc. A/CONF.95/2 (1979).

The wording up to, and including, the phrase 'and to a period required to achieve that purpose' has been adopted by most subsequent conferences. The final phrases of the proposed model rule have not been adopted.

21.1.1 Practice in the UN General Assembly as to Suspension

The Chairman of a committee of the UNGA at its 1950 session ruled that the Committee had no authority to suspend the UNGA rules of procedure.[3]

A memorandum of the Legal Department of the United Nations Secretariat seemed to imply such powers. The memorandum stated that, although there is no provision for suspension of the rules of procedure, 'in the practice of the General Assembly the application of certain rules of procedure has frequently been suspended by common accord'.[4] Blum comments forcefully on this memorandum that the Charter

> does not, however, authorise the Assembly to depart from those rules (as long as they are in force) or to 'amend' them in specific cases, on an *ad hoc* basis, in a manner not provided for by the Charter or the rules of procedure themselves. The approach reflected in the memorandum therefore runs counter to the basic constitutional concept that underlies the activities of the various organs of the United Nations.[5]

Deliberate nonobservance of rules of procedure can be regarded as a form of unofficial suspension, and Castañeda writes that the nonobservance by the UNGA of its own rules, although 'useful on occasion', is 'illegal'. He adds that strict observance of the procedure for amendment of rules of procedure would 'partially guarantee that the decision will be inspired mainly by considerations of general and permanent value'.[6]

The Legal Counsel to the UN, during a discussion in the UNGA at its 1977 session on the possibility of holding a secret ballot, stated that suspension can even be carried by a majority vote. The Legal Counsel's opinion was that a committee could not suspend the rules of procedure but this

> does not exclude the authority of the General Assembly itself to decide by a majority vote to resort to secret ballot, since even if this is considered as

[3] UN GAOR, Ad Hoc Political Committee, 5th Session, 56th Meeting, para. 53, UN Doc. A/AC.38/SR.56 (1950).

[4] 1977 UN Jur. Y.B. 194, 196.

[5] Yehuda Z. Blum, *Eroding the United Nations Charter* (1993), p. 17.

[6] Jorge Castañeda, *Legal Effects of United Nations Resolutions* (1969), p. 32.

> amounting to a suspension or amendment of the rules of procedure, such power is vested in the Assembly by Article 21 of the Charter.[7,8]

A 1984 opinion of the UN Office of Legal Affairs stated, 'An organ that has the explicit or implicit power (e.g., the Plenary of the General Assembly) to suspend its rules can do so for the purpose of holding a secret ballot.'[9]

The Legal Adviser to the UN, at the 1992 session of the UNGA, during a discussion in the Fifth Committee, stated, 'The Fifth Committee, being composed of sovereign Member States, could, of course, decide not to apply rule 160 in the case under consideration. That, however, was a course of action which he, as Legal Counsel, could not recommend.'[10]

It is the practice of the UNGA to waive the application of the rule of procedure requiring that the General Committee of the UNGA approve the inclusion of items in the agenda of the Assembly.[11] The requirement of a quorum for opening meetings has also been waived.[12]

21.1.2 Practice in International Conferences as to Suspension

Conforti comments, I believe correctly, that

> [t]here is no doubt that, just as they are issued by the majority, rules of procedure can be modified by the same majority. However, it is necessary that the modification be general and abstract and that it be made only after an examination of the reasons that objectively make it necessary. On the contrary, the view cannot be held that the majority, which has the power to

[7] Article 21 of the Charter states,

> The General Assembly shall adopt its own rules of procedure. It shall elect its President for each session.

[8] UN GAOR, Plenary, 32nd Session, 103rd Meeting, para. 57, UN Doc. A/32/PV.103 (1977).

[9] Memorandum (from the Office of Legal Affairs) to the Assistant Secretary-General for Human Rights, Center for Human Rights, 16 February 1984. 1984 UN Jur. Y.B. 170.

[10] UN GAOR, 5th Committee, 47th Session, 38th Meeting, para. 14, UN Doc. A/C.5/47/SR.38 (1992). Rule 160 deals with the functions of the Committee on Contributions.

[11] Rule 40 of the UNGA rules of procedure. See, for example, UN GAOR, Plenary, 45th Session, 30th Meeting, p. 8, UN Doc. A/45/PV.30 (Provisional) (1990); UN GAOR, Plenary, 45th Session, 77th Meeting, p. 3, UN Doc. A/45/PV.77 (Provisional) (1990); UN GAOR, Plenary, 47th Session, 95th Meeting, p. 37, UN Doc. A/47/PV.95 (1993); UN GAOR, Plenary, 47th Session, 96th Meeting, pp. 3–5, UN Doc. A/47/PV.96 (Provisional) (1993).

[12] See for example A/62/PV.2 p. 1 (20070. The requirement of a quorum for the taking of decisions has not been waived. The President of the UNGA informed the Assembly that this decision was taken 'on the understanding that such a waiver would not imply any permanent change in the provisions of rules 67 and 108 of the rules of procedure'. UN Doc. A/46/PV.3, pp. 3–4 (Provisional) (1991).

> modify a rule of procedure, may also not apply it in individual cases. The individual failure would constitute a violation of the rules of procedure and mean violation of the rights of the minority.[13]

At the 1950 Conference on Missing Persons, a delegation proposed to suspend the rule of procedure that prohibited the President from participating in the debate.[14] The Legal Adviser to the UN commented that 'all rules of procedure were made for the convenience of the organ applying them and should consequently be flexible and adaptable to circumstances. From the strictly legal point of view, however, it was hardly advisable to suspend a rule of procedure: if it was not satisfactory it was better simply to amend it.'[15] The Conference subsequently decided to suspend the rule 'until the Conference had taken a final decision on it'.[16]

At the 1958 Law of the Sea Conference, the Chairman of a committee stated that a proposed procedure 'would be departing from the rules of procedure which would itself require a separate decision'.[17] The Chairman thus clearly implied that the Committee could depart from the rules of procedure, although the issue was not pursued.

The rules of procedure of the 1963 Tokyo Air Law Conference permitted their suspension by a majority vote.[18] During the Conference, a delegation proposed suspending the rule that prohibited withdrawing a proposal once it had been amended. The motion was put to the vote, and the Conference decided not to suspend the relevant rule of procedure.[19]

During the 1961 Vienna Conference on Diplomatic Relations, the delegate of Ghana proposed to vote directly on the original ILC draft while ignoring amendments that had been submitted to the draft. The delegate of Venezuela objected, quoting the relevant rule of procedure. The Chairman declared that 'the Committee was master of its own procedure'. The delegate of France pointed out that the rules of procedure could only be changed by the Conference as a whole and not by a committee. The Chairman replied that a two-thirds majority could change the rule. When the Ghanaian proposal was put to the vote, it obtained a two-thirds

[13] Benedetto Conforti and Carlo Foracelli, *The Law and Practice of the United Nations*, 4th rev. edn (2010), p. 112.

[14] UN Doc. A/CONF.1/SR.2, para. 81 (1950). [15] *Ibid.* at para. 82. [16] *Ibid.* at para. 83.

[17] Official Records of the 1958 Law of the Sea Conference, 30th Meeting of Committee I, vol. III, p. 88, para. 26, UN Doc. A/CONF.13 (1958).

[18] Rule 28, vol. II, Documents of the 1963 Tokyo Air Law Conference, Doc. No. 3, ICAO Doc. 8565-LC/152–2 (1963).

[19] Vol. I, Minutes of the 17th Meeting of the 1963 Tokyo Air Law Conference, para. 74, ICAO Doc. 8565-LC/152–1 (1963) (published 1966).

majority. The delegates of Yugoslavia, France and Italy strenuously objected to the procedure adopted, calling it extremely dangerous, and the delegate of Ghana summed up by reassuring the delegations that the Conference 'would have recourse to the procedure followed in voting . . . only when it was absolutely necessary'.[20]

At the 1963 Vienna Conference on Consular Relations, the representative of Norway called for suspension of the rules of procedure, but no action was taken.[21]

At the Third Law of the Sea Conference, the Chairman proposed that the question of the extension of a session be 'governed by the rules of procedure of the Conference, also taking into account the traditions of the Conference and the circumstances prevailing at the time'.[22] One delegation protested that this formulation 'left the door open for the possibility of departing from the rules of procedure of the Conference and was tantamount to amending those rules'.[23] After further discussion, the Chairman stated that 'the rules of procedure had primacy, and if it was necessary to resolve a question, they would apply . . . the Conference had always succeeded through consultations in avoiding any need for application of the rules of procedure. It was his hope that that would be possible in the future as well.'[24]

At the 1973 Rome Air Law Conference, the rules of procedure stated,

> *Rule 29*
>
> These Rules may be amended, or any portion of the rules may be suspended, at any time by a decision of the Conference taken by a majority vote of the Representatives present and voting.[25]

This rule was applied in the Conference to suspend the application of the rule that required a majority of two-thirds of the 'total number of States represented at the Conference' in order to adopt a draft convention.[26] Thus a simple majority of members present and voting succeeded in suspending a provision that required the approval of two-thirds of all representatives.

20 Official Records of the 1961 Vienna Conference on Diplomatic Relations, 12th Meeting of the Committee of the Whole, p. 97, paras. 6, 21, 125, UN Doc. A/CONF.20/14 (1961).

21 Official Records of the 1963 Vienna Conference on Consular Relations, Committee II, p. 371, para. 32, UN Doc. A/CONF.25 (1963).

22 Third Law of the Sea Conference, Official Records, vol. XV, General Committee, 63rd Meeting, p. 59, para. 2, UN Doc. A/CONF.62 (1981).

23 *Ibid.* at p. 60, para. 9. 24 *Ibid.* at p. 61, para. 21.

25 ICAO Doc. 9225-LC/178, CAS Doc. No. 3 (1973).

26 Minutes of the 9th Meeting of the Plenary of the 1973 Rome Air Law Conference, para. 10, ICAO Doc. 9225-LC/178 (1973).

21.1.3 *Practice in International Organisations as to Suspension*

The IAEA rules of procedure permit their suspension by a two-thirds majority.[27] Rules of procedure have been suspended, for example, to waive the requirement of a specified number of days' notice for calling a special session of the General Conference.[28] The rule requiring notice has also been waived to allow the Committee of the Whole to consider agenda items prior to the agenda being approved by the General Committee.[29]

The Standing Orders of the Conference of the ILO permit, under stringent safeguards, the suspension of standing orders:

> Subject to the provisions of the Constitution, the Conference, on the unanimous recommendation of the President and three Vice-Presidents, may exceptionally decide to suspend any provision of the Standing Orders, for the purpose of dealing with a specific non-controversial question before it when this will contribute to the orderly and expeditious functioning of the Conference. A decision may not be taken until the sitting following that at which a proposal to suspend the Standing Orders has been submitted to the Conference.[30]

Frequent use is made of this authority, mainly on issues of time limitations and scheduling.[31]

Prior to this rule being introduced, in 1990, ILO Conferences apparently assumed that there was an inherent right to suspend the standing orders. At the 1946 session of the Conference, the President suggested, 'In view of the very heavy agenda with which the Conference has to deal this week, I am prepared to accept a motion that the Standing Orders be suspended to enable this report to be discussed at this sitting.'[32] The President of the 1959 session of the ILO Conference ruled that

[27] Rule 102 of the rules of procedure of the IAEA General Conference, IAEA Doc. GC(XXXI)/INF/245/Rev.1.

[28] IAEA General Conference, 1st Special Session, GC(SPL.1)/OR.1, para. 5 (1987).

[29] For example, Official Records of the 323rd Plenary Meeting of the 34th Regular Session of the IAEA General Conference, IAEA Doc. GC(XXXIV)/OR.323, para. 35 (1991).

[30] Article 76 of the Standing Orders of the International Labour Conference, International Labour Organisation, Geneva, December 1992. Adopted, with slight changes, at the 77th Session of the ILO Conference, Geneva 1990, Record of Proceedings, 20th sitting, p. 19/2.

[31] See for example, *Suspension of various provisions of the standing Orders of the Conference, ILO International Labour Conference*, Provisional Record No. 2, 105th Session, ILO Doc. ILC105-PR2-JUR-160524–1-En-docx (2016).

[32] International Labour Conference, 28th Session, Seattle 1946, Record of Proceedings, 12th sitting, pp. 95, 178. (Such a motion was subsequently proposed and adopted.)

> there is nothing in the Standing Orders that deals with the question of their suspension. It is possible that the Conference itself is the sovereign on this question as to whether it will suspend the Standing Orders or not, that is to say a decision can be taken by a majority of votes cast for or against.[33]

When the amendment on suspension was proposed to the 1990 Conference, the note by the Governing Body stated,

> The aim of such a procedure would be to strengthen the authority of the Standing Orders by removing the temptation to circumvent or ignore their provisions when these stood in the way of action which the Conference wished to take. There was agreement on the need to provide adequate safeguards against the misuse, or ill-considered use, of such a provision.[34]

The Chairman and Rapporteur of the Standing Orders Committee of the 1990 ILO Conference commented on the proposed Rule 76 in his report to the Conference, stating that 'the proposal received the unanimous support of the Committee'.[35]

Although frequent use is made of the aphorism that an assembly is 'master of its own procedure', such 'mastery' is necessarily limited. Mr Baroody, the Saudi representative, at a 1965 meeting of a UNGA committee, commented,

> It was true that the Committee could adopt any procedure it chose, but only on condition that it did not contravene its rules of procedure. It could only depart from the provisions of those rules in cases where their interpretation gave rise to controversy. If it was argued that the Committee could at any time choose new methods of work, then it would be difficult to explain why the rules of procedure had been established and why they were constantly referred to.[36]

COMMENT

There will be times when a conference will wish to waive the application of a technical requirement imposed by the rules of procedure such as a time specification. Rather than spell out the procedure for each such waiver, a general suspension clause seems to be desirable. It is, however, important

[33] ILO Conference, 43rd Session, Geneva 1959, Record of Proceedings, 8th sitting, p. 107.

[34] ILO Conference, 77th Session, Geneva 1990, Record of Proceedings, p. 2/2.

[35] *Ibid.* 20th sitting, p. 19/1.

[36] UN GAOR, 1st Committee, 20th Session, 1418th Meeting, para. 46, UN Doc. A/C.1/20/SR.1418 (1965).

that such right of suspension be regulated and limited so that it will not be used to limit the rights of a minority.

Amending the rules of procedure rather than suspending them may appear to be a more drastic action, but it is inherently more conducive to equitable conduct of business than suspension. An amendment is a general step affecting all participants and does not have the ad hoc characteristic of suspension. Suspension of rules of procedure can be destructive of good conduct of business for it lends itself to being tailored against a specific delegation or process. Practice appears to show that formal suspension of rules of procedure is rarely applied.

21.2 Amendment of Rules of Procedure

The UNGA rules of procedure state,

> *Rule 163*
>
> These rules of procedure may be amended by a decision of the General Assembly, taken by a majority of the members present and voting, after a committee has reported on the proposed amendment.

The UN Model Rules propose,

> *Rule 81*
>
> *Amendment*
>
> These rules may be amended by the General Assembly, upon a report of its Administrative and Budgetary (Fifth) Committee or its Legal (Sixth) Committee.
>
> *Rule 82*
>
> *Supplementary Rules*
>
> These rules may be supplemented by rules adopted by the Conference by a two-thirds majority of the representatives present and voting, on the recommendation of a preparatory organ or of the General Committee, provided that such supplementary rules are not inconsistent with these rules or with applicable decisions of the General Assembly or any other convening organ.

The UN Model Rules, which regard the UNGA as the parent body of all UN-convened conferences, condition amendments to conference rules of procedure on the approval of the UNGA. It appears to this author to be an unacceptable proposal as it negates the independence of international conferences. No conference appears to have adopted the phrase.

Pastuhov, writing in 1945, stated,

> An international conference, as a rule, is at liberty to change its rules of procedure at any time, provided, of course, in the case of an international organization, that the changes made shall not be inconsistent with the charter of the organization. A provision is generally embodied in the rules, however, laying down special conditions for the adoption of any modifications.[37]

21.2.1 Majority Required for Amending Rules of Procedure

Amending the rules of procedure of the UNGA,[38] the IMO Assembly,[39] the IAEA General Conference[40] and the WHO Assembly[41] requires only a simple majority. The UNGA rules of procedure require, however, that they can only be amended 'after a committee has reported on the proposed amendment'.[42] Schermers comments on this that if the rules of procedure 'could easily be overruled, it would create uncertainty'.[43]

The rules of procedure of some earlier UN-convened conferences and the 1954 Hague Conference, the 1974–1977 Geneva Humanitarian Law Conference and conferences convened by the ICAO and the IMO[44] allowed for their amendment by a simple majority.[45] However, later conferences tend to require a majority of two-thirds for such amendments.[46]

[37] Vladimir D. Pastuhov, *A Guide to the Practice of International Conferences* (1945), p. 113.

[38] Rule 163 of the UNGA rules of procedure.

[39] Rule 53 of the rules of procedure of the IMO Assembly.

[40] Rule 101 of the rules of procedure of the IAEA General Conference.

[41] Rule 121 of the rules of procedure of the World Health Assembly.

[42] Rule 163 of the UNGA rules of procedure.

[43] Henry G. Schermers and Niels M. Blokker, *International Institutional Law, Unity within Diversity*, 5th rev. edn, para. 1205 (2011).

[44] Rule 57 of the IMO rules of procedure.

[45] See, for example, the rules of procedure of the 1950 Conference on Missing Persons, Rule 26, UN Doc. A/CONF.1/3 (1950); 1951 Conference on Refugees, Rule 28, UN Doc. A/CONF.2/3/Rev.1 (1951); 1954 Hague Conference, Rule 23, CBC/2/DRAFT and amendments; 1968 Vienna Conference on the Law of Treaties – First Session, Rule 61, UN Doc. A/CONF.39/11/Add.1 (1968); Fourth International Conference on the Peaceful Uses of Atomic Energy, Rule 33, UN Doc. A/CONF.49/3 (1970); UN Conference to Consider Amendments to the 1961 Single Convention on Narcotic Drugs, Rule 63, UN Doc. E/CONF.63/3 (1972); 1975 Vienna Conference on Representation of States, Rule 61, UN Doc. A/CONF.67/8 (1975); Third UN Conference on the Exploitation and Peaceful Uses of Outer Space, Rule 18, UN Doc. A/CONF.184/2 (1999).

[46] See the rules of procedure of the 1986 Conference on Treaties between States and International Organisations, Rule 64, UN Doc. A/CONF.129/7 (1986); 1994 International Conference on Population and Development, Rule 68, UN Doc. A/CONF.171/2 (1994); IMO 1998 Diplomatic Conference on Arrest of Ships, Rule 69, UN Doc. A/CONF.188/2

The rules of procedure of the Third Law of the Sea Conference stipulated that, like substantive issues, amending the rules of procedure required

> two-thirds majority of the representatives present and voting, *provided that such majority shall include at least a majority of the States participating in that session of the Conference.*[47,48] [emphasis added]

Some rules of procedure of UN-convened conferences make no reference to the possibility of their being amended.[49] The absence of any reference to amending the rules of procedure presumably is intended to discourage amendments, but nevertheless, by implication, leaves open the possibility of amendment by a simple majority.

Where a conference adopts its decisions by consensus, this requirement is also applied to amending the rules of procedure.[50] The rules of procedure of a recent WHO conference stipulated that the rules could only be amended by consensus.[51] This was an unusually stringent provision, given that, in the absence of consensus, the rules of the conference allowed for substantive decisions to be taken by a two-thirds majority. The explanation given by the proposers was that the rules of procedure have to be adopted by consensus; hence the same criterion should apply to their amendment.[52]

(1998); 1998 ICC Conference, Rule 65, UN Doc. A/CONF.183/13 (1998); Tenth UN Congress on the Prevention of Crime and the Treatment of Offenders, Rule 61, UN Doc. A/CONF.187/2 (1999); Third UN Conference on Least Developed Countries, Rule 66, UN Doc. A/CONF.191/4 (2001); Second World Assembly on Ageing, Rule 63, UN Doc. A/CONF. 197/2 (2002); 2004 World Conference on Disaster Reduction, Rule 68, UN Doc. A/CONF.206/2 (2004).

47 Rule 67 of the rules of procedure of the Third Law of the Sea Conference, referring back to Rule 39(1). UN Doc. A/CONF.62/30/Rev.3 (1975).

48 The US delegation proposed that the majority required be 'two-thirds of the representatives of States participating in that session of the Conference'. UN Doc. A/CONF.62/7/Rev.1 (1974). The proposal was not adopted.

49 See, for example, rules of procedure of the 1968 Teheran Conference on Human Rights, UN Doc. A/CONF.32/2 (1968); 1971 Stockholm Conference on the Human Environment, UN Doc. A/CONF.48/3 (1971); 1974 Prescription in Sale of Goods Conference, UN Doc. A/CONF.63/8 (1974); 2005 NPT Review Conference, NPT/CONF.2005/1 (2004).

50 See Rule 46 of the rules of procedure of the International Conference on the Relationship between Disarmament and Development, UN Doc. A/CONF.130/1(1987); Rule 56 of the Preparatory Meeting for the Conference of Plenipotentiaries on the Stockholm Convention on Persistent Organic Pollutants, UNEP/POPS/CONF/PM/INF/1 (2001); WHO, Draft rules of procedure for the Conference of the Parties, WHO Framework Convention on Tobacco Control, WHO Doc. A/FCTC/IGWG/1/4 (2004).

51 Rule 60 of the WHO Draft rules of procedure for the Conference of the Parties, WHO Framework Convention on Tobacco Control, WHO Doc. A/FCTC/IGWG/1/4 (2004).

52 Paragraph 23, 'Note by the Secretariat', WHO Doc. A/FCTC/IGWG/1/4 (2004).

COMMENT

Amending a rule of procedure entails a reconsideration of the original adoption of such a rule. The logical inference therefore is that amendment of a rule of procedure should require the majority necessary to reconsider a decision, namely a two-thirds majority. This, nowadays, is in fact the practice in most conferences.

BIBLIOGRAPHY

UN Publications

International Court of Justice, Reports
Répertoire of the Practice of the Security Council
Repertory of Practice of United Nations Organs
United Nations Juridical Yearbooks
Yearbooks of the International Law Commission

Books

Abi-Saab, Georges, and Hazel Fox, eds., *The Changing Constitution of the United Nations* (1997)
Arrow, Kenneth J., *Social Choices and Individual Values*, 2nd edn (1963)
Bailey, Sydney D., *The General Assembly of the United Nations, A Study of Procedure and Practice*, rev. edn (1964)
The Procedure of the UN Security Council, 3rd edn (1998)
Bennet, A. LeRoy, *International Organizations, Principles and Issues*, 5th edn (1991)
Blum, Yehuda Z., *Eroding the United Nations Charter* (1993)
Broms, Bengt, *The United Nations* (1990)
Buckley, William F., *United Nations Journal, A Delegate's Odyssey* (1974)
Buergenthal, Thomas, *Law Making in the International Civil Aviation Organization* (1969)
Cannon, Hugh, *Cannon's Concise Guide to Rules of Order* (1992)
Cassese, Antonio, *International Law* (2001)
Castañeda, Jorge, *Legal Effects of United Nations Resolutions*, 2nd edn (2005)
Clapham, Andrew, ed., *Brierly's Law of Nations*, 7th edn (2012)
Cheng, Bin, ed., *International Law: Treaty and Practice* (1982)
Chiu, Hungdah, *The Capacity of International Organizations to Conclude Treaties, and the Special Legal Aspects of the Treaties so Concluded* (1966)
Ciobano, Dan, *Preliminary Objections Related to the Jurisdiction of the United Nations Political Organs* (1975)
Clark, Grenville, and Louis B. Sohn, *Peace through Disarmament and Charter Revision* (1953)

Conforti, Benedetto, and Focarelli Carlo, *The Law and Practice of the United Nations*, 4th edn (2010)

D'Amato, Anthony A. *The Concept of Custom in International Law* (1971)

Danilenko, G. M., *Law Making in the International Community* (1993)

De Martens, F., *La Conférence de la Paix à la Haye, étude d'histoire contemporaine*, ed. Arthur Rousseau (1900)

Detter, Ingrid, *Law Making by International Organizations* (1965)

Dunn, F. S., *The Practice and Procedure of International Conferences* (1929)

Dupuy, René-Jean, ed., *A Handbook of International Organizations*, 2nd edn (1998)

Eban, Abba, *The New Diplomacy, International Affairs in the Modern Age* (1983)

Feld, Werner J., and Robert S. Jordan with Leon Hurwitz, *International Organizations, A Comparative Approach* (1983)

Feltham, R. G., *Diplomatic Handbook*, 7th edn (1998)

Fox, James, *Dictionary of International and Comparative Law* (1992)

Fox, Maurice W., *Parliamentary Usage* (1945)

Franck, Thomas M., *Nation against Nation* (1985)

Goodrich, Leland M., Edvard Hambro and Anne P. Simons, *Charter of the United Nations*, 3rd rev. edn (1969)

Goodrich, Leland M., and Anne P. Simons, *The United Nations and the Maintenance of International Peace and Security* (1955)

Graham, Norman A., Richard L. Kauffman and Michael F. Oppenheimer, *The United States and Multilateral Diplomacy: A Handbook* (1984)

Gross, Leo, *Selected Essays on International Law and Organization* (1992)

Hadwen, John G., and Johan Kaufmann, *How United Nations Decisions Are Made* (1962)

Hawtrey, S. C., and H. M. Barclay, *Abraham and Hawtrey's Parliamentary Dictionary*, 3rd edn (1970)

Higgins, Rosalyn, *The Development of International Law through the Political Organs of the United Nations* (1963)

Hill, N., *The Public International Conference* (1929)

Jenks, C. Wilfred, *The Common Law of Mankind* (1958)

Law in the World Community (1967)

Kaufmann, Johan, *United Nations Decision Making* (1980)

Conference Diplomacy, An Introductory Analysis, rev. edn (1987); 2nd rev. edn (1988)

Keesey, Ray E., *Modern Parliamentary Procedure* (1974)

Kelsen, Hans, *The Law of the United Nations, A Critical Analysis of its Fundamental Problems* (1951, 6th printing 1966)

Principles of International Law, 2nd rev. edn, ed. Robert W. Tucker (1966)

Kirgis, Frederic L., Jr, *International Organizations in Their Legal Setting*, 2nd edn (1993)

Kolasa, Jan, *Rules of Procedure of the United Nations General Assembly, A Legal Analysis* (1967)
Koo, Wellington, Jr, *Voting Procedures in International Political Organizations* (1947)
Kunz, Josef L., *The Changing Law of Nations* (1968)
Lauterpacht, Sir Hersch, *The Development of International Law by the International Court*, rev. edn (1958)
Leigh, Robert D., *Modern Rules of Parliamentary Procedure* (1937)
Limon, Sir Donald, and W. R. McKay, eds., *Erskine May's Treatise on the Law, Privileges, Proceedings and Usage of Parliament*, eds. 22nd edn (1997)
Lowe, Vaughan, and Colin Warbrick, eds., *The United Nations and the Principles of International Law, Essays in Memory of Michael Akehurst* (1994)
Malanczuk, Peter, *Akehurst's Modern Introduction to International Law*, 7th rev. edn (1997)
Marston, F. S., *The Peace Conference of 1919, Organization and Procedure* (1944)
McWhinney, Edward, *The World Court and the Contemporary International Law-Making Process* (1979)
United Nations Law Making (1984)
Menon, P. K., *The Law of Treaties between States and International Organizations* (1992)
Morgenstern, Felice, *Legal Problems of International Organizations* (1986)
Moynihan, Daniel Patrick, *On the Law of Nations, A Historical and Personal Account of the Role of International Law in Foreign Policy* (1990)
Nicolson, Harold, *The Congress of Vienna: A Study in Allied Unity: 1812–1822* (1946)
Nordquist, Myron H., ed., *United Nations Convention on the Law of the Sea 1982, A Commentary*, vol. I (1985)
O'Connell, D. P., *International Law*, 2nd edn, vol. I (1970)
O'Davoren, William, *Post-War Reconstruction Conferences, The Technical Organisation of International Conferences* (1943)
Oppenheim's International Law, eds. R. Jennings and A. Watts, 9th edn, vol. I (1992)
Pastuhov, Vladimir D., *A Guide to the Practice of International Conferences* (1945)
Pomerance, Michla, *The Advisory Function of the International Court in the League and UN Eras* (1973)
Pratap, D., *The Advisory Jurisdiction of the International Court* (1972)
Randolph, Lillian, *The Fundamental Laws of Governmental Organizations* (1971)
Riches, Cromwell A., *Majority Rule in International Organizations: A Study of the Trend from Unanimity to Majority Decision* (1940)
Rideau, Joël, *Juridictions internationales et contrôle du respect des traités constitutifs des organisations internationales* (1969)
Righter, Rosemary, *Utopia Lost, The United Nations and World Order* (1995)

Robert's Rules of Order, Newly Revised, 11th edn, eds. Sarah Corbin Robert, Henry M. Robert III, William J. Evans, Daniel H. Honemann and Thomas J. Balch (2011)

Rosenne, Shabtai, *The International Court of Justice, An Essay in Political and Legal Theory* (1961)

The Law of Treaties: A Guide to the Legislative History of the Vienna Convention (1970)

Practice and Methods of International Law (1984)

Developments in the Law of Treaties 1945–1986 (1989)

An International Law Miscellany (1993)

The Law and Practice of the International Court 1920–2015, 5th edn (2016)

Rosenne, Shabtai, ed., *League of Nations Committee of Experts for the Progressive Codification of International Law (1925–1928)* (1972)

League of Nations Conference for the Codification of International Law (1975)

Sandifer, Durward V., *Evidence before International Tribunals*, rev. edn (1975)

Schermers, Henry G., and Niels M. Blokker, *International Institutional Law, Unity within Diversity*, 5th rev. edn (2011)

Schwarzenberger, Georg M., *International Law*, 3rd edn, vol. I (1957)

Schwarzenberger, Georg M., and E. D. Brown, *A Manual of International Law*, 6th edn (1967)

Scott, James Brown, ed., *The Declaration of London February 26, 1909, A Collection of Official Papers and Documents Relating to the International Naval Conference held in London, December, 1908–February, 1909* (1919)

Shotwell, James T., ed., *The Origins of the International Labor Organization* (1934)

Simma, Bruno *et al*, eds., *The Charter of the United Nations, A Commentary*, 3rd edn (2012)

Sinclair, Sir Ian, *The Vienna Convention on the Law of Treaties*, 3rd edn (2012)

Singh, N., *The Role and Record of the International Court of Justice* (1989)

Sizoo, Jan, and Rudolph Jurrjens, *The Madrid Experience* (1984)

Sloan, Blaine, *United Nations General Assembly Resolutions in Our Changing World* (1991)

Sørensen, Max, ed., *Manual of Public International Law* (1968)

Sturgis, Alice F., *Standard Code of Parliamentary Procedure* (1950)

Szasz, Paul C., *The Law and Practice of the International Atomic Energy Agency* (1970)

Tabory, Mala, *Multilingualism in International Law and Institutions* (1980)

Thirlway, H. W. A., *International Customary Law and Codification* (1972)

Tung, William L., *International Organization under the United Nations System* (1969)

Villiger, M. E., *Customary International Law and Treaties* (1985)

Werners, S. E., *The Presiding Officers in the United Nations* (1967)

Wolfke, Karol, *Custom in Present International Law*, 2nd edn (1993)
Wolfrum, Rüdiger, and Christiane Philipp eds., *United Nations: Law, Policies and Practice*, new rev. English edn (1995)
Wood, John R., and Jean Serres, *Diplomatic Ceremonial and Protocol, Principles, Procedure and Practices* (1970)
Zacklin, Ralph, *The Amendment of the Constitutive Instruments of the United Nations and Specialized Agencies* (1968)
Zemanek, K., ed., *Agreements of International Organizations and the Vienna Convention on the Law of Treaties* (1971)

Articles and Book Chapters

Abi-Saab, Georges, 'Membership and Voting in the United Nations', in *The Changing Constitution of the United Nations*, eds. Georges Abi-Saab and Hazel Fox (1997) p. 31.
Akehurst, Michael, 'Custom as a Source of International Law', 47 *BYIL* 1 (1974–5)
Anand, R. P., 'Sovereign Equality of States in International Law', 197 *RCADI* 141 (1986 II)
Bernhardt, Rudolph, 'International Organizations. Internal Law and Rules', in *Encyclopedia of Public International Law*, ed. Rudolph Bernhardt, vol. V (1983), p. 142
'Customary International Law', in *Encyclopedia of Public International Law*, ed. Rudolph Bernhardt, vol. I (1983), p. 899
'Custom and Treaty in the Law of the Sea', 205 *RCADI* 247 (1987 V)
Bleicher, Samuel A., 'The Legal Significance of Re-Citation of General Assembly Resolutions', 63 *AJIL* 444 (1969)
Bodansky, Daniel, 'The Legitimacy of International Governance: A Coming Challenge for International Environmental Law?' 93 *AJIL* 596 (1999)
Broms, Bengt, 'The Present Stage in the Work of the Special Committee on the Charter of the United Nations and on the Strengthening of the Role of the Organization', in *International Law at a Time of Perplexity, Essays in Honour of Shabtai Rosenne*, eds. Yoram Dinstein and Mala Tabory (1989), p. 932
Buergenthal, Thomas, 'Self-Executing and Non-Self-Executing Treaties in National and International Law', 235 *RCADI* 303 (1992 IV)
Butler, Harold B., 'The Washington Conference', in *The Origins of the International Labor Organization*, ed. James T. Shotwell, vol. I (1934), p. 305
Buzan, Barry, 'Negotiating by Consensus: Developments in Technique at the United Nations Conference on the Law of the Sea', 75 *AJIL* 324 (1981)
Cahier, Philippe, 'L'ordre juridique interne des organisations internationales', in *A Handbook on International Organizations*, ed. René-Jean Dupuy (1988), p. 244

Chaumont, C., 'The Evolutionary Aspect of International Organizations and International Co-operation', 5 *UNESCO International Social Science Bulletin* 258 (1953 No. 2)

Conforti, Benedetto, 'The Legal Effect of Non-Compliance with Rules of Procedure in the UN General Assembly and Security Council', 63 *AJIL* 479 (1969)

D'Amato, Anthony A., 'Trashing Customary International Law', 81 *AJIL* 101 (1987)

Evensen, Jens, 'Working Methods and Procedures in the Third United Nations Conference on the Law of the Sea', 199 *RCADI* 485 (1986 IV)

Fitschen, Thomas, 'Article 21', in *The Charter of the United Nations, A Commentary*, ed. Bruno Simma *et al*, 3rd edn (2012) p. 688

Gianaris, William N., 'Weighted Voting in the International Monetary Fund and the World Bank', 14 *Fordham Int'l L.J.* 910 (1990–91)

Halberstam, Malvina, 'Excluding Israel from the General Assembly by a Rejection of its Credentials', 78 *AJIL* 170 (1984)

Hambro, Edvard, 'Some Notes on Parliamentary Diplomacy', in *Transnational Law in a Changing Society, Essays in Honour of Philip C. Jessup*, eds. Wolfgang Friedmann, Louis Henkin and Oliver Lissitzyn (1972) p. 281

Hendl, Kurt, 'Reflections on the Role, Functions and Procedures of the Security Council of the United Nations', 206 *RCADI* 319 (1987 VI)

Hill, Norman L., 'Unanimous Consent in International Organizations', 22 *AJIL* 319 (1928)

Hovey, Allan, Jr, 'Voting Procedure in the General Assembly', 4 *UNESCO International Organization* 412 (1950 No. 1)

'Obstructionism and the Rules of the General Assembly', 5 *UNESCO International Organization* 515 (1951 No. 3)

Hudson, Manley O., 'Editorial Comment, Procedure of International Conferences and Procedure for the Conclusion and Drafting of Treaties', 20 *AJIL* 747 (1926)

Hudson, Richard, 'Quick Calculator for Estimating Outcomes of Votes in the UN General Assembly under the Binding Triad System for Global Decision-Making', *Center for War/Peace Studies, Special Study No. 8*, Summer 1995

Jacobs, Stephen, and Marc Poirier, 'The Right to Veto United Nations Membership Applications: The United States Veto of the Vietnams', 17 *Harvard Int'l L.J.* 581 (1976)

Jenks, C. W., 'Unanimity, the Veto, Weighted Voting, Special and Simple Majorities and Consensus: Modes of Decision in International Organisations', in *Cambridge Essays in International Law. Essays in Honour of Lord McNair* (1965) p. 806

Jessup, Philip C., 'Parliamentary Diplomacy, An Examination of the Legal Quality of the Rules of Procedure of Organs of the United Nations', 89 *RCADI* 181 (1956 I)

'International Parliamentary Law, Editorial Comment', 51 *AJIL* 396 (1957)

'International Negotiations Under Parliamentary Procedure', in *Lectures on International Law and the United Nations, Summer Institute on International and Comparative Law, Delivered at University of Michigan Law School June 23–28, 1955* (1986) p. 405

Jhabvala, Farrokh, 'The Credentials Approach to Representation Questions in the United Nations General Assembly', 7 *California Western Int'l L.J.* 615 (1977)

Kaufmann, Johan, 'The Evolving United Nations; Principles and Realities', *ACUNS Reports and Papers 1994 No. 4, The Academic Council on the United Nations System* (1994) p. 27

Kearney, Richard D., 'Sources of Law and the International Court of Justice', in *The Future of the International Court of Justice*, ed. Leo Gross (1976) p. 698

Koh, Tommy T. B. and Shanmugam Jayakumar, 'The Negotiating Process of the Third United Nations Conference on the Law of the Sea', in *United Nations Convention on the Law of the Sea 1982, A Commentary*, ed. Myron H. Nordquist, vol. I (1985) p. 29

Konopczyski, Ladislas, 'Majority Rule', in *Encyclopaedia of the Social Sciences*, vol. X (1953) p. 55

Kunz, Josef L., 'Book Review, "A Guide to the Practice of International Conferences", by Vladimir D. Pastuhov', 40 *AJIL* 230 (1946)

Lachs, Manfred, 'The International Law of Outer Space', 113 *RCADI* 1 (1961 III)

Lang, Winfred, 'Multilateral Negotiations: The Role of Presiding Officers', in *Processes of International Negotiations*, ed. Frances Mautner-Markhof (1989) p. 35

Lateef, Noel, 'Parliamentary Diplomacy and the North–South Dialogue', 11 *Ga. J. Int'l and Comp. L.* 1 (1981)

Lewin, André, 'Le Président', in *La Charte des Nations Unies, commentaire article par article*, eds. Jean Pierre Cot and Allain Pellet (1985) p. 419

Liang, Yuen-li, 'Notes on Legal Questions Concerning the United Nations, What Is an International Conference?', 44 *AJIL* 333 (1950)

Manno, Catherine Senf, 'Selective Weighted Voting in the UN General Assembly: Rationale and Methods', 20 *UNESCO International Organization* 37 (1966)

McDougal, Myres S., 'The Hydrogen Bomb Tests and International Law of the Sea', 49 *AJIL* 356 (1967)

McIntyre, Elizabeth, 'Weighted Voting in International Organizations', 8 *UNESCO International Organization* 484 (1954 No. 1)

McWhinney, Edward, 'The Codifying Conference as an Instrument of International Law-Making: From the "Old" Law of the Sea to the "New"', 3 *Syracuse J. Int'l L. and Commerce* 301 (1975)

Mendelson, Maurice, 'Book Review, "Robbie Sabel, Procedure at International Conferences"', 10 *European J. Int'l L.* 478 (1999)

Morgenstern, Felice, 'Legality in International Organizations', 48 *BYIL* 241 (1976–77)

Nelson, L. D. M., 'The Work of the Drafting Committee', in *United Nations Convention on the Law of the Sea 1982, A Commentary*, ed. Myron H. Nordquist, vol. I (1985) p. 141

Onuf, Nicholas G., 'Book Reviews and Notes', 88 *AJIL* 556 (1994) (reviewing Karol Wolfke, *Custom in Present International Law* (1993))

Osieke, Ebere, 'Majority Voting Systems in the International Labour Organisation and the International Monetary Fund', 33 *ICLQ* 381 (1974)

Plant, G., 'The Third United Nations Conference on the Law of the Sea and the Preparatory Commission: Models for United Nations Law-Making?', 36 *ICLQ* 525 (1987)

Prélot, M., 'Le droit des assemblées internationales', 104 *RCADI* 476 (1961 III)

Rosenne, Shabtai, 'United Nations Treaty Practice', 86 *RCADI* 281 (1954 II)

'Conferences and Congresses, International', in *Encyclopedia of Public International Law*, ed. R. Bernhardt, vol. I (1992) p. 739

'Israel and the First United Nations Conference on the Law of the Sea: The Straits of Tiran', in *An International Law Miscellany* (1993) p. 723

'Article 59 of the Statute of the International Court of Justice Revisited', in *International Law in an Evolving World, Liber Amicorum in Tribute to Professor Eduardo Jiménez de Aréchaga* (1994)

Rosenstock, Robert, 'The United Nations at Forty: The US Policy Perspective', 79 *Proceedings of ASIL* 150 (1985)

Sabel, Robbie, 'The Relevance of Procedure at International Conferences', *Centre for the Study of Diplomacy, Leicester University, Diplomatic Studies Programme* (No. 40) (April 1998)

"Conferences and Congresses, International" in the *Max Planck Encyclopedia of Public International Law* (2009), www.mpepil.com/

Scelle, Georges, 'The Evolution of International Conferences', 5 *UNESCO International Social Science Bulletin* 241 (1953 No. 2)

Schachter, Oscar, 'The Evolving Law of International Development', 15 *Colum. J. Transnat'l L.* 1 (1976)

'Recent Trends in International Law Making', 12 *Australian Y.B. Int'l L.* 1 (1992)

Schaefer, Michael, 'Article 21', in *The Charter of the United Nations, A Commentary*, ed. Bruno Simma (1994) p. 361

Schermers, Henry G., 'Voting Rules in International Conferences and Organizations', in *Encyclopedia of Public International Law*, ed. Rudolph Bernhardt, vol. V (1983) p. 397

'The Chairman of an International Organ', 34 *German Y. B. Int'l L.* 296 (1991)

Senturia, Joseph J., 'Parliamentary Procedure', in *Encyclopaedia of Social Sciences*, vol. XII (1933) p. 455

Sharp, W. R., 'A Check List of Subjects for Systematic Study of International Conferences', 5 *UNESCO International Social Science Bulletin* 322 (1953 No. 2)

Skubiszewski, Krzysztof, 'Enactment of Law by International Organizations', 41 *BYIL* 198 (1965–1966)

'The Elaboration of General Multilateral Conventions and of Non-Contractual Instruments Having a Normative Function or Objective, Resolutions of the General Assembly of the United Nations', 61 *Yearbook of the Institute of International Law* 325 (1984 I) and 154 (1985 I)

Sohn, Louis B., 'Voting Procedures in United Nations Conferences for the Codification of International Law', 69 *AJIL* 310 (1975)

'Editorial Comment, Due Process in the United Nations', 69 *AJIL* 620 (1975)

'Voting Procedure in International Conferences for the Codification of International Law, 1864–1930', in *Jus et Societas, Essays in Tribute to Wolfgang Friedmann*, ed. Gabriel M. Wilner (1979) p. 278

Suy, Eric, 'Consensus', in *Encyclopedia of Public International Law*, ed. R. Bernhardt, vol. I (1992) p. 759

Szasz, Paul C., 'Improving the International Legislative Process', 9 *Ga. J. Int'l & Comp. L.* 519 (1979)

'Reforming the Multilateral Treaty-Making Process: An Opportunity Missed?', in *International Law at a Time of Perplexity, Essays in Honour of Shabtai Rosenne*, eds. Yoram Dinstein and Mala Tabory (1989) p. 932

'Remarks by Paul Szasz', in *The American Society of International Law, The Nederlandse Vereniging voor Internationaal Recht, Contemporary International Law Issues: Opportunities at a Time of Momentous Change, Proceedings of the Second Joint Conference held in the Hague, the Netherlands, July 22–24, 1993* (1993) p. 304

'Centralized and Decentralized Law Enforcement: The Security Council and the General Assembly Acting under Chapters VI and VII', in *Allocation of Law Enforcement Authority, Proceedings of an International Symposium of the Kiel Institute of International Law, March 23 to 25, 1994*, ed. Jost Delbrück (1995) p. 17

'General Law Making Process', in *United Nations Legal Order*, eds. Oscar Schachter and Christopher C. Joyner, vol. I (1995) p. 35

Tammes, A. J. P., 'Decisions of International Organs as a Source of International Law', 94 *RCADI* 306 (1958 II)

Torres Bernárdez, Santiago, 'The Organs of International Organizations', in *A Handbook of International Organizations*, ed. René-Jean Dupuy, 2nd edn (1998) p. 134

Vallat, Francis A., 'Voting in the General Assembly of the United Nations', 31 *BYIL* 273 (1954)

Verhoeven, Joe, 'The Normative and Quasi-Normative Activities', in *A Handbook of International Organizations*, ed. René-Jean Dupuy, 2nd edn (1998) p. 432

Vignes, Daniel, 'Will the Third Conference on the Law of the Sea Work According to the Consensus Rule?', 69 *AJIL* 119 (1975)

Virally, Michel, 'The Sources of International Law', in *Manual of Public International Law*, ed. Max Sørensen (1968) p. 130

Waldock, H., 'General Course in Public International Law', 106 *RCADI* 100 (1962 II)

Weil, Prosper, 'Towards Relative Normativity in International Law', 77 *AJIL* 413 (1983)

Wilcox, Francis O., 'Representation and Voting in the UN General Assembly', in *The Strategy of World Order: The UN*, eds. Richard A. Falk and Saul H. Mendlovitz (1966) p. 274

Wolfrum, Rüdiger, 'Article 18', in *The Charter of the United Nations, A Commentary*, ed. Bruno Simma, 2nd edn (2002) p. 351

INDEX